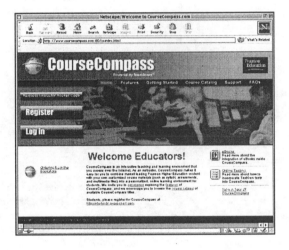

Best-Selling Professional Resources for College Instructors!

As the world's leader in education, Allyn & Bacon understands your interest in continual professional development. From the latest advancements in technology for the classroom to special insights for adjunct professors, these books were written for you! [See the Teaching Tips section at the back of the manual for teaching advice, ideas, and suggestions.]

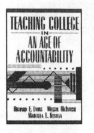     

Instructing and Mentoring the African American College Student: Strategies for Success in Higher Education
Louis B. Gallien, Jr., Regent University and
Marshalita Sims Peterson, Ph.D, Spelman College
©2005 / 0-205-38917-1

Grant Writing in Higher Education:
A Step-by-Step Guide
Kenneth Henson, The Citadel
©2004 / 0-205-38919-8

Using Technology in Learner-Centered Education:
Proven Strategies for Teaching and Learning
David G. Brown and Gordon McCray, both of Wake Forest University,
Craig Runde, Eckerd College and Heidi Schweizer, Marquette University
©2002 / 0-205-35580-3

Creating Learning-Centered Courses
for the World Wide Web
William B. Sanders, University of Hartford
©2001 / 0-205-31513-5

Success Strategies for Adjunct Faculty
Richard Lyons, Faculty Development Associates
©2004 / 0-205-36017-3

The Effective, Efficient Professor:
Teaching, Scholarship and Service
Philip C. Wankat, Purdue University
©2002 / 0-205-33711-2

Emblems of Quality in Higher Education:
Developing and Sustaining High-Quality Programs
Jennifer Grant Haworth, Loyola University, Chicago and
Clifton F. Conrad, University of Wisconsin, Madison,
©1997 / 0-205-19546-6

Faculty of Color in Academe: Bittersweet Success
Caroline Sotello Viernes Turner, Arizona State University
and Samuel L. Myers Jr., University of Minnesota
©2000 / 0-205-27849-3

An Introduction to Interactive Multimedia
Stephen J. Misovich, Jerome Katrichis, David Demers, William B. Sanders, all of the University of Hartford
©2003 / 0-205-34373-2

Learner-Centered Assessment on College Campuses:
Shifting the Focus from Teaching to Learning
Mary E. Huba, Iowa State University and Jann E. Freed,
Central College
©2000 / 0-205-28738-7

The Online Teaching Guide: A Handbook of Attitudes,
Strategies, and Techniques for the Virtual Classroom
Ken W. White and Bob H. Weight, both of University of Phoenix
Online Faculty
©2000 / 0-205-29531-2

The Adjunct Professor's Guide to Success:
Surviving and Thriving in the College Classroom
Richard Lyons, Faculty Development Associates, Marcella L. Kysilka,
and George E. Pawlas, both of University of Central Florida
©1999 / 0-205-28774-3

Teaching Tips for College and University
Instructors: A Practical Guide
David Royse, University of Kentucky
©2001 / 0-205-29839-7

Advice for New Faculty Members
Robert Boice, Emeritus, SUNY Stony Brook
©2000 / 0-205-28159-1

Writing for Professional Publication:
Keys to Academic and Business Success
Kenneth Henson, The Citadel
©1999 / 0-205-28313-6

Teaching College in an Age of Accountability
Richard Lyons, Faculty Development Associates, Meggin McIntosh,
University of Nevada - Reno, and Marcella L. Kysilka, University of
Central Florida
©2003 / 0-205-35315-0

Save 20% on any of these resources when you order online...

www.ablongman.com/highered

Where the classroom comes to life!

What is MyLabSchool?

MyLabSchool is a suite of online tools designed to help your students make the transition from student to teacher. Our new **Lesson Builder** makes it easy to create standards-based lesson plans and our videos are organized by both subject and topic, putting the right information at your fingertips. With easily assigned material for class preparation, you save time out of your busy schedule, and our **new Instructor's Manual** makes integrating MyLabSchool into your course easy.

MyLabSchool is perfect for use in any course where video footage of classroom situations, standards integration, portfolio development and PRAXIS preparation is covered, MyLabSchool meets the individual teaching and learning needs of every instructor and every student. It saves you and your students time, and it helps increase success in your course. What's more, it's EASY!

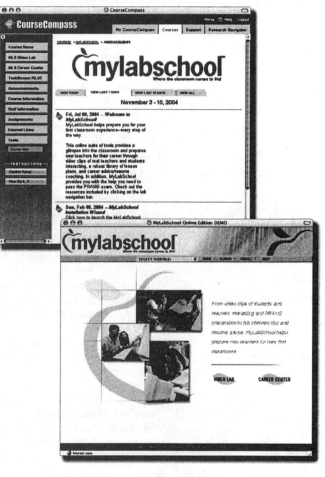

MyLabSchool is available with or without course management tools!

Interested in course management? MyLabSchool is also available in WebCT, Blackboard, and in CourseCompass, Allyn & Bacon's private label course management system.

One place. **Everything** your students need to succeed.
www.mylabschool.com

mylabschool™ — an incredible value!

Resource	Benefit to your Students	Value
MLS VideoLab & Observation Guide	Lets them **see students and teachers interacting in real classroom settings** and connect their observations to what they learn in your course.	$30.00
Research Navigator	Helps them conduct **effective online research** and write better papers.	$15.00
MLS Career Center	Gives them a complete guide to **developing electronic portfolios,** design advice, and a self-survey to help students brainstorm ideas as they plan, prepare, and evaluate their portfolios.	$13.00
	Prepares them for the **PRAXIS exam** with video case studies and practice tests.	$30.00
	Gives them the **advice** they need as they prepare to start their teaching careers.	$25.00
	Gives them access to a **database of proven lesson plans** from TeacherVision.com.	$20.00
MLS Lesson Builder	Guides them, step by step, through creating complete, **standards-based lesson plans**. Lesson Builder includes a comprehensive database of **state and national standards.**	$25.00
Case Archive	Enables them to search a collection of **real-classroom case studies**, drawn from Allyn & Bacon's top education textbooks.	$30.00
Resource Library	Offers them concise, practical information on **what every teacher should know** about eight critical topics, including the updated IDEA law, multicultural education, and classroom management.	$64.00

Total retail value of resources and content **$252.00**

Price of MyLabSchool bundled with an Allyn & Bacon textbook . . . . **FREE!**

Please visit **www.mylabschool.com**
for an online demonstration, or contact your
Allyn & Bacon representative for more information.

THE IRIS CENTER
FOR FACULTY ENHANCEMENT
Peabody College at Vanderbilt University

Enhance your course with these <u>free</u> online resources from IRIS!

 WHAT IS IRIS?
The IRIS Center for Faculty Enhancement is based at Vanderbilt University's Peabody College and supported through a federal grant. The goal of the IRIS Center is to create course enhancement materials for college faculty who teach pre-service general education teachers, school administrators, school counselors and school nurses.

WHAT RESOURCES DOES IRIS HAVE?
IRIS course enhancement materials are designed to better prepare school personnel to provide an appropriate education to students with disabilities. To achieve this goal, IRIS has created free course enhancement materials for college faculty in the following areas:

● Accommodations ● Behavior ● Collaboration ● Disability ● Diversity ● Instruction

These resources include online interactive modules, case study units, information briefs, student activities, an online dictionary, and a searchable directory of disability-related web sites. These resource materials are designed for use as supplements to college classes (e.g., homework assignments) or as in-class activities.

STAR LEGACY MODULES
Challenge-based interactive lessons are provided using *STAR Legacy* modules. The following is a list of some of the many modules available on the IRIS website:
- A Clear View: Setting Up Your Classroom for Students with Visual Disabilities
- Who's in Charge? Developing a Comprehensive Behavior Management System
- You're in Charge! Developing A Comprehensive Behavior Management Plan
- Addressing the Revolving Door: How to Retain Your Special Education Teachers
- What Do You See? Perceptions of Disability
- Teachers at the Loom: Culturally and Linguistically Diverse Exceptional Students
- See Jane Read: Teaching Reading to Young Children of Varying Disabilities

CASE STUDIES
IRIS case studies include three levels of cases for a given topic, with each level requiring higher-level analysis and understanding from students.
- Fostering Student Accountability For Classroom Work
- Effective Room Arrangement
- Early Reading
- Norms and Expectations
- Encouraging Appropriate Behavior
- Reading: Word Identification/Fluency, Grades 3-5
- Reading: Comprehension/Vocabulary, Grades 3-5

WEB RESOURCE DIRECTORY
These online directories help faculty members and college students to search by category to find information about websites on the special education or disability topic of their interest.

All IRIS materials are available to faculty at no cost through the
IRIS website <u>http://iris.peabody.vanderbilt.edu</u>
or on CD by request to the IRIS Center (1-866-626-IRIS).

Instructor's Resource Manual and Assessment Package

for

Slavin

Educational Psychology
Theory and Practice

Eighth Edition

prepared by

Emilie Wright Johnson
Lindenwood University

Catherine McCartney
Bemidji State University

Therese Olejniczak

PEARSON

Boston   New York   San Francisco
Mexico City   Montreal   Toronto   London   Madrid   Munich   Paris
Hong Kong   Singapore   Tokyo   Cape Town   Sydney

Table of Contents

PART ONE:

CHAPTER ANNOTATIONS
AND
RESOURCE REFERENCES

Chapter 1
Educational Psychology: A Foundation for Teaching

CHAPTER OVERVIEW

Chapter 1 introduces the student to the concepts associated with effective teaching and how educational psychology provides a theoretical research base for classroom instruction. The importance of skill development, critical thinking, and life-long learning through self-regulation is addressed in relevance to good teaching. Emphasis is given on the value of research not only as the foundation of good decision making, but also in providing a language by which educators can communicate. The text describes four kinds of educational research commonly used in educational psychology: experimental, descriptive, action research and correlational studies.

While good teaching has to be observed and practiced, there are principles of good teaching that can be taught. Effective teachers are critical thinkers, examining their own teaching practice, identifying and solving problems, and exploring new ideas. Effective teachers are intentional teachers. They believe that what they are doing makes a difference. They are constantly thinking about the outcomes of their lessons and remaining focused on individual student learning goals. They are flexible and include a wide range of methods and resources in their lessons. Intentional teachers take responsibility for their knowledge and skills, setting learning goals, monitoring their progress, assessing mastery of new knowledge, and continually redirecting the course of their own learning. They, in turn, teach their students to respect others, love learning, and accept personal responsibility.

Research in educational psychology focuses on learning and learners, and on teachers and teaching in order to apply principles of learning and teaching to the instructional process. Educational psychology uses objective methods to examine obvious (as well as less than obvious) questions about factors that contribute to learning. Educational researchers use various methods to learn about schools, teachers, students, and instruction.

CHAPTER–AT–A–GLANCE

Chapter Outline	Objectives	Supplements
1.1 What Makes a Good Teacher? • Knowing the Subject Matters (But So Does Teaching Skill) • Mastering the Teaching Skills • Can Good Teaching Be Taught? • The Intentional Teacher	• List characteristics of good teaching. • Identify specific skills of intentional teachers.	• Handout Master 1.1, 1.2, 1.3, 1.4, and 3.6 • Transparency T1 • Video Clip 1, *Veteran Teacher* • Test Bank Items
1.2 What is the Role of Research in Educational Psychology? • Goals of Research in Educational Psychology • The Value of Research in Educational Psychology to the Teacher • Teaching as Decision Making	• Explain how research in educational psychology is applied to teaching and give examples of research findings that contribute to effective teaching.	• Handout Master 1.4, 1.5. & 1.6 • Transparency T2 • Test Bank Items

• Research + Common Sense = Effective Teaching • Research on Effective Programs • Impact of Research on Educational Practice	• Consider the teacher's responsibility in using research to improve student learning and program evaluation.	
1.3 What Research Methods Are Used in Educational Psychology? • Experiments • Correlational Studies • Descriptive Research • Action Research	• Compare and contrast experimental, correlational, descriptive research and action research; provide an example of each type of research, and explain the differences between correlational and causal relationships.	• Transparency T3, T4, T5 • Test Bank Items
1.4 How Can I Become An Intentional Teacher? • Teacher Certification • Beyond Certification • Seek Mentors • Seek Professional Development • Talk Teaching • Talk Teaching on the Web • Keep up with Professional Publications and Associations.	• Become familiar with the requirements for Teacher Certification • Understand the importance of mentors and professional relationships and associations in the lifelong process of developing teacher effectiveness.	• Test Bank Items

ANNOTATED LECTURE OUTLINE

1.1 What Makes a Good Teacher?

Key Terms
> Educational psychology
> Pedagogy
> Intentionality
> Teacher efficacy
> Critical thinking

Lecture Notes and Discussion Questions

> **Discussion Question 1.1** Do good teachers make good students, or do good students make good teachers?

> **Discussion Question 1.2** How do teachers know that what they are doing makes a difference in their classrooms?

Post-Lecture Student Activities

> **Application 1.1** Have students reflect on what makes a good teacher using their own educational experiences. Ask them to brainstorm a list of qualities of good teachers. After reflecting on these qualities ask them to identify one teacher who was especially effective. Have students write a letter to this former teacher who had a positive impact on them. Students should include the specific characteristics of teacher effectiveness they recall this teacher demonstrating.

Application 1.2 Have students discuss, then reach class consensus on the following questions: What are the goals of education, real and ideal? What makes a teacher effective? How do you learn best? What do you hope to gain from this course?

Application 1.3 Using **(HM 1.4)**, assign students to observe a teacher.

Cooperative Learning 1.1 Using the letter written for Application 1.1, have students peer edit letters and discuss their reactions to the effective characteristics noted.

Cooperative Learning 1.2 Have students discuss in pairs or groups of three their experiences with both an effective teacher and a teacher they considered to be ineffective. Students should develop a list of characteristics of both effective and ineffective teachers and share with the class.

Cooperative Learning 1.3 Have students pair up with someone in the class they do not know well and spend 5 minutes interviewing each other about their favorite subject in school. Form groups of four and compare reasons for their choices of favorite subject.

Multicultural Awareness 1.1 Have students reflect on their own school experiences for a census of cultural diversity in their teachers. How many students had African American teachers? Asian American teachers? Hispanic teachers? Native American teachers? Is there a clear absence of cultural diversity in the teaching profession? Have students consider possible reasons why the profession lacks the diversity that is increasing in the student populations.

Multicultural Awareness 1.2 Considering the disparity in the presence of teachers from diverse ethnic backgrounds, have students reflect on the influence multiculturalism might have on teacher efficacy.

Reading 1.1 Beth Hurst, Cindy Wilson, and Genny Cramer, "Professional Teaching Portfolios: Tools for Reflection, Growth, and Advancement," *Phi Delta Kappan (78)(8) (1998)*.

Reading 1.2 Paulo Freire, *Teachers as Cultural Workers: Letters to Those Who Dare To Teach (The Edge: Critical Studies in Educational Theory)*, (1998). This is a brief (100 page) text that views cultural issues in education from the "other side." Freire states that his intention is to demonstrate that the task of teachers as cultural workers in the classroom is both joyful and rigorous. Teaching multicultural students requires seriousness and scientific, physical, emotional, and affective preparation. An excellent resource to look at the issues of welcoming multicultural students into the learning communities in today's schools.

Reading 1.3 Linda Darling-Hammond, "What Matters Most: A Competent Teacher for Every Child," *Phi Delta Kappan* 78, no. 3 (November 1996).

Reading 1.4 Noreen Connell, "Public Education," *Social Policy* (Spring, 1998). The author looks at social injustice issues faced by culturally minority students. She refers to the "stacked deck" that multicultural students encounter in American schools.

Reading 1.5 Cherry A. McGee Banks, "The Challenges of National Standards in a Multicultural Society," *Educational Horizons* (Spring, 1997). This article addresses the interests and needs of multicultural students in the mainstream classrooms where the debate on national standards is being emphasized.

Application 1.4 Refer to Chapter 3 **HM 3.6,** "Adolescent Perceptions of a Good Teacher Interview Guide." Assign these interviews and ask students to summarize and reflect upon Adolescents' Perceptions of a Good Teacher. Are the responses from the adolescents interviewed what the student expected? How so? What was surprising? What do the results of these interviews confirm about the idea of good teaching?

1.2 What is the Role of Research in Educational Psychology?

Key Terms
Principle
Theory

Lecture Notes and Discussion Questions

Critical Thinking 1.1 One of the criticisms of educational psychology is that it is merely common sense. Some believe that the findings of educational research are obvious. What is the danger of this kind of thinking?

Discussion Question 1.3 What distinguishes an intentional teacher from a "good" teacher? Are they the same? Is the use of critical thinking a variable?

Post-Lecture Student Activities

Research and Suggested Reading 1.1 For a real look at who teachers are and what they care about most, have students read A. Meek, "America's Teachers: Much to Celebrate." *Educational Leadership* 55(5), (February 1998).

1.3 What Research Methods Are Used in Educational Psychology?

Key Terms
Treatment
Theory
Variable
Experiment
Random assignment
Laboratory experiment
Internal validity
Randomized field experiment
Experimental group
Control group
External validity
Single-case experiment
Correlational study
Positive correlation
Negative correlation
Uncorrelated variables
Descriptive research
Action research

Lecture Notes and Discussion Questions

Critical Thinking 1.2 In a classroom discussion, have students describe a scientist. Then have them describe an artist. Consider the analogy of teaching as an art and as a science. How do good teachers whom students have known fit the "artist" or "scientist" description?

Critical Thinking 1.3 Have students list the types of skills that might be considered the "art" of teaching. Ask them to consider if they believe these types of skills can be taught to pre-service or practicing teachers? Why or why not? If so, how can they be taught?

Example 1.1 The educational researcher may experiment by changing a variable to see how this change will affect another variable. For example, she might change the amount of sleep students have before three tests (test 1, eight hours; test 2, six hours; test 3, four hours). What do you hypothesize will be the outcome? What else must be controlled?

Example 1.2 With correlational research, the relationship between the two variables is one of the following:

- As one increases, the other increases (positive correlation). Example of a finding: as the number of books a student reads in a year goes up, a student's reasoning achievement score goes up.
- As one increases, the other decreases (negative correlation). Example of a finding: as the teacher-child ratio in a class goes up, student attention goes down.
- They are not related (uncorrelated). Example of a finding: creativity in writing is not related to creativity in drawing.

Discussion Question 1.4 Educational psychologists have long debated whether laboratory research or field experiments are the most relevant and useful to education. What do you think prompts such debate?

Discussion Question 1.5 In looking at good teaching, can correlations be made between student types (cultural diversity, socio-economic status, learning differences, etc.) and effective teaching? What correlations might be made between school type (public, private, charter, home school, etc.) and effective teaching?

Discussion Question 1.6 Give examples of information a teacher would be seeking through action research.

Post-Lecture Student Activities

Application 1.5 Have students design a simple experiment to test the hypothesis that students who spend more hours doing homework have improved test performance.

Application 1.6 Have students cite examples of when an educational researcher might do a single-case experiment. Suggest what the resulting data would (and would not) indicate.

Application 1.7 Have students design a simple descriptive study to determine the types and extent of computer use in an elementary school.

Application 1.8 Ask students to indicate whether each of the following studies is descriptive or experimental.

- Researchers observe teachers of classes that have high achievement to determine how these teachers are alike. (descriptive)
- Teachers give three groups of impulsive children different types of training to determine which type of training is most effective in reducing impulsivity. (experimental)
- Researchers administer IQ tests to a group of boys and girls to determine whether a relationship exists between sex and verbal ability. (descriptive)
- Teachers instruct two similar groups of math students by two different methods to determine which method leads to higher scores on a math achievement test. (experimental)

Application 1.9 Have students interview local educators regarding frequency and types of action research conducted in classrooms.

Reading 1.6 Daniel Tanner, "The Social Consequences of Bad Research," *Phi Delta Kappan* (January 1998).

Application 1.10 Assign students the interviews: "Teachers Using Theory" (**HM 1.6**) Ask students to summarize and reflect upon their findings.

Cooperative Learning 1.4 Assign small group discussions of Application 1.11. Have students develop a list of questions regarding theories mentioned in the interviews. Answer these questions as part of a whole class lecture or discussion or assign them as outside research.

1.4 How Can I Become An Intentional Teacher?

Key Terms
Certified
Intentional
Teacher certification test or licensure test
INTASC
Praxis Series
Mentor

Lecture Notes and Discussion Questions
Discussion Question 1.7 What is the importance of being an intentional teacher?

Discussion Question 1.8 What are the necessary steps in becoming a certified teacher? Why is certification an important issue in the preparation of teachers?

Cooperative Learning 1.5 In pairs or small groups, students should develop a list of qualities they would like in a mentor. Have them also brainstorm a list of characteristics they should bring to a mentoring relationship—for example, open mindedness.

Post-Lecture Student Activities

Application 1.11 Ask students to review the website for the State Department of Elementary and Secondary Education for the state in which they seek certification. Ask them to prepare a list of requirements and to become familiar with the required teacher certification or licensure test.

Application 1.12 Assign students an article abstract from a professional journal and require bibliographic documentation.

Application 1.13 Ask students to research professional organizations that directly relate to their area of interest in education. Encourage them to become a member of any student organizations in their area.

SUGGESTED READINGS

Bigler, P. "A year spent as an ambassador for the profession brings recognition and new insights." *Educational Leadership* (57) (8) (2000): 49.

Burke, J. "How does a teacher surmount fatigue and regain the joy of teaching?" *Educational Leadership* (57) (8) (2000): 8.

Duck, L. "For beginners and the experienced, 12 recommendations for growth, whatever your teaching style." *Educational Leadership* (57) (8) (2000): 42.

Gall, J. P. *Applying Educational Research: A Practical Guide*, 4th ed. Boston: Longman, 1999.

Goddard, R. D. "Collective Efficacy: A Neglected Construct in the Study of Schools and Student Achievement." *Journal of Educational Psychology* (93) (3) (2001).

Hagstrom, D., R. Hubbard, C. Caryl Hurtig, P. Mortola, J. Ostrow, and V. White. "Writing a metaphor that reflects both your chosen work and your avocation can enrich your perspective." *Educational Leadership* (57) (8) (2000): 24.

McLaughlin, J. H., C. Watts, and M. Beard. "Just Because It's Happening Doesn't Mean It's Working: Using Action Research to Improve Practice in Middle Schools." *Phi Delta Kappan 82(4) (2000)*: 284.

Ness, M. "Lessons of a First-Year Teacher." *Phi Delta Kappan 82(9) (2000)*: 700.

Wubbels, T., J. Levy, and M. Brekelmans. "Paying Attention to Relationships." *Educational Leadership* (April 1997): 82–86.

SUGGESTED MEDIA

Institutional Reform and the Future of Schools, video, 30 minutes, 1996. This program looks at why parents and teachers must be left alone to develop the most effective ways of teaching. Host Terry Moe argues that schools must be taken out of politics, and solutions must come from those closest to the students. *From Insight Media.*

Sara Lightfoot, video, 30 minutes. Part of Bill Moyer's *World of Ideas* series. According to Sara Lightfoot, a professor of education at Harvard's Graduate School of Education, "the currency of a good teacher is ideas, as conveyed through relationships." Lightfoot describes what makes certain schools good and some teachers memorable. She highlights the problems and promise of U. S. schools and stresses the need to put learning back into teaching. *From PBS Video.*

Career Close-Ups: School Teacher, video, 27 minutes, 1994, examines the issue of classrooms becoming more dangerous and crowded. Teachers are challenged to find creative ways to motivate their students. Hosted by Whoopi Goldberg, this video profiles extraordinary teachers who entertain as they educate, tailoring their lessons to fit their students' interests. *From Insight Videos.*

The First Year, video, 90 minutes, 2001, follows four first-year teachers in their classrooms, exploring the triumphs and challenges of the profession. Each of the novice teachers reflects on their personal experiences in the classroom, with follow-up on their decisions to return for a second year, or to pursue other career options.

Teacher, video, 20 minutes, 1995, examines what it is really like to be a teacher. This program profiles seven high school teachers and one student teacher who discuss their vocations and roles as educators. It examines the personality and motivation needed to succeed and discusses educational requirements. *From Insight Media.*

American Schools: Catching Up to the Future, video, 30 minutes, 1996. This program raises the question, should American education be more skill-based? In this program Willard Daggett discusses why American schools need to improve instruction in the skills and knowledge necessary for success in today's technological, information-based society. *From Insight Media.*

Teaching the Teachers, video, 22 minutes, 1995. This video showcases a professional development school at which university faculty, current teachers, and student teachers work together in an environment similar to a teaching hospital. *From Insight Media.*

Electronic Companion in Statistics, CD-ROM, 1997. This CD-ROM uses animations, colorful interactive artwork, video segments, and narrations to study such topics in statistics as normal, probability, and sampling distributions; inference; statistical process control; regression; correlation; and the analysis of variance. Students can access topic reviews, quizzes, and a dictionary of terms. *Mac/Windows CD-ROM.*

Chapter 2
Theories of Development

CHAPTER OVERVIEW

This chapter focuses on both traditional and contemporary views of human development. It begins with a look at various issues and aspects of development, including a discussion of the nature-nurture controversy. Major theories of human development included in Chapter 2 are Piaget's and Vygotsky's theories of cognitive development, Erickson's theory of psychosocial development, and Kohlberg's theory of moral development.

Students are presented with the criticisms and revisions of Piaget's theory for relying exclusively on broad, fixed, sequential stages through which all children progress and for underestimating children's abilities. Neo-Piagetians attempt to modify Piaget's theory to overcome its limitations. Constructivist Vygotsky sees systems and relationships as more crucial to learning and development. His ideas of private speech and the zone of proximal development are discussed in detail.

The eight stages of Erikson's psychosocial development are presented with applications to elementary and secondary educational settings. Effective teaching requires an understanding of the characteristics of these stages and the developmental crises associated with each.

Psychologists find that children differ from adults not only in cognitive and personal development but also in their moral reasoning. Piaget's theory of moral development, heteronomous morality, and later autonomous morality are compared to Kohlberg's five stages of moral development. Limitations and implications of Kohlberg's theory point out that his research was initially based only on male subjects. Critics of Kohlberg's theory say that there may be little connection between what children say about moral reasoning and their actual moral behavior. The chapter concludes with how the intentional teacher would apply knowledge of developmental theory to improve teaching.

CHAPTER–AT–A–GLANCE

Chapter Outline	Objectives	Supplements
2.1 What Are Some Views of Human Development? • Aspects of Development • Issues of Development	• Give an overview of important factors involved in human development. • Identify the contributions of each of the following developmental theorists: Piaget, Vygotsky, Erikson, and Kohlberg.	• Handout Master 2.1 • Transparency T7 • Video Clip 2, *A Kolhberg Dilemma* • Test Bank Items
2.2 How Did Piaget View Cognitive Development? • How Development Occurs • Piaget's Stages of Development	• Identify the behaviors and thought processes of preschool, elementary school, middle school, and secondary school children in terms of Piaget's stages of development.	• Handout Master 2.2 • Transparency T8, T9, T10, T11, T12, T13 • Test Bank Items

2.3 How Is Piaget's Work Viewed Today? • Criticisms and Revisions of Piaget's Theory • Neo-Piagetian and Information-Processing Views of Development	• Evaluate the principles of Piaget's theory. • Apply Piagetian principles to appropriate teaching contexts.	
2.4 How Did Vygotsky View Cognitive Development? • How Development Occurs • Applications of Vygotskian Theory in Teaching	• Compare and contrast Vygotsky's views of cognitive development with those of Piaget. • Apply Vygotsky's theory to appropriate teaching contexts.	• Handout Master 2.3, 2.4 • Transparency T14 & T15 • Test Bank Items
2.5 How Did Erikson View Personal and Social Development? • Stages of Psychosocial Development • Implications and Criticisms of Erikson's Theory	• Identify the principles of Erikson's theory and apply them to individuals in each stage of psychosocial development. • Identify ways that teachers can influence positive psychosocial development in the classroom.	• Transparency T16, T17 • Test Bank Items
2.6 What Are Some Theories of Moral Development? • Piaget's Theory of Moral Development • Kohlberg's Stages of Moral Reasoning • Criticisms of Kohlberg's Theory	• Compare and contrast the views of Piaget and Kohlberg on the development of moral reasoning at each stage, and evaluate theories of moral development and their implications for teachers.	• Handout Master 2.5, 2.6 • Transparency T20, T21 • Test Bank Items

ANNOTATED LECTURE OUTLINE

2.1 What Are Some Views of Human Development?

Key Terms

Development
Continuous theory of development
Discontinuous theory of development

Lecture Notes and Discussion Questions

Critical Thinking 2.1 If continuous theories of development were accepted today, what would be the implications for the school curriculum?

Post-Lecture Student Activities

Reading 2.1 Robert Plomin and Stephen A. Petrill, "Genetics and Intelligence: What's New?" *Intelligence* (Jan.–Feb. 1997).

Reading 2.2 Frederick J. Morrison, et. al., "Nature-Nurture in the Classroom: Entrance Age, School Readiness, and Learning in Children," *Developmental Psychology* (March 1997).

Reading 2.3 Susan C. Nurrenbern, "Piaget's Theory of Intellectual Development Revisited," *Journal of Chemical Education* 78, no. 8 (Aug 2001): 1107-10.

2.2 How Did Piaget View Cognitive Development?

Key Terms

Cognitive development
Schemes
Adaptation
Assimilation
Accommodation
Equilibration
Constructivism
Sensorimotor stage
Reflexes
Object permanence
Preoperational stage
Conservation
Centration
Reversibility
Egocentric
Concrete operational stage
Inferred reality
Seriation
Transitivity
Class inclusion
Formal operational thought

Lecture Notes and Discussion Questions

Example 2.1 *Accommodation:* Assimilation occurs when a child whose mother owns a red station wagon first identifies every red car he sees as "Mommy's car." But one day he sees a red convertible sports car driven by his sitter, and his old way of classifying cars does not work. He changes his existing scheme (he accommodates it) to fit the new situation.

Example 2.2 *Object Permanence:* A child is playing with her father's keys. The father, thinking the keys may be unsanitary, puts them away in a traveling bag. The child, remembering where the keys were hidden, searches the bag, finds the keys, and resumes play.

Example 2.3 *Reversibility:* A young child with one sibling may demonstrate trouble with reversibility when asked the simple question "Do you have a brother (sister)?" Young children have difficulty reversing the situation and putting themselves in their sibling's position, so they usually reply, "No."

Example 2.4 *Egocentrism:* A young child may think the snow falls "so I can sled." When playing hide-and-seek, he may hide only his head because he thinks that if he can't see the seeker, the seeker cannot see him. Additionally, young children often believe that the moon follows them around or that the sun goes to sleep and gets up with them.

Critical Thinking 2.2 Class notes are often paraphrases of what the instructor actually said. Ask students to explain the roles of assimilation and accommodation in note taking.

Critical Thinking 2.3 Piaget contended that the most teachable moment for concepts is when a child is crossing from one developmental stage into the next. Give an example of such a teachable moment.

Critical Thinking 2.4 (1) A child's first toy is often a ball. The child learns to throw and bounce the ball with his/her parent. Later the child goes to Grandma's house and sees the pretty orange ball on the table. The child picks up the *orange* and throws it across the floor. Grandma admonishes the child for throwing the fruit. What concepts of Piaget's theory of cognitive development are demonstrated in this example? (2) The teacher asks the class to describe a ball, then to classify the ball by similar characteristics. If the main characteristic of a ball is that it is round, what happens in the schema when footballs are first introduced to the child? How about rugby balls? How many concepts in Piaget's theory are demonstrated in each of these tasks?

Discussion Question 2.1 What are the implications of the Piagetian stages for teaching new math or science concepts to second-graders and to eighth-graders?

Post-Lecture Student Activities

Application 2.1 Ask students to apply their knowledge of Piagetian theory in the following situation: You are a science teacher whose students have just begun to use formal operations. What developmental principles would you keep in mind while forming your lesson plans? What characteristics of children with concrete operations would you also consider?

Application 2.2 Have students imagine that they are teaching the concept of precipitation to third- and tenth-graders. How would their presentations and expectations differ for the two groups? In terms of cognitive development?

Cooperative Learning 2.1 Students often experience difficulties in translating Piagetian concepts and theories to practical teaching methods. In pairs (or with assigned learning partners), have them brainstorm teaching ideas that will capitalize on the cognitive characteristics of students they plan to teach.

Multicultural Awareness 2.1 As a reflection and journal-writing activity, ask students to consider the development of their schemes for understanding human diversity. Ask them to reflect on a fact, incident, or happening that made them rethink a stereotype and maybe change their minds. How do the concepts of schema, disequilibrium, assimilation, accommodation, and equilibration relate to their formation and rejection of stereotypes?

Reading 2.4 Have students read P. S. C. Matthews, "Problems with Piagetian Constructivism," *Science and Education* (January 1997).

Reading 2.5 Lorna C. Endler and Trevor Bond, "Cognitive Development in a Secondary Science Setting," *Research in Science Education* 30, no. 4 (2001): 403-16.

2.3 How Is Piaget's Work Viewed Today?

Post-Lecture Student Activities

Reading 2.6 Have students read Mary Ann Warrington and Constance Kamii, "Multiplication with Fractions: A Piagetian, Constructivist Approach," *Mathematics Teaching in the Middle School* (Feb. 1998). This article concludes that children will go much further with depth, pleasure, and confidence if they are allowed to construct their own mathematics to make sense to them every step of the way. Have students cite examples in their own learning where they have employed constructivism to assist in learning difficult tasks.

2.4 How Did Vygotsky View Cognitive Development?

Key Terms
Sign systems
Self-regulation
Private speech
Zone of proximal development
Scaffolding

Lecture Outline and Discussion Questions

Example 2.5 *Private speech:* A student doing a subtraction problem requiring regrouping may mentally say, "Borrow one ten from the tens group. Make sure I show that the tens group is now one lower. Now check my answer." Research indicates that children who use private speech learn similar tasks more effectively than do those who do not.

Post-Lecture Student Activities

Application 2.3 Using Vygotsky's principle of zone of proximal development, describe the difference between a child's independent reading level and his or her instructional reading level. List some strategies for instruction aimed at the zone of proximal development.

Application 2.4 Imagine a school for professional chefs. Describe the difference between an individual's independent cooking ability and the instructional level for the chef's program.

Application 2.5 Using Vygotsky's theory, have students diagram a seating arrangement to optimize scaffolding and peer assisted learning. Students should discuss whether these arrangements would be fluid and why or why not.

Reading 2.7 Have students read "From Presentation to Programming: Doing Something Different, Not the Same Thing Differently." This article by Cathleen Galas in *Learning and Leading with Technology* (Dec.–Jan. 1997-98) looks at using computer assisted instruction and computer simulation activities to move students from simple knowledge acquisition to a constructivist approach to learning. Students move from simply watching presentations to creating their own.

Reading 2.8 Antoine Alm-Lequeux, "Using the Internet as a Zone of Proximal Development for the Teaching of Indirect Speech: A Vygotskian Approach," *Unterrichtspraxis/Teaching German* 34, no. 1 (Spr 2001): 1-9.

Reflection/Journal Writing 2.1 Have students reflect on a situation in which they were expected to learn something they did not understand. Have them identify ways in which a teacher could have helped (or did help) them become ready for learning.

2.5 How Did Erikson View Personal and Social Development?

Key Terms
Psychosocial theory
Psychosocial crisis

Lecture Outline and Discussion Questions

Critical Thinking 2.5 What aspects of formal operational thought are helpful (or perhaps necessary) in achieving identity formation?

Post-Lecture Student Activities

Application 2.6 Using what you know about Erikson's Stage 1, why might you pick up or not pick up a baby every time he or she cries?

Application 2.7 Using what you know about Erikson's theory, why might a teacher choose to grade an elementary student's quiz paper as "+8" rather than "-2"?

Application 2.8 Identity v. Role Confusion begins in adolescence and continues throughout life. Have students make a list of ten relationships they have that influence their identity. For example, son, brother, employee, etc. To demonstrate that role identity continues throughout life, have them consider ten roles their parents may have as part of their adult identity. Compare lists in a class discussion.

Application 2.9 To better understand the eight stages of Erikson's theory of psychosocial development, have students anonymously identify people from family and friends who fit into each stage of development. A student might consider a family reunion and based on their knowledge of individuals in their family, decide whether family members have positive or negative psychosocial development in the appropriate stage. Have students justify their responses by citing characteristics of the individual in the identified stage.

Multicultural Awareness 2.2 For information on identity formation among minority-group and inner-city children, read M. B. Spencer and C. Markstom-Adams, "Identity Processes Among Racial-and Ethnic-Minority Children in America," *Child Development, 61,* (1990): 290-310; and S. B. Heath and M. W. McLaughlin, *Identity and Inner-city Youth: Beyond Ethnicity and Gender.* (New York: Teachers College, 1993).

2.6 What Are Some Theories of Moral Development?

Key Terms
Heteronomous morality
Autonomous morality
Moral dilemmas
Preconventional level or morality
Conventional level or morality
Postconventional level or morality
Empathic distress
Developmentally appropriate education

Post-Lecture Student Activities

Application 2.10 Assign students the "Parent Interviews on Moral Development" (**HM 2.5**). Following the interviews students should briefly summarize and reflect upon their findings.

Cooperative Learning 2.2 Students should discuss in small groups their findings from the Parent Interviews (**HM 2.5**) and develop a list of recommendations for parents based on their discussion.

Application 2.11 Assign students the "Character Education Teacher Interviews" (**HM 2.6**) and ask them to briefly summarize and reflect upon their findings.

Cooperative Learning 2.3 In small groups, students should discuss their findings from their Character Education Teacher Interviews and develop a list of classroom applications for their future classrooms.

Reading 2.9 Carol Gilligan's work focuses on gender differences in moral reasoning, the perception of violence, the resolution of sexual dilemmas, and abortion decisions. One of the gender biases Gilligan notes in Kohlberg's theory is his statement that the average female reaches Stage 3 (Good Boy-Good Girl), while males reach Stage 4 (Law and Order) and are more likely to move on to postconventional levels. According to Gilligan, men and women follow different voices. Read *Harvard Graduate School of Education Journal* (July/August 1990).

THEORY INTO PRACTICE

Classroom Applications of Erikson's Theory

Applying Erikson's theory to elementary and secondary education requires understanding the characteristics of Stage IV (industry versus inferiority) and Stage V (identity versus role confusion). Stage IV corresponds to the elementary school years (ages 6 to 12), and Stage V corresponds to the middle and high school years (ages 12 to 18).

- **Industry Versus Inferiority Crisis: Beginning Reading to Cursive Writing**

This stage of development consists of a wide range of social and academic challenges. Students begin this stage with a strong self-concept, a sense of self that has been filled with success. Upon starting school, the child adds an extremely important defining characteristic to his or her persona, that of belonging to a particular grade level. Almost all children enter kindergarten or first grade believing that they can and will learn. They fully expect to succeed in school (see Entwistle and Hayduk, 1981); however, the young child experiences for the first time a highly structured learning experience that may challenge these expectations.

Teachers need to promote a positive attitude toward learning, especially during these early school years. The focus should be on the learning style of each student: for instance, some are strong auditory learners, while others are more visual in their approach to learning. In creating a classroom environment that offers various options to the learner, the teacher is allowing each individual student to adapt to the structure of school.

Another element of this structure comes in the various forms of assessment applied to a child's skills. For the first time a child will receive a formal evaluation of performance on a regularly scheduled basis (a.k.a. "the report card"). Given the authority and influence that teachers possess, they must consider the impact their comments have on these young learners. Many school districts have modified the structure of the report card to reflect a more positive outlook on assessment and at the same time to be more specific about what is being evaluated. With the proper feedback, a teacher can enhance the child's self-concept.

- **Identity Versus Role Confusion Crisis: Who Am I? What Will I Be When I Grow Up?**

During this crucial stage of development, the adolescent is faced with a number of serious decisions that will impact his or her future. Remember that the whole idea of having to make decisions is novel to the teenager (see Baron and Brown, 1991). So, not only are these important decisions, but the teen has no experience to call upon for help in such matters.

The teen is faced with the enormous task of balancing the desire to be independent from parents and family with the desire to maintain membership in that same family and in a select peer group. Teens are faced with the question, "How can I be different from my family and friends and still fit in with them?" The adolescent student values the power to decide on topics to be studied within the curriculum, so here is an opportunity for teachers to assist the development of teens' decision-making skills without great cost. Adolescents will feel involved in their education and so this strategy will boost their self-confidence.

Although teachers tend to emphasize classroom curriculum, extracurricular activities and teachers' involvement in these activities begin to become important to the teenage student. The activities the student chooses provide another way for the teenager to define self-identity. Whether the choice is a sport or club, the student is making a statement about his or her interests. Teachers need to attend to students' interests and try, whenever possible, to make connections between these activities and what is happening in the classroom. For instance, the school variety show may give a particular student an opportunity to demonstrate a talent (for example, Irish Step Dancing) to both her peers and teachers. Teachers may draw on this hobby in social studies class when students discuss other cultures or in language arts class when they write about the customs of other peoples. In general, teenagers, who tend to be extremely self-conscience, will more willingly demonstrate the parts of their identities of which they are proud.

SUGGESTED READINGS

Berk, L. E. *Child Development,* 4th ed. Boston: Allyn & Bacon, 1997.

Bukatko, D., and M. W. Daehler. *Child Development: A Thematic Approach*, 3rd ed. Boston: Houghton Mifflin, 1998.

Cottom, C. "A Bold Experiment in Teaching Values." *Educational-Leadership* 53, no. 8 (1996): 54–58.

Dockett, Sue. "Constructing Understandings through Play in the Early Years." *International Journal of Early Years Education* 6, no. 1(1998): 105–16.

Glanzer, Perry L. "The Character to Seek Justice: Showing Fairness to Diverse Visions of Character Education." *Phi Delta Kappan* 79, no. 6 (1996): 434–36,438,448.

Glassman, Michael. "Dewey and Vygotsky: Society, Experience, and Inquiry in Educational Practice." *Educational Researcher* 30, no. 4 (May 2001): 3-14.

Houston, Paul D. "The Centrality of Character Education." *School Administrator* 55, no. 5 (1998): 6–8.

Meacham, Shuaib J. "Vygotsky and the Blues: Re-Reading Cultural Connections and Conceptual Development." *Theory into Practice* 40, no. 3 (Sum 2001): 190-97.

Pascual-Leone, Juan. "Is the French Connection Neo-Piagetian? Not Nearly Enough!" *Child Development* 71, no. 4 (Jul-Aug 2000): 843-45.

Shimoff, Eliot. "Piagetian Conservation in College Students: A Classroom Demonstration." *Teaching of Psychology* 25, no. 1 (1998): 48–49.

Steller, A. W. and W. K. Lambert. "Teach the Children Well." *Executive-Educator* 18, no. 6 (1996): 25–28.

Wolfgang, Charles H. "Another View on 'Reinforcement in Developmentally Appropriate Early Childhood Classrooms.'" *Childhood Education* 77, no. 2 (Win 2000-2001): 64-67.

"Your Children's Values. What Do Parents Need to Know?" *JN: Our-Children* 21, no. 3 (1996): 6–10.

SUGGESTED MEDIA

Adolescent and Adult Development, video, 30 minutes, 2001. This video investigates the central role of peer relationships in adolescent development and presents an overview of Kohlberg's theory of moral development. It examines Erikson's theory of the stages of life and describes Kubler-Ross' theory of the five stages of dying and death. *From Insight Media.*

Infant and Child Development, video, 30 minutes, 2001. This program examines how a newborn acquires the skills to interact with the surrounding world. It presents various theories of child development, focusing on Piaget's stage theory of cognitive development. *From Insight Media.*

Moral Development: Volume 1, video, 25 minutes, 1997. This video discusses the complexities of helping young people develop a sense of right and wrong, presenting key values that are fundamental to most moral codes. The program also present the principal theories of moral development, including psychoanalytic, sociobiological, social learning, and cognitive learning. *From Insight Media.*

Moral Development: Volume 2, video, 25 minutes, 1997. This tape examines the emergence of moral behavior from early infancy through adolescence, discussing the roles of parents, society, schools, and other institutions. The program also considers which experiences and environmental factors impede moral development. *From Insight Media.*

Moral Development in Children, video, 30 minutes, 1996. This program examines the role of values education in modern-day America. It features a discussion with Robert Coles on moral development in education, urging a closer look at the values parents and educators convey.

Chapter 3
Development During Childhood and Adolescence

CHAPTER OVERVIEW

Chapter 3 traces the development of physical and language abilities of children during the preschool years. The important aspects of socioemotional developments during early childhood are described, as well as alternative approaches to early childhood education. Comparative information is presented on daycare centers, nursery schools, compensatory preschool programs, early intervention activities, and kindergartens. Issues relating to the concept of developmentally appropriate practice are discussed.

The development of physical and cognitive abilities in elementary-age children, as well as the key characteristics of socioemotional growth is discussed in this chapter. Likewise, the key issues of physical, social, cognitive, and emotional development during adolescence is discussed, with particular interest in James Marcia's four identity statuses. Attention is given to the problems of adolescence and factors that place adolescents at risk. Finally, information in this chapter demonstrates to the student the relationship of development in childhood and adolescence to the major theories discussed in the previous chapter. Problems of adolescence are examined, with focus on the development of social relationships and responsible decision-making.

CHAPTER–AT–A–GLANCE

Chapter Outline	Objectives	Supplements
31. How Do Children Develop During the Preschool Years? • Physical Development in Early Childhood • Language Acquisition • Socioemotional Development	• Trace the development of physical and language abilities in preschool-age children; describe some important aspects of socioemotional development during early childhood, and relate this information to theories of development.	• Handout Master 3.1, 3.2, 3.4, and 3.5 • Video Clip 3, *Social Development: Learning to Interact with Others* • Test Bank Items
3.2 What Kinds of Early Childhood Programs Exist? • Daycare Programs • Preschools • Compensatory Preschool Programs • Early Intervention • Kindergarten Programs • Developmentally Appropriate Practice	• Consider the various options of early childhood education programs. • Describe alternative approaches to early childhood education and discuss issues relating to the concept of developmentally appropriate education.	• Test Bank Items

3.3 How Do Children Develop During the Elementary Years? • Physical Development During Middle Childhood • Cognitive Abilities • Socioemotional Development in Middle Childhood	• Trace the development of physical and cognitive abilities in elementary-age children. • Describe some key characteristics of socioemotional development during middle childhood, and relate this information to theories of development.	• Transparency T16, T18 • Test Bank Items • Handout Master 3.5
3.4 How Do Children Develop During the Middle School and High School Years? • Physical Development During Adolescence • Cognitive Development • Characteristics of Hypothetical-Deductive Reasoning • Socioemotional Development in Adolescence • Identity Development • James Marcia's Four Identity Statuses • Self-Concept and Self-Esteem • Social Relationships • Emotional Development • Problems of Adolescence	• Trace the development of physical and metacognitive abilities of adolescents. • Describe some key characteristics of socioemotional development during adolescence, relate this information to theories of development, and identify factors that may place adolescents at risk.	• Handout Master 3.3, 3.5 and 3.6 • Test Bank Items

ANNOTATED LECTURE OUTLINE

3.1 How Do Children Develop During the Preschool Years?

Key Terms
> Small muscle development
> Large muscle development
> Emergent literacy
> Whole language
> Peers
> Pro-social behaviors
> Solitary play
> Parallel play
> Associative play
> Cooperative play

Lecture Notes and Discussion Questions

> **Critical Thinking 3.1** How can teachers influence, both positively and negatively, the popularity and friendship development of students through the seating arrangements in their classrooms?

<u>**Post-Lecture and Student Activities**</u>

Application 3.1 Have students conduct the "Caregiver Interview" **(HM 3.5)** and write a brief summary of their experience and discoveries. What did they find surprising? Could they anticipate any of the answers to the interview questions? How do they feel about responses regarding how child rearing practices have changed over time?

Cooperative Learning 3.1 In small groups, have students share their findings from the "Caregiver Interview" **(HM 3.5)** and share highlights on preschool development with the class.

Application 3.2 Ask students to diagram a seating arrangement that would promote positive student interaction and optimize learning. Students should include placement of the chalkboard and the teacher's desk and presentation area in their diagrams. Will they include an area for "time out" or social isolation? Why or why not? Have students include a brief, written justification of the arrangement.

Multicultural Awareness 3.1 Have students read Carol Seefeldt and Alice Galper, "Lessons from the Ukraine." *Childhood Education* (Spring 1998). This is an account of two American University professors who spent time in the Ukraine conducting workshops for preschool teachers. Concludes with lessons to be learned from the Ukraine.

Multicultural Awareness 3.2 Johnetta Wade Morrison and Tashel Bordere, "Supporting Biracial Children's Identity Development," *Childhood Education* 77, no. 3 (Spr 2001): 134-38.

Reading 3.1 Ho Worthy and James Hoffman, "Critical Questions," *Reading Teacher* (Dec.–Jan. 1997-1998). Discusses whether children who have had limited literacy experiences should start reading in whole-language readers and/or trade books or whether they should start in controlled-vocabulary preprimers.

Reading 3.2 Have students read Katy Roberson, "Very Important Preschoolers," *Educational Leadership* (Dec.–Jan. 1997-1998). This article describes a model program for preschoolers in the South Bay Union School District, CA, with impressive comparative results.

Reading 3.3 Saigeetha Jambunathan and Janet A. Norris, "Perception of Self-Competence in Relation to Language Competence among Preschoolers," *Child Study Journal* 30, no. 2 (2000): 91-101.

Reflection and Journal Writing 3.1 Have students reflect on play activities in their childhood by writing about a single incident or day they can remember. Have them describe the activity, the participants, the toys or props, and the feelings associated with the play. Sharing this writing is an interesting activity to increase awareness of cultural and geographic difference among students in the classroom.

3.2 What Kinds of Early Childhood Education Programs Exist?

<u>**Key Terms**</u>

Readiness training
Compensatory preschool programs
Early intervention programs

<u>**Lecture Notes and Discussion Questions**</u>

Critical Thinking 3.2 The issue of daycare is a controversial one for education, partly because educators both provide and use daycare. What is the optimal time for a mother to return to work after a child is born? Should fathers take time off from work to spend time with newborns? What are the possible positive and negative side effects of daycare?

Multicultural Awareness 3.3 Wayne P. Thomas and Virginia P. Collier suggest that educators should develop bilingual programs for all students where students in both languages serve as peer tutors for each other. Implications are that bilingual English learners outperform monolingual students on academic tests. "Two Languages Are Better Than One," *Educational Leadership* (Dec.–Jan. 1997–1998).

Post-Lecture Student Activities

Reading 3.4 "A Decade of School-Based Child Care" summarizes a model program introduced by Yale University's Edward Zigler, the School of the 21st Century. The decade-old program now operates in 500 schools in 17 states. The article by Erin Deemer, Laura Desimone, and Maria Finn-Stevenson appears in *Principal* (Jan 1998).

Reading 3.5 Robert Slavin, "Can Education Reduce Social Inequality?," *Educational Leadership* (Dec.–Jan. 1997-1998), considers academic performance differences among children from varied socioeconomic and ethnic backgrounds. Early-intervention strategies and programs such as Success for All and Reading Recovery hold promise for all children.

Reading 3.6 Carolyn R. Pool, "A Safe and Caring Place," *Educational Leadership* (Dec.–Jan. 1997-1998), reviews a community preschool program in Alexandria, Virginia, that serves over 125 low-income children and their families. The four schools use developmentally appropriate practices, enable parent/community involvement, provide for client health and nutrition needs, and provide easy referrals to social services.

3.3 How Do Children Develop During the Elementary Years?

Key Terms
> Self Concept
> Self-esteem
> Social comparison

Lecture Notes and Discussion Questions

Multicultural Awareness 3.4 *DUSO-Revised: Developing Understanding of Self and Others.* In this program for elementary students are storybooks, audiocassettes, puppets, activities, and a teacher's guide. Topics covered include appreciating individual differences, social skills, making choices, recognizing the consequences of action, communication, and awareness of feelings. American Guidance Service (Publishers' Building, Circle Pines, MN 55014-1796, phone 800-328-2560, in Minnesota 800-247-5053).

Post-Lecture Student Activities

Application 3.3 Have students conduct the "Caregiver Interview" **(HM 3.5)** and write a brief summary of their experience and discoveries. What did they find surprising? Could they anticipate any of the answers to the interview questions? What insights did their caregivers share regarding development during the elementary years? Can they make any recommendations to classroom teachers based on their findings?

Cooperative Learning 3.2 In small groups, have students share their findings from the "Caregiver Interview" **(HM 3.5)** and share highlights regarding the elementary years with the class.

Application 3.4 Have students observe the communication patterns of a small group of early elementary school children. How much real group interaction takes place as compared to more egocentric language? Is imaginary play involved in the group communication?

3.4 How Do Children Develop During the Middle School and High School Years?

Key Terms
> Puberty
> Reflectivity
> Foreclosure
> Identity diffusion
> Moratorium
> Identity achievement

Lecture Notes and Discussion Questions

Critical Thinking 3.3 Research on early and late maturation shows that early-maturing males seem to be more readily accepted by their peers than are early-maturing females. What can education do to help early-maturing adolescent girls weather this difficult transition?

Critical Thinking 3.4 Ask students in what ways a failure to resolve earlier crises might be manifested in an adolescent who is attempting to establish an identity. For example, how might a failure to develop trust (autonomy, initiative, industry) hinder an adolescent in the identity versus role confusion stage of development?

Critical Thinking 3.5 Have your students debate the following viewpoints: a. To establish their identity, adolescents need to separate themselves from their parents so that they can discover who they are, other than being their parents' children. If parents are very strict and controlling, children have to give so much energy to establishing the separation that they don't have the time and effort to give to defining their own identity. For this reason, parents and teachers of adolescents would be more helpful if they were lenient with teenagers. b. Adolescents are similar to large 2-year-olds in that they are egocentric and exhibit out-of-bounds behavior. They are in a transition stage with no clear-cut standards of behavior, since they are neither child nor adult. For this reason, parents and teachers of adolescents should be strict and impose rules to help a teenager make the transition easily and safely.

Discussion Question 3.1 What do you feel are the implications of being relatively small in size in elementary school? Would the effects, if any, differ for girls and boys?

Discussion Question 3.2 Why do you think Erikson called for a psychosocial moratorium in adolescence?

Discussion Question 3.3 Delinquency, emotional disorders, substance abuse, and teen pregnancy each represent a desperate cry for help. Teachers cannot ignore these cries; they need to risk involvement. What are your feelings about accepting an active role? What are the risks?

Post-Lecture Student Activities

Application 3.5 Have students conduct the "Caregiver Interview" **(HM 3.5)** write a brief summary of their experience and discoveries. What did they find surprising? Could they anticipate any of the answers to the interview questions? Did their caregivers share any insights regarding development during adolescence? Can they make any recommendations to secondary teachers based on their findings?

Cooperative Learning 3.3 In small groups, have students share their findings from the "Caregiver Interview" **(HM 3.5)** and share highlights on adolescent development with the class.

Application 3.6 Using the "Adolescent Perceptions of a Good Teacher" (**HM 3.6**), have students conduct several interviews of adolescents and prepare a brief summary of their findings. Are they surprised by what they learned? In what way are adolescents the best source of information on teacher effectiveness? Should they use caution in interpreting adolescent responses to the interview? Why or why not?

Cooperative Learning 3.4 Using the results from the Adolescent Interviews (**HM 3.6**) have students discuss in small groups what they believe adolescents want in a teacher. They can share their results with the class by making a "wanted poster" listing these characteristics.

Multicultural Awareness 3.5 Carrie Rothstein-Fisch, Patricia M. Greenfield, and Elise Trumbull, "Bridging Cultures with Classroom Strategies," *Educational Leadership*, 56 (7): 68–71. The authors assert that assigning children to tell stories while working in pairs will help to address the collective orientation of Latino children.

Multicultural Awareness 3.6 What might be some unique identity or self-concept issues for students who grow up in bilingual households? Ask students who have routinely used more than one language or dialect how this affected their sense of self.

Reading 3.7 Jean Whitney-Thomas and Mairead Moloney, "'Who I Am and What I Want': Adolescents' Self-Definition and Struggles," *Exceptional Children* 67, no. 3 (Spr 2001): 375-89.

Reading 3.8 Gloria S. Wald, "Moving From 'I Think I Can' to 'I Know I Can.'" *Young Children* 55, no. 4 (Jul 2000): 14-15.

Reading 3.9 Meg Kierman, "The Children's Charter." A seventh grader asks, how can we make TV better? *Educational Leadership* 56 (5) (April 1999): 69.

Reading 3.10 Jay Feldman and Peter Gray, "Some Educational Benefits of Freely Chosen Age Mixing Among Children and Adolescents," *Phi Delta Kappan* 80(7) (March 1999): 507–513.

Reflection and Journal Writing 3.2 Ask students to reflect on their friendships in elementary school. How were friendships different than in later years?

SUGGESTED READINGS

Berk, L. E. *Child Development,* 4th ed. Boston: Allyn & Bacon, 1997.

Bukatko, D. and M. W. Daehler. *Child development: A Thematic Approach.* Boston: Houghton Mifflin, 1998.

Collins, Janet. "Are You Talking to Me? The Need To Respect and Develop a Pupil's Self-Image." *Educational Research* 42, no. 2 (Sum 2000): 157-66.

Conard, FranCina and J. William Asher, "Self-Concept and Self-Esteem through Drama: A Meta-Analysis." *Youth Theatre Journal* 14 (2000): 78-84.

Hanson, D. T. "Understanding Students." *Journal of Curriculum and Instruction* 14 (2) (1999).

Verschueren, Karine, Petra Buyck, and Alfons Marcoen. "Self-Representations and Socioemotional Competence in Young Children: A 3-Year Longitudinal Study." *Developmental Psychology* 37 no. 1 (Jan 2001): 126-34.

SUGGESTED MEDIA

The First Years of Life, video, 28 minutes. Newborn and even unborn babies possess abilities that can be observed, measured, and developed. During their first year, infants use skills developed before birth to help them interact with their surroundings. This program examines how infants see and hear, when they are first able to perceive a total image of their mother, and how individuality develops. *From Films for the Humanities and Sciences.*

The First Years: What to Expect, video, 19 minutes. This program covers the critical parent/child relationship in the first 5 years, the effects in adolescence of traits learned in early childhood, how faulty parent-child bonding affects children as they mature, and how parent enrichment classes help parents produce "super-babies." *From Films for the Humanities and Sciences.*

Failures before Kindergarten, video, 28 minutes. Discuss the debate on the screening of preschool children to determine whether they are ready for admission to kindergarten. This specially adapted *Donahue* program discusses the pros and cons of assessing the educational readiness of such young children. Panelists include a teacher who kept back an entire first-grade class. *From Films for the Humanities and Sciences.*

Middle Childhood: Cognitive and Language Development, video, 29 minutes, 1997. This video examines Piaget's theory of concrete operational development and the theory of information processing. It looks at the language abilities of the school-aged child and probes the function of the school in cognitive development, discussing mainstreaming, bilingual education, and standardized assessment tests. *From Insight Media.*

Middle Childhood: Social and Emotional Development, video, 28 minutes, 1997. This program examines how children develop a sense of self and looks at the growth in social cognition. It discusses how changes in family structure affect social development, explores the influence of the peer group, and probes the role of the school in social and emotional development. *From Insight Media.*

Imagine a School: Montessori for Elementary-Age Children, video, 13 minutes. Showing scenes from the urban public schools and one suburban private school, this video shows how the Montessori method is applied at the elementary level. It introduces some of the basic elements of Montessori schools: the use of hands-on materials, self-paced/self-initiated learning, and the presence of a multi-age community of learners. *Insight Media*

Bridge to Adulthood: A Montessori Middle School Model, video, 21 minutes. This video takes viewers inside two model Montessori middle schools. It shows how the schools are based on research and careful observation, with every aspect of the curriculum designed to meet a student's unique needs. *Insight Media.*

Nurturing the Love of Learning: The Montessori Model, video, 9 minutes. Showing children ages three to six, this video introduces the Montessori method of education. Viewers see how children work with hands-on materials that stimulate all of the senses. The video also shows how a Montessori classroom is organized, explaining that multiage grouping is the norm and that competitive pressures are discouraged. *From Insight Media.*

Chapter 4
Student Diversity

CHAPTER OVERVIEW

The complete array of variables that constitute student diversity are presented in Chapter 4. The impact of culture on student learning is discussed with examples of how teachers can address multicultural issues in the classroom. The link between income and achievement is addressed in a discussion on how socioeconomic status affects student academic behavior. The role of schools as middle-class institutions and the role of child-rearing practices as they impact teaching are discussed. A discussion of school and community factors that influence learning is included in this chapter.

Along with the issues of multiculturalism, information is presented on ethnicity and race in relation to student performance. Statistics on the ethnic and racial composition of the United States are given. The academic achievement of students from under-represented groups and the effect of school desegregation precede a section on how language differences and bilingual programs affect student performance.

A final look at multiculturalism is presented with attention given to the broad encompassing features of this issue in school policies and practice. Students are challenged to consider how the outcomes of education might be improved not only for students of different ethnic, social class, and religious backgrounds, but also of different genders and exceptionalities. Bilingual education initiatives are reviewed as part of a discussion on multicultural curricular issues.

Gender and gender bias as they affect students' school experiences are discussed in the context of sex-role stereotyping. Do males and females think and learn differently? Information on differences in intelligence and learning styles follows, with questions raised on the origins and definitions of intelligence, and theories of aptitude-treatment interactions.

CHAPTER–AT–A–GLANCE

Chapter Outline	Objectives	Supplements
4.1 What is the Impact of Culture on Teaching and Learning?	• Discuss several impacts of culture on student learning.	• Handout Master 4.1, 4.2 • Transparency T38, T39 • Test bank items
4.2 How Does Socioeconomic Status Affect Student Achievement? • The Role of Child-Rearing Practices • The Link Between Income and Summer Learning • The Role of Schools as Middle-Class Institutions • School and Community Factors • Is the Low Achievement of Lower-Class Children Inevitable? • Implications for teachers	• Explain how socialized values and normative expectations in schools reflect social class, and how low socioeconomic status may place students at risk of school failure. • Consider the variables associated with at-risk students and suggest ways that communities can provide opportunities for these students that will improve student achievement.	• Handout Master 4.5 • Transparency T40 • Test bank items
4.3 How Do Ethnicity and Race Affect Students' School Experiences?	• Explain how differences in academic achievement among racial and ethnic	• Video Clip 4, *Multiple Intelligence* • Transparency T41

• Racial and Ethnic Composition of the United States • Academic Achievement of Students from Under-represented Groups • Why Have Students from Under-represented Groups Lagged in Achievement? • Effects of School Desegregation	groups can be traced to long-term social and economic inequalities.	• Test Bank Items
4.4 How Do Language Differences and Bilingual Programs Affect Student Achievement? • Bilingual Education • English Immersion • Transitional Bilingual Education • Paired Bilingual Education • 2 Way Bilingual Education	• Discuss the impact of language differences on teaching and learning, and evaluate different approaches to bilingual education.	• Video Clip 5, *Bilingual education* • Transparency T43 • Test bank items
4.5 What is Multicultural Education? • Dimensions of Multicultural Education	• Define multicultural education, and give examples of ways teachers can meet the goals of multicultural education in the classroom.	• Video Clip 6, *Nappy Hair Controversy* • Transparency T44 • Test bank items
4.6 How Do Gender and Gender Bias Affect Students' School Experiences? • Do Males and Females Think and Learn Differently? • Sex-Role Stereotyping and Gender Bias	• Discuss the impact of gender differences on school experiences and achievement, and give examples of ways teachers can detect and avoid gender bias in the classroom.	• Handout Master 4.4 • Transparency T42 • Test bank items
4.7 How Do Students Differ in Intelligence and Learning Styles? • Definitions of Intelligence • Origins of Intelligence • Theories of Learning Styles • Aptitude-Treatment Interactions	• Compare and contrast different theories of intelligence, discuss the significance of debates about the origins of intelligence in relation to education, and give examples of learning style differences and ways teachers can accommodate such differences. • How do aptitude-treatment interactions correlate to improved student achievement?	• Transparency T24, T25 • Test bank items

ANNOTATED LECTURE OUTLINE

4.1 What Is the Impact of Culture on Teaching and Learning?

Key Terms
    Culture

<u>**Lecture Notes and Discussion Questions**</u>

Multicultural Awareness 4.1 What are some specific ways in which cultural differences influence the ways students approach learning tasks? Are these evident in the classroom?

<u>**Post-Lecture Student Activities**</u>

Reflection and Journal Writing 4.1 Stories told in families can play an important role in transmitting culture, values, and knowledge to children as they grow up. Have students reflect on and record in their journals one story they remember being told as a child that exemplifies one of these transmissions.

Research and Suggested Reading 4.1 James and Cherry McGee Banks provide a comprehensive guide for teachers to examine the cultures of their students and the biases in their own teaching. J. A. Banks and C. M. Banks, *Multicultural Education: Issues and Perspectives*, 3rd ed. (Boston: Allyn & Bacon, 1997). Another good resource is K. Cushner, A. McClelland, and P. Safford, *Human Diversity in Education,* 3rd ed. (New York: McGraw-Hill, 1998).

4.2 How Does Socioeconomic Status Affect Student Achievement?

<u>**Key Terms**</u>
Socioeconomic status

<u>**Lecture Notes and Discussion Questions**</u>

Warm-up Distribute (**HM 4.4**) "School, Family and Community Partnerships." Ask students to brainstorm ways to increase communication and collaboration between school, families and community. Students should record ideas directly on the concept map and continue to use the concept map for note taking.

Application 4.1 All students return from summer vacation with decreased academic levels of achievement. However, the decrease is greater for low-income students than for middle-class children. What conditions contribute to this difference?

Cooperative Learning 4.1 Using the material from the (**HM 4.2**), ask students to pair up with a partner and think collaboratively about potential areas of cultural conflict in the classroom. Compare results of the discussion pairs to reach class consensus on areas of potential cultural conflict.

Discussion Question 4.1 Why does the school achievement of low-income students fall below that of middle- and upper-income students?

Discussion Question 4.2 What can be done to make lower-income home environments more educationally stimulating for young children? What kinds of parent training might be effective? What kinds of early intervention programs might be effective?

Discussion Question 4.3 If family background is a key factor in explaining differences in student achievement, then it follows that involving families in their children's educations can be part of the solution. How might you involve families?

<u>**Post-Lecture Student Activities**</u>

Application 4.2 List the ways you will try to involve and invite family and community into your classroom.

Cooperative Learning 4.2 In small groups have students brainstorm interventions mentioned in the text that can positively impact academic achievement of children from low socioeconomic backgrounds.

Application 4.3 Promoting 2 way communication is a key to fostering positive school/family relationships. Draft a letter of introduction to your future students and their families. Outline ways you will communicate throughout the year and ways parents may contact and communicate with you.

Reading 4.1 M. Donald Thomas and William L. Bainbridge, "'All Children Can Learn': Facts and Fallacies." *Phi Delta Kappan* 82, no. 9 (May 2001): 660-62.

Reading 4.2 Jennifer A. Bell, "High-Performing, High-Poverty Schools," *Leadership* 31, no. 1 (Sep.-Oct. 2001): 8-11.

4.3 How Do Ethnicity and Race Affect Students' School Experiences?

Key Terms
    Ethnic group
    Ethnicity
    Race
    Minority-group

Lecture Notes and Discussion Questions

Discussion Question 4.4 Should the following types of books or learning materials be eliminated from school library shelves?
- Those using stereotypical dialects
- Those using pictures of work or activities that stereotype by race or gender
- Those found offensive by one ethnic or gender group

Discussion Question 4.5 What kinds of activities can you use in classes you plan to teach that will promote a sense of "we" and reduce a sense of "us and them"?

Post-Lecture Student Activities

Reading 4. 3 Have students read D. J. Menkart, "Deepening the Meaning of the Heritage Months," *Educational Leadership* 56(7) (April 1999): 19–22. This article raises the question of how to get beyond the annual celebrations that feature food and festivities to enrich students' understanding of values, history, and struggles for freedom.

Reading 4.4 Have students read H. M. Halford, "A Different Mirror: A Conversation with Ronald Takaki," *Educational Leadership* 56(7) (April 1999): 8–14. Historian Takaki discusses the direction of multicultural education and our nation's complex racial and ethnic climate.

Reflection and Journal Writing 4.2 Have students reflect on their own educational histories and recall an experience when they had a teacher from another cultural or ethnic background. Did this teacher bring unique values and skills to the learning setting? How did these affect you? How did they influence you?

Research and Suggested Reading 4.2 For a discussion of issues related to the components of programs that help to prevent, abate, and heal racism in schools and society, have student read S. Parks, "Reducing the Effects of Racism in Schools," *Educational Leadership* 56(7) (April 1999): 14–19.

4.4 How Do Language Differences and Bilingual Programs Affect Student Achievement?

Key Terms
Language minority
Limited English proficient (LEP)
English as a second language (ESL)
Bilingual education
English Immersion
Transitional Bilingual Education
Paired Bilingual Education
Two-Way Bilingual Education

Post-Lecture Student Activities

Reading 4.5 Have students examine the arguments for beginning to teach English earlier and phasing out native language learning sooner by reading R. Gersten, "The Changing Face of Bilingual Education," *Educational Leadership* 56(7) (April 1999): 41–46.

Reading 4.6 Pedro Reyes and Andrea Rorrer, "U.S. School Reform Policy, State Accountability Systems and the Limited English Proficient Student," *Journal of Education Policy* 16, no. 2 (Mar-Apr 2001): 163-78.

Reading 4.7 Luis C. Moll, Ruth Saez, and Joel Dworin, "Exploring Biliteracy: Two Student Case Examples of Writing as a Social Practice," *Elementary School Journal* 101, no. 4 (Mar 2001): 435-49.

Research and Suggested Reading 4.3 For further discussion on language-minority students, have students read B. Alejandro and C. Roseberry-McKibbin, "Turning Frustration into Success for English Language Learners," *Educational Leadership* 56(7) (April 1999): 53–56.

4.5 What Is Multicultural Education?

Key Terms
Multicultural education
Content integration
Knowledge construction
Prejudice reduction
Equity pedagogy
Empowering school culture

Lecture Notes and Discussion Questions

Critical Thinking 4.1 Have student debate the issue "Should school curricula emphasize skills, knowledge, and values of a common culture or emphasis authentic heritage and values?" As a resource, have them read Gisele A. Waters, "ESL Policy and Practice: A Linguistic Human Rights Perspective," *Clearing House* 74, no. 6 (Jul-Aug 2001): 296-300.

Critical Thinking 4.2 In the United States, both legally and socially, there have been long-standing efforts to promote equal educational opportunities for all children regardless of race, ethnicity, socioeconomic status, gender, religion, or disability. Ask students in what ways these efforts have been successful or unsuccessful. What are the persistent obstacles to equal educational opportunities?

Multicultural Awareness 4.2 What are some specific ways in which cultural differences influence the ways students approach learning tasks? Are these evident in the classroom?

Post-Lecture Student Activities

Application 4.4 Have students brainstorm ways they will embrace cultural diversity in their classroom. Create a graphic organizer on the board making connections between the school, home and community.

Application 4.5 One way to overcome cultural differences is to develop a sense of community in the classroom or to become a community of learners. As a teacher, how will you nurture this climate of learning and promote a sense of belonging to a shared community?

Reading 4.8 R. Burroughs, "From the Margins to the Center: Integrating Multicultural Literature into the Secondary English Curriculum," *Journal of Curriculum and Supervision* 14(2) (Winter 1999).

Research and Suggested Reading 4.4 Have students brainstorm how best to prepare themselves for multicultural classrooms they will likely encounter in the future. For an overview of professional preparation for multicultural teaching, have them read Johann Le Roux, "Effective Teacher Training for Multicultural Teaching." *MCT* 19, no. 2 (Spr 2001): 18-22.

4.6 How Do Gender and Gender Bias Affect Students' School Experiences?

Key Terms
Sex-role behavior
Gender bias

Lecture Notes and Discussion Questions

Critical Thinking 4.3 Have students consider the gender ratio in the classes in which they are currently enrolled. Then, consider the gender profile of faculty and administrators of their school. Have them reflect on their high school experience using the same questions. Compare their findings with information in the text. Have them read Michele Knox, Jeanne Funk, Robert Elliott, and Ellen Greene Bush, "Gender Differences in Adolescents' Possible Selves." *Youth & Society* 31, no. 3 (Mar 2000): 287-309.

Discussion Question 4.6 It is generally assumed that some communities (e.g., rural, agriculture-based, non-industrialized, conservatively religious, or immigrant) wish to maintain traditional sex-role behavior for their children. Do you have any experience that would support or refute these assumptions?

Post-Lecture Student Activities

Reading 4.9 For a discussion about gender equity today and updates on gender bias in schools, have students read D. Sadker, "Gender Equity: Still Knocking at the Classroom Door," *Educational Leadership* 56(7) (April 1999): 22–28.

Research and Suggested Reading 4.5 For an interesting look at the effect of siblings on gender issues, have students read Susan M. McHale, Kimberly A. Updegraff, Heather Helms-Erikson, and Ann C. Crouter, *Sibling Influences on Gender Development in Middle Childhood and Early Adolescence: A Longitudinal Study* (2001).

Research and Suggested Reading 4.6 Have students consider differences in academic achievement when considering gender as a variable after reading Thomas Cloer, Jr. and Shana Ross Dalton, "Gender and Grade Differences in Reading Achievement and in Self-Concept as Readers," *Journal of Reading Education* 26, no. 2 (Win 2001): 31-36.

4.7 How Do Students Differ in Intelligence and Learning Styles?

<u>**Key Terms**</u>
> Intelligence
> Intelligence quotient
> Multiple intelligences
> Learning styles
> Field dependence
> Field independence
> Aptitude-treatment interaction

<u>**Lecture Notes and Discussion Questions**</u>

Warm-up Ask students to list the names students give to various academic groups perceived as high or low achievers—for example low achievers may be referred to as "flunkies". What labels have they heard teachers use to refer to different level learners? What are the implications for students who have been given labels?

Discussion Question 4.6 What are the risks to the student of categorizing students by intellectual ability? To the teacher? To the social climate of the school?

Multicultural Awareness 4.3 Glauco De Vita, "Learning Styles, Culture and Inclusive Instruction in the Multicultural Classroom: A Business and Management Perspective," *Innovations in Education and Teaching International* 38, no. 2 (May 2001): 165-74.

<u>**Post-Lecture Student Activities**</u>

Application 4.6 Have students develop a list of classroom activities that address each of the Eight Intelligences. Write suggestions on the chalkboard making connections between content areas.

Reflection and Journal Writing 4.3 Have students reflect on their own cognitive styles.
- Do I seem more field dependent or field independent?
- Am I more impulsive or reflective?
- What are my learning preferences for lighting, seating, noise levels, and time of day?
- Would I choose to work alone or with peers?
- With what mix of auditory, tactile, or visual material do I learn best?
- Are my learning styles effective for me as a learner? As a teacher?

Research and Suggested Reading 4.7 Rebecca Sanchez, "How To Start Somewhere When They All Learn Differently." *Exercise Exchange* 46, no. 2 (Spr 2001): 3-5.

Research and Suggested Reading 4.8 Regina A. Kapusnick and Christine M. Hauslein, "The 'Silver Cup' of Differentiated Instruction." *Kappa Delta Pi Record* 37, no. 4 (Sum 2001): 156-59.

SUGGESTED READINGS

Balfanz, Robert and Doug Mac Iver. *Transforming High-Poverty Urban Middle Schools into Strong Learning Institutions: Lessons from the First Five Years of the Talent Development Middle School.* (2000).

Banks, J. A. and C.A.M. Banks, *Multicultural Education: Issues and Perspectives,* 3rd ed. Boston: Allyn & Bacon, 1997.

Bigelow, B. "Why Standardized Tests Threaten Multiculturalism." *Educational Leadership* 56 (7) (1999): 37–41.

Connell, N. "Public Education." *Social Policy* (Spring, 1998): 68–72.

Fox, S. "The Controversy Over Ebonics." *Phi Delta Kappan* (November 1997): 237–240.

Gandara, Patricia. "Creating Cultures of High Achievement." *Liberal Education* 86, no. 2 (Spr 2000): 14-17.

Gittins, Naomi, ed. "Educating Students with Limited English Skills." *Inquiry & Analysis* (Jan 2001): 1-2 & 7.

Loveless, T. "Will Tracking Reform Promote Social Equity." *Educational Leadership* 56 (7) (1999): 22–28.

Maholmes, Valerie. "Revisiting Stereotype Threat: Examining Minority Students' Attitudes toward Learning Mathematics and Science." *Race, Gender & Class* 8, no. 1 (2001): 8-21.

McGee, C. A. "The Challenges of National Standards in a Multicultural Society." *Educational Horizons* (Spring 1997): 126–132.

Midobouche, E. "Respect in the Classroom: Reflections of a Mexican-American Educator." *Educational Leadership* 56 (7) (1999): 80.

Myers, John and Diane Boothe. "Cultural and Language Diversity in the Middle Grades." *Clearing House* 73, no. 4 (Mar-Apr 2000): 230-34.

Rosen, Lois Matz and Dawn Abt-Perkins. "Preparing English Teachers To Teach Diverse Student Populations: Beliefs, Challenges, Proposals for Change." *English Education* 32, no. 4 (Jul 2000): 251-66.

Quiroz, B., P. M. Greenfield, and M. Altchech. "Bridging Cultures with Classroom Strategies." *Educational Leadership* 56 (7) (1999): 64–68.

Sadker, D. "Gender Equity: Still Knocking at the Classroom Door." *Educational Leadership* 56 (7) (1999): 22–28.

Schick, Jo-Anne E. and Paul B. Nelson. "Language Teacher Education: The Challenge for the Twenty-First Century." *Clearing House* 74, no. 6 (Jul-Aug 2001): 301-04.

Schnur, B. "A Newcomer's High School." *Educational Leadership* 56 (7) (1999): 50–53.

Taylor, E. "Bring in 'Da Noise': Race, Sports, and the Role of Schools." *Educational Leadership* 56 (7) (1999): 75–80.

Taylor, Sheryl V. and Donna M. Sobel. *Addressing the Discontinuity of Students' and Teachers' Diversity: A Preliminary Study of Preservice Teachers' Beliefs and Perceived Skills.* (2001).

Torrez, Nena M. "Incoherent English Immersion and California Proposition 227." *Urban Review* 33, no. 3 (Sep 2001): 207-20.

Waters, Gisele A. "ESL Policy and Practice: A Linguistic Human Rights Perspective." *Clearing House* 74, no. 6 (Jul-Aug 2001): 296-300.

Wilder, Margaret. "Increasing African American Teachers' Presence in American Schools: Voices of Students Who Care." *Urban Education* 35, no. 2 (May 2000): 205-20.

Wolfe, Joanna. "Gender, Ethnicity, and Classroom Discourse: Communication Patterns of Hispanic and White Students in Networked Classrooms." *Written Communication* 17, no. 4 (Oct 2000): 491-519.

SUGGESTED MEDIA

A Teacher's Culture, video, 30 minutes, 2000. Designed for classroom teachers, this video enables viewers to reflect upon their own cultural beliefs and biases through the construction of personalized cultural genograms. It explains the significance of a teacher's cultural background in the classroom environment and discusses the need to treat all cultural differences with respect. *From Insight Media.*

Imagine Yourself: Creative Visualization , video, 20 minutes, 2000. This video teaches the use of creative visualization exercises to increase sensitivity to universal needs. It explores teaching strategies that can facilitate dealings with culturally specific issues and details the attributes of the culturally sensitive teacher. *From Insight Media.*

Learn From the Past, Plan for the Future: Multicultural Value Preference and Dominant U.S. Culture, video, 34 minutes, 2000. This video sensitizes viewers to differences between the dominant U.S. culture and other traditions. It highlights issues pertinent to the relationship between instructor and student, such as family relationships, discipline, and perceptions of teachers. *From Insight Media.*

Understanding the Similarities and Differences Between Your Culture and Other Cultures: Exploring Cultural Differences in Verbal and Nonverbal Communication, video, 77 minutes, 2000. This video offers a comparative summary of cultural value preferences. It includes a cultural genogram activity designed to help faculty reflect upon their personal cultural beliefs and examine how these beliefs impact the classroom. *From Insight Media.*

Whisper and Smile: Verbal and Nonverbal Communication Styles, video, 30 minutes, 2000. This video shows how a knowledge of cultural communication styles can facilitate verbal and nonverbal understanding. It considers the nature of communication styles in the United States and discusses how these styles may be understood by other cultures. *From Insight Media.*

Gender Equity in the Classroom, video, 60 minutes, 1999. This program features three scripted classroom scenes that demonstrate significant gender bias. The scenes are then rewritten to show more equitable and effective teaching. *From Insight Media.*

Gender Nation X, video, 23 minutes, 1998. This video explores whether gender and sexual identity are innate or socially manufactured. Using a series of humorous skits, personal reflections, and interviews with trans-gendered individuals, the program's youth producers raise several thought-provoking questions and challenge some traditional assumptions. *From Insight Media.*

Reviving Ophelia, video, 35 minutes, 1998. This vide explores the pressures and challenges facing today's teenagers—particularly girls. It examines the role of media and popular culture in shaping the identities of teenaged girls, and provides a catalyst for discussion in high school and college classes and in youth groups. *From Insight Media.*

The Student Guide to the Multicultural Classroom, video, 17 minutes, 1998. Designed for schools and classrooms new to multiculturalism, this video answers such questions as what is multiculturalism? and why do we need to understand other cultures? It explores African, Asian, Latino, Native-American, and European cultures, and encourages students to work toward understanding and tolerance. It stresses the value of appreciating multicultural history and recognizing ethnic differences. *From Insight Media.*

Overcoming Prejudice and Discrimination Through Multiculturalism, video, 19 minutes, 1998. The importance of multicultural education lies in the fact that an understanding of other races and cultures can serve to weaken and break the habit of prejudice. This video contains step-by-step instructions for opening viewers' minds to other cultures, races, and nationalities. *From Insight Media.*

The Global Tongue, video, 25 minutes, 1999. This program looks at the different contexts and countries in which the language dominates education pop music, advertising, and the Internet. It explores the pros and cons of this dominance and the ways in which it is factually changing the language. *From Films for the Humanities & Sciences.*

Respecting Diversity in the Classroom, video, 60 minutes, 1999. Rather than viewing the multicultural classroom as a problem to be solved, this program is a "how to" primer offering innovative ideas about exploring the richness of culture and ethnicity. *From Films for the Humanities & Sciences.*

Chapter 5
Behavioral Theories of Learning

CHAPTER OVERVIEW

Learning is defined as a change in an individual caused by experience. The major theories of behavioral learning are presented. The scientific study of learning begun in the late nineteenth century used techniques borrowed from the physical sciences to conduct experiments to understand how people and animals learned. The chapter begins with a review of Pavlov's Theory of Classical Conditioning, E. L. Thorndike's Law of Effect, and B. F. Skinner's Theory of Operant Conditioning. Central principles of behavioral learning include consequences, reinforcement, punishers, and shaping strategies. Important conditions to effective behavioral learning are the schedules of reinforcement, as well as the potency of the reinforcement being used. The use of cues, signals or information to aid discrimination or extinction is discussed. The importance of generalization as a learning variable is discussed at length with practical suggestions for classroom instruction.

The importance of Albert Bandura's Theory of Social Learning through modeling and observational learning is presented, with attention to vicarious learning. Meichenbaum's Model of Self-Regulated Learning focuses on the responsibility of the individual in the learning process and behavioral change. Emphasis is given to the importance of teaching students self-regulated learning skills in order to become independent learners.

CHAPTER–AT–A–GLANCE

Chapter Outline	Objectives	Supplements
5.1 What Is Learning?	• Define learning.	• Handout Master 5.1 • Test bank items
5.2 What Behavioral Learning Theories Have Evolved? • Pavlov: Classical Conditioning • Thorndike: The Law of Effect • Skinner: Operant Conditioning	• Describe experiments that led to the theories of classical and operant conditioning, and distinguish then among these theories.	• Transparency T47 • Test bank items
5.3 What Are Some Principles of Behavioral Learning? • The Role of Consequences • Reinforcers • Intrinsic and Extrinsic Reinforcers • Punishers • Immediacy of Consequences • Shaping • Extinction • Schedules of Reinforcement • Maintenance • The Role of Antecedents	• Define and illustrate several principles of behavioral learning, including reinforcement and punishment, and discuss their applications to teaching. • Give concrete examples of how each of these concepts can be observed in a typical classroom.	• Handout Master 5.2, 5.3, & 5.5 • Video Clip 7, *Consequence Cards* • Transparency T46, T46A, T48, T49 • Test bank items
5.4 How Has Social Learning Theory Contributed To Our Understanding of Human Learning?	• Describe social learning theory, explain how it contributes to our understanding of the way	• Handout Master 5.5 • Transparency T54 • Test bank items

• Bandura: Modeling and Observational Learning • Meichenbaum's Model of Self-Regulated Learning • Strengths and Limitations of Behavioral Learning Theories	people learn, and discuss its application to teaching. • Evaluate the significance and limitations of behavioral learning theories in education.	

ANNOTATED LECTURE OUTLINE

5.1 What is Learning?

Key Terms
Behavioral learning theories
Cognitive learning theories
Learning
Stimuli

Lecture Notes and Discussion Questions

Critical Thinking 5.1 Have students consider what is meant by the statement that "learning is constant." What implications does this have for teachers and planning good lessons?

Application 5.1 Have students list important skills and knowledge typically learned in school that are not part of the curriculum.

5.2 What Behavioral Learning Theories Have Evolved?

Key Terms
Unconditioned stimulus
Unconditioned response
Neutral stimuli
Conditioned stimulus
Classical conditioning
Law of Effect
Operant conditioning
Skinner box

Lecture Notes and Discussion Questions

Warm-up Ask students to brainstorm examples of classical conditioning in the classroom or school setting. Ask them to brainstorm examples of operant condition in the classroom or school setting.

Critical Thinking 5.2 A sixth-grade student is frustrated and embarrassed throughout the year by an insensitive math teacher. In the seventh grade the student becomes extremely anxious every time she goes to math class. What are the unconditioned stimulus, the conditioned stimulus, the unconditioned response, and the conditioned response in this situation?

Discussion 5.1 What examples of classical conditioning commonly occur in schools?

Multicultural Awareness 5.1 Have students consider whether culture has a significant influence on learning. Be sure to have them support their position with concrete examples.

5.3 What Are Some Principles of Behavioral Learning?

Key Terms
Consequences
Reinforcer
Primary reinforcer
Secondary reinforcer
Positive reinforcer
Negative reinforcer
Premack principle
Intrinsic reinforcers
Extrinsic reinforcers
Punishment
Presentation punishment
Aversive stimulus
Removal punishment
Timeout
Shaping
Extinction
Extinction burst
Schedule of reinforcement
Fixed-ratio (FR) schedule
Variable-ratio (VR) schedule
Fixed-interval (FI) schedule
Variable-interval (VI) schedule
Maintenance
Antecedent stimuli
Cues
Discrimination
Generalization

Lecture Notes and Discussion Questions

Application 5.2 Before lecturing, ask students to use **(HM 5.2)** "Classroom Rewards & Consequences" to list rewards and consequences they are considering for their classroom.

Critical Thinking 5.3 Does punishment work? What are some of the negative effects of punishment? If punishment is ineffective and produces negative side effects, why do so many teachers rely on it so much?

Critical Thinking 5.4 How would you use the behavioral principle of shaping to change the behavior of a student who never participated in classroom discussions?

Discussion 5.2 Much observational research reports negative or punitive teacher talk in a typical classroom. Have students brainstorm and correct examples of negative teacher talk.

Discussion 5.3 How would you use the behavioral learning principle of extinction to change the behavior of a student who consistently talked out of turn in class?

Discussion 5.4 Why is it that when a teacher decides to begin ignoring a behavior that he or she wants to extinguish, there is frequently an increase in the behavior for a short time before it decreases.

Example 5.1 Some examples of positive reinforcement are praise for good grades, bonus points on tests, and a class pizza party when everyone makes above 85 on the weekly spelling test.

Example 5.2 An example of the Premack Principle is when a parent allows a child to watch television after completing his or her homework.

Example 5.3 *Cueing*
- *Antecedent:* Teacher giving lecture, taking notes will be rewarded.
- *Antecedent:* Substitute teacher, rule breaking may not be punished in this situation.
- *Antecedent:* Desks in a circle, discussion will be rewarded.

Example 5.4 *Discrimination:* A student learns to distinguish expectations when one teacher demands that specific details of a text be read and another teacher demands that only the main ideas be learned.

Example 5.5 *Generalization:* A student who dreads speaking out in class may experience fear in a reading group when required to read orally. The student may then avoid reading and may eventually avoid all school activities that require reading.

Post-Lecture Student Activities

Wrap-up How can the consequence of being sent to the office actually be a reinforcing experience? What are the "positives" of being sent from class to the office?

Application 5.3 Ask student to review their list from Application 5.2 **(HM 5.2)**. Can they change the headings to read "Reinforcers & Consequences"? Do they feel differently about their list after the lecture? Can they identify any consequences that may inadvertently reinforce undesirable behavior? Do the consequences discourage undesirable behavior?

Cooperative Learning 5.1 Ask students to form small groups to review their lists from Application 5.2. They should develop lists of reinforcers and consequences upon which they all agree. Have them list also the items upon which agreement was not reached. Discuss these lists.

Application 5.4 Describe a situation in which the behavior of other children (e.g., laughter) serves as a reinforcer of a student's inappropriate behavior.

Application 5.5 Match the following examples with the reinforcement schedules that best describe them: (1) Bobby Joe has a habit of sticking his finger in the coin return slot of a pay phone to see whether any change has been left there. He has found change there three or four times. (variable interval) (2) Mr. Wood receives a paycheck every 2 weeks for his work as a maintenance supervisor of the Maplewood Elementary School. He has worked there 20 years. (fixed interval) (3) Zina plays computer games often. The computer game she plays most often gives her an extra game when she has completed five games of 1,000 points or better. (fixed ratio) (4) Amy played "Go Fishing" at the school carnival until all her money was gone, but she never won more than a trinket. She didn't know that Mr. Jones, the concessionaire of the "Go Fishing" booth, was letting every fifth player win big, then every fourth, then every sixth, then every fifth again. (variable ratio)

Application 5.6 A kindergarten teacher used to reward the class with jelly beans for returning from recess on time. By fall break, every student was arriving on time. When she stopped this practice, students again came in late from recess. What learning principle was involved here?

Application 5.7 Have your students suggest the cues or prompts they would use to elicit the following behaviors:

- The class looks at you so as to hear your directions.
- The students open their books to the assigned page when the bell rings.
- The students give you their full attention when you are making an important point.
- A student walks instead of running to the door when the dismissal bell rings.

Reading 5.1 Robert O'Donnell and George P. White, "Teaching Realistic Consequences to the Most Angry and Aggressive Students," *Middle School Journal* 32, no. 4 (Mar 2001): 40-45.

Reflection and Journal Writing 5.1 Ask students to recall an instance of punishment they experienced as students. How did they feel when they were being punished, and what were the consequences?

Reflection and Journal Writing 5.2 To help students become aware of the prevalence of reinforcement in daily life, ask them to keep a log, noting every time they give or receive reinforcement. Remind them to look for positive and negative reinforcement and to record the kind of schedule that is operating.

Application 5.8 Assign **(HM 5.3)** and ask students to summarize and reflect upon the children's responses to reinforcers of choice.

5.4 How Has Social Learning Theory Contributed To Our Understanding of Human Learning?

Key Terms

Social learning theory
Modeling
Observational learning
Vicarious learning
Self-regulation
Cognitive behavior modification

Lecture Notes and Discussion Questions

Critical Thinking 5.5 In Bandura's classic experiment (1965), a group of young children were exposed to a film of adults who punched, kicked, and yelled at an inflated "Bodo" doll. Later, in playing with the doll, these children displayed twice as many aggressive responses as did children who had not seen the aggressive behavior. What does Bandura's work suggest about the effects on children of violence in television shows and movies? What principles of social learning theory support your view?

Application 5.9 Assign "TV Viewing" **(HM 5.5)**. Ask students to summarize and reflect upon their findings.

Example 5.6 Observational learning: In Northern Thailand's teak forests, baby elephant "training camps" are set up, so that when young elephants are of age, they too begin the felling and logging.

Example 5.7 Vicarious learning: A gambler playing a slot machine sees and hears the loud noise, flashing lights, and jingling money announcing that another player has won. His playing of the slot machine increases.

Multicultural Awareness 5.2 The use of corporal punishment in schools as a punisher remains controversial and without consensus among and between ethnic groups. For an exercise to identify cultural differences on this topic, see Handout Master 5.4.

<u>**Post-Lecture Student Activities**</u>

Application 5.10 Assign students **(HM 5.5)** "Television Viewing Guide." Ask students to summarize and reflect upon their findings. Will they have recommendations for parents regarding children and television viewing? How will they communicate these recommendations to parents?

Cooperative Learning 5.2 In small groups or pairs, have students develop lists of recommended television shows based on their research in Application 5.9. Have them develop a second list of television shows they would caution parents to watch before allowing their children to view.

Cooperative Learning 5.3 In pairs (or with learning partners), have students role-play cognitive behavior modification by modeling for a child how to self-guide attention to a specific task through self-talk.

Reading 5.2 Colleen Johnson, "Helping Children To Manage Emotions which Trigger Aggressive Acts: An Approach through Drama in School," *Early Child Development and Care* 166 (Feb 2001): 109-18.

THEORY INTO PRACTICE

Establishing Reinforcement Schedules

The delivery of reinforcement in the classroom should be governed by rules set by you, the teacher. Many different types of schedules of reinforcement exist (Cantania, 1992; Elsmore and McBride, 1994). The most powerful schedules of reinforcement are those that are partial or intermittent schedules of reinforcement. Classroom teachers offer practical tips such as the following for partial reinforcement schedules:

- Treat ratio schedules as good behavior games. *Example:* for younger elementary students, teachers may use cutouts of letters to spell a word, such as T-R-E-A-T, on a bulletin board, one letter at a time next to children's names for good behavior on a daily basis. When a child collects all the letters and spells out the word, he or she gets to choose a treat from the class treat bag. This is an example of a fixed-ration reinforcement schedule. *Example:* for older elementary students, teachers may establish a secret weekly "magic" number, say between 20 and 40. The teacher places good behavior marks on the board for the class collectively, at the same time erasing marks whenever children misbehave. At the end of the week, students tally the marks and check them against the teacher's secret number. If the number is the same or larger, the teacher treats the class to a special event or privilege. This is an example of a variable-ratio schedule.

- Use interval schedules as rewards for the development of study and self-management skills. *Example:* Middle school students benefit from weekly quizzes, especially in subjects that require a good deal of factual knowledge. Weekly quizzes, an example of fixed-interval reinforcement, give students a chance to see what the teacher considers important and to predict what will be on major tests. *Example:* High school teachers may encourage students to prepare for tests or start long-term projects early by making performance assessments unpredictable. Announcing that students will be taking a test "in the next few days" or "sometime this week" forces students to be prepared at all times. This is an example of variable-interval reinforcement.

SUGGESTED READINGS

Cambourne, Brian. "Turning Learning Theory into Classroom Instruction: A Minicase Study." *Reading Teacher* 54, no. 4 (Dec 2000-Jan 2001): 414-17.

Gerber, Sterling. "Where Has Our Theory Gone? Learning Theory and Intentional Intervention." *Journal of Counseling & Development* 79, no. 3 (Sum 2001): 282-91.

Jones, P. "Values Education, Violence Prevention, and Peer Mediation: The Triad Against Violence in our Schools." *Educational Horizons* (Summer 1998): 177–181.

Kauffman, J.M. and H.J. Burbach. "On Creating a Climate of Classroom Civility." *Phi Delta Kappan* (December 1997): 320–325.

Manning, B. H. *Cognitive Self-instruction of Classroom Processes.* Albany, NY: SUNY Press, 1991.

Mazur, J. *Learning and Behavior*, 4th ed. Englewood Cliffs, NJ: Prentice-Hall, 1998.

Raywid, Mary Anne. "What To Do with Students Who Are Not Succeeding." *Phi Delta Kappan* 82, no. 8 (Apr 2001): 582-84.

SUGGESTED MEDIA

Managing Today's Classroom: Elementary Schools, video, 30 minutes. This video shows how to create a positive learning environment that encourages appropriate student behavior and facilitates student achievement. Designed for elementary teachers, it explains how to foster mutual respect, promote self-regulation and autonomy, create a sense of community, and motivate students through the designing of an engaging curriculum. *From Insight Media.*

Classical and Operant Conditioning, video, 56 minutes. This program explains the nature of Behaviorism, and its important applications in clinical therapy, education, and child-rearing The program clearly explains, discusses, and illustrates the complex Classical and Operant conditioning theories, using rats in Skinner boxes, as well as everyday life applications. *From Films for the Humanities & Sciences.*

Discovering Psychology: 8. Learning, video, 30 minutes, on the work of Pavlov, Watson, and Skinner in classical and operant conditioning. *From Annenberg/CPB Collection.*

Chapter 6
Information Processing and Cognitive Theories of Learning

CHAPTER OVERVIEW

This chapter focuses on an information-processing model that addresses the different aspects of memory and learning. Information enters through sensory registers, is held in short-term memory for immediate use, and then is either moved to long-term memory for later use, or discarded. Memory strategies, such as paired-associates, serial and free-recall learning, as well as types of long-term memory are discussed. The importance of schema theory and prior knowledge in making information meaningful is contrasted to rote memory strategies. A look at the role of automaticity in long-term memory processes is discussed, using practical examples to reinforce learning.

What causes people to remember or forget? Data on proactive and retroactive facilitation and inhibition as factors in forgetting is presented. A section on study skills is introduced with material on the importance of metacognitive strategies in helping students remember useful information. Students are presented with specific strategies for improved note-taking skills, and the PQ4R method of study. Organizational tips for relevant learning are discussed as well.

CHAPTER–AT–A–GLANCE

Chapter Outline	Objectives	Supplements
6.1 What Is an Information-Processing Model? • Sensory Register • Short Term or Working Memory • Long Term Memory • Factors That Enhance Long Term Memory • Other Information-Processing Models	• Explain how the information processing model works, and illustrate its processes in a diagram.	• Handout Master 6.1, 6.2, & 6.3 • Transparency T57, T58, T59, T64, T65, & T66 • Video Clip 8, *The Standard Memory Model and Learning* • Test Bank Items
6.2 What Causes People to Remember or Forget? • Forgetting and Remembering • Practice	• Identify factors that lead to forgetting and to retaining information.	• Handout Master 6.4 • Test Bank Items
6.3 How Can Memory Strategies Be Taught? • Verbal Learning • Paired-Associate Learning • Serial and Free-Recall Learning	• Describe several ways in which memory strategies can be directly taught.	• Handout Master 6.6 • Transparency T63 • Test Bank Items
6.5 How Do Metacognitive Skills Help Students Learn?	• Identify the metacognitive skills, and explain how you would teach reciprocal teaching to your students as an example of how metacognitive skills can be taught.	• Handout Master 6.5 & 6.6 • Test Bank Items

6.6 What Study Strategies Help Students Learn? • Note-Taking • Underlining • Summarizing • Outlining and Mapping • The PQ4R Method	• List key study skills, and explain how you would teach cooperative scripting and the PQ4R method as examples of how study skills can be directly taught.	• Transparency T74 • Test Bank Items
6.7 How Do Cognitive Teaching Strategies Help Students Learn? • Making Learning Relevant and Activating Prior Knowledge • Organizing Information	• Define "cognitive teaching," and give examples of classroom strategies teachers can use to make learning relevant to students' prior experiences.	• Transparency T69 • Test Bank Items

ANNOTATED LECTURE OUTLINE

6.1 What Is an Information Processing Model?

Key Terms

> Information-processing theory
> Sensory register
> Perception
> Attention
> Short-term or working memory
> Rehearsal
> Long-term memory
> Episodic memory
> Semantic memory
> Procedural memory
> Flashbulb memory
> Schemata
> Levels-of-processing theory
> Dual code theory of memory
> Parallel distributed processing
> Connectionist models

Lecture Notes and Discussion Questions

Application 6.1 Prior to the lecture, assemble a variety of objects on a small tray. Include objects typically found in a classroom or office and a few novel items. Ask students to clear their desks. Carry the tray around the classroom allowing each student a few seconds to try to memorize the items on the tray. After all students have seen the tray, ask students to get out paper and pencil and list all the items they can remember. Show the tray again and have students compare their lists to the actual items. Discuss the results. Was there a difference for students who had more wait time between seeing the tray and jotting the items on paper? Which items did most people recall? Which items were recalled by the fewest students? Did novelty have a role in remembering? Did anyone remember an item that wasn't on the tray? How might they apply what they have learned to the classroom? At the end of the lecture repeat the process. How have results changed and why?

Critical Thinking 6.1 Are officials who assign telephone numbers mindful of short-term memory capacities? Give some evidence to support your opinion.

Multicultural Awareness 6.1 Ask students to discuss how schemata about differences among individuals, groups, and social contexts can determine how new information about people and situations is interpreted.

Post-Lecture Student Activities

Reading 6.1 Barbara L. McCombs, "What Do We Know about Learners and Learning? The Learner-Centered Framework: Bringing the Educational System into Balance," *Educational Horizons* 79, no. 4 (Sum 2001): 182-93.

Reflection and Journal Writing 6.1 Ask students to recall a vivid memory of an event during their years of elementary school. Prompt them to remember the details of place, time, people, and feelings that make the memory of the event a vivid or lasting one. Ask students to note what images of space and time, so important to episodic memory, helped to facilitate their memory of this event.

Research and Suggested Reading 6.1 Harvette M. Robertson, Billie Priest, and Harry L. Fullwood, "20 Ways To Assist Learners Who Are Strategy-Inefficient," *Intervention in School and Clinic* 36, no. 3 (Jan 2001): 182-84.

Reading 6.2 Rita Smilkstein, "How the Brain Learns: Research, Theory, and Application," *Learning Assistance Review* 6, no. 1 (Spr 2001): 24-38.

6.2 What Causes People to Remember or Forget?

Key Terms
Interference
Retroactive inhibition
Proactive inhibition
Proactive facilitation
Retroactive facilitation
Primacy effect
Recency effect
Automaticity
Massed practice
Distributed practice
Enactment

Lecture Notes and Discussion Questions

Application 6.2 From what you know of part learning, how would you teach the multiplication tables to third-graders: (1) presentation of the squares first, for example, 1 x 1, 2 x 2, 3 x 3, 4 x 4, or (2) presentation of one set, for example, 1 x 1, 1 x 2, 1 x 3, etc., then progress to the 2s?

Critical Thinking 6.2 What did you have for dinner last night? What did you have for dinner exactly one week ago? In answering these questions, what techniques did you use to jog your memory? Could those techniques help you improve your overall ability to remember?

Multicultural Awareness 6.2 An old Turkish proverb illustrates the importance of enactment in memory and learning: "If one could learn by observation alone, then all dogs would be butchers."

Reading 6.3 Neil T. Glazer and Sharron Williams, "Averting the Homework Crisis," *Educational Leadership* 58, no. 7 (Apr 2001): 43-45.

Reading 6.4 Kathleen Vail, "Homework Problems: How Much Is Too Much?" *American School Board Journal* 188, no. 4 (Apr 2001): 24-29.

6.3 How Can Memory Strategies Be Taught?

Key Terms
> Verbal learning
> Paired-associate learning
> Serial learning
> Free-recall learning
> Imagery
> Mnemonics
> Keyword method
> Loci method
> Pegword method
> Initial-letter strategies

Lecture Notes and Discussion Questions

Application 6.3 Have students identify the memory strategy used in each of these situations:
- To help remember the symbol for the number *eight*, the teacher makes a snowman out of the figure 8 while telling a story about the snowman with eight buttons who lives for eight days.
- A student lists the products of Alabama so that the first letters spell *CAPS* (for cotton, apples, paper products, and soybeans).
- Columbus sailed the ocean blue in fourteen hundred and ninety-two.
- A student continues to practice the names of the state capitals long after he can name all perfectly.
- A student divides a list of terms to define into three sections and tries to learn each section separately.

Application 6.4 Assign students one of the memory strategies and ask them to develop a plan to "teach" a grocery list.

Cooperative Learning 6.1 Ask students to teach their grocery list (Application 6.4) to a small group. Which strategies were most effective for remembering groceries? How could they apply this same strategy to remember something from their content area?

Discussion Question 6.1 How might a science teacher use the strategies of rehearsal and mnemonics to teach the anatomical names of human bones?

Discussion Question 6.2 In a test of factual recall, which would generally produce the higher performance, serial recall or free recall? Why?

Multicultural Awareness 6.3 A mnemonic strategy developed in Japan called *Yodai Mnemonics* uses vivid imagery, poems, and songs to aid memory. For example, kindergartners are taught addition of like fractions. The fraction is called a "bug" whose head is the numerator and wings the denominator. Adding fractions is "counting the heads." Relating abstract concepts to well-known images and stories, students can perform complex operations.

6.4 What Makes Information Meaningful?

Key terms
> Rote learning
> Meaningful learning
> Inert knowledge
> Schema theory

<u>Lecture Notes and Discussion Questions</u>

Critical Thinking 6.3 Much of the current emphasis in cognitive research is on problem-solving activities and thinking skills. Ask students to discuss:
- the place for rote memory in the curriculum.
- examples of rote learning that are important in their teaching area.

6.5 How Do Metacognitive Skills Help Students Learn?

<u>Key Terms</u>
       Metacognition
       Metacognitive skills
       Self-questioning strategies

<u>Lecture Notes and Discussion Questions</u>

Critical Thinking 6.4 What advice would a metacognition theorist have for students practicing effective underlining and note-taking?

Multicultural Awareness 6.4 For discussions of metacognitive differences in diverse classrooms, see Roger W. Lee, *"*Encouraging ESL Students to Read," *TESOL Journal 8,* (1) (Spring 1999). Helping students build their self-confidence and develop a positive attitude toward reading can motivate them to pursue and enjoy this lifelong activity.

<u>Post-Lecture Student Activities</u>

Reading 6.5 Xiaodong Lin, "Designing Metacognitive Activities," *Educational Technology Research and Development* 49, no. 2 (2001): 23-40.

Reflection and Journal Writing 6.2 Ask students to reflect on their own cognitive strengths and weaknesses and uses of metacognitive strategies.

Reading 6.6 David K. Pugalee, "Writing, Mathematics, and Metacognition: Looking for Connections through Students' Work in Mathematical Problem Solving," *School Science and Mathematics* 101, no. 5 (May 2001): 236-45.

6.6 What Student Strategies Help Students Learn?

<u>Key Terms</u>
       Note-taking
       Summarizing
       Outlining
       Mapping
       PQ4R

<u>Lecture Notes and Discussion Questions</u>

Application 6.5 Prior to the lecture, distribute copies of **(HM 6.6)** "Activating Prior Knowledge." Ask students to complete the worksheet

Application 6.6 Have students create a concept map of study strategies. Follow-up with a discussion on study strategies that are most effective for different learning tasks. For example, which study strategies are best when learning the symbols for chemical elements? For the causes of the Civil War? For geometric formulas?

Discussion Question 6.3 Ask students to consider why it is important for content teachers to "teach" study skills for students in their classes? Are there differences in study skills for English, history, science, and mathematics classes?

Post-Lecture Student Activities

Application 6.7 Following the lecture and discussion, have students complete **(HM 6.7)** "Noting What I've Learned."

Application 6.8 Following the lecture assign **(HM 6.8)** "T Chart for improving work habits."

6.7 How Do Cognitive Teaching Strategies Help Students Learn?

Key Terms
Advance organizers
Analogies
Elaboration

Lecture Notes and Discussion Questions

Critical Thinking 6.5 What advice would a metacognitive theorist have for students practicing effective underlining and note-taking?

Discussion Question 6.4 What are the best learning strategies to activate prior knowledge before introducing new information to students? Why is it so important to call up prior information before new information is presented? How do teachers accommodate students with limited prior knowledge on a subject? See **(HM 6.6)** "Activating Prior Knowledge" and discuss the benefits of using this handout with students with limited prior knowledge.

Post-Lecture Student Activities

Cooperative Learning 6.2 Have students work in pairs to develop three different types of advanced organizers for a lesson of their choice. Use this text as an example of the variety of advance organizers that can be found in textbooks. Have them brainstorm additional strategies that can be used in advance of teaching the lesson in order to improve student learning.

Cooperative Learning 6.3 Review **(HM 6.6)** "Activating Prior Knowledge" and have students discuss in small groups the benefits of asking students to completed this form prior to instruction. Are there particular topics in which activating prior knowledge is particularly effective? Are there instances when a teacher would not want to use an activity to activate prior learning and why?

THEORY INTO PRACTICE

Teaching Rhyming Pegwords
A very old and quite effective technique for enhancing memory is rhyming. Most of us depend on rhymes such as:
- "Thirty days hath September…"
- "*i* before *e* except after *c*…"
- "When two vowels go walking, the first one does the talking."
- "In fourteen hundred ninety-two, Columbus sailed the ocean blue."

When teaching in any content area, look for opportunities to create rhyming pegwords, and instruct students directly in their use. Your students will also enjoy assignments in which they create rhyming pegwords and other mnemonic devices that they can teach to their classmates.

Several studies have shown that training programs based on these procedures can enhance the "individual's capacity for acquiring and using information" Dansereau, (1985), p.1.

Try developing initial-letter strategies for your students to help with subject area content, procedural knowledge, or metacognitive and study skills.

SUGGESTED READINGS

Davies, Nigel R. "Planning and Teaching To Remember." *Teaching Elementary Physical Education* 12, no. 2 (Mar 2001): 26-30.

Edwards, P., and E. F. Sparapani. "The Thinking/Learning System: A Teaching Strategy for the Management of Diverse Learning Styles and Abilities." *Educational Studies and Research* 14(2) (1996): 2–12.

Hertzog, Christopher and M. Kathryn Bleckley. "Age Differences in the Structure of Intelligence: Influences of Information Processing Speed." *Intelligence* 29, no. 3 (2001): 191-217.

Hill, David. "Showtime!" *Teacher Magazine* 12, no. 4 (Jan 2001): 30-34 & 58.

Fulford, Catherine P. "A Model of Cognitive Speed." *International Journal of Instructional Media* 28, no. 1 (2001): 31-41.

Khoo, Christopher S. G., Sung Hyon Myaeng, and Robert N. Oddy. "Using Cause-Effect Relations in Text To Improve Information Retrieval Precision." *Information Processing & Management* 37, no. 1 (Jan 2001): 119-45.

Kralovac, Etta and John Buell. "End Homework Now." *Educational Leadership* 58, no. 7 (Apr 2001): 39-42.

Morgan, C. and G. Morris. *Good Teaching and Learning: Pupils and Teachers Speak.* Philadelphia, PA: Open University Press, 1999.

Pool, C. R. "Maximizing Learning: A Conversation with Renata Numella Caine." *Educational Leadership* (March 1997): 11–15.

Prescott, Heather M. "Helping Students Say How They Know What They Know." *Clearing House* 74, no. 6 (Jul-Aug 2001): 327-31.

Rivers, William P. *Autonomy at All Costs: An Ethnography of Metacognitive Self-Assessment and Self-Management Among Experienced Language Learners.* (2001).

Sparapani, E.F. "Encouraging Thinking in High School and Middle School: Constraints and Possibilities." *The Clearing House* (May/June 1998): 274–276.

Zelazo, Philip David and Janet J. Boseovski. "Video Reminders in a Representational Change Task: Memory for Cues but Not Beliefs or Statements." *Journal of Experimental Child Psychology* 78, no. 2 (29 Feb 2001): 107.

Zmuda, A. and M. Tomaino. "A Contract for the High School Classroom." *Educational Leadership* 56(7) (1999): 59–62.

SUGGESTED MEDIA

How the Brain Learns, video, 42 minutes, 2000. Featuring the commentary and expertise of David Sousa, this video explores brain-based learning theory and its real-life applications. Using classroom footage, charts, and diagrams, it describes many specific strategies for classroom implementation of brain-based learning methods. *From Insight Media.*

Cognitive Coaching: A Process for Teaching and Learning, video, 39 minutes. This program describes and demonstrates specific examples of instructional conversation and other types of cognitive coaching; identifies instructional arrangements that are used to promote active learning by students; models questioning techniques and student interactions, including the ways in which cognitive coaches keep student discussion focused and productive; and considers the role that authentic and ongoing assessment plays in cognitive coaching. *From Films for the Humanities and Sciences.*

Improving Comprehension, video, 47 minutes. This program illustrates how teachers structure learning activities that foster independent learning around a central concept, identifies student-centered activities that make learning meaningful, models ways for teachers to guide students as they construct meaning and develop strategies for independent learning, and provides examples of how students can work together to develop satisfaction through learning. *From Films for the Humanities and Sciences.*

This Way to an "A" Effective Study Skills, video, 30 minutes. This program stresses the Empty "V" System, which promotes the importance of determining the purpose of each lesson in order to better understand key information. Proven techniques for studying, reviewing, and retaining information are included. Reading and taking notes become easier, more effective, and less time consuming, as students learn how to find key facts and ideas. *From Films for the Humanities and Sciences.*

Discovering Psychology: Remembering and Forgetting, video, 30 minutes, on how people remember, why people forget, and how memory can be improved. *From the Annenberg / CPB Collection.*

Memory: Fabric of the Mind, video, 28 minutes. What kind of brain chemistry can explain memory? Are different types of memory located in different areas of the brain? What is the process of forgetting? Is it possible to improve memory? This program seeks answer to these and other questions about the brain and memory at several memory research labs. *From Films for the Humanities*

Chapter 7
The Effective Lesson

CHAPTER OVERVIEW

This chapter begins with a definition of direct instruction and covers the parts of a direct instruction lesson. Direct instruction is the instructional approach where teachers transmit information, skills, or concepts directly to students, structuring class time to reach a clearly defined set of objectives. The necessary features of an effective direct instruction lesson include stated learning objectives, orienting the students to the lesson, a review of the prerequisites, presentation of new material, learning probes, time for independent practice, performance assessment and timely feedback, and distributed practice and review.

Research suggests that direct instruction methods fall into two distinct categories: Master Teacher models based on the practices of the most effective teachers and Systematic Instruction models. Early supportive research has focused mostly on basic reading and mathematics in the elementary grades. For other grade levels and other subjects, there is weaker evidence supporting direct instruction's impact on student learning.

The final sections of the chapter take a look at how discussions are used in instruction. The introduction of subjective and controversial subjects for class discussion, and tips on the use of difficult and novel concepts are reviewed. The use of affective objectives is discussed, as well as effective use of whole-class and small-group discussions.

CHAPTER–AT–A–GLANCE

Chapter Outline	Objectives	Supplements
7.1 What Is Direct Instruction?	• Define effective instruction	• Handout Master 7.1 • Transparency T78 & T83 • Test Bank Items
7.2 How Is a Direct Instruction Lesson taught? • State Learning Objectives • Orient Students to the Lesson • Review Prerequisites • Present New Material • Conduct Learning Probes • Provide Independent Practice • Assess Performance and Provide Feedback • Provide Distributed Practice and Review	• Describe and illustrate the steps and strategies used in presenting a direct instruction lesson.	• Handout Master 7.2, 7.3, & 7.5 • Transparency T75, T76 & T86 • Video Clip 10, *Concept Mapping* • Test Bank Items
7.3 What Does Research on Direct Instruction Methods Suggest? • Advantages and Limitations of Direct Instruction	• Describe the variants of the direct instruction model, and assess the advantages and limitations of each variation.	• Handout 7.4 • Test Bank Items
7.4 How Do Students Learn and Transfer Concepts? • Concept Learning and Teaching • Teaching for Transfer of Learning	• Using a subject area example for the grade level you plan to teach, illustrate how you would teach a concept for acquisition and transfer of learning.	• Test Bank Items

7.5 How Are Discussions Used In Instruction? • Subjective and Controversial Topics • Difficult and Novel Concepts • Affective Objectives • Whole-Class Discussions • Small-Group Discussions	• Compare and contrast whole-class and small-group discussions in terms of small-appropriate contexts, prerequisites, advantages, and limitations.	• Test Bank Items

ANNOTATED LECTURE OUTLINE

7.1 What Is Direct Instruction?

Key Terms

Direct instruction

Post-Lecture Student Activities

Reading 7.1 Have students read and discuss Don Tapscott , "Educating the New Generation," *Educational Leadership* 56(5), 6–12. The author suggests that students are thriving on the Internet. They create Web sites, do research, manage money, and make friends. How do teachers plan lessons that will meet the learning needs of the current generation of cyber students?

7.2 How Is a Direct Instruction Lesson Taught?

Key Terms

Lesson planning
Mental set
Rule-example-rule
Learning probe
Wait time
Calling order
Choral responses
Independent practice
Seatwork

Lecture Notes and Discussion Questions

Discussion Question 7.1 Because low-achieving students ask fewer and more inappropriate questions than other students do, teachers avoid calling on them. What are the implications of such a finding?

Discussion Question 7.2 Does the appropriateness of using direct instruction as a primary teaching method change according to student age level? If so, how?

Critical Thinking 7.1 Ask students to name some strategies they already know that contribute to lesson organization and clarity of presentation.

Discussion Questions 7.3 Why might a teacher's use of a fast pace of instruction promote learning? Does a fast pace of instruction affect student attention? In what circumstances should a brisk pace be avoided?

Discussion Question 7.4 Can a brisk pace discourage some students from participating? How long should a teacher wait between asking a question and prompting a student? How long should a teacher wait for a student to come up with an answer to a question?

Discussion Question 7.5 Is independent practice appropriate mainly at the pre-college level? What examples, if any, can you identify of college instructors using independent practice in their classes?

Discussion Question 7.6 What are the negative effects of assigning too much homework? How do teachers determine what amount is appropriate?

Discussion Question 7.7 What can teachers do to prevent students from having too much homework? What type of planning is required? Are there implications for staff planning time?

Multicultural Awareness 7.1 In some Asian cultures, the orientation to a lesson is not always verbal. At the beginning of a class, a bell, gong, or singing bowl is sounded to communicate "Come present here" or "Bring your energy to the learning setting."

Post-Lecture Student Activities

Application 7.1 As you discuss different components of the direct instruction model, use examples from your lectures as illustrations. Students enjoy hearing their professors talk about their own teaching.

Application 7.2 Many teachers across the disciplines implement the "1-minute paper" as a check on student comprehension. As an illustration of this concept, ask students to write a 1-minute paper on conducting learning probes and on explaining what a learning probe is and what is its purpose. Allow students exactly 1 minute to perform this task.

Application 7.3 To demonstrate calling order in questioning, ask a question in class, using the various orders: call on the student and then ask the question, ask the question and ask for a volunteer, ask the question and call on a student, ask the question and call for a choral response.

Application 7.4 Assign the "Parent Interviews on Homework" **(HM 7.5)**. Have students summarize and reflect upon their findings.

Cooperative Learning 7.1 Think, Pair, and Share results from Application 7.4. Have pairs join to form groups of four. Each group of four should develop a list of recommendations regarding the use of homework as independent practice.

Multicultural Awareness 7.2 For a discussion of possible modifications in lesson structure, emphases, and clarity for students for whom English is a second language, see "Lesson Structure, Emphasis, and Clarity" in the Instructor's Resource Manual.

Reflection and Journal Writing 7.1 Ask students to observe, reflect on, and note in their journals examples from your teaching that illustrate a particularly effective or ineffective way in which you used emphasis, explanation, or demonstration in a lesson.

Reading 7.2 Beth Hurst, "ABCs of Content Area Lesson Planning: Attention, Basics, and Comprehension," *Journal of Adolescent & Adult Literacy* 44, no. 8 (May 2001): 692-93.

7.3 What Does Research on Direct Instruction Methods Suggest?

Key Terms

Process-product studies

Post-Lecture Student Activities

Reading 7.3 Susan Sandall, Ilene Schwartz, Gail Joseph, "A Building Blocks Model for Effective Instruction In Inclusive Early Childhood Settings," *Young Exceptional Children*, 4, no. 3 (Spr 2001): 3-9.

7.4 How Do Students Learn and Transfer Concepts?

Key Terms
Concept
Transfer of learning

Post-Lecture Student Activities

Application 7.5 Have students brainstorm examples of information learned and transferred in the following contexts:
- Information learned in geometry used in horticulture class.
- Information learned in history used in a literature class.
- Information learned in science used in a geography class.
- Information learned in science used in a history class.

What other examples can students cite that demonstrate transfer of learning in every day activities?

7.5 How Are Discussions Used in Instruction?

Key Terms
Whole-class Discussion
Small-group Discussion

Lecture Notes and Discussion Questions

Critical Thinking 7.2 Ask students whether they agree with John Dewey, who said, "Conflict is the gadfly of thought." To have students think critically about conflict, ask them to identify topics in their fields of interest that might capitalize on students' differences of opinion.

Critical Thinking 7.3 If you knew your next class was a whole class discussion led by your professor, would you prepare more of less than for a lecture? Would this amount of preparation change if the class format was a small group discussion led by a fellow student? Would your preparation and participation level change based on the awarding of class points?

Cooperative Learning 7.2 In small groups, have students discuss and draft a proposal for awarding participation points at the college level. Could they use this strategy at the level they plan to teach? What are the implications for grading?

Post-Lecture Student Activities

Application 7.6 An effective way to teach about the discussion method is to have a whole-class discussion on discussion as an orienting activity. Main questions could include the following:

(1) In which teaching contexts should the discussion method be used? (2) What are the advantages of the discussion method? (3) What are the disadvantages? (4) What are some useful strategies for making the discussion method more effective for learning?

Application 7.7 Have students list the implication for teacher planning and preparation of an effective discussion versus lecture.

Application 7.8 Brainstorm a list of phrases a teacher can use to praise, redirect, and encourage student involvement in a discussion.

SUGGESTED READINGS

Clark, C. M. *Thoughtful Teaching.* New York: Teachers' College Press, 1995.

Duckworth, E. *The Having of Wonderful Ideas and Other Essays on Teaching and Learning.* New York: Teachers' College Press, 1996.

Eanes, R. *Content Area Reading and Literacy: Teaching for Today and Tomorrow.* Albany, NY: Delmar, 1996.

Erickson, H. L. *Stirring the Head, Heart, and Soul.* Thousand Oaks, CA: Corwin Press, 1995.

Popham, W. James. "Teaching to the Test?" *Educational Leadership* 58, no. 6 (Mar 2001): 16-20.

Sherman, Lee. "All in the Family: A Back-to-Basics Charter School Provides Home Schoolers with a Choice They Can Embrace Whole-Heartedly." *Northwest Education* 6, no. 3 (Spr 2001): 12-19.

Sowell, E. J. *Curriculum: An Integrative Introduction.* Upper Saddle River, N.J.: Prentice Hall, 1998.

SUGGESTED MEDIA

How to Teach Study Skills, video, 15 minutes, 2000. Emphasizing the importance of practicing study skills after learning them, this video uses real classroom examples to present effective lessons in a range of study skills. It details strategies for teaching students to manage time, listen, take notes, prepare for tests, and participate actively in classroom activities. *ASCD.*

Teaching Strategies and Techniques That Encourage Learning, video, 27 minutes, 1996. This video illustrates teaching techniques that motivate students and demonstrates how to instill a positive attitude in students. It gives directions that motivate and encourage reluctant learners. It offers tips for communicating positive expectations and for designing lesson plans that capture students' attention. *From Insight Media.*

Teaching Strategies That Promote Interpersonal and Cooperative Learning, video, 150 minutes, 1996. This program teaches ways to ensure that learning is meaningful for students. Using in-depth examples of the "peer practice" and the "jigsaw" strategies, it shows techniques that help students relate their learning to their personal relationships during the learning process. *From Insight Media.*

Teaching Strategies That Promote Organization and Mastery of Content, video, 180 minutes, 1996. This program shows how to help students master content by acquiring knowledge, making connections, and accessing information. It shows the "new American lecture" strategy and the "graduated difficulty" strategy in use in actual classrooms. *From Insight Media.*

Planning Integrated Units: A Concept-Based Approach, video, 65 minutes, 1997. This program offers a step-by-step guide for planning a concept-based integrated unit. It stresses the importance of choosing a theme that incorporates multiple subjects, identifying the branching relationships of the ideas related to the theme and creating instructional activities that actuate the theme. *From Insight Media.*

Empowering At-Risk Youth Through Cooperative Learning and Technology, video, 28 minutes, 1997. This program presents a multi-aged group of at-risk students as they reconnect to school in an innovative and award-winning pilot program. It shows them focusing on formal cooperative learning strategies and technology-infused tasks. The students comment on their improved attitude and attendance and on their goals for the future. *From Insight Media.*

What Is Whole Language? video, 60 minutes. This program deals with the fundamental issues surrounding whole language instruction. It is set in the context of a teacher and parent workshop, including administrators, an educational consultant, school board members, and an education professor. *From Films for the Humanities and Sciences.*

Chapter 8
Student-Centered and Constructivist Approaches to Instruction

CHAPTER OVERVIEW

This chapter begins with a look at the historical roots of constructivism in education and illustrates its basic principles. Starting with a review of top-down processing models, where students begin with complex problems to solve and then discover the basic skills required. It contrasts models, where students begin with basic skills and advance to more complex tasks. The discussion continues with an overview of discovery learning, self-regulated learning, and scaffolding. Vygotsky's concept of scaffolding suggests that a teacher must support a student's progression to more conceptual sophistication in the early phases of learning by modeling, then must decrease its use as learning increases.

Material on the APA's Learner-Centered Psychological Principles offers the idea that the learner is actively seeking knowledge, reinterpreting information and experience for himself or herself, motivated by the quest for knowledge itself (rather than by grades or other rewards), working with others to socially construct meaning, and aware of his or her own learning strategies and in applying them to new problems or consequences.

The use of constructivist methods in the content areas is exemplified with four constructivist approaches to mathematics teaching in the primary grades.

Cooperative learning refers to instructional methods in which students work together in small groups to help each other learn. Most involve students in four-member, mixed-ability groups, but the use of dyads is also discussed. Examples of jigsaw grouping, group investigation, and cooperative scripting is also included in this chapter.

An important topic of this chapter is the focus on problem solving strategies. Strategies, such as the five-step IDEAL program developed by Bransford and Stein illustrate the teaching of problem solving skills as part of the curriculum, through an organized, step by step process.

CHAPTER–AT–A–GLANCE

Chapter Outline	Objectives	Supplements
8.1 What Is the Constructivist View of Learning? • Historical Roots of Constructivism • Top-Down Processing • Cooperative Learning • Discovery Learning • Self-Regulated Learners • Scaffolding • APA's Learner-Centered Psychological Principles • Constructivist Methods in the Content Areas • Research on Constructivist Methods	• Describe the constructivist revolution in education, and illustrate its basic principles. • Differentiate between discovery learning and self-regulated learning. • Develop a hypothetical lesson that uses APA's constructs of learner-centered psychological principles	• Handout Master 8.1 & 8.2 • Video Clip 12, *The Role of Good Planning and Procedures* • Test Bank Items
8.2 How Is Cooperative Learning Used In Instruction? • Cooperative Learning	• Describe some of the benefits of cooperative learning, and provide examples of how it is	• Handout Master 8.3 & 8.4 • Video Clip 11, *Cooperative Learning*

Models • Research on Cooperative Learning	used in the classroom.	• Transparency T84 & T85 • Test Bank Items
8.3 How Are Problem Solving and Thinking Skills Taught? • The Problem Solving Process • Obstacles to Problem Solving • Teaching Creative Problem Solving • Teaching Thinking Skills • Critical Thinking	• Using a subject area example for the grade level you plan to teach, illustrate how you would teach problem solving and critical thinking.	• Video Clip 13, *Hands-On Learning in Elementary Math* • Transparency T71, T72, T73, & T73A

ANNOTATED LECTURE OUTLINE

8.1 What Is the Constructivist View of Learning?

Key Terms
> Constructivist theories of learning
> Cognitive apprenticeship
> Discovery learning
> Self-regulated learners
> Mediated learning
> Reciprocal teaching

Lecture Notes and Discussion Questions

Application 8.1 Have students create examples of the differences in teaching a concept or skill using the bottom-up approach and the top-down approach.

Application 8.2 After presenting a brief definition of generative learning, ask students to write in their own words what generative learning means. After having several students read their descriptions, point out that their paraphrases or elaborations are themselves examples of generative learning.

Application 8.3 Invite students to describe examples of discovery learning and explain their roles as teachers.

Critical Thinking 8.1 Ask students to reflect on learning experiences they have had that reflect a constructive learning approach. How could you use a constructive approach in teaching a particular lesson in your content area? For what types of learning would constructive approaches most likely be inappropriate?

Multicultural Awareness 8.1 Research on scaffolding is limited to Western children. For example, educators in many countries are less likely than Americans to structure young children's learning situations. They expect children to have greater responsibility for their own learning through observation and participation in adult (rather than child-oriented) activities. These findings indicate that effective scaffolding may vary widely from culture to culture. Consider ways that teachers can scaffold learning for Limited English Proficient students and students who use English as their second language for academic tasks.

Research and Suggested Reading 8.1 Liz Suda, "Learning Circles: Democratic Pools of Knowledge," *ARIS Resources Bulletin* 12, no. 3 (Sep 2001): 1-4.

Post-Lecture Student Activities

Cooperative Learning 8.1 Ask students to brainstorm effective scaffolding techniques. Have students pair and share lists. Have pairs form groups of four and share again.

8.2 How Is Cooperative Learning Used in Instruction?

Key Terms
Cooperative learning
Student Teams-Achievement Divisions
Cooperative Integrated Reading and Composition
Jigsaw
Learning together
Group investigation
Cooperative scripting

Lecture Notes and Discussion Questions

Critical Thinking 8.2 What are the challenges of cooperative learning for the teacher and for the students? What can a teacher do to overcome these challenges? When are cooperative learning strategies most appropriate? When are cooperative learning strategies not effective for learners?

Multicultural Awareness 8.2 Cooperative learning has many benefits for social development. Have students consider the benefits to language acquisition for ESL students when working in cooperative learning activities. How are idioms best learned? Can content knowledge be a base for language development for students learning to speak English?

Research and Suggested Reading 8.2 For a broader discussion of Student Teams-Achievement Divisions (STAD) and other cooperative learning strategies used with elementary and secondary students, read R. E. Slavin, *Cooperative Learning: Theory, Research and Practice*, 2nd ed. (Boston: Allyn & Bacon, 1995).

Research and Suggested Reading 8.3 Julie I. Siciliano, "How To Incorporate Cooperative Learning Principles in the Classroom: It's More than Just Putting Students in Teams," *Journal of Management Education* 25, no. 1 (Feb 2001): 8-20.

Research and Suggested Reading 8.4 Ghazi Ghaith, "Learners' Perceptions of Their STAD Cooperative Experience," *System* 29, no. 2 (Jun 2001): 289-301.

Post-Lecture Student Activities

Cooperative Learning 8.2 Assign a specific section of the next chapter to each student. Have them use the jigsaw method to share key concepts and vocabulary. Give students copies of (HM 8.3) "Division of Labor and ask them to document individual contributions.

Cooperative Learning 8.3 Ask small groups of students to match the cooperative learning strategies listed in Chapter 8 with activities and content most appropriate for each individual strategy. Have groups report results to the class.

Cooperative Learning 8.4 You will be modeling a cooperative learning strategy sometimes referred to as "Merry Go Round." On individual sheets of paper list cooperative learning strategies. Divide students into small groups and give each group a different colored pen or marker. Give each group one sheet of paper listing a single cooperative learning strategy and ask them to brainstorm the possible uses or classroom applications of the strategy listed on their piece of paper. Circulate the sheets of paper, giving each group a chance to add comments using the specified color marker. At the end of the activity post these sheets and discuss how the contributions of each group are visible because of the different colors of ink used by each group. Discuss.

Critical Thinking 8.3 Distribute copies of **(HM 8.4)** "Research Plan." Have students discuss the benefits to students and teachers for utilizing a similar form when assigning group investigation.

8.3 How Are Problem Solving and Thinking Skills Taught?

Key Terms

Problem solving
Means-end analysis
Instrumental enrichment
Critical thinking

Lecture Notes and Discussion Questions

Research and Suggested Reading 8.5 A model curriculum for thinking for the upper elementary and middle school grades is the Odyssey Program. It has six components: I. Foundations of Reasoning, the introductory book. It teaches the basic concepts for gathering, organizing, and interpreting information in systematic and critical ways. II. Understanding Language. This book helps students extend their analytical skills to vocabulary, sentences, and paragraphs. III. Verbal Reasoning. Students learn how to recognize, analyze, produce, and evaluate assertions and arguments. IV. Problem Solving. Teaches students graphic representation and simulation of problem statements, use of trial and error, and ways to think through the implications of a solution. V. Decision Making. Teaches how to gather and sort information along the dimensions of relevance, consistency, and credibility. VI. Inventive Thinking. Teaches designs as descriptions, comparisons, and experimentation, plus ways to evaluate, improve, and invent designs.

Research and Suggested Reading 8.6 John Chaffee (1997) offers a taxonomy of key behaviors of critical thinkers: (1) thinking actively, (2) thinking for themselves, (3) being receptive to new ideas, (4) discussing ideas in an organized way, and (5) supporting viewpoints with reasons and evidence. For a good discussion of techniques on teaching students to think critically, read his text *Thinking Critically*, 5th ed. (Boston: Houghton Mifflin, 1997).

Research and Suggested Reading 8.7 Michael D. Mumford, Jack M. Feldman, Michael B. Hein, Dennis J. Nagao, *Tradeoffs between Ideas and Structure: Individual versus Group Performance in Creative Problem Solving*. 2001.

THEORY INTO PRACTICE

Problem Solving through Real-Life Applications

Students often have difficulty applying the skills they have learned in school to real-life situations because those skills were presented in a school context, rather than a real-life context. School tasks often lack context and so are not meaningful to many students because students cannot relate the tasks to what they already know. Teachers can help students to learn problem-solving by placing tasks in a real-life context (Gallagher and Stephen, 1993). Three examples of real-life applications are provided below.

- **Elementary:** Your family is planning on a vacation and has asked you to decide where your family will go, how you will get there, and how long you will be gone, and how much money will be needed. Present a travel and activity schedule, a map, and an estimated budget for all expenses.
- **Middle school:** Imagine that you are an investigative reporter for a local newspaper. Three supermarkets in your community have been running TV commercials in which they claim to have

the lowest prices. How can each store claim to have the lowest prices? Your task is to investigate these claims by designing a way to determine which store actually has the lowest prices. Collect data at each store, and present your findings in an article to be published in your class newspaper.

- **High school:** As an expert on sleep, you have been hired by a law enforcement agency to write a sleep manual. Law enforcement officers must often work for long periods of time with little or no sleep. When an officer is suffering from sleep deprivation, his or her performance may be compromised, sometimes resulting in a risk of loss of life. The agency needs a clear, concise, but comprehensive manual that will give officers the knowledge of sleep that they need to maintain a high level of performance on the job.

Although these problems require more time than most school tasks, they are rich in academic content and skills that are placed in real-life contexts. To solve the problems, students must identify the problem, identify possible solutions, choose a solution, carry out the solution, and analyze and report their findings. But just as importantly, students will learn to apply academic skills such as information gathering, computing, writing, and speaking in a real-life context.

SUGGESTED READINGS

Banks, J. A. "Multicultural Education and Curriculum Transformation." *Journal of Negro Education* 64(4) (1995): 390–400.

Englert, Carol Sue, Ruth Berry, and KaiLonnie Dunsmore. "A Case Study of the Apprenticeship Process: Another Perspective on the Apprentice and the Scaffolding Metaphor." *Journal of Learning Disabilities* 34, no. 2 (Mar-Apr 2001): 152-71.

Fosnot, C. T. *Constructivism: Theory, Perspectives, and Practice.* New York: Teachers' College Press, 1996.

Hee-Won, K. and B. Dutton. "Becoming Multicultural: Focus on the Process." *Multicultural Education* (Summer, 1997): 19–22.

Henderson, J. G. *Reflective Teaching: The Study of Your Constructivist Practices,* 2nd ed. Upper Saddle River, NJ: Prentice Hall, 1996.

Johnston, C. A. *Let Me Learn.* Thousand Oaks, CA: Corwin Press, 1998.

Lambert, L., D. Walker, D.P. Zimmerman, J.E. Cooper, M.D. Lambert, M.E. Gardner, and P.J.F. Slack. *The Constructivist Leader.* New York: Teachers' College, 1996.

Lord, Thomas R.. "101 Reasons for Using Cooperative Learning in Biology Teaching." *American Biology Teacher* 63, no. 1 (Jan 2001): 30-38.

Mueller, Andrea and Thomas Fleming. "Cooperative Learning: Listening To How Children Work at School." *Journal of Educational Research* 94, no. 5 (May-Jun 2001): 259-65.

Nath, Leslie R. and Steven M. Ross. "The Influence of a Peer-Tutoring Training Model for Implementing Cooperative Groupings with Elementary Students." *Educational Technology Research and Development* 49, no. 2 (2001): 41-56.

Scheidecker, D. and W. Freeman. *Bringing Out the Best in Kids: How Legendary Teachers Motivate Kids.* Thousands Oaks, CA: Corwin Press, 1999.

Schifter, D. *What's Happening in Math Class? Reconstructing Professional Identities,* Vol. 2. New York: Teacher's College Press, 1996.

Treagust, D. F., D. Reinders, and B.J. Fraser. *Improving Teaching and Learning in Science and Mathematics.* New York: Teacher's College Press, 1996.

Wiest, Lynda R. "Teaching Mathematics from a Multicultural Perspective." *Equity & Excellence in Education* 34, no. 1 (Apr 2001): 16-25.

SUGGESTED MEDIA

Brainwaves, video, 15 minutes, 2000. This video explores teaching styles designed to engage students' interest and imagination. It discusses how students and teachers relate to curricular material and presents methods that educators can use to encourage participation and creative thinking. It includes segments on constructivism, multiple intelligences, and learning styles. TV Ontario. *From Insight Media.*

Comprehending, Composing, and Communicating, video, 37 minutes. This program models the use of instructional conversations among students and between students and teachers. It demonstrates how cognitive maps are used to present, organize and record information, and shows how authentic assessment is used to determine the direction of learning activities. *From Films for the Humanities & Sciences.*

Integrating Thinking, Reading, and Writing Across the Curriculum, video, 79 minutes. This is a teleconference for teachers, administrators, and parents. It addresses how to improve comprehension, cognitive coaching, and the link between thinking, reading, and writing and the integration of instruction and assessment. *From Films for the Humanities & Sciences.*

Improving Student Achievement: Elementary/Middle School, video, 30 minutes, 1999. Featuring visits to elementary and middle school classrooms, this video shows learner-centered instructional approaches. It also explains how to use class meetings and questioning techniques to promote critical thinking and problem solving. *From Insight Media.*

Building Character Through Cooperative Learning, video, 38 minutes, 1999. This video features Spencer Kagan's discussion of the value of cooperative learning in character education. It explains that cooperative learning is an effective strategy for developing such core virtues as personal responsibility and respect, and illustrates how to incorporate cooperative learning strategies into classroom instruction. *From Insight Media.*

Cooperative Learning Series: A Comprehensive Program, five videos, each 20–45 minutes. Address such topics as planning and implementing cooperative lessons; teaching social skills; teaching strategies, such as STAD, TGT, Jigsaws; and sample lesson plans. *From ASCD.*

A Different Place: The Intercultural Classroom, video, 37 minutes, 1993. Explores both opportunities and challenges created by increased diversity in the classroom. Includes conflicts in the classroom, how insensitivity to different styles of communication reinforces negative perceptions. Also, an interdisciplinary team of experts analyzes vignettes on different ways of building a sense of community in an intercultural classroom. *From Insight Media.*

Chapter 9
Accommodating Instruction to Meet Individual Needs

CHAPTER OVERVIEW

This chapter opens with a look at Carroll's Model of School Learning and the QAIT Model of Effective Instruction. The QAIT Model identifies four elements of instruction beyond a good lesson: quality of instruction, appropriate levels of instruction, incentive to ensure motivation, and time to learn the material. In addition to the presentation of the lesson, material is presented on the way teachers and schools group students to accommodate achievement differences. The chapter looks at between-class and ability grouping, as well as untracking. Traditional grouping activities have related to instruction in math and reading classes. Interest and information in non-graded and cross-age-grouping in elementary schools is discussed, as well as within-class ability grouping.

What is Mastery Learning? Based on instruction that requires that every student meet a pre-established level of skill proficiency before moving on to the next level, mastery learning is most effective with low achievers when teaching basic skills and when corrective instruction is supported outside the classroom.

Suggestions are given for individualizing instruction through tutoring activities. Both peer and adult tutoring strategies are presented, as well as programmed instruction, informal remediation and enrichment activities, and computer-based instruction models. Attention is given to the use of well-trained volunteers using structured materials for teaching reading. The use of computer-based instruction (CBI) is included on the discussion of tutoring. For students identified as at-risk, compensatory education programs and early intervention programs are discussed, including the effects of a comparative study, *Prospects,* on Title I initiatives.

CHAPTER–AT–A–GLANCE

Chapter Outline	Objectives	Supplements
9.1 What are Elements of Effective Instruction Beyond a Good Lesson? • Carroll's Model of School Learning and QAIT	• Give several reasons why effective instruction involves more than giving good lectures, and explain how the QAIT model of effective instruction provides opportunities for accommodating differences in student ability.	• Handout Master 9.1 • Transparency T88 • Test Bank Items
9.2 How Are Students Grouped to Accommodate Achievement Differences? • Between-Class Ability Grouping • Untracking • Regrouping for Reading and Mathematics • Nongraded (Cross-Age Grouping) Elementary Schools • Within-Class Ability Grouping	• Compare between-class ability grouping and within-class ability grouping in terms of advantages, disadvantages, and appropriate use in relation to five general principles of ability grouping.	• Handout Master 9.4 • Test Bank Items
9.3 What Is Mastery Learning?	• Identify the principles on	• Transparency T77

• Forms of Mastery Learning • Research on Mastery Learning	which mastery learning is based, describe some forms mastery learning takes, and plan steps for teaching a unit using mastery learning.	• Test Bank Items
9.4 What Are Some Ways of Individualizing Instruction? • Peer Tutoring • Adult Tutoring	• Evaluate several methods for individualizing instruction, incorporating computer-assisted instruction in the classroom, and providing appropriate levels of instruction.	• Handout Master 9.5 • Transparency T50, T107, T108 • Video Clip 14, *High School Tutors* • Test Bank Items
9.5 How is Technology Used in Education? • Types of Computer Application in the Classroom • Research on Computer-based Instruction	• Compare the ways that teachers used technology in the classroom with ways that students are asked to use it.	• Handout Master 9.2 • Video Clip 16, *Internet Kids* • Video Clip 15, *Laptops for Kids* • Test Bank Items
9.6 What Educational Programs Exist for Students Placed At Risk? • Compensatory Education Programs • Early Intervention Programs • Comprehensive School Reform Programs	• Explain what is meant by "at-risk" students, and evaluate three kinds of educational programs that serve students at-risk.	• Transparency T40 • Test Bank Items

ANNOTATED LECTURE OUTLINE

9.1 What Are Elements of Effective Instruction Beyond a Good Lesson?

Key Terms
>   QAIT model

Lecture Notes and Discussion Questions

>   **Discussion Question 9.1** A common struggle of beginning teachers is timing or pacing of instruction. The challenge of planning for appropriate time for students to learn the new material or complete work is a part of this pacing. What can you do as a new teacher in regard to this challenge?

>   **Discussion Question 9.2** As a teacher, should you allow enough class time for all students to complete the assignment or should unfinished work be assigned as homework? Is it appropriate to have students turn in incomplete work and grade it as such?

>   **Discussion Question 9.3** If you, as an advocate of the Carroll model, were confronted by another educator who argued that students' achievement "results primarily from their aptitude or natural ability for learning," what might be an argument to support another view?

Post-Lecture Student Activities

>   **Application 9.1** To have students apply the principles of the QAIT model to classroom situations, have them observe a lesson in an elementary or secondary classroom and evaluate the quality of the lesson, the appropriate levels of instruction for the students, the incentive for student learning,

and the amount of time students are given to learn the material. Compare observations in an in-class discussion to determine the effectiveness of the "QAIT Model of Instruction."

Application 9.2 Have students keep an "instructional diary" for one week in their college classes to quietly observe if the QAIT model is being implemented in university teaching. Is learning at the university level affected by the same teaching models as for elementary and secondary students? Do the same principles of good teaching apply to all instructional settings? Why or why not?

Multicultural Awareness 9.1 Eileen Dugan Waldschmidt, "Alma's Unfinished Play: Bilingual Playwriting in a Summer School Program," *Language Arts* 78, no. 5 (May 2001): 442-48.

9.2 How Are Students Grouped to Accommodate Achievement Differences?

Key Terms
Tracks
Between-class ability grouping
Within-class ability grouping
Untracking
Regrouping
Joplin Plan
Nongraded programs

Lecture Notes and Discussion Questions

Critical Thinking 9.1 To encourage students to listen actively and think critically about grouping students for learning, have students recall classes where grouping was done both within and between groups. Have them consider tracking programs in their high school classes. Were students tracked for college? For vocational programs?

Discussion Question 9.4 What might be the negative and positive effects on the achievement, self-esteem, or life options of a high school student enrolled in a vocational track? A college preparatory track? A remedial math track?

Discussion Question 9.5 Distribute copies of **(HM 9.4)**. What might be the effects of mixed-ability grouping, within-class ability grouping, and between-class ability grouping on student achievement? On student motivation? On your interest or motivation as a teacher?

Post-Lecture Student Activities

Cooperative Learning 9.1 The Joplin Plan, a cross-grade ability-grouping scheme in reading, avoids some of the problems of ability grouping. In every group there are high-, middle-, and low-ability students. Have students discuss in groups of four how such a plan might be useful to them.

Cooperative Learning 9.2 In groups of two, have students describe the circumstances under which they might do the following in their classrooms: set up cooperative learning activities using mixed-ability teams, use within-class ability groups, and send a high achiever in math to a more advanced class.

Critical Thinking 9.2 If mastery learning requires that a student master one skill before moving on to the next, identify one subject or content area that would be easily adapted to mastery learning and one that would not.

Reflection and Journal Writing 9.1 Discuss your personal experiences with between-class ability grouping, or tracking. What advantages and/or disadvantages did tracking have for you?

Research and Suggested Reading 9.1 Have students read and discuss Jay Feldman and Peter Gray, "Some Educational Benefits of Freely Chosen Age Mixing Among Children and Adolescents" *Phi Delta Kappan* 80(7), 507–513.

Research and Suggested Reading 9.2 For a comprehensive review of research on the effects of ability grouping on achievement in secondary schools read Slavin (1995).

Research and Suggested Reading 9.3 Teachers should keep the number of ability groups within an elementary class quite small (usually no more than two or three). Grouping in math has shown positive effects on overall achievement. For more information, read T.L. Good and J.E. Brophy, *Looking Into Classrooms*, 7th ed. (Boston: Addison Wesley, 1997).

9.3 What Is Mastery Learning?

Key Terms
Mastery learning
Mastery criterion
Corrective instruction
Enrichment activities
Formative evaluation
Summative evaluation

Lecture Notes and Discussion Questions

Discussion Question 9.6 You plan to set up a mastery learning program in math. What do you think is an adequate mastery level that a student should achieve before being allowed to pass to the next skill level?

Discussion Question 9.7 In mastery learning, students are often encouraged to increase their learning time by doing homework. Educators, parents, and students fiercely debate the amount of time students should spend doing homework. How much homework do you believe is an appropriate amount for one class (e.g., in this class, in a third-grade class, in a high school English class) for one night?

Post-Lecture Student Activities

Application 9.3 Describe a class you have seen or taken that was taught with the mastery learning approach. In your opinion, was the method more or less effective than more traditional methods? Consider the amount of material you learned, your retention of that material, and the amount of time spent studying and taking tests. Did you experience mastery learning? Why or why not?

Application 9.4 Brainstorm strategies a teacher might use with a student who is not reaching mastery?

9.4 What Are Some Ways of Individualizing Instruction?

Key Terms
Individualized instruction
Peer tutoring
Cross-age tutoring

Lecture Notes and Discussion Questions

Critical Thinking 9.3 Why is individualizing instruction a significant part of curricular planning and assessment in today's classrooms? Identify five hypothetical scenarios where individualized instruction would be important for student success.

Application 9.5 Some parents object to their students serving as peer tutors. What do you say to these parents? Summarize your comments and rationale for peer tutoring.

Discussion Question 9.8 What are some benefits of cross-age tutoring? Can you think of any potential drawbacks?

Multicultural Awareness 9.2 Think of ways in which reciprocal teaching strategies can be used in paired learning activities with mixed-culture students in supporting individualized instruction.

Reading 9. 1 Rudolf Van den Berg, Peter Sleegers, and Femke Geijsel, "Teachers' Concerns about Adaptive Teaching: Evaluation of a Support Program," *Journal of Curriculum and Supervision* 16, no. 3 (Spr 2001): 245-58.

Reading 9.2 Leaunda Hemphill, "Providing Learners with Individualized Learning Strategies," *TechTrends* 45, no. 1 (Jan-Feb 2001): 40.

Reading 9.3 Charles R. Greenwood, Carmen Arreaga-Mayer, Cheryl A. Utley, Karen M. Gavin, Barbara J. Terry, *Classwide Peer Tutoring Learning Management System: Applications with Elementary-Level English Language Learners.* (2001).

9.5 How Is Technology Used in Education?

Key Terms
Computer-based instruction (BCI)
Drill and practice
Tutorial programs
Simulation software
Word processing
CD-ROM
Videodisc
Integrated learning system
Internet World Wide Web

Lecture Notes and Discussion Questions

Application 9.6 Assign students **(HM 9.5)** "Evaluating Quality of Internet Source." Ask students to evaluate a website based on the criteria presented. What are the benefits of using such a form when requiring internet research?

Critical Thinking 9.4 Why would you be or not be reluctant to use computers instructionally? Are you receiving the training you need to use computer technologies effectively? What computer peripherals enhance student learning and how?

Critical Thinking 9.5 What research skills will students need to acquire in order to use the World Wide Web in scholarly ways that differ from using traditional print resources?

Discussion Question 9.9 How might you use CBI methods in your teaching as substantive aids to teaching and learning?

Cooperative Learning 9.3 One challenge of technology based learning is student access to technology. With a partner, brainstorm ways you could increase student access to technology.

Multicultural Awareness 9.3 For an article that discusses Mexican students studying English who link up with peers in English-speaking countries to improve their language skills and insights into their own culture, read M.E. Meagher, "Learning English on the Internet," *Educational Leadership* 53(2) (October 1995): 88–90.

Reading 9.4 Have students read John G. Conyers, Toni Jappel, and Joanne Rooney, "How Technology Can Transform A School," *Educational Leadership* (February 1999). This article looks at how a school staff revamped its culture and curriculum to take advantage of the positive effects technology can have on student learning.

Reading 9.5 Kim Moyer, "Where Technology Use Is Second Nature: Old Meets New at a Minnesota Charter School," *Converge* 4, no. 2 (Feb 2001): 18-20 & 22.

Reflection and Journal Writing 9.2 What are your thoughts, attitudes, and fears about the future use of computer technology in your classrooms? Is classroom technology keeping up with the pace of technology in the business world, leisure technology, and other areas of life where students use computer skills. Are students better prepared to use technology than teachers?

Research and Suggested Reading 9.4 For an in-depth look at concerns parents have regarding tutorial services to improve their students' performance in schools, have students read Jerry Adler, "The Tutor Age," *Newsweek* (March 30, 1998).

Research and Suggested Reading 9.5 L. Buschman, "Katie's Computer," *Instructor* 101(33) (February 1992); L. Olson, "Profiles in Technology and State of the Art," *Teacher* (Winter, 1992); E. Schulz, "Back to the Future," *Teacher* (January 1992).

Research and Suggested Reading 9.6 To find out what can really happen to a school when levels of technology are significantly increased, that is, the effects on staff and students, read R. Buckley, "What Happens When Funding is Not an Issue?," *Educational Leadership* 53(2) (October 1995): 64–66.

9.6 What Educational Programs Exist for Students Placed At Risk?

Key Terms

> Student at risk
> Compensatory education
> Title I
> Pull-out programs
> Early intervention
> Reading Recovery
> Success for All

Lecture Notes and Discussion Questions

Critical Thinking 9.6 Instead of the term *at-risk students*, some educators use the term *students placed at risk*. What do you think is the distinction?

Discussion 9.10 All students return from summer vacation with decreased academic levels of achievement. For low-income students, however, the decrease is greater than that for middle-class children. What conditions may contribute to this difference?

Multicultural Awareness 9.4 Have students react to the findings in *The Condition of Education 1991*, prepared by the U.S. Department of Education, that the percentage of children living in poverty is 2 to 3 times greater for minorities than whites.

Cooperative Learning 9.4 Discuss in pairs how you as a teacher can build rapport with an at-risk learner. How might you develop rapport with at an-risk learner's family? Share your ideas with another pair. Develop a list you can all agree upon and share with the class.

Reading 9.6 Sandra Feldman, "Closing the Achievement Gap," *American Education* 25, no. 3 (Fall 2001): 7-9.

Research and Suggested Reading 9.7 For a synthesis of research on effective interventions for students who are at risk for school failure, see Slavin et al. (1995).

SUGGESTED READINGS

Conyers, J. G. "How Technology Can Transform a School." *Educational Leadership* 56(5) (1999): 84–87.

Fisher, C., ed. *Education and Technology.* San Francisco: Jossey-Bass, 1996.

Fritzberg, Gregory J. "From Rhetoric to Reality: Opportunity-to-Learn Standards and the Integrity of American Public School Reform." *Teacher Education Quarterly* 28, no. 1 (Win 2001): 169-87.

Fritzberg, Gregory J. "Less Than Equal: A Former Urban Schoolteacher Examines the Causes of Educational Disadvantagement." *Urban Review* 33, no. 2 (Jun 2001): 107-29.

Goldberg, Mark F. "Balanced Optimism: An Interview with Linda Darling-Hammond." *Phi Delta Kappan* 82, no. 9 (May 2001): 687-90.

Good, T.L. and J.E. Brophy. *Looking Into Classrooms,* 7th ed. Boston: Addison Wesley, 1997.

Heron, E. and C.M. Jorgeson. "Addressing Learning Differences Right From the Start." *Educational Leadership* 52(4) (1995): 56–59.

Jonassen, D. H. *Computers in the Classroom: Mindtools for Critical Thinking.* Upper Saddle River, NJ: Prentice Hall, 1996.

Juarez, T. "Why Any Grades at All, Father?" *Phi Delta Kappan* 77(5) (1996): 374–378.

Maddux, C.D., D.L. Johnson, and J.W. Willis. *Educational Computing: Learning with Tomorrow's Technologies,* 2nd ed. Boston: Allyn & Bacon, 1997.

Oakes, J. and A.S. Wells. "Detracking for High Student Achievement." *Educational Leadership* 55(6) (1998): 38–42.

Slavin, R.E. *Cooperative Learning: Theory, Research, and Practice,* 2nd ed. Boston: Allyn & Bacon, 1995.

Smith, Frank. "Just a Matter of Time." *Phi Delta Kappan* 82, no. 8 (Apr 2001): 572-76.

Stingfield, S. C. "What We Must Do For Students Placed At Risk." *Phi Delta Kappan* 77(1) (1995): 73–76.

Tapscott, D. "Educating the Net Generation." *Educational Leadership* 56(5) (1999): 6–12.

Testerman, J. "Holding At-risk Students: The Secret is One-on-One." *Phi Delta Kappan* 77(7) (1996): 364–366.

SUGGESTED MEDIA

Technology and the Writing Process, video, 28 minutes, 2000. This video demonstrates how technology can transform writing instruction, showing how to use technologies at all stages of the writing process while honoring diverse student ability levels. It shows students using electronic stationery, publishing a class book, and discussing writing techniques on the Internet. *From Insight Media.*

Technology and the Role of the Teacher: How to Integrate Technology Into the Classroom, video, 20 minutes, 1996. This video addresses technology not as a cure but as a tool for effective instruction. It shows how to restructure a classroom to incorporate technology and discusses pedagogical and emotional issues raised by its growing use in schools. *From Insight Media.*

Multimedia Dropout Prevention, CD-ROM. This is an interactive program that uses video, audio, and narration to highlight options and alternatives available to students who are thinking about dropping out of school. The dismal real-life experiences of high school dropouts reinforce the relationship between education and job opportunities. A Cambridge Education Production. *From Insight Media.*

Superhighway and You: Navigating the World Wide Web. Video, 22 minutes. 1999. This program defines the Web, differentiates it from the Internet, discusses the various browsers and how servers bring files and pages to the screen, and describes the services available and how to access them. Other topics include the differences between BBS and commercial providers, different databases, the composition of Internet addresses, and an analysis of digital forms. *From Films for the Humanities and Sciences.*

Supporting Students at Risk, video, 26 minutes. No matter how well planned the lesson or how skilled the teacher, there will always be some unhappy and disruptive students. This program examines how a school can support its teachers in dealing with particularly difficult students. *From Films for the Humanities and Sciences.*

Surfing the Internet: Practical Ideas for K-12 Classrooms, video, 20 minutes, 1995. Identifying student, teacher, and administrative resources on the Internet, this video suggests how to integrate information resources into classroom activities. It teaches how to create lessons for exploring the Internet and offers such ideas as initiating e-mail exchange programs with schools around the world. *From Insight Media.*

Chapter 10
Motivating Students to Learn

CHAPTER OVERVIEW

Motivation is the product of personality and ability factors of the student and the characteristics of learning tasks and settings. Contemporary theories of motivation include a discussion on motivation and behavioral learning theories, motivation and human needs, motivation and attribution theory, and motivation and expectancy theory. Teachers can emphasize learning goals and positive or empowering attributions. Motivation and goal orientations differ in that some are oriented toward learning goals or mastery goals, while others are oriented toward performance goals. Anxiety can block student performance by causing difficulties in initial learning, in using or transferring knowledge, and in demonstrating knowledge on tests.

Interest aroused by the fascination of the material itself, or intrinsic motivation, cannot sustain student interest indefinitely; therefore, schools apply a variety of reinforcers not inherent in the material, or extrinsic motivation. Teachers can enhance intrinsic motivation by arousing interest, maintaining curiosity, using a variety of interesting presentation modes, and helping students set their own goals.

Incentive systems can focus on individual or group performance (task mastery or grades) or focus on student effort and recognize student improvement over past performance by using praise effectively or using grades as incentives. Individual Learning Expectations (ILE) increase student achievement by rewarding improvements over past performance as a means to develop and maintain student effort. Incentives based on goal structure permit students to work in cooperation or competition. A student's success depends on the group performance, or individual performance is not dependent on the success/failure of others.

CHAPTER-AT-A-GLANCE

Chapter Outline	Objectives	Supplements
10.1 What Is Motivation?	• Define motivation and discuss its importance to teaching and learning.	• Handout Master 10.1 • Transparency T 87 • Test Bank Items
10.2 What Are Some Theories of Motivation? • Motivation and Behavioral Learning Theory • Motivation and Human Needs • Motivation and Attribution Theory • Motivation and Expectancy Theory	• Identify and describe the characteristics of four theories of motivation. • Explain and illustrate some implications of these theories for education.	• Transparency T89, T90, & T93 • Test Bank Items
10.3 How Can Achievement Motivation Be Enhanced? • Motivation and Goal Orientations • Learned Helplessness and Attribution Training • Teacher Expectations and Achievement • Anxiety and Achievement	• Define achievement motivation • Analyze ways that teachers can encourage intrinsic motivation and provide incentives for extrinsic motivation.	• Transparency T91 & T94 • Test Bank Items
10.4 How Can Teachers Increase Students' Motivation to Learn?	• Differentiate intrinsic and extrinsic motivation.	• Handout Master 10.2 • Transparency T92 & T95

• Intrinsic and Extrinsic Motivation • How Can Teachers Enhance Intrinsic Motivation? • Principles for Providing Incentives to Learn	• Analyze ways that teachers can encourage intrinsic motivation and provide incentives for extrinsic motivation.	• Video Clip 17, *Encouraging Involvement* • Test Items
10.5 How Can Teachers Reward Performance, Effort, and Improvement? • Using Praise Effectively • Teaching Students to Praise Themselves • Using Grades as Incentives • Incentive Systems Based on Goal Structure	• Describe five specific ways that teachers can enhance motivation to learn by rewarding performance effort, or improvement.	• Handout Master 10.4 • Transparency T51 • Chapter 10 Video Clip • Test Bank Items

ANNOTATED LECTURE OUTLINE

10.1 What Is Motivation?

Key Terms
Motivation

Lecture Notes and Discussion Questions

Discussion Question 10.1 Ask the class the following questions: What motivates teachers? Why do they teach? What motivates students? What motivates you? Write responses on the chalkboard.

Multicultural Awareness 10.1 Have students consider if cultural and gender factors influence motivation to attend college. Have them give specific examples. Where do these examples fit into the clusters from the previous discussion question? Do students see any trends in the clustering of motivation?

Post-Lecture Student Activities

Reflection and Journal Writing 10.1 Have students list everything they can think of that they did during the last 24 hours. Ask them to reflect during the next 24 hours on why they did each of the things they listed. Were possible rewards or punishments associated with an action?

10.2 What Are Some Theories of Motivation?

Key Terms
Deficiency needs
Growth needs
Self-actualization
Attribution theory
Locus of control
Expectancy theory
Expectancy-valence theory

Lecture Notes and Discussion Questions

Discussion Question 10.2 On the basis of Maslow's hierarchy, what is the rationale for the school breakfast program? If a student is afraid of being scolded or ridiculed by a teacher, which of Maslow's needs is not being met? Would such a fear affect a child's need to achieve?

Discussion Question 10.3 Why is a sense of belonging so important to students? How can you increase students' feelings of acceptance and belonging?

Discussion Question 10.4 The common attributions for failure and success are ability, effort, task difficulty, and luck. Are there others?

Discussion Question 10.5 On the basis of expectancy theory, ask students to predict the level of motivation in each of the following situations:
- Perceived probability of success under minimum effort is high; incentive value is high.
- Perceived probability of success under maximum effort is high; incentive value is moderate.
- Perceived probability of success under maximum effort is low; incentive value is moderate.

Example10.1 Fifty low-achieving and fifty high-achieving fifth-graders were given a task that they failed. Their reasons for the failure were recorded. All the low-achieving children ascribed failure to an internal cause, and 30 percent of this group expressed an illness or mood attribution. In contrast, the high-ability students attributed failure to bad luck, task difficulty, or experimenter unfairness

Post-Lecture Student Activities

Application 10.1 Maslow stated that growth is most likely to occur "when the delights of growth and anxieties of safety are greater than the anxieties of growth and delights of safety." From Maslow's perspective, how might a teacher best help a student who arrives in class on October 5 from a distant state? A student who presents a report in class? A student who claims to have been abused by another student?

Critical Thinking 10.1 If motivation, as a personality characteristic, is stable and difficult to alter, explain the implications for a student's efforts toward mastery learning.

Cooperative Learning 10.1 In pairs or with learning partners, have each student list a specific instance in the last month when he or she experienced a success or a failure. Applying attribution theory, have students indicate the attribution they gave at the time to account for their performance. After they share these accounts with their partners, ask students, "What are some ways in which attributions influence motivation? Can attribution explanations be modified?" To expand this activity, have students work together to modify one of their original attributions to model motivation for a successful outcome.

Cooperative Learning 10.2 Think, pair and share: What is an ideal classroom environment for nurturing student motivation? What are the characteristics of a motivating teacher?

Multicultural Awareness 10.2 Marcelle D. Christian and Oscar A. Barbarin, "Cultural Resources and Psychological Adjustment of African American Children: Effects of Spirituality and Racial Attribution," *Journal of Black Psychology* 27, no. 1 (Feb 2001): 43-63.

Research and Suggested Readings 10.1 Have students read "The effects of classroom perceptions on motivation: Gender and ethnic differences," by Lorrie A. Powdrill, Helen D. Just, Teresa Garcia, and Nicole A. Amador, University of Texas at Austin. This is a paper session, "Gender differences in motivation, self-regulation, and learning," at the annual meeting of the American Educational Research Association, Chicago IL, March 1997. This research was supported by grants awarded to Teresa Garcia from the University Research Institute and the Center of Applied Research and Development in Education at the University of Texas.

10.3 How Can Achievement Motivation Be Enhanced?

Key Terms
Learning goals
Performance goals
Learned helplessness

Lecture Notes and Discussion Questions

Discussion Question 10.6 When, if ever, is anxiety helpful to performance? Give an example from your own experience.

Post-Lecture Student Activities

Application 10.2 Assume that the students in your class have adopted the behavior pattern of learned helplessness to avoid failure. Design a three-point program that you, as the teacher, would implement to change that pattern of behavior and motivate your students to learn.

Cooperative Learning 10.3 In pairs, have students discuss the ways a teacher can increase a student's anxiety level through the use of questioning techniques. Are there appropriate and inappropriate approaches to increasing student anxiety? Is student anxiety sometimes a good thing? Why?

Research and Suggested Reading 10.2 Harald Valas, "Learned Helplessness and Psychological Adjustment: Effects of Age, Gender and Academic Achievement." *Scandinavian Journal of Educational Research* 45, no. 1 (Mar 2001): 71-90.

10.4 How Can Teachers Increase Students' Motivation to Learn?

Key Terms
Intrinsic incentive
Extrinsic incentive
Feedback

Lecture-Notes and Discussion Questions

Discussion Question 10.7 How can these typical student interests be used as motivators in different subject areas?
- Shooting pool
- T-shirt logos
- Song lyrics
- Human interest news stories
- Sports heroes

Teaching Suggestion 10.1 Divide the class into groups according to students' teaching level of interest (e.g., elementary school, middle school, high school, adult). Ask each group to generate a list of the classroom rewards that appear to serve as the strongest motivators for the age level concerned. Have the groups present their lists. Compare and discuss them.

<u>Post-Lecture Student Activities</u>

Research and Suggested Reading 10.3 John R. Todorovich, "Managing Success for Motivated Student Learning in Secondary Physical Education," *Journal of Physical Education, Recreation & Dance* 72, no. 2 (Feb 2001): 24-27.

Reflection and Journal Writing 10.2 Ask students to remember a teacher who motivated them or helped them to set goals. Ask them to create a conversation in which this teacher offers advice on ways to promote intrinsic motivation among students in the classroom.

10.5 How Can Teachers Reward Performance, Effort, and Improvement?

<u>Key Terms</u>
Contingent praise
Individual Learning Expectations
Goal structure

<u>Lecture Notes and Discussion Questions</u>

Discussion Question 10.8 What can you do as a teacher to encourage play-it-safe students to take risks and seek new educational experiences such as making a presentation in class, trying to type a report on the computer, writing about feelings in a journal, participating in special math classes, or taking a leadership role in a school club or activity?

<u>Post-Lecture Student Activities</u>

Application 10.3 Assign "Motivation Interviews" **(HM 10.3)**. Ask students to provide a brief summary and reflection.

Cooperative Learning 10.4 In small groups, have students share the results of the "Motivation Interviews" **(HM 10.3)**. Ask them to develop a poster titled "Wanted: A Motivating Teacher" based on the results of their discussions. The posters should list the characteristics of a motivating teacher.

Multicultural Awareness 10.3 Have students consider how cultural variables can interfere with learning expectations for academic tasks. What are the issues related to cultural differences that teachers need to keep in mind when setting up contingency reinforcements?

SUGGESTED READINGS

Chen, Ang. "A Theoretical Conceptualization for Motivation Research in Physical Education: An Integrated Perspective." *Quest* 53, no. 1 (2001): 35-58.

Graham, S., A.Z. Taylor, and C. Hudley. "Exploring Achievement Values Among Ethnic Minority Early Adolescents." *Educational Psychology* 90(4) (1998).

Hurst, Beth. "ABCs of Content Area Lesson Planning: Attention, Basics, and Comprehension." *Journal of Adolescent & Adult Literacy* 44, no. 8 (2001): 692-93.

McInerney, D.M., J. Hinkley, M. Dawson, and S. Van Etten. "Aboriginal, Anglo, and Immigrant Australian Students' Motivational Beliefs About Personal Academic Success: Are There Cultural Differences?" *Journal of Educational Psychology* 90(4) (1998).

Murdock, T. B. "The Social Context of Risk: Status and Motivational Predictors of Alienation in Middle School." *Murdock Journal of Educational Psychology* 91(1) (1999): 62-75.

Pool, Carolyn R. "Up with emotional health." *Educational Leadership* (May 1997): 12-14.

Noels, Kimberly A., Richard Clement, and Luc G. Pelletier. "Intrinsic, Extrinsic, and Integrative Orientations of French Canadian Learners of English." *Canadian Modern Language Review* 57, no. 3 (2001): 424-42.

Rea, Dan. "Maximizing the Motivated Mind for Emergent Giftedness." *Roeper Review* 23, no. 3 (2001): 157-64.

Wagner, Tony. "Leadership for Learning: An Action Theory of School Change." *Phi Delta Kappan* 82, no. 5 (2001): 378-83.

Wentzel, K. R. "Social-Motivational Processes and Interpersonal Relationships: Implications for Understanding Motivation at School." *Journal of Educational Psychology* 91(1) (1999): 76-97.

SUGGESTED MEDIA

Motivation, video, 2001. This program offers an in-depth exploration of the biological and social theories of motivation. Albert Bandura discusses his research on self-efficacy. *From Insight Media.*

Understanding the Unmotivated Child, video, 2000. Many students who appear intellectually and developmentally capable in non-academic activities seem to struggle with schoolwork, exams, and report cards. This video helps instructors understand the discrepancy between ability and performance. It considers early warning signs, the dangers of mislabeling a learning disability, and constructive communication strategies that can rectify a lack of motivation. *From Insight Media.*

Before Students Will Learn, video, 1996. Designed for teachers at all levels, this video explains the nature of motivation. It teaches how to identify and understand the primary needs (food, water, sex, air, rest, escape from pain, and elimination of waste) and examines the role they play in students' lives. It also explains why these needs may interfere with motivation. *From Insight Media.*

Increasing Motivation Through Gender Equity, video, 50 minutes, 1995. This program identifies unintentional gender biases that can hamper motivation and classroom performance for girls. It discusses instructional inequities and presents strategies for assuring equal motivation and learning opportunities for all students. *From Insight Media.*

Using Nine Powerful Motivators in the Classroom, video, 23 minutes, 1996. This video teaches how to use such powerful classroom motivators as personal gain, prestige, pleasure, imitation, and convenience. It shows how students' motivation changes over time and discusses ways to plan lessons at the correct level of difficulty. *From Insight Media.*

Increasing Motivation Through Active-Learning Strategies, video, 80 minutes, 1995. The more students think and respond during instruction, the greater their motivation and retention will be. This video offers techniques for enlisting students' active participation in learning. It shows how to adapt these techniques to personal teaching styles and how to apply them to various activities. *From Insight Media.*

Increasing Motivation Through Dynamic Presentation Skills, video, 45 minutes, 1995. This video shows how to grab and hold students' attention with fast-paced lessons and fresh communication techniques. It demonstrates how to create anticipatory sets that "hook" students on a lesson and shows how to use expressive and animated communication to maintain students' interest.

Motivating Underachievers, video, 28 minutes. Linus Pecaut and Larry Hawkins discuss motivational factors and effective interventions with low-achievers. *From Films for the Humanities and Sciences.*

Increasing Student Learning through Motivation, video. Raymond Wlodkowski explains how teachers can incorporate motivation strategies into instructional plans. *From 10X Assessment Associates.*

Increasing Student Effort: The Role of attribution Theory, video on using attribution theory to improve student effort and self-esteem. *From 10X Assessment Associates.*

Chapter 11
Effective Learning Environments

CHAPTER OVERVIEW

Maintaining an effective learning environment is key to learning. The use of time and how it impacts student achievement is considered. Allocated and engaged time are differentiated. Allocated time is defined as that time during which students have the opportunity to learn. Engaged time is the time students spend actually learning; same as time on task. Instructional time is often lost to testing, field trips, and other relevant activities, leaving approximately 60 percent of class time for learning.

Research has consistently shown that effective classroom management, based on commonsense planning, can prevent discipline problems from developing. Teachers need to be equipped with not only effective lessons and a positive learning environment, but also the class structure to reduce the frequency of behavior problems as well as strategies to deal with behavior problems when they occur.

Behavioral learning theories have direct applications to classroom management, with most strategies based on the notion of strengthening appropriate and weakening inappropriate behaviors. The school has an important role to play in preventing serious discipline problems. However, delinquent behavior often involves the police, courts, and social service agencies, as well as students' parents and peers. The chapter suggests judicious application of consequences, coupled with guided peer mediation.

CHAPTER-AT-A-GLANCE

Chapter Outline	Objectives	Supplements
11.1 What Is an Effective Learning Environment?	• Describe some of the resources teachers have for effective classroom management.	• Handout Master 11.1, 11.2, & 11.3 • Test Bank Items
11.2 What Is the Impact of Time on Learning? • Using Allocated Time for Instruction • Using Engaged Time Effectively • Can Time On Task Be Too High? • Classroom Management in the Student-Centered Classroom	• Describe ways that teachers maximize the use of allocated time and engaged time.	• Transparency T96 • Video Clip 18, *Expect Respect* • Test Bank Items
11.3 What Practices Contribute to Effective Classroom Management? • Starting Out the Year Right • Setting Class Rules	• Apply elements of teacher planning and classroom organization that help prevent discipline problems.	• Handout Master 11.4 • Transparency T97, T100, & T101 • Test Bank Items
11.4 What Are Some Strategies for Managing Routine Misbehavior? • Principle of Least Intervention • Prevention • Nonverbal Cues	• Analyze examples of classroom management strategies for managing routine misbehavior that illustrate the principle of least intervention.	• Handout Master 11.6 • Transparency T98 & 99 • Video Clip 19, *Using Rewards and Reinforcements* • Test Bank Items

• Praising Behavior That is Incompatible with Misbehavior • Praising Other Students • Verbal Reminders • Repeated Reminders • Applying Consequences		
11.5 How Is Applied Behavior Analysis Used to Manage More Serious Behavior Problems? • How Student Misbehavior Is Maintained • Principles of Applied Behavior Analysis • Applied Behavior • Analysis Programs • Ethics of Behavioral Methods	• Explain the basic procedure and appropriate use of applied behavior analysis in individual and group behavior modification programs.	• Test Bank Items
11.6 How Can Serious Behavior Problems Be Prevented? • Preventive Programs • Identifying Causes of Misbehavior • Enforcing Rules and Practices • Enforcing School Attendance • Avoiding Tracking • Practicing Intervention • Requesting Family Involvement • Using Peer Mediation • Judiciously Applying Consequences	• Discuss and evaluate alternative prevention methods and interventions against serious school discipline problems.	• Handout Master 11.5 • Transparency T102 • Video Clips • Test Bank Items

ANNOTATED LECTURE OUTLINE

11.1 What Is An Effective Learning Environment?

Key Terms

    Classroom management

    Discipline

Lecture Notes and Discussion Questions

    Discussion Questions 11. 1 How do the learning environments of elementary, middle, and high school classes differ? Do these differences influence attitudes of learning as students progress through the different levels of school? Does more learning take place in elementary, middle, or high school?

Post-Lecture Student Activities

    Multicultural Awareness 11.1 Have students read "Supporting Visual and Verbal Learning Preferences in a Second-Language Multimedia Learning Environment," by Jan L. Plass, Dorothy

M. Chun, Richard E. Mayer, and Detlev Leutner, *Journal of Educational Psychology, 90* (1) (March 1998).

11.2 What Is The Impact of Time on Learning?

Key Terms

Discipline
Engaged time
Time on-task
Allocated time
Accountability
Group alerting
Withitness
Overlapping
Mock participation

Lecture Notes and Discussion Questions

Computer Resources 11.1 Many computer programs have been written to help teachers manage their own activities inside and outside the classroom. Typical activities include on-line standard forms, individual education plans, student home and school databases, student reports, letters to parents, archiving and locating information, electronic mail, financial planning, and scheduling. Complete classroom management systems and computer-managed instruction are also available. For more information, see P. Geisert and M. Futrell, *Teachers, Computers, and Curriculum.* (Boston: Allyn & Bacon, 1995).

Discussion Question 11.2 What actions should a high school or college teacher take in dealing with students who come late to class?

Discussion Question 11.3 Which events or conditions commonly interrupt instruction in school classrooms?

Discussion Question 11.4 What strategies have students observed in their own school experiences that minimized interruptions, such as restroom breaks, roll call, returning class assignments, establishing cooperative groups, etc.

Discussion Question 11.5 What types of behavior problems are most likely to occur during seatwork activity?

Post-Lecture Student Activities

Application 11.1 Because lag time at the beginning and end of tasks eats up instructional time, have students brainstorm as many strategies as they can think of to avoid late starts and early finishes.

Application 11.2 Have students keep a journal of how allocated time is used in their college courses. Maintaining appropriate anonymity of the instructors, have students discuss their findings and compare ways that time is used in efficient and non-efficient ways.

Research and Suggested Readings 11.1 "Taking Time Seriously: A Theory of Socioemotional Selectivity," by Laura L. Carstensen, Derek M. Isaacowitz, and Susan T. Charles, *American Psychologist* 54(3) (March 1999). Why has psychology devoted so little time to time? Our perception of time is fundamental to motivation. Whether knowledge and novel cognitive pursuits take priority over social and emotional goals depends largely upon one's perception of time.

Lecture Notes and Discussion Questions

Discussion 11.6 What are the different routines in which teachers begin the school year? Are rules established on the first day? Does the teacher involve the students in rule-setting? Have students respond to these questions in a class discussion prior to reviewing this material.

Post-Lecture Student Activities

Cooperative Learning11.1 Have students work in pairs to develop appropriate rules for an elementary, middle, and high school class. Have them consider whether classroom rules are needed in college courses.

11.3 What Practices Contribute to Effective Classroom Management?

11.4 What Are Some Strategies for Managing Routine Misbehavior?

Key Terms
Nonverbal cues
Assertive discipline

Lecture Notes and Discussion Questions

Critical Thinking 11. 1 Some educators argue that an effective teacher is a good manager, but others object to this metaphor. These critics suggest that the image brings with it notions of manipulation and detachment. Ask your students whether they find the manager metaphor an appropriate choice. What other metaphors can they suggest for teachers acting to maintain order and discipline?

Discussion Question 11.7 Why do good teachers have fewer discipline problems than do poor teachers?

Discussion Question 11.8 What are appropriate types of consequences for the age level you plan to teach

Post-Lecture Student Activities

Application 11.3 Ask students what strategies they might use in these situations: Joanne is usually tardy for class because she and the teacher of the class before yours often chat. Eduardo is usually tardy for class because he is being held after the class before your class to receive a reprimand from the teacher. Mem is punctual but visits with her best friend in class and does not ready her materials for the start of class.

Application 11.4 List all the ways a teacher can discourage inappropriate behavior. Begin by listing the least disruptive techniques a teacher can use. Develop a continuum of disciplinary action using **(HM 11.4)** "Disciplinary Action Continuum."

Application 11.5 (HM 11.5) "Teacher Expectations Interviews." Ask students to summarize and reflect upon their findings.

Application 11.6 (HM 11.6) "Teacher Discipline Interviews." Ask students to summarize and reflect upon their findings.

Cooperative Learning 11.2 Divide the class into two groups. Ask one group to summarize their findings from the Teacher Expectations Interviews and have the other group summarize findings from the Teacher Discipline Interviews. Have elected group members share results with the class. Discuss the connections between the two reports.

Research and Suggested Readings 11.2 Edward Brainard, "Classroom Management: Seventy-Three Suggestions for Secondary School Teachers," *Clearing House* 74, no. 4 (Mar-Apr 2001): 207-10.

11.5 How Is Applied Behavior Analysis Used to Manage More Serious Behavior Problems?

Key Terms

> Applied behavior analysis
> Group contingencies
> Behavior modification
> Time-out
> Home-based reinforcement strategies
> Group contingency program

Lecture Notes and Discussion Questions

Critical Thinking 11.2 In what contexts, if any, do you think corporal punishment in school would be justified? How, if at all, would you carry out a time-out policy in your class? What are some causes and consequences of increased violence among children and youths? How would you respond to an act of violence between your students?

Application 11.7 Describe an effective time out. What behaviors must the teacher demonstrate? What classroom conditions are necessary for effective time outs? Why don't time outs work in some instances?

Discussion Question 11.9 Despite an obvious advantages of home-based reinforcement programs, a problem in many cases is ensuring that the parents will participate fully. What are some things that teachers can do to encourage their involvement.

Post-Lecture Student Activities

Application 11.8 Have students reflect on the following student responses and identify one stimulus that is in their control that might provoke this response or one reward that is in their control that might reinforce this behavior: a high achiever's boredom, mocking of praise by a low achiever, nonparticipation in class discussion, reading a book that is below the appropriate reading level.

Application 11.9 Have students suggest select reinforcers of praise, privileges, and tangible rewards that would be and would not be appropriate for elementary school students and for high school students.

Application 11.10 Reuben sometimes roughly pushes other students in line. You have chosen to punish him swiftly each time you see this pushing by promptly returning him to the classroom. The principal objects to this punishment and fears that it will only lead to more aggressive behavior. Defend your choice of action for modifying Reuben's behavior.

Application 11.11 Try this scenario on your students: Almost every day in your sixth-grade class, Rod talks out of turn and loses the reward for his group. The other group members are giving Rod a difficult time, and the parents of two students have called you to complain that the group reward system is unfair. What would you do to resolve this problem?

Application 11.12 There is one student in your class who is never prepared to do her work. She doesn't have a pencil, has misplaced her book, left her homework at home, doesn't understand the assignment, forgot to buy notebook paper, and so on. The result of all this is that she seldom hands in her homework assignments. As you approach this problem, how might you use rewards? Punishments? Shaping? Home-based reinforcement? Contingency contracting?

Cooperative Learning 11.3 Role play with another student a phone conversation with a parent of the student described in Application 11.12. Take turns being the parent and teacher.

Application 11.13 Draft a letter to the parents of the student in Application 11.12.

Cooperative Learning 11.4 For an instructional strategy to have students problem solve collaboratively and apply principles of behavioral management, see Handout Master 11.5, "Managing Serious Misconduct."

Multicultural Awareness 11.2 Discuss with your students any cultural differences in the verbal and nonverbal ways in which students show respect, pay attention, bid for a turn in conversation, and so on. How can cultural differences in interaction styles and expectations make classroom management more challenging?

Multicultural Awareness 11.3 JoAnn (Jodi) Crandall, "Rethinking Classroom Management: Creating an Effective Learning Community," *ESL Magazine* 4, no. 3 (May-Jun 2001): 10-13.

11.6 How Can Serious Behavior Problems Be Prevented?

Lecture Notes and Discussion Questions

Discussion Question 11.10 A child continually acts aggressively toward other children, pushing in line and hitting and kicking others during recess. Ask your students how they would set up a behavior management program to eliminate this behavior.

Discussion Question 11.11 With the recent increase in the incidents of school violence, ask your students if they think it is possible to identify serious behavior problems—both aggressive and non-aggressive in today's classrooms. Can they cite incidents of serious behavior problems in their high school classes where appropriate intervention may have prevented school tragedies such as those being discussed in the media today?

Post-Lecture Student Activities

Discussion Question 11.12 What are potential challenges and pitfalls of working with families of aggressive kids?

Multicultural Awareness 11.4 For a review of how cultural issues influence aggression in adolescents, have students read "A Cross-Cultural Study of family and Peer Correlates of Adolescent Misconduct," by Chuansheng Chen, Ellen Greenberger, Julia Lester, Oi Dong, and Miaw-Sheue Guo (1998), in *Developmental Psychology,* 34 (5).

Research and Suggested Readings 11.3 Have students read "Adolescent Storm and Stress, Reconsidered," by Jeffrey Jensen Arnett in *American Psychologist,* 54(5) (1998). Nearly 100 years after G. Stanley Hall characterized adolescence as a time of storm and stress, that view is ripe for reevaluation. What do we know about turmoil during adolescence?

SUGGESTED READINGS

Adelman, N., B. Haslam, B. Pringle, and K. Walking-Eagle. *Teachers' uses of time in the context of reform: A casebook of teacher experiences.* Washington, DC: Policy Studies Associates, 1995.

Albert, P.A. and A.C. Troutman. *Applied behavior analysis for teachers,* 5th ed. Columbus, OH: Merrill, 1999.

Arnold, D. H., McWilliams, L. and Arnold, E. H. "Teacher Discipline and Child Misbehavior in Day Care: Untangling Causality With Correlational Data." *Developmental Psychology,* 34(2) (1998).

Egan, S. K., T.C. Monson, and D.G. Perry. "Social–Cognitive Influences on Change in Aggression Over Time." *Developmental Psychology,* 34(5) (1998).

Emmer, E.T., C.M. Evertson, J.P. Sanford, B.B. Clements, and M.E. Worsham. *Classroom Management for Secondary Teachers,* 4th ed. Boston: Allyn & Bacon, 1997.

Evertson, C.M., E.T. Emmer, B.S. Clements, J.P. Sanford, and M.E. Worsham. *Classroom Managements for Elementary Teachers,* 4th ed. Boston: Allyn & Bacon, 1997.

Freidberg, H.J. *Beyond Behaviorism: Changing the Classroom Management Paradigm.* Boston: Allyn & Bacon, 1999.

Hyman, I.A. *School Discipline and School Violence: The Teacher Variance Approach.* Boston: Allyn & Bacon, 1997.

Larrivee, B. *Authentic Classroom Management: Creating A Community of Learners.* Boston: Allyn & Bacon, 1999.

Logan, Kent R. and Sue S. Stein. "The Research Lead Teacher Model: Helping General Education Teachers Deal with Classroom Behavior Problems." *TEACHING Exceptional Children* 33, no. 3 (2001): 10-15.

McCormack, Ann Carolyn. "Investigating the Impact of an Internship on the Classroom Management Beliefs of Preservice Teachers." *Professional Educator* 23, no. 2 (2001): 11-22.

Zimmerman, Joy. "How Much Does Time Affect Learning?" *Principal* 80, no. 3 (2001): 6-11.

SUGGESTED MEDIA

Collaborative Classroom Management, video, 43 minutes, 2001. In this video, best-selling author Bob Sylwester discusses the benefits of using knowledge about cognition and culture in classroom management.

Preventing Classroom Discipline Problems, CD-ROM, 2001. This CD-ROM offers individual training exercises for handling and preventing disruptive classroom behavior. Based on the video version, this CD-ROM features the advice of national consultant Howard Seeman.

Interactive Cases in Teacher Education: Classroom Management, CD-ROM, software, 1995, designed by Peter Desberg, Joel Colbert, and Kimberly Trimble. *From Allyn & Bacon.*

Catching Them Early, video, 1999. This video cites a program in Richmond, California, where gang violence, drug abuse, and teen pregnancy are daily realities for at-risk youth. Together with several civic organizations and school programs, their mission is to provide wholesome activities that build confidence resolution, show teen parents how to take care of their children, teach life skills, and above all, offer love and emotional support so that the children and teenagers can learn to live better lives. *From Films for the Humanities and Sciences.*

What to Do When Students Act Out, 2 volume, video, 120 minutes total, 1999. This set offers a continuum of strategies for decreasing student misbehavior that teachers can tailor to the context and level of student development. It shows how to vary disciplinary approach, prevent disruptive behavior, and guide students to correct their own behavior. *From Insight Media.*

Managing Today's Classroom: Elementary Schools, video, 30 minutes, 1998. This video shows how to create a positive learning environment that encourages appropriate student behavior and facilitates student achievement. Designed for elementary teachers, it explains how to foster mutual respect, promote self-regulation and autonomy, create a sense of community, and motivate students through the design of an engaging curriculum. *From Insight Media.*

Dealing With Discipline Problems, 3 volumes, 71 minutes total, 1995. Elementary: Cheating, Refusing to Work, Not Responding. Illustrates strategies for handling cheating, willfulness, and unresponsiveness at the elementary level. It presents vignettes of a usually well-behaved high-achiever who cheats on a test, a chronically difficult student, and a trouble student who refuses to open up to her teacher. *From Insight Media.*

Dealing With Discipline Problems, 3 volumes, 65 minutes total, 1995. Elementary: Excuses, Arguing, Repeated Misbehavior. Uses three elementary school vignettes to illustrate issues of commitment, conflict resolution, and behavior modification. *From Insight Media.*

Chapter 12
Learners with Exceptionalities

CHAPTER OVERVIEW

When students need special programs other than compensatory programs, early intervention, or prevention programs, they are called exceptional learners. Definitions and prevalence of students with mental retardation; learning disabilities; speech and language disorders; emotional disorders; autism; sensory, physical and health impairments; as well as those who are gifted and talented are presented. Consideration of students with disabilities as "people-first" is discussed early in the chapter to set the tone of discussions that follow on inclusion and other instructional topics.

In accordance with Public Law 101-476, IDEA (Individuals with Disabilities Education Act), every school district must provide a range of special education services. Those services, referred to as a continuum of services, include: general education classroom placement, consultation and itinerant services, resource room placement, special class with part-time mainstreaming, self-contained special education classes, and other special services, such as speech, physical therapy, or psychological services. A discussion on the 1997 amendments that revised IDEA are also included.

A discussion on inclusion provides clarity to what is meant by "full inclusion" for students with special needs in the school. Current trends in special education encourage the importance of collaboration and working with special education teams. In addition, the importance of social integration of students with disabilities is emphasized.

CHAPTER–AT–A–GLANCE

Chapter Outline	Objectives	Supplements
12.1 Who Are Learners With Exceptionalities? • "People-First" • Types of Exceptionalities and the Numbers of Students Served • Students with Mental Retardation • Students with Learning Disabilities • Students with Communication Disorders • Students with Emotional and Behavioral Disorders • Students with Sensory, Physical, and Health Impairments • Students Who Are Gifted and Talented	• Define what is meant by "people-first" as a concept in serving learners with exceptionalities. • Explain what is meant by "exceptional" students. • Distinguish between the terms "disability" and "handicap." • Describe the characteristics of students who are mentally retarded, those who have specific learning disabilities, those who are gifted and talented, and those students who have emotional disorders, sensory or physical disabilities, speech and language impairments, and students with autism.	• Handout Master 12.1, 12.3, 12.4, & 12.5 • Transparency T26, T28, T29, T30, T31, & T32 • Test Bank Items
12.2 What Is Special Education? • Public Law 94-142 and IDEA • An Array of Special Education Services		
12.3 What Is Inclusion?	• Distinguish between the terms	• Handout Master 12.7, 12.8,

• Research Inclusion • Adapting Instruction • Teaching Learning Strategies and Metacognitive Awareness • Prevention and Early Intervention • Computers and Students with Disabilities • Buddy Systems and Peer Tutoring • Special-Education Teams • Social Integration of Students with Disabilities	"mainstreaming" and "inclusion." • Illustrate four approaches to accommodating instruction for student who are mainstreamed or in inclusion programs.	12.9, & 12.10 • Transparency T37 • Video Clip 20, *Inclusion* • Test Bank Items

ANNOTATED LECTURE OUTLINE

12.1 Who Are Learners with Exceptionalities?

Key Terms

Learners with Exceptionalities
Disability
Handicap
Mental retardation
Intelligence quotient (IQ)
Learning disabilities
Attention-deficit/hyperactivity disorder (ADHD)
Speech disorders
Language disorders
Emotional and behavioral disorders
Conduct disorders
Autism
Sensory impairment
Vision loss
Hearing disabilities
Giftedness
Acceleration Programs
Enrichment Programs

Lecture Notes and Discussion Questions

Critical Thinking 12.1 Invite to class a school psychologist or educational diagnostician whose job is to test students and make special-education placement recommendations. Have students ask questions about the uses and misuses of IQ tests and testing. After the visit, discuss with students how they will use information from these tests in their classrooms.

Discussion Question 12.1 What are some reasons the number of students classified as learning disabled has increased dramatically in recent years? What are some reasons why boys might be identified as learning disabled more often than girls? What are some reasons why many more fourth-graders than second-graders are identified as learning disabled?

Discussion Question 12.2 What would you do as a teacher if you observed students mocking a student who stuttered in class?

Discussion Question 12.3 If you had an epileptic child who was prone to tonic-clonic seizures in your class, how would you prepare other students?

Discussion Question 12.4 Which idea do you think has more merit as a strategy for educating gifted students: acceleration or enrichment? Why?

Post-Lecture Student Activities

Application 12.1 Introduce this section on exceptional students by using the instructional strategy "Who Are Exceptional Learners?" described in the Instructor's Resource Manual, Handout Master 12.2, "Myths and Facts about Special Education," in the Instructor's Resource Manual that supports this activity.

Application 12.2 For an activity to introduce the concept of mental retardation, see "Mental Retardation: Myth and Facts" in the Instructor's Resource Manual, Handout Master 12.3. "Myths and Facts about People with Mental Retardation," in the Instructor's Resource Manual supports this activity.

Multicultural Awareness 12.1 Students with speech and communication disorders consistently report that people treat them as if they were stupid. Why do you think we equate intelligence with language usage? Does this attitude also have an impact on children for whom English is a second language?

Multicultural Awareness 12.2 Have students read Guoping Zhao, "A Cross-Cultural Approach towards Students with Disabilities," *Educational Foundations* 15, no. 1 (Win 2001): 25-38.

Multicultural Awareness 12.3 For a discussion on the influence of multicultural variables on learning disabilities in bilingual education classrooms, read Todd V. Gletcher, Candace S. Bos, and Lorri M. Johnson, "Accommodating English Language Learners With Language and Learning Disabilities in Bilingual Education Classrooms," *Learning Disabilities Research and Practice* *14*(2) (Spring 1999): 80–92.

Reading 12.1 Belva C. Collins and Meada Hall, "Just Say 'No!' and Walk Away: Teaching Students with Mental Disabilities to Resist Peer Pressure," *Teaching Exceptional Children* 31(6) (July/August 1999).

Reading 12.2 Jean Whitney-Thomas and Mairead Moloney, "'Who I Am and What I Want': Adolescent' Self-Definition and Struggles," *Exceptional Children* 67, no. 3 (Spr 2001): 375-89.

Reading 12.3 Claire E. Hughes and Wendy A. Murawski, "Lessons from Another Field: Applying Coteaching Strategies to Gifted Education," *Gifted Child Quarterly* 45, no. 3 (Sum 2001): 195-204.

Reading 12.4 Sean Joseph Smith, LuAnn Jordan, Nancy L. Corbet, and Ann S. Dillon, "Teachers Learn About ADHD on the Web: An Online Graduate Special Education Course," *Teaching Exceptional Children* 31(6) (July/August 1999).

Reading 12.5 Candace S. Bos, Maria L. Nahmias, and Magda A. Urban, "Targeting Home-School Collaboration for Students with AD/HD," *Teaching Exceptional Children* 31(6) (July/August 1999).

Reading 12.6 Evonn N. Welton, "Getting the Homework Back from the Dog: How to Help Inattentive Students Find Success in School," *Teaching Exceptional Children* 31(6) (July/August 1999).

Reading 12.7 Kathy Loechler, "Frequently Asked Questions About ADHD and the Answers from the Internet," *Teaching Exceptional Children* 31(6) (July/August 1999).

Reading 12.8 For a discussion on the use of technology in teaching mentally retarded students, have students read Micheal L. Wehmeyer, "Assistive Technology and Students With Mental Retardation: Utilization and Barriers," *Journal of Special Education* 14(1) (Winter 1999): 48–58.

Readings and Reflection 12.1 Timothy E. Morse, "Designing Appropriate Curriculum for Special Education Students in Urban Schools," *Education and Urban Society* 34, no. 1 (Nov 2001): 4-17.

Readings and Research 12.1 Marleen C. Pugach and Cynthia L. Warger, "Curriculum Matters: Raising Expectations for Students with Disabilities," *Remedial and Special Education* 22, no. 4 (Jul-Aug 2001): 194-96 & 213.

Reflection and Journal Writing 12.1 Ask students who experienced any articulation, stuttering, or other speech problem as children to write about any experience in their school or personal life that was affected by this problem. Have other students recall a person they knew with such a problem and write a description of their observations and how they reacted to the person's speech problem.

Research and Suggested Reading 12.1 For good general references to all the exceptionality areas, see M. Hardman, et al., *Human Exceptionality: Society, School, and Family*, 5th ed. (Boston: Allyn & Bacon, 1996); and D. Hallahan and J. Kauffman, *Exceptional Children: An Introduction to Special Education*, 8th ed. (Boston: Allyn & Bacon, 2000).

Research and Suggested Reading 12.2 Mitchell L. Yell, Michael E. Rozalski, and Erik Drasgow, "Disciplining Students with Disabilities," *Focus on Exceptional Children* 33, no. 9 (May 2001): 1-20.

Research and Suggested Reading 12.3 Phil Foreman, Sid Bourke, Gita Mishra, and Rick Frost, "Assessing the Support Needs of Children with a Disability in Regular Classes," *International Journal of Disability, Development and Education* 48, no. 3 (Sep 2001): 239-52.

Research and Suggested Reading 12.4 Rachel F. Quenemoen, "IEPs within Standards-based Reform," *Assessment for Effective Intervention* 26, no. 2 (Win 2001): 75-76.

Research and Suggested Reading 12.5 Festus E. Obiakor, "Multicultural Education: Powerful Tool for Preparing Future General and Special Educators," *Teacher Education and Special Education* 24, no. 3 (Sum 2001): 241-55.

12.2 What Is Special Education?

Key Terms

> Special education
> Public Law 92-142
> Individuals with Disabilities Education Act (IDEA)
> IDEA '97
> Least restrictive environment
> Mainstreaming
> Individual Education Program (IEP)
> collaboration

Lecture Notes and Discussion Questions

Discussion Question 12.5 Use the analogy of the small fish, caught but too small to keep, thrown back into the "mainstream" to sink or swim. What are its chances of survival? Does it depend on the condition of the fish following its "catch"? Does the probability of success of the mainstreamed student similarly depend on the degree and type of disability?

Discussion Question 12.6 When considering what special education really is, should the emphasis be placed on "special" or "education"? Explain.

Post-Lecture Student Activities

Critical Thinking 12.2 Not all students with disabilities receive special education services in public schools. Explain.

Critical Thinking 12.3 Special Education remains a critical shortage area for classroom supply. There are always positions available for teachers in special education programs. Consider the reasons why this is the case. Is it because of a continuous increase in identified students? Is it related to teacher satisfaction? For a discussion on this topic, have students read M. David Miller, Mary T. Brownwell, and Stephen W. Smith, "Factors That Predict Teachers Staying In, Leaving, or Transferring From the Special Education Classroom," *Exceptional Children* 65(2) (Winter, 1999): 201–219.

Reading 12.9 Diane Torres Raborn and Mary Jo Daniel, "Oobleck: A Scientific Encounter of the Special Education Kind," *Teaching Exceptional Children* 31(6) (July/August 1999).

Reading 12.10 Helen Hammond, "Identifying Best Family-Centered Practices in Early-Intervention Programs," *Teaching Exceptional Children* 31(6) (July/August 1999).

12.3 What Is Inclusion?

Key Terms
Full inclusion

Lecture Notes and Discussion Questions

Discussion Question 12.7 What are some similarities and differences between mainstreaming and mixed-ability grouping? What are the benefits of mainstreaming mildly disabled and gifted students to the student? To the teacher? To the social climate of the school?

Post-Lecture Student Activities

Application 12.3 Assign "Teacher Interviews" **(HM 12.10)**. Ask students to summarize and reflect upon their findings.

Cooperative Learning 12.1 In small groups, students should list the concerns they have regarding meeting the needs of exceptional learners. Have students brainstorm a list of resources available to teachers of special need students. Encourage creativity and "out of the box" thinking.

Reading 12.11 Kathleen Cage Mittag and Anthony K. Van Reusen, "One Fish, Two Fish, Pretzel Fish! Learning Estimation and Other Advanced Math Concepts in an Inclusive Class," *Teaching Exceptional Children* 31(6) (July/August 1999).

Reading 12.12 Paula J. Stanovich, "Conversations About Inclusion," *Teaching Exceptional Children* 31(6) (July/August, 1999).

Reading 12.13 Dean Corrigan defends mainstreaming, and W. N. Bender raises criticisms. Proponents of mainstreaming can also obtain literature on full inclusion by writing to Schools Are For Everyone (SAFE), 360 South Third Street, Suite 101, Columbus, OH 43215. *Teaching Exceptional Children* 31(6) (July/August 1999).

Reading 12.14 Stephanie Wasta, Margaret Grant Scott, Nancy Marchand-Martella, and Robert Harris, "From the Great Wall to a Great Inclusive Classroom: Integrated Instruction at Work," *Teaching Exceptional Children* 31(6) (July/August 1999).

Research and Suggested Reading 12.6 Liv Randi Opdal, Siri Wormnaes, Ali Habayeb, "Teachers' Opinions about Inclusion: A Pilot Study in a Palestinian Context," *International Journal of Disability, Development and Education* 48, no. 2 (Jun 2001): 143-62.

Research and Suggested Reading 12.7 Margaret E. King-Sears, "Teacher and Researcher Co-Design Self-Management Content for an Inclusive Setting: Research Training, Intervention, and Generalization Effects on Student Performance," *Education and Training in Mental Retardation and Developmental Disabilities* 34(2) (June 1999): 134–157.

THEORY INTO PRACTICE

Fostering Social Integration of Students with Special Needs
More and more, students with special needs are becoming an integral part of the general education classroom experience. Regardless of the student's age or the grade level being taught, teachers have many ways to foster positive social integration of students with regular and special needs. Several suggestions follow.

- By being caring and accepting, model the attitude that all students belong in your classroom.
- Explain to students that everyone is capable of learning and some learn in different ways.
- Use the Individualized Education Plan (IEP) to guide instruction of students with special needs.
- Have expectations of students that are developmentally appropriate and achievement oriented.
- Use cooperative leaning strategies in which all students are given a chance to work together to solve common problems.
- Use peer tutors or peer helpers when assistance is needed.
- Provide opportunities for all students to participate in classroom routines and responsibilities.
- Set aside time for students to communicate and develop relationships with each other.
- Capitalize on students' academic and leisure interests to bring students together.

SUGGESTED READINGS
Yell, Mitchell L. and Antonis Katsiyannis. "Legal Issues. Promises and Challenges in Education Law: 25 Years of Legal Developments." *Preventing School Failure* 45, no. 2 (Win 2001): 82-88.

Birely, M. *Crossover Children: A Sourcebook for Helping Children Who are Gifted and Learning Disabled,* 2nd ed. CEC, 1995.

Bos, C.S. and S. Vaughan. *Strategies For Teaching Students With Learning and Behavior Problems,* 4th ed. Boston: Allyn & Bacon, 1998.

Bryan, W. V. *In Search of Freedom: How Persons with Disabilities Have Been Disenfranchised from the Mainstream of American Society.* Springfield, IL: Charles C. Thomas, 1996.

Davis, G.A. and S.B. Rimm. *Education of the Gifted and Ttalented,* 4th ed. Boston: Allyn & Bacon, 1998.

Ford, B.A., ed. *Multiple Voices for Ethnically Diverse Exceptional Learners.* CEC, 1995.

Friend, M. and W.D. Bursock. *Including Students With Special Needs: A Practical Guide for Classroom Teachers*, 2nd ed. Boston: Allyn & Bacon, 1999.

Hallahan, D.P. and J.M. Kauffman. *Exceptional children,* 7th ed. Boston: Allyn & Bacon, 1997.

Higgins, P.C. and J.E. Nash. *Understanding Deafness Socially: Continuities in Research and Theory,* 2nd ed. Springfield, IL: Charles C. Thomas, 1996.

Miles, T.R. and E. Miles. *Dyslexia: A Hundred Years On,* 2nd ed. Philadelphia, PA: Open University Press, 1999.

Miller, R. *The Developmentally Appropriate Inclusive Classroom Early Education.* Albany, NY: Delmar, 1996.

O'Neill, Paul T. "Special Education and High Stakes Testing: An Analysis of Current Law and Policy." *Journal of Law and Education* 30, no. 2 (Apr 2001): 185-222.

Peetsma, Thea, Margaretha Vergeer, Sjoerd Karsten, and Jaap Roeleveld. "Inclusion in Education: Comparing Pupils' Development in Special and Regular Education." *Educational Review* 53, no. 2 (Jun 2001): 125-35.

Skirtic, T.M. *Disability Democracy: Reconstructing (Special) Education for Postmodernity.* New York: Teachers' College Press, 1995.

Strichart, S.S., C.T. Mangrum II, and P. Ianuzzi. *Teaching Study Skills and Strategies to Students With LD, ADD, or Special Needs*, 2nd ed. (1998).

Taylor, R. *Assessment of Exceptional Students: Educational and Psychological Procedures,* 4th ed. Boston: Allyn & Bacon, 1997.

Vlachou, A. *Struggles for Inclusive Education: An Ethnographic Study.* Philadelphia, PA: Open University Press, 1997.

Yell, Mitchell L. and Antonis Katsiyannis. "Legal Issues. Promises and Challenges in Education Law: 25 Years of Legal Developments." *Preventing School Failure* 45, no. 2 (Win 2001): 82-88.

SUGGESTED MEDIA

Special People, Special Needs, video, 51 minutes, 2000. Designed to increase caregivers' awareness of the nature of special needs, this video explains some of the causes of disabilities. It describes characteristics, capabilities, and expectations for children with mental retardation, physical or neurological impairments, sensory deficits, physical disabilities, communication limitations, and emotional/behavioral disorders. It discusses cerebral palsy, arthritis, muscular dystrophy, mental retardation, hearing loss, vision impairment, language impairment, aggression, anxiety, and withdrawal, and demonstrates the use of specialized equipment. *From Insight Media.*

A New I.D.E.A. for Special Education: Understanding the System and the New Law, video, 40 minutes. This video examines recent changes to the Individuals with Disabilities in Education Act (IDEA), the law governing special education. It explains the new law, the referral process, the evaluation process, placement and related services, and standardized testing. It also offers tips from parents with children in special education and advice from experts in the field. *From Insight Media.*

What's Best for Matthew? CD-ROM, 2000. This video walks users through the process of writing an IEP. It presents the history of Matthew's case, offers access to knowledgeable sources, and shows how to record and prioritize impressions. It teaches how to set short and long-term goals, determine measurable objectives, decide upon evaluation criteria, and identify necessary resources. *From Insight Media.*

Attention Deficit Disorder and Self-Esteem, video, 15 minutes, 1998. This video examines the symptoms of ADHD, its possible causes, common treatments, and its psychological and social effects. Stressing the importance of diagnosis, educators and medical professionals discuss different treatment methods for ADHD. *From Insight Media.*

Linking Medicine and Education for the Child With Special Needs, video, 34 minutes, 1998. This program examines how advances in neuroscience, diagnostic procedures, prescription medication, and treatment approaches can help special educators, classroom teachers, and school nurses meet the health care requirements of special-needs students. The video examines how teachers can approach students with special needs, including students with autism, ADD, and fetal alcohol syndrome. *From Insight Media..*

Standards and Inclusion: Can We Have Both? video, 40 minutes, 1998. The debate between including students with disabilities in a regular classroom and maintaining academic standards is explored. *From Insight Media.*

Breakthrough: How to Reach Students With Autism, video, 25 minutes, 1998. Actual classroom footage is used to present issues in teaching autistic students. The program also covers self-abuse. *From Insight Media.*

Assistive Technology: Meeting the Needs of All our Students, video, 2 volumes, 30 minutes each, 1997. A panel of education professionals discusses assistive technology and considers which special-needs students benefit from it. Communication boards, auditory trainers, closed captioning, and picture-exchange systems are featured. *From Insight Media.*

Learning Disabilities and Discipline, video 60 minutes, 1997. Produced by the Learning Disabilities Project at WETA in Washington, DC, this program addresses preventive discipline to resolve behavioral conflicts and the role of a stable environment in helping students achieve in the classroom. *From Insight Media.*

Without Pity: A Film about Abilities, video, 56 minutes, 1998. The HBO award winning film, hosted by Christopher Reeve, celebrates the abilities of persons with disabilities. A variety of both moderate and severe disabilities are addressed in this very informative and positive film. *From Films for the Humanities and Sciences.*

Understanding the Disabled: Dances with the Dinosaur, video, 40 minutes, 1999. Told from the point of view of the physically challenged, this film realistically depicts problems and triumphs of a high school student in a wheel chair. It raises awareness of stereotyping, inaccessibility, and constant pressure of crossing into the mainstream. *From Films for the Humanities and Sciences.*

Epilepsy: The Storm Within, video, 27 minutes, 1999. This film addresses the second most common neurological disorder in the U.S. and examines its causes, seizure activity and what should and should not be done. Sufferers of epilepsy describe what it is like living with this disorder. *From Films for the Humanities and Sciences.*

Chapter 13
Assessing Student Learning

CHAPTER OVERVIEW

Instructional or behavioral objectives are clear statements about what students should know and be able to do at the end of a lesson, unit, or course. Objectives state the conditions under which learning will be assessed and criteria for success. The use of the taxonomies or instructional objectives, such as Bloom's Taxonomy, helps to classify and organize instructional activities.

Formal measures of student performance are important as feedback, information, and incentives. To be useful as feedback, evaluations should be as specific as possible. Evaluation provides valuable information about teaching outcome. Evaluation can motivate students to give or improve a certain level of performance. Formative evaluations are given to discover strengths and weakness in learning or to make midcourse corrections in pace or content of instruction. In contrast, summative evaluation refers to end measure, final tests, of student knowledge.

Norm-referenced evaluations focus on comparisons of a student's scores, while criterion-referenced evaluations focus on assessing a student's mastery of specific skills, without comparison to other student performance. Authentic assessment refers to a student's actual performance or demonstration of skills. Teachers must choose different assessment tools for different purposes in order to match evaluation strategies with goals.

In addition, this chapter focuses on test construction and important elements that address bias, grading options, writing effective test items, and using tables of specification to organize assessment. Authentic assessment and portfolios as evaluation options are presented with scoring rubrics for performance assessments. Finally, there is a comprehensive discussion on grading options and the use of alternative assessment in assigning report card grades.

CHAPTER–AT–A–GLANCE

Chapter Outline	Objectives	Supplements
13.1 What Are Instructional Objectives and How Are They Used? • Planning Lesson Objectives • Linking Objectives and Assessment • Using Taxonomies of Instructional Objectives • Research on Instructional Objectives	• Write appropriate, specific, and clear objectives of various taxonomic types, and practice using backward planning to develop a unit of study.	• Handout Master 13.1 & 13.2 • Transparency T53, T75, T76, T105, & T119 • Test Bank Items
13.2 Why Is Evaluation Important? • Evaluation as Feedback • Evaluation as Information • Evaluation as Incentive	• Discuss six main reasons for the importance of evaluating student learning.	• Test Bank Items
13.3 How Is Student Learning Evaluated? • Formative and Summative Evaluations • Norm-Referenced and	• Compare and contrast different kinds of classroom assessment and their appropriate use, including formative and summative	• Handout Master 13.6 • Transparency T109 • Test Bank Items

Criterion-Referenced Evaluations • Matching Evaluation Strategies with Goals	tests and norm-referenced and criterion-referenced tests.	
13.4 How Are Tests Constructed? • Principles of Achievement Testing • Using a Table of Specifications • Writing Selected Response Test Items • Writing Constructed-Response Items • Writing and Evaluating Essay Tests • Writing and Evaluating Problem-Solving Items	• Construct an appropriate student test with a variety of selected response test items, such as well-written multiple-choice, true-false, completion, matching, essay, and problem-solving items.	• Handout Master 13.3, 13.4 & 13.5 • Transparency T118, T120, & T121 • Test Bank Items
13.5 What Are Authentic Portfolio and Performance Assessment? • Portfolio Assessment • Performance Assessment • How Well Do Performance Assessments Work? • Scoring Rubrics for Performance Assessments	• Define assessment and show how portfolio and performance assessment can be used in elementary, middle, and secondary school classrooms for effective student evaluation.	• Handout Master 13.6 • Transparency T122 & T123 • Video Clip 21, *Portfolio Assessment* • Test Bank Items
13.6 How Are Grades Determined? • Establishing Grade Criteria • Assigning Letter Grades • Performance Grading • Other Alternative Grading Systems • Assigning Report Card Grades	• Express an appropriate grading policy and defend it in relation to criteria or standards; describe the conventions or reporting grades.	• Handout Master 13.6 • Transparency T112, T127, & T128 • Video Clip 22, *Grading Student Work* • Test Bank Items

ANNOTATED LECTURE OUTLINE

13.1 What Are Instructional Objectives and How Are They Used?

Key Terms
       Instructional objective
       Task analysis
       Backward planning
       Assessment
       Teaching objectives
       Learning objectives
       Taxonomy of educational objectives
       Behavior content matrix
       Affective objectives

<u>**Lecture Notes and Discussion Questions**</u>

Discussion Question 13.1 What level of objectives seems most important in your teaching area? Are the levels clearly distinguishable (e.g., comprehension versus application)? Do they seem to form a true hierarchy?

Discussion Question 13.2 Are analysis, synthesis and evaluation objectives reserved only for upper level students? Give an example of these objectives as used in a primary class. (Suggestion: This concept can be applied to the process of making applesauce or mixing primary paint colors for easel painting.)

<u>**Post-Lecture Student Activities**</u>

Application 13.1 Using transparency T75, "Mager's Three-Part Objectives," have students write "yes" if all three parts are present in an objective; otherwise, they should identify the missing part or parts by letter, as follows: A = Behavior, B = Conditions of performance, C = Performance criteria. Suggested answers: 1.C, 2.B, 3.Yes, 4.Yes, 5.C, 6.B, 7.Yes.

Application 13. 2 Have students write a cognitive behavioral objective (using Mager's format) for their teaching area. Indicate which level of Bloom's taxonomy of the cognitive domain their objective represents.

Critical Thinking 13.1 Mr. Pallitino, an art teacher, is adamantly opposed to the use of instructional objectives. He argues that they stifle creativity and spontaneity and promote low-level learning. Have students role-play a dialogue they might have with Mr. Pallitino arguing for the use of objectives.

Critical Thinking 13.2 Should there be objectives for schools that are shaped by a state or national agenda? If so, who should set that agenda?

Critical Thinking 13.3 What kinds of instructional objectives would be involved if you wanted students to be able to identify the distinguishing features of a human skeleton, explain the relationships among its parts, and hypothesize what the person would have looked like in the flesh?

Multicultural Awareness 13.1 Affective objectives differ for different communities depending on ethnicity, culture, religion, and socioeconomic orientation. Think of an example of an affective objective that might be given priority in one community and be highly controversial in another.

13.2 Why Is Evaluation Important?

<u>**Key Terms**</u>
Evaluation

<u>**Lecture Notes and Discussion Questions**</u>

Discussion Question 13.3 If all forms of evaluating students were eliminated in schools, what would be the impact on students? On teachers? On parents? What might teachers use to motivate students to complete assignments?

<u>**Post-Lecture Student Activities**</u>

Application 13.3 Ask students what the disadvantages of the following would be: (1) returning student test results after several weeks, (2) posting test grades without returning the actual test papers, (3) returning the answer sheets promptly but without reviewing the correct answers.

Reading 13.1 Robert Stake, "The Goods on American Education," *Kappan* 80(9) (May 1999): 668–672.

Reflection and Journal Writing 13.1 Have students reflect on their evaluation experiences in the early grades and in middle school. Have them consider both academic and extracurricular activities (e.g., sports, plays, music performances, and service projects). Was there a particular competence that they discovered because of positive and supportive feedback or attention given to them by a teacher? Have them describe it.

13.3 How Is Student Learning Evaluated?

Key Terms
Norm-referenced evaluations
Criterion-referenced evaluations

Lecture Notes and Discussion Questions

Discussion Question 13.4 Which type of grading orientation—norm-referenced or criterion-referenced—would be best understood by parents? Which would they favor? How might the choices vary depending on grade level?

Post-Lecture Student Activities

Application 13.4 Ask students how they are likely to use formative evaluation in their classrooms.

Application 13.5 A time-honored method that teachers have used to promote preparation for class is the pop quiz. Ask students how they might use pop quizzes to encourage learning while minimizing the anxiety that tests often provoke.

Application 13.6 Assign students the "Teacher Interviews on Classroom Assessment" (**HM 13.6**). Ask them to summarize and reflect upon their findings.

Cooperative Learning 13.1 Have students think, pair, and share results of Application 13.6 and present their findings in small groups.

Critical Thinking 13.4 List the incentives and disincentives of (1) being graded on the curve, (2) receiving cooperative group grades, (3) having to get 90 percent to make an A.

Multicultural Awareness 13.2 Have students consider the implications of comparing scores of students who do not speak English as their native language with scores of students born in the United States. Is the norm the same for these students? What types of students are typically used to establish the norms of standardized testing? Is it simply a matter of translating the test to the spoken language of the ESL student? Where do the norms for those students come from? Does it make a difference as to *why* the ESL student is now in this country? What about immigrants versus migrants? Rural versus metropolitan backgrounds? Why is this an important issue for assessing ESL students?

Reading 13.2 John Read and Carol A. Chapelle, "A Framework for Second Language Vocabulary Assessment," *Language Testing* 18, no. 1 (Jan 2001): 1-32.

Reading 13. 3 G. Delandshere and J. H. Jones, "Elementary Teachers' Beliefs About Assessment in Mathematics: A Case of Assessment Paralysis," *Journal of Curriculum and Supervision* 14(3) (1999).

Research and Suggested Reading 13.1 Ann W. Wright, "The ABCs of Assessment. Science Teacher," 68, no. 7 (Oct 2001): 60-64.

13.4 How Are Tests Constructed?

Key Terms

Reliability
Table of specifications
Multiple-choice items
Stem
Distractors
True-false items
Completion items
Matching items
Short essay items
Problem-solving assessment

Lecture Notes and Discussion Questions

Discussion Question 13.5 On an essay question to evaluate a student's content understanding, should a teacher take off points for grammar, spelling, or technical errors? If so, how much?

Discussion Question 13.6 Imagine that you have just handed back a test on which students were asked to solve problems. Several students complain when they see their scores. What do you say to them? How might the use of evaluation descriptors be helpful in minimizing such complaints?

Post-Lecture Student Activities

Application 13.7 For an activity requiring students to use a table of specifications, see Handout Master 13.4, "Devising an Evaluation Plan."

Application 13.8 What is wrong with the following multiple-choice question? Question: Which of the following is false? a. Chicago is the capital of Tennessee. b. Los Angeles is the largest city in Utah. c. Nashville is the capital of Florida. d. All of the above.

Application 13.9 Ask your students whether an objective test or an essay test would be more appropriate under these circumstances: (1) You wish to test the students' knowledge of the terminology used in lab experiments. (2) The test must be given and graded in the 2 days before the end of the 6-week grading period. (3) You want to test the students' ability to present a logical argument. (4) Your aim is to balance subjective judgments with a highly reliable measure. (5) You are seeking to test student understanding of a few major principles. (6) You want to test students' knowledge of foreign countries' major export goods. (7) You have limited time to construct the test. (8) You are interested in students' ability to differentiate between the major philosophies of democracy and socialism.

Critical Thinking 13.5 In recent years an approach to evaluating essays, known as *holistic scoring*, has become increasingly popular. Rather than assigning separate grades for style, content, organization, and the like, the holistic approach involves giving one grade for the overall quality of the answer. What do you think are the advantages and disadvantages of this kind of scoring?

Reflection and Journal Writing 13.2 Some students will avoid or drop classes that involve writing assignments or essay exams. Do you know students who fit that description? Why might students avoid writing assignments that will be evaluated?

13.5 What Are Authentic Portfolio and Performance Assessment?

Key Terms
Portfolio assessment
Performance assessment

Lecture Notes and Discussion Questions

Discussion Question 13.7 Would you choose to use portfolio assessment, performance assessment, or course-end test scores for assigning report card grades in your class? Why?

Post-Lecture Student Activities

Critical Thinking 13.6 The National PTA once identified the U.S. educator's passion for evaluation as "pulling carrots to see if they are growing." Have students discuss the question "Does measurement and evaluation drive instruction in the schools?"

Reading 13.4 George F. Madaus and Laura M. O'Dwyer, "A Short History of Performance Assessment: Lessons Learned," *Kappan* 80 (9) (May 1999): 688.

Reading 13.5 E. Eisner, "The Uses and Limits of Performance Assessment," *Kappan* 80(9) (1999): 658–660.

Research and Suggested Readings 13.2 Lizabeth Berryman and David R. Russell, "Portfolios Across the Curriculum: Whole School Assessment in Kentucky," *English Journal* 90, no. 6 (Jul 2001): 76-83.

Research and Suggested Readings 13.3 Samuel J. Meisels, Yange Xue, Donna DiPrima Bickel, Julie Nicholson, Sally Atkins-Burnett, "Parental Reactions to Authentic Performance Assessment." *Educational Assessment* 7, no. 1 (2001): 61-85.

13.6 How Are Grades Determined?

Key Terms
Relative grading standard
Mastery grading

Lecture Notes and Discussion Questions

Discussion Question 13.8 Some high school and college courses use a pass/fail method to grade performance in elective courses. What are some of the advantages and disadvantages of such a method?

Post-Lecture Student Activities

Application 13.10 Assign students the "Teacher Interviews on Classroom Assessment" (**HM 13.6**). Ask them to summarize and reflect upon their findings.

Cooperative Learning 13.2 Have students think, pair, and share results of Application 13.6 and present their findings in small groups.

Critical Thinking 13.7 There is an obvious discrepancy between a child's IQ score and academic performance. Which would you consider more valid? Why?

Chapter 14
Standardized Tests

CHAPTER OVERVIEW

The final chapter of the text introduces the student to the issues and uses of standardized tests for effective and useful student evaluation. Standardized tests are typically constructed by experts in curriculum and assessment to provide accurate, meaningful information on a student's levels of performance. Standardized tests are typically used for selection and placement, diagnosis, evaluation, school improvement, and accountability.

Three kinds of standardized tests are commonly used in school settings: aptitude tests, norm-referenced achievement tests, and criterion-referenced achievement tests. Tests (whether sent away for computer scoring or scored by users) usually yield raw scores that are translated into one or more types of derived scores, each with its own meaning and purpose. Students are given opportunities to examine percentile scores, grade equivalent scores, standardized scores, including standard deviation, stanine scores, normal curve equivalents, and Z scores.

Issues around testing and standards are among the most hotly debated in American education. In recent years there have been many developments and proposals for change in testing. Key issues of concern related to standardized testing are validity, reliability, and test bias.

CHAPTER–AT–A–GLANCE

Chapter Outline	Objectives	Supplements
14.1 What Are Standardized Test and How Are They Used? • Selection and Placement • Diagnosis • Evaluation • School Improvement • Accountability	• Discuss five significant uses of standardized tests and ways to prepare students for taking standard and formal classroom tests.	• Handout Master 14.1, 14.2, 14.3, &13.5 • Transparency T111 • Test Bank Items
14.2 What Types of Standardized Tests Are Given? • Aptitude Tests • Norm-Referenced Achievement Tests • Criterion-Referenced Achievement Tests • Standard Setting	• Compare and contrast the types of standardized tests and ways to prepare students for taking standard and formal classroom tests.	• Transparency T26 & T109 • Video Clip 23, *Using Standardized Assessments* • Test Bank Items
14.3 How Are Standardized Tests Interpreted? • Percentile Scores • Grade-Equivalent Scores • Standard Scores	• Interpret the meaning of standardized test scores including percentiles, grade equivalents, and the different types of standard scores.	• Transparency T110, T113, T114, T115, T116, & T117 • Test Bank Items
14.4 What Are Some Issues Concerning Standardized and Classroom Testing? • Test Validity • Test Reliability • Test Bias	• Argue issues concerning standardized and classroom testing (including issues of validity, reliability, bias, and ethics) and alternate testing (including the use of portfolios and performances	• Video Clip 24, *School Report Cards* • Test Bank Items

• Computer Test Administration	as forms of authentic assessment).	

ANNOTATED LECTURE OUTLINE

14.1 What Are Standardized Tests and How Are They Used?

Key Terms
   Standardized tests
   Norms
   Minimum competency tests

Lecture Notes and Discussion Questions

Brainstorming/Warm-up/Discussion Question 14.1 How are results from standardized tests used? Let's brainstorm all the standardized tests you have taken yourself. What other standardized tests do you know? How are the results from these tests used? What concerns do you have about the use of these test results? Why is it critical for classroom teachers to understand and be able to explain standardized test results?

Post-Lecture Student Activities

Critical Thinking 14.1 In some school districts the accountability movement has resulted in teachers trying to "teach to the test" so that their students will achieve required passing scores. How does this relate to earlier discussions on student learning? What lasting effects, if any, will this have on overall student performance? What are the risks of teaching to the test? What are the risks of not teaching to the test? As a teacher, what would you do?

Critical Thinking 14.2 Competency tests for high school graduation hold local educators accountable for educational performance. Ask students to identify implications for students, for teachers, and for the curriculum.

Reading 14. 1 Norbert Schwarz, "Self-Reports: How the Questions Shape the Answers," *American Psychologist Volume* 54(2) (February 1999). The author discusses how questionnaires are sources of information to respondents as well as to the researchers who use them. Researchers are not always fully aware of the extent to which the questions they ask determine the answers they are given.

Reflection and Journal Writing 14.1 Have students write examples from their own experience of how standardized tests have been used (e.g., retention, accelerations, special class placements, college admissions, scholarships, honors).

Research and Suggested Reading 14.1 For a discussion on the use of tests for evaluation, read R. D. Bingham, "Evaluating schools and teachers based on student performance: Testing as an alternative methodology." *Evaluation Review* 15(2) (1991): 191–218.

Research and Suggested Reading14.2 Mary L. Trepanier-Street, Shannan McNair, Mary M. Donegan, "The View of Teachers on Assessment: A Comparison of Lower and Upper Elementary Teachers," *Journal of Research in Childhood Education* 15, no. 2 (Spr-Sum 2001): 234-41

Reading 14.2 Pamela A. Moss and Aaron Schutz, "Risking Frankness in Educational Assessment," *Kappan* 80(9) (May 1999): 680.

Application 14.1 Assign students the interviews on "Standardized Testings" (**HM 14.3**). Ask them to summarize and reflect upon their findings.

Cooperative Learning 14.1 Have students think, pair and share their results from the interviews in Application 14.1. Ask them to develop a list of concerns they have regarding standardized testing and share with the class.

Application 14.2 Assign both the interviews from Chapter 13 (HM 13.6) and Chapter 14 (HM 14.3). Ask students to summarize and compare/contrast findings.

Cooperative Learning 14.2 Small groups should discuss results of teacher interviews (HM13.5, HM 14.3) and determine the key points presented by the teachers interviewed. Small groups should then draft "An Assessment Primer" for pre-service teachers. They should be sure to include key vocabulary and concepts from both chapters.

14.2 What Types of Standardized Tests Are Given?

Key Terms

> Aptitude test
> Achievement tests
> Intelligence
> Mental age
> Chronological age
> Multifactor aptitude battery
> Achievement batteries
> Diagnostic tests
> Cutoff score

Lecture Notes and Discussion Questions

Discussion Question 14.2 This is a good time to have students reflect on the types of standardized tests they have taken and on their attitudes regarding administration, results, and use of results of those tests.

Post-Lecture Student Activities

Application 14.3 One of your seventh-grade students does poorly on the arithmetic-reasoning section of a standardized test. How would your interpretation of these results differ if the test were a criterion- referenced type (discussed in Chapter 13) rather than a norm-referenced type?

Application 14.4 Ask students how they would interpret the academic skills and grade placement of a seventh-grader who had a grade-equivalent score on an achievement test of 11.6 in reading and 10.2 in math.

Research and Suggested Reading 14.3 Robert L. Linn, "A Century of Standardized Testing: Controversies and Pendulum Swings," *Educational Assessment* 7, no. 1 (2001): 29-38.

14.3 How Are Standardized Tests Interpreted?

Key Terms

> Derived scores
> Percentile score
> Grade-equivalent scores
> Normal distribution
> Standard deviation
> Stanine scores
> Normal curve equivalent
> z-score

Lecture Notes and Discussion Questions

Discussion Question 14.3 What factors might contribute to the "Lake Wobegon Effect," named for a popular radio show's mythical town, where "all the children are above average"? Are students getting smarter today and thus making old norms too easy?

Discussion Question 14.4 At a PTA meeting, parents were complaining because half of the students in the district scored below the district average on the achievement tests that were given. Is this a valid argument?

Post-Lecture Student Activities

Application 14.5 In third grade, a high-achieving student receives a grade equivalent (GE) score in math of 4.3. A low-achieving student receives a GE score of only 2.3. Is it likely that this difference between two GE scores will be maintained as the two students progress through higher grades?

Application 14.6 Present students with this question: What conclusions would you draw about a test with a possible score ranging of 1 to 50 on which your class mean was 40 with a standard deviation of 3? You gave the same test to another class whose mean was 26 with standard deviation of 7. How would you characterize the second class? What is the difference between the classes?

Application 14.7 Which math class, *A* or *B* is probably easier to teach, judging from the following standard score results (50 = national average)? Class *A*: Mean = 55, SD = 13. Class *B*: Mean = 53, SD = 4.

Application 14.8 Ask students how they would interpret the academic skills and grade placement of a student who had a stanine score of 5 on a standardized achievement test.

Research and Suggested Reading 14.4 Kenneth A. Wesson, "The 'Volvo Effect'—Questioning Standardized Tests," *Young Children* 56, no. 2 (Mar 2001): 16-18.

14.4 What Are Some Issues Concerning Standardized and Classroom Testing?

Key Terms
Validity
Content evidence
Criterion-related evidence
Predictive validity
Readiness tests
Concurrent evidence
Convergent evidence
Discriminant evidence
Reliability
Bias
Computer adaptive

Lecture Notes and Discussion Questions

Discussion Questions 14.5 Have students compare their attitudes toward classroom tests versus standardized tests. Which do they prepare for? Which do they believe reflect learning best? Which do they prefer? Why?

Post-Lecture Student Activities

Critical Thinking 14.3 What influence do you think standardized testing has on the teaching of prep courses? On the curriculum? How should test content be determined? How would you describe an instance of culture, class, or gender bias that you may recall from your own experience?

Readings and Reflection 14.1 Janet McClaskey, "Who's Afraid of the Big, Bad TAAS? Rethinking Our Response to Standardized Testing," *English Journal* 91, no. 1 (Sep 2001): 88-95.

Multicultural Awareness 14.1/Research and Suggested Reading14.5 Information is available from a national clearinghouse of advocacy groups working on standardized test reform: The National Center for Fair and Open Testing (FAIRTEST), 342 Broadway, Cambridge, MA 02139-1802 (617-864-4810).

SUGGESTED READINGS

Adkison, Stephen and Stephen Tchudi. "Reading the Data: Making Supportable Claims from Classroom Assessment." *English Journal* 91, no. 1 (Sep 2001): 43-50

Baker, Eva L. "Testing and Assessment: A Progress Report." *Educational Assessment* 7, no. 1 (2001): 1-12

Beiger, G.R. *Educational Research: A Practical Approach.* Albany, NY: Delmar, 1996.

Broadfoot, P. *Education, Assessment and Society: A Sociological Analysis.* Philadelphia, PA: Open University Press, 1996.

Goodson, Ivor and Martha Foote. "Testing Times: A School Case Study." *Education Policy Analysis Archives* 9, no. 2 (Jan 2001).

Lyman, H.B. *Test Scores and What They Mean,* 6th ed. Boston: Allyn & Bacon, 1998.

Maki, Peggy L. "From Standardized Tests to Alternative Methods: Some Current Resources on Methods To Assess Learning in General Education." *Change* 33, no. 2 (Mar-Apr 2001): 28-31.

SUGGESTED MEDIA

Alternatives to Standardized Testing, video, 30 minutes, 1996. This program argues that standardized testing is harmful to the educational health of most public school students. The video, hosted by Monty Neil, also discusses alternative assessment systems. *From Insight Media.*

Redefining Intelligence, video, 30 minutes, 1996. Arguing that "smart is something you get, not something you are," Jeff Howard explains why beliefs about intelligence need to be reexamined. *From Insight Media.*

How to Use Standards to Inform Assessment and Instruction in the Classroom, video, 35 minutes, 1997. This video explores the educational value of implementing performance and content standards. It shows that the use of standards can enhance assessment and instruction at all grade levels and in all subject areas. *From Insight Media.*

Reporting Results, video, 28 minutes. Today's parents have a difficult time understanding alternative assessment strategies. This program looks at techniques schools might adopt in order to communicate better with parents, the media, and the community regarding student performance and expectations. Presenters address the pitfalls of relying to heavily on data as the sole indication of student success. *From Films for the Humanities and Sciences.*

Norm-Referenced Tests: Uses and Misuses, video. *From 10X Assessment Associates.*

Criterion-Referenced Tests: Today's Alternative to Traditional Testing, video. *From 10X Assessment Associates.*

PART TWO:

ANSWER KEY TO
CHAPTER
SELF-ASSESSMENTS
&
HANDOUT MASTERS

CHAPTER 1

SELF-ASSESSMENT ANSWERS

1. In the first paragraph, Ellen Mathis does not understand why her students are nonproductive and unimaginative. According to educational psychology research, which of the following teacher characteristics is Ellen most likely lacking?

ANSWER: c) Ellen most likely lacked *intentionality*. Although Ellen is a knowledgeable teacher, she did not know how to tailor her teaching style to meet her teaching goals with the current set of students. Nor did Ellen take into account student motivation (e.g., writing about something one is interested in is much more intrinsically motivating than writing about one's summer experience). Finally, Ellen did not apply the lessons of educational psychology to her classroom.

2. Leah Washington talks with Ellen Mathis about getting students to write interesting compositions. Which of the following statements summarizes Leah's approach to teaching writing?

ANSWER: a) Leah employs a variety of activities that are motivating to her students. For instance, she began by having her students listen to interesting stories written by other students, then gave her students the chance to write their own personally meaningful stories.

3. According to research on expertise development, what characteristic separates novice teachers from expert teachers?

ANSWER: d) Expert teachers are critical thinkers; they evaluate their conclusions through logical and systematic examination of the problem, the evidence, and the solution.

4. Educational psychologists are often accused of studying the obvious. However, they have learned that the obvious is not always true. All of the following statements demonstrate this idea except one. Which one is obvious *and* supported by research?

ANSWER: d) There is research evidence from numerous programs—from methods for specific school subjects to strategies for the reform of entire schools—that intentional teachers balance competing goals according to the needs of particular students and situations.

5. Leah Washington discusses many of her teaching strategies with Ellen Mathis. One can easily see that Leah views teaching as a decision-making process. She recognizes problems and issues, considers situations from multiple perspectives, calls upon her professional knowledge to formulate action and

ANSWER: a) She selects the most appropriate action and judges the consequence. As such, her teaching style is dynamic, fitting the constraints of her current teaching environment while remaining consistent with her knowledge of educational psychology and her goals as an instructor.

6. The products of research are principles, laws, and theories. Leah Washington describes many principles and theories of educational psychology as she speaks with Ellen Mathis about teaching students to write compositions. First, describe an instruction with which Ellen Mathis is having difficulties, and then describe principles and theories she can use to engage her students in exciting and meaningful lessons.

ANSWER: According to the introduction, Ellen Mathis was having difficulty motivating her students to write imaginative material in creative writing. Further, her students' papers were full of errors. As a result, Ellen wondered if her students were developmentally ready to write creative papers. However, after speaking to Leah Washington, Ellen learned that she too could apply lessons learned from research on motivational processes to stimulate student curiosity.

7. The goal of research in educational psychology is to examine questions of teaching and learning using objective methods. These research methods include experiments, correlational studies, descriptive research, and action research. Think of a research question, and then describe how you would go about answering your question using the above methods.

ANSWER: One possible research question is: "Does academic performance affect self-esteem?"
- Experimental method: Create student groups with one *failure* and the other the *success* group, with a third *control* group for comparison, if desired. A second strategy would be to compare a group of students tracked in a remedial learning class to a group of students in traditional classes.
- Correlational method: The correlational method can be employed by having students complete age-appropriate measures of self-esteem, and then correlating self-esteem scores with academic performance.
- Descriptive method: A researcher interested in self-esteem and academic performance can observe students with different levels of academic performance and log behaviors indicative of high and low self-esteem.
- Action method: Instructors can assess strategies in their classrooms designed to enhance academic performance (e.g., rewarding effort rather than grades) and monitor the impact of those strategies on student self-esteem. This information can then be used to facilitate change locally.

8. Intentional teachers are aware of resources available for professional learning. They continually refine their practices to address the needs of all students. List four actions you could take to find information to help you teach your students with limited English proficiency.

ANSWER: Possible answers include:
- Contact the school counselor and ask about district programs for limited English proficiency students.
- Ask the building Administrator to connect you with teachers who have had success working with students with limited English proficiency.
- Contact the Department Chair of Special Education and ask for resources or personnel available to teachers of students with limited English proficiency.
- Contact District Central Office and ask for resources, personal, or workshops available to teachers of students with limited English proficiency.
- Contact an area Community College or University and ask for resources or instructors with knowledge of teaching students with limited English proficiency.
- Research the internet for classroom materials or instructional techniques for teaching students with limited English proficiency.

CHAPTER 2

SELF-ASSESSMENT ANSWERS

1. Mr. Jones, in the first section of the chapter-opening vignette, is perplexed when he asks his students to follow his example by raising their right hands; instead, they raise their left hands. According to developmental theory, why did this happen?

ANSWER: c) According to Piaget, children of first grade age have entered the concrete operations stage of cognitive development. Concrete operational children are egocentric; they are not yet capable of seeing the perspective of others. Therefore, they did not understand that because Mr. Jones was facing them, they would have to see what is their right as his left, and their left as his right.

2. What simple solution might work to help Mr. Jones to get his students to raise their right hands?

ANSWER: b) Mr. Jones can turn around, his back facing his students, so that they share the same perspective.

3.   In the opening-chapter vignette, why did Ms. Lewis's students refuse to allow the girl with the ill mother to go on the field trip?

ANSWER: d) According to Piaget's theory of moral development, children of this age are judging morality of behavior based on the consequences of actions, and see rules as irreversible, regardless of circumstances.

4.   According to Kohlberg's theory of moral development, how can Ms. Lewis help her students move past their beliefs that "rules are rules with no exceptions"?

ANSWER: a) Kohlberg proposed that the way to advance moral reasoning is by having children interact with others one or, at most, two stages above their own level of moral reasoning.

5.   According to Erikson's theory of personal development, why did Frank react the way he did to Ms. Quintera's praise of his poetry?

ANSWER: a) Highlighting Frank's achievement placed him in the role of *teacher's pet*, a role unfavorable to the early adolescent.

6.   Write a brief description of a typical (i.e., fits the theories) student at one of the following grade levels: K-6, 5-9, or 7-12. Use the ideas of each theorist from this chapter to guide your description.

POSSIBLE ANSWER: If there is a typical student at the 7th–12th grade level, the student is most likely capable of reasoning at Piaget's formal operations level of cognitive reasoning, provided appropriate environmental stimuli are present and scaffolding (see Vygotsky's theory) is provided. This individual can think abstractly, reasoning about counterfactual phenomena. Morally speaking, the adolescent, if challenged appropriately, is beginning to reason at a stage 5 level of moral reasoning; s/he believes that what is right is what is favored by the majority of people, yet protects individual rights. It is highly unlikely, though possible, that an adolescent can reason at stage 6 of Kohlberg's stages of moral reasoning. Finally, emotionally speaking, this adolescent is searching for his/her identity, experimenting with a variety of facades, both in terms of lifestyle and career. If all goes well, s/he will emerge from this stage prepared to form an interpersonal relationship in stage 6 of Erikson's psychosocial theory of development.

7.   Make a list of developmentally appropriate teaching strategies for one of the following grade levels: K-5, 5-9, and 7-12.

POSSIBLE ANSWER: If I were teaching a group of 5th through 9th graders, I'd be focusing on developing their ability to reason over concrete issues, as children in this group fall within Piaget's concrete operations stage. However, because they are also emerging as abstract thinkers during this period, I'd mix students by different levels of ability so that developmentally more advanced thinkers can challenge their less advanced peers to their zones of proximal development. I would also be careful to insure that children focus on developing their skills rather than social comparison, even though social comparison is of utmost importance in older children and young adolescents. The goal here is to have children feel industrious rather than inferior and eventually attain a strong sense of identity in stage 5. Finally, I'd challenge moral reasoning so that children and adolescents learn to reason at Kohlberg's stage five reasoning. I'd highlight moral dilemmas as they emerge during daily class interactions, and ask students to discuss their opinions about the dilemmas.

CHAPTER 3

SELF-ASSESSMENT ANSWERS

1.   As noted in the interaction between Sam and Billy, there are enormous differences between students of varying ages. According to the information presented in the chapter, which of the following behaviors is more likely to be exhibited by Billy than by Sam?

ANSWER: a) Morally speaking, Billy sees obedience to parents as critical, as parents are key sources of social support and guidance.

2.   According to the information presented in the chapter, which of the following behaviors is more likely to be exhibited by Sam than by Billy?

ANSWER: b) Sam is more likely to defy convention in order to fit in with his adolescent peers, who are also defying convention at this stage.

3.   Typically, a young child's social life evolves in relatively predicable ways. The social network grows from an intimate relationship with parents or guardians to:

ANSWER: d) other family members, nonrelated adults, and peers, who eventually become extremely important during middle childhood and adolescence.

4.   For students like Sam Stevens, who is entering what Piaget terms "formal operations," which of the following instructional strategies would be considered developmentally appropriate?

ANSWER: d) The best solution is to require Sam to write assignments that encourage debate, as formal operational thinking allows for abstract reasoning.

5.   One of the first signs of early adolescence is the appearance of reflectivity. What is this?

ANSWER: c) Reflectivity refers to the ability to think about one's own mind.

6.   Design a lesson that would be considered developmentally appropriate for someone Billy's age. Include an explanation as to why you believe it is appropriate

POSSIBLE ANSWER: Billy is just entering concrete operations. Therefore, he is likely beginning to conduct operations mentally. The best lessons for a child his age involve tasks that stretch his cognitive ability within his zone of proximal development. I would have Billy work with a classmate to write a grocery list for a family of otters, based on a set budget. Therefore, Billy and his classmate would strengthen their ability to take the perspective of others by imagining what the family of otters would eat. Further, they would practice arithmetic, involving errors requiring reversibility, such as if too much money is spent and some groceries need be taken off the list. Finally, having Billy work with a peer, particularly a girl, would encourage social-emotional development and cooperation.

7.   Design a lesson that would be considered developmentally appropriate for someone Sam's age. Include an explanation as to why you believe it is appropriate.

POSSIBLE ANSWER: Sam is an adolescent. Therefore, the best lessons would involve formal operational thinking. As Sam's instructor, I'd present him a moral dilemma involving common adolescent problems, such as what to do if a friend is drinking and driving. I would ask Jake and his classmates for the pros and cons of turning his friend in to the principal.

8.   One of the most serious problems of adolescence is delinquency. Delinquents are usually

Answer: c. low achievers who feel they can't succeed in school.

CHAPTER 4

SELF-ASSESSMENT ANSWERS

1. Marva Vance and John Rossi discuss their students' diverse norms, traditions, behaviors, languages, and perceptions. Which of the following terms best describes the essence of their conversation?

ANSWER: d) culture: Multiculturalism encompasses a variety of factors, including race, socioeconomic status, and intelligence.

2. In regard to the students of Marva Vance and John Rossi, which of the following statements on socioeconomic status is most likely true?

ANSWER: b) Students from disadvantaged homes are more likely to have inadequate access to health care, due to the generally lower levels of parental education and less health insurance coverage.

3. Marva Vance and John Rossi discuss their students' tendencies to accept the stereotypical roles assigned to them by society. According to research, what should the teachers do about stereotyping?

ANSWER: d) Write a Thanksgiving play that includes the contributions of all under-represented groups, so that all children can feel like they are valued members of American culture.

4. José, a student in Marva Vance's class, wants to be the narrator of the Thanksgiving pageant, even though he is not proficient in English. According to the research on the effectiveness of bilingual programs, which strategy might Ms. Vance use to improve all her students' English speaking and writing skills?

ANSWER: c) Ms. Vance should support bilingual education since researchers have found that students in bilingual programs ultimately achieve in English as well as or better than students taught only in English. Therefore, allowing José the opportunity to participate in this pageant as a narrator will likely continue his progress in language competence, consistent with the findings of researchers in bilingual education.

5. Marva Vance and John Rossi discuss stereotypical gender roles in the Thanksgiving pageant. From the research reported in this section, how should the teachers assign male and female students to the roles of the pageant?

ANSWER: a) Teachers should encourage students to select roles for which the students have interest, not roles that society expects them to play. Teachers can assign atypical roles. However, that may be offensive to some students. It is better to teach children freedom of choice, instead of imposing values upon them.

6. What is multicultural education? What steps can teachers, administrators, and other school personnel take to reach their students from underrepresented groups?

POSSIBLE ANSWER: Multicultural education is teaching children to understand and respect diversity. To reach students from underrepresented groups, instructors and administrators should seek to diversify their staff first. They should provide parental education programs and parental counseling to help parents find needed services. Administrators should train instructors in multicultural awareness and promote cooperative learning while de-emphasizing unnecessary competition.

7. Students differ in their prior learning and their cognitive learning styles. What strategies can teachers use to reach all of their students?

POSSIBLE ANSWER: It is very difficult to teach to the level of every student, as students come to school with vast differences in experience as well as learning styles. To enhance each student's learning experience, teachers should urge cooperative learning, which enhances scaffolding, pushing group members to their zones of proximal development in a variety of dimensions of learning. Multifaceted lessons that tap visual as well as auditory learning styles and field independence and dependence strengthens weaknesses while taking advantage of strengths. The goal should be that no student suffers low self-esteem from negative education experience; instead, students strengthen their feelings of self-worth through education.

8. List six strategies that a teacher could implement to involve parents or caregivers to help students meet their potential.

POSSIBLE ANSWERS:
- Positive phone calls home
- Voicemail announcements
- Homework notebooks
- Home visits
- Newsletters
- Frequent parent conferences
- Invite parents to volunteer
- Plan activities that welcome parents

CHAPTER 5

SELF-ASSESSMENT ANSWERS

1. Julia Esteban, first-grade teacher at Tanner Elementary School, calls on her students when they do not raise their hands, a practice that goes against the established rule in the class. Which of the following types of conditioning can Ms. Esteban use to teach her students about appropriate hand-raising behavior?

ANSWER: b) Operant conditioning employs reinforcement to increase the likelihood that a desired behavior, like raising one's hand, will be repeated.

2. Which of the following explanations best summarizes Julia Esteban's problem with her students' failure to raise their hands before speaking?

ANSWER: d) Ms. Esteban is experiencing a common problem among new instructors; she is losing control of a class by failing to apply the principles of operant conditioning appropriately. Instead of rewarding appropriate behaviors, she is unknowingly rewarding inappropriate behavior, the exact behavior she desires to curb.

3. According to the research on behavioral learning theories, which strategy might Ms. Esteban use to get her students to raise their hands before speaking?

ANSWER: a) The best strategy is to reward students who follow the rules.

4. Imagine that Ms. Esteban's students have a difficult time breaking their habit of speaking out of turn. Which of the following techniques might she use to reinforce close approximations of the behaviors she wants her students to exhibit?

ANSWER: c) Shaping occurs when learners are reinforced for successive approximations of desired behaviors.

5. Which type of reinforcement schedule is Ms. Esteban using if she reinforces her students' appropriate behavior after so many behaviors, but the students do not know when the reinforcement will be applied?

ANSWER: d) Ms. Esteban would be using a variable ratio schedule for which only she knows the average number of correct responses preceding reinforcement.

6. Explain how classical conditioning and operant conditioning are alike and different. Give at least one example of each.

QUESTION 1: Explain how classical conditioning and operant conditioning are alike and different.

POSSIBLE ANSWER: Classical conditioning and operant conditioning refer to forms of learning that require experience to initiate. Once learned, both forms are subject to stimulus generalization and discrimination, as well as extinction. Both forms of learning are also predictive, so that their formation implies that some environmental stimulus or behavior indicates impending reward. Therefore, they persist as long as rewards are predictable and degrade only when reward is no longer predictable. They differ, however, in that operant conditioning relies on behavioral consequences, whereas classical conditioning relies on stimulus pairing.

QUESTION 2: Give at least one example of each.

POSSIBLE ANSWER: Phobias are examples of classically conditioned responses that generalize. Studying to get high marks is an example of the power of operant conditioning to elicit desirable behavior.

7. Describe Albert Bandura's social learning theory. Bandura's analysis of observational learning involves four phases—describe each phase.

QUESTION 1: Describe Albert Bandura's social learning theory.

POSSIBLE ANSWER: Albert Bandura hypothesized that learning does not require occurrence of direct reinforcement. Rather, people can learn vicariously, observing the consequences of behaviors to models. Furthermore, just because a behavior is learned does not necessarily foretell its enactment; motivation is required for a behavior learned vicariously to be enacted. If negative consequences are observed, the behavioral enactment is not as likely as when positive consequences are observed. Even if positive consequences are observed, and the individual is motivated to enact the behavior, the observer must feel efficacious that the behavior can be enacted successfully. Therefore, according to Bandura, the time between learning and behavioral enactment depends on a variety of personal factors.

QUESTION 2: Bandura's analysis of observational learning involves four phases—describe each phase.

POSSIBLE ANSWER: The four phases involved are:
*   Attention: Observational learning cannot occur without adequate attention paid to the model. Attention is facilitated by factors like attractiveness, similarity, and popularity of the model to the observer.
*   Retention: Behavioral reproduction is facilitated by retention of modeled behavior. Retention occurs when teachers give students a chance to rehearse learned material and when material is presented in a form conducive to retention.
*   Reproduction: Reproduction refers to the learner's ability to reproduce the modeled behavior. Reproduction increases the possibility of reward. Failure to reproduce decreases possibility of reward.
*   Motivation: Behaviors are reproduced only when students are motivated to do so. Motivation increases when a modeled behavior is rewarded sufficiently to peak the learner's interest.

CHAPTER 6

SELF-ASSESSMENT ANSWERS

1. According to information-processing theory, which component of the memory system did Verona Bishop's students first use during the 3-second experiment?

ANSWER: a) They first registered the visualized material in their visual-sensory memory.

2. Verona Bishop asks her students, "[I]magine that you could keep everything that ever entered your mind. What would that be like?" One student responds, "You'd be a genius!" Another responds, "You'd go crazy!" Why does Ms. Bishop side with the second student?

ANSWER: c) Learning would be very difficult if one were bombarded by too much information

3. During the 3-second memory experiment, Verona Bishop asks her students to recall things not associated with the overhead information she presented. What type of memory are students using when they recall smells, sounds, and details of the classroom and the people in it?

ANSWER: d) Episodic memory is the type of long-term memory that stores images of our personal experience, such as the sounds of a truck going by or details of a classroom and the people in it.

4. Cheryl, one of Verona Bishop's students, recalled seeing the word *learning* on the overhead screen, even though it was not there. How does Ms. Bishop explain this phenomenon?

ANSWER: c) Learning and memory are closely related concepts, and are likely stored closely together in memory.

5. Consider that some of Verona Bishop's students attempted to memorize the information on the overhead screen in a random fashion. Which of the following learning strategies are they using?

ANSWER: a) Free-recall learning is learning a list of items in any order.

6. Verona Bishop summarizes her experiment by telling her students that they will forget some details of the experiment but remember others. Why is this so?

ANSWER: a) Students remember information they process deeply and give meaning to.

7. Review the current research on the brain. What do we know about how it works? What is the connection between brain function and memory?

POSSIBLE ANSWER: Research on the brain has been very fruitful. For instance, we know that the human brain is divided in two hemispheres that function asymmetrically yet always share information. For example, for most people language is housed in the left hemisphere along with many logical-mathematical tasks, whereas visual-spatial tasks tend to reside in the right hemisphere. Regarding learning and memory, information processing of newly learned information is cumbersome, but becomes far more efficient over time, ignoring useless and redundant information while employing far fewer brain processes.

8. Describe several memory strategies that you can teach your students to help them remember facts, concepts, and ideas presented to them in a lesson.

POSSIBLE ANSWER: First, I would teach them note-taking skills, especially learning to paraphrase rather than seeking to write down all material presented. Second, I would teach them to summarize facts learned in reading and prepare to teach learned material to other students, as teaching is a terrific method to solidify difficult concepts in memory. I would also tell them to relate material to concepts they already know, so they can form associations between old and new concepts. Furthermore, I would tell them to make learning meaningful by having them reflect upon their learning in relation to daily life events outside of class. This step would make difficult concepts learned in class meaningful. Finally, I would ask them to ask themselves many questions while reading material and to remind themselves to employ all the strategies I asked them to employ, thereby teaching them to reflect upon their own thinking (metacognition).

CHAPTER 7

SELF-ASSESSMENT ANSWERS

1. In the chapter-opening vignette, Ms. Logan uses a variety of instructional strategies in the lesson on sound. Which of the following statements from the vignette is an example of Ms. Logan using direct instruction?

ANSWER: b) Ms. Logan whet her students' appetites for learning about sound by having them experiment independently, filling bottles with different amounts of liquid to produce sounds. Then, she called them back for the lesson.

2. If Ms. Logan were to use a direct instruction approach to a science lesson on gravity, which of the following steps would come first?

ANSWER: b) Ms. Logan would begin by stating the learning objective.

3. According to research on direct instruction, why should Ms. Logan conduct learning probes during her lesson on sound?

ANSWER: c) Ms. Logan should conduct learning probes to get feedback on student comprehension, thereby allowing her to make adjustments in her lesson plan as necessary to insure students apprehend the lesson.

4. Ms. Logan plays a flute and a piccolo to demonstrate how sound waves travel through air. She hopes this demonstration will help her students understand the experiment with bottles of water. What principle of instruction is she using?

ANSWER: c) Ms. Logan is hoping her demonstration will result in transfer of learning by example.

5. After Ms. Logan's students work in groups to finish the lesson on sound, she tells them they will be tested individually to demonstrate their knowledge; however, their group can only be called "superteam" if everyone knows the material. What instructional strategy is the teacher using?

ANSWER: b) Small group discussion. The group leader is responsible for keeping the group on task to complete the lesson on sound in order to become a superteam. The group works cooperatively, though, to ensure all students attain sufficient task mastery.

6. Create a lesson using all the steps of a direct instruction lesson.

POSSIBLE ANSWER:
*   State learning objectives and orient students to the lesson: For example, I will say, "The objective of today's lesson is to understand the heart's function under stress." I will follow the objective by telling students I'm giving them a pop-quiz on the basic structure of the heart, a topic already studied. To whet their appetites, I will have them calculate a classmate's heart rate by palpating the radial artery on the wrist near the thumb and calculating beats per minute. I will use the results to demonstrate how the heart rate increases during stress. Then, I will relax them with a brief imagery exercise and have classmates re-calculate each other's heart rates.

- Review prerequisites: I will give students a worksheet with a drawing of the heart and ask student to identify different structures. Students will exchange worksheets and grade them. We will then briefly review prerequisite knowledge.
- Present new material: The lesson will be presented, paying close attention for student comprehension. If I detect student confusion, I will stop and ask for clarification of understanding. I will also use examples to help transfer concepts learned in class to outside of classroom settings, like giving a presentation in front of a club.
- Conduct learning probes: To ensure comprehension of new material, I will pose questions to a variety of students by randomly selecting student names from the class list until all students have had a chance to answer. If I detect confusion, I will have students apprehending the concepts to clarify the concepts for students failing to apprehend the concepts.
- Provide independent practice: I will have students work on interpreting a vignette by discussing the physical processes underlying a stress-provoking situation. I will have students exchange worksheets for correction.
- Assess performance and provide feedback: Student work on the aforementioned vignette will be assessed in a large group discussion, after students have exchanged their papers with classmates for grading. In this manner, feedback will be almost immediate.
- Finally, to ensure that students retain knowledge beyond the classroom, I will assign homework that requires students to collect their own heart rate information at set intervals, recording the surrounding circumstances occurring at the time of the recordings. This material will be presented to class, in a non-threatening fashion, to ensure compliance.

7. What are some advantages and disadvantages of small-group discussions and whole-group discussions?

POSSIBLE ANSWER: Both small and whole-group discussions have several advantages and disadvantages. A key advantage of large group discussions for the instructor is the ability to maintain control over the course of the discussion and to include a variety of students. However, this advantage can easily turn into a disadvantage if teachers fail to pursue fertile topics or ignore all but the most motivated students. For students, large group discussions allow opinions to be voiced to a larger audience and perhaps build competence in public speaking. A drawback, however, applies to the socially anxious student for whom public speaking is a dreadful event. As such, some teachers or students may come to see the quiet student as lacking motivation or loafing.

Small-group discussions also have a variety of advantages and disadvantages. The advantages are a less-threatening environment for students to speak their minds, and if arranged correctly, the ability for a variety of students of different abilities to work together, encouraging scaffolding. A disadvantage is lack of control, particularly among younger students. Therefore, student maturity is a big issue. Further, because each group needs a leader, teachers may discriminate and make only the highest-achieving students leaders.

CHAPTER 8

SELF-ASSESSMENT ANSWERS

1. Mr. Dunbar, in his lesson on the volume of a cylinder, asks his students to figure out how to measure volume through experimentation. What type of learning strategy is he using?

ANSWER: c) Discovery learning. Mr. Dunbar's students are being encouraged to learn on their own in small groups, conducting experiments that permit them to discover principles for themselves.

2. Why didn't Mr. Dunbar just tell his students that the formula for finding the volume of a cylinder is $\Pi r^2 h$?

ANSWER: a) He believes that discovery learning provides for deeper understanding because students work out problems for themselves. Discovery learning also encourages critical thinking, problem solving, and cooperation, pushing students to their zones of proximal development.

3. In which of the following examples is Mr. Dunbar demonstrating Vygotsky's "zone of proximal development" concept?

ANSWER: c) Mr. Dunbar acknowledged the group's discovery but now pushes them to a higher level of cognitive development.

4. Mr. Dunbar effectively uses cooperative learning strategies in his lesson on the volume of cylinders. He does all the following except

ANSWER: b) Mr. Dunbar didn't select students for group membership by ability. Doing so would diminish the power of group processes to stretch cognition within students' zones of proximal development.

5. Which of the following cooperative learning strategies is Mr. Dunbar using?

ANSWER: b) Students worked together in small but heterogeneous groups on solving the assigned problem, providing a group product.

6. Describe an example of discovery learning. What is the teacher's role in a discovery lesson? What strengths and limitations exist with discovery learning?

QUESTION 1: Describe an example of discovery learning.

POSSIBLE ANSWER: One example of discovery learning is learning a foreign language by immersion in the culture in which the language is spoken. Students wishing to learn Spanish, for instance, learn different grammatical rules by necessity, as daily life in Spanish-speaking countries forces students to use different tenses. Therefore, learning these tenses is facilitated by immersion.

QUESTION 2: What is the teacher's role in a discovery lesson?

POSSIBLE ANSWER: The teacher's role in discovery learning is scaffolding, providing appropriate clues that help organize student understand and bring students closer to understanding. An alternative approach to comprehending the teacher's role in discovery learning is the operant conditioning principle of shaping. In shaping, desired student outcomes are shaped by rewarding successive approximations of the desired outcome.

QUESTION 3: What strengths and limitations exist with discovery learning?

POSSIBLE ANSWER: Discovery learning helps students learn to solve problems by organizing their thought processes so that appropriation of concepts is possible. Further, discovery learning enhances metacognition by teaching students to focus on their thought processes. Finally, it is useful in the enhancement of efficacy beliefs, as students learn they can achieve cognitively.

7. How can teachers improve students' problem-solving abilities?

POSSIBLE ANSWER: Teachers can improve problem-solving ability by assigning discovery learning tasks and using strategies like *Jigsaw*, *Learning Together*, *Group Investigation*, and *Cooperative Scripting*, which encourage students to solve problems actively by investigating assignments cooperatively, reaching solutions, and thinking critically about solutions and revising responses as necessary.

CHAPTER 9

SELF-ASSESSMENT ANSWERS

1. How does Mr. Arbuthnot, the fourth-grade teacher in the chapter-opening vignette, incorporate John Carroll's Model of School Learning into his lesson?

ANSWER: a) Mr. Arbuthnot tries to match the time actually spent learning with the time students need to learn when he goes over long division for a second day to help all students grasp the concept.

2. Imagine that Mr. Arbuthnot decides to divide his class into three groups: those who know long division, those who know some long division, and those who do not know long division. What type of ability group would he be using?

ANSWER: c) Mr. Arbuthnot is using a strategy known as within-class ability grouping because students are being divided into ability groups within his classroom, rather than across classrooms.

3. If Mr. Arbuthnot were to use a "mastery learning" approach to continue his lesson on long division, what would he most likely do next?

ANSWER: d) Mr. Arbuthnot would arrange students by ability level within the classroom so that all students can learn at their own pace.

4. In the opening of the vignette, Mr. Arbuthnot teaches an engaging lesson on long division and then gives students a quiz about the content. What type of evaluation is this?

ANSWER: d) Formative evaluation. Mr. Arbuthnot evaluated his students to see if additional instruction is needed.

5. Mr. Arbuthnot decides that he cannot work individually with all the students who have not yet mastered long division. He decides that some sort of tutoring might solve his problem. If he selects the type of tutoring that is most effective, according to the research, which of the following will he use?

ANSWER: c) Research findings indicate that adult tutoring (by certified teachers) is most effective, although it is generally costly.

6. Explain how you can use technology in the classroom. What does the research on computer-based instruction say?

QUESTION 1: Explain how you can use technology in the classroom.

POSSIBLE ANSWER: There are a variety of technologies available for the classroom. The simplest but most mundane is drill and practice. Tutorial programs actually are intended to teach material and can even substitute for teachers. Instructional games are highly entertaining and can be used to supplement instruction and even improve attention ability. Other uses of technology include simulation games, word processing packages, and the Internet.

QUESTION 2: What does the research on computer-based instruction say?

POSSIBLE ANSWER: Most research findings indicate that computer-based instruction has a small to moderate positive effect on learning. Most agree that computer-based learning is best if used as an adjunct to traditional instruction (e.g., using the Internet to conduct research).

7. Describe programs that exist for students placed at risk.

POSSIBLE ANSWER: Several options exist for students at risk of poor educational outcomes.
- Compensatory Education Programs are designed to prevent or remediate learning problems among students from lower socioeconomic status families. Examples of Compensatory Education Programs are Head Start and Follow Through.
- Early Intervention Programs, like the Carolina Abecedarian program, are designed to provide early stimulation to children, from infancy to around the age of five, and parent training in hopes of preventing later learning difficulties.
- Comprehensive School Reform Programs (CSRP) are a recent form of school reform that attempts to bring research findings into every aspect of education, such as curriculum, assessment, instruction, grouping, accommodation for students having difficulties, parent involvement and other elements of education. One example of a CSRP is the Success for All program, designed to prevent learning difficulties in schools serving lower income students. This program addresses every relevant area of education, including one-on-one tutoring and reading programs for pre-school children, kindergartners, and first through eighth graders, among others.

8. How does No Child Left Behind change what teachers do with their students?

POSSIBLE ANSWERS:
- Raises teacher expectations for all learners.
- Holds teachers accountable for academic achievement of all students.
- Requires teachers to know students as individual learners.
- Requires teachers to address deficiency needs of individual learners.
- Emphasizes the importance of testing procedures.
- Emphasizes the importance of student attendance.
- Emphasizes the importance to engage all students in learning activities.
- Requires remediation for non-achieving students.

CHAPTER 10

SELF-ASSESSMENT ANSWERS

1. According to behavioral learning theorists, why are Cal Lewis's students motivated to learn about the Constitutional Convention?

ANSWER: a) Behavioral learning theorists believe behavior is motivated by the opportunity to attain valuable reinforcers, like grades.

2. Mr. Lewis's students see the purpose of lessons about the Constitutional Convention as a way to gain information about the history of the United States. What type of goal orientation is this?

ANSWER: b) Students see the purpose of the lesson being to gain knowledge about history of the United States. Although one can conceptualize this as a performance goal, it is more likely that students were intrinsically interested in learning because of the way Mr. Lewis structured the lesson.

3. Beth Andrews, a shy girl in Mr. Lewis's class, proposes elements of the Bill of Rights to the convention members. If Beth has an internal locus of control, she is most likely to attribute her successful presentation to which of the following factors?

ANSWER: c) Beth would attribute her success to an internal source within her own control, careful preparation.

4. Mr. Lewis wants his students to work hard regardless of their ability level or task difficulty. What type of attribution will he attempt to instill in his students?

ANSWER: b) Mr. Lewis wants his students to realize that with effort, they are capable of high achievement. Conversely, with little effort, achievement would be low.

5. Under what circumstances is it most important for Cal Lewis to avoid the use of external incentives?

ANSWER: c) Researchers have found that extrinsic rewards undermine intrinsic motivation.

6. Analyze Mr. Lewis's lesson and his students' willingness to participate from the four theories of motivation presented in the chapter: behavioral, human needs, attributions, and expectancy.

POSSIBLE ANSWER:
- From the *behavioral* approach, Mr. Lewis's students were motivated to achieve praise from group members and Mr. Lewis. Further, students were motivated to perform well to not be ridiculed by peers for lack of preparation, should their number be called. Therefore, student motivation was to achieve rewards and avoid punishment.
- From the *human needs* perspective, students were motivated by the deficiency needs of belongingness and esteem, as well as the growth need of knowledge and understanding. Belongingness is attained from positive group involvement. Esteem is achieved through social praise. Finally, knowledge and understanding are attained through mastery efforts. Although these goals may appear out of order, there is no evidence that higher goals must occur in a specific order.
- From the *attributions* perspective, students are learning to attribute success to internal and unstable sources, such as effort and changing ability.
- From an *expectancy-value* perspective, students' perceptions of competence increase with practice organizing thoughts for presentation, argument, and debate, thereby increasing the expectancy of success. Increases in competence, when paired with valued goals like high grades and praise from teachers and peers, leads to motivation to participate and succeed.

7. Describe ways in which a teacher can increase students' motivation to learn.

POSSIBLE ANSWER: Teachers can increase student motivation to learn by creating competence opportunities for students. Teachers should structure activities so that results are not emphasized over task mastery. When students succeed at sub-tasks, they gain feelings of competence. With gains in perceptions of competence, students begin to value learning.

Student perceptions of competence are also influenced by teacher feedback. Teachers must learn to provide feedback that is contingent on performance. Therefore, when students perform well, they should be lauded and told why they are being rewarded. When students perform poorly, however, they should be told why they performed poorly and told how to improve future performance. In no circumstances should students be punished undeservedly. Positive behaviors should be rewarded so that desired educational outcomes are shaped. Therefore, a good instructor increases student motivation employing a variety of approaches supported by research and theory.

CHAPTER 11

SELF-ASSESSMENT ANSWERS

1. Ms. Cavalho works hard to prevent behavior problems and disruption in her classroom. Which of the following terms refers to her interaction with Mark?

ANSWER: a) Management. Ms. Cavalho is employing techniques designed to prevent future negative behaviors rather than punish him directly.

2. According to research, how could Ms. Cavalho increase student achievement in her classroom?

ANSWER: c) It appears that increasing the amount of time students spend engaged in learning has the greatest effect on learning, more so than merely increasing allocated time, which does not guarantee all students will use it for learning. However, increasing engaged time too much may have detrimental effects.

3. Ms. Cavalho continues her lesson on writing style even as Mark attempts to interrupt. This is called

ANSWER: c) Momentum. Ms. Cavalho prevents the disruption of momentum, as other students are engaged in learning and the disruption of Ms. Cavalho's flow would destroy momentum.

4. Ms. Cavalho uses the "Principle of Least Intervention" in her classroom. She works to prevent inappropriate behavior first, then if that does not work, she gives nonverbal cues and verbal reminders about how to act. She has used these strategies with Mark. Assume that Mark's behavior does not change after their discussion. What should she do next?

ANSWER: a) The final step is to apply consequences.

5. Daily report cards, group contingency programs, home-based reinforcement programs, and individual behavior management programs are all based on

ANSWER: c) All these strategies are based on the principles of behavioral learning theory.

6. Discuss ethical considerations in the use of individual and group behavior management techniques

POSSIBLE ANSWER: The employment of behavior management techniques is useful in dealing with highly disruptive students and classrooms. However, their use has been criticized because some teachers focus more on preventing disruption than fostering learning. Therefore, individual and group behavior management techniques should be used judiciously and only after preventative or less obvious discipline techniques have failed.

7. Explain how you would prevent the following misbehaviors: speaking out of turn, teasing, and physical fighting.

POSSIBLE ANSWER: Probably the best way to prevent negative behaviors is to not reward negative behaviors inadvertently. For instance, speaking out of turn may easily be rewarded when teachers allow students to continue speaking once the student has started, even if the student did not raise a hand and get teacher permission to speak. Instead, teachers must not reward speaking out of turn, and must praise students only when they raise their hands, following class protocol. Teasing and physical abuse are rewarded inadvertently because they tend to achieve their effects on the victim, either bring one to tears or visible sadness or physically hurting the victim. The beginning of the school year should be spent discussing rules, what is considered appropriate behavior, and the consequences of behavioral transgressions. One behavior to be discussed is demonstrating respect for others. Failing to demonstrate respect by either teasing or physically abusing students must be punished swiftly and firmly, but justly and consistently. It is hoped that once students know administration and teachers are serious about rules, teasing and physical abuse will cease.

CHAPTER 12

SELF-ASSESSMENT ANSWERS

1. Elaine Wagner, assistant principal at Pleasantville Elementary School, meets with Helen Ross about her son, Tommy, who is having a difficult time in another school. She explains to Ms. Ross that

Tommy would need to meet certain criteria to receive special education services. Which of the following examples is an indication that some one needs special education services?

ANSWER: b) The student must have at least one of a small number of categories of disabilities.

2. Suppose you are going to be Tommy's new teacher. If his mother were to ask you about the difference between a handicap and a disability, what would you say?

ANSWER: c) A disability is a functional limitation a person has that interferes with functioning. A handicap, on the other hand, refers to an external limitation placed on an individual.

3. Which of the following public laws gave parents like Helen Ross an increased role in making decisions about the education of their children?

ANSWER: d) P.L. 105-17 increased the involvement of parents in the special education of their children.

4. Assistant principal Elaine Wagner tells Helen Ross that even if Tommy needs special education services, he will be placed in the "least restrictive environment." What does this mean for Tommy?

ANSWER: a) Tommy will be placed in a general education environment and be pulled out on a very limited basis for special education.

5. Helen Ross, Tommy's mother, asks Elaine Wagner, "Your school's philosophy on inclusion sounds just right for Tommy. Why don't all schools adopt it? What disadvantages are there?" Ms. Wagner, who is current on her knowledge about inclusion, would most likely make which of the following responses?

ANSWER: c) Opponents of special education argue that teachers are already too overburdened to pay adequate attention to children with disabilities in general education classrooms.

6. How would you go about developing an individualized learning plan for Tommy if it is determined that he has a reading disability?

POSSIBLE ANSWER: If specialists indicate that Tommy has a reading disability, a meeting would be organized with the special education teacher, the classroom instructor, and any other specialist (such as a reading specialist) whose feedback would be appropriate at the time. Each specialist would conduct independent assessment of Tommy and report back in a special team meeting. Next, a draft of Tommy's IEP would be prepared by the classroom instructor or special education teacher. A meeting would be held with all experts and Tommy's parents/guardians. If agreement is received, the parent/guardian will be asked to sign the IEP, and the IEP will be initiated.

7. Describe the advantages and disadvantages that might occur when students with special needs are enrolled in the general education classroom.

POSSIBLE ANSWER: Inclusion is beneficial for both students with disabilities and students without disabilities. For the former, education is provided that helps the student with a disability meet the school's curricular goals. Further, inclusion allows students social interaction with other students, increasing social competence and possibly feelings of esteem. The possible disadvantages of inclusion are poor teacher instruction, as already precious time is divided further by the inclusion of a student with special needs beyond the teacher's training. A second disadvantage occurs if the student's presence is somehow disruptive to other students, such as if the student in question has ADHD. Finally, the potential for social ridicule against the student with special needs exists, as some students may say or do something that is psychologically hurtful to the student with special needs.

CHAPTER 13

SELF-ASSESSMENT ANSWERS

1. Mr. Sullivan is having a difficult time connecting what he is teaching and what he is testing. Which of the following evaluation tools will most likely help Mr. Sullivan make the connection?

ANSWER: b) Instructional objectives may include material that will be tested, so students are better prepared to face the material on Mr. Sullivan's tests.

2. Mr. Sullivan might use a chart showing how a concept or skill will be taught at different cognitive levels in relation to an instructional objective. What is this chart called?

ANSWER: a) A task analysis breaks down tasks into fundamental subskills.

3. Mr. Sullivan might improve the connection between what he teaches and what he tests by following which of the following pieces of advice?

ANSWER: a) Mr. Sullivan presented an array of fun activities that increased his students' interest. However, his test was not very related to the learning activities in class. He should have included all instructional content on the test, rather than just traditional test questions, especially since his lessons were not very traditional.

4. Which of the following types of evaluation is Mr. Sullivan using?

ANSWER: a) The test was summative, testing the students' knowledge at the end of the instructional unit.

5. Why would Mr. Sullivan construct a table of specification?

ANSWER: a) Tables of specification are lists of instructional objectives and expected levels of understanding that guide test development, something Mr. Sullivan did not do in choosing the single item he did and not relating it to the lessons learned in class.

6. Write a brief essay describing why evaluation is important.

POSSIBLE ANSWER: There seems to be a growing trend of opposition against standardized forms of evaluation. The chief argument is that the traditional A - F grading system discriminates against students with learning disabilities or those who are disadvantaged in socioeconomic status. However, evaluation by itself is not necessarily a negative practice. Evaluation provides feedback to teachers, parents, administration, and lawmakers about the efficacy of education. Further, evaluation provides feedback to students about progress. This feedback is useful for improving the quality of education, as well as student mastery. Therefore, the problem is not with evaluation but with how evaluations are used and the forms of testing used to evaluate student abilities and capabilities. Conducted properly, evaluation should increase student competence and eliminate waste in educational funding.

7. Write instructional objectives, create a table of specifications using Bloom's Taxonomy, develop a lesson plan, and write a short test for a topic of study.

POSSIBLE ANSWER:

Type of objective	Cognitive objective: Maslow's hierarchy of needs	Affective objective: Self-actualization
Knowledge	Know the levels of Maslow's hierarchy	Define self-actualization
Comprehension	Give examples of each	Provide an example of a self-actualization goal of your own
Application	Be able to relate Maslow's hierarchy to your current life circumstance	When would you consider yourself actualized?
Analysis	Be able to explain how lower level of Maslow's hierarchy relate to higher levels	Be able to explain how lower level of Maslow's hierarchy relate to self-actualization
Synthesis	Why is Ghandi considered a self-actualized person?	What do you have to do in order to consider yourself actualized one day?
Evaluation	Evaluate Maslow's theory by comparing and contrasting it to Freud's psychosexual theory of personality development	Is self-actualization possible for people of different socio-economic statuses?

The objective then is mastery of Maslow's hierarchy of needs.

Knowledge of terms	Knowledge of facts	Knowledge of rules and principles	Skills in using processes and procedures	Ability to make translations	Ability to make applications
Humanism, biological needs, safety needs, attachment needs, esteem needs, and self-actualization needs	Know the temporal relationship of Maslow's theory to psychodynamic theory, behaviorism, and other forms of humanism	Understand movement toward actualization	Being able to compare and contrast humanistic theory to other theories of personality	Understand how Maslow's theory can be applied to motivation and individuals living in under-developed nations	Ability to apply the principles of Maslow's theory to goal setting

Test:
1. List Maslow's hierarchy of needs in order from most basic to most advanced need.
2. Define each need in relation to the other needs, and provide an example of each.
3. Compare and contrast humanistic theory of personality with psychodynamic theory and learning theory, in relation to personality development.
4. Discuss how Maslow's hierarchy relates to motivation in countries suffering from droughts and food shortages.
5. Discuss the temporal relationship between Maslow's theory, psychodynamic theory, behaviorism, and cognitive theory.

CHAPTER 14

SELF-ASSESSMENT ANSWERS

1. Ms. Tranh speaks to Anita's parents about the many measures of achievement she has to assess Anita's academic ability. Which of the following types of assessment would Ms. Tranh use to predict Anita's future performance?

ANSWER: c) Aptitude tests are designed to assess student potential, measuring general abilities and predicting future performance.

2. Which of the following interpretations would Ms. Tranh make if Anita were to score at the mean of a standardized test?

ANSWER: b) The arithmetic mean is equivalent to 50 for NCE, 0 for z, and 50 for percentile ranking.

3. Ms. Tranh tells Mr. and Mrs. McKay that Anita's grade equivalent score on the CAT is 6.9. What does this mean?

ANSWER: c) A grade equivalent score of 6.9 means that Anita's score is the equivalent of a student in the ninth month of the sixth grade.

4. Ms. Tranh compares her students' scores on a math test with those of another class. She finds that the student's average score in both classes is 75, but the students in her class have scores that are much more spread out. This means that Ms. Tranh's results will have a larger

ANSWER: c) Standard deviation. Standard deviation is a measure of the dispersion of scores.

5. If Anita scored consistently on the CAT over multiple applications, it can be said that the test has

ANSWER: d) Reliability. Reliability refers to the consistency of test scores obtained from the same student at different times.

6. Write a short essay describing the advantages and major criticisms of standardized tests.

POSSIBLE ANSWER: Standardized tests are popular because they provide teachers, parents, and those involved in the selection process with an easy method to compare students to normative samples. For instance, SAT tests are employed by many colleges to determine suitability for admission, on the premise that SAT test scores are valid predictors of future academic performance. However, while standardized tests like the SAT make the selection processes easier, they are not necessarily the most reliable measure of future performance, as other factors like student motivation, subjective value of success, and previous success determine academic success. Further, standardized tests tend to discriminate unwittingly against the economically disadvantaged students, students attending poor quality schools, and ethnic minorities. Therefore, they should be employed with a battery of other sources in determination of college admission.

7. What are the advantages and disadvantages of absolute grading and relative grading standards?

POSSIBLE ANSWER: An advantage of absolute grading standards is student knowledge, in advance, of criteria for attainment of specific grades. One disadvantage of absolute grading standards is that student scores may depend on the difficulty of tests given. A second disadvantage is the range of grades is typically different, particularly for failure, such as 0-60 for an F, versus only 61 to 70 for a D.

Relative grading standards have the advantage of placing students' scores in relation to other students in class, without regard to test difficulty. Relative grading standards also have some disadvantages. For instance, attaining an A is much more difficult in high achieving classes than low achieving classes, when teachers grade on a curve. Further, relative grading standards increase competition for high grades, as each time a student receives an A, the lot of A's available decreases by one, making an already scarce resource even more scarce.

CHAPTER ONE CONCEPT MAP
EDUCATIONAL PSYCHOLOGY:
A FOUNDATION FOR TEACHING

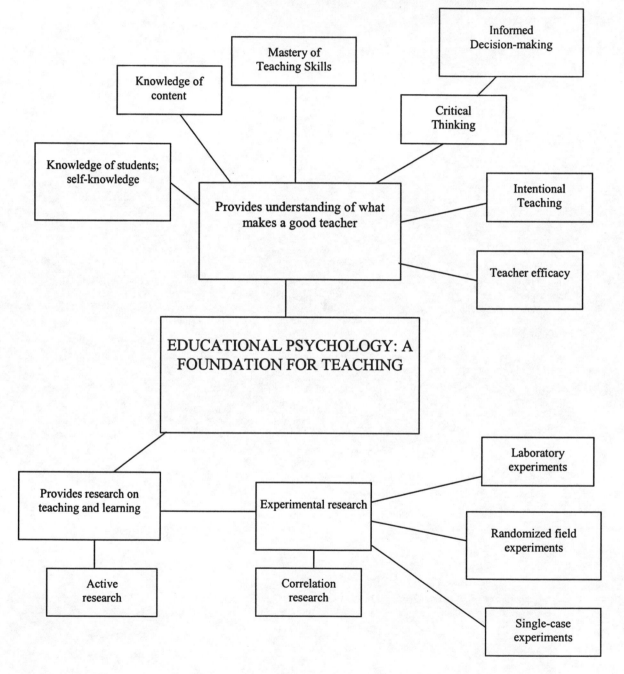

COMPONENTS OF GOOD TEACHING

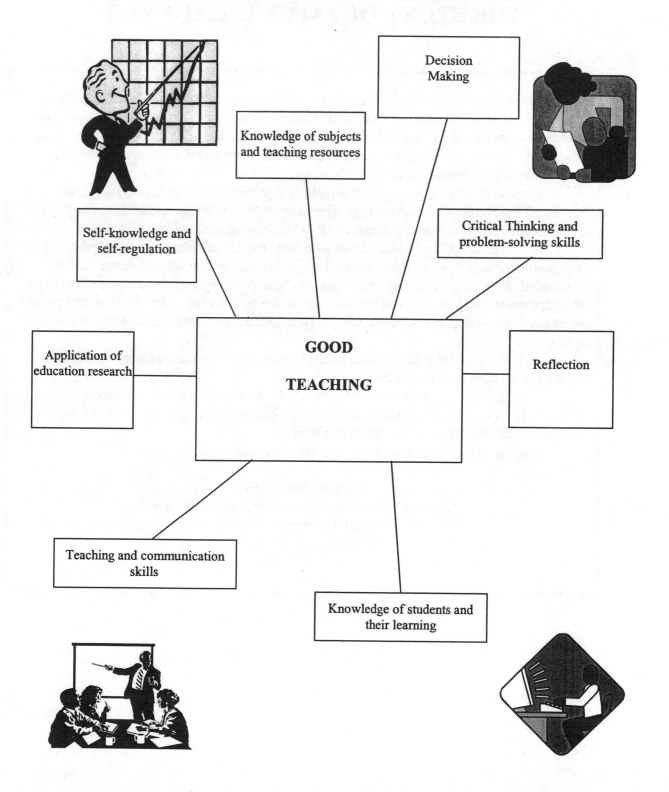

SHOOTING FOR SUCCESS:
THE STORY OF JAIME ESCALANTE

"Shooting for Success," a 22-minute video narrated by actor Edward James Olmos portrays the remarkable success of Jaime Escalante and his students at Garfield High School in East Los Angeles. The video depicts Escalante's determination to teach Advanced Placement Calculus to inner city students whose past successes in learning basic math skills were minimal.

Predominantly Hispanic, Garfield High is presently ranked fourth in the nation in Advanced Placement calculus testing. The exam, which qualifies students for college credit, is taken by less than 2 percent of all public high school students each year.

In 1982, all 18 Garfield students who took the AP calculus exam passed it. The Princeton University-based Educational Testing service, which administered the test, questioned the high pass rate by inner-city students, pointing mainly to similarities in an incorrect answer to one question by 14 of the students. Twelve of the 14 took and passed the exam again. Of the two others, one had joined the Army and one had already entered college.

In 1986, 80 of the 93 Garfield students who took the exam passed. In 1990, a record 160 student took the exam.

"Ganas"–the Spanish word for "desire"–is the key factor in the students' achievement, explains Escalante in the video. When a student has the desire to learn and then puts forth the effort, great things can happen.

Copies of the video may be borrowed at no cost by contacting:

Shooting for Success
National Education Association Communications
1201 16th Street, N. W.
Washington, DC 20036
(202) 822-7200

CATEGORIES OF TEACHING EFFECTIVENESS

1. MANAGEMENT OF INSTUCTIONAL TIME
- ❑ Teacher has lesson materials ready.
- ❑ Teacher gets the lesson started quickly.
- ❑ Teacher gets students on-task quickly.
- ❑ Teacher maintains a high level of student time-on-task.

2. MANAGEMENT OF STUDENT BEHAVIOR
- ❑ Teacher has established routine for administrative matters.
- ❑ Teacher has established rules for verbal participation.
- ❑ Teacher has established rules governing student movement in the classroom.
- ❑ Teacher frequently surveys the class visually.
- ❑ Teacher stops inappropriate behavior promptly and consistently.

3. INSTRUCTIONAL PRESENTATION
- ❑ Teacher introduces the lesson.
- ❑ Teacher begins lesson with a review of previous material.
- ❑ Teacher presents the lesson using understandable concepts and language.
- ❑ Teacher speaks fluently and precisely.
- ❑ Teacher provides relevant examples.
- ❑ Teacher conducts lesson at a brisk pace.
- ❑ Teacher makes sure that the assignment is clear.
- ❑ Teacher assigns tasks and asks questions that students handle with a high rate of success.
- ❑ Teacher summarizes the main point(s) of the lesson at the end.
- ❑ Teacher makes smooth transitions between lessons.

4. INSTRUCTIONAL MONITORING
- ❑ Teacher assesses the student performance.
- ❑ Teacher moves around and checks students' independent work.
- ❑ Teacher maintains deadlines and standards for student work.

5. INSTRUCTIONAL FEEDBACK
- ❑ Teacher provides student with feedback on correctness of class work.
- ❑ Teacher affirms a correct oral answer quickly.
- ❑ Teacher probes; repeats cues.

The Intentional Teacher

- Constantly thinks about the outcomes of the lesson.

- Has a clear purpose for the lesson.

- Is flexible without losing the focus of the lesson.

- Uses a wide variety of instructional methods, experiences, assignments, and materials.

- Incorporates a variety of cognitive objectives in the lesson.

TEACHER INTERVIEW—THEORY & PRACTICE

Interview teachers, counselors, or principals who are currently working in a public or private school. Use this form to record responses. Develop a few questions of your own.

We are studying theories of educational psychology and learning about the importance of developing our own theory and philosophy. It would really be helpful if you could talk with me a little bit about your understanding of the role of educational theory in actual classroom practice. In your work, do you use any theory or model?

I understand that a teacher makes a great number of independent decisions every day. Do you have a theory or model that helps you make decisions relating to instruction, student discipline, etc.?

Have you developed any classroom practices/techniques based on theories/models?

Have you had any in-service training that is based on a particular theory/model and/or does the administration/board in your district support/encourage the use of a particular model or theory?

In faculty meetings or during performance based teacher evaluations are any theories or models discussed?

Do you have friends or colleagues in other districts, buildings, or disciplines who develop practices based on a theory or model?

Is there any particular theory/model you are interested in learning more about?

What words of wisdom do you have for me?

CHAPTER TWO CONCEPT MAP
THEORIES OF DEVELOPMENT

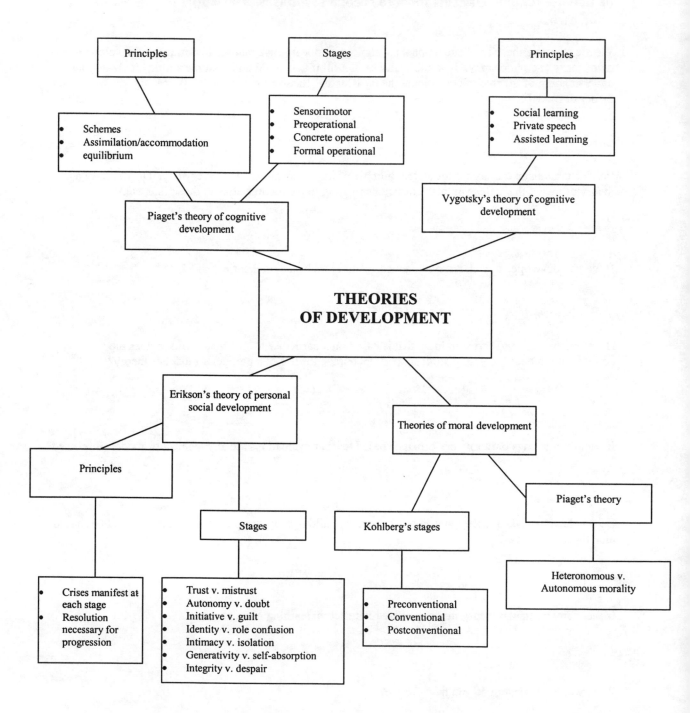

Principles

- Schemes
- Assimilation/accommodation
- equilibrium

Stages

- Sensorimotor
- Preoperational
- Concrete operational
- Formal operational

Principles

- Social learning
- Private speech
- Assisted learning

Piaget's theory of cognitive development

Vygotsky's theory of cognitive development

THEORIES OF DEVELOPMENT

Erikson's theory of personal social development

Theories of moral development

Principles

Stages

Kohlberg's stages

Piaget's theory

- Crises manifest at each stage
- Resolution necessary for progression

- Trust v. mistrust
- Autonomy v. doubt
- Initiative v. guilt
- Identity v. role confusion
- Intimacy v. isolation
- Generativity v. self-absorption
- Integrity v. despair

- Preconventional
- Conventional
- Postconventional

Heteronomous v. Autonomous morality

TASKS THAT ASSESS DEVELOPMENTAL DIFFERENCES IN CHILDREN'S THINKING

INTERPRETATION OF STORIES

Read children *Aesop's Fables* and ask, "What do you think this story means?"

- <u>Preoperational</u>: Response will likely mention something that happened in their own life. They will probably explain or justify their answer.
- <u>Concrete operational</u>: Response is based on the literal content of the story.
- <u>Formal operational</u>: Response goes beyond the literal content of the story and indicates some understanding of the meaning of the moral.

CLASSIFICATION

Give children the following objects and ask them to group things that go together. (Objects: a magazine picture, marker chalk, notebook paper, typing paper, thumb tack, straight pin, tape, and a paper sack)

- <u>Early operational</u>: Grouping is based on some perceptual feature – color, shape, etc. The paper and chalk may be grouped because they are both white.
- <u>Late preoperational</u>: Grouping is based on a functional relationship. Pencil and paper may be grouped because you write on the paper with a pencil. The tack and the picture, because you use the tack to put the picture on the wall.
- <u>Concrete operational</u>: Grouping is based on a common element. For example, a group may include things made of paper, things you can write with, or things you can use to put things on a bulletin board.

CONSERVATION

Line two sets of wooden beads side by side. Ask the children, "Does each set have the same amount or does one set have more?" If they answer "same," then spread out one set and ask again. Return them to their original position, but bunch up one set. Then ask again. Create two equal balls of clay. Ask children, "Do the balls have the same amount of clay or does one have more?" Make a "snake" or a "pancake" out of one ball and ask again.

- <u>Preoperational</u>: Responds that one set has more than the other when changes are made.
- <u>Concrete operational</u>: Responds that each set has the same amount and explains the answer by counting, 1:1 correspondence, or reversibility as rationale.

COMBINATION LOGIC

Give the children five different one-digit numbers on separate small pieces of paper. Ask them to make as many different 3-digit numbers as they can.

- <u>Concrete operational</u>: Task is approached in a random, haphazard manner.
- <u>Formal operational</u>: Task is approached in an orderly and systematic way

TEACHING MODEL BASED ON VYGOTSKY'S THEORY

Peer or teacher

Assisted Learning

Learner's private speech

Learned tasks

Scaffolding: support for learning and problem *solving*

Zone of Proximal Development: level of development immediately above a *person's present level.*

Unlearned tasks not yet within learner's ability and cultural *tools for learning.*

INTERACTION

HOW PRIVATE SPEECH
REFLECTS COGNITIVE DEVELOPLEMENT

Vygotsky (1978) described his idea of the development of "private speech" as a child going through the following cognitive and linguistic stages:

1. The child's thoughts are nonverbal and speech is nonintellectual (e.g., crying and babbling). Vocabulary is social rather than cognitive.

2. The child uses external signs (e.g., counting on fingers) and talks aloud to herself as she solves problems.

3. The child internalizes the external signs and uses speech to communicate with others.

4. The child has soundless language and uses it as a psychological tool for structuring thought, i.e., he has "private speech."

Using Vygotsky's idea of the development of private speech, pretend you observe a group of preschool-aged children playing in a sandbox. Match them with Vygotsky's principle and order the children by age based on these brief observations:

_____ A girl working alone building a sand-castle says, "No that won't fit. I'll try it here."

_____ A girl chatters with some other girls about how to dig a tunnel under the sand-castle she is building.

_____ One boy's thinking is done silently.

_____ One girl talks to another about how to dig a tunnel under the sand-castle she is building.

_____ A boy's speech is less social and more focused on building the castles.

_____ One boy's phrases are muttered aloud but are unintelligible to the other children or observer.

For more information about the idea of private or inner speech, read Vygotsky, L. (1978). <u>Mind in Society: The development of higher mental process.</u> Cambridge, MA: Harvard University Press.

HM 2.5

Moral Development Parent Interview Guide

Interview several parents and speak to them about their beliefs and efforts to guide the moral development of their child(ren). Your research team can use these questions as a guide. You will want to adapt this form to fit your needs and to obtain the type of information you are looking for regarding moral development. *Develop a few questions of your own.*

As a parent, what goals do you have for your child?

Do you, or have you, given any thought to the moral development of your child?

What values do you try to teach?

What family traditions do you try to maintain, and what is the importance of these traditions to you?

When do you have discussions about values?

What are your concerns or worries about your child's moral development?

How do you feel about our society/media and moral development?

How do you feel about character education programs in schools?

What words of advice would you give teachers?

Character Education Interview Guide

You will want to interview several teachers, principals, counselors, central office administrators in public and/or private schools. Your research team can use these questions as a guide. You will want to adapt this form to fit your needs and develop a few question of your own to obtain the type of information you are looking for regarding character education.

Tell me about character education in your classroom/school/district.

In your opinion, is character education a new initiative of schools?

Do you believe character education should be left up to the family/church?

What has been the reaction of parents and community members to character education programs?

Please tell me a little bit about any resistance you have found to character education.

Which types of programs or activities do you believe are most successful in promoting a sustained character education program?

Which type of activities or programs do you feel are least successful?

Are there any noticeable changes in student behavior or morale since you have started character education?

What words of wisdom, advice, or caution do you have regarding character education?

CHAPTER THREE CONCEPT MAP
CHANGES DURING CHILDHOOD AND ADOLESCENCE

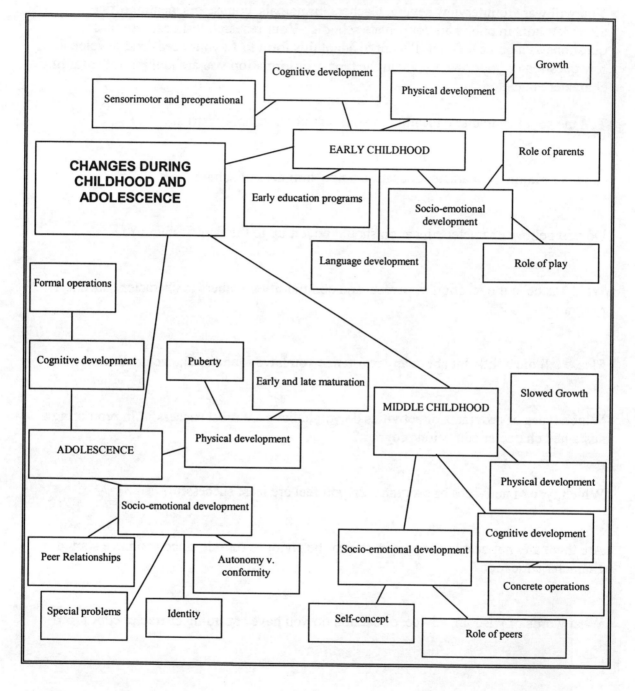

CENTRAL ISSUES IN DEVELOPMENT DURING EARLY CHILDHOOD, MIDDLE CHILDHOOD AND ADOLESCENCE

Early Childhood

Cognitive Development
language acquisition
development

Physical Development
large and small muscle skills

Socioemotional Development
prosocial behaviors

Middle Childhood

Cognitive Development
memory and metacognitive skills

Physical Development
physical growth

Socioemotional Development
self-concept
self-esteem
peer relationships

Adolescence

Cognitive Development
hypothetical and deductive reasoning
identity
intimacy
social responsibility

Physical Development
puberty

Socioemotional Development
identity formation
social responsibility
intimacy

COMPARING CONCRETE AND FORMAL OPERATIONS

Non-Hypothetical-Deductive Reasoning (Concrete-Operational Thinkers)

- Can form limited hypotheses, reasons with reference to actions, objects, and properties that are familiar or that can be experienced.

- May memorize prominent words, phrases, formulas, and procedures but will apply them with little understanding of the abstract meaning or principles underling them.

- Has problems reasoning logically about ideas that are contrary to fact or personal beliefs, or that are arbitrary.

- Needs step-by-step instructions when planning a lengthy, complex procedure.

- Is unaware of inconsistencies and contradictions within own thinking.

Hypothetical-Deductive Reasoning (Formal Operational Thinkers)

- Can form multiple hypotheses, has concrete and formal abstract concepts and relationships, reasons about intangible properties and theories.

- Can understand the abstract meaning and principles underlying formal concepts, relationships, and theories.

- Can argue logically about ideas that are contrary to fact or personal belief or that are arbitrary; can reason based on testimonials.

- Can plan a lengthy, complex procedure given a set of conditions, goals, and resources.

- Is aware and critical of own reasoning; can reflect on the problem-solving process and verify conclusions by checking sources, using other known information, or seeking a solution from another perspective.

FIELD OBSERVATION: CHILDREN AT PLAY

Instruction: *Observe preschool aged children in a freeplay activity at a day-care, park, or home. Record your field notes on this observation sheet.*

I. **PLAY SETTING**
   A. Describe the play setting:_____
   _____
   _____
   B. Describe the play activity:_____
   _____
   _____
   C. What are the toys or props?:_____
   _____
   _____

II. **ACTORS**
   A. Identify the participants:_____
   _____
   _____
   B. Who initiated the play?:_____
   _____
   _____
   C. Describe the interactions of the players. (Do they play alone? Side by side? Take turns? Play together?):_____
   _____
   _____

III. **PLAY LANGUAGE**
   A. Do children talk to themselves (monologues) or to each other (dialogues)?:_____
   _____
   _____
   B. Give examples of the language:_____
   _____
   _____

IV. **SYMBOLIC PLAY**
   A. Do children play identifiable roles (e.g. daddy, teacher, etc.)?_____
   _____
   _____
   B. What are the elements of fantasy and reality in the play?_____
   _____
   _____

CAREGIVER INTERVIEW

Call your parent or caregiver or another adult who was involved in your life as a baby or young child. If you have difficulty connecting with someone to interview, try interviewing someone who is about the same age as your parent.

Use these questions only as a guide for your discussion. You will want to adapt the questions to fit your discussion and to explore areas of interest to you. Be sure to develop a few questions of your own.

1. What were your goals for raising me?

2. What were special challenges in raising me?

3. What were special joys in raising me?

4. How do you think times have changed in regard to child rearing?

5. What is your advice for new parents and students of human development?

6. Do you recall any areas of development in which I was either "ahead of" or "behind" other children my age? Can you give some examples?

Develop a few questions of your own.

ADOLESCENT INTERVIEWS: PERCEPTIONS OF GOOD TEACHERS

You can use these questions as a guide. You will want to adapt this form to fit your needs and to obtain the type of information you are looking for regarding adolescents and their perceptions of teachers.

Obtain permission to interview several high school or junior high school students. Explain to your subjects that we will be using their responses in a classroom discussion and their feedback can help us become better, more effective teachers. Gather background information about your subject: grade level, age, type of school attended, success in school etc....

In your opinion, what is the most important characteristic of a good teacher?

When you are having trouble with a concept, what is the best way a teacher can help you?

What kinds of testing procedures does a good teacher use?

What can a teacher do to motivate you in an area?

How does a good teacher handle the classroom?

What are some other traits, techniques, or behaviors of a good teacher?

Without using the teacher's name, tell me something about a teacher you did not like/respect. What was it this teacher did or didn't do that caused you to form this opinion of him or her?

What final words of advice on teaching would you like to give our class?

Be sure to thank your subject for his/her time and let him/her know we appreciate it.

CHAPTER FOUR CONCEPT MAP
STUDENT DIVERSITY

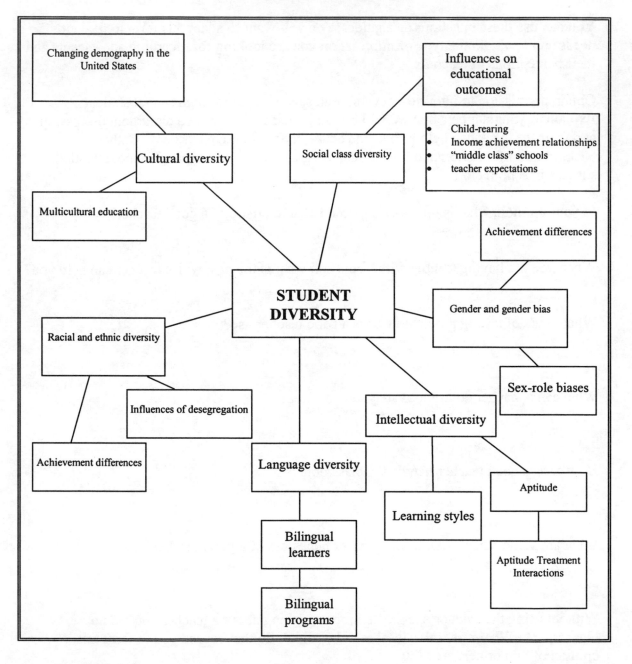

CULTURAL DIVERSITY AND INDIVIDUAL IDENTITY

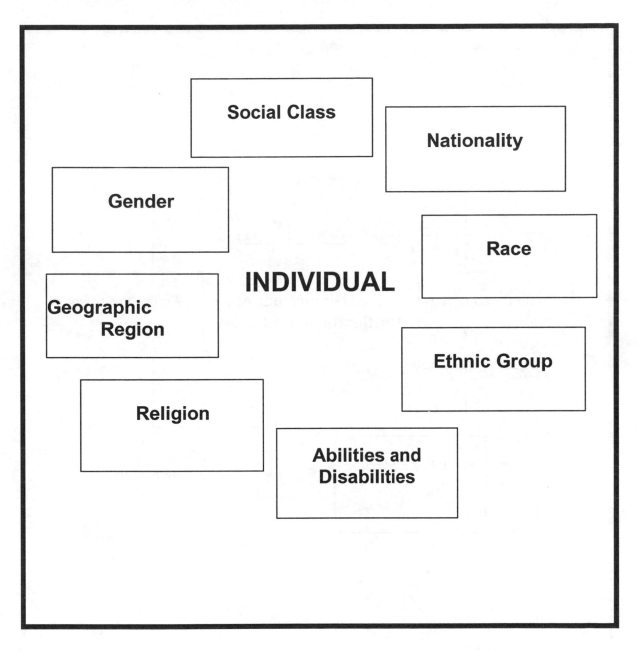

HM 4.3

FIVE KEY DIMENSIONS TO MULTICULTURAL EDUCATION

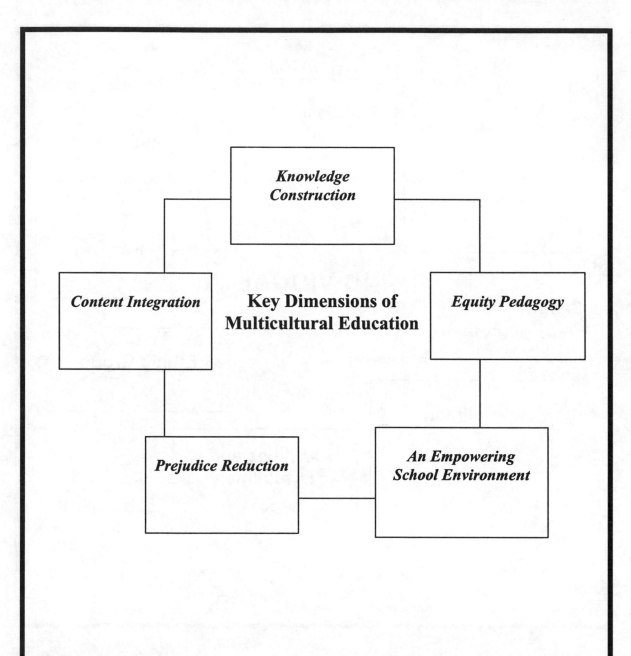

FIELD OBSERVATION:CHILDREN'S TELEVISION & GENDER

PROGRAM OBSERVED:
    A. Describe the type of program observed:_____

_____

    B. Describe the story setting:_____

_____

_____

I.   ACTORS
    A. Identify the actors and note their genders:_____

_____

    B. Describe the roles of the actors:_____

_____

    C. Describe the activities of the players:_____

_____

    D. Is any activity gender typical? Non-typical?_____

_____

_____

II.   LANGUAGE OF THE ACTORS
    A. Give examples of the language that may be gender stereotypical:_____

_____

_____

    B. Note any stereotypical "names" (e.g. "Ace" or "Doll baby"): _____

_____

_____

III.   COMMERCIAL INTERLUDES
    A. Describe the advertisements aimed at children during the program:_____

_____

_____

    B. Note when commercial advertisements target gender specifically:_____

_____

_____

    C. Describe how they might reinforce gender stereotypes:_____

_____

_____

School, Family & Community Partnerships

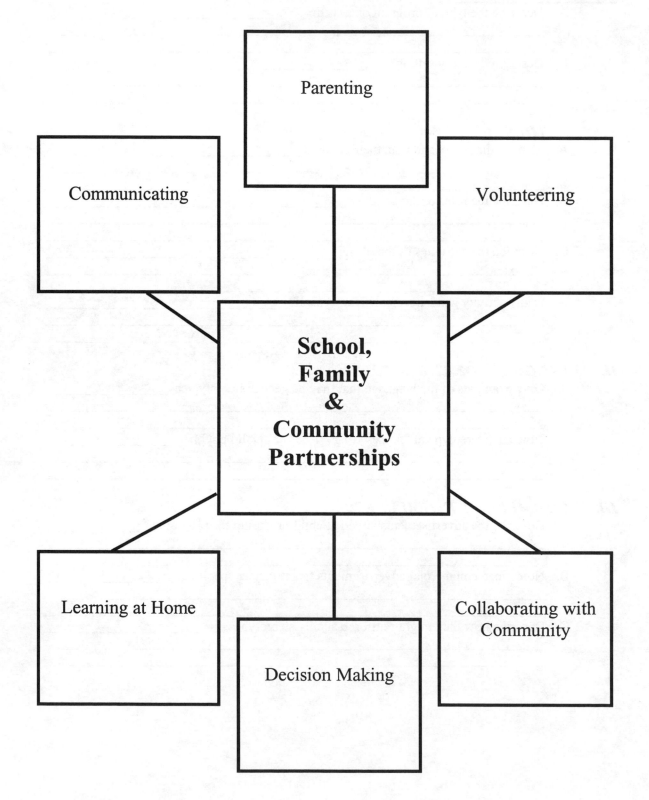

Parenting

Communicating

Volunteering

School, Family & Community Partnerships

Learning at Home

Decision Making

Collaborating with Community

CHAPTER FIVE CONCEPT MAP
BEHAVIORAL THEORIES OF LEARNING

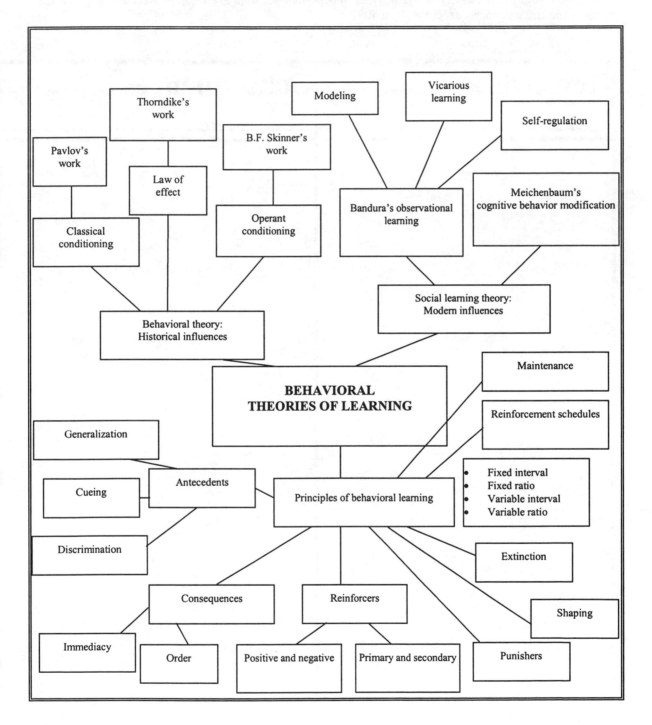

REWARDS & CONSEQUENCES

Think about your future classroom and the types of behaviors you wish to encourage and discourage. What types of rewards and consequences will you use?

Rewards ————	Consequences ————
1.	1.
2.	2.
3.	3.
4.	4.
5.	5.
6.	6.
7.	7.
8.	8.

FIELD INTERVIEW: CHILDREN'S CHOICES OF REINFORCERS

Interview a student in or near the grade level you hope to teach to determine what kinds of reinforcers he/she thinks are meaningful rewards.

II. REWARDS FOR HOMEWORK COMPLETION
   A. What rewards, if any, do you receive at home after completing your homework?

   _____
   _____
   _____

   B. Which of these rewards would you like best for completing homework? Rank them.
      _____praise from parents
      _____snack
      _____television time
      _____outdoor play / recess
      _____talking with classmates
      _____library time
      _____phone visits with friends
      _____personal reading time
      _____free play time (toys, crafts, etc.)
      _____money

II. REWARDS FOR SCHOOL WORK COMPLETION AND ACCURACY
   A. What of these rewards do you receive when you complete assignments at school?

   _____
   _____
   _____

   B. Which of these rewards would you like best for completing classwork? Rank them.
      _____praise or acknowledgement from teacher(s)
      _____smiley face, sticker, or star
      _____snack
      _____outdoor time / recess
      _____talking with classmates
      _____library time
      _____personal reading time
      _____free time (games, crafts, etc.)
      _____a token to collect and cash in for a prize
      _____computer time
      _____a high grade

III. TEACHER PRAISE
   A. How does your teacher tell you that you have done something correctly?

   _____
   _____
   _____

   B. Would you prefer another kind of praise? If so, what?

   _____
   _____
   _____

   C. Do you like it when the teacher praises your work and others can hear?

   _____
   _____
   _____

CULTURAL DIFFERENCES IN DISCIPLINE CHOICE

Interview an individual from each of the following groups to determine if there are cultural differences in discipline choices of parents and teachers.

Ethnic Background	(FORMER GENERATION) *My Parent or Teacher's Discipline Choice*	(PRESENT GENERATION) *My Discipline Choice as a Parent Or Teacher*
African American		
Anglo American		
Hispanic		
Other Ethnic Groups		
Other Immigrant Groups		

FOCUS QUESTIONS:

1. Are there patterns of differences in discipline choices by ethnic or cultural group?

2. Are there marked differences in discipline choices between our parents' generation and our own?

3. What other factors might account for differences in discipline choices? (e.g., class, rural v. urban background, geographic region, legal traditions, etc.)

CHILDREN'S TELEVISION—MODELING AGGRESSION

Your task in this project is to compare the amounts of aggressive and prosocial behavior children will observe if watching children's programs on commercial networks versus PBS. Use copies of this worksheet to note each instance of physical aggression, verbal aggression, physical prosocial behavior, and verbal prosocial behavior. Observe at least one commercial show that children watch (for example *Rugrats*, *Superman*, *Bugs Bunny*, *Power Rangers*, *Teen Titans*) and at least one PBS program.

Aggressive acts are those intending to harm or agitate. Physical aggression includes but is not limited to biting, hitting, smashing, and shooting. Verbal aggression includes but is not limited to name calling, yelling, and putting down. Prosocial acts are those with intent to aid such as helping, sharing, complimenting, and reinforcing verbally.

Also count how many minutes per half hour show are devoted to actual show versus commercials. Evaluate the type of product promoted and its appropriateness for children. You will want to summarize your findings, draw some conclusions, and make some recommendations for parents and teachers in regard to children and television viewing.

1. NAME OF SHOW:
2. TV NETWORK AND TIME:
3. BRIEF SUMMARY OF SHOW:

4. TOTAL NUMBER OF ADVERTISEMENTS:
5. LENGTH OF SHOW:
6. MAJOR CATEGORY OF ADS:
7. LIST ADVERTISERS OR SPONSORS:

8. NUMBER OF VERBAL AGGRESSIVE ACTS:
9. EXAMPLE:

10. NUMBER OF PHYSICAL AGGRESSIVE ACTS:

11. EXAMPLE:

12. NUMBER OF PROSOCIAL ACTS:
13. EXAMPLE:

14. MAJOR CHARACTER:
15. NUMBER OF TIMES EPISODE OUTCOMES WERE POSITIVE FOR MAIN CHARACTER?
16. NUMBER OF TIMES EPISODE OUTCOMES WERE NEGATIVE FOR MAIN CHARACTER?

NOTEWORTHY QUOTES FROM THE SHOW:

CONCLUSIONS:

RECOMMENDATIONS:

CONCERNS:

CHAPTER SIX CONCEPT MAP
COGNITIVE THEORIES OF LEARNING:
BASIC CONCEPTS

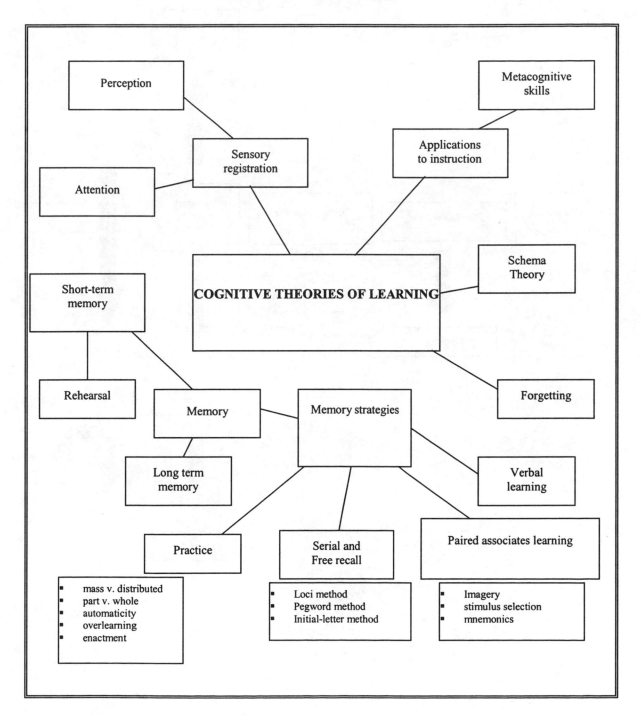

HM 6.2

THE SEQUENCE OF INFORMATION PROCESSING

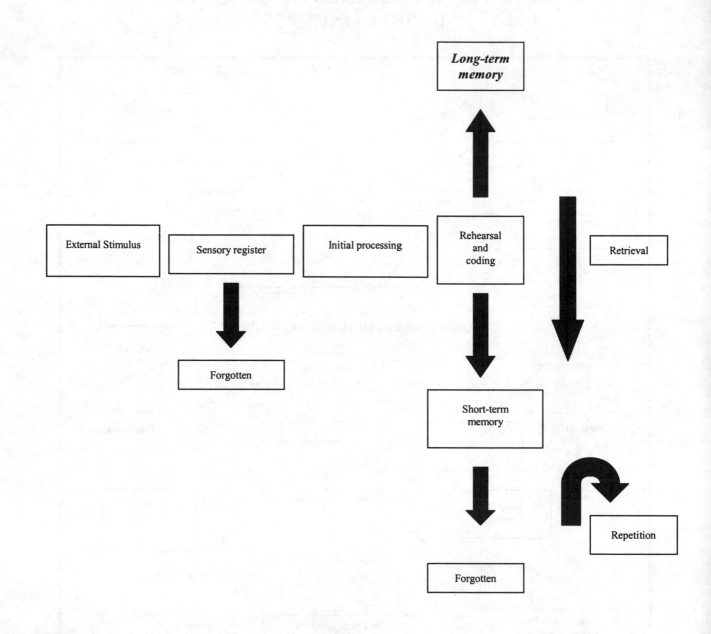

THREE TYPES OF MEMORY

Three Types of Memory: Recalling soccer practice is an example of episodic memory. The example of semantic memory shows the meaningful associations that might be part of your understanding of the concept of "library." Using a computer involves procedural memory.

PROCEDURES FOR MEASURING PROACTIVE AND RETROACTIVE INHIBITION

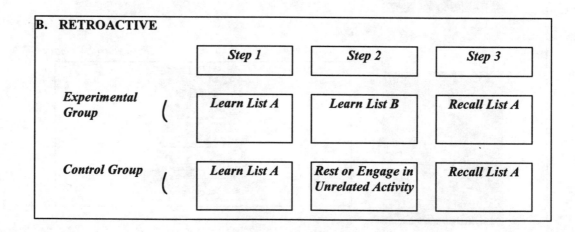

A. PROACTIVE

	Step 1	Step 2	Step 3
Experimental Group	Learn List A	Learn List B	Recall List B
Control Group	Rest or Engage in Unrelated Activity	Learn List B	Recall List B

B. RETROACTIVE

	Step 1	Step 2	Step 3
Experimental Group	Learn List A	Learn List B	Recall List A
Control Group	Learn List A	Rest or Engage in Unrelated Activity	Recall List A

HM 6.5

Teaching Metacognitive Awareness

Instructions: Students, to be self-regulated learners, must have knowledge about their own strategies for learning. Observe when and how teachers ask their students to monitor and evaluate their own thinking and learning processes.

I. TALKING TO ONE'S SELF

    A. Note when and how a teacher instructs the student to talk to themselves:

_____

_____

_____

    B. What behaviors or strategies is the teacher promoting in the student?

_____

_____

_____

    C. Note ways the teacher suggests that the student monitor his/her behavior or performance for appropriateness or accuracy:

_____

_____

_____

II. KNOWLEDGE OF "what to do" AND "when to do it"

    A. Which of these content strategies does the teacher remind students to do:
        (Give an example)

      1. Use a memory strategy_____

      2. Form an association_____

      3. Identify a main idea_____

      4. Use an organizational strategy_____
        (e.g., outline, concept map)

    B. Which of these procedural strategies does the teacher remind them to do:
        (Give an example)

      1. Check to see if you
        understand the instructions_____

      2. Predict your answers/outcome_____

      3. Plan how to do the task_____

      4. Brainstorm for ideas_____

      5. If unsuccessful, find
        another way_____

KNOWLEDGE CHART

Name: _____

Prior Knowledge About _____ _____	New Knowledge About _____ _____
1.	1.
2.	2.
3.	3.
4.	4.
5.	5.
6.	6.
7.	7.
8.	8.

NOTING WHAT I'VE LEARNED

Topic: _____

Main Ideas/Key Words/
Questions/Drawings

What I've learned:

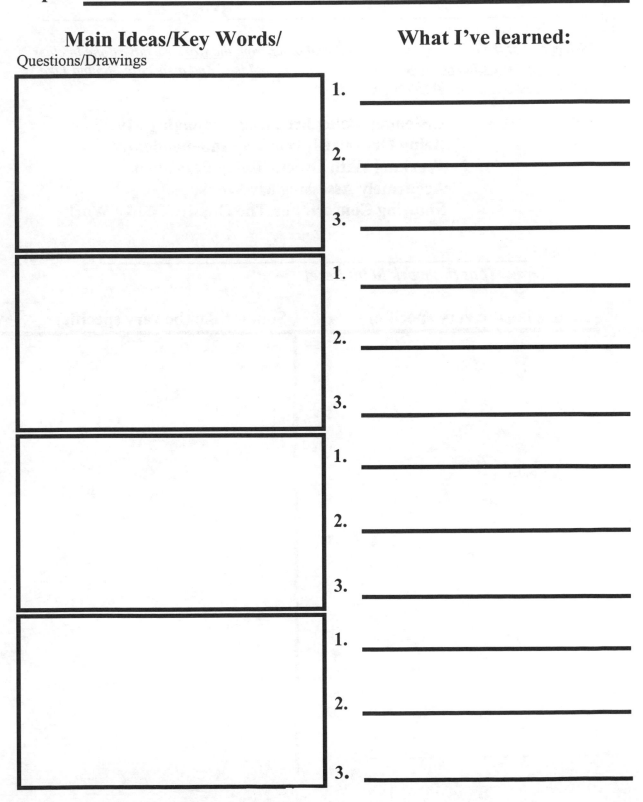

1. _____

2. _____

3. _____

1. _____

2. _____

3. _____

1. _____

2. _____

3. _____

1. _____

2. _____

3. _____

T CHART PLAN FOR IMPROVING WORK HABITS

Name:

_____**Date:**_____

Select one of the following work habits or another from the work we have done in class.
Complete the T Chart. Then select a specific "Look Like" and a specific "Sound Like"
behavior as you focus for improvement.

Work Habits: **Listening, Being Prepared, Managing My Time,**
Being Organized, Working Independently,
Working With Others, Being Persistent,
Accurately Assessing My Work,
Showing Concern For The Quality Of My Work

When I_____**, it would:**
        (put the work habit here)

Look Like (be very specific)   **Sound Like (be very specific)**

CHAPTER SEVEN CONCEPT MAP
THE EFFECTIVE LESSON

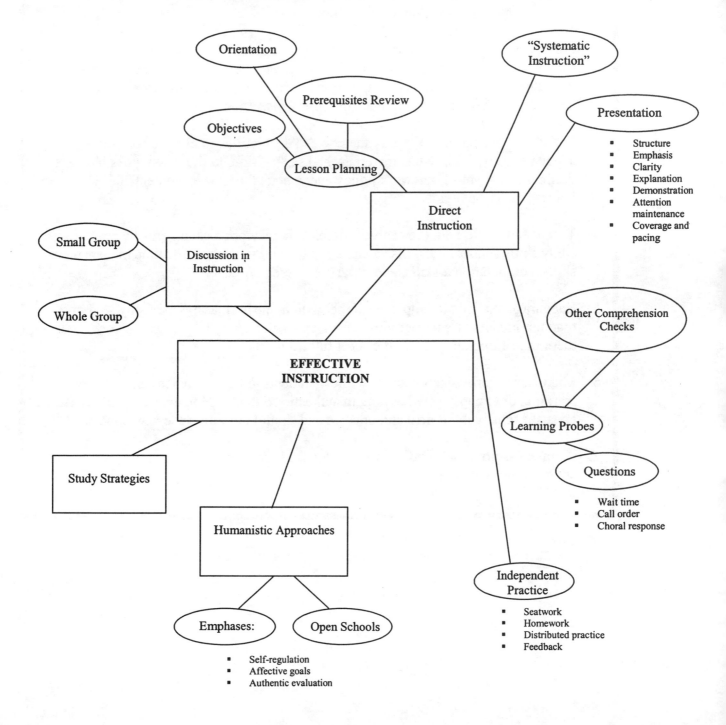

MAKING HOMEWORK COUNT

1. Regularly assign, collect, assess, and review homework in all subjects and all grade levels. Give students feedback about their homework and include homework assessments in your system of evaluation.

2. For the amount of homework to assign, observe the guidelines established by your school district. Guidelines are usually expressed in terms of a number of minutes per subject, per day, graduated upward according to grade level. Homework is generally not effective if too much or too little is assigned.

3. Enlist the cooperation of family members. Ask families to allow or provide adequate study time, space, materials, and supervision, to the extent possible. Let families know your homework policy and contact them when students fail to turn in homework assignments.

4. Teach students to help themselves complete homework assignments by practicing study skills and related skills, such as reading and writing skills, time management skills, computational skills, and library and research skills.

5. Encourage students to help one another with homework assignments by studying together in pairs or small groups. If students still need help with homework, assist them in teaming up with adult or peer tutors.

6. Make homework assignments that allow students to be creative, to extend new learning, or to apply new learning in authentic contexts. Homework should not consist exclusively of drill and practice and should not introduce new concepts.

7. As much as possible, modify or individualize homework assignments to meet students' particular abilities, interests, or needs.

HM 7.3

Parent Interview: Homework Concerns

1. How much homework does your child have on an average evening?

2. What benefits do you see for your child from completing homework?

3. What types of homework assignments do you feel are most effective in increasing your child's learning?

4. Do you find some homework assignments to be ineffective in increasing student learning?

5. How does homework impact your family life?

6. Do you routinely assist your child with homework?

7. What suggestions do you have for future teachers regarding the assigning of homework?

FIELD OBSERVATION: PARTS OF A LESSON

Instruction: Using this observation sheet, observe a lesson in a classroom. Indicate which of the seven parts of the lesson are effectively accomplished.

DESCRIBE THE LESSON OBSERVED: _____
_____
_____

I.   Teacher States Learning Objectives and Orients Students to the Lesson.
  - a) Tells students what they will be learning ☐
  - b) Tells what performance will be expected of students ☐
II. Teacher Reviews Prerequisites.
  - a) Goes over skills or concepts needed to understand the lesson ☐
III. Teacher Presents New Material.
  - a) Presents information ☐
  - b) Gives examples ☐
  - c) Demonstrates concepts ☐
  - d) Uses these features:
    - i.   Clear lesson structure ☐
    - ii.   Good emphasis ☐
    - iii. Simple, well organized language ☐
    - iv. Good explanations ☐
    - v.   Effective demonstrations, models, and illustrations ☐
    - vi. Attention maintenance ☐
    - vii. Adequate content coverage ☐
    - viii. Brisk pacing ☐
IV. Teacher Conducts Learning Probes.
  - a) Poses questions to students throughout the lesson ☐
  - b) Checks for understanding ☐
  - c) Varies questioning technique to maximize accuracy and responses ☐
V. Teacher Provides Independent Practice.
  - a) Provides guided practice to demonstrate the task ☐
  - b) Assigns appropriate independent work for practice ☐
VI. Teacher Assesses Performance and Provides Feedback.
  - a) Monitors the accuracy and completeness of independent work ☐
  - b) Gives feedback on accuracy and mid-course correction ☐
VII. Teacher Provides Distributed Practice and Review.
  - a) Assigns homework or other distributed practice ☐

EVALUATION:
Which parts were most effectively accomplished?_____
_____
_____
_____

Which parts were omitted?_____
_____
_____
_____

FIELD OBSERVATION:
USING EXAMPLES IN TEACHING CONCEPTS

Instruction: Observe a lesson when a teacher uses similar and diverse examples to teach concepts.

NATURE OF THE LESSON:

I.   *CONCEPTS AND SIMILAR EXAMPLES*
    A.   First Key Concept taught: _____
_____
_____

        List the examples used to teach the concept: _____
_____
_____

        Describe how similar these examples are: _____
_____
_____

    B.   Another Key Concept taught: _____
_____
_____

        List the examples used to teach the concept: _____
_____
_____

        Describe how similar these examples are: _____
_____
_____

II.   *CONCEPTS AND DIVERSE EXAMPLES*
    A.   Describe when a concept (from I) is broadened to include diverse examples: _____
_____
_____

    B.   Give the example: _____
_____
_____

    C.   Did the student transfer the learning to the new, diverse example?

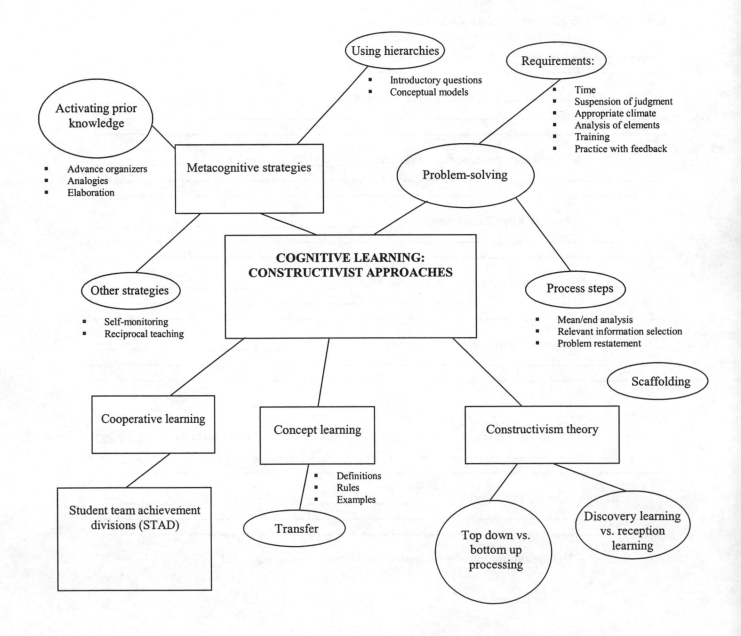

HM 8.1

CHAPTER EIGHT CONCEPT MAP
STUDENT-CENTERED AND CONSTRUCTIVIST APPROACHES TO INSTRUCTION

Using hierarchies
- Introductory questions
- Conceptual models

Requirements:
- Time
- Suspension of judgment
- Appropriate climate
- Analysis of elements
- Training
- Practice with feedback

Activating prior knowledge
- Advance organizers
- Analogies
- Elaboration

Metacognitive strategies

Problem-solving

COGNITIVE LEARNING: CONSTRUCTIVIST APPROACHES

Other strategies
- Self-monitoring
- Reciprocal teaching

Process steps
- Mean/end analysis
- Relevant information selection
- Problem restatement

Scaffolding

Cooperative learning

Concept learning
- Definitions
- Rules
- Examples

Constructivism theory

Student team achievement divisions (STAD)

Transfer

Top down vs. bottom up processing

Discovery learning vs. reception learning

HM 8.2

STORY PROBLEMS FOR TEACHING MULTIPLICATION

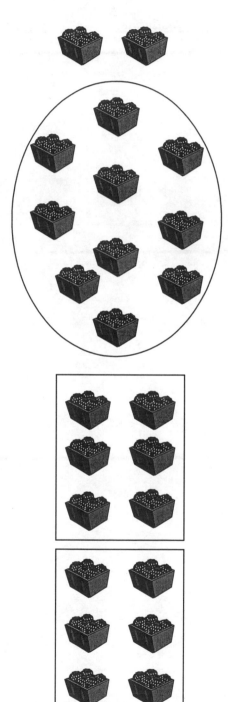

T: Can anyone give me a story that could go with this multiplication…12 x 5?

S: There were twelve baskets, and each had 5 strawberries in it.

T: And if I did this multiplication and found the answer, what would I know about these baskets and strawberries?

S: You would know you had that many strawberries altogether.

T: Okay, here are the baskets. [Draws a picture to represent the baskets of strawberries – see diagram.] Now, it will be easier for us to count how many strawberries there are altogether if we think of the baskets in groups. And as usual, the mathematician's favorite number for thinking about groups is?

S: 10

T: Each of these 10 baskets has 5 strawberries in it. [Draws a loop around 10 jars.]

T: Suppose I erase my circle and go back to looking at the 12 baskets again together. Is there any other way I could group them to make it easier for us to count all the strawberries?

S: You could do 6 and 6.

T: Now, how many do I have in this group?

S: 30

T: How did you figure that out?

S: 10 and 10 and 10. [He put the 6 baskets together into 3 pairs, intuitively finding a grouping that made the figuring easier for him.]

T: That's 3 x 10. It's also 6 x 5. Now how many are in this group?

S: 30. It's the same. They both have 6 baskets.

T: How many are there all together?

S: 30 and 30 is 60.

T: Do we get the same number of strawberries as before? Why?

S: Yes, because we have the same number of baskets, and they still have 5 strawberries in each.

DIVISION OF LABOR CHART

Name	*Role*	*Responsibilities*

RESEARCH PLAN

Name: _____ Date: _____

RESEARCH

Topic: _____

Sources I will use

1.

2.

3.

4.

QUESTIONS I want answered:

1.

2.

3.

4.

CHAPTER NINE CONCEPT MAP
ACCOMMODATING INSTRUCTION TO MEET INDIVIDUAL NEEDS

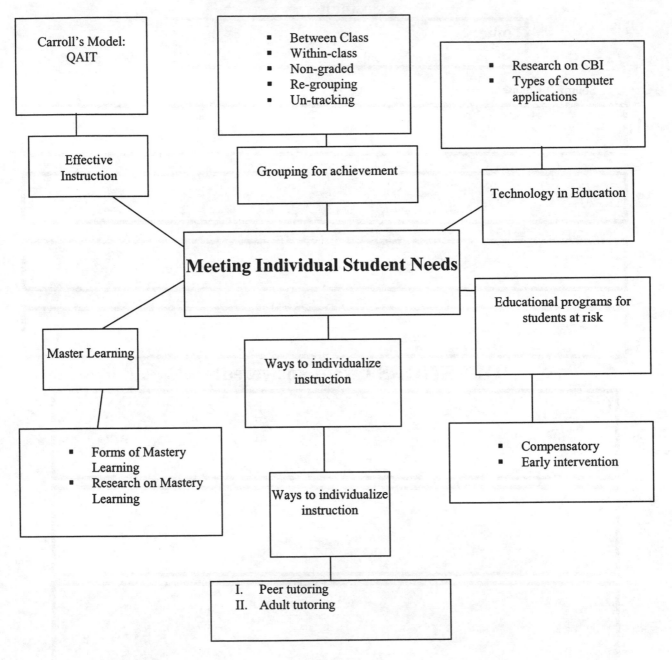

Carroll's Model: QAIT

- Between Class
- Within-class
- Non-graded
- Re-grouping
- Un-tracking

- Research on CBI
- Types of computer applications

Effective Instruction

Grouping for achievement

Technology in Education

Meeting Individual Student Needs

Educational programs for students at risk

Master Learning

Ways to individualize instruction

Compensatory
Early intervention

- Forms of Mastery Learning
- Research on Mastery Learning

Ways to individualize instruction

I. Peer tutoring
II. Adult tutoring

FIELD OBSERVATION: CLASSROOM COMPUTER USE

Instruction: Increasingly, instructional strategies include computer use in both teaching and learning. Observe and discuss with a classroom teacher how computers are used in his/her classroom.

I. COMPUTER HARDWARE AND SOFTWARE

    A.   Describe the type of computer equipment available to students and teachers in the regular classroom:_____

_____

    B.   What are the software programs typically available to the students for use on this equipment?_____

_____

    C.   What computer equipment or training is a regular feature of the instructional program for the students? (e.g., labs, computer instruction, etc.)_____

_____

_____

II. COMPUTER LEARNING

    A.   How much time does each student have on the classroom computer per week?_____

_____

          In the computer instruction lab?_____

_____

    B.   How are students trained to use the classroom hardware and software?_____

_____

_____

    C.   Describe the frequency of the following computer uses in the classroom:

          1)   Drill and practice:_____

          2)   Keyboarding and typing tutorials:_____

          3)   Computer games:_____

          4)   Computer simulations:_____

          5)   Instructional management tasks:_____

III. SUMMARY OBSERVATIONS

    A.   Are computers linked well to the school curricula?_____

_____

    B.   Do students have ample time working with computers to use them independently?_____

_____

    C.   Are the computer resources in the classroom put to good use?_____

_____

_____

HM 9.3

MATCHING PROGRAMS TO INDIVIDUALIZED NEEDS

In the following situations choose one of the following programs to accommodate instruction to individual needs:

- ☐ **Keller Plan**
- ☐ **Cooperative Integrated Reading and Composition**
- ☐ **Independent Study**
- ☐ **Tutoring**
- ☐ **CAI**
- ☐ **AGAT**
- ☐ **Programmed Instruction**
- ☐ **TAI**

I.   You have a fifth grade social studies class. The students seem unmotivated and quite dependent on the teacher for structure. You would like them to do their social studies work and also to learn to be less dependent on the teacher.

_____

_____

_____

_____

II.   You have a highly motivated college-bound high school group that has requested a special class that is not currently being offered. You have already organized material for the course, but you just do not have time to meet them regularly to present it.

_____

_____

_____

_____

III.   You are a book publisher with considerable resources. You have authors who have written some programmed materials and you want to conduct extensive national tryouts of the materials by collecting and analyzing the responses of many students.

_____

_____

_____

_____

<u>Ability Grouping</u>
<u>Comparing Between-Class and Within-Class Ability Grouping</u>

Refer to Chapter 9. Compare Between-Class and Within-Class Ability Grouping in terms of advantages and disadvantages in relation to five general principles of ability grouping.

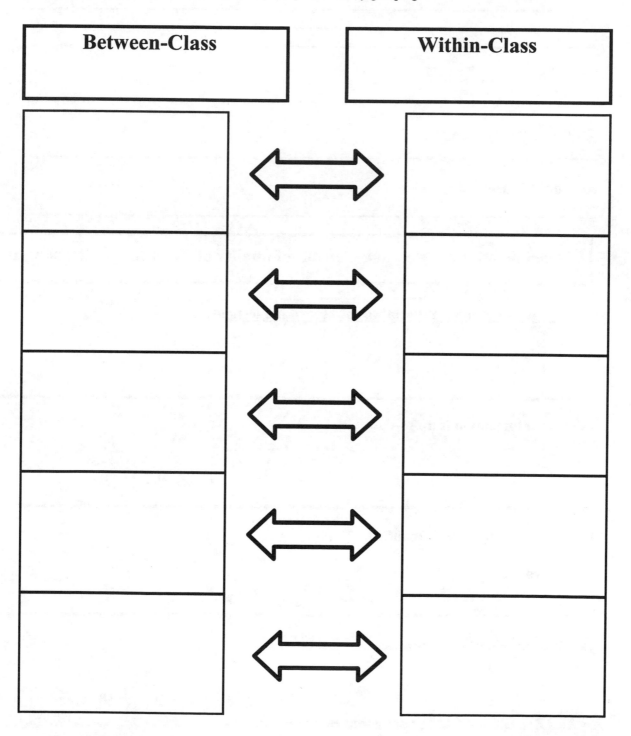

JUDGING THE QUALITY OF AN INTERNET INFORMATION SOURCE

Name: _____   Date: _____

My research question is:

_____

_____

_____

The website address is:

_____

Title of website is:

_____

Author(s) is/are:

_____

Circle one numeral for each element of quality of the information source.

A. **The information is relevant to my research questions.**

No									Yes
1	2	3	4	5	6	7	8	9	10

B. **The information is up-to-date.**

No									Yes
1	2	3	4	5	6	7	8	9	10

C. **The author(s) is/are qualified.**

No									Yes
1	2	3	4	5	6	7	8	9	10

D. **The information is objective and unbiased.**

No									Yes
1	2	3	4	5	6	7	8	9	10

Explain your judgment about this element.

CHAPTER TEN CONCEPT MAP
MOTIVATING STUDENTS TO LEARN

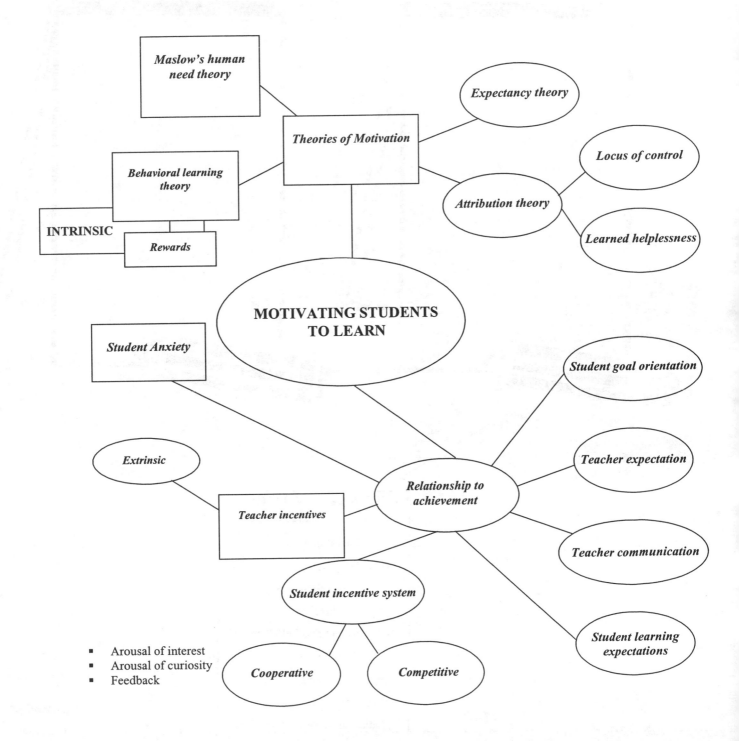

SOME FACTORS AFFECTING MOTIVATION

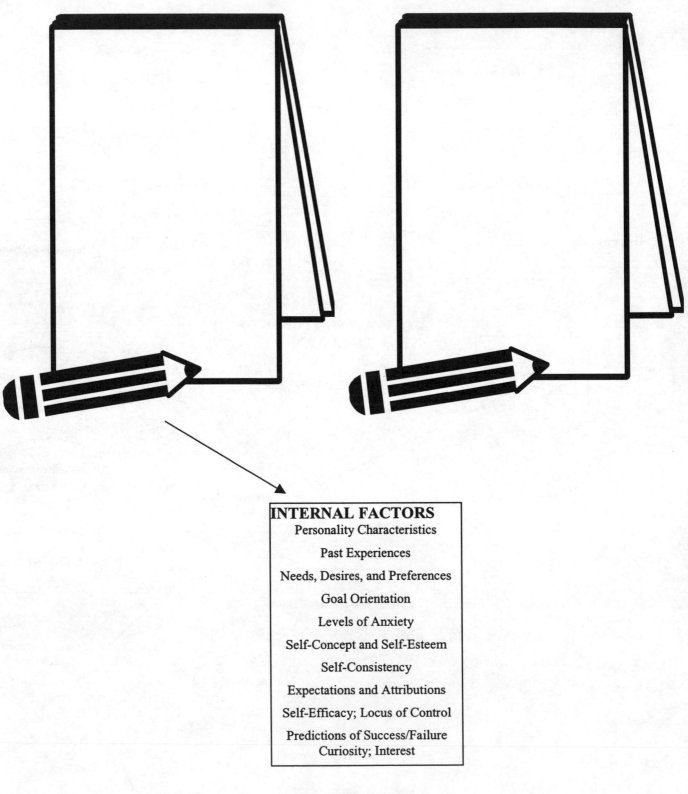

INTERNAL FACTORS

Personality Characteristics

Past Experiences

Needs, Desires, and Preferences

Goal Orientation

Levels of Anxiety

Self-Concept and Self-Esteem

Self-Consistency

Expectations and Attributions

Self-Efficacy; Locus of Control

Predictions of Success/Failure
Curiosity; Interest

MOTIVATION: TEACHER INTERVIEWS

This form is suitable for **elementary** and **secondary** teacher interviews. Using the following questions as your guide, interview several teachers, counselors or administrators. You will want to develop a few questions of your own and perhaps delete a few of the questions provided. Inform the person you are interviewing that all information will remain confidential and will be used strictly for classroom discussion/learning purposes. Gather background information about your subject: grade level/subject taught, years experience, type of school, etc....

In your opinion/experience, is motivation of students a major concern?

What factors do you think may be contributing to problems with student motivation?

How do you motivate your students to participate in instruction?

Do you have any techniques, strategies, or classroom rewards that you find to be effective in motivating students to complete assignments/comply with rules?

Do you have a system of classroom rules and punishments to encourage compliance with rules or completion of assignments? What concerns do you have about your system?

In general, what is your greatest concern regarding motivation of students?

In your opinion/experience are there any techniques or strategies that can backfire or undermine motivation?

Do you have any surefire motivators?

Can you share with me an experience with a student or one of your teachers that comes to mind when you consider these questions?

How do you motivate yourself, or what motivates you to continue teaching?

FIELD OBSERVATION: TEACHER EXPECTATION

Instruction: Observe these five instructional behaviors in a learning setting. Do you think they communicate expectations to students?

A.   GROUPING BY ABILITY

1.   Are students in the class grouped by ability? If so, is it within class or between class or both?

_____

_____

2. How does the teacher make differential instructions or assignments?

_____

_____

3. Are cooperative or cross group strategies employed?

_____

_____

B.   ASKING QUESTIONS

1. How does the teacher solicit responses to questions?

_____

_____

2. Is the wait time ample for all students' responses?

_____

_____

3. Are all students equally called upon? Describe how this is or is not done.

_____

_____

C.   ORGANIZING INSTRUCTION

1. Does the material show ethnic and/or gender diversity? Give examples:

_____

_____

D.   GIVING FEEDBACK AND REINFORCEMENT

1. Does the teacher communicate the "difficulty level" of the task? If so, how?

_____

_____

2. Does the teacher praise correct responses or accurate work? If so, how?

_____

_____

E.   RESPONDING NONVERBALLY

1. Describe any non-verbal behavior that might communicate expectations (e.g., smiles, tone of voice, proximity to a student, touching.)

_____

_____

CHAPTER ELEVEN CONCEPT MAP
EFFECTIVE LEARNING ENVIRONMENTS

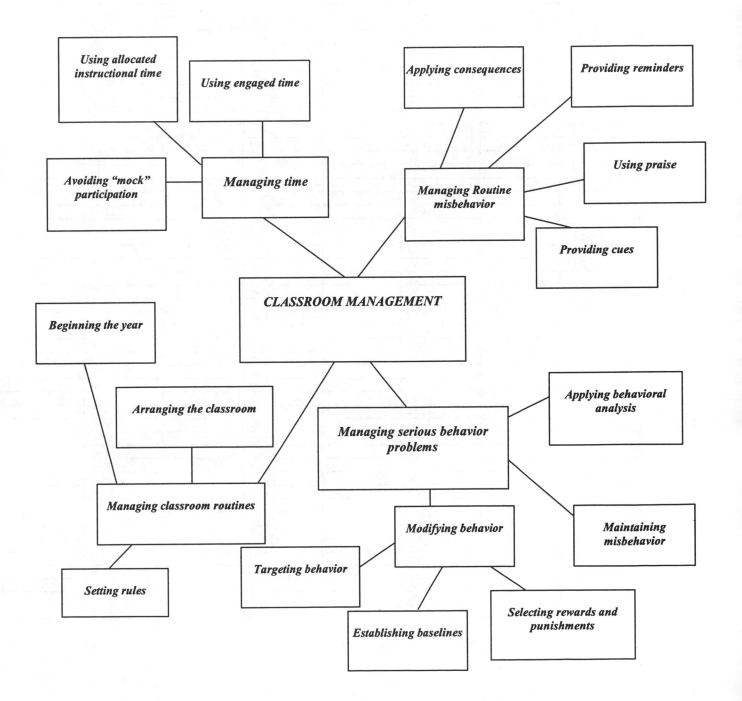

FIELD OBSEVATION: ON-TASK CODE SHEET

Instructions: *Check the box at each ten second interval when the class is involved in "on-task" instructional time. Do not check when there are interruptions, routine procedures, lag time, late starts, early finishes, chaos, etc.*

TIME	CHECK ON-TASK	TIME	CHECK ON-TASK	TIME	CHECK ON-TASK	TIME	CHECK ON-TASK
0:00		7:30		15:00		22:30	
0:10		7:40		15:10		22:40	
0:20		7:50		15:20		22:50	
0:30		8:00		15:30		23:00	
0:40		8:10		15:40		23:10	
0:50		8:20		15:50		23:20	
1:00		8:30		16:00		23:30	
1:10		8:40		16:10		23:40	
1:20		8:50		16:20		23:50	
1:30		9:00		16:30		24:00	
1:40		9:10		16:40		24:10	
1:50		9:20		16:50		24:20	
2:00		9:30		17:00		24:30	
2:10		9:40		17:10		24:40	
2:20		9:50		17:20		24:50	
2:30		10:00		17:30		25:00	
2:40		10:10		17:40		25:10	
2:50		10:20		17:50		25:20	
3:00		10:30		18:00		25:30	
3:10		10:40		18:10		25:40	
3:20		10:50		18:20		25:50	
3:30		11:00		18:30		26:00	
3:40		11:10		18:40		26:10	
3:50		11:20		18:50		26:20	
4:00		11:30		19:00		26:30	
4:10		11:40		19:10		26:40	
4:20		11:50		19:20		26:50	
4:30		12:00		19:30		27:00	
4:40		12:10		19:40		27:10	
4:50		12:20		19:50		27:20	
5:00		12:30		20:00		27:30	
5:10		12:40		20:10		27:40	
5:20		12:50		20:20		27:50	
5:30		13:00		20:30		28:00	
5:40		13:10		20:40		28:10	
5:50		13:20		20:50		28:20	
6:00		13:30		21:00		28:30	
6:10		13:40		21:10		28:40	
6:20		13:50		21:20		28:50	
6:30		14:00		21:30		29:00	
6:40		14:10		21:40		29:10	
6:50		14:20		21:50		29:20	
7:00		14:30		22:00		29:30	
7:10		14:40		22:10		29:40	
7:20		14:50		22:20		29:50	
						30:00	

Nature of task: Nature of task: Nature of task:

Tally: <u>(# checks on task)</u>   = % time on task   %
        (total observation)   180

HM 11.3

<u>RESOURCES FOR EFFECTIVE CLASSROOM MANAGEMENT</u>

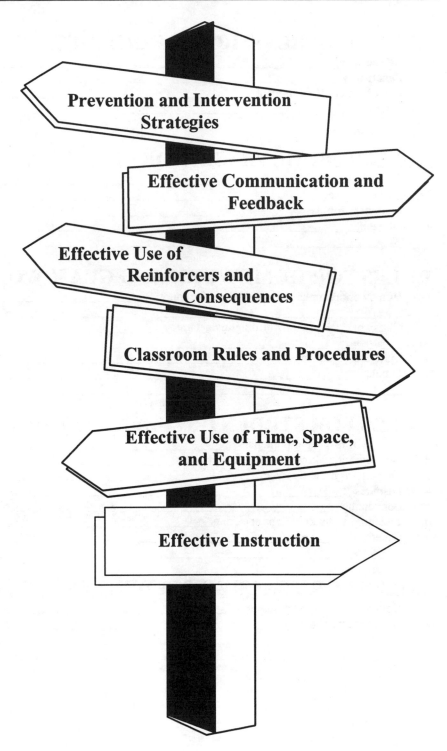

FIELD OBSERVATION: CLASS RULES

A.   RULES FOR CLASSROOM ROUTINES
1. Attendance_____
2. Punctuality_____
3. Use of material/ Equipment_____
4. Others:_____
_____

B.   RULES FOR MOVEMENT OF STUDENTS
1. Entering and leaving room_____
2. Bathroom use_____
3. Readiness for class_____
4. Others:_____
_____

C.   RULES FOR HOMEWORK AND CLASSWORK
1. Homework completion / turning in / accuracy_____
_____
2. Classwork completion / turning in / accuracy_____
_____
3. Materials specified_____
4. Others:_____
_____

D.   RULES FOR STUDENT-STUDENT INTERACTION
1. Degree of respect or politeness_____
2. Collaboration allowed or disallowed_____
3. Property rights and respect_____
4. Disputes_____
5. Socializing_____
6. Listening and taking turns speaking_____
7. Others:_____
_____

E.   RULES FOR TEACHER-STUDENT INTERACTION
1. Degree of respect or politeness_____
2. Help seeking signals_____
3. Others:_____
_____

Teacher Interview on Teacher Expectations

Interview several teachers or administrators at various levels regarding teacher expectations. These questions are just a guide. Your research team will want to develop some of your own questions and change these questions if necessary to fit your needs.

Gather background information about your subject: grade level/subject taught, years experience, type of school etc....

What methods do you use during the first few weeks of class to establish control in the classroom? (Probe for specifics if the answers are very general; ask about what rules are established, how students are informed of them, what expectations the teacher holds for students, what expectations the students have.)

What kinds of events or forces coming from outside the classroom make teaching difficult? Are they periodic or continual problems? What do you do to counter such forces?

How do other teachers' behaviors, expectations, and attitudes, and the attitudes and behaviors of the principal affect your classroom?

How do you monitor student behavior?

What kinds of outside classroom supports are available to you if there is a student whose behavior is consistently unacceptable? How effective are these supports? How is a teacher who occasionally requests help with a student perceived by peers? students? administrators?

How have your beliefs about establishing and maintaining rapport with students changed over the course of your career? What accounts for these changes?

What are the problems associated with teachers who lack the ability to build rapport with students? Do you believe teachers can be "too friendly" with students? What problems do beginning teachers have in this area of teaching? What advice do you have for a new teacher?

TEACHER INTERVIEW – DISCIPLINE

What is your approach to discipline in your classroom?

Does your school have discipline guidelines you must follow?

What kind of support do you receive from your administration regarding your discipline approach?

When and how do you introduce your discipline plan to your classroom?

Do your students participate in setting rules and consequences in the classroom? Why or Why not?

How do you modify your discipline approach for those students who are special education and ESL?

How do you involve parents in your discipline approach? Are they supportive?

How do you handle students who do not respond to your discipline approach?

What has been your biggest discipline challenge?

MANAGING SERIOUS MISCONDUCT

Earth science class began this October morning with the usual handing in of assignments and then a whole class discussion on the upcoming soil sample project. Ten minutes into the discussion (twenty minutes after class began), Steven walks in and the following interaction takes place:

Ms. Terrell:	*(approaches Steven and quietly speaks with him)* Steven, you're late again. Go get a tardy slip from the office.
Steven:	*(slowly leaves the room and pauses outside the door)* Not fair! You bitch. You don't make any other late students go to the office!
Ms. Terrell:	*(follows Steven into the hall and speaks firmly)* Steven, keep your voice down. Go directly to the office and come back with a tardy slip. You know the rules!

After another insistence from Ms. Terrell for Steven to go to the office and him refusing, she closes and locks the hall door. He yells a few more defiant obscenities and is silent.

Ms. Terrell, a bit flustered, continues describing the procedures for the soil sample project to the class. She looks at her watch. After class, she walks the halls looking for Steven, but he is nowhere to in sight.

FOCUS QUESTION:
1. Evaluate Ms. Terrell's actions at each step.
2. What should Ms. Terrell do when Stephan comes to class next?

HM 11.8

Disciplinary Action Continuum

Beginning with the least disruptive method and progressing to more direct methods, list the actions a teacher can take to discourage inappropriate student behavior.

Least

Most

CLASSROOM MANAGEMENT OBSERVATION SHEET

Seatwork: varied, interesting, on student's ability level
Rating: _____
Observation: _____

Organization: use of student helpers, smooth transitions between
activities, lessons well organized and well paced, materials are
readily available, quickly takes care of routine activities
Rating: _____
Observation: _____

Supervision: teacher monitors class, spots potentially disruptive
situations, reacts calmly in problem situations, moves around
classroom
Rating: _____
Observation: _____

Assignments: clearly presented, procedure for getting help, work is
checked, student knows what to do when finished
Rating: _____
Observation: _____

Rules: few and general (not too specific), reasons for rules
explained by teacher, flexible and may change as class develops
Rating: _____
Observation: _____

Overall classroom management rating:_____
What changes would you suggest that the teacher make?

_____
_____

CHAPTER TWELVE CONCEPT MAP
LEARNERS WITH EXCEPTIONALITIES

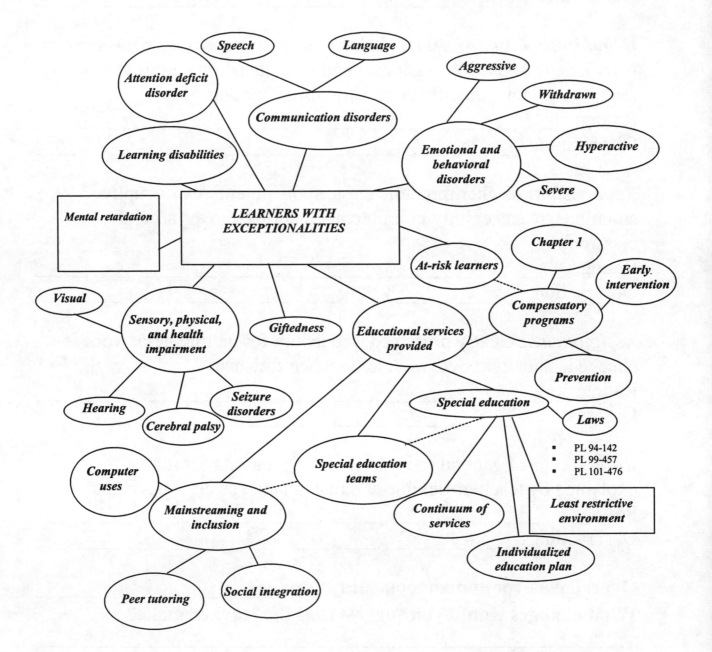

MYTHS AND FACTS ABOUT SPECIAL EDUCATION

From Exceptional Children, Fifth Edition, Daniel Hallahan and James Kauffman (Englewood Cliffs, NJ: Prentice Hall, 1991), p. 3.

MISCONCEPTIONS ABOUT EXCEPTIONAL CHILDREN

<u>Myth</u>	<u>Fact</u>
Public schools may choose not to provide education for some children.	Federal legislation specifies that to receive federal funds, every school system must provide a free, appropriate education for every child regardless of any disabling condition.
By law, the handicapped child must be placed in the least restrictive environment (LRE). The LRE is always the regular classroom.	The law does require the handicapped child to be placed in the LRE. However, the LRE is not always the regular classroom. What the LRE does mean is that the handicapped child shall be segregated as little as possible from home, family, community, and the regular class setting while appropriate education is provided. In many, but not all instances this will mean placement in the regular classroom.
The causes of most disabilities are known, but little is known about how to help children overcome or compensate for their disabilities.	In most cases, the causes of children's disabilities are not known, although progress is being made in pinpointing why many disabilities occur. More is known about the treatment of most disabilities than about their causes.
People with disabilities are just like everyone else.	First, no two people are exactly alike. People with disabilities, just like everyone else, are unique individuals. Most of their abilities are much like those of the "average" person who is not considered to have a disability. Nevertheless, a disability is a characteristic not shared by most people. It is important that disabilities be recognized for what they are, but individuals with disabilities must be seen as having many abilities—other characteristics that they share with the majority of people.
A disability is a handicap.	A disability is an inability to do something, the lack of a specific capacity. A handicap, on the other hand, is a disadvantage that is imposed on an individual. A disability may or may not be a handicap, depending on the circumstances. For example, inability to walk is not a handicap in learning to read, but it can be a handicap in getting into the stands at a ball game. Sometimes handicaps are needlessly imposed on persons with disabilities. For example, a student who cannot write with a pen but can use a typewriter or word processor would be needlessly handicapped without such equipment.

MYTHS AND FACTS ABOUT MENTAL RETARDATION

MISCONCEPTIONS ABOUT PERSONS WITH MENTAL RETARDATION
From Hallahan and Kauffman, 1991, p. 79.

Myth	Fact
Once diagnosed as mentally retarded, a person remains within this classification for the rest of his or her life.	The level of mental functioning does not necessarily remain stable, particularly for those in the mild classification.
In most cases, we can identify the cause of retardation.	In most cases (especially within the mild classifications) we cannot identify the cause. For many of the children in the mild classification, it is thought that poor environment may be a causal factor. However, it is usually extremely difficult to document.
Most mentally retarded children look different from nondisabled children.	The majority of mentally retarded children are mildly retarded, and most mildly retarded children look like nondisabled children.
If a person achieves a low score on an IQ test, this means that his or her adaptive skills are also sure to be subnormal.	It is possible for a person to have a tested subnormal IQ and still have adequate adaptive skills. Much depends on the individual's training, motivation, experience, social environment, etc.
Most mental retardation can be diagnosed in infancy.	Because the majority of retarded children are mildly retarded, because infant intelligence tests are not as reliable and valid as those used in later childhood, and because intellectual demands on the child greatly increase upon entrance to school, most children eventually diagnosed as retarded are not so identified until they go to school.
Retarded individuals go through different learning stages compared to nondisabled individuals.	Many studies indicate that the learning characteristics of retarded individuals, particularly those classified as mildly retarded, do not differ from those of nondisabled people. That is, retarded people go through the same stages, but at a slower rate.
Children classified as moderately retarded (once called "trainable") require a radically different curriculum from that appropriate for children classified as mildly retarded (once called "educable").	Although academic subjects are generally stressed more with mildly retarded students, and vocational skills are stressed more with moderately, severely and profoundly retarded students, there is actually a great deal of overlap in curricular goals for all retarded students.
When a worker with mental retardation fails on the job it is usually because he or she does not have adequate job skills.	There is substantial research indicating that when mentally retarded workers fail on the job, it is more often because of poor job responsibility (e.g., poor attendance and lack of initiative) and social competence (e.g., not interacting appropriately with co-workers) than because of competence in task production.
Transition programming for students with mental retardation begins in secondary school.	Although the degree of emphasis should be greater for older students, most authorities agree that transition programming for students with mental retardation should begin in elementary school.
Severely retarded people are helpless.	With appropriate educational programming, many severely retarded people can lead relatively independent lives. In fact, with appropriate professional support, some can live in the community and even enter competitive employment.

MYTHS AND FACTS ABOUT VISION IMPARIMENT

MISCONCEPTIONS ABOUT PERSONS WITH VISION IMPAIRMENT
From Hallahan and Kauffman, 1991, p. 303.

Myth	Fact
Legally blind people have no sight at all.	Only a small percentage of those who are legally blind have absolutely no vision. The majority have a useful amount of functional vision.
Most legally blind people use Braille as their primary method of reading.	The majority of legally blind individuals use print (even if it is in large type) as their primary method of reading. In addition, a recent trend shows that more blind people who cannot benefit from the use of print are now using aural methods (listening to tapes or records) rather than Braille.
Blind people have an extra sense that enables them to detect obstacles.	Blind people do not have an extra sense. They can develop an "obstacle sense" provided they have the ability to hear.
Blind People automatically develop better acuity in their other senses.	Through concentration and attention, blind individuals learn to make very fine discriminations in the sensations they obtain. This is not automatic but rather represents a better use of received sensations.
Blind people have superior musical ability.	The musical ability of blind people isn't necessarily any better than that of sighted people. Apparently many blind individuals pursue musical careers because this is one way in which they can achieve success.
Blind people are helpless and dependent.	With a good attitude and favorable learning experiences, a blind person can be as independent and possess as strong a personality as a sighted person,
If people with low vision use their eyes too much, their sight will deteriorate	Only in rare conditions is this true; visual efficiency can actually be improved through training and use. Wearing strong lenses, holding books close to the eyes, and using the eyes as much as possible cannot harm vision.
Blind children automatically develop superior powers of concentration that make them good listeners.	Good listening is primarily a learned skill. Although many visually impaired individuals do develop good listening skills, this is the result of work on their part because they depend on these skills for so much of the information they gain from the environment.
Guide dogs take blind people where they want to go.	The guide dog does not "take" the blind person anywhere; the person must first know where he or she is going. The dog is primarily a safeguard against unsafe areas or obstacles.
The long cane is a simply constructed device that is easy to use.	The National Academy of Sciences has drawn up specifications for the manufacture of the long cane, and to use it properly, most visually impaired individuals require extensive instruction from mobility specialists.

MYTHS AND FACTS ABOUT HEARING IMPARIMENT

MISCONCEPTIONS ABOUT PERSONS WITH HEARING IMPAIRMENT
From Hallahan and Kauffman, 1991, p. 265.

Myth	*Fact*
Deafness leads automatically to inability to speak.	Even though hearing impairment, especially with greater degrees of hearing loss, is a barrier to normal language development, some deaf people can be taught some understanding of oral language and the ability to speak.
Deafness is not as great a handicap us blindness.	Although it is impossible to predict the exact consequences of a handicap on a person's functioning, in general deafness is a greater handicap than blindness. This is due in a large degree to the effects hearing loss can have on the ability to understand and speak oral language.
The deaf child is inherently lower in intellectual ability.	It is generally believed that unless they are born with additional handicaps, deaf infants have the same intellectual capacities as hearing infants. Deaf individuals, however, may perform more poorly on some tasks because of their difficulty in communicating with those who hear.
In learning to understand what is being said to them, deaf individuals concentrate on reading lips.	*Lipreading* refers only to visual cues arising from movement of the lips. Some deaf people not only learn to lipread but also learn to make use of a variety of other visual cues, such as facial expressions and movements of the jaw and tongue. They thus engage in what is referred to as *speechreading*, a term that covers all visual cues associated with speaking.
Teaching American Sign Language is harmful to a child and may hamper development of oral language.	Most authorities today recognize the value of American Sign Language as a means of communication.
American Sign Language is a loosely structured group of gestures.	American Sign Language is a true language in its own right with its own set of grammatical rules.
American Sign Language can only be used to convey concrete ideas.	American Sign Language can be used at any level of abstraction.
A hearing aid is of no use to a person with a sensorineural loss.	Although not as useful as with conductive hearing losses, hearing aids can help some people with sensorineural impairments.

FLOW CHART FOR THE INDIVIDUALIZED PROGRAM PROCESS

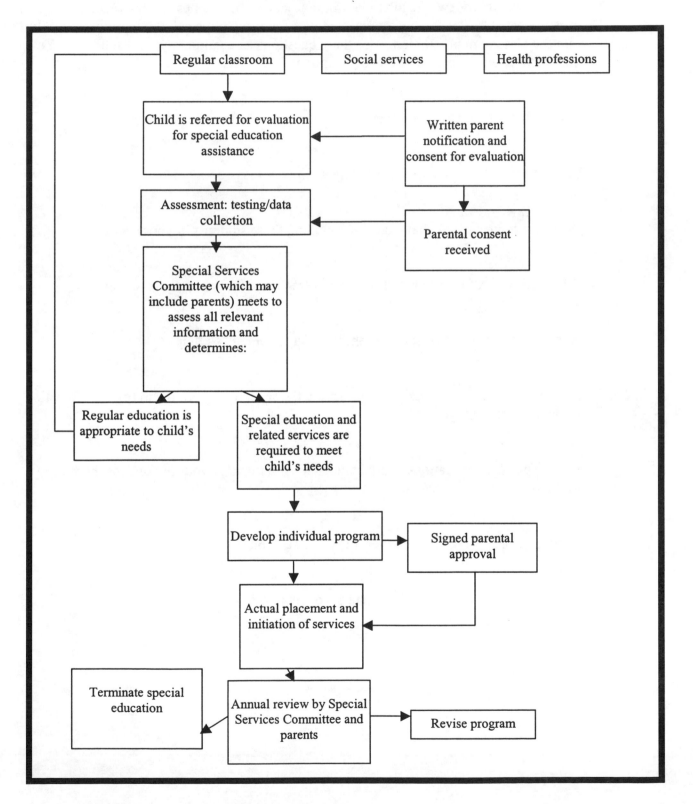

Regular classroom → Social services → Health professions

Child is referred for evaluation for special education assistance

Written parent notification and consent for evaluation

Assessment: testing/data collection

Parental consent received

Special Services Committee (which may include parents) meets to assess all relevant information and determines:

Regular education is appropriate to child's needs

Special education and related services are required to meet child's needs

Develop individual program

Signed parental approval

Actual placement and initiation of services

Terminate special education

Annual review by Special Services Committee and parents

Revise program

Inclusion: Teacher Interview

Instructions: Interview a regular classroom teacher who teaches "mainstreamed" students or is impacted by "inclusion" of children with learning, physical, or emotional disabilities into the classroom population. Use these questions as a guide to your discussion. You may want to add a few questions of your own.

Do you have students in your class receiving special education services?

In what ways do these students participate in your classroom?

What are some special challenges of including these students in your classroom?

What are some of the rewards for you as a teacher in including these students?

How do other students respond to these "mainstreamed" students?

Have you found any unique ways to getting the special education and regular education students working together?

What type of modifications or adaptations do you make to your lessons for these students?

Do you have special education teachers to assist you?

In what ways do they provide assistance or support?

INDIVIDUALIZED EDUCATION PROGRAM: CONFIDENTIAL INFORMATION

From Hallahan and Kauffman, 1991.

INDIVIDUALIZED EDUCATION PROGRAM

School Year _94-95_

Confidential Information

Name __Patrick Milton__ DOB _11/7/82_ School __Field__ Grade _6_

Handicapping condition __Learning Disability__ Date of IEP meeting _10/15/94_ Notification to parent _11/12/94_

Initiation and anticipated duration of services _11/94 11/95_ Eligibility/Triennial _10/12/94_ Plan to be reviewed no later than _3/95_
M-Y to MY   M-D-Y   M-Y

Educational/Vocational Program

Special Education Services

Work with LD resource teacher on reading and language arts; may be taught in group of up to five students; summer school (1995) recommended.

Total Amount   Times/Wk. _5_   Hrs./Day ____

Regular Education Services

Regular sixth grade

Total Amount   Times/Wk. _5_   Hrs./Day _5_

Related Services

Type   Amount

Speech-language sessions with speech-language therapist for 30 minutes 2 times/ week to work on lateral lisp and improve oral fluency.

Adapted Class   Amount _None_

Regular Class   Amount _As scheduled_

Transportation

Special _NA-walk to sch._   Regular ____

Current Level of Performance

Reading: Second grade, first semester; special difficulty with word-attack skills; knows 70 basic sight words.
Language Arts: Cursive writing mostly illegible; not able to construct sentences in composition; mostly phonetic spelling; poor ability to give verbal descriptions.
Math and other areas: Completes work with 80% or better accuracy at grade level.
Work Habits: Consistently completes about 20% of language arts assignments with about 50% accuracy.

Participants in Plan Development

Name	Title
Marie Milton	Mother
Melissa Borden	LD resource teacher
Tim Triumph	Sixth grade teacher
Evan Gorley	Principal
Kate Nona	Speech-language therapist
Ron Horsely	School psychologist

For High School Students ONLY (to be initially completed at 9th grade IEP meeting and reviewed annually).

This student is a candidate for: High School Diploma _____ : Special Ed. Certificate _____ : GED Equivalency Diploma _____

Is the Minimum Competency Test to be administered this school year? Yes _____ No _____ If yes, attach addendum.

White: Confidential Folder Yellow: Parent Copy

INDIVIDUALIZED EDUCATION PROGRAM:
ANNUAL GOAL

From Hallahan and Kauffman, 1991.

INDIVIDUALIZED EDUCATION PROGRAM — School Year __94-95__

ANNUAL GOAL: The student __Patrick Milton__ will complete all assigned work in language arts and reading with 90% or better accuracy at Fifthgrade level by September 1985 **PROGRESS REPORTS**

SHORT TERM OBJECTIVES	Grading Periods		COMMENTS
Objective: Given 200 sight words from his reader, Pat will read them with 90% accuracy.	1	✕	
	2	12/94	
Beginning Skill Level: 2² (Ginn); knows 70 Dolch words	3	3/95	P-Learning average of 2 new sight words/school day
Date Initiated: 11/21/94	4		M-Now knows all Dolch words and all words in reader
Objective: Given a topic with which he is familiar, Pat will write at least 5 complete sentences on the topic within 30 minutes.	1	✕	
	2	12/94	P-will write 2 or 3 sentences before refusing to continue; tells sentence from nonsentence with 75% accuracy.
Beginning Skill Level: Does not know sentence from non sentence.	3	3/95	P-
Date Initiated: 11/21/94	4		
Objective: Given instructions to copy 5 lines of printed material from a book, Pat will write the material on lined paper using cursive letters so that another teacher can immediately decipher at least 90% of the material.	1	✕	
	2	12/94	P-Most written work now 60% legible; 75% legible when copying.
Beginning Skill Level: Only letters legible 80% of the time are e,p,w	3	3/95	M-Nearly all written work is legible
Date Initiated: 11/21/94	4		
Objective: Given 50 sight words from his reading book and 50 CVCE words, Pat will read them with 100% accuracy; given the same words from dictation, he will spell them with 95% accuracy.	1	✕	
	2	12/94	P--Reads CVCE words with 95% accuracy and writes them with 80% accuracy.
Beginning Skill Level: Tested spelling grade level = 2'.	3	3/95	
Date Initiated: 11/21/94	4		

Evaluation Procedures: Annual goals will be evaluated during the annual review. Short term objectives will be monitored at each nine week marking period. Beginning skill level indicates the sutdent's performance prior to instruction.

Progress Key: No mark-Objective not initiated **P**-Progressing on the Objective **D**-Having difficulty with the objective (comment to describe difficulty)

M-Objective mastered   **M/R**-Objective mastered, but needs review to maintain mastery

White: Confidential Folder   **Yellow:** Parent Progress Report   **Pink:** Teacher Working Copy   **Goldenrod:** Parent Original

CHAPTER THIRTEEN CONCEPT MAP
OBJECTIVES AND CLASSROOM ASSESSMENT

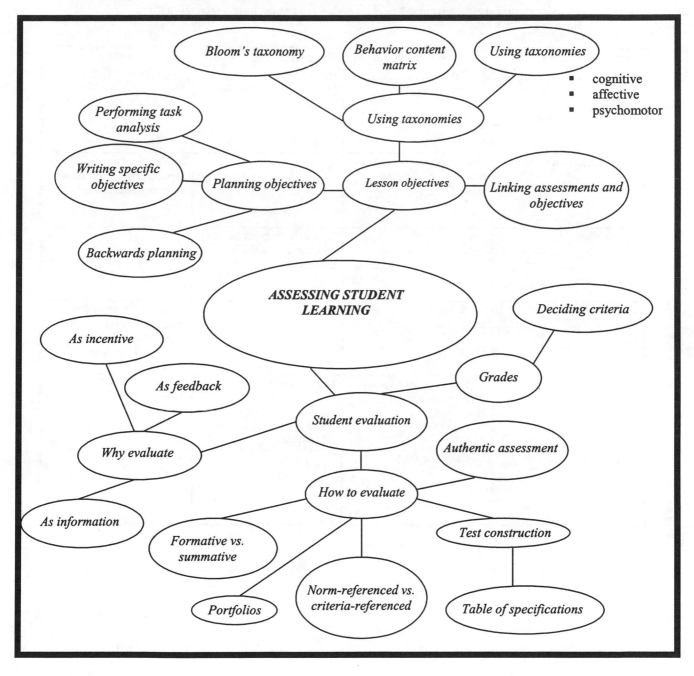

Bloom's taxonomy

Behavior content matrix

Using taxonomies

- cognitive
- affective
- psychomotor

Performing task analysis

Using taxonomies

Writing specific objectives

Planning objectives

Lesson objectives

Linking assessments and objectives

Backwards planning

ASSESSING STUDENT LEARNING

Deciding criteria

As incentive

Grades

As feedback

Student evaluation

Why evaluate

Authentic assessment

As information

How to evaluate

Formative vs. summative

Test construction

Portfolios

Norm-referenced vs. criteria-referenced

Table of specifications

EXAMPLES OF OBJECTIVES
IN A BEHAVIOR CONTENT MATRIX

A behavior content matrix can remind teachers to develop instructional objectives that address skills at various cognitive levels.

Type of Objective	Example 1: Main Idea of the Story	Example 2: The Area of the Circle	Example 3: The Colonization of Africa
Knowledge	Define "main idea."	Give the formula for the area of a circle.	Make a timeline showing how Africa was divided into colonies.
Comprehension	Give examples of ways to find the main idea of a story.		Interpret a map of Africa showing its colonization by European nations.
Application		Apply the formula for area of a circle to real life problems.	
Analysis	Identify the main idea of a story.		Contrast the goals and methods used in colonizing Africa by different European nations.
Synthesis	Write a new story based on the main idea of the story read.	Use knowledge about the areas of circle and volumes of cubes to derive a formula for the volume of a cylinder.	Write an essay on the European colonization of Africa from the perspective of a Bantu chief.
Evaluation	Evaluate the story.		

COMPARISONS OF TWO APPROACHES
TO ACHIEVMENT TESTING

Adapted from Gronlund, "Constructing Achievement Tests," (3rd Edition) (Englewood Cliffs, NJ: Prentice Hall, 1982).

Norm-referenced tests and criterion-referenced tests serve different purposes and have different features.

	Norm-Referenced Testing	Criterion-Referenced Testing
Principal Use	Survey Testing	Mastery Testing
Major Emphasis	Measures individual differences in achievement.	Describes tasks students can perform.
Interpretation of Results	Compares performance to that of other individuals.	Compares performance to a clearly specified achievement domain.
Content Coverage	Typically covers a broad area of achievement.	Typically focuses on a limited of learning tasks.
Nature of Test Plan	Table of specifications is commonly used.	Detailed domain specifications are favored.
Item Selection Procedures	Items are selected that provide maximum discrimination among individuals.	All items needed to adequately describe performance are included.

DEVISING AN EVALUATION PLAN

I.   PURPOSE

To provide students with supervised practice in developing instructional objectives, writing test items, and specifying an evaluation and grading plan.

II.   OBJECTIVES

When the assignment is complete, the student will be able to:
1. Describe the group of students to whom your lesson is directed, specifying their age, grade level, and other pertinent characteristics;
2. Write general instructional objectives for the topic selected;
3. Write specific instructional objectives in appropriate form for the topic selected;
4. Describe the instructional method(s) you would use to reach the objectives;
5. Describe the procedures to be followed in evaluating the attainment of the objectives and communicating the results to appropriate audiences.

III.   PROCESS

1. Choose a unit of study appropriate to the grade level/subject matter area you plan to teach. Write a brief topic outline of the content.
2. Develop at least three general objectives for the unit of study.
3. Write at least six instructional objectives for the unit. Use the Mager format and remember to specify various levels of the Bloom taxonomy, as appropriate.
4. Determine the overall evaluation plan for the unit, which for most purposes should include:
    a) Table of specifications
    b) Test items—Items should fit the objectives and content. You are encouraged to use several item formats.
5. Describe your performance standards and the method(s) you will use to score and interpret the results of the appropriate audiences.

IV.   COMPLETED ASSIGNMENT

Turn in the following components:
1. Brief description of the student group
2. Brief description of the unit of study
3. General objectives
4. Behavioral objectives
5. Table of specifications
6. Items: 15 objectives, 2 essay or problem-solving
7. Grading plan.

Classroom Assessment: Teacher Interview Questions

Interview several teachers, counselors, and/or principals currently working or recently retired from the public, private, and/or alternative schools. You can use these questions as a guide and develop a few questions of your own. You will want to adapt this form to fit your needs and to obtain the type of information you are looking for regarding assessment.

Tell your subject we are studying educational psychology and one of our topics is classroom assessment. We are particularly interested in learning how teachers in the "real world" use assessments and how they figure grades etc....

What types of student assessment do you use in your classroom? (Types of tests/quizzes/authentic assessment etc. you use on a regular basis throughout the year.)

Do you communicate results of classroom assessments with students/parents, and how much do regular classroom assessments count as a part of the overall grade?

How do you calculate grades? (Daily work, homework, tests, attendance etc.) Does the administration give you any guidelines or restrictions in calculating grades?

Do you use a computer program to help you manage your gradebook?

How do you report grades to administration? Are you responsible for recording grades in permanent records?

How do you prepare students for your regular classroom assessments?

What suggestions, comments, or words of wisdom do you have for our class in our study of assessment, test question development, etc...?

Be sure to thank your subject for his or her time and remind him or her that all answers will be kept confidential and used for classroom learning only.

CHAPTER FOURTEEN CONCEPT MAP
STANDARDIZED TESTS

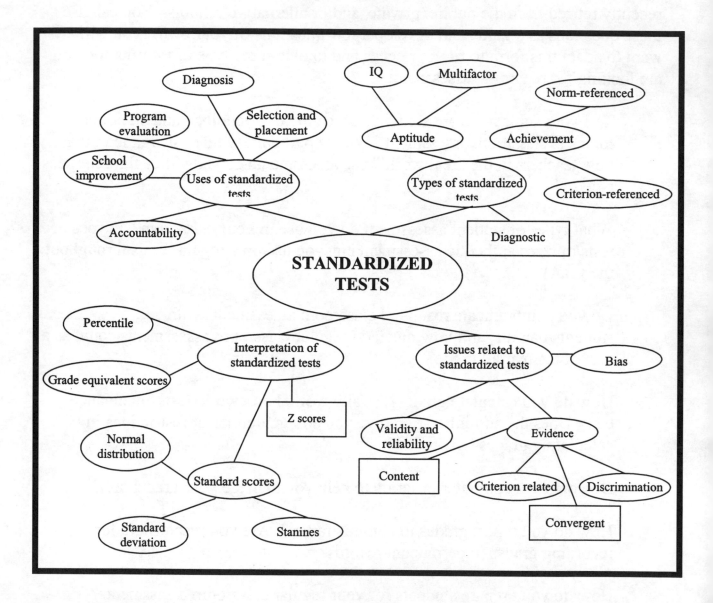

HM 14.2

FIELD INTERVIEW:
ATTITUDES TOWARD STANDARDIZED TESTING

I.   USEFULNESS OF STANDARDIZED TESTS FOR INSTRUCTION
1.   Is standardized test information useful to you for planning regular classroom instruction?

_____

_____

2.   How important are test scores in your individualizing instruction for one particular child?

_____

_____

3.   Do you get test data aggregated for your class? How useful is it?

_____

_____

4.   Are there any local trends toward "authentic testing?" (e.g. portfolios, performance-based assessment that might be useful to you?

_____

_____

II.   USES AND MISUSES OF STANDARDIZED TESTS
1.   How are test scores used for grouping? For special services?

_____

_____

2.   How are test scores used for promotion and retention?

_____

_____

3.   In your experience, are test scores ever misused for making educational decisions?

_____

_____

III.   TESTING AND TEACHER ACCOUNTABILITY
1.   Should teachers be evaluated using a standardized teacher competency test? Why?

_____

_____

2.   Should teachers be evaluated using their students' standardized tests performance? Why?

_____

_____

Standardized Testing: Teacher Interview Questions

Interview several teachers, counselors, and/or principals currently working or recently retired from the public, private, and/or alternative schools. You can use these questions as a guide and develop a few questions of your own. You will want to adapt this form to fit your needs and to obtain the type of information you are looking for regarding standardized assessment.

What types of standardized assessments are used in your grade level?

How do you prepare students for standardized testing?

Do you feel a great deal of pressure regarding standardized testing and how does this impact the classroom?

How are standardized test scores communicated to parents?

Do you feel comfortable discussing and interpreting the standardized test scores of your students with parents?

What suggestions, comments or words of wisdom do you have for our class in our study of assessment, test question development, etc.?

Be sure to thank your subject for his or her time and remind them that all answers will be kept confidential and used for classroom learning only.

Assessment Package

for

Slavin

Educational Psychology
Theory and Practice

Eighth Edition

Contents

Chapter 1 Educational Psychology: A Foundation for Teaching

Multiple-Choice Questions

1) Which of the following statements about the role of educational psychology in teacher education is accurate?

   A) Educational psychology tells teachers what to do in order to be effective in the classroom.

   B) Educational psychology is the study of learning theory without regard to classroom application.

   C) Educational psychology course work focuses on subject matter knowledge rather than pedagogical knowledge.

   D) Educational psychology provides teachers with research-based principles to guide their teaching.

   Answer: D

   Explanation: D) Educational psychology is the study of learners, learning, and teaching. Educational psychologists do not tell teachers what to do, but rather they carry out research on the nature of students, principles of learning, and methods of teaching in order to give educators the information they need to think critically about their work.

   Page Ref: 3

2) Which of the following statements best expresses the text author's view of the importance of subject matter knowledge in effective teaching?

   A) It is the single indispensible ingredient in effective teaching.

   B) It is a good start; necessary, but not sufficient.

   C) It is more important than communicating knowledge to students.

   D) It is of little importance when compared to qualities such as self-discipline, leadership, and enthusiasm.

   Answer: B

   Explanation: B) Subject matter knowledge is essential, but skill in communicating knowledge to students is of equal, if not greater importance.

   Page Ref: 3

3) According to the text author, knowledge of how to transmit information and skills to students is

    A) not as important as knowledge of what to teach.

    B) no different from knowing the subject matter well.

    C) at least as important as knowledge of what to teach.

    D) sufficient for effective teaching.

Answer: C

Explanation: C) Both knowledge of the subject and skill in communicating information are critical to teaching effectively.

Page Ref: 4

4) Teachers who demonstrate skill in communicating with students possess

    A) pedagogical knowledge.   B) teaching licenses.

    C) advanced degrees in their disciplines.   D) tenure status.

Answer: A

Explanation: A) Pedagogical knowledge requires the effective transmission of information and skills from the teacher to the learner.

Page Ref: 4

5) All of the following teacher actions are pedagogically sound **EXCEPT**

    A) considering prerequisite skills needed to understand new ideas.

    B) engaging students in active learning that leads to understanding.

    C) taking into account the intellectual characteristics of students.

    D) concluding that the required subject matter will not interest the students.

Answer: D

Explanation: D) Effective instruction requires teachers to peek students' interest in the subject.
Page Ref: 4

6) Content knowledge is to "what to teach" as _____ is to "how to teach."

    A) prerequisite   B) discipline   C) pedagogy   D) ethnography

Answer: C

Explanation: C) The relationship between subject matter being "what is taught" is the same as the relationship between pedagogy being "how to teach."
Page Ref: 4

7) According to your text author, can good teaching be taught?

    A) No, teachers are born, not made.

    B) No, there are too many personality factors to be considered.

    C) Yes, good teaching strategies can be learned and applied.

    D) Yes, but it can only be taught to those who demonstrate above average intelligence.

Answer: C

Explanation: C) Research over the last two decades, especially that related to expertise development, has identified specific skills and dispositions that make up effective teaching. These skills and dispositions can be observed and practiced by preservice and novice teachers.

Page Ref: 5

8) During a social studies class, two students at the back of the room whisper to each other about the dance on Saturday night. The teacher moves near the two students, but does not stop the discussion about President Johnson's Great Society. The students stop whispering to each other. Which principle of effective teaching is being used?

    A) Wait until minor problems become major before intervening.

    B) Use the discipline problem as a teaching tool.

    C) Use the mildest intervention possible.

    D) State rules, give examples, and then restate rules.

Answer: C

Explanation: C) Maintaining momentum, dealing with behavior problems using the mildest intervention possible, and resolving minor problems before they become major are effective management strategies.

Page Ref: 5

9) Teachers who think about the outcomes they want for their students and how each decision they make moves students toward those outcomes

    A) are novice teachers.

    B) are focused mainly on subject matter knowledge.

    C) will lose students' attention.

    D) are intentional teachers.

Answer: D

Explanation: D) Intentionality is one attribute that is shared by all outstanding teachers.
Page Ref: 7

10) Ms. Marano has a strong sense of teacher efficacy. Which of the following is she most likely to believe?

A) A teacher's actions are a major influence on a student's level of success.

B) Success will come when a teacher is lucky enough to get a "good class".

C) Students with a negative home environment cannot be reached.

D) Students' potential for academic achievement comes down to how much ability they inherited.

Answer: A

Explanation: A) Teacher efficacy involves the belief that student achievement depends on factors that are under a teacher's control.

Page Ref: 7

11) According to Bandura (1997), teachers who have strong **teacher efficacy** are likely to

A) accept the fact that some students will never succeed.

B) persist in their efforts, even when students fail.

C) blame students' failure on parents.

D) decrease the amount of effort invested in teaching, when students fall short of academic goals.

Answer: B

Explanation: B) Bandura's research showed a high degree of persistence among teachers possessing teacher efficacy.

Page Ref: 7

12) Intentional teachers become expert by engaging in all of the following activities **EXCEPT**

A) upgrading and examining their teaching practices.

B) reading and attending conferences to learn new ideas.

C) using their own students' responses to guide instructional decisions.

D) unquestioning adherence to the methods learned during teacher training.

Answer: D

Explanation: D) Expert teachers examine their own teaching critically by keeping up with new ideas and receiving feedback from students.

Page Ref: 8

13) According to the text author, what is most likely the major difference between teachers with 20 years of experience and teachers with one year of experience 20 times?

    A) content knowledge   B) ability to reflect

    C) relationships with principals   D) age

Answer: B

Explanation: B) Teachers with 20 years of experience constantly upgrade and examine their teaching strategies, stay current in their disciplines, and reflect on their own and students' reactions to the instructional environment. Teachers with one year of teaching experience 20 times fail to reflect upon their performance.

Page Ref: 8

14) From studies in educational psychology, we know that

    A) mixed–ability grouping is more effective than same–ability grouping.

    B) scolding students for misbehavior will result in better behavior.

    C) whole group instruction is better than individual instruction.

    D) student achievement increases when independent study strategies are used.

Answer: A

Explanation: A) Although it might seem that same–ability groupings would be more effective than mixed–ability groupings, since the teacher works with a narrower range of abilities and skills, research shows the opposite to be true.

Page Ref: 9

15) Ideas that explain relationships between factors are called

    A) hypothesis.   B) theories.   C) principles.   D) laws.

Answer: C

Explanation: C) A principle explains the relationship between factors, such as the effects of alternative grading systems on student motivation.

Page Ref: 10

16) What is the main purpose of theory development?

    A) Theories synthesize laws and principles.

    B) Theories explain relationships between two factors.

    C) Theories identify principles that have been thoroughly tested.

    D) Theories gather data that prove cause and effect.

Answer: A

Explanation: A) Theories tie facts and principles together to give us the big picture.
Page Ref: 10

17) Which one of the following statements about educational psychology is accurate?

A) Progress in how we come to understand behavior and learning is a slow and uneven process.

B) Often, a single study will provide breakthrough evidence to extend theories.

C) An example of a theory would be that discovery learning increases student learning.

D) Theories break down laws and principles so that they can be studied in their most pure form.

Answer: A

Explanation: A) As in any science, progress in educational psychology is slow and uneven. While single breakthroughs are rare, evidence accumulates over time on a subject and allows theorists to refine and extend theories.

Page Ref: 10

18) It is probably true that the most important things that teachers learn about teaching take place

A) in departments of education.   B) in liberal education programs.

C) while on the job.   D) in graduate school.

Answer: C

Explanation: C) While course work is an important factor in learning about teaching, on–the–job training is fundamental.

Page Ref: 10

19) Which of the following statements about theories is accurate?

A) Theories are based on clearly established outcomes and are thus rarely changed once formulated.

B) Theories evolve and gain acceptance relatively quickly.

C) Theories are common in the hard sciences but not appropriate for education.

D) The quality, accuracy, and usefulness of theories are what determine, ultimately, a teacher's success.

Answer: D

Explanation: D) Theories are broader and more general in scope than laws or principles. Theories are formulated from sets of related principles and laws, but they tend to change over time as new evidence is accumulated.

Page Ref: 10

20) One aim of educational psychology is to

  A) turn laws into useful theories.

  B) test theories that guide the actions of teachers.

  C) find a unified method of teaching all learners.

  D) eliminate rigorous teaching licensing policies.

Answer: B

Explanation: B) Teachers make hundreds of decisions every day. Educational psychology tests
                  the theories behind these decisions.

Page Ref: 10

21) When you combine objective research with common sense, the result is

  A) decreased quality in decision making.   B) inconsistent student achievement.

  C) self-regulated learning.   D) effective teaching.

Answer: D

Explanation: D) Research + Common Sense = Effective Teaching. This formula suggests that it is
                 best to apply results of research with common sense and a clear view of what is
                 being taught to whom and for what purpose.

Page Ref: 13

22) Which of the following statements best sums up the role of research in teaching?

  A) Educational psychology research can be translated directly into instructional
     effectiveness.

  B) Decision making, when based on research, is free of context.

  C) Common sense has no place in instructional decision making.

  D) No theory, research, or book can tell teachers what to do in a given situation.

Answer: D

Explanation: D) There is no single theory that fits all situations.

Page Ref: 13

23) Which of the following components of sound teacher decision–making is **FALSE**?

  A) Sound decision making depends on the situation within which a problem arises.

  B) Sound decision making depends on the objectives the teacher has in mind.

  C) It is necessary to combine principles and theories with common sense when making
     decisions.

  D) Principles and theories should be isolated from context.

Answer: D

Explanation: D) Sound decision making depends on the context in which it is to be made, the
                 objectives to be addressed, and the use of principles and theories as guides,
                 along with common sense.

Page Ref: 13

24) Based on your textbook author's conception of effective teaching, which of the following statements is true?

A) More weight should typically be given to the teacher's informed judgment of a classroom situation, than to direct prescriptions from research findings.

B) Knowing what research prescribes will ensure that the most effective teaching decisions will be made.

C) Common sense may be appealing, but it usually results in poor judgment and lower student success.

D) What were effective strategies 10 years ago will not work well today.

Answer: A

Explanation: A) For effective teaching to occur, more weight should typically be given to what the teacher thinks is logical. This is because research provides only general guidelines regarding what usually works.

Page Ref: 14

25) The essence of a variable is that it

A) creates special treatments and examines their effects.

B) can have more than one value.

C) ensures that two groups are equivalent.

D) synthesizes principles and laws.

Answer: B

Explanation: B) A variable in research is anything that can have more than one value such as age, gender, achievement, etc. It can be manipulated to demonstrate treatment effect.

Page Ref: 16

26) A researcher wants to study the effects of rewards on motivation. Two groups of students are set up; one group receives rewards for its efforts and the other group does not. In order to ensure that the two groups are essentially equivalent, what procedure should the researcher use?

A) Randomly assign students to groups.

B) Have students count off by twos.

C) Let students choose the group to which they would like to belong.

D) Put all students who are motivated by awards in one group.

Answer: A

Explanation: A) Random assignment ensures that two groups are essentially equivalent before the experiment begins. If a researcher does not use random assignment, there is no way to know if the treatment was the cause of the differences found between or among the groups.

Page Ref: 16

27) Which of the following is an example of random assignment?

   A) Students whose last name begins with the letters A – L are assigned to one group; the remainder are assigned to another group.

   B) The first half of the class that enters the classroom is put in one group; the remaining students are assigned to another group.

   C) Students who roll an odd number on a die are assigned to one group; those who roll an even number are assigned to another.

   D) Students are allowed to choose the group to which they prefer to belong.

   Answer: C

   Explanation: C) The example of random assignment is using the roll of the die to form groups. Random assignment requires that each participant has an equal chance of being assigned to either group.

   Page Ref: 16

28) A math teacher randomly assigns one group of students to use computers and one group to use work sheets when learning fractions. The teacher then compares the two groups by giving both groups a test of fractions knowledge. What type of research was conducted?

   A) experiment   B) correlational study

   C) descriptive study   D) ethnography

   Answer: A

   Explanation: A) The type of research being performed is an experiment. The research is creating two treatments and comparing them to determine the effects.

   Page Ref: 16

29) Studies demonstrating that differences in findings can be attributed to the treatment given are said to have high

   A) correlational coefficients.   B) internal validity.

   C) generalizabilty.   D) applicability.

   Answer: B

   Explanation: B) Internal validity refers to the amount of confidence one can place in attributing the differences in results to treatments: the higher the degree of internal validity, the greater the confidence that the treatment is the cause of the observed differences.

   Page Ref: 17

30) Which of the following research types attempts to control all factors except those created by the treatment, while remaining relevant to real life?

    A) correlational study   B) laboratory experiment

    C) randomized field experiment   D) single case study

Answer: C

Explanation: C) Randomized field experiments are similar to laboratory experiments except they have a higher degree of external validity. This is because they attempt to remain relevant to real life situations at the expense of internal validity.

Page Ref: 17

31) A teacher experimented with different approaches to instruction in a class. Although all of the conditions of the experiment could not be controlled, the teacher's study was meaningful to real students in real classrooms because it followed all the rules of good research. Therefore, the

    A) study can be replicated with consistent results.

    B) results would be the same across cultures and contexts.

    C) findings will predict effective instruction in all third grade classrooms.

    D) results show a high degree of external validity.

Answer: D

Explanation: D) With a high degree of external validity, it may be more difficult to attribute differences in results to treatment; however, at the same time, the findings are more relevant to real life.

Page Ref: 17

32) In a study, students were randomly assigned to classes receiving individual tutoring or no tutoring. The students who did not receive tutoring are called the

    A) control group.   B) experimental group.

    C) pilot group.   D) placebo group.

Answer: A

Explanation: A) The students who do not receive the tutoring represent the control group. They will be compared to the experimental group (the tutored students) to determine treatment effects.

Page Ref: 17

33) In one study, teachers were assigned to either group A, which received additional training in teaching strategies, or group B, which received no training. Group A is called the

    A) control group.   B) experimental group.

    C) pilot group.   D) placebo group.

Answer: B

Explanation: B) Group A would be considered the experimental (or treatment) group. Group B would be the control group.

Page Ref: 17

34) In some situations a randomized field experiment may not be possible, because teachers cannot be assigned to treatments. In such cases equivalence of experimental and control groups may be established using **matching**, rather than random assignment. Compared with the randomized field experiment, the field experiment that uses matching has

    A) lower external validity.   B) higher external validity.

    C) lower internal validity.   D) higher internal validity.

Answer: C

Explanation: C) A study has internal validity when we can confidently attribute differences observed in the results, to the treatments themselves. Random assignment ensures that groups compared are essentially equal at the start of the study. But when matching is used in forming groups, the groups may differ, from the start, in ways unknown to the researcher. This possibility of uncontrolled differences between treatment groups gives the **matching** study lower internal validity.

Page Ref: 18

35) After a new hand-raising rule was implemented, a special education teacher collects data on a student's hand-raising behavior. What type of research is this?

    A) correlational study   B) laboratory experiment

    C) randomized field experiment   D) single case experiment

Answer: D

Explanation: D) A single case study is a detailed study of a single person's or a group's behavior over time.

Page Ref: 18

36) A teacher notes the average number of students who clean up their materials each day for one week. The teacher then implements a reinforcement program for neatness and observes the students' neatness behavior for another week. What type of research is this?

A) laboratory experiment
B) randomized field study
C) correlational study
D) single case experiment

Answer: D

Explanation: D) This is a single case study. The teacher uses the control group (before treatment) and the experimental group (treatment) to investigate the effects of the neatness program on student behavior.

Page Ref: 18

37) A researcher can understand the results of a single case study by

A) graphing the results and analyzing the graphs.

B) talking to the participants and noting their ideas.

C) statistically comparing the experimental and control groups.

D) statistically comparing the results from the lab and the field.

Answer: A

Explanation: A) Usually, results of a single-case study can be graphed and analyzed. If the differences are meaningful, they should be detectable and describable without formal statistical testing.

Page Ref: 19

38) In single-case experiments, examination of graphed results would generally be used for

A) deciding about whether results are clear enough to accept.

B) selecting experimental methodologies that "meet the eye."

C) situations in which common sense is at odds with research.

D) determining whether a correlation is statistically significant.

Answer: A

Explanation: A) In looking at graphs, researchers may be "hit in the eye" by obvious differences that preclude the need for more formal statistical validation.

Page Ref: 19

39) A researcher found that students who scored high on a test of reading achievement also scored high on a self-esteem inventory. The researcher can say that reading achievement and self-esteem are

A) negatively correlated.
B) positively correlated.
C) internally correlated.
D) externally correlated.

Answer: B

Explanation: B) Positively correlated variables show relationships that rise together.
Page Ref: 20

40) Which of the following examples depicts a negative correlation?

A) Students who studied for the greatest length of time prior to a math test received the highest scores.

B) The amount of time students studied for a math test was unrelated to the scores they received.

C) Students who were absent the least prior to a math test had the highest scores.

D) Students who had the highest grade point averages received the highest math scores.

Answer: C

Explanation: C) Negatively correlated variables show relationships that move in opposite directions. As one variable increases, the other decreases.

Page Ref: 20

41) A researcher has completed a study correlating middle school students' science interests and science achievement. The results of the study will show

A) what happens when one of the two variables is kept constant for two or more groups.

B) the degree of relationship between the two variables.

C) how one variable causes the other.

D) how a single student who is low or high on one variable scores on the other.

Answer: B

Explanation: B) The results of this correlational study will show the relationship between the two variables. Unlike an experiment, these results will not imply that one variable causes the other.

Page Ref: 20

42) When the values of one variable are high, the values of the other are also high. What type of correlation is being described?

A) positive   B) negative   C) neutral   D) uncorrelated

Answer: A

Explanation: A) A positive correlation exists when high values on one variable occur in association with high values on the other variable. In contrast, negative correlations occur when high values on one variable occur in association with low values on the other.

Page Ref: 20

43) A music teacher finds that the amount of time students spend listening to rap music is negatively correlated with grades in music class. Based on these results, the teacher might conclude that listening to rap music

    A) causes the high grades.   B) causes the low grades.

    C) is associated with high grades.   D) is associated with low grades.

Answer: D

Explanation: D) The teacher can conclude that a lot of time spent listening to rap music is associated with low grades. Cause and effect cannot be determined by correlational studies.

Page Ref: 20

44) A positive correlation would most likely exist between

    A) school achievement and ability to ride a bicycle.

    B) motivation to learn and academic achievement.

    C) singing ability and academic achievement.

    D) hours spent playing video games and writing ability.

Answer: B

Explanation: B) Generally, the greater the students' motivation, the more likely they are to achieve.

Page Ref: 20

45) A student has been absent for many days during a semester; so, the teacher meets with the student's parents. The teacher remarks that the more days absent from school, the worse students' grades tend to be. What type of correlation is the teacher suggesting there is between attendance and achievement?

    A) positive   B) negative   C) neutral   D) uncorrelated

Answer: B

Explanation: B) The teacher is implying that a negative correlation exists between absences and grades. The more you are absent, the lower your grades are likely to be.

Page Ref: 20

46) A teacher suspects that students who take more time to complete examinations will tend to earn higher scores. If the teacher is correct, the resultant correlation between completion time and performance will be

    A) positive.   B) zero.   C) negative.   D) causal.

Answer: A

Explanation: A) The correlation should be positive. More time will be associated with higher scores. The fact that some cases are exceptions does not eliminate the overall relationship between the two variables.

Page Ref: 20

47) You are reading a description of a correlational study in which the author concludes that aggression in class causes poor grades. Which of the following reactions to the author's conclusion is appropriate?

    A) The author is correct in making the conclusion.

    B) The author's conclusion is wrong since a correlational study cannot demonstrate a relationship between two factors.

    C) The author is incorrect since aggression cannot be measured.

    D) The author may be correct but cannot make a cause-effect conclusion from a correlational study.

Answer: D

Explanation: D) The author may be correct, but cannot make such a statement from this study. The fact that aggression and grades are correlated does not necessarily mean that one causes the other.

Page Ref: 20

48) A type of research in which an observer studies natural events as they occur in a social setting is called

    A) cause-and-effect research.   B) descriptive research.

    C) quantitative research.   D) correlational research.

Answer: B

Explanation: B) Ethnographic or descriptive studies consist of naturalistic observations of social events.

Page Ref: 21

49) Why would a researcher conduct an ethnographic study?

    A) to prove a theory

    B) to explore a new context for conducting research

    C) to validate a principle or law

    D) to establish cause-and-effect relationships between variables

Answer: B

Explanation: B) An ethnographic study is a descriptive study. It would be most valuable in exploring new contexts (e.g., classroom events) for research. It describes the natural environment rather than manipulating or treating it.

Page Ref: 21

50) An experimenter sits in the back of a classroom for three months in a school for students with special needs. Students' behaviors are observed as a new teaching method is used. What type of study is this?

    A) correlational   B) ethnography

    C) experimental   D) lab experiment

Answer: B

Explanation: B) Ethnographies are descriptive studies that involve observing particular social contexts over extended time periods.

Page Ref: 21

51) Which of the following procedures is used in descriptive research?

    A) control groups   B) random assignment

    C) interviews   D) treatments of variables

Answer: C

Explanation: C) Surveys and interviews help researchers to understand what is occurring naturally in the environment.

Page Ref: 21

52) A developmental psychologist observes and then synthesizes observations into a theory showing how individuals develop cognitively over time. What type of research is being conducted?

    A) experimental   B) laboratory   C) correlational   D) descriptive

Answer: D

Explanation: D) Ethnographies have been helpful in developing theoretical ideas since they describe naturally occurring events. Ideas can then be tested using designs with a greater degree of internal validity.

Page Ref: 22

53) A benefit of **action research** is that

    A) it gives pupils a more active role in research design, than they have in other types of descriptive research.

    B) it has higher internal validity than experiments.

    C) the data gathering process meets the highest standards of objectivity.

    D) professionals are directly involved in the program under study, which may bring great insight to the investigation.

Answer: D

Explanation: D) Action research is research conducted by professionals such as teachers, who are directly involved in the process they are studying.

Page Ref: 21

True/False Questions

1) Educational psychology is the study of learners, learning, and teaching.

   Answer: TRUE
   Page Ref: 3

2) Pedagogy is the study of academic content knowledge.

   Answer: FALSE
   Page Ref: 4

3) Effective instruction is simply a matter of one person with more knowledge transmitting it to another.

   Answer: FALSE
   Page Ref: 4

4) According to the text author, good teaching can be taught.

   Answer: TRUE
   Page Ref: 5

5) One attribute that is characteristic of outstanding teachers is intentionality.

   Answer: TRUE
   Page Ref: 5

6) Intentional teachers keep instructional goals in mind when making decisions about students.

   Answer: TRUE
   Page Ref: 5

7) Critical thinking skills for teachers include the use of logical and systematic approaches to educational practices.

   Answer: TRUE
   Page Ref: 8

8) Laws are principles that have yet to be thoroughly tested.

   Answer: FALSE
   Page Ref: 10

9) Principles, theories, and laws are the products of research.

   Answer: TRUE
   Page Ref: 10

10) Research + Effective Teaching = Common Sense.

Answer: FALSE
Page Ref: 13

11) A variable is anything that has just one value.

Answer: FALSE
Page Ref: 16

12) Laboratory experiments may have little relevance to real–life situations.

Answer: TRUE
Page Ref: 17

13) If achievement in reading goes up as does achievement in math, the variables can be said to be negatively correlated.

Answer: FALSE
Page Ref: 20

14) Descriptive research has less objectivity than experimental research.

Answer: TRUE
Page Ref: 21

15) Surveys, ethnographies, and action research are all examples of descriptive research.

Answer: TRUE
Page Ref: 21

Short Answer Questions

1) The discipline or field about learners, learning and teaching.

Answer: educational psychology
Page Ref: 3

2) The study of teaching and learning with application to the instructional process.

Answer: pedagogy
Page Ref: 4

3) Teachers who do things for a reason, on purpose.

Answer: intentional teachers
Page Ref: 5

4) The degree to which teachers feel that their own efforts determine the success of their students.

Answer: teacher efficacy
Page Ref: 7

5) Sets of principles and facts that attempt to explain some phenomenon.

Answer: theories
Page Ref: 10

6) Individual principles that have been thoroughly tested.

Answer: laws
Page Ref: 10

7) These explain relationships between factors.

Answer: principles
Page Ref: 10

8) A systematic procedure used to study the effects of a treatment.

Answer: experiment
Page Ref: 16

9) The degree to which the results of a laboratory experiment can be directly attributed to the treatment studied rather than other factors.

Answer: internal validity
Page Ref: 17

10) A type of research in which a single participant's behavior may be observed over a period of time.

Answer: single-case experiment
Page Ref: 18

11) A type of research that explores the degree to which two variables are related.

Answer: correlational study
Page Ref: 20

12) A type of nonexperimental study aimed at systematically identifying and gathering detailed information about something.

Answer: descriptive study
Page Ref: 21

Essay Questions

1) What personal and professional characteristics are necessary for effective teaching?

   Answer: First and foremost, teachers need to possess subject matter knowledge (knowing what to teach) and pedagogical knowledge (knowing how to teach). Other personal qualities, such as warmth, humor, empathy, hard work, leadership, enthusiasm, a contagious love of learning, and speaking ability, are highly desirable, but are not enough. A meshing of all these professional and personal characteristics will most likely produce the strongest teachers.
   Page Ref: 3

2) A teacher wants to know: Do students behave better in class when they help to create classroom rules or do they behave better when teachers create the rules alone? How would you go about setting up a study to answer this question?

   Answer: The first step in the research process would be to create two groups using random assignment. Group one would consist of students who help make classroom rules. Group two would consist of students who did not participate in rule making. The teacher could then count the number of rule violations for each group, draw conclusions from the data, and answer the question as to which strategy is most effective.
   Page Ref: 17

3) Define and compare external validity and internal validity. Given your personal values, which do you feel is more important to emphasize in educational research? Explain the rationale for your choice.

   Answer: Internal validity, which is established in laboratory experiments, allows the researcher to conclude that experimental outcomes are due to the effects of treatments and not of extraneous factors. High internal validity sometimes comes at the cost of external validity, which is the applicability of the findings to some real-life problem.
   Page Ref: 17

4) You are interested in how teacher feedback on homework (e.g., "good going" or "more detail needed") influences the quality of subsequent homework. Describe how this question might be studied using each of the following: 1) laboratory experiment; 2) single-case experiment; and 3) randomized field experiment.

   Answer: 1) Laboratory experiments require tight control. Students would be randomly assigned to an experimental group (comments) or a control group (no comments). Comments would be systematically given to the first group over time. The second group would complete identical assignments, but not receive comments. The assignments of both groups would be evaluated. 2) Single case experiments would involve one group of students. No comments on homework would be given. Results would be evaluated. Then, comments would be introduced and analyzed. 3) A randomized field experiment would involve two classes. The design would be the same as for the laboratory experiment, but methods would be more natural and less controlled.
   Page Ref: 17-18

5) Give examples of relationships in the educational environment that would likely yield a positive correlation, a negative correlation, and no correlation. For each example, specify what kind of change in one variable is associated with what change in a second variable.

Answer: An example of a positive correlation might be students whose achievement level increases as their hours of study increase. A negative correlation might be students whose achievement level decreases as their number of days absent increases. There is most likely no relationship between student achievement and shoe size.
Page Ref: 20

6) Describe a study you might conduct using a descriptive research design.

Answer: A study could be conducted of life in well-funded and poorly-funded schools, or of tracked or untracked middle schools. Research in developmental psychology is often descriptive in nature.
Page Ref: 21

7) For this question consider the following research finding:
   Finding A: It was reported that students who receive more homework obtain higher grades.
   • Why is this research called correlational rather than experimental
   • How strongly does the Finding A support the conclusion that spending time on homework causes students to obtain higher grades?

Now compare Finding A to the following finding:
   Finding B: It was reported that students who own cell phones obtain higher grades.
   • How strongly does Finding B support the conclusion that owning cell phones results in more learning?
   • In what way do these two findings differ? Does one tell us more than the other about how students achieve higher grades?

Answer: Both findings are correlational, because they show only that a change in one variable is associated with a change in another. They cannot show a cause/effect connection because they do not manipulate any treatment.
   Neither finding tells us what causes students to obtain high grades. The difference between the studies is that a causal connection between spending time on homework and getting good grades (the incorrect interpretation of Finding A) is **plausible**, whereas the idea that owning cell phones causes high grades (incorrect interpretation of Finding B) is implausible. It is easier to see, looking at finding B, that correlation does not prove causation; looking at Finding A it is very tempting to conclude (incorrectly) that a causal relationship has been demonstrated.
Page Ref: 20

8) Mr. Duvall enters his classroom on the first day of the fall semester. This is his first year of teaching 10th grade English at Southview High School. Although he is a little nervous, he believes that his training at the state university and his student teaching experience have prepared him well for this day.

As he attempts to introduce himself to his new students, a group of students at the back of the room begins talking to each other in voices loud enough to disturb the class. He moves to the back of the classroom, thinking that his presence near the students will quiet them; however, when he gets within a short distance of the students, they talk louder.

There are several actions that Mr. Duvall can take and several theories to support his decision. Based on theories presented in the chapter, what do you think he should do and why? Write an ending to the story that demonstrates a positive solution to the problem.

Answer: Mr. Duvall could reprimand the students (a reprimand is a form of punishment and the students would behave to avoid punishment), ignore their talking (calling attention to the talking could be a punishment), send the students to the office (depriving the students of their audience), or punish the whole class (get other students to be concerned about the talking).

Page Ref: 12

9) Below is a chart for experimental, correlational, and descriptive research. Fill in the missing information, which is indicated by an X.

EXPERIMENTAL RESEARCH

Goals	Forms	Examples
	laboratory study	X
test effectiveness of a treatment	randomized field study	Teaching math using manipulatives is effective than using traditional approaches
	single case study	X

CORRELATIONAL RESEARCH

Goals	Forms	Examples
	positive correlation	X
look for relationships between variables	X	The fewer days students are absent from school, the higher their math scores.
	no correlation	Student achievement in social studies and musical ability.

DESCRIPTIVE RESEARCH

Goals	Forms	Examples
	surveys	Students are in favor of an open lunch.
X	interviews	Adolescent females describe themselves in positive terms.
	ethnography	Study the meaning and consequence of desegregation at three high schools.

Answer: A laboratory study example could be to study the effects of two groups; one group is rewarded for using felt markers while the other is not.

A single case study example could be to study how one student's behavior changes over time after the introduction of a contract for grade system.

An example of a positive correlation could be the increase in test scores with an increase in praise for hard work.

The fewer the days students are absent from school the higher their math scores is an example of a negative correlation.

The goal of descriptive research is to observe and describe events in a natural environment.

Page Ref: 18-21

Chapter 2   Theories of Development

Multiple-Choice Questions

1) Development refers to how people

    A) use context to nurture social relationships.

    B) learn from clues in their environment.

    C) grow, adapt, and change over the course of their lifetimes.

    D) process environmental information.

Answer: C

Explanation: C) Development refers to how and why people grow, adapt, and change over the course of their lifetimes. These changes occur through physical development, personality development, emotional development, cognitive development (thinking), and language development.

Page Ref: 30

2) Which of the following statements about development is accurate?

    A) Children are not miniature adults; their thinking is qualitatively different.

    B) Biological factors influence moral development more than environmental factors.

    C) Continuous theories of development suggest distinct stages at which individuals must complete tasks.

    D) One requirement of effective teaching is that all students receive the same learning activities, regardless of their developmental characteristics.

Answer: A

Explanation: A) Children are not miniature adults. They think differently, see the world differently, and live by different moral and ethical principles than do adults.

Page Ref: 30

3) Which one of the following developmental characteristics is affected by nurture to a greater degree than nature?

    A) eye color   B) reflexes

    C) moral character   D) height

Answer: C

Explanation: C) Most developmental psychologists believe that nature and nurture combine to influence development, with biological factors playing a stronger role in some aspects of development such as physical development, and environmental factors playing a stronger role in others such as moral development.

Page Ref: 31

4) According to discontinuous theorists, all of the following statements are true **EXCEPT**

   A) Individuals progress through predictable and invariant developmental stages.

   B) Individuals acquire developmental skills in the same way and at the same rate.

   C) Skipping stages is impossible.

   D) Developmental changes occur over time.

Answer: B

Explanation: B) According to discontinuous theorists, individuals progress through distinct stages, over time, that cannot be skipped.
Page Ref: 31

5) Developmental psychologist Jean Piaget introduced terms to psychology drawn directly from

   A) biology.   B) the lives of his children.

   C) history.   D) observation.

Answer: A

Explanation: A) After receiving his doctorate in biology, Piaget became more interested in psychology, basing his earliest theories on careful observation of his own three children and others. Piaget thought of himself as applying biological principles and methods to the study of human development.
Page Ref: 31

6) According to Piaget, "knowledge comes from action." Which of the following statements best explains Piaget's adage?

   A) Piaget assumes that cognitive development is a smooth progression from less knowledge to more knowledge.

   B) Development depends in large part on an individual's manipulation of and interaction with the environment.

   C) Children are miniature adults. This means knowledge is quantitative rather than qualitative.

   D) Inactivity is an indicator of intelligence, especially during childhood.

Answer: B

Explanation: B) Knowledge comes from action—or interaction—with the environment.
Page Ref: 31

7) Piaget's theory of cognitive development proposes that children's intellect (cognitive ability) progresses through four stages in which individuals

    A) demonstrate thinking patterns called scaffolds.

    B) process information patterns by scaffolding.

    C) demonstrate thinking abilities through repetition of modeled behaviors.

    D) organize and process information as cognitive structures called schemes.

Answer: D
Page Ref: 31

8) Piaget believed that all individuals are born with an innate tendency to interact with and make sense of their environments by creating

    A) an identity.   B) moral dilemmas.

    C) schemes.   D) discontinuous theories.

Answer: C

Explanation: C) According to Piaget, all children are born with an innate tendency to interact with and make sense of their environments. His reference to schemes details patterns of behavior or thinking that children and adults use in dealing with objects in the world.

Page Ref: 32

9) The process of using or adjusting schemes in response to the environment by means of assimilation and accommodation is called

    A) organization.   B) construction.   C) adaptation.   D) structuring.

Answer: C

Explanation: C) Accommodation involves varying existing schemes to adapt to changing situations. This adaptation brings about a modification of the individual's existing cognitive developmental stage as a response to new events.

Page Ref: 32

10) The process of understanding a new object or event using existing schemes is called

    A) assimilation.   B) accommodation.

    C) conservation.   D) memorization.

Answer: A

Explanation: A) As new situations and problems face individuals, they draw from what they already know. Assimilation is understanding new experiences in terms of existing schemes.

Page Ref: 32

11) If Piaget were to say that you **assimilate** your new pen into your writing–scheme, he would mean that

    A) you are able to apply existing skill in using the new pen, because you had developed that writing ability (writing–scheme) earlier.

    B) you are unable to apply previous knowledge, because the pen is so novel.

    C) you make adjustments in the scheme so it will work with the new pen.

    D) the pen elicits a reflex reaction.

Answer: A

Explanation: A) Assimilation and accommodation both take place in this situation, but "assimilate" refers to applying the previously–learned scheme.

Page Ref: 32

12) An infant has always used one hand to pick up a small ball but now, when faced with a large beach ball, picks it up with two hands. In Piaget's terms, the change from one hand to two is called

    A) conservation.   B) equalization.

    C) accommodation.   D) assimilation.

Answer: C

Explanation: C) Accommodation is a process by which the individual, during periods of disequilibrium, self–regulates in order to attain high levels of cognitive stability. Eventually, new ways of thinking about the world emerge and individuals advance to a new stage of development.

Page Ref: 33

13) Which of the following best describes Piaget's idea of equilibrium?

    A) You do something and feel uncomfortable about it.

    B) You find that what you expect to happen actually does happen.

    C) You know what to do, but your response doesn't work.

    D) You need to respond, but can't think of what to do.

Answer: B

Explanation: B) When you find that what you expect to happen actually does happen, equilibrium takes place. Equilibrium is a state of comfort or balance that we try to restore when dissonant outcomes occur.

Page Ref: 33

14) A teacher often begins his lectures by presenting students with two ideas or observations that apparently conflict. He feels that this works because presenting a paradox arouses students' interest. From Piaget's point of view, the teacher is making use of the students' natural response to

    A) scaffolding.   B) egocentrism.

    C) transitivity.   D) disequilibrium.

Answer: D

Explanation: D) Conflict between ideas upsets equilibrium. Piaget's theory holds that human beings are motivated, spontaneously, to restore equilibrium.

Page Ref: 33

15) Piaget divided cognitive development into which of the following sequences of stages?

    A) preoperational, concrete operational, formal operational, sensorimotor

    B) concrete operational, preoperational, formal operational, sensorimotor

    C) sensorimotor, preoperational, formal operational, concrete operational

    D) sensorimotor, preoperational, concrete operational, formal operational

Answer: D

Explanation: D) A child begins to represent objects and events mentally at the sensorimotor stage. Piaget believed that all children are born with an innate tendency to interact with and make sense of their environments. During the preoperational stage, children's language and concepts develop quickly; however, much of their thinking remains primitive. Elementary school students move from here into the concrete operational stage. Their thinking is rooted in the world as it is and they have difficulty with abstract thought. Children's thinking begins to develop into the form that is characteristic of adults at the formal operation stage. The preadolescent begins to take on the ability to deal with potential or hypothetical situations.

Page Ref: 34

16) Which of the following adages depicts Piaget's belief that infants lack object permanence?

    A) Have your cake and eat it too.   B) Six of one, half dozen of another.

    C) A stitch in time saves nine.   D) Out of sight, out of mind.

Answer: D

Explanation: D) The saying "out of sight, out of mind" directly captures the meaning of object permanence. When the sensorimotor child can no longer see the object, he/she loses interest in it, acting as if it no longer exists.

Page Ref: 34

17) Four-year-old Kenny visits the lecture hall and says "Daddy's classroom is bigger than the whole world!" Piaget would attribute this preschool child's "illogical" thinking to

    A) incomplete development of object permanence.

    B) difficulty focusing on two ideas at once.

    C) inability to apply formal operations in some contexts.

    D) failure to separate form from content.

Answer: B

Explanation: B) To grasp the contradiction the child must pay attention simultaneously to the bigness of the classroom, and to its status as only a part of the world (conservation).

Page Ref: 34

18) Which one of the following cognitive characteristics explains why preoperational children have difficulty with the beaker-of-water problem (conservation of volume)?

    A) centration   B) object permanence

    C) hypothetical thought   D) egocentricism

Answer: A

Explanation: A) Conservation tasks require decentration—paying attention to more than one aspect of a problem at one time.

Page Ref: 35

19) A child knows that if 7 + 5 = 12, then 12 – 5 = 7. This requires which one of the following cognitive characteristics?

    A) situational thought   B) reversibility

    C) transitivity   D) formal thought

Answer: B

Explanation: B) For Piaget, reversibility means the ability to change direction in one's thinking so that one can return to a starting point. We know that if 7 + 5 = 12, then 12 – 5 = 7. If we add five things to seven things and then take the five things away (reverse what we've done), we're left with seven things.

Page Ref: 35

20) Which cognitive stage and characteristic are children showing when they believe that everyone sees the world exactly as they do?

    A) concrete operational stage; egocentric thought

    B) concrete operational stage; centration

    C) preoperational stage; egocentric thought

    D) preoperational stage; centration

Answer: C

Explanation: C) Preoperational thought is egocentric. Children at this stage believe that everyone sees the world exactly as they do. Preoperational children also interpret events entirely in reference to themselves.

Page Ref: 37

21) Which of the following is most likely to help a concrete operational child solve conceptual problems?

    A) The child is older than the typical concrete operational learner.

    B) The child is taught to solve the problems.

    C) The problems are explained several times.

    D) The problems involve objects and situations that are familiar (to the child).

Answer: D

Explanation: D) The concrete operational child is rooted in the world as it is and has difficulty with abstract thought that is beyond her or his familiarity. The child can form concepts, see relationships, and solve problems only as long as they involve objects and familiar situations.

Page Ref: 38

22) Which of the following statements best defines the term seriation?

    A) arrangement of things in a logical progression

    B) ability to infer a relationship between two objects

    C) method of solving problems by forming concepts and recognizing relationships

    D) ability to change direction in one's thinking

Answer: A

Explanation: A) When children learn how to arrange things in a logical progression, it is said that they are demonstrating seriation. This takes place in the concrete operational stage. In order to do this, they must be able to order or classify objects according to some criterion or dimension.

Page Ref: 38

23) Once children learn the concept of seriation in the concrete operational stage, they can begin to infer relationships between two objects on the basis of knowledge of their respective relationship with a third object. This ability is known as

A) reversibility.   B) centration.   C) conservation.   D) transitivity.

Answer: D

Explanation: D) Transitivity refers to the ability to infer a relationship between two objects based on knowledge of their respective relationships with a third object. Logical progressions like this are not possible until the stage of concrete operations, during which school-aged children develop the ability to make mental transformations that require reversible thinking.

Page Ref: 38

24) Which of the following descriptions best represents Piaget's notion of class inclusion?

A) Think about groups of objects and their relationships.

B) Mentally arrange and compare objects.

C) Arrange objects according to a particular property.

D) Reason hypothetically.

Answer: A

Explanation: A) Class inclusion is defined as a skill learned during the concrete operational stage of cognitive development, in which individuals can think simultaneously about a whole class of objects, and relationships among its subordinate classes.

Page Ref: 39

25) According to Piaget, which of the following cognitive tasks requires formal operational thought?

A) Fixate on the perceivable.

B) Infer relationships between groups of objects.

C) Arrange objects in a sequential order.

D) Reason about imagined situations and conditions.

Answer: D

Explanation: D) Hypothetical thought is a formal operational skill.
Page Ref: 39

26) You are ready to teach a lesson to a tenth grade class. Your lesson involves some abstract principles. Which of the following would be the most accurate assumption you could make about your students as you plan your learning activities?

    A) All of the students are ready to apply formal thought to your lesson.

    B) All of the students have mastered hypothetical reasoning, although some may not yet understand conservation.

    C) You can't be sure that all who have reached formal operations will be able to apply formal thought to your lesson.

    D) Most of the students have not reached the concrete operational stage.

Answer: C

Explanation: C) Whether or not an individual is able to use formal operations, depends on the situation.

Page Ref: 39

27) Reassessment of children's egocentricity has been put forth by researchers who have found that in simple, practical contexts, children demonstrated their ability to

    A) verbalize around a central point or theme.

    B) rely on other people for direction.

    C) consider the point of view of others.

    D) demonstrate counting skills.

Answer: C

Explanation: C) In simple and practical contexts, children have demonstrated their ability to consider the views of others. While this is a different perspective on Piaget's theory, the point to keep in mind is that very simple, practical circumstances allow this to occur.

Page Ref: 41

28) Which of the following is an argument used by critics of Piaget's theory?

    A) The theory is based too heavily on the concept that children can be taught almost anything if the teaching method is appropriate.

    B) There is some evidence that children can be taught to master skills such as conservation at an earlier age than Piaget thought possible.

    C) Piaget overestimated children's abilities and used tasks that were too easy.

    D) The stage idea is based too much on the result of experimental-type research rather than descriptive research.

Answer: B

Explanation: B) One criticism of Piaget's ideas is based on findings that children can be taught conservation at earlier ages than Piaget proposed. Piaget, therefore, appears to have underestimated children's abilities.

Page Ref: 41

29) Which is a conclusion of contemporary evaluations of Piagetian theory?

    A) Piaget underestimated children's cognitive abilities.

    B) Piaget credited cultural differences for most developmental differences among children and adolescents.

    C) Piaget did not go far enough in describing cognitive changes that occur in young children.

    D) Piaget was remarkably accurate in his assessment of learners' abilities at all ages.

Answer: A

Explanation: A) Children are more competent than Piaget originally thought, especially when their practical knowledge is being assessed.

Page Ref: 42

30) How have neo-Piagetian theorists modified Piaget's original work?

    A) Neo-Piagetians have demonstrated that individuals' abilities to operate at a particular stage depend on the specific task involved.

    B) Neo-Piagetians emphasize the importance of basic skills instruction as the foundation for the curriculum.

    C) Neo-Piagetian theories are more behavioral in orientation than Piaget's original theory.

    D) Neo-Piagetian theory favors teacher-centered approaches over discovery approaches to learning.

Answer: A

Explanation: A) Neo-Piagetians have demonstrated that children's abilities to operate at a particular stage depend a great deal on the specific tasks involved; training and experience, including social interactions, can accelerate children's development.

Page Ref: 43

31) On which of the following points do Piagetian and information processing theorists agree?

    A) The development of cognitive skills is stage-like.

    B) Development of cognition can be described in terms of changes in logical skills.

    C) Thinking skills can be directly taught.

    D) Short-term memory skills decrease with age.

Answer: B

Explanation: B) Information processing theorists tend to agree with Piaget's description of cognition but, unlike Piaget, believe that thinking skills can be directly taught.

Page Ref: 43

32) Information processing theorists argue that learners acquire powerful directions and procedures for problem solving, and can be stimulated to discover deficiencies in their logic and to apply new logical principles. What is this approach to learning called?

A) inferred reality

B) rules–assessment

C) self–regulation

D) constructivism

Answer: B

Explanation: B) Some researchers believe, unlike Piaget, that thinking skills can be directly taught. Children have been observed to acquire increasingly powerful rules or procedures for solving problems and can be stimulated to discover deficiencies in their logic and to apply new logical principles. Children have the ability to discern rules and assess their application. The implications of the rule-assessment approach for education is that stimulating new methods of instruction may actually enhance children's thinking abilities.

Page Ref: 43

33) Neo–Piagetian modifications of Piaget's theory include Case's (1998) idea that

A) developmental change is based on a learner's capacity to process and remember information.

B) learners whose thought processes are decentered are able to learn that events may be governed by physical laws.

C) development is a smooth progression, uniform across tasks.

D) developmental change is unaffected by practice and instruction.

Answer: A

Explanation: A) According to a neo–Piagetian, Case, this short term memory capacity increases with physical maturity of the brain, but it also becomes more efficient with practice and instruction.

Page Ref: 43

34) What term does Vygotsky use to designate the symbols, created by cultures, that help people to think, communicate, and solve problems?

A) conventions

B) cognitive structures

C) proximal zone

D) sign system

Answer: D

Explanation: D) Sign systems refer to symbols that cultures create to help people think, communicate, and solve problems—for example, a culture's language, writing system, or counting system.

Page Ref: 44

35) One step in developing internal structures and self-regulation involves

    A) intimacy.   B) programmed instruction.

    C) practice.   D) self-absorption.

Answer: C

Explanation: C) The second step in developing internal structures and self-regulation involves practice. The infant practices gestures that will get attention. The preschooler will enter into conversations with others to master language.

Page Ref: 44

36) Self-regulation refers to the condition whereby individuals internalize cultural language signs so that they can

    A) think and solve problems without the help of others.

    B) reference complex information.

    C) focus on the systematic development of discrete skills.

    D) work in cooperative groups.

Answer: A

Explanation: A) Self-regulation refers to the acquisition and internalization of signs by means of instruction and information from others. This allows the learner to think and solve problems without the help of others.

Page Ref: 44

37) The role of private speech, in Vygotsky's view, is to

    A) guide one's activities in solving a problem.

    B) satisfy the egocentric needs of preoperational children.

    C) call attention to oneself during play.

    D) stimulate the development of language from telegraphic speech to full sentences.

Answer: A

Explanation: A) According to Vygotsky, private speech serves the beneficial function of guiding activities in solving a problem. Research has shown that private speech by children facilitates the learning of complex tasks.

Page Ref: 44

38) The basic implication of the zone of proximal development concept is to

    A) have students at the same cognitive stages work together in cooperative dyads.

    B) teach just beyond students' present understanding.

    C) teach just below students' present understanding.

    D) accept adolescents' approximate answers to essays and open-ended questions as correct.

Answer: B

Explanation: B) An application of Vygotsky's zone of proximal development is to teach just beyond the learner's current level of understanding. With support or scaffolding from others where needed, this orientation will help the child progress to new levels of thinking.

Page Ref: 44

39) According to Vygotsky, external support that teachers provide to help learners solve problems just beyond their reach is referred to as

    A) self-regulation.   B) scaffolding.

    C) sign systems.   D) criterion-referenced achievement.

Answer: B

Explanation: B) Scaffolding refers to the assistance that is provided by more competent peers or adults. It usually means providing an individual with a great deal of support during the early stages of learning and then diminishing support and having the learner take on increasing responsibility as soon as he or she is able.

Page Ref: 45

40) An example of the Vygotsky notion of scaffolding would be

    A) a teacher passing out new supplies.

    B) students taking a test.

    C) a mother helping a child learn to ride a bike.

    D) a father taking his children for a ride in the car.

Answer: C

Explanation: C) According to Vygotsky, scaffolding represents the external support that teachers should provide in order to help students solve problems just beyond their reach. Such scaffolding, when provided in the zone of proximal development, can help a child acquire higher levels of learning.

Page Ref: 45

41) During which type of learning do student peers operate within each others' zones of proximal development, providing models for each other of slightly more advanced thinking?

    A) cooperative learning   B) discovery learning

    C) mediated learning   D) vicarious learning

Answer: A

Explanation: A) Because peers are usually operating within each others' zones of proximal development, they provide models for each other of slightly more advanced thinking.

Page Ref: 45

42) From Vygotsky's viewpoint, which would be the best description of developmentally appropriate activities?

    A) Teach the concept of object permanence.

    B) Focus on what students can't yet do (even with help).

    C) Reflect on what students are capable of doing on their own.

    D) Select tasks that range from those that students can learn with the help of others to those they can learn alone.

Answer: D

Explanation: D) Vygotsky's concept of the zone of proximal development is based on the idea that development is defined both by what a learner can do independently and by what the learner can do when assisted by an adult or more competent peer. Knowledge of both levels is useful for teachers since these levels indicate not only where the learner is at a given moment, but also where she or he is going.

Page Ref: 47

43) Erik Erikson, in stage two of his theory of psychosocial development, asserts that parents who are overly restrictive and harsh give their children

    A) a sense of power that can provide the child with independence.

    B) a sense of powerlessness and incompetence, that can lead to shame and doubt in one's abilities.

    C) a new sense of self- or ego-identity that leads to confusion about the role played by each parent.

    D) sound guidance as they move into adulthood.

Answer: B

Explanation: B) Parents who are flexible enough to permit their children to explore freely and do things for themselves, while at the same time providing a guiding hand, encourage the establishment of a sense of autonomy. When parents are overly restrictive and harsh, they give their children a sense of powerlessness and incompetence. This can lead to shame and doubt in one's abilities.

Page Ref: 49

44) During which of the following stages of Erikson's theory of psychosocial development do teachers and peers take on increasing importance while the influence of parents decreases?

    A) trust versus mistrust   B) initiative versus guilt

    C) industry versus inferiority   D) intimacy versus isolation

Answer: C

Explanation: C) During the industry vs. inferiority stage, teachers and peers take on increasing importance for the learner, while the influence of parents decreases.

Page Ref: 49

45) The positive psychosocial outcome of the teenage years is a sense of

    A) integrity.   B) initiative.   C) identity.   D) generativity.

Answer: C

Explanation: C) The positive psychosocial outcome of the teenage years is a sense of identity. During this stage (from 12 to 18 years), adolescents struggle with the questions of who they are and what they should become. Unsuccessful resolution of this crisis results in role confusion.

Page Ref: 49

46) Which one of Erikson's stages is likely to be experienced as Piaget's formal operations unfolds?

    A) initiative versus guilt   B) identity versus role confusion

    C) intimacy versus isolation   D) generativity versus self-absorption

Answer: B

Explanation: B) The Eriksonian stage of identity vs. role confusion (11 to 18 years) is likely to correspond with the Piagetian stage of formal operations (12 years to adulthood). Both stages create pressures and significant new changes for adolescents.

Page Ref: 49

47) According to Erikson, a young adult who does not seek out close relationships with other people may develop a sense of

    A) isolation.   B) inferiority.   C) mistrust.   D) guilt.

Answer: A

Explanation: A) A young adult who does not seek out close relationships with other people may develop a sense of isolation. Having successful relationships creates the positive state of intimacy.

Page Ref: 50

48) If individuals do not grow during the generativity stage, a sense of stagnation and interpersonal impoverishment develops. This leads to

A) confusion.

B) doubt.

C) self-absorption or self-indulgence.

D) intimacy or competition.

Answer: C

Explanation: C) Generativity refers to the interest in establishing and guiding the next generation. Usually, this comes through raising one's own children. During this stage people should continue to grow; if they don't, a sense of stagnation and interpersonal impoverishment develops, leading to self-absorption or self-indulgence.

Page Ref: 50

49) A student is caught walking about during a test, a behavior that breaks a class rule. Another student in Piaget's autonomous stage of morality is likely to react in which of the following ways?

A) Protect the offender, regardless of circumstances.

B) View any punishment as deserved.

C) Listen to the offender's rationale for the behavior.

D) Side with the teacher's decision.

Answer: C

Explanation: C) As children progress from Piaget's heteronomous morality stage to the autonomous morality stage, they become less likely to judge behavior absolutely while giving more consideration to the circumstances that may have prompted the change. Accordingly, a child in the autonomous morality stage would be likely to give the offender a chance to defend herself or himself before deciding on the consequences.

Page Ref: 52

50) According to Piaget, between the ages of six and ten, children believe that the rules of a game

A) can be altered with the consent of all players.

B) are set by a higher authority and cannot be altered.

C) can be altered by older children in the group, but not by younger ones.

D) are flexible.

Answer: B

Explanation: B) According to Piaget, between the ages of 6 and 10, children believe that rules are set by a higher authority and cannot be altered. Piaget labeled this first stage of moral development "heteronomous morality."

Page Ref: 52

51) According to Piaget, children in the heteronomous stage of moral development believe that rules

    A) are relative.   B) and punishment are unrelated.

    C) bring about ethical challenges.   D) bring automatic punishment.

Answer: D

Explanation: D) Children in the heteronomous stage believe that rule–breaking brings automatic punishment. This occurs during the first stage of moral development (heteronomous morality). Justice is seen as automatic and people who are bad will eventually get theirs.

Page Ref: 52

52) Kohlberg studied individuals' responses to hypothetical problems called

    A) moral dilemmas.   B) ethical challenges.

    C) behavioral incidents.   D) clinical ambiguities.

Answer: A

Explanation: A) Kohlberg tested individuals' responses to a series of hypothetical situations called moral dilemmas. Based on this work, he proposed that people pass through a series of six stages of moral reasoning.

Page Ref: 53

53) Children at the preconventional level of moral reasoning concentrate on

    A) respecting the laws of society.

    B) understanding the meaning of rules for a group.

    C) how to further their own interests and avoid being punished.

    D) how to adapt rules to fit the condition of their situations.

Answer: C

Explanation: C) According to Kohlberg, individuals at the preconventional level of moral reasoning concentrate on how to avoid being punished and further their own interests. This level is followed by conventional reasoning, which gives more consideration to the feelings of others.

Page Ref: 54

54) According to Kohlberg, for individuals operating at which level of moral development is morality defined in terms of cooperation with peers?

    A) postconventional   B) conventional

    C) preconventional   D) unconventional

Answer: B

Explanation: B) The conventional level of morality, according to Kohlberg, begins at Stage Three. This is the stage at which individuals have an unquestioning belief in the Golden Rule. Here, morality is defined in terms of cooperation with peers.

Page Ref: 54

55) One student sees another cheat on a test. The first student reasons that cheating is acceptable because the teacher wasn't looking. What level of moral reasoning is the student exhibiting?

    A) postconventional   B) conventional

    C) unconventional   D) preconventional

Answer: D

Explanation: D) The student is exhibiting preconventional moral reasoning. Such reasoning, representing the lowest of three levels, determines morality on the basis of the consequences—whether or not the person gets caught.

Page Ref: 54

56) The third grade teacher has told a group of students to go to the cabinet and take a box of crayons that they may use during the year. A student who is the last one in line is faced with the moral dilemma of whether to take several boxes, since no one is watching. The student makes the decision that it would not be proper because the rule did not allow for anyone to take more than one box. This behavior reflects which level of moral reasoning?

    A) preconventional   B) conventional

    C) nonconventional   D) postconventional

Answer: B

Explanation: B) The student is exhibiting conventional moral reasoning—adherence to following rules and "doing what is right." Conventional reasoning, as contrasted with the earlier preconventional level, places greater emphasis on societal "law and order."

Page Ref: 54

57) A student does not really think about plagiarism as a true injustice to her fellow students. She believes it's acceptable because her close friends say that plagiarism is just a survival skill that everybody uses. Applying Kohlberg's theory of moral development, what level best identifies the student's judgment about plagiarism?

    A) preconventional (stage 1 or 2)   B) conventional (stage 3 or 4)

    C) postconventional (stage 5 or 6)   D) neoconventional (stage 4 or 5)

Answer: B

Explanation: B) Conventional moral judgment involves conforming to the beliefs of a group or person.

Page Ref: 54

58) A criticism of both Piaget's and Kohlberg's work is that they did not observe that young children can often reason about moral situations in

A) more sophisticated ways than than the theories would suggest.

B) abstract terms.

C) ways similar to adults.

D) hypothetical dilemmas.

Answer: A

Explanation: A) A criticism of Kohlberg's work is that young children can often reason about moral situations in more sophisticated ways than the theory would suggest. For example, researchers have found that although young children often consider consequences to be more important than intentions when evaluating conduct, under certain circumstances young children use intentions to judge the behavior of others. Six to ten year–olds have also been shown to make distinctions between rules that parents are justified in making and enforcing, and rules that are under personal or peer jurisdiction. It has also been suggested that young children make a distinction between moral rules such as lying and stealing that are based on principles of justice, and social–conventional rules, which are based on social consensus and etiquette.

Page Ref: 57

59) Two limitations of Kohlberg's theory are that it

A) deals only with actual behavior, and it involves only males.

B) addresses only individual rights, and focuses only on females.

C) deals with moral reasoning rather than actual behavior, and involves only males.

D) focuses on moral reasoning rather than moral behavior, and, because of its complexity, is not so predictable.

Answer: D

Explanation: D) One limitation of Kohlberg's theory is that it deals with moral reasoning rather than with actual behavior. That leads to a second limitation—moral behavior is very complex and not nearly as predictable as Kohlberg's stages suggest.

Page Ref: 58

True/False Questions

1) Development refers to how and why people grow, adapt, and change over the course of their lifetimes.

Answer: TRUE
Page Ref: 30

2) Most developmental psychologists believe that nature alone influences development.

Answer: FALSE
Page Ref: 30

3) Discontinuous development is a smooth and orderly progression.

Answer: FALSE
Page Ref: 31

4) According to Piaget, assimilation is the process of understanding a new object or event in terms of an existing scheme.

Answer: TRUE
Page Ref: 32

5) Piaget divided the cognitive development of children and adolescents into five stages: sensorimotor, preoperational, concrete operational, formal operational, and postoperational.

Answer: FALSE
Page Ref: 32

6) Piaget's theory of cognitive development represents constructivism, a view of cognitive development as a process in which people actively build systems of meaning and understandings of reality through their experiences and interactions.

Answer: TRUE
Page Ref: 33

7) Many of the changes in cognitive functioning described by Piaget are now known to take place earlier under certain circumstances.

Answer: TRUE
Page Ref: 31

8) Alternatives to Piagetian views of cognitive development include information–processing approaches, which are based on the idea that cognitive development is based on the internalization of acquired signs.

Answer: FALSE
Page Ref: 43

9) According to Vygotsky, people process information in ways similar to computers.

Answer: FALSE
Page Ref: 44

10) A Vygotskian approach to instruction emphasizes scaffolding, with students taking more and more responsibility for their own learning.

Answer: TRUE
Page Ref: 45

11) Erikson believed that during the stage of autonomy versus doubt, children have the dual desire to "hold on" and to "let go."

Answer: TRUE
Page Ref: 49

12) According to Erikson, elementary school students generally want to shock their parents, at the expense of parents' approval.

Answer: FALSE
Page Ref: 49

13) Piaget observed that at the first of two stages of moral development, children judge behavior as bad if it results in negative consequences, even if the actor's original intentions were good.

Answer: TRUE
Page Ref: 52

14) Individuals operating at the postconventional level of moral reasoning tend to decide what is moral according to whether or not they get caught doing the questionable behavior.

Answer: FALSE
Page Ref: 54

15) A study of adolescents found that moral reasoning is affected by context.

Answer: TRUE
Page Ref: 60

Short Answer Questions

1) The descriptive term that refers to how and why people grow, adapt, and change over their lifetimes.

Answer: development
Page Ref: 30

2) A set of principles and laws that suggests that, at a fairly early age, children are capable of thinking and acting like adults, given the proper experience and education.

Answer: continuous theory of development
Page Ref: 31

3) Theories that draw on inborn factors more than environmental influences, in explaining the sequence of changes in development.

Answer: discontinuous theories of development
Page Ref: 31

4) The patterns of behavior or thinking that children and adults use in dealing with objects in the world.

Answer: schemes
Page Ref: 32

5) The process of adjusting schemes in response to the environment by means of assimilation and accommodation.

Answer: adaptation
Page Ref: 32

6) The process of understanding a new object or event in terms of an existing scheme.

Answer: assimilation
Page Ref: 32

7) In Piagetian theory, the process of restoring balance between present understanding and new experiences.

Answer: equilibration
Page Ref: 33

8) In the sensorimotor stage of development, all infants have inborn behaviors that are described by this term.

Answer: reflexes
Page Ref: 33

9) This is the descriptive term used when infants understand that objects exist even if they cannot be seen.

Answer: object permanence
Page Ref: 34

10) During this stage children are no longer infants, and their language and concepts develop at incredible rates.

Answer: preoperational stage
Page Ref: 34

11) A term used to describe a characteristic of preoperational thinking observed when children focus on only one dimension of an object, such as height or length, but ignore others such as width.

Answer: centration
Page Ref: 35

12) The ability to change direction in one's thinking so that one can return to a starting point.

Answer: reversibility
Page Ref: 35

13) The kind of preoperational thought children show when they interpret events entirely in reference to themselves.

Answer: egocentric
Page Ref: 37

14) The Piagetian stage in which conservation abilities merge and develop.

Answer: concrete operations
Page Ref: 38

15) With this stage comes the ability to deal with potential or hypothetical situations; the form of a problem can now be seen as separate from the content.

Answer: formal operational stage
Page Ref: 39

16) Instruction based on student's physical and cognitive abilities, as well as their social and emotional needs (rather than just on their age alone) is called

Answer: developmentally appropriate education
Page Ref: 2

17) Vygotsky's view that development involves the internalization of signs so that the child can think and solve problems without the help of others.

Answer: self-regulation

Explanation:
Page Ref: 44

18) According to Vygotsky, this is a mechanism for turning shared knowledge into personal knowledge.

Answer: private speech
Page Ref: 44

19) During this stage, Erikson saw children as expanding their social worlds, as teachers and peers take on increasing importance.

Answer: industry vs. inferiority
Page Ref: 49

20) Erikson believed that during this psychosocial stage, the individual questions and redefines the psychosocial identity established during the earlier stages.

Answer: identity vs. role confusion
Page Ref: 49

21) Piaget's first stage of moral development that has been called the stage of moral realism or morality of constraint.

Answer: heteronomous
Page Ref: 52

22) The level of morality, according to Kohlberg, where moral behavior is defined in terms of cooperation with peers.

Answer: conventional
Page Ref: 54

23) The level of morality, according to Kohlberg, where moral behavior is defined in terms of self interest.

Answer: preconventional
Page Ref: 54

Essay Questions

1) The following are examples of Piaget's concept-equilibration. Analyze **two** of the following scenarios, identifying in each one:
   a) the source of disequilibrium,
   b) a change in skill or understanding (the accommodation taking place),
   c) the resulting new skill, concept, or level of understanding.

   Baby scenario: Baby Warren can get applesauce to his mouth with his hand, pretty efficiently. But now, he tries to eat with a spoon. He scoops up the applesauce successfully, but what goes to his mouth is the spoon handle; the applesauce goes onto his forehead. Later, after weeks of practice, he can eat successfully with the spoon.

   Preschool scenario: Emily sees some groups of numbers on a gravestone (1899–1950). She assimilates them (attempts to understand them based on what she already knows about numbers grouped that way). Then she looks perplexed and says, "But you can't really call them up, can you, if they're dead?" Her mom helps her out by explaining how dates are written.

   College scenario: As Ravi begins reading his textbook, he "knows" that in cognitive development we form our first operations in the "formal operations" stage. But now he reads that children first develop operations in the Concrete Operations stage. After some thought and re-reading, he learns the correct sequence.

   Answer: a) sources of disequilibrium: Warren's applesauce goes awry; Emily cannot reconcile being dead with having a phone number; Ravi finds that the textbook contradicts his "knowledge."
   b) accommodation: Warren adjusts his movements so that the food goes to his mouth; Emily learns that the numbers on the gravestones are dates, not phone numbers; Ravi learns about the emergence of Piaget's operations.
   c) new skill: Warren now has an eat-with-spoon scheme; next time Emily sees numbers on a gravestone, she will assimilate them to a dates-scheme, not to a phone-numbers scheme; Ravi's development-of-cognitive-operations-scheme has differentiated into a more complex, correct conceptualization
   Equilibration has moved each learner forward.
   Page Ref: 33

2) Describe four educational beliefs or practices that are grounded in the developmental ideas presented by Piaget.

   Answer: There are four main teaching implications drawn from Piaget's work. The first is the focus on the process of children's thinking, not just its products. The second is recognition of the crucial role of children's self-initiated, active involvement in learning activities. The third is a de-emphasis on practices aimed at making children adult-like in their thinking. And, the fourth is an acceptance of individual differences in developmental progress.
   Page Ref: 42

3) A teacher believes in discipline: students sit in neat rows of desks, one in front of the next. They are quiet and attentive during lectures; however, they do not ask questions or discuss ideas. After lectures, the teacher has students work independently on assignments. According to Lev Vygotsky, will this teaching style be effective? Give at least two reasons why it would or would not be.

Answer: According to Lev Vygotsky, this teaching style would not be effective. Vygotsky saw cooperative learning in which students of differing levels of ability are grouped together as most effective in promoting learning. Also, he emphasized scaffolding, with students taking more and more responsibility for their own learning through the use of private speech.

Page Ref: 45

4) Use Erikson's theory to draw a contrast between children of high school age and children of elementary school age. How do their day–to–day concerns differ?
For each of these age groups, describe a scenario in which a teacher's awareness of how Erikson's stages affect individuals might be beneficial to a student.

Answer: Both elementary and high school students are expanding their involvement with peers. But while the younger children are focused on measuring up in their abilities, adolescents are focused on finding an identity in the face of unsettling personal change. Teachers who are aware of the developmental changes in these periods can be more understanding, for instance, less likely to take students' egocentric behavior personally.

Page Ref: 49

5) Erik Erikson's theory describes the basic issues that individuals confront as they progress through life; however, he has been criticized about several of his ideas. What are some of these criticisms?

Answer: Erikson has been criticized because his theory is based more on his impressions of development than on scientific investigation. He does not explain how or why individuals progress from one stage to the next and, although he considered cultural differences in development, his theory is most representative of western, white males.

Page Ref: 50

6) Describe a moral dilemma, then explain how an individual might reason at each stage of Kohlberg's theory of moral development.

Answer: At a preconventional level, decisions are made to avoid punishment and to serve the self. At the conventional level, decisions are made to please others or to conform. At the postconventional level, decisions are made based on self–chosen ethical principles.

Page Ref: 53

7) Analyze the following scenarios from Kohlberg's point of view. For each scenario, identify the moral judgment as either preconventional or conventional. Explain why Kolhberg would classify them at the levels you select.

Seven–year–old–Adam scenario: Adam (7 yrs.) and Clarice (4 yrs.) are decorating the picture window for Halloween. Adam wishes to have total artistic control. He offers Clarice two pieces of candy if she will give up all participation in the decorating. Clarice thinks two pieces of candy sounds great! It's a deal. Adam decorates the whole window and then produces Clarice's payoff: 2 Smarties (not two rolls of Smarties—only two aspirin–sized candy pills). Adam sees the deal as fair.

In time, Clarice (being very young) forgets the deal and tampers with the decorations. Adam expresses outrage and righteous indignation, asserting that Clarice BROKE the deal! Classify Adam's level of moral reasoning.

Heidi's–grandfather scenario: Heidi lives in the mountains with her grandfather. Grandfather values the wholesome surroundings and feels the mountain life is all the education anyone could need. When relatives come from the city to take Heidi for schooling, he resists, arguing that she just doesn't need to learn the school subjects. But at last the city-aunt says, "But Grandfather, it's the LAW!" That settles it; Heidi is sent away with her grandfather's complete consent. Classify the moral judgment of Grandfather, when he changes his mind, accepting compulsory education.

Young–teen scenario: Mom insists on limiting junk food, based on nutritional considerations. Her young teenager asserts that the other kids all get unlimited junk food. Mom sticks to her position and puts fruit in the lunch bag. Young teen is outraged and accuses Mom of "setting your own standards!" The teenager believes that it is wrong to go against the group and follow your own standard.
Classify the moral judgment of the young teen.

Answer: As individuals develop from preconventional to conventional moral judgment, the tendency to base what's right on self–interest gives way to a view that what's right is what pleases an important person or group.

Seven–year–old Adam shows preconventional self–interest (Kohlberg Stage 2) in holding the younger child to the letter of the "deal." Heidi's–grandfather showed conventional morality when he believed that if it's the Law it must be right (Kohlberg Stage 4). The young–teen is basing moral judgment on the group's norm, believing her mother is wrong to adopt an independent standard.

Page Ref: 54

8) Dr. Lapovich, superintendent of a mid-size school district, walked into the faculty meeting on the first day of school with some apprehension. The state legislature had recently voted to make all public schools standards-based—a system in which all students must demonstrate competence in a variety of ways to graduate from high school.

As she began her address to the faculty, Dr. Lapovich sensed the apprehension in the room. "We have two years to become a standards-based school," she told her faculty. "This means we need to adopt the state Board of Education's Standards for Graduation plan."

A voice from the back of the room said, "I've been teaching in this district for 20 years. We've gone through these changes before. The way I teach now suits me fine and my students think so too." Dr. Lapovich recognized the speaker. He was Ansel Green, the 10th grade English teacher at the high school. Dr. Lapovich also noticed that many of Mr. Green's colleagues were nodding in agreement with his remarks. This was something she feared; some teachers were going to argue against the new standards.

A second voice came from the crowd, "I've talked with parents and they're concerned too. One of my student's parents complained that her daughter had special learning needs and that she would most likely have difficulties in passing the standards."

Dr. Lapovich politely reminded the faculty, "We have to think of the students first. We have to be able to say that we are doing everything we can to help students learn. If the first teaching method we try doesn't work, then we try another, then another; whatever it takes. Isn't that why we are here—to help students learn?"

One of the district's elementary teachers replied, "Don't you think we're removing some of the incentive for doing well by threatening them with possible failure? Might this not increase cheating if standards are too rigorous? And how will my students feel when some try hard but aren't successful? How will we explain to them that effort doesn't matter?" Dr. Lapovich sighed as she realized that this would be a very long year of change.

Consider some of the arguments made for and against standards-based education. Would cognitive development theorists (e.g., Piaget and Vygotsky), psychosocial developmental theorists (e.g., Erikson), and moral developmental theorists (e.g., Kohlberg) argue for or against this teaching-learning approach?

Answer: There are several possible avenues to pursue, both positive and negative, when considering how standards-based education might be viewed from a developmental perspective. Possible considerations might include, but not be limited to: 1) standards-based education might seem effective because all learners are to demonstrate competence; 2) standards-based education could be considered ineffective because it ignores students' individual needs, interests, and abilities.

Page Ref: 59

9) Below is a lesson plan on data collection and interpretation. Decide on a developmental level for which the lesson would be most appropriate. Using the cognitive, psychosocial, and moral developmental theories from the chapter, support your decision.

Lesson: Data Collection and Interpretation

1. Ask students to conduct a survey of teachers and parents, about whom they will support in an upcoming election (e.g., school, city council, state or national). Questions are to include a list of reasons why a candidate is supported.

2. Have students record the number of support votes a candidate receives and the rationale given for the support.

3. In groups, ask students to make interpretations about the results of the survey.

Candidate A		Candidate B		Candidate C	
X	healthy environment	X	pro–business	X	fewer taxes
X	healthy environment				
X	better education				

Answer: The lesson is most likely best suited for learners who need abstract ideas tied to the concrete, are self–regulated learners, can consider the views of others, have a sense of industry, and can consider group needs over individual needs.

Page Ref: 59

Chapter 3   Development During Childhood and Adolescence

Multiple–Choice Questions

1) An example of a gross motor activity is

    A) zipping a coat.   B) reading a book.

    C) writing a letter to a friend.   D) climbing a tree.

Answer: D

Explanation: D) An example of a gross motor activity would be climbing a tree. This activity depends upon large muscle development as opposed to fine motor activities, using smaller muscles, such as zipping, reading, and writing.

Page Ref: 67

2) Which of the following reflects small muscle development?

    A) paddling a canoe   B) taking a leisurely walk on the beach

    C) typing words on a keyboard   D) raking the leaves

Answer: C

Explanation: C) Fine motor or small muscle development would be needed for typing words on a keyboard. Large or gross muscle development, by comparison, would be needed for running and walking.

Page Ref: 67

3) The research on emergent literacy asserts that very young children

    A) are receptive to reading when taught formal rules of writing.

    B) have more knowledge about reading than previously thought.

    C) are not able to grasp that reading goes from left to right.

    D) normally develop basic language skills after entering school.

Answer: B

Explanation: B) Research on emergent literacy has suggested that young children have much more knowledge about reading than has been thought in the past. Specifically, they know many of the letters, are familiar with story plots, and can predict what will happen next in simple stories. They can, therefore, benefit from exposure to reading in preschool.

Page Ref: 70

4) By the time children start school, they have:
   1) mastered most of the grammatical rules of language.
   2) developed preoperational thought.
   3) mastered vocabulary consisting of thousands of work.
   4) a vocabulary consisting on 900 words.

   Which of the preceding statements are true?

   A) 1, 2 and 4 (not 3)   B) 1 and 4 (not 2 and 3)

   C) 1, 2 and 3 (not 4)   D) 2 and 3 (not 1 and 4)

   Answer: C

   Explanation: C) During preschool years, children's vocabulary increases along with their
                    knowledge of the rules of spoken language. By the time they start school,
                    children have mastered most of the grammatical rules of language and their
                    vocabulary consists of thousands of words. They have reached Piaget's
                    preoperational stage.
   Page Ref: 70

5) Research has shown that before entering school many young children have learned that print
   is arranged from left to right, and that books are read from front to back. This knowledge
   about reading is know as

   A) whole language.   B) associative play.

   C) emergent literacy.   D) word attack skills.

   Answer: C

   Explanation: C) Emergent literacy refers to awareness of reading as a system of communication,
                    not the acquisition of specific reading skills.
   Page Ref: 70

6) Regarding reading and language development in preschoolers, researchers believe

   A) a child's knowledge about reading does not contribute to success in formal reading
      instruction.

   B) whole language is the best way to teach formal learning.

   C) preschoolers often play with language by experimenting with its patterns and rules.

   D) there is no relationship between children learning to read and being read to at an early
      age.

   Answer: C

   Explanation: C) Preschoolers often plan with language or experiment with its patterns and rules.
                    Frequently, this experimentation involves changing sounds, patterns, and
                    meanings. Children often rearrange word sounds to create new words, rhymes,
                    and funny sentences.
   Page Ref: 70

7) A speaker at a conference concludes a speech by saying, "And, as the research shows, whole language approaches are clearly superior to phonics for developing reading skills." How should you react?

   A) Disagree; research findings appear to show benefits for both.

   B) Disagree; research findings have shown that neither whole language nor phonics approaches are effective.

   C) Disagree; research findings have shown that phonics is clearly superior to whole language approaches.

   D) Agree; the speaker is essentially correct.

Answer: A

Explanation: A) Many students appear to perform best if taught word attack skills using a phonics approach in a meaningful (whole language) context.

Page Ref: 71

8) Which of the following statements about young children and writing are true?
   1) Children's writing follows a developmental sequence.
   2) Preschool children cannot see features that distinguish one letter from another (they see "c" as "o", and "D" as "O").
   3) Children's writing emerges out of early scribbles and at first is spread randomly across a page.
   4) Letter reversal for young children is not an indication of reading or writing problems if other development in these areas is normal.

   A) 2, 3 and 4 (not 1)   B) 1, 3 and 4 (not 2)

   C) 1 and 3 (not 2 and 4)   D) 1, 2, 3 and 4

Answer: B

Explanation: B) Children's writing follows a developmental sequence. It emerges out of early scribbles and at first is spread randomly across a page. This reflects an incomplete understanding of word boundaries as well as an inability to mentally create a line for placing letters. They do perceive distinctive features of letters.

Page Ref: 72

9) According to Erikson, children's socioemotional development involves resolving the personality crisis of initiative versus guilt (understanding the permissible). Early educators can facilitate by giving children all of the following **EXCEPT**

   A) opportunities to take initiative.   B) challenges.

   C) opportunities to succeed.   D) punishment.

Answer: D

Explanation: D) Preschool children's successful resolution to the personality crisis of initiative versus guilt can be encouraged by early educators who give children opportunities to take initiative, to be challenged, and to succeed.

Page Ref: 73

10) Erikson once used the word "exhilarated" to describe the preschool (stage 3) child. This description is consistent with the text's statement that, when the child resolves the crisis of initiative vs. guilt, the outcome is a sense of

    A) ambition.   B) identity.   C) integrity.   D) authority.

Answer: A

Explanation: A) Erikson's theory of personal and social development suggests that during early childhood children must resolve the personality crisis of initiative versus guilt. The child's successful resolution of this stage results in a sense of initiative and ambition.

Page Ref: 73

11) A nursery school teacher tells a mother that her child engages in parallel play. The mother might see her child frequently playing

    A) by acting out different social roles with others.

    B) along side of others but with little interaction.

    C) in competitive games in which only one child can be the winner.

    D) by modeling play behaviors observed in older children.

Answer: B

Explanation: B) Parallel play involves children who are engaged in the same activity side by side but with very little interaction or mutual influence.

Page Ref: 74

12) Solitary play is often carried out

    A) by modeling peers' behavior.

    B) by those children who have the most secure relationships with their parents.

    C) with toys.

    D) as children begin to engage in more complex pretend-play.

Answer: C

Explanation: C) Solitary play is play that occurs alone, often with toys, and independent of what other children are doing.

Page Ref: 74

13) Play that is much like parallel play, but with increased levels of interaction in the form of sharing and turn-taking, is

    A) cooperative play.   B) solitary play.

    C) parallel play.   D) associative play.

Answer: D

Explanation: D) Associative play is much like parallel play, but with increased levels of interaction in the form of sharing, turn-taking, and general interest in what others are doing.

Page Ref: 74

14) Prosocial behavior is promoted by all of the following **EXCEPT**

   A) parents who stress the consequences of the child's behavior for others.

   B) contact with adults who let children know that aggression is unacceptable and that there are alternatives.

   C) contact with parents who show concern for others.

   D) parents who maintain a cool, businesslike relationship with their children.

   Answer: D

   Explanation: D) Prosocial behaviors are positive actions voluntarily taken toward others. Such actions show caring, empathy, and warmth. prosocial behaviors are promoted by parents who stress consequences of behavior and by contact with good adult role models.

   Page Ref: 75

15) Day-care programs exist primarily to

   A) teach readiness skills for entering school.

   B) teach remedial skills for entering school.

   C) provide an alternative to excessively academic kindergartens.

   D) provide child-care services for working parents.

   Answer: D

   Explanation: D) Day-care programs exist primarily to provide child-care services for working parents. Typically such programs serve lower income families and provide less academic instruction than do nursery schools.

   Page Ref: 75

16) A key concept in preschool education is readiness training, in which children learn skills that are supposed to prepare them for formal instruction. Which of the following best describes these readiness skills?
   1) follow directions;
   2) cooperate with others;
   3) stick to a task;
   4) display good manners.

   A) 1 and 3 (not 2 and 4)   B) 2, 3 and 4 (not 1)

   C) 1 and 2 (not 3 and 4)   D) 1, 2, 3 and 4

   Answer: D

   Explanation: D) A key concept in nursery school education is readiness training. Students learn skills that are supposed to prepare them for formal instruction later, such as how to follow directions, stick to a task, cooperate with others, and display less structured activities, ranging from art projects to group discussion to unstructured indoor and outdoor play.

   Page Ref: 76

17) Head Start was part of President Lyndon Johnson's war on poverty, an attempt to break the cycle of poverty. This is an example of what kind of program?

    A) program for disadvantaged elementary students

    B) Montessori

    C) readiness program for the middle-class

    D) compensatory preschool

Answer: D

Explanation: D) Head Start is an example of a compensatory preschool program. These are programs offered to disadvantaged children to increase school readiness.

Page Ref: 76

18) Evaluations of the Head Start program indicate that it

    A) is a large and costly failure since disadvantaged children show no academic gains.

    B) is successful since disadvantaged children who attend such programs do better throughout their schooling than those who do not participate in the program.

    C) is unsuccessful because positive effects on children have no measurable impact beyond first grade.

    D) cannot be deemed either successful or unsuccessful since no scientifically valid studies on children attending Head Start have been performed.

Answer: B

Explanation: B) Evaluations of Head Start indicate that it is successful since disadvantaged children who attend such programs do better than those who do not. However, preschool programs are much more effective when followed up by high-quality programs in the early elementary grades.

Page Ref: 77

19) When researchers assert the need for early intervention programs for children who are at the greatest risk for school failure, they are looking at beginning the process as early as the age of

    A) six months.   B) one year.   C) three years.   D) four years.

Answer: A

Explanation: A) Although most compensatory preschool programs, including Head Start, have begun working with children and their parents when the children are three or four, there are numerous early intervention programs that work with children as young as six months.

Page Ref: 77

20) Regarding a discussion of kindergarten programs, which of the following statements are true?
   1) The original purpose of kindergarten was to prepare students for formal instruction by encouraging development of their social skills;
   2) The kindergarten has increasingly focused on academics.
   3) Full-day kindergarten is offered only to children of a lower socioeconomic status.

   A) 1 and 2 (not 3)   B) 1 and 3 (not 2)

   C) 2 and 3 (not 1)   D) 1, 2 and 3

   Answer: A

   Explanation: A) The original purpose of kindergarten was to prepare students for formal instruction by encouraging the development of their social skills. But in recent years this function has increasingly been taken on by nursery schools and preschool programs. Kindergarten has increasingly focused on academics, emphasizing pre-reading and pre-mathematical skills, as well as behaviors that are appropriate in school (such as raising hands, lining up, and taking turns).

   Page Ref: 77

21) Research on kindergarten indicates that students of a lower socioeconomic status gain more from

   A) half-day programs.   B) full-day programs.

   C) licensed preschool programs only.   D) loosely structure programs.

   Answer: B

   Explanation: B) Research on kindergarten indicates that students of a lower socioeconomic status gain more from well-structured, full-day kindergarten programs than from half-day programs.

   Page Ref: 78

22) Which of the following orientations would be most consistent with the idea of developmentally appropriate practice for children in the primary grades?

   A) Allow for considerable allowance for individualized learning activities.

   B) Use teacher-directed instruction supplemented with workbooks.

   C) Select teaching strategies that ensure all children receive identical instruction.

   D) Adhere to a standard pacing schedule and curriculum.

   Answer: A

   Explanation: A) Consistent with the idea of developmentally appropriate practice would be considerable allowance for individualized learning activities. The philosophy supported is that each learner is unique and, regardless of chronological age, has different needs and levels of readiness from his/her peers. The curriculum must, therefore, be responsive by accommodating individual differences.

   Page Ref: 78

23) Developmentally appropriate practice, which allows learners to move at their own pace in acquiring important skills, is instruction based on students' individual characteristics and needs,

    A) as well as the teacher's interests.   B) not their ages.

    C) not personal likes and dislikes.   D) as well as their biological age.

Answer: B

Explanation: B) In developmentally appropriate practice, each child is viewed as a unique person with an individual pattern and timing of growth. Curriculum and instruction are responsive to individual differences in ability and interests. Different levels of ability, development, and learning styles are expected, accepted, and used to design curriculum.

Page Ref: 78

24) By the end of fifth grade, a distinguishing characteristic of girls in comparison to boys is that they are

    A) shorter.   B) more ambitious.

    C) heavier.   D) weaker.

Answer: C

Explanation: C) By the end of the fifth grade, the typical female is heavier than the typical male. Females start puberty about a year and half earlier than males and thus begin the associated growth spurt earlier (usually toward the end of fourth grade).

Page Ref: 79

25) Between the ages of five and seven, children experience significant changes in a period of transition from

    A) a phase of gradual development to one of rapid growth.

    B) a shift from mental development to social development.

    C) the stage of sensorimotor to the stage of preoperational thought.

    D) the stage of preoperational thought to the concrete operational stage.

Answer: D

Explanation: D) Between the ages of five and seven, children's thought processes undergo significant changes. This is a period of transition from the stage of preoperational thought to a stage of concrete operations.

Page Ref: 79

26) Elementary students have developed ideas about their strengths and weaknesses. Their perception of these qualities is referred to as

A) decentered thought.

B) self-concept.

C) self-actualization.

D) self-absorption.

Answer: B

Explanation: B) An individual's perception of his/her own strengths and weaknesses is called self-esteem. Self-esteem has important implications for personal and social development, and is influenced by experiences at home and at school.

Page Ref: 81

27) Multidimensional classrooms are intended to

A) give top students the opportunity to experience cultural activities.

B) give top students the opportunity to take part in unique field trip experiences.

C) build self-concept by providing alternative ways to succeed.

D) build self-concept by providing enrichment activities.

Answer: C

Explanation: C) Multidimensional classrooms are specifically intended to build self-concept for providing alternative ways to succeed. In contrast, unidimensional classrooms establish one way of doing things and one standard of success.

Page Ref: 81

28) A child's experiences in the primary grades can contribute to her or his sense of accomplishment, if that child has developed trust during infancy, autonomy during the early years, and

A) initiative during the preschool years.

B) a sense of identity during the preschool years.

C) concrete operations by age five.

D) has attended transitional first grade.

Answer: A

Explanation: A) Assuming that a child has developed trust during infancy, autonomy during the early years, and initiative during the preschool years, the child's experiences in the primary grades can contribute to her or his sense of industry and accomplishment. During this stage, children start trying to prove that they are grown up; in fact, this is often described as the "I-can-do-it-myself" stage.

Page Ref: 82

29) In research on peer acceptance, an individual who is frequently named as someone who is liked but also frequently named as someone who is disliked is called

    A) rejected.   B) controversial.   C) neglected.   D) average.

Answer: B

Explanation: B) Status among peers is typically studied with respect to specific categories of acceptance. One of these is controversial children, who are frequently named as someone who is liked but also frequently named as someone who is disliked.

Page Ref: 82

30) What term describes children who are neither frequently named as someone who is liked, nor someone who is disliked?

    A) popular children   B) rejected children

    C) neglected children   D) controversial children

Answer: C

Explanation: C) Neglected children are neither frequently named as someone who is liked nor someone who is disliked.

Page Ref: 82

31) Which of the following growth patterns would a sixth grade teacher expect to observe?

    A) Girls will be ready for a major growth spurt.

    B) Boys' growth spurt will have peaked.

    C) Late-maturing boys have caught up to the early-maturing boys.

    D) Girls will be closer to reaching puberty than boys.

Answer: D

Explanation: D) They should expect to observe that females will reach puberty before males. Females typically begin the growth spurt associated with puberty by the end of the fourth grade or beginning of fifth grade. For males, the spurt is likely to start in sixth grade.

Page Ref: 83

32) Which of the following best describes the sequence of events at puberty?

    A) From individual to individual, the beginning of pubertal changes can vary by as much as six years.

    B) The timing of changes at puberty is generally the same for each person.

    C) Females tend to begin pubertal change two years later than males.

    D) The order in which changes take place is a largely individual variable.

Answer: A

Explanation: A) Although the sequence of events at puberty is generally the same for each person, the timing and the rate at which they occur vary widely.

Page Ref: 83

33) In Piaget's theory, adolescence is the stage of transition from the use of concrete operations to the application of formal operations in reasoning. At this time, adolescents

    A) wrestle with concepts, but only those that are part of their own experience.

    B) shy away from exchange and contradiction of ideas with peers.

    C) begin to be aware of the limitations of their thinking.

    D) experience a period of intellectual stability.

Answer: C

Explanation: C) In Piaget's theory of cognitive development, adolescence is the stage of transition from the use of concrete operations to the application of formal operations in reasoning. Adolescents begin to be aware of the limitations of their thinking. They wrestle with concepts that are removed from their own experience.

Page Ref: 84

34) Which of the following strategies would **NOT** be recommended for developing adolescent students' hypothetical–deductive reasoning skills?

    A) timed learning tasks   B) cooperative learning

    C) self–critiques of work   D) arguing both sides of an issue

Answer: A

Explanation: A) Timed learning tasks would not be helpful to the development of hypothetical–deductive reasoning. Students need time to absorb ideas and to use formal thought patterns. Other good strategies would be cooperative learning, self–critiques, and arguing both sides of an issue.

Page Ref: 85

35) One thing that a teacher might do to promote students' hypothetical–deductive reasoning is to

    A) have students fill out a worksheet.

    B) assign labwork in which students follow specific instructions from a manual.

    C) ask students to memorize.

    D) have students defend their opinions.

Answer: D

Explanation: D) Hypothetical–deductive reasoning is one of the characteristics that marks the development of formal operational thinking, which emerges by the time learners are about 12 years old. A teacher can have students discuss ideas, purposefully picking specific opposing positions.

Page Ref: 85

36) Which of the following statements are true concerning the implications of hypothetical–deductive reasoning for educational practice?
1) Students who have not yet attained formal operational thought may need more support for planning complex tasks;
2) When introducing new information, particularly involving abstract concepts and theories, allow students enough time to absorb the ideas and to use formal thought patterns;
3) Encourage students to state principles and ideas in their own words and to search for the meaning behind abstract ideas;
4) Never pair students who can plan with those who need support.

A) 2 and 3 (not 1 and 4)   B) 2, 3 and 4 (not 1)

C) 1, 2 and 3 (not 4)   D) 1, 3 and 4 (not 2)

Answer: C

Explanation: C) The following guidelines should be considered when educational practice is in place using hypothetical–deductive reasoning:
1) When introducing new information, particularly involving abstract concepts and theories, allow students enough time to absorb the ideas and to use formal thought patterns. Begin with more familiar examples and encourage them to apply hypothetical–deductive reasoning;
2) Students who have not yet attained formal operational thought may need more support for planning complex tasks. Pairing children who can plan with those who need support is one way of handling the situation;
3) Encourage students to state principles and ideas in their own words and to search for the meaning behind abstract ideas and theories; and
4) Incorporate a variety of activities that promote the use of hypothetical deductive thinking.

Page Ref: 85

37) Students' relationships with teachers go from being easily accepting and dependent to becoming more complex during the

A) lower elementary years.   B) kindergarten years.

C) nursery school years.   D) upper elementary years.

Answer: D

Explanation: D) The middle school years often bring changes in the relationship between children and their teachers. In primary school, children easily accept and depend on teachers. During the upper elementary years, this relationship becomes more complex. Sometimes students will tell teachers personal information they would not tell their parents. Some preadolescents even choose teachers as role models.

Page Ref: 86

38) What is the term used to describe the tendency to think about what is going on in one's own mind and to study oneself, in early adolescence?

    A) reflectivity   B) deduction   C) foreclosure   D) diffusion

Answer: A

Explanation: A) One of the first signs of early adolescence is the appearance of reflectivity, the tendency to think about what is going on in one's own mind, and to study oneself.

Page Ref: 86

39) Which of Marcia's identity status levels describes an adolescent who experiments with occupational and ideological choices, but has not yet made definite commitments?

    A) diffusion   B) autonomy   C) foreclosure   D) moratorium

Answer: D

Explanation: D) Moratorium occurs when adolescents are exploring roles and values, but have not yet made the commitments that would define an identity.

Page Ref: 87

40) The identity status that signifies a state of identity consolidation is

    A) diffusion.   B) foreclosure.   C) achievement.   D) moratorium.

Answer: C

Explanation: C) Marcia's achievement status signifies a state of identity consolidation in which adolescents have made their own decisions.

Page Ref: 87

41) Which of Marcia's Identity Status levels is associated with the highest degree of anxiety?

    A) identity achievement status   B) identity diffusion status

    C) moratorium status   D) foreclosure status

Answer: C

Explanation: C) The category of moratorium is reserved for those who have begun to experiment with occupational and ideological choices, but who have not yet made definitive commitments to either. These individuals are directly in the midst of an identity crisis and are currently examining alternate life choices. Levels of anxiety tend to be highest for adolescents with a moratorium status and lowest for those in foreclosure.

Page Ref: 87

42) Adolescents attempt to develop a sense of identity by

   A) ignoring any indications by others that they are being viewed negatively.

   B) focusing on their present experiences, without much concern about past or future.

   C) hiding feelings that are not complimentary toward another person.

   D) trying out a variety of roles to test their fit.

Answer: D

Explanation: D) Adolescents need, according to Slavin, to develop a sense of ego–identity by trying out a variety of roles to test their fit. Conflicts that arise during this process are identity diffusion (failing to develop a clear sense of identity) and identity foreclosure (premature acceptance of an identity).

Page Ref: 88

43) Adolescents seek to share their inner feelings most often with

   A) parents more than peers.   B) popular peers.

   C) close friends.   D) school teachers.

Answer: C

Explanation: C) During adolescence the capacity for mutual understanding and the knowledge that others are unique individuals with their own feelings contribute to an increase in self-disclosure, intimacy, and loyalty among friends. Early adolescents seeking independence of parents look increasingly to peers for security and social support.

Page Ref: 89

44) Emotional problems related to the physical, cognitive, and social development of upper elementary learners are

   A) rare.

   B) common.

   C) greater among boys than girls.

   D) the basis of this group's pervasive unhappiness.

Answer: B

Explanation: B) Emotional problems related to the physical, cognitive, and social development of upper elementary children are common. Though preadolescents are generally happy and optimistic, they also have many fears, such as not being accepted into a peer group.

Page Ref: 89

45) Which of the following correctly describes the substance use of contemporary adolescents, as they complete high school?

   A) About 1/3 drink alcoholic beverages.

   B) Eighty percent drink alcoholic beverages.

   C) Most have tried marijuana.

   D) Fewer than 10% have tried marijuana.

Answer: B

Explanation: B) Eighty percent of high school seniors drink alcoholic beverages.
Page Ref: 90

46) Pregnancy and childbirth are major concerns for all groups of female adolescents, but particularly among those from

   A) white middle-class families.

   B) middle-class families.

   C) lower-income families.

   D) upper-middle class families in rural communities.

Answer: C

Explanation: C) Pregnancy and childbirth are increasing among all groups of female adolescents, but particularly among those from lower income homes. Just as adolescent males often engage in delinquent behavior to try to establish their independence from adult control, adolescent females often engage in sex and in many cases have children to force the world to see them as adults. Since early childbearing makes it difficult for adolescent females to continue their schooling or obtain jobs, it is a primary cause of the continuation of the cycle of poverty into which many adolescent mothers were themselves born.
Page Ref: 90

47) Delinquency in adolescence is overwhelmingly

   A) an individual phenomenon.

   B) a group phenomenon.

   C) one of the least dangerous problems of adolescence.

   D) more common among females than males.

Answer: B

Explanation: B) Delinquency in adolescence is overwhelmingly a group phenomenon; most delinquent acts are done in groups or with the active support of a delinquent subgroup.
Page Ref: 90

48) According to your text author, which of the following problems is still very rare during adolescents today?

    A) emotional disorders   B) drug use

    C) delinquency   D) symptoms of AIDS

Answer: D

Explanation: D) AIDS, though a growing concern, presently affects fewer adolescents than do problems associated with drugs, delinquency, and emotional disorders. Only time will tell how many adolescents actually have AIDS, since it may take several years for symptoms to develop.

Page Ref: 91

49) During adolescence people begin to explore their

    A) sexual identity.   B) environmental ecology.

    C) academic integrity.   D) civic orientation.

Answer: A

Explanation: A) It is during adolescence that people begin to explore their sexual identity, including young people who begin to identify with a gay or lesbian orientation.

Page Ref: 91

True/False Questions

1) Large muscle development is also referred to as fine motor development.

Answer: FALSE
Page Ref: 67

2) In addition to there being individual differences in the rates at which children acquire language abilities, the sequence of accomplishments is also different for all children.

Answer: FALSE
Page Ref: 69

3) The quality of day care services provided to disadvantaged children is better than the quality of day care available to middle-class children .

Answer: FALSE
Page Ref: 75

4) In recent years, kindergarten has increasingly focused on academics.

Answer: TRUE
Page Ref: 77

5) Research on kindergarten indicates that students of lower socioeconomic status gain less from full–day programs.

Answer: FALSE
Page Ref: 78

6) With developmentally appropriate practice, children are allowed to move at their own pace in acquiring important skills including those of reading, math, art, science, music, and health.

Answer: TRUE
Page Ref: 78

7) The period of transition from the stage of preoperational thought to the stage of concrete operations allows children to do mentally what previously was done emotionally.

Answer: FALSE
Page Ref: 79

8) Children's self–concept and self–esteem are strongly influenced by experiences at home, school, and with peers.

Answer: TRUE
Page Ref: 81

9) Scores on intelligence tests obtained over several years from the same individual fluctuate most during the period from 12 to 15 years of age.

Answer: TRUE
Page Ref: 84

10) Hypothetical–deductive reasoning is one of the characteristics that marks the development of concrete operational thinking.

Answer: FALSE
Page Ref: 84

11) Using the developing intellectual skills that permit them to consider possibilities, adolescents are prone to be satisfied with themselves.

Answer: FALSE
Page Ref: 84

12) Eighty percent of high school seniors drink alcohol.

Answer: TRUE
Page Ref: 90

Short Answer Questions

1) The idea that the process of reading begins well before formal schooling is supported by research on this type of literacy.

   Answer: emergent
   Page Ref: 70

2) The reference to a broad range of teaching practices that attempt to move away from teaching reading as a set of discrete skills.

   Answer: whole language
   Page Ref: 73

3) Voluntary actions toward others such as caring, sharing, comforting, and cooperation are referenced by these types of behaviors.

   Answer: prosocial
   Page Ref: 73

4) Play that occurs alone, often with toys, and independent of what other children are doing.

   Answer: solitary
   Page Ref: 74

5) The type of play that involves children engaged in the same activity side-by-side, but with very little interaction or mutual influence.

   Answer: parallel
   Page Ref: 74

6) The type of play that involves increased levels of interaction, relative to parallel play, in the form of sharing, turn-taking, and general interest in what others are doing.

   Answer: associative
   Page Ref: 74

7) A key concept in preschool education whereby students learn skills that are supposed to prepare them for later formal instruction.

   Answer: readiness training
   Page Ref: 76

8) The compensatory preschool program that was started in 1965 to increase school readiness.

   Answer: Head Start
   Page Ref: 76

9) A general term used to describe compensatory preschool programs that work with children and their parents when the children are very young.

Answer: early intervention
Page Ref: 77

10) This term refers to how individuals evaluate their skills and abilities.

Answer: self esteem
Page Ref: 81

11) A term used to describe children who are those named most often by their peers as being someone they like, and least often as someone they dislike.

Answer: popular
Page Ref: 82

12) A series of physiological changes that render the immature organism capable of reproduction.

Answer: puberty
Page Ref: 83

13) One of the characteristics that marks the development of the kind of operational thinking that emerges by the time students are about 12 years old.

Answer: hypothetical-deductive reasoning, or another characteristic of formal operational thought.
Page Ref: 84

14) This is the tendency to analyze oneself and one's own thoughts.

Answer: reflectivity
Page Ref: 86

15) An adolescent's adoption of a role, when it is taken on prematurely, to escape conflict.

Answer: identity foreclosure
Page Ref: 87

16) The term used to describe the adolescent's inability to develop a clear sense of self.

Answer: identity diffusion
Page Ref: 87

17) This category is reserved for those who have begun to experiment with occupational and ideological choices, but who have not yet made definitive commitments.

Answer: moratorium
Page Ref: 87

18) The state of identity in which the individual is convinced that decisions concerning occupation and ideology were autonomously and freely made.

Answer: identity achievement
Page Ref: 87

19) An area of adolescent exploration that may lead to distress for parents and tension with peer groups.

Answer: sexual identity
Page Ref: 91

Essay Questions

1) Reading to young children before they can do so for themselves is important, according to most educators. What types of differences exist between children who have been exposed to print prior to entering school and those who have not?

Answer: Research on emergent literacy shows that children who have been read to prior to entering school have learned that print ideas are arranged from left to right, that spaces between words have meaning, and that books are read from front to back. Many can interpret pictures, understand story plots, and recognize logos. If students have not been read to prior to school, they may still have ideas about print, but preschools or kindergartens can help them catch up with their reading-ready peers.

Page Ref: 70

2) An elementary school has a large population of non-English speaking students. The faculty at the school are divided about how to teach these students. Explain how you would approach this problem, using arguments presented in the text to support your position.

Answer: The debate over how to best educate students who do not speak English involves, for the most part, two sides. Proponents of bilingual education say that students should be taught in their native language and in English. In this way, they will not fall behind in their studies. Those opposed to bilingual education believe that students are to be assimilated into "American" culture and will best learn English if they are exposed to it more often.

Page Ref: 71

3) At your first job interview, the principal of the school says to you, "We follow the National Education Association's guidelines for developmentally appropriate practice here. What does developmentally appropriate practice mean to you?" How would you respond?

Answer: Each student is viewed as a unique person with an individual pattern and timing of growth. Curriculum and instruction are responsive to individual differences in ability and interests. Different levels of ability, development, and learning styles are expected, accepted, and used to design curriculum. Students are allowed to move at their own pace in acquiring important skills.

Page Ref: 78

4) You are planning curriculum for a preschool class. Describe an example of what you want the children to learn. Make your learning objective one that would be developmentally appropriate for preschoolers, but not for fourth grade children. Explain why your learning content fits the grade level.

Answer: Examples should include concrete tasks that allow preschoolers to explore properties of objects, but do not call for concrete operational conceptual abilities, such as class inclusion or conservation.

Page Ref: 78

5) Describe the major issue absorbing a child during Erikson's third stage of personal and social development. How does this stage differ from the previous one?
   Think about the whole child, entering the preschool years. This child has developed preoperational thought. Explore the connection between the young child's cognitive development, and personal/social development. Discuss how attaining preoperational thought might relate to the child's progression from Erikson's stage 2, to Erikson's stage 3. In other words, how could an advance from sensorimotor to preoperational thought processes, make it possible for a child to advance from the confines of *autonomy vs. shame*, to the broader horizons of *initiative vs. guilt*?

Answer: The sensorimotor child lives in the here–and–now. Accordingly, the act of *autonomy* is of the moment (e.g., climbing–into–the–carseat–myself), and *shame* is also of the moment (e.g., I am grabbing Spot's tail, and getting scolded).
   In contrast, the preoperational child uses words and other symbols in play and in thinking, manipulating ideas from the past ("let's play orphanage like we saw in 'Annie' "), and projecting thoughts into the future ("I'll get dressed all by myself and surprise Daddy"). The ability to think about future events enables a child to make plans, or, in Erikson's terms, take *initiative*, which reaches into the future. The ability to think about the past allows the preoperational child to experience *guilt*—a painful reflection on one's past behavior. Thus, advances in cognitive development as the child enters the preschool years, lay groundwork for progression from Erikson's stage 2, to stage 3.

Page Ref: 79

6) A teacher has taught second grade at an elementary school for ten years. Due to changes in staff, this year the teacher will teach sixth grade. What types of changes in students' development can be expected?

Answer: During second grade, students are beginning the concrete operational stage. They have developed complex thought, action, and social influence; however, they are largely egocentric since their worlds have been that of home, family, and some schooling. By sixth grade, they are entering formal operations and beginning to prove they are "grown–up." Students' powers of concentration are stronger, they can spend more time on chosen tasks, and often take pleasure in completing projects. They will also become more independent, cooperate in groups, perform in socially acceptable ways, and possess a concern for fair play.

Page Ref: 79

7) Most students in elementary schools are at the concrete operational stage of cognitive development. What types of classroom activities would be appropriate for these students? Give examples in several subject areas.

　　　Describe one activity that would be developmentally *inappropriate* for these students, and explain why you consider it inappropriate.

Answer: Science lessons should involve touching, building, manipulating, experimenting, and tasting. Social studies lessons should include field trips, guest speakers, role playing, and debates. Language arts and reading activities should include creating, imagining, acting out, and writing. Mathematics lessons should use concrete objects to show concepts, and allow students to manipulate objects to represent mathematical principles and operations.

Page Ref: 79

8) Describe a lesson that would be developmentally appropriate for formal operational learners but not for concrete operational learners. Provide several reasons why you believe the lesson to be appropriate.

Answer: There are numerous lessons appropriate for formal operational thinkers; however, they should expose students to complex problems and the exchange and contradiction of ideas, hypothetical or otherwise.

Page Ref: 84

9) Develop a list of activities that promote the use of hypothetical–deductive thinking.

Answer: Have students write a paper that requires debate between two arguments, pro and con, and a discussion of the evidence that supports the two perspectives. Have students participate in mock trials. Have students participate in cooperative activities that require planning and organization. Have students give testimonials that may be contradictory. Have students critique their own work.

Page Ref: 84

10) A teacher of high school social studies has planned an activity in which students will produce a commercial on video that attempts to sell one product over another. Students will be evaluated by their peers on how convincing their arguments are. Is this, according to Piaget, an appropriate activity for formal operational students? Why or why not?

Answer: Piaget asserted that experiences with complex problems, especially the exchange and contradiction of ideas with peers, facilitates formal operational thinking. Therefore, this lesson would be appropriate.

Page Ref: 85

11) Compare a child in the elementary grades to the same individual in high school, focusing on Erikson's stages of social and personal development. What changes has this student undergone?

    Briefly describe two examples of how the high school teacher's awareness of these types of changes might benefit students.

Answer: Changes include physiological, cognitive and social revolutions in the adolescent's life and search for identity. Teachers who recognize these changes can understand emotional reactions to rates of physical change, to new intellectual awareness and to changes in social priorities.

Page Ref: 81

12) Based on Erikson's work, James Marcia identified four identity statuses from in-depth interviews with adolescents. The statuses reflect the degree to which adolescents have made firm commitments to occupational, religious, and political values. Identify each status and give examples of the characteristics of that status.

Answer: The four statuses are foreclosure, identity diffusion, moratorium, and identity achievement. Individuals in a state of foreclosure have never experienced an identity crisis. Rather, they have prematurely established an identity on the basis of their parents' choice. Individuals experiencing identity diffusion have found neither an occupational direction nor an ideological commitment of any kind. Individuals experiencing moratorium have begun to experiment with occupational and ideological choices, but have not yet made definite commitments. Individuals experiencing identity achievement have made conscious, clear-cut decisions about occupation and ideology.

Page Ref: 87

13) Secondary educators need to be sensitive to problems that face adolescents. What are some of the problems, and how can teachers help adolescents who are experiencing them?

Answer: Some problems that face adolescents include emotional disorders, drug and alcohol abuse, and delinquency. First, secondary educators should be sensitive to the stresses faced by adolescents and should realize that emotional disturbances are common. Alerting the school counselor may be a way to help students with emotional problems or drug and alcohol abuse. To help delinquent students, secondary educators should try to develop programs in schools that recognize adolescents' needs for independence and self-esteem.

Page Ref: 90

14) Based on Erik Erikson's work, James Marcia created four categories of identity development during adolescence. Each category reflects the degree to which adolescents have made firm commitments to occupational, religious, and political values. Below are descriptions of four adolescents, each of whom fits one of Marcia's categories. Read the description of the adolescent, then label the individual as *identity foreclosure*, *identity diffusion*, *moratorium*, or *identity achievement*. Provide an explanation for your selection.

Adolescent	Analysis
Suzette comes from a family of teachers. Her parents dream is that she become a teacher. Suzette agrees that teaching is the only occupation that she can pursue since it would break her parents' hearts if she did anything else.	
Makki finds the political debate that his teachers, parents, and peers engage in to be boring. He couldn't care less who is in office and who is not.	
Caitlin is a good student, a strong athlete, and an excellent musician. She has ideas about a future career, but hasn't yet decided which of her many interests to pursue.	
After winning a contest to be a guest announcer at a large radio station, Tim decides that he will go to college to study broadcasting.	

Answer: Suzette is in a state of foreclosure, having established an identity on the basis of her parents' choices for her future and not her own. Makki is in a state of identity diffusion; he has no ideological commitment and has made no progress toward having one. Caitlin is in a state of moratorium. She has begun to experiment with occupational choices, but has not yet made one. Tim's behavior signifies a state of identity achievement; he has made his own conscious, clear-cut decision concerning his future occupation.

Page Ref: 87.

15) James Callahan is the assistant principal at DuBois Elementary School in a large urban school district. During his seven years at the school, he has come to know children from many different backgrounds and with many different types of problems. He has also seen many bright and successful students come and go.

One fall afternoon, Elaine Hersh, a high school guidance counselor from the school located a few blocks from DuBois Elementary, stops by James' office. She sits down and tells James that she has an idea. "James, you know I've been working with a group of kids from my school who have completed drug treatment programs. They are good kids and need some activities that will keep them off the streets. I would like to have them tutor some of your students. They could walk over during the day and read to your students or help them with homework. Or, they could help your teachers to grade papers or run other errands. What do you think of my idea?"

James' first reaction was negative. "I don't know, Elaine. We have problems with the high school students coming over here offering to sell drugs to our students already. Why would I want to invite trouble?"

"But these kids don't use drugs anymore," argued Elaine. "They are trying to put their lives back together and need to know that we trust them." James tells Elaine he will have to think about her idea.

From the information presented in this chapter, what advantages might exist for elementary children who are exposed to adolescents? What disadvantages might exist? What advantages might exist for adolescents who work with children? What disadvantages might exist? If you were James Callahan, what would you do?

Answer: James Callahan might consider that elementary students interacting with adolescents who are drug-free are exposed to good role models. They learn that drugs do not have to be a part of everyday life. However, if any of the adolescents returns to drugs, serious problems could arise. Parents might accuse James of bringing drug abusers into the school. On the other hand, Elaine makes a good point when she says that adolescents need healthy activities and encouragement as they learn to live without drugs. Working with elementary students might convince them that planning for the future and setting goals are important endeavors.

Page Ref: 90

Chapter 4   Student Diversity

Multiple-Choice Questions

1) All of the following terms refer to socioeconomic status **EXCEPT**

    A) occupation.   B) income.   C) education.   D) intelligence.

Answer: D

Explanation: D) Socioeconomic status, or social class, is commonly defined on the basis of an individual's income, education, and prestige in society. Intelligence or IQ is not a relevant factor.

Page Ref: 99

2) The culture of most schools in the United States tends to reflect

    A) upper class values.   B) lower-class values.

    C) middle-class values.   D) the full range of class values.

Answer: C

Explanation: C) The culture of most schools in the United States tends to reflect middle-class values. This orientation may place lower-class and minority students at a disadvantage, since their cultures may promote behaviors considered inappropriate in school settings.

Page Ref: 99

3) You are a teacher working with students from a low-income neighborhood. Based on findings from research on academic progress and SES, you should expect your students, relative to middle-class students of the same age, to achieve

    A) more when given special reinforcers during the school year.

    B) the same during the school year, but to gain during the summer.

    C) the same during the school year, but to lose ground over the summer.

    D) less during the school year, but to gain during the summer.

Answer: C

Explanation: C) You should expect your students to perform the same as middle-class students during the school year, but to lose ground during the summer. The main problem for many disadvantaged learners is not receiving academically relevant stimulation at home. Thus, compared to middle-class students, they are more likely to forget what they learned in school and are less likely to learn new academic skills during their summer vacations.

Page Ref: 101

4) Children from low socioeconomic status families are more likely to have limited access to health care, which may lead to _____, affecting school readiness.

    A) delayed cognitive development
    B) accelerated verbal development

    C) delayed visual development
    D) accelerated motor development

Answer: A

Explanation: A) Children from disadvantaged homes are more likely to have poor access to health care, and to suffer from diseases such as lead poisoning. Their mothers are less likely to have received good prenatal care. These factors can delay cognitive development, which affects school readiness.

Page Ref: 101

5) The structural bias in traditional classrooms works against lower-class and minority-group students because

    A) lower-income learners are less intelligent.

    B) of the mismatch between the cooperative orientation of these students, and the competitive orientation of the school.

    C) lower-income students are not receiving enough support from their teachers.

    D) these students are more disposed toward competitive activities.

Answer: B

Explanation: B) Because of the mismatch between the cooperative orientation of many lower-class and minority-group students and the competitive orientation of the school, Kagan et al. have argued that there is a structural bias in traditional classrooms that works against these learners. Kagan recommends the use of cooperative learning strategies at least part of the time.

Page Ref: 102

6) Relative to middle-class students, lower-class students

    A) are more disposed toward competitive activities.

    B) have less difficulty with delaying gratification.

    C) have more of a future time orientation.

    D) have greater difficulty pacing themselves.

Answer: D

Explanation: D) Middle-class students have more of a future time orientation than do lower-class students. Schools are geared to reward behavior sometime in the future. Lower-class families, concerned with day-to-day survival, may not provide as much support for their children in making and following through on long-term plans. Their children may, therefore, have difficulty pacing their work so that they can complete the project when required.

Page Ref: 102

7) Which of the following statements is **NOT** true, regarding schools attended by children from low-income families?

    A) Children attending these schools may be affected by neighborhood problems, such as crime, that interfere with their educational development.

    B) The educational budget of schools in low-income neighborhoods is reduced by the need to devote resources to unusual expenses, such a s security.

    C) Lack of resources (such as textbooks) can lower children's achievement at these schools.

    D) The teacher pay at these schools is higher than at schools serving students from middle-income families.

Answer: D

Explanation: D) Middle-class children, not lower-class children, are likely to attend schools with greater resources, including better-paid teachers.

Page Ref: 103

8) There is a modest positive correlation between social class and achievement. Which interpretation of this finding is most valid?

    A) Lower-class families cannot provide home environments supportive of their children's success in school.

    B) It can NOT be assumed that this relationship holds for all students from lower-class families.

    C) Lower-income students receive the most educational support.

    D) It should be assumed that this relationship holds for all students from working-class families.

Answer: B

Explanation: B) While there is a modest positive correlation between social class and achievement, it should not, by any means, be assumed that this relationship holds for all children from lower-class families. There are many exceptions. Lower-class families can provide home environments quite supportive of their children's success in school.

Page Ref: 103

9) Which of the following characteristics may help define an individual's ethnicity?

    A) race   B) eye color

    C) language   D) place of origin

Answer: D

Explanation: D) An ethnic group is one in which individuals have a shared sense of identity because of common place of origin, religion or race; but ethnicity is not the same as race, which refers only to physical characteristics.

Page Ref: 106

10) Which of the following groups of people will show dramatic increases in their U.S populations by 2010?

    A) African Americans and Native Americans

    B) Hispanics and Asians

    C) Caucasians and Asians

    D) Hispanics and African Americans

Answer: B

Explanation: B) After African Americans, the largest minority group is Hispanics. The Hispanic population under 25 may be as much as 40 percent higher in 2010 than in 1990. There may be 14 percent more African Americans under 25, and almost 7 percent fewer whites.

Page Ref: 107

11) The differences in achievement levels between whites and members of under-represented groups

    A) remain high, although the gap has been reduced somewhat.

    B) remained constant since 1970.

    C) narrowed for Native Americans only.

    D) increased on the SAT.

Answer: A

Explanation: A) Although African American and Latino students are gaining in achievement more rapidly than whites, the gap between whites and members of under-represented groups remains high.

Page Ref: 107

12) The academic self-concepts of African Americans, and the expectations they have of themselves, tend to be

    A) at least as high as those of their white classmates.

    B) lower than those of their white classmates.

    C) higher than their Asian American classmates.

    D) lower than those of their Native American classmates.

Answer: A

Explanation: A) Although African American students often suffer from low expectations from teachers and others, their expectations for themselves and their academic self-concepts tend to be at least as high as those of their white classmates. The low achievement of these students may well be a temporary problem; in a decade or two, minority groups will increasingly achieve economic security and enter the middle-class.

Page Ref: 108

13) In the textbook-author's discussion of ethnic group differences in achievement, which of the following was **NOT** identified as a cause for minority group students' relatively lower performance?

   A) fewer resources at home

   B) inferior schools

   C) cultures that have values different from those of schools

   D) lower intelligence

Answer: D

Explanation: D) According to your textbook, the main causes of the lower academic achievement of minority groups are external factors and not lower intelligence. Specifically, minority group students tend to have fewer resources at home, attend inferior schools, and belong to cultures that may value behaviors different from those expected by schools.

Page Ref: 108

14) Which of the following was a direct result of the *Brown vs. the Board of Education of Topeka* case?

   A) Junior kindergartens were established.

   B) Title I programs were funded to provide compensatory education.

   C) Schools were desegregated.

   D) African American teachers received higher pay.

Answer: C

Explanation: C) The *Brown vs. Board of Education of Topeka* case abolished legal segregation. Unfortunately, the flight of white students from desegregated schools has left some districts just as segregated as before. Although the effects of desegregation have been small, they are positive nonetheless.

Page Ref: 110

15) According to the text, what is the impact on desegregation when students from under-represented groups are sent early in life to high quality schools attended by middle-class students?

    A) There is none; the effectiveness remains unchanged.

    B) As a result of the students (from under-represented groups) having contact with middle-class students, a significant positive effect is observed.

    C) As a result of the students (from under-represented groups) receiving better educational experiences, a significant positive effect is observed.

    D) As a result of the students (from under-represented groups) having to compete with middle-class students, a negative effect of desegregation occurs.

Answer: C

Explanation: C) When students from under-represented groups are sent to high quality high schools attended by middle-class students, the effectiveness of desegregation increases mainly as a result of the students attending better schools. That is, the key factor does not appear to be mere contact with middle-class students, but having the resources that higher quality schools provide.

Page Ref: 110

16) Research shows that as a result of desegregation, achievement of students from under-represented groups

    A) increased substantially.   B) surpassed expectations.

    C) remained constant.   D) increased to a small degree.

Answer: D

Explanation: D) Research on school desegregation shows that, in general, desegregation practices have raised the achievement scores of students from under-represented groups by a small degree. While positive in direction, the results are disappointing. A key factor seems to be that the quality of the desegregated schools is often not better than the segregated schools formerly attended.

Page Ref: 110

17) African American and Latino students who attend desegregated schools are more likely than their peers from segregated schools, to attend

    A) segregated colleges.   B) desegregated colleges.

    C) small colleges.   D) technical colleges.

Answer: B

Explanation: B) African American and Latino students who attend desegregated schools are more likely to attend desegregated colleges, work in integrated settings, and attain higher income.

Page Ref: 111

18) By 2026, what percentage of U.S. students is expected to come from homes in which the primary language is not English?

    A) 5 percent   B) 10 percent   C) 25 percent   D) 40 percent

Answer: C

Explanation: C) Projections forecast that by 2026, 25 percent of all students will come from homes in which the primary language is not English. Most of these students' families speak Spanish, and are located primarily in the Southwest and in the New York City, Miami, and Chicago areas.

Page Ref: 113

19) English language learners are typically taught in the most common instructional placement, which is called

    A) English immersion, referred to as a "sink-or-swim" approach.

    B) transitional bilingual education in which children are taught in both their native tongue and English together.

    C) paired bilingual education is which students study with a partner.

    D) three-way bilingual education, which involves English speaking and non-English-speaking students and their teachers.

Answer: A

Explanation: A) English language learners are typically taught in one of four types of programs, the most common of which is English immersion. This "sink or swim" approach is most common when the number of English language learners is small.

Page Ref: 113

20) What has research told us about the use of cooperative learning in bilingual education programs?

    A) Cooperative learning is not very effective.

    B) This approach has about the same success rate as other approaches.

    C) This approach helps students make a successful transition to English-only instruction.

    D) Cooperative learning will keep bilingual students in bilingual classes until they finish school.

Answer: C

Explanation: C) Cooperative learning programs have been particularly effective both in improving the outcomes of Spanish reading instruction and in helping bilingual students make a successful transition to English-only instruction in the upper elementary grades.

Page Ref: 115

21) Which of the following is the most valid reason for continuing bilingual education programs?

    A) It offers a lower risk of school failure than leaving non-English-speaking students in a regular class.

    B) Transition from bilingual programs to English-only programs is no longer a problem.

    C) Staffing for such programs is easier than keeping students in Spanish-only or English-only classes.

    D) Language-minority students cannot be ready for English-only classes until eighth grade.

Answer: A

Explanation: A) The most valid reason (of the choices listed) for maintaining bilingual education is that it is superior to the alternative of placing non-English speaking students in regular classes where they must "sink or swim." In many cases, these students will "sink" in the regular class due to inability to understand the teacher or to read English text.

Page Ref: 116

22) Which of the following statements about bilingual education is true?

    A) Recently there has been a movement to abandon bilingual education in favor of English-only instruction.

    B) Proposition 227 was passed in California in 1998 requiring all students to learn a second language.

    C) Most bilingual programs serve students throughout their academic careers.

    D) Bilingualism has been found to interfere with academic achievement in both languages.

Answer: A

Explanation: A) Recently there has been a movement to abandon bilingual education in favor of English-only instruction. In California, which has the largest number of language minority students in the U.S., a referendum called Proposition 227 was passed in 1998. It mandates a maximum of one year for limited English proficient students to receive intensive assistance in learning English. After that, students are expected to be in mainstream classes.

Page Ref: 116

23) Which of the following is a problem with bilingual education?

   A) Bilingualism seems to interfere with students' performance in at least one of the two languages.

   B) Bilingual instruction is distracting for students who speak English as their first language.

   C) The curriculum tends to be less academically oriented than the standard curriculum.

   D) It is inconsistent with desegregation since language–minority students often end up separated from students whose native language is English.

Answer: D

Explanation: D) A problem with bilingual education is that it conflicts with the goals of desegregation since language minorities are often grouped together. Thus, in essence, a tracking system is created in which students who are low achievers (in this case, due to limited English proficiency) spend most or all of their time in school with other low achievers.

Page Ref: 116

24) Language minority children who experience academic difficulties due to a lack of proficiency in English

   A) are sometimes assigned to special education.

   B) have been shown to have low intelligence.

   C) will never find a group with which to identify.

   D) usually come from single-parent families.

Answer: A

Explanation: A) Language minority children are sometimes assigned to special education because of academic difficulties that are, in fact, due to lack of proficiency in English.

Page Ref: 116

25) Researchers define multicultural education in a variety of ways. Of the following statements, which reflect contemporary positions on the topic?
   1)   Include non–European perspectives in the curriculum.
   2)   Teach more about the cultures and contributions of non–western societies.
   3)   Revise school policies and practices to improve educational outcomes for students of different genders and exceptionalities.

   A) 1 and 2 (not 3).   B) 1 and 3 (not 2).

   C) 2 and 3 (not 1).   D) All three statements.

Answer: D

Explanation: D) The simplest definitions of multicultural education emphasize the inclusion of non–European perspectives in the curriculum, such as including the works of African, Latino, and Native American authors in English curricula, teaching about Columbus from the point of view of Native Americans, and teaching about the cultures and contributions of non–western societies.

Page Ref: 116

26) The basic idea supported in your text regarding multicultural education is to emphasize

    A) identical treatment of students, regardless of culture or ethnicity.

    B) separate instructional activities for students with different cultural backgrounds.

    C) the aptitude–treatment interaction approach to instructional design and delivery.

    D) equal treatment of students, with sensitivity to cultural or ethnic differences.

Answer: D

Explanation: D) In discussing multicultural education, the text supports the idea of treating students equally, with sensitivity to differences in cultural or ethnic background. The idea is to promote harmony, not increase divisiveness. Yet, treating everyone exactly the same is not reasonable, since students of different backgrounds have different needs and expectations.

Page Ref: 116

27) What is the term used to describe teachers' use of examples, data, and information from a variety of cultures?

    A) multicultural bias   B) equity pedagogy

    C) content integration   D) Eurocentricism

Answer: C

Explanation: C) Content integration refers to teachers' use of examples, data, and information from a variety of cultures. This is what most people think of as multicultural education: teaching about different cultures and about contributions made by individuals from diverse cultures.

Page Ref: 117

28) According to Banks, all of the following are key dimensions of multicultural education **EXCEPT**

    A) equity pedagogy.   B) prejudice reduction.

    C) knowledge construction.   D) mainstreaming.

Answer: D

Explanation: D) Banks identifies five key dimensions of multicultural education: content integration, knowledge construction, prejudice reduction, equity pedagogy, and empowering school culture.

Page Ref: 117

29) The first step in multicultural education is for teachers, administrators, and other school staff to

    A) learn about the cultures from which their students come.

    B) learn to speak Spanish.

    C) begin American cultural enrichment programs.

    D) acquaint the white students with multilingual lesson plans.

Answer: A

Explanation: A) The first step in multicultural education is for teachers, administrators, and other school staff to learn about the cultures from which their students come and to carefully examine all the policies, practices, and curricula used in the school to identify any areas of possible bias (i.e., exclusively or Eurocentric teaching).

Page Ref: 118

30) One of the efforts that teachers can undertake to have their classrooms reflect cultural diversity is to

    A) have the bulletin boards consistently indicate an appreciation for one culture.

    B) allow different students to stifle diverse opinion.

    C) try to understand culturally diverse parents and extended families.

    D) provide organizational patterns that result in segregation.

Answer: C

Explanation: C) According to the text, teachers, administrators, and other school staff need to learn about the cultures—including the world views of parents and extended families.

Page Ref: 118

31) A school principal is interested in promoting multicultural education at school. Which of the following practices would **NOT** be consistent with that goal?

    A) Use a variety of teaching methods rather than concentrating on those that work best for most students.

    B) Confront instances of racism.

    C) Use bilingual education on a school–wide basis.

    D) Maintain artwork throughout the building that reflects one culture.

Answer: D

Explanation: D) For promoting multicultural education, the principal would not want to emphasize the dominance of one culture over another.

Page Ref: 118

32) Studies of achievement and ability differences between males and females indicate that

   A) males tend to score higher in general verbal ability.

   B) females tend to score higher in spatial reasoning.

   C) there are more females than males who are gifted in mathematics.

   D) male scores vary more than female scores in quantitative reasoning.

Answer: D

Explanation: D) Studies of achievement and ability differences between males and females show that males tend to be more variable in quantitative reasoning. This means that there are more very high-achieving males and more very low achieving males than there are females in either category.

Page Ref: 119

33) Which of the following statements concerning gender roles is **FALSE**?

   A) Most gender roles are based upon biological differences.

   B) Males and females are treated differently from birth on.

   C) All societies treat children differently on the basis of their gender.

   D) Learning is the major determinant of gender roles.

Answer: A

Explanation: A) It is not true that most gender roles are based upon biological differences between males and females. Although biological factors may contribute to gender roles, socialization effects appear much more influential.

Page Ref: 119

34) The overall findings from research on gender differences in intelligence and academic achievement show

   A) noticeable differences favoring males in both areas.

   B) noticeable differences favoring females in both areas.

   C) noticeable differences favoring males in intelligence.

   D) inconsistent differences of questionable meaning.

Answer: D

Explanation: D) Research on gender differences in intelligence and academic achievement shows inconsistent differences of questionable meaning. In some comparisons, females score higher; in others, males are superior. The important issue is the influence of cultural norms in encouraging one sex more than the other to excel in certain subjects (e.g., mathematics).

Page Ref: 119

35) High school females tend to

A) overestimate their skills in language and math.

B) overestimate their skills in social studies and English.

C) estimate their skills as being the same as males.

D) underestimate their skills in language and math.

Answer: D

Explanation: D) In actual school achievement, females start out with an advantage over males and maintain this advantage into high school. Even in math and science, where females score somewhat lower on tests, they still get better grades in class. Despite this, high school males tend to overestimate their skills in language and math (as measured by standardized tests) while females underestimate their skills.

Page Ref: 119

36) Gender–role behavioral differences occur because of all of the following **EXCEPT**

A) genetic differences between males and females.

B) reinforcement by adults.

C) socialization throughout life.

D) school contributions of reinforcement.

Answer: A

Explanation: A) Behavioral differences originate from different experiences, including reinforcement by adults for different behaviors, socialization into approved sex–role behavior throughout life, and schools' contributions through socialization experiences and achievement interactions.

Page Ref: 120

37) All of the following are ways that schools differentiate between the sexes **EXCEPT**

A) males receive more attention than do females.

B) teachers punish females more promptly and explicitly for aggressive behavior than they do males.

C) gender bias is often found in curriculum materials.

D) females engage in more interactions with their teachers in such areas as approval and instruction giving.

Answer: D

Explanation: D) In general, males receive more attention than females from their teachers. Males receive more disapproval and blame from their teachers than do females. However, males also engage in more interactions with their teachers in such areas as approval, instruction giving, and being listened to. Teachers tend to punish females more promptly and explicitly for aggressive behavior than males.

Page Ref: 120

38) Regarding gender differences, which of the following implications is correct for teachers?

   A) Make students pursue interests that are appropriate for their gender.

   B) Treat males and females similarly wherever appropriate.

   C) Use masculine-oriented modeling to increase female assertiveness.

   D) Have more classes in which males and females are separated.

Answer: B

Explanation: B) The main implication for teachers, with regard to gender differences, is to treat males and females similarly wherever appropriate. Gender differences are increased through biases, stereotyping, and differential treatment of males and females in class. It is up to teachers to avoid promoting sexual stereotypes.

Page Ref: 121

39) Charles Spearman's conception of intelligence is that

   A) intelligence is only weakly related to school achievement.

   B) there are several different types of intelligences.

   C) there is one overall type of intelligence, called a g factor.

   D) intelligence is accumulated knowledge.

Answer: C

Explanation: C) In 1927, Charles Spearman claimed that while there were variations in a person's ability from task to task, there was one general intelligence factor, or g, that existed across all learning situations.

Page Ref: 122

40) Binet's work advanced the science of intelligence assessment, but it also began to establish the idea that

   A) there were multiple intelligences.

   B) intelligence could be improved with motivation.

   C) there were smart people who could be expected to do well in a broad range of learning situations.

   D) there were smart people who could be expected to do well in a narrow range of learning situations.

Answer: C

Explanation: C) Binet's work greatly advanced the science of intelligence assessment. But it also began to establish the idea that intelligence was one thing and that there were "smart" people who could be expected to do well in a broad range of learning situations.

Page Ref: 122

41) Which of the following is not one of the intellectual abilities described by Sternberg?

    A) general   B) practical   C) analytical   D) creative

Answer: A

Explanation: A) Sternberg proposed that there are three types of intellectual ability: practical, analytical, and creative.

Page Ref: 123

42) Studies showing the effects of schooling in raising intelligence scores support an interpretation of intelligence as

    A) environmentally influenced.   B) an aptitude rather than an ability.

    C) general ability.   D) genetically influenced.

Answer: A

Explanation: A) The effects of schooling on intelligence support an environmental interpretation of intelligence differences by showing that positive experiences can raise IQ scores. This idea supports the concept of intelligence as changeable rather than fixed.

Page Ref: 125

43) Which position regarding the use of intelligence scores is supported by your text author?

    A) Knowing students' general intelligence scores can be helpful to teachers in planning lessons.

    B) Intelligence scores are basically invalid and should not be used for educational decision making.

    C) Intelligence should be measured and reported as a linguistic score and a mathematical score.

    D) Teachers should be more concerned with students' specific abilities than with their general intelligence.

Answer: D

Explanation: D) The position the textbook author supports is that teachers should be more concerned with specific areas of ability and less with general intelligence. Thinking about general intelligence results in classifying students as "smart" or "dumb," when in fact each may have particular areas of strengths and weaknesses.

Page Ref: 125

44) French studies of children of low SES parents adopted into high SES families find strong

A) negative effects on the children's IQs compared to non-adopted children raised in low SES families.

B) positive effects on the children's IQs compared to non-adopted children raised in low SES families.

C) positive effects on the children's IQs compared to non-adopted children raised in high SES families.

D) negative effects on the children's IQs compared to adopted children raised in low SES families.

Answer: B

Explanation: B) It is clear that children of high achieving parents are, on average, more likely to be high achievers themselves; but, this is due as much to the home environment created by high achieving parents as to genetics. For example, French studies of children of low SES parents adopted into high SES families find strong positive effects on the children's IQs compared to non-adopted children raised in low SES families.

Page Ref: 125

45) What might a teacher expect from a field dependent learner?

A) problems in working carefully and deliberately

B) shyness in social situations

C) complications in learning subjects such as history and literature

D) difficulty with complex, analytical tasks

Answer: D

Explanation: D) A field dependent individual has particular difficulty with complex tasks, while being at ease in social situations and preferring subjects such as literature and history. Having difficulty in analyzing patterns places the field dependent individual at a disadvantage with complex tasks.

Page Ref: 126

46) When compared with field independent learners, field dependent individuals tend to be

A) less oriented toward people and social relationships.

B) less able to recall conversations and relationships.

C) more oriented toward people and social relationships.

D) more likely to do well with problem solving tasks.

Answer: C

Explanation: C) Field dependent people tend to be more oriented toward people and social relationships than are field independent learners.

Page Ref: 126

47) Based on the work of Dunn and Dunn, students may differ in preferences associated with surroundings, and these differences

    A) necessitate individualized learning environments for all children.

    B) cannot predict which learning environment will be most effective for each student.

    C) can sometimes predict which learning environment will be most effective for each student.

    D) can predict the students who are in need of remedial education.

Answer: C

Explanation: C) Students may vary in preferences for different learning environments or conditions. For example, Dunn and Dunn (1987) found that students differ in preferences regarding such things as the amount of lighting, hard or soft seating, quiet or noisy surroundings, for working alone or with peers, and so on, and that these differences can predict, to some extent, which learning environments are most effective for each child.

Page Ref: 126

48) Research designed to show an impact on learning due to aptitude-treatment interactions

    A) are not taken seriously due to invalid research designs.

    B) yield inconclusive results.

    C) yield uniformly positive results.

    D) are conducted in the area of motor skills development.

Answer: B

Explanation: B) Research studies designed to show an impact on learning due to aptitude-treatment interactions generally yield inconclusive results. This limits the usefulness of the aptitude-treatment interaction paradigm for affecting educational practice.

Page Ref: 126

True/False Questions

1) Middle-class parents are likely to expect and demand high achievement from their children, while lower-class parents are more likely to demand good behavior and obedience.

Answer: TRUE
Page Ref: 101

2) Several studies have found that while low-SES and high-SES children make similar progress in academic achievement during the school year.

Answer: TRUE
Page Ref: 101

3) Research findings on the relationship between SES and rates of academic progress imply that offering summer school programs to lower-class students would be desirable for improving their academic achievement.

Answer: TRUE
Page Ref: 101

4) Students from middle-class white families are less willing to compete and more interested in cooperating with their peers than are students from lower-class groups.

Answer: FALSE
Page Ref: 102

5) Helping poor parents engage in more enriching interactions with their children can have a substantial impact on their children's cognitive performance.

Answer: TRUE
Page Ref: 103

6) Often, teachers hold low expectations for disadvantaged children, affecting their motivation and reasoning.

Answer: TRUE
Page Ref: 106

7) The U.S. is becoming less ethnically diverse as larger numbers of minority groups leave each year.

Answer: FALSE
Page Ref: 106

8) The gap in academic achievement between youth from under-represented groups and their Caucasian peers is increasing.

Answer: FALSE
Page Ref: 107

9) A disadvantage faced by students from under-represented groups is that they often attend academically inferior, overcrowded urban schools.

Answer: TRUE
Page Ref: 108

10) In the 1970s, a series of supreme court decisions found that the continued segregation of many schools was due to past discriminatory practices.

Answer: TRUE
Page Ref: 110

11) Typically, bilingual programs offer some instruction in Spanish. The programs differ in the degree to which the Latino culture is taught to all students.

Answer: TRUE
Page Ref: 113

12) Research on bilingual education is focusing on the identification of effective forms of bilingual instruction, rather than on the question of which is the best language of instruction.

Answer: TRUE
Page Ref: 115

13) Multicultural education is easily implemented because it can be fully accomplished by adding facts and examples, representing different cultures, to the existing curriculum.

Answer: FALSE
Page Ref: 116

14) High school males tend to underestimate their skills in language and math (as measured by standardized tests) while females overestimate their skills.

Answer: FALSE
Page Ref: 119

15) Teachers tend to punish males more promptly and explicitly for aggressive behavior than they do females.

Answer: FALSE
Page Ref: 120

16) Spearman claimed that there is an intelligence factor, g, that affects performance on geometrical reasoning tasks, exclusively.

Answer: FALSE
Page Ref: 122

17) Today, most researchers believe that intelligence is both environmentally and genetically determined.

Answer: TRUE
Page Ref: 125

18) Field dependence as a learning style is generally associated with high academic performance in science and math.

Answer: FALSE
Page Ref: 126

19) There are a few studies that find positive effects for programs that adapt instruction to an individual's learning style.

Answer: TRUE
Page Ref: 125

Short Answer Questions

1) The term used to describe different families' levels of income, occupation, prestige, and education.

Answer: socioeconomic status
Page Ref: 99

2) Despite many risk factors, many at–risk children develop the ability to succeed, which is referred to by this term.

Answer: resilience
Page Ref: 103

3) A type of group in which individuals share a sense of identity, usually because of a common place of origin.

Answer: ethnic
Page Ref: 106

4) The two groups that are gaining more rapidly than whites on SATs.

Answer: African American and Latino
Page Ref: 107

5) This refers to programs for students with limited use of English that teach students in their own language part of the time while English is being learned.

Answer: bilingual education
Page Ref: 113

6) The type of programs that have been particularly effective in improving the outcomes of Spanish reading instruction.

Answer: cooperative learning
Page Ref: 115

7) The inclusion of non–European perspectives in the curriculum, plus policies and practices that improve education for students of diverse abilities and backgrounds.

Answer: multicultural education
Page Ref: 116

8) Early socialization into this kind of behavior continues throughout life.

   Answer: sex-role behavior
   Page Ref: 119

9) Stereotypical views and differential treatment of males and females, often favoring one gender over the other.

   Answer: gender bias
   Page Ref: 120

10) Although Binet's test of intelligence can assess a broad range of abilities, it was designed to yield this single score.

    Answer: intelligence quotient
    Page Ref: 123

11) Contrasting Binet's and Spearman's intelligence theories, in recent years, Sternberg, Guilford, Gardner, and others have proposed the existence of these.

    Answer: multiple intelligence
    Page Ref: 123

12) The type of learning style through which individuals tend to see patterns as a whole.

    Answer: field dependent
    Page Ref: 126

13) The term used to describe the learning style of people who are more likely to do well with numbers, science, and problem-solving tasks.

    Answer: field-independent
    Page Ref: 126

14) The finding that student learning is better when teaching style is matched to the student's learning style.

    Answer: aptitude-treatment interaction
    Page Ref: 126

Essay Questions

1) David and Luke are starting kindergarten. They both have loving and supportive parents, but their backgrounds are different. David's social-class background would be classified as "low SES", while Luke's is "high SES".

What do researchers mean by "SES"? What are its components?

Using examples, illustrate how differences in David's and Luke's backgrounds may influence how readily they will adapt to the middle-class school environment.

Answer: Researchers usually measure SES as a combination of a family's income and parents' years of education. SES stands for socioeconomic status. Children of different SES backgrounds may differ in their exposure to experiences that resemble school life or school tasks. Some examples are:
- learning skills such as counting or using a scissors.
- following directions; language skills in listening or speaking.
- meeting expectations for intellectual development.
- observing models for reading and verbal expression.
- experience with learning materials.
- educational trips.
- experiences affected by poor access to health care, and by mothers' prenatal care.

Page Ref: 99

2) *A teacher's low expectations of some students can become a self-fulfilling prophecy.* What does this statement mean and how does it apply to social class?

Answer: A teacher's low expectations of students can become a self-fulfilling prophecy, causing students to perform less well than they could have. While there is a modest positive correlation between social class and achievement, it should not be assumed that this relationship holds for all children from lower-social-class families. There are many exceptions.

Page Ref: 106

3) Trace the history of school desegregation beginning before 1954, to the present.

Answer: Before 1954, black, white, and Latino students were legally required to attend separate schools in many states and the District of Columbia. Minority group students were often bused miles past their nearest public school to separate schools. The doctrine of "separate but equal" education was upheld in several Supreme Court decisions. However, in 1954 the Supreme Court struck down this practice in the landmark Brown vs. Board of Education of Topeka case, on the grounds that separate education was inherently unequal. In the 1970s a series of Supreme Court decisions found that continued segregation of many schools throughout the United States was due to past discriminatory practices such as the drawing of school boundary lines deliberately to separate neighborhoods along racial lines.

Page Ref: 110

4) Reviews of research focusing on the best-designed studies of quality bilingual programs yield positive results. What are they?

Answer: Researchers have never found bilingual programs to be harmful to students, and the programs are often beneficial for the achievement of Latino students in English as well as in subjects they learned in Spanish. Bilingual education can also increase students' self-esteem. Also, the learning of a second language is facilitated by skills in one's native language. Cooperative learning programs have been particularly effective both in improving the outcomes of Spanish reading instruction and in helping bilingual students make a successful transition to English-only instruction.
Page Ref: 113

5) Make lists of multicultural classroom activities that would be appropriate for elementary, middle level, and secondary students.

Answer: Be sure that assignments are not offensive or frustrating to students of cultural minorities. Ask individuals who are knowledgeable about multicultural topics to be guest speakers in your class. Take a cultural census of the class to find out what cultures are represented; let students be the ethnographers. Select a theme to tie various multicultural activities together. Hold a multicultural fair or food festival. Have multicultural celebrations. Supplement textbooks with authentic material from different cultures taken from newspapers, magazines, and other media. Use community resources. Study works in science, art, music and literature of various cultures. Take field trips to multicultural sites. Establish pen pal or video exchange programs.
Page Ref: 117

6) Researchers claim that few genetically based differences exist between males and females; however, differences are still observed. What types of differences exist and to what are the differences attributed?

Answer: First, it should be noted that differences between males and females are small when compared with the variability within each sex. However, some differences are observed. Males tend to score higher on the quantitative section of the Scholastic Aptitude Test, tests of general knowledge, mechanical reasoning, and mental rotations, while females score higher on language measures and on attention and planning tasks. In actual school achievement, females start out with an advantage over males and maintain this advantage through high school. Even in math and science, where females score somewhat lower on tests, they still get better grades in class. Differences in scholastic achievement between females and males are due in part to how they are treated. Sex-role teaching begins early and continues throughout the lifespan. Differences in approved sex roles between females and males is stronger in lower socioeconomic level families than high socioeconomic families.
Page Ref: 118

7) Historically, a great debate has focused on whether intelligence is a product of heredity or a product of an individual's environment. Using supporting evidence from the text, argue one of these two points of view.

Answer: The origins of intelligence have been debated for decades. Some believe that intelligence is overwhelmingly a product of heredity. Children of high achieving parents are, on average, more likely to be high achievers themselves. Others believe that intelligence is overwhelmingly a product of the environment. Schools clearly affect intelligence. There is evidence that intelligence can be changed by programs designed to do so. Most likely, intelligence is a combination of both heredity and the environment.

Page Ref: 125

8) You have a student in your class who is field independent. Write a description of how this student might act.

Answer: A field independent individual tends to see parts that make up a pattern rather than the pattern as a whole. They are most likely to do well with numbers, science, and problem solving tasks.

Page Ref: 126

9) Think about the following observations in the light of learning styles.

Alicia takes part in an experiment in which her task is simply to adjust the orientation of a bar, until it is vertical (a knob is used to control the bar's position). The challenge is that the bar is surrounded by a misleading background—the background pattern can make the bar appear vertical when in fact it is tilted.

Some of Alicia's friends performed the task, doing their best to set the bar at vertical, but had found out afterwards that what looked vertical to them, was in fact slightly tilted—the surrounding pattern had influenced their perception. Alicia, on the other hand, adjusted the bar to its true vertical every time, in spite of the misleading pattern.

Later, at the diner, Alicia and friends were working on their "find the hidden animals" placemats. Alicia noticed that she was able to separate these figures from the whole picture very quickly and easily, however cleverly they were hidden.

• What learning style do these observations of Alicia illustrate? Explain how the characteristics of this learning style are manifested in Alicia's behavior.

• If Alicia is similar to other students with this learning style, what would her teachers notice about her academic and social tendencies?

Answer: Alicia appears to be field independent. Field independent individuals are able to see parts within a pattern, as Alicia does with the hidden animals. They do not have difficulty isolating aspects of a situation, as Alicia shows when she judges the orientation of the bar, independent of its background.
If Alicia shares the characteristics of many other field independent individuals, she will tend to do well on quantitative tasks, science and problem solving, and be less inclined toward history and literature. Socially, Alicia may not prefer working in groups; she may be less socially-oriented than some of her classmates.

Page Ref: 125

10) Meg Campbell teaches high school physics in a private Christian school in a middle class, suburban community. Her best friend and roommate, Chris Gustafson, teaches second grade in a public elementary school in the same community. Today, both are planning to attend a meeting in which the state's governor will propose that the state adopt a school vouchers program.

Meg meets up with Chris just outside the high school auditorium, which is filled to capacity. They find seats just as the governor is being introduced. "Thank you, Principal Ledderman, for that fine introduction," the governor begins. "Let me say that I am here to tell you about a proposal I will take to the legislature—a proposal for school vouchers. I think that a school vouchers program will revolutionize education in this state because it holds schools accountable. Because tax payer dollars are given directly to parents to give to a school of their choice, school vouchers will increase competition, thus making all schools, or those that survive, better institutions. We practice this in business, why not our schools? In addition, vouchers will give money to poor kids who need to escape from ineffective urban schools. It will give them a chance to get away from schools that aren't making it."

Chris, who is opposed to school vouchers, raises her hand. She asks the governor, "Aren't public schools held to different standards than private schools? We have to be licensed by the state, meet state and federal mandates about, for example, special education, and we have to accept all students. How can public schools compete with schools that have fewer regulations?"

"The differences shouldn't matter," replied the governor. "You've been trained to teach under a variety of circumstances; at least that's what the university people tell us. Public schools have been able to do what they want for too long. Some healthy competition would make them better. How could you be against that?"

Meg questions the governor next. "I work in a Christian school. What about the separation of church and state? Would vouchers for my school be constitutional?"

Before he can reply, others speak up. "How can you say that poor kids will benefit? If the state gives them a couple of thousand dollars, but it costs $10,000 to attend a private school, how can this help?"

Using information from the text, continue the discussion by listing advantages and disadvantages of vouchers. Include in your discussion information from the text about special populations who might be affected by such a practice.

Answer: Advantages cited for school vouchers include increased competition, parental choice, and accountability. Disadvantages cited include unfair competition, loss of quality control, and tax payer dollars supporting religious schools.
Page Ref: 98

11) Below is a list of individual characteristics. Discuss whether you believe each is a characteristic of the dominant group in the United States or whether it might be a characteristic of a non–dominant group. Explain how dominant and non–dominant characteristics can affect learning.

competitive	future oriented	meditative
respectful of nature	individualistic	group focused
assertive	quiet	religious
spiritual	monolingual	scientific

Answer: While there is much diversity in and among various groups, western culture tends to be competitive, assertive, future oriented, individualistic, religious, and scientific.
Page Ref: 102

Chapter 5   Behavioral Theories of Learning

Multiple-Choice Questions

1) Which of the following definitions best fits a behaviorist's conception of learning?

    A) Learning is a change in an individual caused by experience.

    B) Learning is a change in an individual's knowledge structures.

    C) Learning is synonymous with development.

    D) Learning is synonymous with cognition.

Answer: A

Explanation: A) Learning is usually defined as a change in an individual caused by experience.
Page Ref: 134

2) A central goal of instruction is

    A) how to get students to learn.

    B) to help students learn particular information, skills, and concepts.

    C) how to help students memorize data.

    D) how to get students to pay attention to roles and strategies.

Answer: B

Explanation: B) The problem educators face is not how to get students to learn. Rather, it is how to help students learn particular information, skills, and concepts that will be useful in adult life. We present students with the right stimuli on which to focus their attention and mental efforts so they will acquire important skills.
Page Ref: 135

3) In Pavlov's experiments with dogs, which of the following identifies the role of the bell (or tone), prior to conditioning?

    A) conditioned response   B) neutral stimulus

    C) unconditioned response   D) unconditioned stimulus

Answer: B

Explanation: B) In Pavlov's classical conditioning experiment, the bell (or tone) served as the neutral stimulus (it has no effect on a particular response).
Page Ref: 136

4) In classical conditioning, the object or event that automatically elicits a behavior before the conditioning takes place is referred to as the

    A) conditioned response.
    B) neutral stimulus.

    C) unconditioned response.
    D) unconditioned stimulus.

Answer: D

Explanation: D) In classical conditioning, the event that automatically evokes a behavior before conditioning takes place is the unconditioned stimulus. In Pavlov's experiment, the unconditioned stimulus was the meat powder; it naturally caused the dog to salivate.

Page Ref: 136

5) Pavlov's experiments show that if a previously neutral stimulus is paired with an unconditioned stimulus, the neutral stimulus becomes a(n)

    A) unconditioned response.
    B) conditioned stimulus.

    C) conditioned response.
    D) unconditioned stimulus.

Answer: B

Explanation: B) Pavlov's experiments showed that if a previously neutral stimulus is paired with an unconditioned stimulus, the neutral stimulus becomes a conditioned stimulus and gains the power to prompt a response similar to that produced by the unconditioned stimulus.

Page Ref: 136

6) Which of the following examples demonstrates Thorndike's Law of Effect?

    A) A child learns how to ride a bicycle once larger pedals are added.

    B) After spending 10 minutes in a biology classroom, students no longer smell any chemical odor.

    C) Students frequently stay after school because the teacher rewards them with treats.

    D) A student becomes excited and angry after someone shouts out the correct answer to a puzzle.

Answer: C

Explanation: C) If an act (staying after school) is followed by a favorable effect (treats), it is likely to be repeated.

Page Ref: 136

7) Thorndike's Law of Effect states that

    A) the last response to a stimulus becomes the one to be repeated.

    B) the more a response is practiced, the more proficient one becomes at making that response.

    C) the association between a stimulus and a response is unimportant.

    D) if a response is followed by something satisfying, its likelihood of being repeated increases.

Answer: D

Explanation: D) Thorndike's law states that an act that is followed by a favorable effect is more likely to be repeated in similar situations and an act that is followed by an unfavorable effect is less likely to be repeated. This idea extended Pavlov's classical conditioning paradigm by emphasizing the importance of consequence on future behavior.

Page Ref: 136

8) Classical conditioning focuses on physiological changes that occur due to the pairing of a neutral stimulus with an unconditioned stimulus. What is the focus of operant conditioning?

    A) the relationship between a behavior and its consequence

    B) animal learning rather than human learning

    C) treating learning as associating stimuli, rather than acting on one's surroundings.

    D) reflexive types of responses

Answer: A

Explanation: A) Operant conditioning differs from classical conditioning by focusing on the relationship between a behavior and its consequences. In contrast, reinforcement and punishment are not directly considered in classical conditioning, in which the role of associations between stimuli is emphasized.

Page Ref: 137

9) Behavioral learning theorists tell us that

    A) pleasurable consequences reduce the frequency of behavior.

    B) unpleasant consequences strengthen a behavior.

    C) behavior changes according to its immediate consequences.

    D) consequences have little impact on behavior.

Answer: C

Explanation: C) Perhaps the most important principle of behavioral learning theories is that behavior changes according to its immediate consequences. Pleasurable consequences strengthen a behavior, while unpleasant consequences weaken it.

Page Ref: 138

10) Which of the following is a secondary reinforcer?

    A) food   B) sex   C) security   D) money

Answer: D

Explanation: D) The secondary reinforcer is money, since it acquires reinforcing properties as a result of being associated with primary (natural) reinforcers such as food, safety, security, etc. That is, money would not be reinforcing to a person from a primitive society who is unaware of its value.

Page Ref: 139

11) All of the following are examples of secondary reinforcers **EXCEPT**

    A) food.   B) tokens.

    C) words of praise.   D) social events.

Answer: A

Explanation: A) There are three categories of secondary reinforcers: social (e.g., praise), activity (e.g., games), and token (money or grades). Food is a primary reinforcer.

Page Ref: 139

12) A secondary reinforcer takes on value

    A) by directly satisfying basic human needs.

    B) when it is associated with primary reinforcers.

    C) when reinforcement is withheld.

    D) when a primary reinforcer loses its value.

Answer: B

Explanation: B) Secondary reinforcers are reinforcers that acquire their value by being associated with primary reinforcers or well-established secondary reinforcers.

Page Ref: 139

13) All of the following stimuli are primary reinforcers **EXCEPT**

    A) warmth.   B) grades.   C) security.   D) food.

Answer: B

Explanation: B) Primary reinforcers satisfy basic human needs. Examples include food, water, security, warmth, and sex.

Page Ref: 139

14) Of the following statements about reinforcers, which are true?

    1)   A reinforcer is any consequence that strengthens a behavior.

    2)   Rewards (e.g., praise and grades) can be assumed reinforcing for everyone under all conditions.

    3)   A reward can be classified as a reinforcer for a particular individual only if there is evidence that it strengthened a behavior for that individual.

    4)   The effectiveness of the reinforcer must be determined.

    A) 1, 2, and 4 (not 3).   B) 2, 3 and 4 (not 1).

    C) 1, 3, and 4 (not 2).   D) All four statements.

Answer: C

Explanation: C) A reinforcer is defined as any consequence that strengthens (that is, increases the frequency of) behaviors. Note that the effectiveness of the reinforcer must be demonstrated. It cannot be assumed that a particular consequence is, in fact, a reinforcer until there is evidence that it strengthens a behavior for a particular individual.

Page Ref: 140

15) The three basic categories of secondary reinforcers are

    A) social, activity, and token.   B) social, mediation, and symbolic.

    C) activity, token, and metacognition.   D) social, token, and unconditioned.

Answer: A

Explanation: A) There are three basic categories of secondary reinforcers. One is social reinforcers, such as praise, smiles, hugs, or attention. Other types of secondary reinforcers are activity reinforcers such as access to toys, games, or fun activities, and token (or symbolic) reinforcers such as money, grades, stars, or points.

Page Ref: 140

16) Whenever students turn in their homework, a teacher rewards them with computer time. The more often they turn in their homework, the more they are allowed to use the computers. Students have been turning in their homework with increasing frequency. Thus, the computer time is serving as a(n)

    A) aversive stimulus.   B) unconditioned stimulus.

    C) reinforcer.   D) punisher.

Answer: C

Explanation: C) A reinforcer is defined as any consequence that strengthens (i.e., increases the frequency of) a behavior. In this case, the computer is serving as a reinforcer since it serves to increase the frequency of students turning in their homework assignments.

Page Ref: 140

17) A reinforcer that allows a student to escape from an unpleasant situation is called a(n)

A) secondary reinforcer.

B) primary reinforcer.

C) negative reinforcer.

D) unconditioned reinforcer.

Answer: C

Explanation: C) A reinforcer that allows a student to escape from an unpleasant situation is called a negative reinforcer.

Page Ref: 140

18) The Premack Principle links less-desired activities to

A) enjoyable activities.

B) punishment.

C) misbehavior.

D) positive participation.

Answer: A

Explanation: A) The Premack Principle of behavior promotes less-desired (low strength) activities by linking them to more-desired activities. Access to something desireable is made contingent on doing something less desireable. This principle is sometimes call "Grandma's Rule" from the old statement, "Eat your vegetables, and then you may play."

Page Ref: 140

19) What type of reinforcer is being encountered when students enjoy taking a field trip (which is the reward itself)?

A) extrinsic   B) intrinsic   C) primary   D) negative

Answer: B

Explanation: B) Intrinsic reinforcers are activities or behaviors that a person enjoys engaging in for their own sake, without any other reward.

Page Ref: 141

20) What type of reinforcer is a gold star that a student receives as a reward for completing her homework?

A) extrinsic   B) intrinsic   C) primary   D) negative

Answer: A

Explanation: A) Extrinsic reinforcers are motivational praise or rewards given to people who engage in behavior that they might not engage in without them. Evidence shows that reinforcing children for certain behaviors they would have done anyway can undermine long-term intrinsic motivation.

Page Ref: 141

21) Which of the following examples best illustrates removal punishment? (assume that the undesirable behavior decreases after the consequence occurs).

    A) scolding a student for misbehavior

    B) embarrassing a student in front of peers

    C) making students do extra work

    D) sending a student to the principal

Answer: D

Explanation: D) Consequences that weaken behavior are called punishers. Removal punishers will decrease a targeted behavior by withdrawing the pleasant consequences that are reinforcing a behavior. Sending a student to the principal is removing a student from his or her social environment (the classroom). Note that if an apparently unpleasant consequence does not reduce the frequency of the behavior it follows, it is not necessarily a punisher. Some students like being sent to the principal's office.

Page Ref: 143

22) The belief behind this discipline strategy is that students want to be part of the social setting.

    A) fixed ratio reinforcement   B) points for attendance

    C) time out   D) Premack Principle

Answer: C

Explanation: C) Time out is used when teachers believe that the attention of other students is serving to reinforce misbehavior; so, the student is deprived of the reinforcer, in which case time out would be considered removal punishment.

Page Ref: 143

23) Which of the following terms is defined as follows: applying unpleasant stimuli to decrease a target behavior?

    A) presentation punishment   B) positive reinforcement

    C) negative reinforcement   D) removal punishment

Answer: A

Explanation: A) Presentation punishment decreases a targeted behavior by adding some aversive stimulus as a consequence for undesirable behavior.

Page Ref: 143

24) Consequences that weaken behavior are called

    A) secondary consequences.   B) anticipatory consequences.

    C) punishers.   D) negative reinforcers.

Answer: C

Explanation: C) Punishers are consequences that weaken a targeted behavior.

Page Ref: 143

25) On what grounds is physical punishment (such as spanking) in schools almost universally opposed by behavioral learning theorists?

A) economic

B) ethical and scientific

C) religious and economic

D) historic

Answer: B

Explanation: B) Physical punishment in schools (such as spanking) is illegal in most places and is almost universally opposed by behavioral learning theorists on ethical as well as scientific grounds.

Page Ref: 145

26) Which of the following reinforcement procedures would be most appropriate for the classroom?

A) As students begin a new task, praise the desired final behavior only, ignoring any approximations to the response you are seeking.

B) Delay punishment following a misbehavior.

C) Increase the frequency of the reward over time.

D) Give immediate reinforcement when a desired behavior is observed.

Answer: D

Explanation: D) Immediate consequences are more effective than delayed consequences. Effective practice includes reinforcing approximations to desired behaviors, and, decreasing the frequency of a reward over time.

Page Ref: 145

27) Which of the following positions regarding punishment have behavioral learning theorists taken?
1) Some theorists have claimed that the effects of punishment are temporary.
2) Punishment produces aggression.
3) Punishment causes individuals to avoid settings in which it is used.
4) When punishment is necessary it should take the mildest possible form.

A) 1, 3, and 4 (not 2).

B) 2 and 4 (not 1 and 3). .

C) 1, 2, and 3 (not 4).

D) All four positions.

Answer: D

Explanation: D) Behavioral learning theorists have claimed that the effects of punishment are only temporary, that punishment produces aggression, and that punishment causes individuals to avoid settings in which it is used. However, even behavioral learning theorists who do support the use of punishment generally agree that it should be resorted to only when reinforcement for appropriate behavior has been tried and failed, that when punishment is necessary it should take the mildest form possible, and that punishment should always be used as part of a careful plan.

Page Ref: 145

28) A coach is using a shaping technique to help a student work on a figure skating routine. According to behaviorists, all of the following strategies can be applied to assist the skater **EXCEPT**

    A) immediate reinforcement of approximations to the desired skill.

    B) adapting the reinforcement criteria to the student's needs.

    C) withholding feedback.

    D) using a step–by–step sequence.

Answer: C

Explanation: C) The coach should not consider restricting the provision of feedback. Shaping involves reinforcing the acquisition of subskills that lead to mastery of a more complex skill. It uses a systematic step-by-step approach in which the provision of feedback is important.

Page Ref: 146

29) A teacher reinforces a child first for recognizing two letters of the alphabet, then for recognizing four, then six, and so on. The teacher is using a technique called

    A) negative reinforcement.   B) "Grandma's Rule."

    C) generalization.   D) shaping.

Answer: D

Explanation: D) The teacher is using shaping by teaching the alphabet in small steps (a few letters at a time). This approach allows students to learn the letters in small enough segments to experience success and obtain reinforcement.

Page Ref: 146

30) An English teacher wants students to begin writing paragraphs on various topics. How should the teacher proceed in explaining the parts of paragraph construction?

    A) Have students write entire paragraphs, then hand them in so the teacher can score them on grammar, punctuation, and spelling.

    B) Teach the skills step-by-step, gradually shaping the final skill.

    C) Allow the student to write in whatever manner he or she chooses.

    D) Reinforce only the behaviors that demonstrate the final skill.

Answer: B

Explanation: B) The teacher might teach the skills step–by–step, gradually shaping the final skill. Students might first be taught how to write topic sentences, then supporting details, and then concluding sentences.

Page Ref: 146

31) A student is used to getting the attention of the teacher by making annoying sounds. One day the teacher decides to ignore the sounds by showing no reaction. Based on behavioral theory, what would be the expected outcome, assuming the teacher's attention was the reinforcer?

A) The behavior will be immediately extinguished.

B) The behavior will immediately decrease in frequency, but then increase over time.

C) The behavior will immediately increase in frequency, but then decrease over time.

D) There will be very little change, since the teacher did not apply an aversive stimulus.

Answer: C

Explanation: C) The student's behavior may immediately increase in frequency, but then decrease over time. This is a typical effect of extinction. Here, the teacher is using extinction by withholding the reinforcement (attention) following the misbehavior (annoying sounds). The student's initial response, then, is to try even harder to be annoying (and receive attention).

Page Ref: 147

32) A student calls out answers in a social studies class instead of following the hand-raising rule. The teacher decides to ignore the student until the appropriate behavior is observed; however, when the teacher begins to ignore the misbehavior, the student increases the calling out. This is an example of

A) negative reinforcement.   B) shaping.

C) extinction burst.   D) combination approach.

Answer: C

Explanation: C) The characteristic extinction burst—the increase in levels of behavior in the early stages of extinction—has important consequences for classroom management. At first, ignoring the student is likely to increase the calling out behavior, a classic extinction burst. Eventually, the behavior should be weakened and the teacher will be able to call on the student, who should exhibit the proper behavior when it is realized that this is the only way to be recognized.

Page Ref: 152

33) Students receive a reward every third time they score 90 percent or higher on a test. What schedule is being used to reinforce the students?

A) fixed interval   B) fixed ratio

C) variable interval   D) variable ratio

Answer: B

Explanation: B) The students are being reinforced on a fixed ratio schedule. This schedule reinforces a behavior after a fixed number of correct responses (in this case, doing well on a test, three times).

Page Ref: 148

34) Students do not know when a reinforcer is coming, but know that if they continue to do their work, it will eventually appear. The students are being reinforced on what type of schedule?

    A) fixed interval   B) variable ratio   C) continuous   D) fixed ratio

Answer: B

Explanation: B) The students are being reinforced on a variable ratio schedule. A variable ratio schedule is one in which the number of behaviors required for reinforcement is unpredictable, although it is certain that the behaviors will eventually be reinforced.

Page Ref: 149

35) A teacher is teaching a new math skill with which the students are having great difficulty. Which schedule of reinforcement should the teacher try to use with the students until they show some progress?

    A) fixed interval   B) variable ratio

    C) continuous   D) variable interval

Answer: C

Explanation: C) The teacher should use continuous reinforcement. Since the students are having great difficulty with the math concepts, they need constant reinforcement, for both motivation and feedback purposes.

Page Ref: 149

36) A teacher spot-checks how students are doing by walking around the room, selecting students to observe at random and then reinforcing those who are working well. What type of schedule is being used?

    A) fixed interval   B) fixed ratio

    C) variable interval   D) variable ratio

Answer: C

Explanation: C) The teacher is using a variable interval schedule. Since the teacher is selecting students at random, their cumulative responses make no difference. All that matters is that at the time a student is selected to be observed, she or he is doing the right thing.

Page Ref: 149

37) All of the following positions regarding the maintenance of learned behavior are believed to be true **EXCEPT**

    A) A teacher has used reinforcement to establish a variety of behaviors; continued reinforcement by the teacher is necessary for maintaining the behavior in some, but not all, cases.

    B) Maintenance of a behavior without continued reinforcement occurs when learners are engaging in behaviors that are pleasurable-in-themselves.

    C) Schedules requiring many behaviors to earn reinforcement are more resistant to extinction than are schedules under which reinforcement is easily obtained.

    D) Once behaviors are established, reinforcement for correct responses should become frequent and predictable.

Answer: D

Explanation: D) When new behaviors are being introduced, reinforcement for correct responses should be frequent and predictable. However, once the behaviors are established, reinforcement for correct responses should become less frequent and less predictable. The reason for this is that variable schedules of reinforcement, and schedules of reinforcement that require many behaviors before reinforcement is given, are much more resistant to extinction than are fixed schedules.

Page Ref: 151

38) A student yells at another student for interrupting a response to a teacher's question, but remains silent when the teacher does the same. This is an example of

    A) generalization.   B) discrimination.

    C) negative reinforcement.   D) extinction burst.

Answer: B

Explanation: B) Discrimination is making distinctions between situations in which consequences (reinforcement versus punishment) are likely to differ for the same behavior.

Page Ref: 152

39) At his locker, Rick is describing his exciting weekend to Tony, using very colorful and inappropriate language. Tony gestures down the hall to let Rick know that Sherri is approaching. Rick continues his story but instantly cleans up his language, sounding like a completely different person while Sherri walks by. Rick's adjustment of his behavior is based on

    A) shaping.   B) immediate primary reinforcement.

    C) discrimination.   D) a fixed interval schedule.

Answer: C

Explanation: C) Rick discriminates between different kinds of friends. His responses in Tony's presence are altered by Sherri's presence. Sherri is a discriminative stimulus for clean language. Clean language is reinforced in Sherri's presence, but not in Tony's.

Page Ref: 152

40) A student learns to add blocks and later transfers this skill to adding sticks, and checkers. Educational psychologists would say that the student is demonstrating

    A) the Premack Principle.   B) discrimination.

    C) generalization.   D) shaping.

Answer: C

Explanation: C) Generalization involves demonstrating previously learned behaviors in a new situation. Specifically, what was learned with blocks is now being applied with sticks and checkers.

Page Ref: 153

41) As the similarity between two sets of stimuli increases,

    A) both generalization and discrimination become easier.

    B) generalization becomes more difficult and discrimination easier.

    C) both generalization and discrimination become more difficult.

    D) discrimination becomes more difficult and generalization easier.

Answer: D

Explanation: D) As the similarity between two stimuli increases, discrimination will become more difficult and generalization easier. The reason is that very similar stimuli will be more difficult to distinguish.

Page Ref: 153

42) Which of the following is the correct sequence of phases for understanding observational learning?

    A) attention, retention, motivation, reproduction

    B) motivation, attention, reproduction, retention

    C) attention, retention, reproduction, motivation

    D) motivation, retention, reproduction, attention

Answer: C

Explanation: C) The correct sequence of phases in observational learning is paying attention, retaining what was observed, being able to reproduce the behavior, and being motivated to do so.

Page Ref: 154

43) One student sees another being praised for working hard. The first student begins to work in the same manner. This is an example of

    A) a fixed ratio schedule of reinforcement.

    B) vicarious learning.

    C) classical conditioning.

    D) negative reinforcement.

Answer: B

Explanation: B) Vicarious learning involves learning from observing the consequences of others' behaviors.

Page Ref: 155

44) In Bandura's classic study on modeling, children who observed a film of an aggressive adult being punished

    A) showed less desire to see movies in later classes.

    B) engaged in fewer aggressive acts during subsequent play than did the control group.

    C) appeared unaffected by the film.

    D) engaged in more aggressive acts in subsequent play than did the control group.

Answer: B

Explanation: B) In Bandura's classic study on modeling, children who observed a film showing an aggressive adult being punished engaged in significantly fewer aggressive acts during subsequent play. This illustrates vicarious learning, which is learning by observing the consequences of others' behaviors.

Page Ref: 155

45) Which of the following illustrates Bandura's concept of self-regulation?

    A) A student engages in a desired activity after judging previous work as well done.

    B) A teacher is in charge of creating and enforcing all class rules.

    C) Standard grading criteria are applied to all members of a class.

    D) Reinforcement is based on improvement.

Answer: A

Explanation: A) People observe their own behavior, judge it against their own standards, and reinforce or punish themselves. This is called self-regulation.

Page Ref: 156

46) Attempts to train students to monitor their own behavior have

    A) been failures since the only effective reinforcers were those administered by others.

    B) not succeeded because the teachers and researchers involved have lacked the technical ability to teach these skills.

    C) shown success in helping students regulate their own behavior.

    D) been successful with social interactions, but failed to influence classroom behavior or achievement.

Answer: C

Explanation: C) Programs designed to train students to monitor and change their behavior have shown success in helping students regulate their own behavior.

Page Ref: 157

47) Meichenbaum's self-regulated learning strategy and Vygotsky's scaffolded instruction strategy both emphasize modeling private speech and

    A) gradually moving from teacher-controlled to student-controlled behaviors.

    B) quickly moving from teacher-controlled to student-controlled behaviors.

    C) encouraging teacher-regulated learning.

    D) discouraging student regulated learning.

Answer: A

Explanation: A) Michenbaum's self-regulated learning strategy and the Vygotskian approach to scaffold instruction emphasize modeling private speech and gradually moving from teacher-controlled to student-controlled behaviors, with the students using private speech to talk themselves through their tasks.

Page Ref: 157

48) One way to help children engage in self-regulated learning is to provide them with this when assigning long or complex tasks.

    A) student models of expectation   B) a task completion checklist

    C) a detailed paragraph of instructions   D) a stack of blank paper

Answer: B

Explanation: B) One example of a way to help children engage in self-regulated learning is to provide a form for monitoring their progress—such as a checklist—when assigning long or complex tasks.

Page Ref: 158

49) Which of the following statements about behavioral learning theories are correct?
1) Behavioral learning theories are limited in scope.
2) With the exception of social learning theories, behavioral learning theorists focus exclusively on observable behavior.
3) Examples of behavioral learning theories often involve the management of behavior.
4) The basic principles of behavioral learning theories are questionable, that is, not yet well-established by research.

A) 1 and 3 (not 2 and 4).

B) 1, 3, and 4 (not 2).

C) 1, 2, and 3 (not 4).

D) All four statements.

Answer: C

Explanation: C) The basic principles of behavioral learning theories are as firmly established as any in psychology and have been demonstrated under many different conditions. The principles are useful for explaining much of human behavior and they are even more useful in changing behavior. It is important to recognize, however, that behavioral learning theories focus almost exclusively on observable behavior.

Page Ref: 159

50) Which of the following conditions best describes what behavioral and cognitive theories of learning have in common?

A) Both include concepts that overlap with social learning theory.

B) Both place primary emphasis on conditioning.

C) The major application of both is classroom management.

D) Both were heavily influenced by E.L. Thorndike.

Answer: A

Explanation: A) A link between behavioral and cognitive learning theories is that both share concepts with social learning theory. The bridge provided by social learning theory derives from its emphasis on the influence of thought (cognition) on actions (observable behavior).

Page Ref: 159

True/False Questions

1) The meat powder in Pavlov's experiment served as the conditioned stimulus.

Answer: FALSE
Page Ref: 136

2) Pavlov linked behavior to physical reflex.

Answer: TRUE
Page Ref: 136

3) B.F. Skinner proposed a class of behaviors called operant behaviors because they operate on the environment in the apparent absence of any unconditioned stimulus.

Answer: TRUE
Page Ref: 136

4) An important principle of behavioral learning theories is that behavior changes according to its immediate consequence.

Answer: TRUE
Page Ref: 138

5) A reinforcer is a pleasurable consequence that maintains or increases a behavior

Answer: TRUE
Page Ref: 139

6) Secondary reinforcers are reinforcers that acquire their value by being associated with primary reinforcers or other well established secondary reinforcers.

Answer: TRUE
Page Ref: 139

7) A negative reinforcer is equivalent to punishment.

Answer: FALSE
Page Ref: 140

8) Consequences that are reinforcing are called punishers.

Answer: FALSE
Page Ref: 140

9) The Premack Principle, also called Grandma's Rule, is based on associating enjoyable activities with less enjoyable activities.

Answer: TRUE
Page Ref: 140

10) Consequences that follow behaviors closely in time affect behavior far more than delayed consequences.

Answer: TRUE
Page Ref: 145

11) When using reinforcers to strengthen behaviors, always use the most elaborate or tangible rewards.

Answer: FALSE
Page Ref: 145

12) The principle of shaping asserts that students should be reinforced when they can perform the desired final behavior.

Answer: FALSE
Page Ref: 145

13) Extinction is rarely a smooth process. When reinforcers are withdrawn, individuals often decrease their rate of behavior immediately.

Answer: FALSE
Page Ref: 147

14) Every Friday, the teacher collects and evaluates assignments. The type of reinforcement schedule being used is fixed interval.

Answer: TRUE
Page Ref: 149

15) To maintain behaviors, teachers should use reinforcers indefinitely.

Answer: FALSE
Page Ref: 151

16) The final step of Bandura's theory involves being motivated to imitate the model in order to obtain extrinsic or intrinsic reinforcement.

Answer: TRUE
Page Ref: 155

Short Answer Questions

1) This is defined as a change in an individual caused by experience.

Answer: learning
Page Ref: 134

2) This term refers to the dog's salivating in Pavlov's experiment.

Answer: unconditioned response
Page Ref: 136

3) In Pavlov's experiments, this is what the neutral stimulus becomes, after it has been paired with an unconditioned stimulus.

Answer: conditioned stimulus
Page Ref: 136

4) In Pavlov's research, the name of the process through which a neutral stimulus, when paired with an unconditioned stimulus, becomes capable of producing a conditioned response.

Answer: classical conditioning
Page Ref: 136

5) The role the food plays in Pavlov's classical experiment with salivating dogs.

Answer: unconditioned stimulus
Page Ref: 136

6) Thorndike's idea that any act followed by pleasant circumstances is likely to be repeated, and any act followed by unpleasant circumstances, is not.

Answer: Law of Effect
Page Ref: 136

7) The use of pleasant and unpleasant consequences to change behaviors.

Answer: operant conditioning
Page Ref: 137

8) Skinner is famous for his development and use of this apparatus.

Answer: Skinner box
Page Ref: 138

9) Any consequence that strengthens (increases) the frequency of behaviors.

Answer: reinforcer
Page Ref: 139

10) The type of reinforcer that satisfies basic human needs.

Answer: primary
Page Ref: 139

11) Money is an example of this kind of reinforcer.

Answer: secondary
Page Ref: 139

12) The behavioral strategy that is sometimes called "Grandma's Rule."

Answer: Premack Principle
Page Ref: 140

13) The name given to the type of reinforcer that is built into a behavior, leading a person to perform the activity for its own sake.

Answer: intrinsic
Page Ref: 141

14) Decreasing the frequency of a targeted behavior by adding an unpleasant consequence.

Answer: presentation punishment
Page Ref: 143

15) Form of removal punishment in which the teacher has a student who misbehaves sit away from the rest of the class.

Answer: time out
Page Ref: 143

16) Type of consequence teachers use when they believe an undesirable behavior is being reinforced by attention from the misbehaving student's classmates.

Answer: removal punishment; time out
Page Ref: 143

17) Another name for an unpleasant consequence used in presentation punishment.

Answer: aversive stimulus
Page Ref: 143

18) Consequences that are not reinforcing, that is, that weaken behaviors.

Answer: punishers
Page Ref: 143

19) The technique in use when teachers guide students toward goals by reinforcing the many steps that lead toward success.

Answer: shaping
Page Ref: 145

20) The process of eliminating a behavior by withdrawing reinforcement.

Answer: extinction
Page Ref: 147

21) The reinforcement schedule in which rewards follow a set number of correct responses.

Answer: fixed ratio
Page Ref: 148

22) Schedule under which the number of behaviors required to earn reinforcement is unpredictable.

Answer: variable ratio
Page Ref: 149

23) Under this kind of schedule, the opportunity to earn reinforcement occurs at random times.

Answer: variable interval
Page Ref: 149

24) The type of schedule under which reinforcement is available only at certain regular times.

Answer: fixed interval
Page Ref: 149

25) Events preceding behaviors

Answer: antecedent stimuli
Page Ref: 152

26) The perceptions of and responses to differences using cures and signals.

Answer: discrimination
Page Ref: 152

27) The imitation of someone else's behavior.

Answer: modeling
Page Ref: 154

Essay Questions

1) Using Pavlov's classical conditioning terms, explain how test anxiety develops. Develop your explanation using an example of an individual learner. Use that learner's experiences to illustrate *neutral stimulus, unconditioned stimulus, unconditioned response, conditioned stimulus* and *conditioned response*.

    Extended thinking: Apply the concept of *generalization* to classical conditioning. Expand on your example by illustrating how the learner's test anxiety might generalize beyond the original stimuli.

Answer: According to Pavlov's theory, test anxiety develops in the following way: the test begins as a neutral stimulus that had been paired with an unconditioned stimulus—perhaps a humiliating or embarrassing feeling created by a failing grade—that produces anxiety. If the unconditioned stimulus is paired enough times with a test, the test becomes the conditioned stimulus that elicits anxiety, even when the unconditioned stimulus is absent.

    Test anxiety developed in 6th grade math class may appear in other situations. A situation that involves stimuli similar to those that evoke test anxiety, will elicit a similar response, through generalization.Thus, other math classes, other objective tests, or other assessments of performance, could effect generalization.

Page Ref: 136

2) What role do consequences play in strengthening or weakening behaviors, according to operant conditioning theory? Give an example that supports your response.

Answer: According to operant conditioning theory, behavior changes according to its immediate consequences. Pleasurable consequences strengthen behavior, while unpleasant consequences weaken it. That is, pleasurable consequences increase the frequency with which an individual engages in behavior, while unpleasant consequences reduce the frequency of a behavior. For example, if students enjoy reading books, they will probably read more often. If they find stories boring and are unable to concentrate, they may read less often, choosing other activities instead.

Page Ref: 138

3) Below are four examples of behavior changes that occurred as a result of some consequence. Read each example; then identify it as positive reinforcement, negative reinforcement, presentation punishment, or removal punishment. Explain your classifications.

Rita is caught cheating on her English exam. The teacher, in a loud voice, threatens Rita with an F. Rita starts to cry, then fabricates a story about hardships at home. The teacher stops the threats and lets Rita finish the exam with no penalty. In the future, Rita uses the same ploy when caught cheating in her other classes.
Targeted Behavior: Cheating

Raul repeatedly gets into heated arguments with students during his physical education class basketball game. As a result, the teacher removes Raul from the game. He spends the rest of the class period sitting on the bench. During future games, Raul does not argue with officials.
Targeted Behavior: Arguing with Officials

Stan gets caught passing a note to Marilyn describing his plans for their date that evening. The teacher sees this, grabs the note, and reads it to the class. In the future, Stan does not pass notes.
Targeted Behavior: Note Passing

Suzette shouts out to the teacher, "Why do we have to learn this stuff, anyway? I'll never use it." The teacher, who has been assisting another student, stops to explain why the information is important. With increasing frequency throughout the term, Suzette shouts out questions.
Targeted Behavior: Shouting

Answer: 1) negative reinforcement; 2) removal punishment;
3) presentation punishment; 4) positive reinforcement

Page Ref: 138

4) A teacher makes the following statement: *I reinforce my students with praise, but it doesn't always work.* Using Skinner's definition of reinforcement, how would you respond to the teacher?

Answer: The teacher is misusing the term reinforcement. According to Skinner, a reinforcer is any consequence that strengthens (increases the frequency of) behaviors. If the teacher praises a student and the targeted behavior decreases, then the praise is not a reinforcer; instead, it is a punisher. In addition, reinforcers and punishers cannot be determined until there is evidence that the behavior has increased or decreased.

Page Ref: 139

5) Using the guidelines below, analyze an example of *punishment*. Use an example based on your personal observations; choose an example in which punishment was used to control a student's (or a child's) behavior.

What consequence was used in your "case"? Classify the consequence—what type of punishment was used? Explain any operant-conditioning terms used in your answer.

Explain why the punisher might have chosen the form of punishment used. Evaluate the effectiveness of the punishment, including any unintentional effects on the learner.

Suggest an alternative to punishment that could be used in a situation like the one in your example. Identify any consequences or techniques used in your alternate solution. Identify at least one drawback or pitfall that might be encountered in implementing your alternative.

Answer: Examples are classified as either removal punishment, or presentation punishment. Effectiveness of the punishment may be limited by factors such as duration of effect, side-effects such as aggression and avoidance of the punishing setting. Immediacy of consequences, severity of punishment, ethical status of the punishment and availability of alternative methods are relevant variables.

Page Ref: 143

6) Use a classroom example to illustrate the technique Skinner called *shaping*. Include a brief description of the learners and the setting. Specify:
    1) the reinforcement used,
    2) the target behavior,
    3) what the learners are capable of at the outset, and
    4) several responses that function as successive *approximations* to the desired behavior.

Answer: Examples of simple operant conditioning are not considered *shaping*. Shaping is useful when the response the teacher wants to reinforce does not exist. The approximations to the desired behavior identified, and reinforced by, the teacher, are critical to an example of shaping.

Page Ref: 145

7) Below are three different schedules of reinforcement. Identify which schedule is depicted and predict the effect of the schedule on behavior.
    1) An elementary school has a policy that prohibits students from running in the halls. The hall monitor waits by the cafeteria doors every morning from 8:00 until 8:30 looking for runners.
    2) A teacher has his students complete all problems at the end of the chapter in their math text; however, he only grades the even ones.
    3) A teacher gives unannounced quizzes, usually once per week, but sometimes more often.

Answer: The first example depicts a fixed interval schedule. Most likely, students in the hall by the cafeteria will not run from 8:00 until 8:30, but after that they may. The second example depicts a fixed ratio schedule. Most likely, students will try hard on the even problems while paying less attention to the odd ones. The third example is a variable interval schedule. Students do not know when a quiz will occur, so they will study each night, just in case.

Page Ref: 149

8) Using an example of classroom learning, illustrate both generalization and discrimination. Identify the important stimuli and responses in your example.
Explain the text author's statement that "generalization cannot be taken for granted." Indicate two ways in which the teacher in your example could facilitate generalization.

Answer: In art class, children need to generalize skills such as drawing shapes, across varied media (pastels, paints; paper, ceramics). At the same time they need to discriminate, for example, using a forceful stroke with crayon, and a lighter touch with felt-tips.
Students may be less apt than the teacher assumes, when expected to transfer skills from one set of materials to another. Generalization would be facilitated by, for example, exposing students to a wide variety of materials as they practice their skills, and by reinforcing successful generalization.
Page Ref: 152

9) Much has been said about violence in the media and its effect on children and adolescents. According to Bandura's social learning theory, can humans learn to be violent by watching violence? Explain.
Identify two factors that could influence modeling of violent behavior; use an example to illustrate the effect of each factor.

Answer: According to Bandura's social learning theory, humans can become violent when they watch violence if four factors are present. If individuals pay attention to a violent model, remember how a violent act was committed, are physically capable of reproducing the act, and are motivated to imitate the behavior, they can become violent.
Factors that influence modeling might include the model's attractiveness, success or social status. Observed consequences to the model are also important factors.
Page Ref: 154

10) Recall a behavior you have learned through observation, in a cooperative learning situation. Use this learning experience to illustrate Bandura's four phases of observational learning. Explain how the concept of vicarious learning relates to your example.

Answer: Students in cooperative groups may learn academic skills, study strategies, appropriate or inappropriate behaviors, social skills, and attitudes. In each case: 1) the model gets the learner's attention, 2) the learner retains a representation of the behavior, usually through practice, 3) the learner reproduces the model's behavior, and 4) the learner's level of motivation is affected by characteristics of the model, and by vicarious learning.
Page Ref: 154

11) Evaluate behavioral learning theories (as a group), identifying both strengths and weaknesses.

Answer: The basic principles of behavioral learning theories are as firmly established as any in psychology and have been demonstrated under many different conditions. These principles are useful for explaining much of human behavior, and they are even more useful in changing behavior. However, behavioral learning theories are limited in scope. With the exception of social learning theorists, behavioral learning theorists focus almost exclusively on observable behavior.
Page Ref: 159

12) How does social learning theory bridge the gap between behavioral and cognitive learning theories?

Answer: A link between behavioral and cognitive learning theories is that both draw on social learning theory. The bridge provided by social learning theory derives from its emphasis on the influence of thought (cognition) on actions (observable behavior).
Page Ref: 159

13) Mr. Swan had made it through his first semester of teaching industrial technology at Lindberg Middle School. For the most part, he felt good about his teaching relationships with students and other faculty, and the support he received from his principal. One problem kept him from being completely pleased with this job, however. Two students who were difficult to handle during his first semester computer drafting class had signed up to take his electronics class for the second semester. Mr. Swan's concern was that the two might continue to talk loudly, use tools inappropriately, hit at each other, and bother other students as they had done in the drafting class. Talking to them didn't seem to help.

When the lunch bell rang, Mr. Swan headed for the teachers' lounge as he did every day. He appreciated having time to talk with other adults and today he had a question for his colleagues. "Stewart Bell and Annie Hanks are in my electronic class this term. When I had them last term, they were difficult. Can you give me some ideas about what to do with them when they misbehave?" Several of the teachers had ideas for Mr. Swan, so he grabbed a paper and pencil and proceeded to write down their suggestions. After school he took out the paper and looked at the ideas he had listed:

- Make a contract with them. Tell them they have three times to misbehave, then you will send them to the principal.
- The contract idea is good, but reward their good behavior rather than punish their bad behavior.
- Make them come to your class before or after school to do extra assignments.
- If you ignore their behavior, it will stop.
- Give them detention, then call their parents.
- Talk to them privately about their behavior. Explain how they will be punished, then follow through.
- Give them a failing grade for the day.

Using a behaviorist's perspective, identify strategies (from the above list) that you would consider effective and those you would consider ineffective. Explain your rationale.

Answer: Mr. Swan's list includes both effective and ineffective discipline strategies, according to behaviorists. Contracting is an effective strategy; however, focusing on appropriate behavior is often more effective than focusing on inappropriate behavior. Allowing students three opportunities to misbehave can be problematic, especially if safety issues are involved. While some would argue that it may take students a few times to get their behavior under control, having a stated consequence that is used each time a behavior is inappropriate is easiest to manage. Punishing inappropriate behaviors with learning (doing extra assignments) will most likely teach students that learning is something to be avoided. Ignoring inappropriate behavior will only work if nothing else is reinforcing it. Involving parents when there is a concern is effective, but care should be taken to ensure that the parents are not excessively punitive. Talking to students intervention." Also, some evaluation experts may say that grades are indicators of achievement and that failing students for inappropriate behavior jeopardizes the validity of the grade.

Page Ref: 159

Chapter 6   Information Processing
and Cognitive Theories of Learning

Multiple-Choice Questions

1) The cognitive theory of learning that describes how individuals take in, work with, store, and retrieve information about the world is called

   A) behaviorism.

   C) dual code.

   B) information processing.

   D) serial learning.

   Answer: B

   Explanation: B) Information processing theory describes how information is taken in, processed, stored, and retrieved.
   Page Ref: 166

2) Which component of memory best fits the description "in one ear and out the other"?

   A) sensory register

   C) episodic memory

   B) working memory

   D) permanent memory

   Answer: A

   Explanation: A) "In one ear and out the other" best describes the sensory register. The sensory register receives a large amount of information from the senses and holds it for a very short period of time. Unless it is processed, it is lost.
   Page Ref: 167

3) One of the educational implications of the sensory register is that

   A) without attention, information received by the senses is quickly lost, and will not be remembered.

   B) reinforcement is necessary if learners are to retain information.

   C) learning is a slow process because the sensory register holds only a few items.

   D) learning difficulties occur when we are conscious of all the information stored in our sensory registers.

   Answer: A

   Explanation: A) An educational implication of the sensory register is that attention is necessary if learners are to remember information. In addition, it takes time to bring all the information attended to into consciousness. If too much information is presented at once, very little may be learned.
   Page Ref: 168

4) When the senses receive stimuli, the mind immediately begins working on some of them. Therefore, the sensory images of which we are conscious are not exactly the same as what we saw, heard, or felt. Which of the following terms relates most closely to these statements?

A) registration   B) reception   C) attention   D) perception

Answer: D

Explanation: D) Perception is a person's interpretation of stimuli.
Page Ref: 168

5) Which of the following statements about attention is accurate?

A) Attention is the tendency to organize stored memories.

B) Attention is the mental repetition of information.

C) Attention is a limited resource.

D) One way to gain attention is to reduce emotional content of subject matter.

Answer: C

Explanation: C) Attention is the process of focusing on certain stimuli while screening out others.
Page Ref: 168

6) What is the name for the component of memory that holds current thoughts?

A) sensory register   B) working memory

C) episodic memory   D) permanent memory

Answer: B

Explanation: B) Short-term or working memory is the component of memory in which limited amounts of information can be stored, consciously, for a brief amount of time.
Page Ref: 169

7) Two words are used to define one type of memory: short-term and working. "Short term" refers to duration while "working" refers to

A) importance.   B) capacity.   C) location.   D) function.

Answer: D

Explanation: D) Another term for short term memory is working memory. This term emphasizes that the most important aspect of short term memory is not its duration, but the fact that it is active. Working memory is where the mind operates on information, organizes it for storing or discarding, and connects it to other information.
Page Ref: 169

8) The process of maintaining a thought in working memory is called

    A) repository.   B) rehearsal.   C) automaticity.   D) elaboration

Answer: B

Explanation: B) The process of maintaining an item in working memory by repetition is called rehearsal. Rehearsal is important in learning because the longer an item remains in working memory, the greater the chance that it will be transferred to long term memory.

Page Ref: 169

9) Which of the following statements about working memory is **FALSE**?

    A) The limited capacity of working memory is one aspect of information processing that has important implications for instruction.

    B) Working memory is where the mind operates on information.

    C) Working memory is where the mind organizes information for storage or discarding.

    D) On a given learning task, working-memory capacity is the same from individual to individual.

Answer: D

Explanation: D) Individuals do differ in the capacity of their working memories when attempting to accomplish a given learning task.

Page Ref: 170

10) Which of the following terms describes the capacity of working memory?

    A) long-term   B) limited   C) random   D) network

Answer: B

Explanation: B) Working memory can be thought of as a bottleneck due to its limited capacity. Only so much information can be held there at a given time. Teachers, therefore, need to limit the amount of material presented to students at one time.

Page Ref: 170

11) Human beings often complain about having poor memories. This inadequacy of the memory system is primarily due to

    A) difficulties in gaining access to information in long-term memory.

    B) the small capacity of long-term memory.

    C) the limited storage capacity of the sensory registers.

    D) too many items permanently stored in working memory.

Answer: A

Explanation: A) Long-term memory seems to have unlimited capacity, but people often have difficult retrieving information from long-term storage.

Page Ref: 171

12) A teacher tries to help a student recall an event that took place during a field trip to the natural history museum by saying, "Remember, it was the time when you went off to see the skeletons." Which memory component was most directly involved?

A) episodic memory

B) massed practice

C) semantic memory

D) short term memory

Answer: A

Explanation: A) The teacher is mainly using long term episodic memory with the student by relating events to be recalled to personal experience. This experience is most likely stored as images in the order in which they occurred.

Page Ref: 172

13) Theorists divide long-term memory into three parts that include all of the following **EXCEPT**

A) episodic.   B) strategic.   C) semantic.   D) procedural.

Answer: B

Explanation: B) Theorists divide long-term memory into at least three parts: episodic memory, semantic em memory, and procedural memory.

Page Ref: 172

14) Semantic memory would be most directly involved in trying to remember

A) which classes you took last semester.

B) information from a textbook.

C) the names of one's new classmates as they are introduced.

D) how to drive a car with a stick shift.

Answer: B

Explanation: B) Semantic memory would be most directly involved in trying to remember information from a text. This memory system stores the concepts and information learned.

Page Ref: 172

15) Schemata consist of

A) strategies or game plans for solving problems.

B) frameworks for organizing ideas in memory.

C) recall strategies through which episodic memory is accessed.

D) whatever information we are conscious of at a given moment.

Answer: B

Explanation: B) Schemata consist of frameworks for organizing ideas in semantic memory. Data that fit into schemata are retained more readily than data that do not fit.

Page Ref: 173

16) Two students are shown a variety of tools in a wood working class. The first one is asked to name the tools and the second is asked to indicate several possible uses of each tool. Later, they are asked to recall which tools they were shown. What would be predicted by levels–of–processing theory?

   A) The first student will remember more tools.

   B) The second student will remember more tools.

   C) They will remember the same amount of tools.

   D) There is no way to determine who will remember more tools.

Answer: B

Explanation: B) Levels–of–processing theory would predict that the second student would later remember more of the tools than the first. The reason is that the second student is more engaged with the material by having to think of uses for the tools. This activity requires deeper processing.

Page Ref: 175

17) A seventh grade middle school science teacher wants students to know a particular organism they studied under a microscope. Based on the dual code theory, what is the best strategy for students to use?

   A) touching it

   B) viewing it at different magnifications under the microscope

   C) naming it and repeating the name

   D) seeing it and naming it

Answer: D

Explanation: D) The best strategy for students to use, based on the dual coding theory, is seeing the organism and naming it. The dual code theory hypothesizes that information is stored in memory in two forms, visual and verbal.

Page Ref: 176

18) An implication of the parallel distributed processing model is that

   A) successful storage in short term memory is essential for transfer of information to long term memory.

   B) long term memory is actually limited in capacity.

   C) the sensory register, like long term memory, consists of semantic episodic components.

   D) transfer of new information to long term memory may be more immediate than was formerly believed.

Answer: D

Explanation: D) An implication of the parallel distributed processing model is that transfer of new information to long term memory may be more immediate than was once believed. The basic idea is that information is processed simultaneously by all memory systems rather than in sequence (from one system to the next).

Page Ref: 176

19) Which of the following statements regarding connectionist models are accurate?
   1) The implications of connectionism for teaching and learning are not clear;
   2) The connectionist model does have a place for rule-based teaching;
   3) Connectionism is inconsistent with current research on the brain;
   4) Connectionism can be modeled mathematically and simulated in artificial intelligence computer experiments.

   A) 2 and 4 (not 1 and 3).   B) 1, 2, and 3 (not 4).

   C) 1, 2, and 4 (not 3).   D) 3 and 4 (not 1 and 2)

   Answer: C

   Explanation: C) Connectionist models are consistent with current research on the brain, which has established that information is not held in any one location, but is distributed to many locations and connected by intricate neural pathways.
   Page Ref: 177

20) One brain research study finds that the amount of stimulation early in a child's development relates to the

   A) number of neural connections, or synapses.

   B) length of neural connections, or synapses.

   C) incidences of seizures.

   D) duration of seizures.

   Answer: A

   Explanation: A) Many findings from brain research might have importance for education and child development. One has to do with early development where studies find that the amount of stimulation early in a child's development relates to the number of neural connections, or synapses, which are the basis for higher learning and memory.
   Page Ref: 178

21) In the classic Peterson and Peterson (1959) study, subjects were asked to count backwards by threes while trying to memorize nonsense letters. A major implication of the findings was

   A) a mechanical task such as counting cannot be performed if long term memory is filled to capacity.

   B) interference does not occur if two sets of stimuli are unrelated.

   C) interference occurs when people are unable to rehearse information in short term memory.

   D) short term memory involves random rather than sequential access.

   Answer: C

   Explanation: C) The implication of the Peterson and Peterson study was that interference occurs when people are unable to rehearse information in short term memory. For Peterson and Peterson's subjects, counting backwards created the interference that hindered their recall.
   Page Ref: 181

22) All of the following statements are examples of retroactive inhibition **EXCEPT**

   A) a student forgets an old telephone number after learning a new one.

   B) a student has difficulty remembering how to get around her old high school once she transfers to a new school.

   C) a student forgets the name of last year's teacher after meeting new teachers.

   D) a student can recite all of the counties in the state after studying.

Answer: D

Explanation: D) Retroactive inhibition occurs when a student forgets the name of last year's teacher while meeting new teachers. New learning (present names) interferes with previous learning (old names).

Page Ref: 182

23) Which of the following is an example of proactive inhibition?

   A) A North American driver who is used to driving on the right side of the road has difficulty driving in England where they drive on the left.

   B) Emily can play her first song on the violin very well, until she learns a second song. After learning the second song she has trouble remembering the first.

   C) A student forgets the name of last year's teachers when meeting this year's instructors.

   D) A student says each letter of the alphabet while trying to think of an old friend's last name.

Answer: A

Explanation: A) An example of proactive inhibition is when the North American driver has difficulty driving in England. Previous learning (driving on the right side) is interfering with new learning (driving on the left side).

Page Ref: 183

24) Which of the following is an example of retroactive facilitation?

   A) A student is able to remember the name of each teacher she had from kindergarten through high school.

   B) After taking a music theory course, a student finds that his piano playing improves.

   C) A student starts playing racquetball and finds that her tennis skills decline.

   D) A student finds that his old typing skills give him a real advantage in learning to use a word processor.

Answer: B

Explanation: B) The student experienced retroactive facilitation when his piano playing improved after he took the music course. Subsequent learning (music course) had the effect of improving performance on something previously learned (piano playing).

Page Ref: 183

25) An example of proactive facilitation would be

   A) learning Spanish first, which may help an English-speaking student learn Italian (a language similar to Spanish).

   B) learning piano first, which may help a student later learn conducting.

   C) learning Spanish, which may help an English-speaking student better understand English.

   D) learning the wrong spelling of a name first, which later creates difficulty in learning the correct spelling.

Answer: A

Explanation: A) Learning one thing can often help a person learn similar information. For example, learning Spanish first may help an English-speaking student later learn Italian, a similar language.

Page Ref: 183

26) Which of the following is a major reason that the recency effect occurs?

   A) Proactive facilitation takes place.   B) Fatigue is reduced.

   C) Automatization occurs.   D) Retroactive inhibition is reduced.

Answer: D

Explanation: D) Items introduced toward the end of a list benefit from the recency effect because retroactive inhibition is reduced. That is, no subsequent items are present to create retroactive interference.

Page Ref: 183

27) An educational application of the primacy and recency effect is to

   A) cover the most important or most difficult concepts in the middle part of a lecture.

   B) provide a preview of the next period, at the end of class, rather than a review of what was covered today.

   C) teach important materials at the beginning or end of class and deal with administrative tasks in the middle.

   D) whenever possible, start a class with seatwork, teach new material and then end the class with seatwork.

Answer: C

Explanation: C) An educational implication of the primacy and recency effects is to start teaching important materials at the beginning or end of class and deal with administrative tasks in the middle. Simply put, students are better able to remember (due to primacy and recency) what they learn at the beginning and end of a lesson (or class period).

Page Ref: 183

28) How can teachers help their students to develop automaticity?

    A) Make some parts of a task more noticeable so that they stand out.

    B) Integrate motor skills with cognitive skills in learning new material.

    C) Draw on multiple memory components rather than on selected components only.

    D) Be sure that certain parts of a task are practiced until they become second nature, so that more concentration can be given to other parts.

Answer: D

Explanation: D) The basic function of automaticity is to make parts of certain tasks second nature so that more concentration can be given to difficult parts. Through automaticity, students can perform tasks (e.g., spelling familiar words) without much attention or concentration.

Page Ref: 184

29) Which term refers to a teacher's assigning students a few problems for homework each day, over the semester?

    A) distributed practice   B) massed practice

    C) elaboration   D) metacognition

Answer: A

Explanation: A) Assigning a few problems as homework each night takes direct advantage of distributed practice. Students are given the opportunity to practice over time rather than all at once. Better retention should result.

Page Ref: 185

30) Researchers have identified three types of verbal learning tasks typically seen in the classroom. These tasks include all of the following **EXCEPT**

    A) free-recall learning.   B) paired-associate learning.

    C) dual code learning.   D) serial learning.

Answer: C

Explanation: C) Researchers have identified three types of verbal learning: 1) free-recall learning, 2) paired-associate learning, and 3) serial learning.

Page Ref: 186

31) As the chair of the language department, you suggest that your new teacher of Chinese consider introducing a process to help students learn the vocabulary more easily. Which approach would be most appropriate for you to suggest, according to the text author?

    A) initial letter strategy   B) loci method

    C) keyword method   D) pegword method

Answer: C

Explanation: C) The keyword method is designed for learning vocabulary. The pegword, initial letter, and loci strategies are all used for serial recall.

Page Ref: 187

32) A student remembers a long list of outdoor sculptures by imagining each piece on top of a different campus building, along Campus Drive. What memory strategy is being used?

    A) loci method

    B) combinational approach

    C) keyword method

    D) free-recall strategy

Answer: A

Explanation: A) The student is using the loci method by associating the names of sculptures to be memorized with a series known locations (loci) in a familiar context.

Page Ref: 188

33) A student is asked to write down the names of all the mid-western states in any order. This type of assignment is an example of

    A) paired-associate learning.

    B) serial learning.

    C) prose learning.

    D) free-recall learning.

Answer: D

Explanation: D) The student is using free-recall. The key feature is being able to recall the words in any order rather than in a particular sequence.

Page Ref: 188

34) Which of the following learning tasks and memory strategies make an appropriate match?

    A) free-recall and pegword method

    B) paired-associate and loci method

    C) serial and pegword method

    D) free recall and keyword method

Answer: C

Explanation: C) The correct matching is serial learning and the pegword method. By memorizing certain pegwords, and associating new words with them, students can remember the serial order of the new words using the memorized sequence of the pegwords.

Page Ref: 189

35) A student uses the term ROY G BIV to remember the colors of the spectrum: red, orange, yellow, green, blue, indigo, and violet. What type of memory strategy is this?

    A) loci   B) pegword   C) rhyming   D) initial-letter

Answer: D

Explanation: D) The student has used the initial-letter strategy. This strategy involves making up a catchy expression or saying that incorporates the first letter from each word to be memorized.

Page Ref: 189

36) Initial–letter strategies include

    A) keywords.   B) locations.   C) acronyms.   D) imagery.

Answer: C

Explanation: C) Initial–letter strategies are strategies for learning in which initial letters of items to be memorized are made into a more easily remembered word or phrase.
Page Ref: 189

37) Rote learning can be characterized as

    A) involving arbitrary associations.

    B) involving innate knowledge.

    C) relating new material to existing knowledge.

    D) underused in the traditional classroom.

Answer: A

Explanation: A) Rote learning can be characterized as involving arbitrary associations. This means that the new information must be learned as given and cannot be meaningfully related to what the learners already know. Learning the term "arbitrary association" may be rote learning for many students.
Page Ref: 190

38) A visiting curriculum evaluation team criticized a school district for teaching too much inert knowledge. A disadvantage, they said, is that, according to educational psychologists, inert knowledge is

    A) highly difficult for teachers to present.

    B) at too high a level for students in the various grades.

    C) only one point of view, not necessarily the correct one.

    D) useless due to the student's inability to apply it outside the classroom.

Answer: D

Explanation: D) A disadvantage of inert knowledge is that it is less meaningful to students. Students have difficulty applying it to events in their lives.
Page Ref: 190

39) About half of the class (group A) knows more about the Democratic party while the other half (group B) knows more about the Republicans. The teacher presents a week long lesson on both parties. Which of the following is likely, based on schema theory?

 A) Group A will learn more about the Democrats than will group B.

 B) Group B will have a better attitude than group A about the parts dealing with the Republicans.

 C) Group B will learn more about the democrats than will group A.

 D) Both groups should learn the same amount about both parties.

Answer: A

Explanation: A) Group A should learn more than group B about the Democrats. They have more prior knowledge about Democrats and, thus, better developed schemata for relating what is taught to what they already know.

Page Ref: 191

40) Schemata are believed to be organized hierarchically with

 A) general categories grouped under specific information.

 B) specific information grouped under general categories.

 C) recent events grouped under earlier events.

 D) earlier events grouped under more recent events.

Answer: B

Explanation: B) Schemata are believed to be organized hierarchically with specific information grouped under general categories. Information that fits into this existing framework will be easier to process and retain.

Page Ref: 191

41) In which situations are fourth-graders displaying developed metacognition?
  1) Mary, who does not recognize a word, looks for clues in familiar affixes to help her pronounce it.
  2) Anne, who does not recognize a word, asks her teacher to tell her.
  3) Elisa, who does not recognize a word, uses her dictionary to find the pronunciation and meaning.
  4) Libby, who does not recognize a word, looks at the illustrations for clues to its meaning.

 A) 1, 2, and 3 (not 4). B) 2, 3, and 4 (not 1).

 C) 1, 3, and 4 (not 2). D) 1, 2, and 4 (not 3).

Answer: C

Explanation: C) The term metacognition means knowledge about one's own learning, or about how to learn. Thinking skills and study skills are examples of metacognitive skills.

Page Ref: 192

42) According to research, which of the following statements about note taking are true?
   1) It can be effective for certain types of material because it can require mental processing of main ideas;
   2) The effects of note taking have been found to be inconsistent;
   3) Note taking that requires some mental processing is more effective than simply writing down what was read;
   4) Positive effects are less likely when note taking is used with complex, conceptual material in which the critical task is to identify the main ideas.

   A) 1, 2, and 4 (not 3).   B) 1 and 3 (not 2 and 4).

   C) 1, 2, and 3 (not 4).   D) All four statements.

Answer: C

Explanation: C) Positive effects are most likely when note taking is used with complex, conceptual material in which the critical task is to identify the main ideas.
Page Ref: 194

43) The strategy that involves writing brief statements that represent the main idea of the information being read is referred to as

   A) mapping.   B) summarizing.

   C) PQ4R method.   D) combinational strategy.

Answer: B

Explanation: B) Summarizing involves writing brief statements that represent the main idea of the information being read. The effectiveness of this strategy depends on how it is used.
Page Ref: 205

44) What is the term for the process in which students identify main ideas and then diagram connections between them?

   A) summarization   B) PQ4R method

   C) note taking   D) mapping

Answer: D

Explanation: D) In mapping, students identify main ideas and then diagram connections between them.
Page Ref: 195

45) The four Rs in the acronym PQ4R stand for

   A) repeat, react, recite, and respond.   B) recite, react, reflect, and remedy.

   C) read, reflect, recite, and review.   D) ready, recite, respond, and repeat.

Answer: C

Explanation: C) One of the best known study techniques for helping students understand and remember what they read is a procedure called the PQ4R method. The acronym means preview, question, read, reflect, recite, and review.
Page Ref: 195

46) A teacher planned to take a class to the art museum for the first time. Before the trip, the teacher shared prints illustrating how the artwork at the museum is grouped into historical periods. When the actual visit took place, students saw many works of art (for the first time) and were amazed at how readily they were learning to recognize them . The orientation process students experienced is referred to as

    A) an analogy.   B) loci method.

    C) outlining.   D) an advance organizer.

Answer: D

Explanation: D) David Ausubel developed advance organizers to orient students to material they are about to learn and to help them recall related information that could be used to assist in incorporating the new information. An advance organizer is an initial statement about a subject to be learned that provides a structure for the new information and relates it to information students already possess.

Page Ref: 198

47) What is the term used by cognitive psychologists to refer to the process of thinking about material to be learned in a way that connects the material to information or ideas already in the learner's mind?

    A) elaboration   B) metacognition

    C) free recall   D) compacting

Answer: A

Explanation: A) Elaboration refers to the process of thinking about material to be learned in a way that connects the material to information or ideas already in the learner's mind.

Page Ref: 199

48) The Halpern study found that these work best for students when they are most different from the process being explained.

    A) advance organizers   B) keywords

    C) analogies   D) levels of processing

Answer: C

Explanation: C) Like advance organizers, use of explanatory analogies can contribute to an understanding of the lessons or the text. Analogies can help students learn new information by relating it to concepts they already know. In the Halpern study it was found that analogies work best when they are different from the process being explained.

Page Ref: 199

49) According to the text author, which of the following strategies facilitates learning and remembering?

    A) organizing information into a hierarchy

    B) isolating new learning from the students' established schemata

    C) using analogies that are similar to the information being learned

    D) avoiding the use of advance organizers

Answer: A

Explanation: A) Material that is well organized is much easier to learn and remember than material that is poorly organized. Hierarchical organization, in which specific issues are grouped under more general topics, seems particularly helpful for student understanding.

Page Ref: 199

50) Which of the following is a variation on conceptual models, that uses graphic representation of concepts and their connections?

    A) PQ4R

    B) knowledge map

    C) prior knowledge

    D) analogy

Answer: B

Explanation: B) A variation on conceptual models, knowledge maps, can be used to teach a wider variety of content. A knowledge map graphically shows the main concepts of a topic of study and the links between them. Giving students knowledge maps after a lesson has been shown to increase their retention of the lesson's content.

Page Ref: 201

True/False Questions

1) What makes the sensory register different from other components of the memory system is that it holds information for long periods of time.

Answer: FALSE
Page Ref: 167

2) The process of maintaining an item in working memory by repetition is called rehearsal.

Answer: TRUE
Page Ref: 169

3) The most important aspect of working memory (or short-term memory) is not its duration, but that it is active.

Answer: TRUE
Page Ref: 169

4) Long-term memory is thought to be a very limited capacity store of information.

Answer: FALSE
Page Ref: 171

5) Semantic memories are stored in networks of connected ideas called schemata.

Answer: TRUE
Page Ref: 172

6) Research suggests that extensive training can not increase brain structure after attainment of adulthood.

Answer: FALSE
Page Ref: 179

7) Individuals with learning disabilities have been found to use less efficient brain processes than other learners.

Answer: TRUE
Page Ref: 179

8) An example of proactive facilitation is learning a second language that can improve your grasp of an already established language.

Answer: FALSE
Page Ref: 183

9) Paired-associate learning involves learning a list of terms in a particular order.

Answer: FALSE
Page Ref: 186

10) One of the most important determinants of how much you can learn about something is how much you already know about it.

Answer: TRUE
Page Ref: 193

11) One effective means of increasing the value of students' note-taking is for the teacher to provide "skeletal" notes before a lecture or reading, which give students categories to direct their own note-taking.

Answer: TRUE
Page Ref: 194

12) Examples of topics that lend themselves to use of conceptual models include the study of mechanics and electricity.

Answer: TRUE
Page Ref: 201

Short Answer Questions

1) The part of the memory system that is most directly involved in receiving incoming information.

Answer: sensory register
Page Ref: 167

2) The process that occurs when we select stimuli from the sensory register, to attend to. This activity is more than reception of stimuli, and is influenced by our mental state, past experience, knowledge, motivations, and other factors.

Answer: perception
Page Ref: 168

3) This is the process of focusing on certain stimuli while screening out others.

Answer: attention
Page Ref: 168

4) A storage system that can hold a limited amount of information for a few seconds.

Answer: short-term memory
Page Ref: 169

5) The conscious part of memory.

Answer: short-term memory
Page Ref: 169

6) Short-term memory is also called working memory because we often maintain an item through this process.

Answer: rehearsal
Page Ref: 169

7) A phenomenon in which the occurrence of an important event fixes mainly visual and auditory memories in a person's mind.

Answer: flashbulb memory
Page Ref: 173

8) The part of long term memory from which we try to recall personal experiences.

Answer: episodic memory
Page Ref: 172

9) A concept, related to levels-of-processing theory, that hypothesizes that information is retained in long term memory in two forms: visual and verbal.

Answer: dual code
Page Ref: 176

10) This happens when information gets mixed up with or pushed aside by other information in working memory.

Answer: interference
Page Ref: 181

11) When prior learning makes it more difficult to learn something new, this type of inhibition is said to occur.

Answer: proactive
Page Ref: 183

12) The tendency to learn things more easily when they occur at the end of a presentation is referred to as what kind of effect?

Answer: recency
Page Ref: 183

13) The type of practice that occurs when new information is practiced intensely within a short period of time.

Answer: massed practice
Page Ref: 184

14) Technique in which items to be learned are repeated at intervals over a period of time.

Answer: distributed practice
Page Ref: 184

15) Type of learning tasks that may involve memorizing a list, but not in a special order.

Answer: free-recall
Page Ref: 186

16) One of the most extensively studied methods of using imagery and mnemonics to help students with paired-associate learning.

Answer: keyword method
Page Ref: 187

17) A mnemonic device for serial learning in which the student thinks of a very familiar set of ordered locations, and then mentally places each item on the list into a consecutive location.

Answer: loci method
Page Ref: 188

18) A memory strategy that involves using the first letter of each word in order to remember a number of items.

Answer: initial-letter strategy
Page Ref: 189

19) An imagery method useful for learning ordered lists. To use this mnemonic the student creates mental images that relate items on the list to a well–learned set of words, such as a nursery rhyme.

Answer: pegword method
Page Ref: 198189

20) Refers to the memorization of facts or associations. Much of this type of learning involves associations that are essentially arbitrary.

Answer: rote learning
Page Ref: 190

21) The most important principle of this theory is that information that fits into an existing framework is more easily understood.

Answer: schema theory
Page Ref: 191

22) In this form of note taking students identify main ideas and then diagram connections between them.

Answer: mapping
Page Ref: 195

23) An initial statement about a subject to be learned that provides structure for the new information and relates it to information students already possess.

Answer: advance organizer
Page Ref: 198

24) The process of thinking about material to be learned in a way that connects the material to information or ideas already in the learner's mind.

Answer: elaboration
Page Ref: 19

25) This method of facilitating learning helps students absorb new information by relating it, through comparisons or parallels, to concepts they already understand.

Answer: analogies
Page Ref: 199

Essay Questions

1) Characterize working memory in terms of its limitations. With two examples from your experience or personal observation, illustrate how an excessive load on working memory can cause problems in learning tasks, skills (such as reading or writing) or problem solving.

    Describe a situation in which a learner could use practice, or a learning strategy, to help overcome learning problems caused by working memory overload. Using concepts from the information–processing model, explain how the practice or learning strategy aids learning.

    Answer: Working memory is limited in both capacity and duration. In reading a long sentence or paragraph, comprehension is hindered if, in order to grasp the meaning, the learner must store a large amount of information in working memory (more than about seven items).

        One possible example is: reading a long sentence repeatedly helps to ease the load on working memory. The repeated reading involves practice. The practice enables the learner to make use of information from long–term–memory, to reorganize the smaller units of the sentence into larger ideas, reducing the number of items in working memory, and thus easing comprehension/learning.

Page Ref: 169

2) Explain the basic ideas of levels–of–processing theory, using an example to illustrate your explanation. How do the research findings that support levels–of–processing theory help us understand why some study strategies, such as highlighting, are not always effective?

    Answer: The levels–of–processing theory holds that people subject stimuli to different levels of mental processing and retain only the information that has been subjected to the most thorough processing. For example, you might perceive a tree, but pay little attention to it. Since this is the lowest level of processing, you are unlikely to remember the tree. Second, you might give the tree a name such as "tree" or "oak." Once named, the tree is somewhat more likely to be remembered. The highest level of processing, however, is giving meaning to the tree. You might have climbed the tree, for example.

        Study strategies such as highlighting are ineffective when students use them at a shallow level of processing. A student who highlights "everything," for instance, is omitting the deep processing of meaning that would occur if important ideas were being selected before highlighting.

Page Ref: 175

3) Does practice make perfect? Include in your response a discussion about massed vs. distributed practice, automaticity, and enactment.

    Answer: Practice is important at several stages of learning. First, massed practice (learn intensively at one time) allows for faster initial learning, but distributed practice (learning a little each day) is better for retention. Also, if students practice just long enough to learn something and then do no more, they are likely to forget much of what they have learned. However, if they continue to practice beyond the point where they can recall the answers, and thus develop automaticity, retention will increase. Performing a task, rather than just hearing about it or observing it, also improves learning.

Page Ref: 184

4) Three types of verbal learning tasks are typically seen in classrooms. What are they? Give several examples of each.

The choice of a learning strategy should depend on the nature of the material to be learned. For two of the types of tasks you described above, suggest strategies that would be effective for classroom learning, and explain why each of these strategies suits its task.

Answer: Three types of verbal learning tasks typically seen in classrooms are paired-associate learning, serial learning, and free recall learning. Paired-associate learning tasks involve learning to respond with one member of a pair when given the other member of the pair. For example, learning the multiplication table would be an example of paired-associate learning. Serial learning involves learning items in a particular order. The alphabet, poetry and songs are serial learning tasks. Free recall learning tasks may also involve memorizing a list, but not in a special order. Recalling state capitals is an example of a free recall task.

A mnemonic such as keyword method would be an appropriate learning strategy for Paired-associate learning, whereas organizing a list into categories would be helpful on a free recall task.

Page Ref: 186

5) A teacher was excited when all of his fourth grade students were able to reduce fractions to their lowest common denominator. On a test he had given, the students were able to reduce, for example, 18/20 to 9/10 and 18/24 to 3/4 correctly. The teacher told his class how pleased he was with their performance, then he said, "For a review, let me ask you which you would prefer: 18 pieces of a cake that has been cut into 24 pieces or 3 pieces of a cake that has been cut into 4 pieces?" To his astonishment, the teacher listened as half the class said they would prefer 18 pieces because there were more pieces, and the other half said they would prefer 3 pieces because they were bigger. Explain what happened with the students, by discussing rote versus meaningful learning.

Answer: The teacher's students used rote learning to complete the fraction test. There was little connection between the reduction of fractions and real world experiences. The exercise of reducing fractions was meaningless to the students outside of memorizing to take the test.

Page Ref: 190

6) Think about a schema for a familiar idea, such as types-of-punishment, or Erickson's 5th stage. Draw a representation of that schema, using the "bison" example in Figure 6.3 as a model.

Now imagine that you are going to teach that idea to someone younger, or less-informed about the subject. Draw a representation of what that learner's schema might be like. Summarize the difference between these two individuals' schemata.

If you were in fact teaching the concept to the learner whose schema you described, how would you address the differences between the learner's schema, and your own? Specifically, what are two things you would do as a teacher, that take into account the limited schema of your student?

Answer: Schemata should include a network of related ideas, not necessarily in a neat hierarchy. The new learner's schema may be less elaborate, and less tightly organized. The "teacher" might use a wide variety of strategies, for instance, use of advance organizers, imagery, increased awareness of background knowledge, outlining and mapping, activating prior knowledge and organizing information.

Page Ref: 191

7) What does the research say about note taking, underlining, and summarizing as effective or ineffective study strategies?

Answer: Note taking can be effective for material that requires mental processing of main ideas, especially if the teacher provides skeletal notes before a lecture or reading. Research on underlining generally finds few benefits because students fail to make decisions about what material is most critical. They simply underline too much. Summarizing can be effective if it is used correctly. One effective way to use summarizing is to write one sentence summaries after reading a paragraph of text.
Page Ref: 197

8) List the steps of the PQ4R method and describe its usefulness.

Answer: Steps of the PQ4R method include preview, question, read, reflect, recite, and review. Research has shown the effectiveness of the PQ4R method for older learners because it focuses them on the meaningful organization of information and involves them in other effective strategies such as question generation, elaboration, and distributed practice.
Page Ref: 195

9) As a teacher, what classroom strategies could you use to help students memorize either of the following lists:

Dinosaur

protoceratops	tyrannosaur	triceratops	brachiosaur	iguanodon
trachodon	rhamphorhyncus	allosaur	archeopteryx	brontosaur

Food

tortilla	crepe	tortellini	baguette	enchilada	ravioli
croissant	fritata	fajita	ziti	lasagna	fondue

Extended thinking. Increasing the meaningfulness of material must involve the use of information already stored in the learner's long-term memory. Using the information processing model, explain why one strategy you described above would involve both: 1) the flow of information from short-term memory to long-term memory, AND 2) the flow of information from long-term memory to short-term memory.

Answer: When a list of random terms is presented, it is difficult to memorize, partly because it contains too many items to be held in working memory all at once. However, when the list is organized in a logical way, it is made meaningful, thus, easier to learn and recall. For example, the list of dinosaurs could be divided into meat eaters, plant eaters, flying reptiles, etc.

The learner stores items from the list in STM (having selected them from information in the sensory registers). Any information that will be learned from the list, must flow from short-term memory into long-term memory. But if meaningful categories (e.g., plant eaters) are to be used in working memory (to organize the list, lightening the load on working memory), then knowledge of those categories must be activated. Activating these organizing concepts for use in short-term memory amounts to a flow of category-information from long-term memory, to short-term memory.
Page Ref: 200

10) Elaine Hanley teaches at Maple Hills High School in a large suburban community. Her third period advanced placement history students completed their first exam of the year and they were not happy with the results.

Mrs. Hanley knew the students would be concerned. Most of them were applying at competitive colleges across the nation, so grades and grade point averages were a part of their daily discussions.

"I'm doomed!" cried a student who Mrs. Hanley knew was applying to Carlston University, a prestigious nearby institution. "I'll never get into Carlston now!"

"Mrs. Hanley, what can we do?" asked another member of the class. "I'm not sure it's worth taking this advanced placement class if all I can get is a C on the exam. I'd be better off in the regular history class getting As."

"Instead of changing classes," declared Mrs. Hanley, "let's figure out some study strategies that will help you get high grades on my tests. First of all, what's different about my tests? Why are they more difficult for you?"

"You make us know the stuff. In most classes we just write down what the teacher says, memorize it, then take the exam."

Mrs. Hanley replied, "Well, you're right, I want you to do more than memorize history. What study strategies do you use? Monica?"

"First of all, I take notes in class, then rewrite them when I get home. I underline important points, which is just about everything I write down. Then I read and reread until I think I have a page of notes memorized."

Next Mrs. Hanley asks, "Alex, how do you study for tests?"

"I don't take many notes, but listen carefully to what the teacher says. When I study my text, I just start from the beginning and read until I'm finished. That usually works for me."

After listening to other students about their study habits, Mrs. Hanley announced, "I think I can help you study for my tests by suggesting some different strategies than those you are now using."

Using the information from the chapter, discuss whether or not the strategies suggested by the students are effective. If they are effective strategies, what makes them effective? If they are ineffective, what makes them so? What additional strategies do you think Elaine Hanley will suggest to her students?

Answer: The strategies suggested by the students work effectively if they need to memorize information without attaching meaning to it. However, Elaine Hanley's tests require students to consider the information in meaningful ways. Strategies that work to make learning relevant include: activating and meshing prior knowledge with new knowledge, elaborating on to–be–learned concepts, using simple or known analogies to learn complex or new information, organizing information into some meaningful order, using questioning techniques, drawing conceptual models, and using the PQ4R method when reading new material.

Page Ref: 197

11) From what you know about storing semantic or declarative information in long term memory, explain what would happen if an individual reads:

Mary had a little lamb

which activates the schema to the right, but next reads:

along with some mint jelly and potatoes.

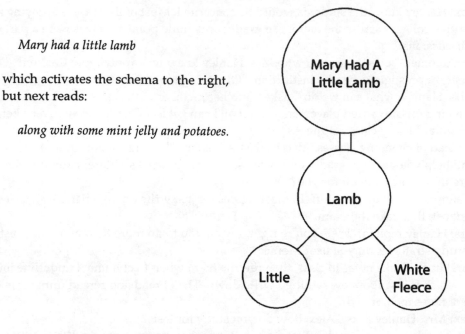

Answer: As the individual reads Mary had a little lamb, she or he activates a "Mary had a Little Lamb" poetry schema. However, when the individual next reads along with some mint jelly and potatoes, she or he cannot, at first, make sense of the information because it does not fit what was expected. The individual will need to select "Mary had a little lamb" as a meal schema in order to understand the second statement.

Page Ref: 172

Chapter 7   The Effective Lesson

Multiple-Choice Questions

1) Which of the following statements about direct instruction is correct?

    A) In a direct instruction lesson, teachers transmit information directly to students.

    B) Direct instruction is a teaching approach in which lessons are designed by students.

    C) Direct instruction requires students to reverse roles with the teacher.

    D) Cooperative learning and discovery are two types of direct instruction.

Answer: A

Explanation: A) Direct instruction is a teaching approach in which the teacher transmits information directly to students. Lessons are goal-oriented and structured by the teacher.

Page Ref: 209

2) What idea about direct instruction does recent research support?

    A) Direct instruction alone is the most effective teaching method.

    B) Direct instruction is the most efficient method of teaching.

    C) Direct instruction can be more efficient than discovery in conceptual development.

    D) Direct instruction is the least efficient method to student development of concepts.

Answer: C

Explanation: C) Recent research has supported the idea that direct instruction can be more efficient than discovery in conceptual development. Students who received direct instruction in how to do experiments performed better in setting up new experiments than students who carried out their own experiments without direct instruction.

Page Ref: 210

3) What is the first step of a direct instruction lesson?

    A) State the learning objectives and orient students to the lesson.

    B) Present students with new learning material.

    C) Give students learning probes and provide feedback.

    D) Give students time for independent practice.

Answer: A

Explanation: A) The first step of a direct instruction lesson is to state learning objectives or outcomes and orient students to the lesson.

Page Ref: 210

4) Which step in a direct instruction lesson focuses on obtaining a brief student response to lesson content, in order to assess level of understanding and correct students' misconceptions?

   A) Orient students to the lesson.

   B) Provide distributed practice and review.

   C) Conduct learning probes.

   D) Present new material.

Answer: C

Explanation: C) Conducting learning probes involves the teacher posing questions to students to assess their level of understanding and correct their misconceptions.

Page Ref: 210

5) Which of the following procedures is recommended for communicating objectives to students?

   A) List objectives that students have already met.

   B) Take steps to avoid establishing "mental set."

   C) State objectives at the beginning of a lesson.

   D) Introduce objectives at the end of the lesson.

Answer: C

Explanation: C) Setting out objectives at the beginning of the lesson is an essential step in providing a framework into which information, instructional materials, and learning activities will fit.

Page Ref: 213

6) To establish a positive mental set (the attitude of readiness) in students, a teacher needs to arouse student curiosity by

   A) emphasizing the subject's seriousness.

   B) making the subject personally relevant to students.

   C) having students open textbooks to the proper page.

   D) waiting at least five minutes to allow for late comers to arrive.

Answer: B

Explanation: B) At the beginning of a lesson, the teacher needs to establish a positive mental set, or attitude of readiness in students by arousing students' curiosity or interest in a lesson. The teacher may help student understanding by making the lesson personally relevant to students.

Page Ref: 214

7) After students have been oriented to the lesson, the next major task in a lesson is to

  A) wait several minutes before talking so that the class can get focused.

  B) be sure that students have mastered prerequisite skills.

  C) tell students that they will be tested on the material at a later time so they can prepare themselves accordingly.

  D) be positive in your approach, but resist the temptation to add humor to the lesson.

Answer: B

Explanation: B) After students have been oriented to the lesson the next major task in a lesson is to be sure that students have mastered prerequisite skills and to link information already in their minds to the information about to be presented.

Page Ref: 215

8) A teacher, in conducting a lesson, draws attention to what students had learned previously by saying, "Yesterday we learned how to find the area of a rectangle. Who will remind us how this is done?" The teacher believes that this brief reminder is sufficient because today's lesson —finding the area of a triangle—is a direct continuation of yesterday's. Which of the following strategies does the example reflect?

  A) evaluating student work   B) using wait time

  C) applying a rule–example–rule pattern   D) reviewing prerequisites

Answer: D

Explanation: D) If today's lesson is a continuation of yesterday's, and students understood yesterday's lesson, then the review may just remind them about the earlier lesson. Ask a few quick questions before beginning the new lesson.

Page Ref: 215

9) A teacher begins a lesson in chemistry by discussing the symbols for each of the elements. Part way into the lesson the teacher refers to chapters and classwork the students will have in six months. At another point the teacher expresses dissatisfaction with the administration's new policy regarding equipment security, which will now require more paperwork. The teacher then talks about an event that took place during spring vacation. The class period ends before the teacher finishes the lesson. What appears to be the overriding problem of the teacher's lecture style?

  A) The teacher does not vary the topics.

  B) There is a lack of clarity in the lesson presentation.

  C) The teacher should not share personal information with students.

  D) The lesson includes abstract elements.

Answer: B

Explanation: B) One consistent feature of effective lessons is clarity, which is the use of direct, simple, and well-organized language to present concepts. Wandering off into digressions or irrelevant topics or otherwise interrupting the flow of the lesson detracts from clarity.

Page Ref: 217

10) Research on this finds that it helps children to learn and retain information.

    A) embedded video lessons   B) verbal repetition of facts by students

    C) lengthy homework assignments   D) video documentaries

Answer: A

Explanation: A) Research on embedded video finds that it helps children learn and retain information to the degree that it is easy to understand and clearly links to the main content. Examples include brief animations and puppet videos.

Page Ref: 218

11) Research on instructional pace implies that most teachers could

    A) slow down considerably.

    B) slow down a moderate amount in their instruction.

    C) increase their pace of instruction as long as degree of understanding is not sacrificed.

    D) increase their pace of instruction considerably, even if that means that some students will not be able to be successful.

Answer: C

Explanation: C) In general, students of teachers who cover more material learn more than other students. Research on instructional pace does imply that most teachers could increase their pace of instruction as long as degree of understanding is not sacrificed.

Page Ref: 219

12) Which of the following roles is most emphasized by your text author's discussion of effective lecturing techniques?

    A) performer   B) scholar   C) guide   D) tutor

Answer: A

Explanation: A) The role that is most emphasized of the choices listed is performer. Good lecturers are active, continually striving to keep the attention of their audience (students). They accomplish this through clarity, organization, and enthusiasm.

Page Ref: 218

13) Using humor in an introduction to a lesson is generally

   A) negative, since it gets students off task.

   B) negative, since it compromises the authority of the teacher.

   C) positive, since it can establish a positive learning set.

   D) positive, because it adds lesson clarity.

Answer: C

Explanation: C) The textbook author's position on using humor in an introduction to a direct instruction lesson is generally positive, since it can establish a positive set to learn. Getting students motivated and interested in learning is an important aspect of a lesson orientation.

Page Ref: 218

14) Which is most often the appropriate amount of time for a teacher to wait after asking a question?

   A) 1 second   B) 3 seconds   C) 10 seconds   D) 20 seconds

Answer: B

Explanation: B) An appropriate amount of wait time is approximately three seconds. One second would be much too short, conveying a negative expectancy. Ten or 20 seconds would seem an eternity and make everyone uncomfortable.

Page Ref: 221

15) The length of time a teacher allows a student to answer a question, before moving the class along, is called

   A) mental set.   B) delay interval.

   C) attention span.   D) wait time.

Answer: D

Explanation: D) Wait time is the length of time a teacher allows a student to answer a question. The recommended wait time is about three seconds.

Page Ref: 221

16) A teacher calls on a student and waits (about three seconds) for an answer. The teacher stays with the student who is having difficulty responding. How would your text author evaluate this approach?

   A) It is not a good approach because it places the student and teacher in a power struggle.

   B) It is not a good approach because it communicates negative expectations to the student.

   C) It is a good approach because it communicates positive expectations to the student.

   D) It is a good approach because it shows the teacher's authority.

Answer: C

Explanation: C) The textbook author would evaluate the teacher's approach as positive because it communicates positive expectations to students. Often what occurs, particularly with low achievers, is that teachers quickly move to someone else when a student hesitates with an answer. This communicates the expectancy that the first student will not succeed in answering.

Page Ref: 221

17) Which of the following is true about choral responding?

   A) It is overused by teachers.

   B) It should be oral and audible, not conveyed through gestures.

   C) It is more effective for learning than individual questioning.

   D) It is recommended primarily for questions having only one correct answer.

Answer: D

Explanation: D) Choral responding is recommended primarily for questions having one correct answer. If multiple answers were possible, the "chorus" could get rather chaotic. Gestures or hand signals as well as oral responses can be used.

Page Ref: 222

18) A teacher uses frequent questioning of students, calling on those who raise their hands to respond. Your textbook author would evaluate this procedure as

   A) effective, because it avoids having to call on people and possibly embarrassing them.

   B) effective, because it treats all students equally across a wide range of ability.

   C) limited, because students who do not volunteer will escape having to respond.

   D) effective, because volunteers usually give correct responses.

Answer: C

Explanation: C) The textbook author would evaluate the teacher's procedure as limited because students who don't volunteer will escape having to respond. A better procedure is to call on students at random so that all participate and are kept attentive during the recitation.

Page Ref: 222

19) What is the best way for teachers to ask questions of students?

    A) Ask the question first, then call on a student at random.

    B) Call on a student at random, then ask the question.

    C) Ask for a volunteer to answer, then ask the question.

    D) Ask the question first, then ask for a volunteer to answer.

Answer: A

Explanation: A) The best way to ask questions in class is to ask the question first, then call on students at random. This procedure keeps all students attentive to the question since they don't know who will be asked. If the question were asked after calling on a student, the rest could tune out.

Page Ref: 222

20) For which lesson would independent practice probably be **LEAST** necessary?

    A) multiplying two-digit numbers   B) examining ethics in our society

    C) learning rules of grammar   D) learning how to use a word processor

Answer: B

Explanation: B) Independent practice would probably be least necessary for a lesson on ethics in our society. Such practice is more essential where there are specific skills involved such as in mathematics, grammar, and word processing.

Page Ref: 222

21) In conducting learning probes, a drawback of factual questions is that they

    A) are unsuitable for use with choral response.

    B) are not effective for developing conceptual skills.

    C) have little effect on students' factual skills.

    D) require longer wait times than do conceptual questions.

Answer: B

Explanation: B) Factual questions help with factual skills, but not with conceptual skills. They are often suitable for choral response. The text gives no indication that factual questions would call for longer wait times than conceptual questions.

Page Ref: 222

22) Which of the following recommendations regarding independent practice is appropriate?

   A) Keep the assignments fairly short.

   B) Make the assignments highly challenging.

   C) Orient much of the assignment around new material that will soon be introduced.

   D) Limit the amount of instructions and directions, to encourage student independence.

Answer: A

Explanation: A) It is recommended that independent practice assignments be kept fairly short. Distributed practice is more effective than massed practice. Also, such assignments should not be overly challenging or deal with new material. Adequate instructions are needed.

Page Ref: 223

23) Which of the following is **NOT** recommended in assigning independent practice?

   A) Teachers should monitor student work by walking around the room.

   B) Teachers should intermittently lecture during seatwork.

   C) Students' work should be collected and checked.

   D) Students' work should be counted toward their grades.

Answer: B

Explanation: B) Once independent practice begins it should not be interrupted. A poor procedure, therefore, would be for teachers to intermittently provide brief lectures or explanations during the seatwork period. Teachers should monitor individual work, collect it, and grade it.

Page Ref: 223

24) Which of the following statements on seatwork are accurate, according to research?
   1) Seatwork is typically both overused and misused.
   2) Student time spent receiving instruction directly from the teacher is more productive than time spent during seatwork.
   3) Seatwork is a productive solution for students who lack the motivation to work well on their own.
   4) Studies of elementary mathematics find students spending 50 to 70 percent of their class time doing seatwork.

   A) 1, 2, and 3 (not 4).   B) 3 and 4 (not 1 and 2).

   C) 2 and 4 (not 1 and 3).   D) 1, 2, and 4 (not 3).

Answer: D

Explanation: D) Anderson et al, (1985) have noted that time spent on seatwork is often wasted for students who lack the motivation, reading skill, or self-organization skills to work well on their own.

Page Ref: 223

25) A high success rate on independent practice work can be accomplished in two ways. First, assignments should be clear and self-explanatory covering content appropriate for the students. Second,

    A) assignments should be at least 30 minutes long, to allow students to get involved.

    B) students should be given independent practice worksheets so that the teacher can determine whether or not they have mastered the material.

    C) students should rarely be given independent practice worksheets until the teacher has determined, through learning probes, that they can handle the material.

    D) to minimize student anxiety, teachers should avoid such actions as walking around the room, or evaluating students' work.

Answer: C

Explanation: C) A high success rate on independent practice work can be accomplished in two ways. First, assignments should be clear and self-explanatory and should cover content on which all students can succeed. Second, students should rarely be given independent practice worksheets until they have indicated in learning probes that they can handle the material.

Page Ref: 223

26) What changes in typical current practices are suggested by the direct teaching model described in your textbook?

    A) Increase the amount of independent practice.

    B) Decrease the amount of feedback provided to students.

    C) Slow the instructional pace.

    D) Increase the frequency of testing.

Answer: D

Explanation: D) The direct instruction model described in your textbook suggests increasing the frequency of testing to provide more feedback to students and the teacher. Instructional pacing should be increased where appropriate and the amount of independent practice should be reduced.

Page Ref: 224

27) Which of the following statements regarding the assessment of students' work is accurate?
    1) It may be done informally by questioning students;
    2) It may use performance on independent work as an assessment;
    3) It may involve a quiz;
    4) In general, less testing results in greater achievement than frequent testing.

    A) 1 and 4 (not 2 and 3).   B) 2, 3, and 4 (not 1).

    C) 1 and 2 (not 3 and 4).   D) 1, 2, and 3 are accurate (not 4).

Answer: D

Explanation: D) In general, more frequent testing results in greater achievement than less testing.
Page Ref: 224

28) According to researchers, how many minutes of homework per subject is recommended for fourth graders?

    A) 5–10 minutes   B) 15–20 minutes

    C) 20–25 minutes   D) at least 30 minutes

Answer: A

Explanation: A) Good and Brophy (2003) recommend five to ten minutes of homework per subject for fourth graders, increasing to 30 minutes or more for college-bound high school students.

Page Ref: 225

29) Retention of learned material is increased when practice is spaced, over time. What implication does that statement have for teachers?

    A) Reviewing and recapitulating important information from earlier lessons enhances learning.

    B) When teachers plan lessons they will have to set aside time for students to respond to questions.

    C) Students who are in year-round school programs will find homework to be difficult.

    D) Reviewing and recapitulating important information from earlier lessons will not interest students.

Answer: A

Explanation: A) Retention of many kinds of knowledge is increased by practice or review spaced out over time. This has several implications for teaching. First, it implies that reviewing and recapitulating important information from earlier lessons enhances learning. Reviews of important material at long intervals are particularly important to maintain previous skills.

Page Ref: 226

30) Studies of the Direct Instruction (DI, or DISTAR) program have shown that it is

    A) effective in increasing long-term success of students at risk for low achievement.

    B) somewhat damaging for lower-ability students' self-esteem.

    C) successful in raising math scores for females and reading scores for males.

    D) successful in teaching problem-solving strategies and in raising IQ scores.

Answer: A

Explanation: A) Studies of the DISTAR program have shown strong positive effects on achievement, especially with low achievers.

Page Ref: 226

31) Outside of school, how are we most likely to learn concepts?

   A) through television and magazines

   B) through family members' help in interpreting formal(dictionary-like) definitions.

   C) from tutors

   D) by observing how others name things.

Answer: D

Explanation: D) Most concepts that we learn outside of school we learn by observation. For example, a child learns the concept "car" by hearing certain vehicles referred to as a "car."

Page Ref: 227

32) Which of the following uses a rule-example-rule pattern?

   A) Present a few instances, state a definition, and then restate the definition.

   B) State a definition, present several instances (and non-instances, if appropriate), and then restate the definition showing how the instances typify the definition.

   C) State a definition, restate the definition, present several instances, and then restate the definition showing how the instances typify the definition.

   D) State a definition, present non-instances, and then restate the definition.

Answer: B

Explanation: B) For most concepts taught in school, it makes most sense to state a definition, present several instances (and non-instances, if appropriate), and then restate the definition showing how the instances typify the definition. Use of this pattern, called rule-example-rule, has been found to be characteristic of effective teachers.

Page Ref: 228

33) All of the following are effective ways to teach concepts **EXCEPT**

   A) order the examples from easy to difficult.

   B) select examples that differ from one another.

   C) start with unusual examples.

   D) compare and contrast examples and non-examples.

Answer: C

Explanation: C) Effective ways to teach concepts include ordering examples from easy to difficult, selecting examples that differ from one another, and comparing examples and non-examples.

Page Ref: 228

34) An important thing to know about the transfer of learning is that it

   A) always occurs when the degree of similarity between concepts is low.

   B) never occurs when the degree of similarity between concepts is high.

   C) cannot be assumed to have occurred.

   D) can be assumed to have occurred, as long as the teacher has presented the lesson clearly.

Answer: C

Explanation: C) We cannot simply assume that students will be able to transfer their school learning to practical situations. So we must teach them to use skills in situations similar to those they are likely to encounter in real life or in other situations to which we expect learning to transfer.

Page Ref: 228

35) Transfer of learning principles specify that the ability to apply knowledge in new circumstances depends on all of the following **EXCEPT**

   A) whether the subject matter is drawn from the sciences, or from language arts.

   B) the similarity between the situation in which information is learned, and that in which it is applied.

   C) the variety of circumstances in which students learn or practice the information or skill.

   D) the depth of processing of the original learning.

Answer: A

Explanation: A) According to research, one important principle of transfer is that the ability to apply knowledge in new circumstances depends in part on the variety of circumstances in which we have learned or practiced the information or skills. Successful transfer also depends on whether the material was learned in a meaningful way (not by rote), and the degree of similarity between the original learning situation and the setting targeted for transfer.

Page Ref: 228

36) The classic experiments by Nitsch (1977) illustrate which of the following principles?

   A) Students can increase their understanding of concepts by applying them to situations that they have shared with other students.

   B) Students learn best when they have the opportunity to apply knowledge to past situations.

   C) One way to increase the chance that the concepts will be applied to new situations is to expose students, during learning, to non-examples from a new situation.

   D) One way to increase the chance that the concepts will be applied to new situations is to expose students, during learning, to examples from a range of situations.

Answer: D

Explanation: D) In teaching concepts, one way to increase the chance that the concepts will be appropriately applied to new situations is to give examples from a range of situations. A set of classic experiments by Nitsch (1977) illustrated this principle.

Page Ref: 230

37) Which of the following statements regarding transfer versus initial learning are accurate?
   1) Teaching a concept in many different contexts is confusing to students
      if it is done at the beginning of a sequence of instruction;
   2) The tricky aspect of teaching for transfer is that some of the most effective
      procedures for enhancing transfer are exactly the opposite of those for initial
      learning;
   3) When introducing a new concept, it is important to use similar examples until
      the concept is well understood, and only then use diverse examples;
   4) Teaching a concept in many different contexts decreases transfer if done after
      students understand the concept in one setting.

   A) 1, 2, and 3 (not 4).   B) 1 and 4 (not 2 and 3).

   C) 2 and 3 (not 1 and 4).   D) All four statements.

   Answer: A

   Explanation: A) Teaching a concept in many different contexts enhanced transfer when done
                    after students understood the concept in one setting.
   Page Ref: 231

38) The evaluation of an "explicit transfer" technique in third-grade math classes found that

   A) students can be taught explicitly to transfer skills to new circumstances.

   B) students at this level cannot be taught to transfer learned skills to new circumstances.

   C) students can be taught the transfer technique if their IQs were above average.

   D) only students above the third grade level can learn the technique.

   Answer: A

   Explanation: A) Students can be taught explicitly to transfer skills to new circumstances, as
                    shown by Fuchs et al. (2003) in their evaluation of an "explicit transfer"
                    technique in third grade math classes. Children were taught what transfer
                    means and were given examples of how similar story problems could be
                    changed using different language, context, and numbers.
   Page Ref: 231

39) During whole-class discussions, the teacher functions as a(n)

   A) information giver.   B) censor.

   C) moderator.   D) performer

   Answer: C

   Explanation: C) During whole-class discussions, the teacher normally functions as a moderator.
                    In this role, the teacher is careful not to dominate or intervene too much, while
                    focusing on stimulating the discussion when it slows down or gets off track.
   Page Ref: 233

40) A teacher is planning to have a whole-class discussion on the effects of television violence on children. Before beginning the discussion, what should the teacher do?

    A) The teacher should list the students to be called upon.

    B) The teacher should question students about their understanding of the effects of television violence on children.

    C) The teacher should take a position on this issue in order to set the tone for the discussion.

    D) The teacher should give students the opportunity to choose members of their groups.

Answer: B

Explanation: B) It is important for the teacher to ensure that the students are somewhat familiar with the subject of the discussion (TV violence). Otherwise, they will have little to discuss and end up giving mostly opinions or not talking much at all.

Page Ref: 234

41) A teacher has been using whole-class discussion but decides to try small-group discussion. What change will the teacher have to make?

    A) The teacher will have to appoint group leaders.

    B) The teacher will need less time to prepare students for the topic to be discussed.

    C) Small-group discussion will require more direct teacher involvement.

    D) With small-group discussion, the topics will have to be less controversial.

Answer: A

Explanation: A) One change the teacher should anticipate with small-group discussion is to have group leaders appointed to guide their respective groups. Students will still need preparation, often in the form of teacher presentations.

Page Ref: 234

42) Which of the following statements about small-group discussion is true?

    A) Leaders should be the highest-achieving students.

    B) Discussion topics may vary from group to group.

    C) The ideal group size is three, regardless of the ages of the participants.

    D) Younger students benefit from small-group discussions as much as older students do.

Answer: B

Explanation: B) Groups may not necessarily discuss the same question. Often, each group is assigned one subtopic from a larger topic. Small-group discussions seem best suited for older students, with group size maintained at from four to six students.

Page Ref: 234

43) Based on research results, small-group discussions have greater effects on student achievement when the subject selected

    A) generates different viewpoints.

    B) is beyond the grasp of the students.

    C) is unrelated to normal curriculum objectives.

    D) conveys a high-consensus idea.

Answer: A

Explanation: A) Research indicates that discussion is most effective for achievement when the subject selected generates different viewpoints. In other words, engaging in controversy seems more beneficial than seeking consensus.

Page Ref: 235

True/False Questions

1) The first step of a lesson, stating learning objectives or outcomes, represents a condensation of much advance lesson planning.

Answer: TRUE
Page Ref: 210

2) An appropriate task to begin a lesson with is the assessment of students' performances and to provide them with feedback.

Answer: FALSE
Page Ref: 210

3) Students' readiness requires lesson introductions that arouse student curiosity and personal relevance.

Answer: TRUE
Page Ref: 214

4) One reason to review prerequisites is to provide advance organizers.

Answer: TRUE
Page Ref: 216

5) According to research, too much variation in mode of presentation can decrease achievement if it distracts students from the lesson content.

Answer: TRUE
Page Ref: 217

6) A rule-example-rule approach is inconsistent with good teaching practices, according to the text author.

Answer: FALSE
Page Ref: 217

7) The method of calling on students randomly defies common sense, but has been supported overwhelmingly in the research findings.

Answer: FALSE
Page Ref: 222

8) In cognitive terms, practice serves as rehearsal for transferring information from working memory to long term memory.

Answer: TRUE
Page Ref: 222

9) Frequent testing results in greater achievement than in frequent testing.

Answer: TRUE
Page Ref: 224

10) Research on homework shows that it does not increase achievement of secondary school students.

Answer: FALSE
Page Ref: 224

11) The prescriptions derived from studies of effective teachers cannot be expected to make a substantial difference in student achievement, when applied in the classroom uncritically.

Answer: TRUE
Page Ref: 226

12) When introducing new concepts, it is best to use similar examples until the concept is well understood, and only then to use diverse examples.

Answer: TRUE
Page Ref: 228

13) What differentiates a whole–class discussion from a usual lesson is that in discussions the teacher plays more of a dominant role.

Answer: FALSE
Page Ref: 233

14) Poorly organized students may not be able to benefit from small–group discussion.

Answer: TRUE
Page Ref: 234

15) Research on small–group discussions indicates that these activities can increase student achievement more than traditional lessons.

Answer: FALSE
Page Ref: 235

Short Answer Questions

1) The term used to describe lessons in which the teacher transmits information directly to students, structuring class time to reach a clearly defined set of objectives as efficiently as possible.

   Answer: direct instruction
   Page Ref: 209

2) The procedure that includes stated learning objectives, information, and activities the teacher will provide, and time and materials needed.

   Answer: lesson planning
   Page Ref: 213

3) Like drama, this aspect of a teacher's "performance" is one way to establish a positive mental set in students.

   Answer: humor
   Page Ref: 214

4) An attitude reflected by students that indicates their eagerness to learn the important information or skills the teacher is about to present.

   Answer: mental set
   Page Ref: 214

5) The term that refers to a variety of ways of asking for brief student responses to lesson content.

   Answer: learning probe
   Page Ref: 219

6) The length of time the teacher hesitates for a student to answer a question, before giving the answer or going on to another student.

   Answer: wait time
   Page Ref: 221

7) An approach that is used when there is only one possible answer and the teacher asks the class to respond in unison.

   Answer: choral response
   Page Ref: 222

8) Component of instruction in which students work by themselves to demonstrate and rehearse new knowledge.

   Answer: independent practice
   Page Ref: 222

9) A term that refers to in-class independent practice.

Answer: seatwork
Page Ref: 223

10) Research on direct instruction has mostly focused on the elementary grades in these subject areas.

Answer: basic reading and mathematics
Page Ref: 226

11) A general idea abstracted from specific instances. It may be a category under which specific elements are grouped.

Answer: concept
Page Ref: 227

12) The application of skills learned in one setting, to performance in a new context.

Answer: transfer of learning
Page Ref: 228

Essay Questions

1) Make a list of questions you need to answer before you teach a lesson.

Answer: What will students know or be able to do after the lesson? What will be the outcomes of their learning? How will you know when the students have achieved the outcomes? What information, activities, and experiences will help students acquire the knowledge and skills needed to demonstrate the outcomes? How much time will be needed? How will in-class and out-of-class time be used? How will seatwork and homework assignments help students? What books and materials are needed? Are the materials accurate, pedagogically sound, fair to different cultures, and appropriate in content and grade level? How should the material be presented? What learning tasks will students perform? How will students be organized, monitored, and evaluated?

Page Ref: 223

2) A teacher has spent the week teaching about women's suffrage in the United States during the late 1800s. Below is an outline of a lesson for today. Read the lesson, then write a short description of a lesson that might have preceded this one and one that might follow.

    I. Women's Suffrage (late 19th century)

        A. National Women Suffrage Association worked to increase congressional support for a constitutional amendment.

        B. Suffragists attempted to cast ballots in elections and to test voting rights in the courts.

            1. Susan B. Anthony attempted to vote (early 1970s) and suedwhen she was prevented from doing so, but lost.

            2. Sojourner Truth was turned away before she could obtain a ballot.

        C. Congress did not seem to be moving toward support for an amendment.

Answer: A preceding lesson most likely contained events that explained how the Women's Suffrage Movement arrived at where it was in the late 1800s. It probably addressed major players and their activities before this time, issues associated with why women were not allowed to vote, and other major events of the day. A lesson that follows this one would most likely contain events that explain how the Women's Suffrage Movement finally succeeded in passing an amendment giving women the right to vote.
Page Ref: 215

3) Based on the text's discussion of direct instruction, develop a set of 3–5 guidelines for teachers, on presenting new material. For each guideline, explain how it will help students learn, and give an example of how a teacher would implement it.

Answer: Guidelines for presenting new material might include logical organization, emphasis of important points, avoidance of vague terms (for lesson clarity), use of explanatory words, techniques for maintaining attention, and appropriate pacing.
Page Ref: 216

4) In teaching by direct-instruction, at what steps in the lesson will a teacher need to assess students' skills or knowledge? At each of these steps, what is the purpose of the assessment?

Answer: Assessment is involved in reviewing prerequisites, conducting learning probes, monitoring independent practice, and in the overall evaluation of student mastery of lesson objectives.
Page Ref: 224

5) How well do findings from research support the effectiveness of the direct instruction approach? What research questions still need to be considered?

Answer: It is clear that direct instruction methods can improve the teaching of certain basic skills, but it is equally clear that there is much yet to be learned about how and for what purposes they should be used. Direct instruction research has focused on basic reading and mathematics, mostly in the elementary grades. For other subjects and grade levels, we have less of a basis for believing that direction instruction methods will improve student learning.
Page Ref: 226

6) Classroom lessons often focus on teaching concepts—categories under which specific elements may be grouped—in two ways. What are the ways? Give an example of each.

   If you were teaching the concept of positive reinforcement, you would be selecting examples to aid student learning. Describe the sorts of examples you would use: to ease initial learning, and then to maximize students' ability to apply the concept to new situations.

   Answer: Concepts are generally learned in one of two ways. Most concepts that we learn outside of school we learn by observation. For example, a child learns the concept car by hearing certain vehicles referred to as cars. Other concepts are learned by definition. For example, it is difficult to learn the concepts of aunts and non-aunts without understanding the definition of aunt.

   For initial learning, a selection of same-context examples would be effective. After the basic concept is grasped, varied-context examples will work to promote transfer.

   Page Ref: 227

7) A teacher is a firm believer in teaching for transfer. If the teacher is to teach a lesson on grammar for fifth graders, what activities might be included?

   Answer: The teacher will give students the skills and knowledge necessary for them to function effectively as adults in the real world. The teacher might have them write letters to friends, submit an editorial to the school newspaper, keep a journal, or write a composition about a hero.

   Page Ref: 228

8) How is a whole-class discussion activity different from a typical (e.g., direction instruction) lesson? What type of information is learned best through discussion?

   Answer: What differentiates a whole-class discussion from a usual lesson is that in discussions the teacher plays a less dominant role. Teachers may guide the discussion and help the class avoid dead ends, but the ideas should be drawn from the students. A type of information that is well suited to discussion would be exploring points of view. A teacher does not have a specific principle in mind, but rather wants students to explore and develop their own ideas about a topic, using information they have learned.

   Page Ref: 233

9) How is small-group discussion different from whole-class discussion? What is the role of the leader during a small group discussion activity?

   Answer: In small-group discussions, students work in four- to six-member groups to discuss a particular topic. Small-group discussions require students to work independently of the teacher most of the time; therefore, students under fourth grade may have difficulties with this instructional strategy. The leader's role in a discussion group is to make sure that the group stays on task and to ensure that all group members participate.

   Page Ref: 234

10) After three years of declining achievement test scores, the West Rockaway school board voted 12-1 in favor of adopting a standard direct instruction model for use by all teachers in the district. Their rationale was that if all teachers were trained and were required to use the model, student achievement would improve. During the fall inservice, teachers received training, were told to post the steps of the model in their classrooms, and use it for all their lessons.

Dr. Feinman, an elementary principal in the district who attended the inservice, thought to herself, "This is a great idea. I can evaluate my teachers on how well they can follow the steps of the model. No more heated discussions with teachers who argue that a poor evaluation is just a difference of opinion in teaching philosophies."

Across the table from Dr. Feinman sat Mr. Casey, a third grade teacher at West Rockaway Elementary School where Dr. Feinman was principal. His thoughts were the opposite of his supervisor. "This is a sad day for teachers. First we're given curriculum guides from the state, lesson plans from textbook manufacturers, and now we're being told that we have to teach in one way and one way only. What was the point of all those years of college to learn how to teach. Doesn't anyone trust me to be professional?"

From what you have learned in the chapter, discuss the school board's plan. Do you think the plan will work? Why or why not? Discuss what the school might be like after six months, a year, and five years after implementation of the plan.

Answer: There is no evidence that direct instruction should be used as the sole method of instruction. In fact, there is evidence that it is not always appropriate. For example, researchers know that whole-class and small-group discussions are effective tools for some learning situations as are dozens of other methods. Using one method only will most likely frustrate teachers who are not comfortable with its underlying philosophy and with students who could become bored with the routine. Direct instruction is a useful strategy; however, it is not a teacher's only strategy.

Page Ref: 226

11) Rank order the following steps of a direct instruction lesson.

_____ present new material
_____ provide independent practice
_____ orient students to the lesson
_____ assess performance and provide feedback
_____ state learning objective
_____ provide distributed practice and review
_____ review prerequisites
_____ conduct learning probes

Answer: 4 present new material
        6 provide independent practice
        2 orient students to the lesson
        7 assess performance and provide feedback
        1 state learning objective
        8 provide distributed practice and review
        3 review prerequisites
        5 conduct learning probes

Page Ref: 210

12) An integral component of learning is readiness. Name the term for an "attitude of readiness," and describe ways that teachers can establish an attitude of readiness in students. When should this be done?

Answer: An attitude of readiness is referred to as a positive mental set in which students are prepared to focus on the topic presented. Teachers can establish this mental set by beginning a lesson promptly to convey a sense of seriousness, but also need to arouse students' curiosity or interest. This can be accomplished by making the lesson personally relevant to students with an introduction connecting the lesson to events, people, or objects students are familiar with or close to. Humor or drama can also prompt students' interest or curiosity. Teachers need to establish the mental set during the lesson introduction.

Page Ref: 214

Chapter 8   Student–Centered and Contructivist Approaches to Instruction

Multiple–Choice Questions

1) The essence of constructivist theory is the idea that learners

   A) participate in bottom–up instruction.

   B) individually discover and transform complex information.

   C) are passive and teachers are active.

   D) should be placed in ability groups.

   Answer: B

   Explanation: B) The essence of constructivist theory is the idea that learners must individually discover and transform complex information if they are to make it their own. Constructivist theory sees learning as constantly checking new information against old rules than revising rules when they no longer work. This suggests a far more active role for students.

   Page Ref: 243

2) Which of the following teacher roles best captures the philosophy of the constructivist approach?

   A) guide on the side   B) sage on the stage

   C) knowledge imparter   D) drill instructor

   Answer: A

   Explanation: A) In a student–centered classroom the teacher becomes the "guide on the side" instead of the "sage on the stage," helping students to discover their own meaning instead of lecturing and controlling the classroom.

   Page Ref: 243

3) According to constructivist thought, as it draws on Vygotsky's theories, four key concepts for classroom instruction are zone of proximal development; cognitive apprenticeship; scaffolding or mediated learning; and

   A) rote learning.   B) shaping.

   C) social learning.   D) computer–based learning.

   Answer: C

   Explanation: C) One of Vygotsky's key principles from his theories is his emphasis on the social nature of learning. Students learn, he proposed, through joint interactions with adults and more capable peers.

   Page Ref: 244

4) Which of the following learning strategies would a constructivist be **LEAST** likely to advocate?

    A) cooperative learning

    B) discovery

    C) inquiry

    D) drill and practice

Answer: D

Explanation: D) A constructivist would be least likely to advocate drill and practice. In contrast, the constructivist would favor strategies that give learners the opportunity to explore new ideas and concepts on their own (through discovery or inquiry) or in cooperative groups. Active learning rather than memorization (drill) is stressed.

Page Ref: 245

5) Constructivist approaches to teaching typically make extensive use of cooperative learning. Why is this?

    A) It is easy for teachers to assign drill and practice activities.

    B) There is less need to challenge students' misconceptions.

    C) Students understand concepts better if they can talk with each other.

    D) It allows teachers time to work on non-instructional duties.

Answer: C

Explanation: C) Constructivist approaches to teaching typically make extensive use of cooperative learning, on the theory that students will more easily discover and comprehend difficult concepts if they can talk with each other about the problems.

Page Ref: 245

6) Which of the following applies to discovery learning?

    A) Teachers encourage students to experiment and discover.

    B) Math and reading are the most suitable subjects for this approach.

    C) Knowledge is a product, not a process.

    D) No teacher input is permitted during a discovery lesson.

Answer: A

Explanation: A) In using discovery learning, students may learn individually or in groups. Teachers will give direction from time to time, but mainly they provide encouragement. Students may also explore ideas not directly related to the lesson.

Page Ref: 245

7) What type of instruction is emphasized by constructivist approaches?

    A) bottom-up   B) individualized

    C) teacher-led   D) top-down

Answer: D

Explanation: D) Constructivist approaches to teaching emphasize top-down rather than bottom-up instruction, meaning that students begin with complex problems to solve and then work out or discover the basic skills required with the teacher's guidance.

Page Ref: 245

8) A student knows how to break complex problems into simpler steps, how and when to skim, and how and when to read for deep understanding. What key concept of constructivist theories of learning defines this student?

    A) impulsive thinker   B) dependent learner

    C) reflective thinker   D) self-regulated learner

Answer: D

Explanation: D) Self-regulated learners are those who have knowledge of effective learning strategies and how and when to use them. For example, they know how to break complex problems into simpler steps or to test out alternative solutions.

Page Ref: 248

9) Which of the following statements best characterizes scaffolding?

    A) As a set of lessons progresses, students are give more and more structure.

    B) The teacher gradually assigns the students more responsibility for their learning.

    C) The teacher initially gives the students major responsibility for their learning, and then tunes it downward, as needed.

    D) The teacher's role is consistent throughout a set of lessons.

Answer: B

Explanation: B) In scaffolding, the structure given to students gradually decreases as the teacher turns over increasing responsibility to students, to operate on their own.

Page Ref: 248

10) While discovery learning promotes the advantage of arousing student curiosity and motivation, pure discovery learning is less common than

    A) regulated discovery learning where the teacher requires students to follow strict rules.

    B) guided discovery learning where the teacher gives clues and structures portions of an activity.

    C) approximate discovery learning where students theorize approximate details.

    D) self–discovery learning where students use their own schemata and perceptions.

Answer: B

Explanation: B) Discovery learning has the advantages of arousing student curiosity and motivation, and helping students' independent problem solving and critical–thinking skills. However, discovery learning can lead to errors and wasted time; so guided discovery learning—where the teacher plays a more active role by giving clues and structuring portions of an activity—is more common than pure discovery learning.

Page Ref: 248

11) In assisted (or mediated) learning, who is the primary cultural agent guiding instruction?

    A) a student

    B) an outside resource person (e.g., librarian)

    C) the teacher

    D) an author

Answer: C

Explanation: C) The teacher will be the main mediating agent. Once students begin to develop internal mediators, they will be given more freedom to learn on their own.

Page Ref: 249

12) Based on the APA's document Learner–Centered Psychological Principles, which of the following statements are true of the learner?

    1)   actively seeking knowledge;

    2)   motivated by the quest for knowledge;

    3)   working with others to socially construct meaning;

    4)   reinterpreting information and experience for himself or herself.

    A) 1 and 2 (not 3 and 4) .   B) 1, 3, and 4 (not 2).

    C) 2 and 4 (not 1 and 3).   D) All four statements.

Answer: D

Explanation: D) The Learner–Centered Psychological Principles paint a picture of the learner as actively seeking knowledge, reinterpreting information and experience for himself or herself, motivated by the quest for knowledge itself (rather than by grades or other rewards), working with others to socially construct meaning, and aware of his or her own learning strategies—strategic in applying them to new problems or circumstances.

Page Ref: 249

13) Which of the following best describes reciprocal teaching?

    A) Students discover principles by conducting experiments on their own.

    B) After the teacher has presented a lesson, students work in teams, making sure that all team-members learn the material.

    C) Each student from a group becomes an "expert" on a different segment of the overall assignment. Then they put the segments together, like a puzzle.

    D) The teacher asks a small group of students questions about material they have just read. Later, the students model the teacher's behavior, generating their own questions for the group.

Answer: D

Explanation: D) Unlike discovery learning, STAD and jigsaw, reciprocal teaching involves students in asking their group members questions, modeled after the teacher's questioning.

Page Ref: 251

14) Students are using the reciprocal teaching method in a small reading group. They would use all of the following procedures **EXCEPT**

    A) thinking of important questions that might be asked.

    B) predicting what the author might discuss next.

    C) completing a test and rereading the passage if unsuccessful.

    D) pointing out when something is unclear about the passage.

Answer: C

Explanation: C) Important activities in using reciprocal teaching are questioning, predicting, and pointing out when something is unclear. Not included is completing a self-quiz and rereading the passage if unsuccessful.

Page Ref: 251

15) A teacher is initiating reciprocal teaching with a group of six students of high, average, and low ability. Who should be the teacher for the first segment of learning?

    A) a student of high ability   B) a student of average ability

    C) a student of low ability   D) the teacher

Answer: D

Explanation: D) The classroom teacher would serve as the teacher until students demonstrate that they can initiate the activities themselves. Typically, teachers will remove themselves from directing the group gradually over time.

Page Ref: 252

16) What is the first step for students (after reading a passage) when using a reciprocal teaching approach in reading?

    A) Develop a list of goals.   B) Complete a pretest.

    C) Predict what will happen.   D) Generate questions.

Answer: D

Explanation: D) The first step in reciprocal teaching is to think of questions a teacher might ask about what is being read. This step is followed by summarizing, predicting what the author might discuss next, and pointing out when something is unclear.

Page Ref: 252

17) In the constructivist writing process model and mathematics instruction approach, students work

    A) individually on assigned lessons.

    B) in small groups or teams working together.

    C) with tutors who scaffold them.

    D) with detailed outlines of expectations.

Answer: B

Explanation: B) A widely used set of approaches to the teaching of creative writing, writing process models engage students in small peer-response teams in which they work together through the writing steps. In approaches to early mathematics instruction, students also work together in small groups. Children review each other's work and give helpful ideas for improvement.

Page Ref: 253

18) The Student Teams–Achievement Division involves

    A) competition between individuals, within their small groups.

    B) cooperative learning within small groups.

    C) small-group preparation for standardized tests.

    D) computer–assisted instruction.

Answer: B

Explanation: B) Student Teams– Achievement Division (STAD) is a cooperative learning method whereby students are assigned to four–member learning teams that are mixed in performance level, gender, and ethnicity. The teacher presents a lesson, and then students work within their teams to make sure that all team members understand the lesson.

Page Ref: 256

19) What component of STAD is designed to give each team member an equal opportunity to contribute to the team points?

   A) Teams are composed of like–ability members.

   B) Points are based on improvement rather than absolute score.

   C) Students take the quizzes in groups.

   D) Any student who passes earns the maximum number of points.

Answer: B

Explanation: B) The component of STAD that gives each team member an equal opportunity to contribute to the team points is that points are based on improvement rather than the absolute score. Thus, a low achiever can earn as much as a high achiever by showing a comparable level of improvement.

Page Ref: 256

20) Which of the following statements about STAD are true?

   A) Low achievers are assigned to special teams that work more closely with the teacher.

   B) The team score is equal to the single highest improvement–score achieved within a four–person group.

   C) Students take quizzes as a group, helping each other answer difficult questions.

   D) Students are intermittently assigned to new teams through the year.

Answer: D

Explanation: D) After five or six weeks of STAD, students are assigned to new teams. This gives students who were on low–scoring teams a new chance, allows students to work with other classmates, and keeps the program fresh.

Page Ref: 258

21) Which of the following types of objectives is best suited for cooperative learning methods such as STAD?

   A) affective   B) unspecific   C) psychomotor   D) well–defined

Answer: D

Explanation: D) The STAD method is most appropriate for teaching well–defined objectives with single right answers, such as mathematical computations and applications, language usage and mechanics, geography, and map skills, and science facts and concepts.

Page Ref: 256

22) A comprehensive program for teaching reading and writing in the elementary grades, described by Stevens and Slavin (1995), is called

   A) ABC   B) LRC   C) CIRC   D) TGT

Answer: C

Explanation: C) Cooperative Integrated Reading and Composition or CIRC is a comprehensive program for teaching reading and writing in the upper elementary grades.
Page Ref: 258

23) According to Slavin, each student in a Jigsaw II cooperative learning group receives a topic on which to

   A) write an essay.   B) become an expert.

   C) teach the whole class.   D) develop an outline.

Answer: B

Explanation: B) In a modification of the Jigsaw approach called Jigsaw II, Slavin proposes that students work in four- or five-member teams as in TGT and STAD. Instead of each student being assigned a unique section, all students read a common text, such as a book chapter, a short story, or a biography. However, each student receives a topic on which to become an expert.
Page Ref: 259

24) Learning Together, a model of cooperative learning developed by David and Roger Johnson, involves students working in four- or five-member

   A) heterogeneous groups, on assignments.

   B) randomly-assigned groups.

   C) teams, to compete for points.

   D) cooperative scripting groups.

Answer: A

Explanation: A) A model of cooperative learning developed by David and Roger Johnson involves students working in four- or five-member heterogeneous groups on assignments. The groups hand in a single completed assignment, and receive praise and rewards based on the group product. Their methods emphasize team building activities before students begin working together.
Page Ref: 259

25) Cooperative learning methods fall into two broad categories. One category might be called group study methods, while the other category is often called project-based learning, collaborative learning or

　　A) passive learning. 　　　　　　　　　　B) observational learning.

　　C) active learning. 　　　　　　　　　　D) well-structured problem solving.

Answer: C

Explanation: C) One category of cooperative learning methods is called group study methods, while the other category is often called project-based learning or active learning. Project-based learning methods involve students working in groups to create a report, experiment, or other product.

Page Ref: 259

26) Research has favored cooperative learning in cases where two essential conditions are met. First, there must be some kind of recognition or small reward provided to groups that do well so that group members can see that it is in their interest to help their group-mates learn. What is the second essential condition?

　　A) group accountability 　　　　　　　　B) individual accountability

　　C) teacher accountability 　　　　　　　D) whole class accountability

Answer: B

Explanation: B) Research studies have consistently favored cooperative learning as long as two essential conditions are met. First, there must be some kind of recognition or small reward provided to groups that do well, so that group members can see that it is in their interest to help their group-mates learn. Second, there must be individual accountability. That is, the success of the group must depend on the individual learning of all group members, not on a single group product.

Page Ref: 260

27) One study (Stevens and Slavin, 1995) found that students in schools that used a variety of cooperative learning methods in all subjects, for a two-year period, differed from students in schools using traditional teaching approaches. How did they differ?

   A) Students from cooperative learning schools achieved less than students from traditional schools.

   B) High- and low-achieving students from cooperative learning schools were not helped by cooperative learning, but those with average achievement levels benefitted dramatically.

   C) Students from cooperative learning schools achieved significantly better than students from traditional schools.

   D) Students from cooperative learning schools achieved less in reading and math than students from traditional schools.

Answer: C

Explanation: C) While cooperative learning methods are usually used for only a portion of student's school
day and school year, a recent study found that students in schools that used a variety of
cooperative learning methods in almost all subjects for a two-year period achieved
significantly better than students in traditionally organized schools.

Page Ref: 260

28) In the general problem-solving strategy IDEAL, what does the A stand for?

   A) Analyze possible strategies.   B) Answer the question.

   C) Argue the point.   D) Anticipate outcomes and act.

Answer: D

Explanation: D) In the five-step IDEAL problem solving strategy, the A stands for anticipate outcomes and act.

Page Ref: 262

29) Given a problem to solve, beginners tend to jump right into proposing solutions, while experts tend to spend time thinking about the underlying causes of the problem, and interpreting it from different perspectives. Which step in the IDEAL model are the beginners **NEGLECTING**?

   A) Define goals and represent the problem.

   B) Explore possible strategies.

   C) Anticipate outcomes and act.

   D) Look back and learn.

Answer: A

Explanation: A) The second step in IDEAL involves developing an understanding of the problem, before moving to solutions.

Page Ref: 263

30) The question "What is the difference between where I am now and where I want to be?" is a critical step in

   A) discovery learning.   B) means-ends analysis.

   C) expository learning.   D) inductive reasoning.

Answer: B

Explanation: B) The question of the difference between where one is and where she or he needs to be is a critical step in means-end analysis. The problem-solving steps will then involve progressively reducing this difference.

Page Ref: 263

31) Often, mathematics textbooks include problems that fail to make students think about context and which calculation method is call for. But students who learn to solve different kinds of problems requiring thinking

   A) have a better chance of being able to transfer skills and knowledge to new situations.

   B) will succeed with neat categories of problems.

   C) will find it more difficult to transfer skills and knowledge to new situations.

   D) have no chance of being able to succeed in transferring skills to new situations.

Answer: A

Explanation: A) The more different kinds of problems students learn to solve, and the more they must think to solve the problems, the greater chance they will be able to transfer learned skills or knowledge to new situations.

Page Ref: 264

32) In general, people who do well on tests of creative problem solving

   A) seek short cuts to the solution.

   B) resist change.

   C) resolve issues by giving in to the group.

   D) do not worry about making mistakes.

Answer: D

Explanation: D) People who do well on tests of creative problem solving seem to be less afraid of making mistakes and appearing foolish than those who do poorly. They also seem to treat problem-solving situations more playfully. This implies that a relaxed, fun atmosphere may be important when teaching problem solving.

Page Ref: 264

33) One important principle of creative problem solving is to

   A) quickly find a solution.

   B) seek the expertise of those who have greater knowledge of the problem.

   C) realize that the solution may be impossible.

   D) avoid rushing to a solution.

Answer: D

Explanation: D) Creative problem solving is quite different from the analytical, step-by-step process used to solve problems. In creative problem solving, one important principle is to avoid rushing to a solution, but rather to pause and reflect on the problem and think through, or incubate, several alternative solutions before choosing a course of action.

Page Ref: 365

34) What is the term for considering all possibilities before trying out a solution?

   A) STAD   B) suspension of judgment

   C) means-ends analysis   D) Instrumental Enrichment

Answer: B

Explanation: B) In creative problem solving students should be encouraged to suspend judgment, and to consider all possibilities before trying out a solution.

Page Ref: 265

35) During the incubation period of problem solving teachers must avoid

   A) putting time pressures on students.

   B) interacting with students.

   C) letting students work together.

   D) providing information that could foster additional in-depth thinking.

Answer: A

Explanation: A) In teaching the incubation process teachers must avoid putting time pressure on students. Instead of speed, they should value careful thought.

Page Ref: 265

36) Which of the following is a motivational factor that enhances students' creative problem solving, by affecting their feelings?

   A) incubation   B) means-ends-analysis

   C) appropriate climate.   D) Instrumental Enrichment

Answer: C

Explanation: C) Creative problem solving is enhanced by a relaxed, even playful environment. Perhaps even more importantly, students engaging in creative problem solving must feel that their ideas will be accepted.

Page Ref: 265

37) Providing students with a great deal of practice on a wide variety of problem types is essential for their skill development, but not sufficient unless the practice includes

    A) decontextualization.

    B) feedback on their solutions, and on the process by which they arrived at the solutions.

    C) extensive direct instruction.

    D) experience with the strategy of cooperative scripting.

Answer: B

Explanation: B) The role of practice with feedback in solving complex problems cannot be overemphasized. Perhaps the most effective way to teach problem solving is to provide students with a great deal of practice on a wide variety of problem types, giving feedback not only on the correctness of their solutions but also on the process by which they arrived at the solutions.

Page Ref: 266

38) Students are given the opportunity to come up with as many solutions to a problem as they can think of, no matter how seemingly ridiculous. What is this problem solving process called?

    A) feedback   B) wasted time

    C) critical thinking   D) brainstorming

Answer: D

Explanation: D) In creative problem solving students should be encouraged to suspend judgment and to consider all possibilities before trying out a solution. The idea of brainstorming is to avoid focusing on one solution too early and perhaps ignoring better ways to proceed.

Page Ref: 265

39) During the incubation period teachers should value

    A) ingenuity and careful thought.

    B) individual accountability.

    C) the speed at which students can finish problems.

    D) superficial responses.

Answer: A

Explanation: A) During the incubation period, teachers should value ingenuity and careful thought and allow students to take their time in coming up with solutions to the problem.

Page Ref: 265

40) The Instrumental Enrichment program is meant to be administered over a period of at least two years at the rate of how many hours per week?

    A) less than 1 hour per week   B) at least 15 hours per week

    C) 20–30 hours per week   D) 3–5 hours per week

Answer: D

Explanation: D) In this program, called Instrumental Enrichment, students work through a series of paper–and–pencil exercises intended to build such intellectual skills as categorization, comparison, orientation in space, and numerical progressions. The Instrumental Enrichment treatment is meant to be administered for three to five hours per week over a period of at least two years, usually to underachieving or learning–disabled adolescents.

Page Ref: 266

41) Studies of the Instrumental Enrichment treatment have found that the program has positive effects on

    A) achievement, but not on tests of aptitude.

    B) tests of aptitude, but generally not on achievement.

    C) both achievement and tests of aptitude.

    D) tests of emotional intelligence.

Answer: B

Explanation: B) Studies of the Instrumental Enrichment treatment have found that the program has positive effects on tests of aptitude, such as IQ tests, but generally not on achievement.

Page Ref: 266

42) Which of the following phrases best characterizes critical thinking?

    A) tolerates misleading interpretations of facts

    B) focuses on correct answer rather than reasons for an answer

    C) recognizes logical inconsistencies

    D) tends to be irrational

Answer: C

Explanation: C) Critical thinking can be characterized as open, divergent, rational, and analytical. It is not closed, convergent, negative, or irrational.

Page Ref: 269

43) Which of the following statements accurately describe the process of teaching critical thinking?
    1) depends on setting a classroom tone that encourages the acceptance of divergent perspectives and free discussion;
    2) should place more emphasis on opinions and correct answers, than on the reasons behind them;
    3) requires practice;
    4) best acquired in relationship to topics with which students are familiar.

    A) 1, 3, and 4 (not 2).   B) 2 and 3 (not 1 and 4).

    C) 1 and 4 (not 2 and 3).   D) All four statements.

Answer: A

Explanation: A) During the teaching of critical thinking there should be an emphasis on giving reasons for correct opinions rather than only for answers.
Page Ref: 269

True/False Questions

1) Vygotsky noted that successful problem solvers talk themselves through difficult problems.

Answer: TRUE
Page Ref: 243

2) Key elements of Piaget's and Vygotsky's conceptions of cognitive change involve transmission of knowledge in which the learner's role is passive.

Answer: FALSE
Page Ref: 243

3) A central assumption of constructivist approaches is that learning is a process of discovery.

Answer: TRUE
Page Ref: 243

4) During discovery learning students learn independent problem solving and critical-thinking skills.

Answer: TRUE
Page Ref: 245

5) Self-regulated learners have a difficult time using learning strategies, for instance, breaking complex problems into simpler steps.

Answer: FALSE
Page Ref: 248

6) Scaffolding may include giving students less structure at the beginning of a set of lessons.

Answer: FALSE
Page Ref: 248

7) In STAD, students work in four–member learning teams that are mixed in performance level, gender, and ethnicity.

Answer: TRUE
Page Ref: 256

8) Project–based learning methods involve students working in groups to create a report, experiment, mural, or other product.

Answer: TRUE
Page Ref: 259

9) For many kinds of problems, graphic representation may be an effective aid to finding a solution.

Answer: TRUE
Page Ref: 265

10) People who do well on tests of creative problem solving seem to treat problem–solving situations less playfully than most individuals.

Answer: FALSE
Page Ref: 265

11) Students can be taught specific strategies for approaching creative problem solving, such as mapping possibilities and thinking of unusual ideas.

Answer: TRUE
Page Ref: 266

12) Skills in critical thinking are best acquired in relationship to topics with which students have little familiarity.

Answer: FALSE
Page Ref: 269

Short Answer Questions

1) A concept derived from Vygotsky's emphases, both on the social nature of learning and on the zone of proximal development, that refers to a learner's development of skill through extensive interaction with an expert.

Answer: cognitive apprenticeship
Page Ref: 244

2) Constructivist approaches to teaching typically make extensive use of this method on the theory that students will more easily discover and comprehend difficult concepts if they can talk with each other about the problems.

Answer: cooperative learning
Page Ref: 245

3) The term used to describe learning that takes place in real–life, authentic tasks.

Answer: situated learning
Page Ref: 244

4) Learners who have knowledge of effective learning strategies and how and when to use them.

Answer: self-regulated learners
Page Ref: 248

5) In the context of Vygotsky's views: learning in which the teacher is the cultural agent who guides instruction so that students will master and internalize skills that permit higher cognitive functioning.

Answer: mediated learning
Page Ref: 249

6) Principles published by A.P.A. that affirm the active nature of the human learner, and a constructivist viewpoint on acquisition of knowledge.

Answer: Learner–Centered Psychological Principles
Page Ref: 249

7) This constructivist approach, designed primarily to help low achievers learn reading comprehension, involves the teacher working with small groups of students. The teacher models behaviors such as making–up questions based on the reading material, and then allows the students to perform those behaviors independently.

Answer: reciprocal teaching
Page Ref: 251

8) A cooperative learning approach in which students play games with members of other teams to add points to their team scores.

Answer: teams–games–tournaments
Page Ref: 256

9) The letters STAD refer to this cooperative learning method.

Answer: Student Teams Achievement Division
Page Ref: 256

10) A comprehensive program that uses cooperative learning for teaching reading and writing in the upper elementary grades.

Answer: cooperative integrated reading and composition
Page Ref: 258

11) According to the work of Aronson, students in this cooperative learning method are assigned to six-member teams to work on academic material that has been broken down into sections. This method also features "expert" groups, made up of students who have prepared the same sections of the material.

Answer: Jigsaw
Page Ref: 258

12) A process reported by Sharan & Sharan (1992) whereby students work in small groups using cooperative inquiry, group discussion, and cooperative planning and projects. In this method each small group of students works on a subtopic from the unit's material, and communicates the results of their efforts to the whole class.

Answer: group investigation
Page Ref: 259

13) A model of cooperative learning developed by David and Roger Johnson that involves students working in four- or five-member heterogeneous groups on assignments. Each group hands in a single completed assignment, and receives praise and rewards based on the group product.

Answer: learning together
Page Ref: 259

14) Trying to progressively reduce the difference between the current problem state and the required solution state describes this problem-solving method.

Answer: means-ends analysis
Page Ref: 263

15) In this program students work through a series of paper and pencil exercises intended to build such intellectual skills as categorization, comparison, orientation in space, and numerical progressions.

Answer: instrumental enrichment
Page Ref: 266

16) The ability to make rational decisions about what to do or what to believe.

Answer: critical thinking
Page Ref: 269

Essay Questions

1) Explain how Vygotsky's theories of learning and development have influenced constructivism.

   Answer: Modern constructivist thought draws heavily on Vygotsky's theories, which have been used to support classroom instructional methods that emphasize cooperative learning, project based learning, and discovery. Four key principles derived from his theories have played an important role. First is his emphasis on the social nature of learning. Students learn, he proposed, through joint interactions with adults and more capable peers. A second key concept is the idea that individuals learn best concepts that are in their zone of proximal development (i.e., when they are engaged in tasks they could not do alone but can do with assistance). A third concept borrowed from Vygotsky is cognitive apprenticeship. This refers to the process by which a learner gradually acquires expertise in interaction with an expert. Finally, Vygotsky's emphasis on scaffolding or mediated learning is important in modern constructivist thought.
   Page Ref: 243

2) How do cooperative learning approaches fit a constructivist model? More specifically, identify features of cooperative learning that incorporate a constructivist view of the learner, and explain how those features reflect constructivism.

   Answer: Constructivist approaches to teaching typically make extensive use of cooperative learning, on the theory that students will more easily discover and comprehend difficult concepts if they can talk with each other about the problem. With both, the emphasis is on the social nature of learning.
   Page Ref: 245

3) Create a dialogue in which you introduce reciprocal teaching in order to help students attend to what they are reading.

   Answer: For the coming weeks we will be working together to improve your ability to understand what you read. Sometimes we are so busy figuring out what the words are that we fail to pay much attention to what the words and sentences mean. We will be learning a way to pay more attention to what we are reading. I will teach you to think of important questions, summarize, predict, and point out unclear passages as you read.
   Page Ref: 251

4) A teacher assigned each student in the class to a six-member group to work on a lesson. Each group is assigned to a section of the text chapter. The teacher then reassigns each group member to another group in which each student knows about the same section of the chapter. This group reviews together; then each member returns to her or his original group. What type of classroom activity is this? Explain how the characteristics of the scenario described above correspond to the defining features of the method you identified.

Describe one change the teacher could make in this lesson while maintaining the same method.

Indicate one way in which this lesson reflects a constructivist approach to learning.

Answer: The teacher has involved the class in a Jigsaw cooperative learning activity. In Jigsaw, students are assigned to six-member teams to work on academic material that has been broken down into sections. Each team member reads her or his section. Next, members of different teams who have studied the same sections meet in expert groups to discuss their section. Then the students return to their teams to teach their teammates about the section.

The teacher could assign each group member a poem or article, instead of a chapter-section, and still follow the jigsaw procedure.

Active learning and social learning are two constructivist approaches seen in jigsaw.

Page Ref: 258

5) A teacher wants to encourage team building in students. What type of cooperative learning method would you recommend the teacher use? Explain your choice.

Answer: Although many cooperative learning activities involve teamwork, the learning together model specifically emphasizes teamwork. It involves students working in four- or five-member heterogeneous groups on assignments. The groups hand in a single completed assignment, and receive praise and rewards based on the group product.

Page Ref: 259

6) What does the research say about the effectiveness of cooperative learning as compared with more traditional teaching methods?

Answer: Most studies comparing cooperative learning to traditional teaching methods have consistently favored cooperative learning over traditional methods as long as two essential conditions have been met. First, there must be some kind of recognition or small reward provided to groups that do well so that group members can see that it is in their interest to help their groupmates learn. Second, there must be individual accountability.

Page Ref: 259

7) Ms. Aretti likes her 7th graders this year, but there is one student, Mira, who is very shy. Mira never speaks up in class. Ms. Aretti can only get her to whisper an answer when called on. There are many ways that Ms. Aretti could try to help Mira, but the problem calls for creative problem solving—it is not well structured.

Illustrate how two of the following might be helpful to Ms. Aretti's thinking, as she tries to solve her classroom problem: incubation; suspension of judgment, appropriate climates; analysis.

Think of the two strategies you illustrated, as they relate to the IDEAL model of problem solving. For each strategy, explain why it would be relevant when performing one of the steps in IDEAL.

Answer: Ms. Aretti's first reactions to the problem may not be good solutions. She needs to pause and reflect to give alternative solutions a chance to incubate. She can suspend judgment and list a great many possible solutions, as in brainstorming, before narrowing down the solutions with critical thinking. If Ms. Aretti can find a relaxed atmosphere in which she can analyze the problem, looking at it from different points of view, she will increase her chances of success.

The strategies considered are most likely to be helpful in defining and representing the problem, and in exploring possible strategies. At both of these steps it can be important to maintain a reflective, flexible thought process.

Page Ref: 262

8) How is creative problem solving different from traditional, analytical problem solving?

Answer: Creative problem solving is quite different from the analytical, step–by–step process used to solve problems. In creative problem solving, one important principle is to avoid rushing to a solution, but rather to pause and reflect on the problem and think through several alternative solutions before choosing a course of action.

Page Ref: 265

9) How would you create a "culture of thinking" in your classroom?

Answer: In order to integrate thinking skills into daily lessons, teachers deliberately teach generic problem solving strategies to students. An example of a problem solving strategy might be to state, search, evaluate, and elaborate. This could be used for a lesson on what caused a classroom plant to die, for example.

Page Ref: 265

10) Davis Brookline is the newly appointed chair of the history department at Cool Ridge High School, which is a large, under-funded, urban school. On the first day of the new academic year, Davis meets with his 10 history colleagues. Some of them are seasoned teachers, some are new to the district, and some are new to teaching. "We're going to do things differently this year, people," he tells his colleagues. "Over the summer, I attended a workshop about taking the classroom back from students. We talked about teachers' rights, teacher control, and assertive and firm discipline. Things have gotten out of control here at Cool Ridge—students have too much power—and I intend to regain control!"

One of Davis Brookline's colleagues asks, "What do you mean you intend to regain control? You sound a little like a drill sergeant, Davis."

"Exactly!" stated Davis. "This history department is going to be tough. Students will have to earn each and every grade they get the hard way—through drill and practice and weekly written tests, which we will grade on a curve. Those students who don't get in line will pay the consequences."

"Don't we have any say about how we want to teach?" asked another colleague. "I don't agree that your method is the best way to reach students, especially some who have outside problems to deal with."

"We're not helping students by letting them off the hook. Yes, some have problems, but getting tough is the only way to teach them to survive in this city."

What are some of the issues raised in the above scenario? How do Davis Brookline's beliefs about teaching compare to constructivist approaches to instruction?

Answer: Mr. Brookline believes that teachers need to be in control in classrooms, an approach that might fit more closely with direct instruction techniques. Constructivist views of learning focus on active student involvement in the learning process.
Page Ref: 243

11) Ms. MacIver asked her senior math students to solve the following problem:
Make three rows of three dots on a piece of paper. Without lifting your pencil, and using four straight lines, connect all of the dots.

The students tried to solve the problem, but could not. Ms. MacIver then said to her students, "I'll show you how to connect the dots." She then drew the following solution on the overhead.

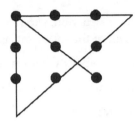

"You have to go outside the boundaries of the dots in order to solve the problem," explained Ms. MacIver.

How did the students initially represent the problem? In other words, state how the students described the problem to themselves—how they pictured it, interpreted it or defined it?

Explain how the students' representation of the problem interfered with finding the solution. What could students learn from this experience that might help in solving problems in the future?

Answer: Ms. MacIver's students represented the problem as limited, in space, to the boundaries of the dots. This confining representation required them to change direction at the dot boundaries, making too many lines. A representation such as "a large parking lot where there is plenty of room for 3–point turns," may have allowed them to find the solution. Through experience, students may learn to be more flexible in looking at a problem from different perspectives, i.e., exploring different ways of representing a problem.

Page Ref: 264

Chapter 9   Accommodating Instruction
to Meet Individual Needs

Multiple–Choice Questions

1) In order to bring about effective instruction, excellent lesson preparation is not sufficient. Teachers must also accomplish all of the following **EXCEPT**

    A) make the correct assumptions about what students know coming into a lesson.

    B) make informed decisions about whether and how to place students in ability groups.

    C) nourish students' motivation to learn.

    D) measure students' progress in learning.

Answer: A

Explanation: A) Teachers should find out what their students know, not rely on assumptions.
Page Ref: 276

2) Which of the following strategies would be the most direct application of Carroll's model?

    A) Reward students when they complete assignments correctly.

    B) Group students according to ability.

    C) Make it possible for students to work at their own pace.

    D) Define instructional objectives at the beginning of each unit.

Answer: C

Explanation: C) Carroll's model would most directly support allowing students to complete lessons at their own pace. This strategy is consistent with the idea that student aptitude determines the amount of time it takes to learn material
Page Ref: 277

3) A teacher who is dissatisfied with student achievement wants to use more effective teaching strategies. Which element from Carroll's model would the teacher be able to control most directly?

    A) attitude   B) opportunity

    C) perseverance   D) ability to understand

Answer: B

Explanation: B) The teacher would want to work on changing opportunity because it is an alterable element directly under the teacher's control. Aptitude is a student characteristic, whereas perseverance and ability to understand instruction are student variables over which the teacher has only partial control.
Page Ref: 277

4) The difference between Carroll's Model of School Learning and Slavin's QAIT model is that

    A) Carroll's model deals with the learner whereas Slavin's deals with the teacher.

    B) Slavin's model deals with changeable elements, while Carroll's includes factors that cannot be directly addressed by the teacher.

    C) Carroll's model emphasizes abstract learning whereas Slavin's model emphasizes concrete learning.

    D) Slavin's model emphasizes elementary school education whereas Carroll's model emphasizes secondary school education.

Answer: B

Explanation: B) Carroll's model contains some elements that are directly alterable (e.g., opportunity) by teachers and some that are student characteristics (e.g., aptitude). In contrast, in Slavin's QAIT model are all directly changeable by the teacher.

Page Ref: 277

5) Which of the following statements about elements in the QAIT model are true?
    1)   Quality of instruction refers to those aspects most people first think of when they consider teaching, such as clear presentation of material.
    2)   The elements are arranged in a series, so that the Q is the simplest and the T is the most complicated;
    3)   The home situation of the student is considered to be of paramount importance;
    4)   Time is the last element put forth in this model.

    A) Statements 2 and 3 are true (not 1 and 4).

    B) Statements 1, 3, and 4 are true (not 2).

    C) Statements 1 and 4 are true (not 2 and 3).

    D) Statements 1 and 3 are true (not 2 and 4).

Answer: C

Explanation: C) The common feature of the four elements in the QAIT model is that all must be adequate for instruction to be effective. For example, if students have little incentive to learn, the impact of high quality instruction, additional time to learn, and/or appropriate levels of instruction will be greatly diminished.

Page Ref: 277

6) A teacher is very disorganized and presents confusing lessons to students. Which of the following is a correct interpretation, based on Slavin's QAIT model, of what is happening?

    A) The students lack the aptitude needed to learn.

    B) Students will perform poorly regardless of the level of incentives.

    C) Incentive to learn will increase significantly.

    D) High student motivation can compensate for ineffective instruction.

Answer: B

Explanation: B) An assumption of the QAIT model is that all four elements must be adequate for instruction to be effective. Thus, if a lesson is confusing (poor quality of instruction), students will probably perform poorly regardless of incentives or their motivation.

Page Ref: 278

7) Based on research reviewed by the text author, which group of students is likely to experience damaging effects of between–class ability grouping?

    A) students in classes for academically gifted learners

    B) students in high–track classes

    C) students in middle–track classes

    D) students in low–track classes

Answer: D

Explanation: D) Research on between–class ability grouping or tracking suggests that it is ineffective for low–ability students who may receive poorer quality instruction and develop low self-esteem.

Page Ref: 280

8) Which of the following statements reflects a limitation of between-class ability grouping?
   1) Quality of instruction tends to be lower in low track classes;
   2) The selection process for grouping may not be based directly on relevant achievement criteria, resulting in groups that don't truly differ much in achievement potential;
   3) Low track students are exposed to too few positive role models;
   4) Teachers' reactions to low-ability classes may convey low expectations to the students.

   A) Statements 1, 2, and 4 are true (not 3).

   B) Statements 2 and 4 are true (not 1 and 3).

   C) Statements 1 and 3 are true (not 2 and 4).

   D) All four statements are true.

   Answer: D

   Explanation: D) All of the factors listed are limitations of between-class ability grouping. That is, quality of instruction and exposure to positive role models tends to be reduced in low-track classes. Also, the reduction in the range of differences is usually relatively small, and teachers of low-track classes may have low expectations.

   Page Ref: 280

9) Your text author reviewed research on low-ability track classes, showing that teachers in these classes teach fewer concepts than teachers of high-ability classes. Which element of the QAIT model would incorporate this finding?

   A) time   B) quality of instruction

   C) incentive   D) within-class tracking

   Answer: B

   Explanation: B) An analysis of the elements of the QAIT model and of the results of research on between-class ability grouping would suggest quality of instruction to be the main problem in low-track classes. Seemingly, students in those classes would receive adequate time (opportunity) to learn and appropriate levels (adaptation) of instruction. But a tendency to stress facts rather than concepts reflects quality of teaching.

   Page Ref: 281

10) What is often one outcome of tracking, or varied academic levels, for students from lower socioeconomic backgrounds and minority groups?

   A) Given a free choice of academic levels, African-American and Latino students disproportionally end up in low-level classes.

   B) Tracking creates unrealistically high expectations for lower-socioeconomic students.

   C) Tracking promotes the needs of low-achieving students to the detriment of high-achieving students.

   D) Given a free choice of academic levels, African-American and Latino students are enrolled proportionally across class levels.

Answer: A

Explanation: A) The textbook stresses the stigma placed on low-track students as the most damaging aspect of tracking. Low-tracks classes are often predominantly composed of students from lower socioeconomic backgrounds and minority groups, while upper-track classes are more often composed of children from higher socioeconomic levels. A study found that even in high schools in which students are given a free choice of academic levels, African-American and Latino students disproportionately ended up in low-level classes.

Page Ref: 283

11) Research on between-class ability grouping shows that it is

   A) harmful for students assigned to high track and to low track programs.

   B) harmful for students assigned to high track programs, but beneficial for those assigned to low track programs.

   C) harmful for students assigned to low track programs, but somewhat beneficial for those assigned to high track programs.

   D) beneficial for students assigned to high track and to low track programs.

Answer: C

Explanation: C) Researchers have found between-class ability grouping to be harmful for low-ability students, but slightly beneficial for high-ability students. The limitations for low-achieving students include less exposure to positive role models, lower-quality instruction, and reduced self-esteem.

Page Ref: 281

12) How does a low-ability student benefit when a school uses a regrouping strategy, rather than tracking?

   A) The student has a special teacher for the entire day.

   B) The student receives services in a separate class oriented toward individualized instruction.

   C) The teaching style the student encounters is consistent throughout the day.

   D) The student has less chance of losing self-esteem, than with all-day between-class grouping.

Answer: D

Explanation: D) If regrouping is used, a student will spend only part of the day (perhaps one period, such as math) with other low-achievers. The rest of the day will be spent in a heterogeneous (mixed) classroom. Thus, compared to whole-day tracking, regrouping will be less likely to damage self-esteem.

Page Ref: 284

13) Untracking often runs into serious opposition from the parents of

   A) high achievers.   B) middle class students.

   C) lower socioeconomic status students.   D) low achievers.

Answer: A

Explanation: A) Untracking often runs into serious opposition from the parents of high achievers. Oakes and Wells have pointed out that untracking requires changes in thinking about student potential, not only changes in school or classroom practices. Teachers, parents, and students themselves, they claim, must come to see the goal of schooling as success for every learner, not as sorting students in categories, if untracking is to take hold.

Page Ref: 284

14) A student reads far below grade level. If the Joplin Plan is used at the student's school, which of the following is most likely to occur?

   A) The student will take reading in a mixed-ability class.

   B) The student will spend the day in a cross-graded class.

   C) The student will receive special education services.

   D) The student will take reading in a same-ability class, and most other subjects in mixed-ability classes.

Answer: D

Explanation: D) Use of the Joplin Plan will result in students taking, for example, reading in a cross-graded ability-grouped class. Other subjects are to be taken in a mixed-ability class.

Page Ref: 284

15) Which of the following terms most precisely describes non-graded programs?

    A) cross-age grouping   B) regrouping

    C) within-class ability grouping   D) between-class ability grouping

Answer: A

Explanation: A) Nongraded programs combine students of different ages in the same classes. Most often, students ages 5-7 or 6-8 might be mixed in a nongraded primary program. Students work across age lines, but are often flexibly grouped for some instruction according to their needs and performance levels.

Page Ref: 284

16) What does the research say about within-class ability grouping?

    A) It is beneficial for high ability students only.

    B) It is beneficial for low ability students only.

    C) It is beneficial for both low and high ability students.

    D) It is ineffective for both high and low ability students.

Answer: C

Explanation: C) According to the research, students of high, average, and low achievement levels seem to benefit equally from within-class ability grouping.

Page Ref: 285

17) Typical uses of within-class ability grouping reflect the tendency of teachers to

    A) make group assignments less flexible than they are with between-class ability grouping.

    B) use the groups for most of the school day rather than only for targeted subjects.

    C) allow groups to proceed at their own pace, so high-performing groups cover more material.

    D) expect and demand less of the high ability group than occurs with between-class ability grouping.

Answer: C

Explanation: C) Teachers often allow groups to proceed at their own rates in the same book, so the higher-performing group will cover more material.

Page Ref: 285

18) In the lower elementary grades, for which of the following subjects has within–class ability grouping been used the most, for accommodating differences in student abilities?

    A) science   B) social studies   C) mathematics   D) music

Answer: C

Explanation: C) It is important to note that the research finding benefits of within–class grouping in elementary mathematics was mostly done many years ago with traditional teaching methods primarily intended to teach computations rather than problem solving. As mathematics moves toward use of constructivist approaches more directed at problem solving, discovery, and cooperative learning, within–class grouping may become unnecessary.

Page Ref: 285

19) What is the basic idea behind mastery learning?

    A) Students become masters of at least one subject prior to graduation.

    B) Students learn to teach a particular subject to other students.

    C) Students learn a particular skill before moving on to the next one.

    D) Students learn from established experts in the field.

Answer: C

Explanation: C) Students who fail to meet a preestablished mastery criterion following a lesson are given this extra corrective instruction until they can score at a mastery level on a similar quiz. Research on mastery learning programs that provide corrective instruction in addition to regular class time has generally found achievement gains, particularly for low–achievers.

Page Ref: 286

20) Mastery learning was first proposed by Benjamin Bloom to address which of the following issues?

    A) individual differences   B) the drop–out rate

    C) overpopulation in schools   D) low test scores

Answer: A

Explanation: A) Mastery learning was first proposed as a solution to the problem of individual differences by Benjamin Bloom, who based his recommendation in part on the earlier work of John Carroll.

Page Ref: 286

21) A standard that students must meet to be considered proficient in a skill is called a mastery

    A) corrective.   B) criterion.   C) summation.   D) adaptation.

Answer: B

Explanation: B) A master criterion is a standard that students must meet to be considered proficient in a skill.

Page Ref: 286

22) A teacher, using mastery learning, is about to give one group corrective instruction. Based on the recommendation given in your text, it is desirable that the teacher

    A) use a different teaching approach from the one originally used.

    B) select group members on the basis of summative quiz results.

    C) present the instruction in individualized five minute tutorial sessions.

    D) use a direct instructional method regardless of the approach originally used.

Answer: A

Explanation: A) When a group is to receive corrective instruction, it is desirable to use a different teaching approach than the one originally used. The rationale is that a different strategy might provide different perspectives and reach students better than the first (apparently unsuccessful) strategy.

Page Ref: 287

23) In a mastery learning context, which of the following classroom activities serves as an enrichment activity?

    A) Students who received a 90 percent on a quiz on volcanoes and earthquakes go to the library to find out about the San Francisco earthquake and the Mount Vesuvius eruption.

    B) Students who received less than 90 percent on a fractions quiz are given extra instruction.

    C) Students who did not finish the biology assignments are expected to come to class before school starts or stay in class after school is over for the day.

    D) Students who built their end tables to a satisfactory degree in industrial technology class are asked to clean up the shop while the other students continue working.

Answer: A

Explanation: A) At the end of a lesson, students are quizzed. Those who score less than acceptable will be given corrective instruction, while the remaining students do enrichment activities, such as finding out about the San Francisco earthquake or the Mount Vesuvius eruption.

Page Ref: 288

24) What is a basic problem in mastery learning?

    A) motivating students to be independent learners

    B) providing the extra time necessary for slower students to learn

    C) deciding what types of skills are necessary to teach

    D) convincing teachers to use the strategy

Answer: B

Explanation: B) The basic problem in mastery learning is how to provide the extra time needed for slower students to learn the material. Thus, mastery learning works fine as a concept, but is often impractical to implement within normal school schedules.

Page Ref: 288

25) Research on mastery learning indicates that its effects are

    A) positive when corrective instruction is used in addition to regular class time instruction.

    B) positive when corrective instruction is given as part of regular class time instruction.

    C) positive when corrective instruction is avoided.

    D) negative for low ability students, but positive for high ability students.

Answer: A

Explanation: A) Research on mastery learning indicates that its effects are positive when corrective instruction is given in addition to regular class time. This outcome makes sense because students would receive supplementary instruction rather than having time removed from regular lessons.

Page Ref: 288

26) What is the central problem of mastery learning?

    A) It must be used with other instructional strategies to be effective.

    B) It is a difficult strategy for novice teachers to use.

    C) The teacher has no control over the content to be learned.

    D) It involves a trade-off between the amount of content that can be covered and the degree to which concepts are mastered.

Answer: D

Explanation: D) The central problem of mastery learning is that it involves a tradeoff between the amount of content that can be covered and the degree to which students master each concept. The time needed to bring all or almost all students to a preestablished level of mastery must come from somewhere. If corrective instruction is provided during regular class time, it must reduce content coverage. And, content coverage is one of the most important predictors of achievement gain.

Page Ref: 288

27) Tutors who have been taught specific tutoring strategies

    A) produce better results than those without such training.

    B) do not do well, since they have limited training.

    C) produce the same results as those without training.

    D) do not do as well as those without training.

Answer: A

Explanation: A) Tutors who have been taught specific tutoring strategies produce much better results than those without such training. Also, involving parents in support of a tutoring program enhances its effectiveness.

Page Ref: 289

28) Cross-age tutoring is

   A) rarely recommended.

   B) recommended less than same-age tutoring.

   C) recommended by researchers more often than same-age tutoring.

   D) not recommended because teachers often have to re-teach material.

Answer: C

Explanation: C) Sometimes peer tutoring is used with students in need of special assistance, in which case a few older students may work with a few younger students. Cross-age tutoring is more often recommended by researchers than same-age tutoring because students may accept an older student as a tutor, but resent having a classmate appointed to tutor them.

Page Ref: 289

29) Research on the effects of tutoring on learning indicates that

   A) the results are much the same regardless of the expertise of the tutor.

   B) the tutors benefit, but the tutees do not.

   C) both the tutors and the tutees benefit.

   D) neither tutors nor tutees benefit significantly.

Answer: C

Explanation: C) Research on the effects of tutoring indicates that both the tutors and the tutees benefit from the activities.

Page Ref: 290

30) A particular one-to-one tutoring program, in which highly trained certified teachers work with first graders who are at risk for failing to learn to read, is called

   A) Reading for Success.   B) Reading Recovery.

   C) Challenge Reading.   D) Reading Readiness.

Answer: B

Explanation: B) Reading Recovery uses highly trained, certified teachers to work with first graders who are at risk for failing to learn to read. Research on this strategy has found that students who received tutoring in first grade were still reading significantly better than comparable students at the end of third grade.

Page Ref: 290

31) Meeting students' diverse needs has been an impetus leading educators to

   A) breakthroughs in early childhood health and education.

   B) interest in technology, which increasingly costs less and is more widely available.

   C) requests for larger special education staffs and record-setting budgets.

   D) less interest in technology, which increasingly costs more and is less available.

Answer: B

Explanation: B) The decreasing costs and increasing availability of microcomputers and other technologies in schools have led educators at all levels to become more interested in technology, particularly as a means of meeting students' diverse needs.

Page Ref: 292

32) According to the author, three general types of technology applications in education are all of the following EXCEPT

   A) Teachers plan instruction and present content using technology.

   B) Students explore, practice, and prepare papers using technology.

   C) Staffs monitor weather, bus routes, and sports schedules using technology.

   D) Teachers and administrators accomplish assessment, record keeping, reporting and management tasks using technology.

Answer: C

Explanation: C) There are three general types of technology applications in education: A, B, and D.

Page Ref: 292

33) Increasingly, technology is being used to combine text and visual content, which has been found to enhance students' learning as long as

   A) the students' attention is held for consistent time periods.

   B) the text and visuals entertain the students.

   C) the students are only allowed to watch 10 to 15 minute segments.

   D) the text and visuals directly support each other.

Answer: D

Explanation: D) A multimedia approach to teaching has been found to enhance students' learning as long as the text and visuals directly support each other. Adding diagrams or animations to show how something works, for example, has been found to enhance the text, but adding non-explanatory, motivational text adds little.

Page Ref: 293

34) Word processing applications provide students

    A) less advantage in facilitating revision of compositions.

    B) greater concern about mechanics of compositions.

    C) spell checkers and other utilities.

    D) a neat way to present work, but great concern over organization.

Answer: C

Explanation: C) A key advantage of word processing over paper–and–pencil composition is that word processing facilitates revision. Spell checkers and other utilities help students to worry less about mechanics and focus on the meaning and organization fo their compositions.

Page Ref: 295

35) Studies of word processing show that students using computers

    A) take greater pride in their writing than paper–and–pencil writers.

    B) take as less pride in their writing than paper–and–pencil writers.

    C) write the same amount as paper–and–pencil writers.

    D) revise less than paper–and–pencil writers.

Answer: A

Explanation: A) A key advantage of word processing over paper–and–pencil composition is that word processing facilitates revision. Studies of word processing show that students using computers write more, revise more, and take greater pride in their writing than paper–and–pencil writers. Writing quality tends to be somewhat better when students have access to word processors.

Page Ref: 295

36) Which of the following is a computer program having a large amount of information contained on a CD–ROM?

    A) a memory chip   B) a database

    C) a fact sheet   D) a spread sheet

Answer: B

Explanation: B) A database is a computer program that keeps a lot of information to be referred to later on and sometimes manipulated. Students can learn to search CD–ROM (ROM stands for "read–only memory") databases such as encyclopedias, atlases, road maps, catalogs and other information needed for instructional purposes which can be particularly important in project–based learning.

Page Ref: 295

37) In many databases, students may use hypertext and hypermedia, which allows them to

   A) link to keyboards and cameras.

   B) link to their school's book and video resources.

   C) search a database by clicking on a word or picture.

   D) print out text and photos.

Answer: C

Explanation: C) In many databases, students can use hypertext and hypermedia to search a database (such as an encyclopedia) by clicking on a word or picture. This leads to related or more detailed information on a specific portion of the text, allowing learners to follow their interests or resolve gaps in understanding more efficiently than with traditional texts.

Page Ref: 295

38) Although computer experts refer to drill-and-practice on computers as "electronic page-turning," the program's major advantages include which three of the following?
   1)   immediate feedback
   2)   increased motivation
   3)   independent learning
   4)   skill reinforcement

   A) 1, 2, and 3   B) 1, 3, and 4   C) 1, 2, and 4   D) 2, 3, and 4

Answer: C

Explanation: C) Once common application of microcomputers in education is to provide students with drill-and-practice on skills or knowledge. Computer experts often frown on drill-and-practice programs as "electronic page-turning," and less than exciting. They do replace seatwork, however, and provide several major advantages over seatwork: immediate feedback, record keeping, and appealing graphics, and variations in pace or level that can increase student motivation and reinforce skills or knowledge that students have learned elsewhere.

Page Ref: 296

39) How are most children first introduced to computers?

   A) through courses that apply concepts to the real world

   B) by their teachers

   C) through video games

   D) through "programmed instruction"

Answer: C

Explanation: C) Most children are first introduced to computers through video games; and, many educators (and parents) have wondered whether the same intensity, motivation, and perseverance they see in Nintendo could have applications to the classroom.

Page Ref: 297

40) The Jasper series is a CAI program designed specifically to assist in developing which student skills?

    A) communication

    B) creative thinking

    C) social studies

    D) critical thinking

Answer: B

Explanation: D) The goal of developing students' critical thinking skills has led to the creation of numerous CAI programs that are designed as problem-solving activities. One innovative problem-solving is the Jasper series, developed and researched at Vanderbilt University.

Page Ref: 297

41) Well-designed computer tutorial programs

    A) are useful in the elementary grades but inappropriate for secondary students.

    B) ask few questions of students.

    C) avoid the use of graphics to engage students' attention.

    D) mimic a patient human tutor.

Answer: D

Explanation: D) The best tutorial programs come close to mimicking a patient human tutor. Very sophisticated tutorial programs that simulate the behaviors of expert human tutors are being developed and applied in a variety of settings.

Page Ref: 300

42) Research on computer usage in public schools indicates that

    A) males and females spend equal amounts of time at computers.

    B) females tend to spend more time on computers than males.

    C) middle class females spend more time on computers than middle class males.

    D) males tend to spend more time on computers than females.

Answer: D

Explanation: D) Within schools boys tend to spend much more time on computers than girls, according to research.

Page Ref: 300

43) Students who are subject to school failure because of characteristics they possess, or from inadequate responses to their needs by school, family, or community are called

    A) students at risk.   B) special education students.

    C) remedial learners.   D) formative students.

Answer: A

Explanation: A) Students who come from impoverished or single-parent homes, those who have marked developmental delays, or those who exhibit aggressive or withdrawn behavior are more likely to experience problems in school than are other students. These individuals are often referred to as students at risk.

Page Ref: 302

44) What is the name given to educational programs designed to help children overcome problems that stem from growing up in low-income communities?

    A) Joplin Plan   B) special education

    C) cross-age tutoring   D) compensatory education

Answer: D

Explanation: D) Programs designed to overcome the problems associated with being brought up in low-income communities are called compensatory education. Compensatory education programs supplement the education of students from disadvantaged backgrounds who are experiencing trouble in school or who are felt to be in danger of having school problems.

Page Ref: 303

45) All of the following educational programs are considered compensatory **EXCEPT**

    A) Title I.   B) Head Start.

    C) Remediation and Enrichment.   D) Follow Through.

Answer: C

Explanation: C) Compensatory education programs, designed to prevent or remediate learning problems among students from low-income families, include Title I, Head Start, and Follow Through.

Page Ref: 303

46) Programs in which students attend separate classes for purposes such as remediation are called

    A) Success for All.   B) simulation programs.

    C) pull-out programs.   D) mastery learning programs.

Answer: C

Explanation: C) In pull-out programs students are removed from regular classes, to receive special instruction.

Page Ref: 303

47) Research on effective practices in Title I pullout classes finds that what works best in these classes are

A) practices that are effective in regular classes.

B) methods that emphasize drill and practice.

C) methods that use computer-based instruction.

D) infant stimulation and parent training.

Answer: A

Explanation: A) Research on effective practices in Title I pullout classes finds that, in general, practices that are effective in regular classes are also effective in Title I classes. For example, more instructional time, high time on task, and other indicators of effective classroom management are important predictors of achievement gain in Title I classes.

Page Ref: 303

48) Which of the following is a provision of the No Child Left Behind Act (NCLB) passed by the U.S. Congress in December 2001?

A) increase teacher wages

B) improve reading scores

C) provide scientifically -based report cards

D) hold schools accountable for their students' achievement

Answer: D

Explanation: D) In December 2001, the U.S. Congress passed the No Child Left Behind Act (NCLB) to supplement state and local efforts to improve education for all children and eliminate the achievement gap between students from differing backgrounds. NCLB has provisions for increasing teacher quality, improving reading instruction, providing scientifically-based practices, and holding schools accountable for their students' achievement.

Page Ref: 305

49) Under the No Child Left Behind Act (NCLB), all states must administer tests to determine levels of proficiency in reading, language arts, and math to what percentage of students in grades three through eight?

A) 100 percent   B) at least 95 percent

C) at least 85 percent   D) at least 75 percent

Answer: B

Explanation: B) Under NCLB, each year all states must administer tests in reading, language arts, and math to students in grades three to eight and one year in high school. Performance on these tests determines students' level of proficiency—Basic, Proficient, or Advanced. In each school, at least 95 percent of all students must take these high-stakes tests, including special subgroups of students.

Page Ref: 306

50) Criticisms of the No Child Left Behind Act (NCLB) make all of the following arguments **EXCEPT**

   A) NCLB presents real obstacles because it focuses on sanctions rather than assistance.

   B) Since the federal government provides only seven percent of the total funding for public schools, it should only have a seven percent say in how it is spent.

   C) Severe accountability measures can lead schools to focus on a limited set of skills at the expense of enriching classes including social studies, art, and music.

   D) Severe accountability pressures will lead to cheating or the use of practices that increase scores without increasing learning.

Answer: B

Explanation: B) Criticisms include A, C, and D. Also, the Center on Education Policy (2003) determined that since the federal government provides only seven percent of the total funding for public schools, it may be impossible for poor school districts to make all the changes necessary to meet the NCLB requirements.

Page Ref: 306

51) In recent years, in place of efforts to undo the school failure of students placed at risk, there has been an increasing emphasis on

   A) integrated learning systems.   B) incentives.

   C) disability screening.   D) early intervention.

Answer: D

Explanation: D) In recent years there has been an increasing emphasis on prevention and early intervention rather than remediation in serving children placed at risk of school failure.

Page Ref: 307

52) What is Success for All?

   A) It is a teacher training program started in New York that takes recent college graduates from various academic disciplines and gives them a minimal teacher training program for teaching in the inner-city.

   B) It is a comprehensive approach to early intervention for disadvantaged students, that works to prevent students from falling behind in the early grades.

   C) It is a reading program that gives middle school students incentives for improvement of their reading skills.

   D) It is a national program aimed at raising the scores in mathematics.

Answer: B

Explanation: B) Success for All is a comprehensive approach to prevention and early intervention for elementary schools serving disadvantaged students. Longitudinal studies of Success for All have shown that students in this program read substantially better than do students in matched control schools throughout the elementary grades.

Page Ref: 308

53) Which of the following best describes the types of reform recently developing in Title I schools?

   A) programs such as Success for All, that introduce research-based methods into a wide array of practices throughout the school.

   B) more frequent assignment of disadvantaged students to special-education classes.

   C) a focus on programs that make sure students have fallen behind significantly, before providing remedial services.

   D) a more intense focus on pull-out programs.

Answer: A

Explanation: A) The recent trend in Title I reform, is toward comprehensive, schoolwide programs.

Page Ref: 308

True/False Questions

1) The researcher John Carroll proposes that learning is partly a function of time actually spent on learning.

Answer: TRUE
Page Ref: 277

2) A feature of Slavin's QAIT model is that only three of its four elements must be adequate, for instruction to be effective.

Answer: FALSE
Page Ref: 277

3) Between-class ability grouping is more common in elementary schools than in secondary schools.

Answer: FALSE
Page Ref: 280

4) Within-class ability grouping is far more common in secondary schools than elementary schools.

Answer: FALSE
Page Ref: 280

5) Research has indicated that untracking requires changes in thinking about students' potential, not just changes in school or classroom practices.

Answer: TRUE
Page Ref: 284

6) The term regrouping refers to a type of within-class ability grouping, in which students stay with the same teacher for all subjects.

Answer: FALSE
Page Ref: 284

7) The problem inherent in any mastery learning strategy is how to provide the additional instructional time to students who need it.

Answer: TRUE
Page Ref: 286

8) In mastery learning the teacher emphasizes that every student can achieve mastery, that mastery, not grades, is the most important goal, and that each student who attains the standard will receive an A.

Answer: TRUE
Page Ref: 286

9) The central problem of mastery learning is that it involves a tradeoff between the amount of content that can be covered and the degree to which students master each concept.

Answer: TRUE
Page Ref: 288

10) A teaching approach in which each student works at her or his own level and rate is called individualized instruction.

Answer: TRUE
Page Ref: 288

11) Same-age tutoring is more often recommended by researchers than cross-age tutoring.

Answer: FALSE
Page Ref: 289

12) The three general populations in education that use technological applications are teachers, parents, and administrators.

Answer: FALSE
Page Ref: 292

13) The most common use of computers in elementary and secondary schools is for word processing.

Answer: TRUE
Page Ref: 295

14) One of the most common applications of computers in education is to provide students with practice on skills or knowledge.

Answer: TRUE
Page Ref: 296

15) The best tutorial programs are helpful but do not come close to mimicking a patient human tutor.

Answer: FALSE
Page Ref: 296

16) Recent evidence regarding computer simulations, such as Oregon Trail, indicates they can improve achievement compared to traditional teaching methods.

Answer: TRUE
Page Ref: 297

17) Computer-based instruction (CBI) is often effective when used without any other form of instruction.

Answer: FALSE
Page Ref: 299

18) According to federal guidelines, Title I funds must be used to replace, not to supplement, local educational efforts.

Answer: FALSE
Page Ref: 303

19) Research on effective practices in Title I pull-out classes finds that practices that are effective in regular classes are also effective in Title I classes.

Answer: TRUE
Page Ref: 303

20) In a recent study of the effects of Title I, called Prospects, findings indicate no overall effects on students who received Title I services, but suggest that integrating Title I services with schoolwide projects may improve effectiveness.

Answer: TRUE
Page Ref: 304

21) Some critics of No Child Left Behind (NCLB) believe that it presents real obstacles to helping students and strengthening public schools because it focuses on sanctions rather than assistance.

Answer: TRUE
Page Ref: 306

Short Answer Questions

1) Slavin's model that focuses on the alterable elements of Carroll's model—those that the teacher or school can directly change.

Answer: QAIT
Page Ref: 277

2) Curriculum sequences to which students of specified achievement or ability level are assigned.

Answer: tracks
Page Ref: 280

3) Another name given to the use of college preparatory or general tracks in high school.

Answer: between-class grouping
Page Ref: 280

4) One specific method of regrouping for reading that groups students across grade lines.

Answer: Joplin Plan
Page Ref: 284

5) Type of program that combines students of different ages in the same class, generally at the primary level. It is also called cross-age grouping.

Answer: nongraded program
Page Ref: 284

6) A system of instruction that seeks to enable all students to achieve instructional objectives by allowing learning time to vary as needed.

Answer: mastery learning
Page Ref: 286

7) Students who fail to meet a pre-established mastery criterion following a lesson are given this.

Answer: corrective instruction
Page Ref: 287

8) Assessments that are not a final measure of learning, but give the teacher ongoing feedback about the student's progress.

Answer: formative evaluation
Page Ref: 287

9) In mastery learning, while some students receive corrective instruction on concepts they had problems with, the remaining students work on this.

Answer: enrichment activities
Page Ref: 288

10) The method in which a tutor is several years older than the student being taught.

Answer: cross–age tutoring
Page Ref: 289

11) This type of instruction uses a well–designed program that is nearly perfect at providing appropriate levels of instruction, because it can analyze student responses immediately to determine whether to spend more time on a particular topic or skill.

Answer: computer based instruction
Page Ref: 296

12) Application of computer technology to provide students with extensive practice of skills and knowledge.

Answer: drill-and-practice
Page Ref: 296

13) Software that comes close to mimicking a patient human giving one–to–one instruction.

Answer: tutorial
Page Ref: 296

14) The medium for an all–information database containing such information as encyclopedias.

Answer: CD–ROMs
Page Ref: 298

15) Compensatory education programs in which students are placed in separate classes for remedial instruction.

Answer: pull-out programs
Page Ref: 303

Essay Questions

1) Define each element of the QAIT model of school learning, illustrating each step with a classroom example. Explain how the elements interact to produce effective instruction.

Answer: Slavin's QAIT model includes the following elements: 1) quality of instruction; 2) appropriate levels of instruction; 3) incentive; and 4) time. Quality of instruction refers to lecturing, calling on students, discussion, helping students with seatwork, and so on. Appropriate levels of instruction include levels of student knowledge, skills, learning rate, and motivation. Incentive is the degree of willingness of students to pay attention, conscientiously perform tasks required of them, and study. Time, in the QAIT model, is the amount of time teachers schedule for instruction versus the amount of time they actually use to teach.

If any one of the elements of the QAIT model does not function well, instruction can not succeed.

Page Ref: 277

2) What is between-class ability grouping? How is it different from within-class ability grouping? Explain how either regrouping or nongraded programs can function as an alternative to regular between-class and within-class grouping.

Answer: Between-class ability grouping is the practice of grouping students together according to their abilities. Within-class ability grouping is accommodating students individual needs while keeping a group intact. Regrouping and nongraded programs offer alternatives that allow students to have instruction matched to their ability level, without establishing all-day "tracks."

Page Ref: 281

3) Despite its widespread use, between-class ability grouping is ineffective, according to many research studies. Why is this so and why do schools continue to use the practice?

Answer: The primary purpose of ability grouping is to reduce the range of student performance levels teachers must deal with so they can adapt instruction to the needs of a well-defined group. However, grouping is often done on the basis of standardized test scores or other measures of general ability rather than performance in a particular subject. As a result, the reduction in the range of differences that are actually important for a specific class may be too small to make much difference.

Page Ref: 281

4) A teacher uses mastery learning in an advanced placement chemistry class. All students must receive 90 percent on a weekly quiz. If they fail to do so, they are given individual instruction on the material. They then re-take the quiz.
   Why would the teacher select this method? What challenges will the teacher encounter in implementing mastery learning?

Answer: The teacher is using a form of mastery learning. Students must meet a preestablished mastery criterion (90 percent on the quiz). If not, students receive corrective instruction.
   Mastery learning may be selected because it can potentially motivate all students to succeed. The teacher will meet significant challenges in ongoing assessment (formative evaluation) and in finding time to implement corrective instruction.

Page Ref: 286

5) As a teacher, you are trying to decide whether to use cross-age tutors or same-age tutors for your reading program. Assuming you want to do what is most effective, what does the research tell you to do?

Answer: Cross-age tutoring is more often recommended by researchers than same-age tutoring. This is partly because of the obvious fact that older students are more likely to know the material and partly because students may accept an older student as a tutor but resent having a classmate appointed to tutor them.

Page Ref: 289

6) In what ways can computers be used in the classroom? Make a list of the most common purposes. Give an example of an effect, shown in research, of a classroom computer application. Evaluate student access to computers, from the perspective of social equality.

Answer: Common uses of computers include: 1) drill and practice; 2) tutorial programs; 3) instructional games; 4) simulations; 5) word processing; 6) spreadsheets and databases; 7) CD-ROMs; 8) hypertext and hypermedia; 9) videodiscs; 10) integrated learning systems; 11) programming; and 12) Internet.

Examples of effects include findings such as those from word processing (students using computers write and revise more), and from Jasper (students using Jasper showed improved performance on word problems).

Students do not have equal access to computers. Both gender and class differences are concerns.

Page Ref: 294

7) Can computers teach? What research evidence exists that says they can or cannot?

Answer: Most reviews on the effects of computer-based instruction conclude that there is a small to moderate sized positive effect on achievement when computers are used in the classroom. It is most effective when it is used in addition to—rather than in place of—regular instruction.

Page Ref: 299

8) What are compensatory programs? Give two examples of compensatory educational programs. Describe one type of compensatory education that has produced disappointing results. Describe one solution that may improve compensatory education.

Answer: Compensatory educational programs are designed to help students overcome the problems associated with being brought up in low-income communities by supplementing the regular school program. Two such programs are Head Start and Follow Through, which are designed to give disadvantaged preschool and primary school children the skills necessary for a good start in school. The largest compensatory program is called Title I, a federally funded program that gives schools money to provide extra services for students who are having trouble in school.

Title I pull-out programs have been criticized for lack of effectiveness. Programs that place a greater emphasis on early intervention, and on schoolwide, researched-based innovation, appear promising today.

Page Ref: 303

9) Briefly describe Title I programs: what are they and why do they exist? Describe two forms that Title I programs have taken. What problems have been associated with these approaches?

Describe one positive, and one negative research finding evaluating recent Title I programs. Explain the reasoning behind one recent trend in Title I programming , that is supported by research.

Answer: Title I programs are federally funded; they give schools money to provide extra services for students placed at risk. Title I programs have taken the form of pull-out programs, which place students in separate classes for remediation, and in-class models, which place a Title I teacher in the regular classroom. Neither of these programs have helped students enough, perhaps because they begin after the student has already fallen behind.

Recent Title I studies include Sustaining Effects, which found reading and math gains for first graders, and Prospects, which failed to find overall achievement benefits. Recent trends include early intervention, which hopes to help students more by focusing on prevention, and comprehensive school reform programs, which introduce research-based strategies on a school-wide basis.

Page Ref: 303

10) In preparing for the opening of the new Southwest Canyon Elementary School, it quickly becomes obvious to the principal, Ms. Gomez, that "something different" will be needed with instructional strategies. Southwest Canyon is drawing its highly diverse student population from several local communities. Individual differences in educational backgrounds and home environments are substantial. Ms. Gomez decides to approach her faculty.

"What is the best way to address our problem of such diverse learners?" begins Ms. Gomez.

Ms. Joplin, a seasoned sixth grade teacher, suggests that classes at each grade level be organized into tracks to create high, average, and low groups. Each group then works with the same teacher throughout the day. "The plan makes sense," declares Ms. Joplin. "Teachers can work with students who have similar academic backgrounds. And, students who do poorly will not be frustrated as they are left behind, while students who do well will not have to feel like they need to wait for others."

Mr. Compro, one of the kindergarten teachers disagrees. "Students need to be exposed to a wide range of individual abilities, characteristics, talents, and so on. How can we ever help our students appreciate their own uniqueness and diversity if we continually group them together in a way that is more convenient for us than for them?"

Discuss the ideas presented by Ms. Gomez, Ms. Joplin, and Mr. Compro regarding between-class and within-class grouping.

Answer: Each of the solutions presented in the case has its benefits, but each introduces problems. Research does not generally support its use; however, this is because grouping occurs as a result of standardized test scores rather than real academic needs. When grouped according to academic needs, students can do better, in part, because teachers can customize lessons to the group's needs. Additionally, the quality of instruction in low-track groups tends to be less effective than that found in high-track groups. Finally, one of the most insidious aspects of tracking is that it often creates low-track classes that are predominately composed of students from lower socioeconomic groups and from minority groups.

Page Ref: 279

11) Below are several examples describing how computers can be used in the classroom. On the line next to the example, identify the type of application being used.

1. electronic page turning _____
2. virtual environment _____
3. desktop publishing _____

Answer: 1. electronic page   turning drill and practice
          2. virtual environment   simulations
          3. desktop publishing   word processing
Page Ref: 292

Chapter 10   Motivating Students to Learn

Multiple-Choice Questions

1) According to behavioral learning theory, a person's motivation to engage in a particular activity is a function of

    A) the type of attributions the person has made in response to past failures.

    B) the perceived difficulty of the activity.

    C) the degree to which the activity was reinforced in the past.

    D) an individual's self-esteem needs.

Answer: C

Explanation: C) According to behavioral learning theory, a person's motivation to engage in a particular activity is a function of the degree to which the activity has proven reinforcing in the past. Behavioral theories link motivation to an individual's personal history of reinforcement and punishment.

Page Ref: 318

2) Ms. Frey has been rewarding Marcia with praise but Marcia's behavior has not improved. Ms. Frey needs to consider that

    A) praise may not be a reinforcer for Marcia in this situation.

    B) praise is not a primary reinforcer.

    C) the consensus from research is that praise is not effective as a reward.

    D) praise will be effective only after any other reinforcers are removed from the situation.

Answer: A

Explanation: A) The value of potential reinforcers is determined by personal and situational factors.

Page Ref: 319

3) A student participates frequently and enthusiastically in class question and answer sessions. From the viewpoint of behavioral theory, one can confidently conclude that the student is motivated to

    A) increase learning of the subject.   B) demonstrate knowledge to classmates.

    C) obtain recognition from the teacher.   D) answer or ask questions.

Answer: D

Explanation: D) All that we can conclude confidently is that the student is motivated to participate in class. Internal motives remain in question.

Page Ref: 319

4) In Maslow's hierarchy of needs,

    A) each need functions independently of all others.

    B) safety needs must be satisfied before a person can move on to higher needs.

    C) reinforcement is more important than avoiding punishment during early childhood, while avoiding punishment is more important during middle childhood.

    D) maintaining a positive self-concept is the most basic need.

Answer: B

Explanation: B) In Maslow's hierarchy, basic needs must be satisfied before individuals attend to higher-level needs. For example, if an individual were hungry (physiological need), she or he might not be very interested in school work (esteem need).

Page Ref: 319

5) According to Maslow, self-actualization can be described as

    A) the need most critical to good adjustment in academic situations.

    B) a deficiency need.

    C) a need requiring adequate satisfaction of all other needs.

    D) the motivation to avoid failure in relationships with others.

Answer: C

Explanation: C) Self-actualization is placed at the top of Maslow's hierarchy. The desire to become everything that one is capable of becoming requires satisfaction of all other needs.

Page Ref: 319

6) Nicole was kept awake half the night because her brother and parents were fighting. Nicole's motivation to perform school tasks will be low today, not only because she is upset about her family, but because her _____ needs have not been met.

    A) higher   B) esteem   C) growth   D) physiological

Answer: D

Explanation: D) Lack of sleep is one of the lower, physiological needs. According to Maslow, when lower needs are not met, a person will not be inclined to satisfy the higher needs that would motivate school learning.

Page Ref: 319

7) Maslow's deficiency needs are those that are critical to physical and psychological well-being. When they are satisfied,

    A) the individual's motivation to satisfy them increases.

    B) the individual has achieved self-actualization.

    C) motivation to satisfy them decreases.

    D) a student will be unable to focus on school work.

Answer: C

Explanation: C) Maslow's deficiency needs are those that are critical to physical and psychological well-being. They include physiological, safety, love, and esteem. Once these needs are satisfied, motivation to perform them temporarily decreases. Self-actualization is not a deficiency need; it is a growth need.

Page Ref: 320

8) Which of the following is a correct implication of Maslow's hierarchy of needs?

    A) A student who is feeling ill or unsafe may show little interest in academic performance.

    B) Students who are self-actualized must be taught to have respect for their fellow students who are not so fortunate.

    C) Students who have skipped a need level on the hierarchy must be helped to complete it.

    D) Educators should design lessons that teach students to ignore unmet deficiency needs, and concentrate on higher needs.

Answer: A

Explanation: A) An implication for educators of Maslow's hierarchy of needs is that a student who is feeling ill or unsafe may show little interest in academic performance. As deficiency needs, feeling ill or unsafe will be attended to first before the learner becomes interested in the high level need, esteem (doing well on academic tasks).

Page Ref: 320

9) Which of the following theories most directly seeks to understand how people view causes, in explaining both their successes and failures?

    A) behavioral learning theory   B) attribution theory

    C) achievement motivation theory   D) expectancy valence theory

Answer: B

Explanation: B) Attribution theory seeks to understand explanations and excuses, particularly when applied to success or failure. Such explanations view causes as internal or external, stable or unstable, and controllable or uncontrollable.

Page Ref: 321

10) According to attribution theory, people are most likely to attribute

A) both successes and failures to luck.

B) successes to luck and failures to their own inadequacies.

C) successes to their own abilities and failures to (bad) luck.

D) both successes and failures to their own abilities.

Answer: C

Explanation: C) Attribution theory assumes that most people strive to maintain a positive self-image. To do this, they tend to attribute successes to their own abilities and failures to bad luck.

Page Ref: 322

11) A category of attributions that are internal and stable is

A) effort.   B) task difficulty.

C) luck.   D) ability.

Answer: D

Explanation: D) An internal stable attribution is ability because it is perceived as intrinsic to the learner (i.e., unaffected by outside factors) and enduring (stable from day to day). In contrast, effort is internal-unstable, meaning it can vary from situation to situation.

Page Ref: 322

12) A student says, "I did well because of some lucky guessing." The type of attribution being demonstrated is

A) internal, stable.   B) external, stable.

C) internal, unstable.   D) external, unstable.

Answer: D

Explanation: D) Luck is seen as outside the learner's control (external) and varying from situation to situation (unstable).

Page Ref: 322

13) A student believes that her reason for success in reading is the effort put into the task. The student's locus of control is

A) external.   B) internal.   C) dimensional.   D) luck-based.

Answer: B

Explanation: B) People with an internal locus of control tend to attribute success or failure to their own efforts or abilities (i.e., internal factors).

Page Ref: 322

14) A student with an internal locus of control is likely to blame poor performance on

    A) the teacher's difficult tests.   B) parents' pressures to succeed.

    C) lack of effort.   D) bad luck.

Answer: C

Explanation: C) People with an internal locus of control tend to attribute success or failure to their own efforts or abilities (internal factors) rather than to luck or task difficulty (external factors).

Page Ref: 322

15) Ice skating was a new experience for Leonard. He found that he had trouble keeping up with his friends, who had skated a lot before. After his first evening on the ice a friend asked him to go skating again. Leonard flatly refused, insisting that "It's not for me—I stink at skating." Which of the following best describes the attribution Leonard is making to explain his failure at skating?

    A) internal, stable   B) external, stable

    C) internal, unstable   D) external, unstable

Answer: A

Explanation: A) Leonard is saying that his ability level is low. Lack of ability is a cause that is located within the individual—internal, and that is seen as unchangeable—stable.

Page Ref: 322

16) Studies have shown that the most successful students

    A) are not affected by the difficulty of a task.

    B) correctly estimate the degree to which their success is due to their own effort.

    C) tend to overestimate the degree to which their own behavior leads to success.

    D) have an external locus of control.

Answer: C

Explanation: C) Studies have shown that successful students actually overestimate the degree to which their own behavior leads to success. These perceptions are a product of having an internal locus of control.

Page Ref: 324

17) Students who are highly motivated to learn are more likely than other students to consciously do which three things?

    1) plan their learning
    2) carry out a learning plan
    3) set specific study times
    4) retain the information they obtain

    A) 1, 2, and 3.   B) 1, 2, and 4.   C) 1, 3, and 4.   D) 2, 3, and 4.

Answer: B

Explanation: B) Self-regulated learning is closely related to students' goals. Students who are highly motivated to learn something are more likely than other students to consciously plan their learning, carry out a learning plan, and retain the information they obtain.

Page Ref: 324

18) Self-regulated students receive motivation from many sources, including all of the following **EXCEPT**

    A) social modeling.   B) feedback.

    C) goal-setting.   D) punishment.

Answer: D

Explanation: D) Motivation can come from many sources. One is social modeling, such as seeing other students using self-regulated strategies. Another is goal-setting, where students are encouraged to establish their own learning goals. A third is feedback that shows students that they are making good progress toward their learning goals, especially if their effort and ability are emphasized.

Page Ref: 324

19) The expectancy valence model views motivation as dependent on the person's expectation of reward and

    A) external attributions for past successes.

    B) internal attributions for past successes.

    C) past reinforcement of the behavior in question.

    D) the value placed on success.

Answer: D

Explanation: D) The expectancy valance model views motivation as dependent on the person's expectations of success and the value placed on success. The relationship is multiplicative, meaning that if the value of one of these factors is zero, overall motivation will be zero.

Page Ref: 325

20) Which of the following formulas is representative of expectancy theory?

   A) UCS → UCR

   B) a + b = b + a

   C) M = Ps × Is

   D) M = ability + effort + task difficulty + luck

Answer: C

Explanation: C) Motivation (M) = perceived probability of success (Ps) × incentive value of success (Is).

Page Ref: 325

21) Expectancy theory supports the idea that grading systems should be

   A) extremely difficult so that only a small percentage earn the highest grade.

   B) challenging, but not extremely difficult.

   C) bimodal, such that half the students receive low grades and half receive high grades.

   D) fairly easy so that most students earn the highest grade.

Answer: B

Explanation: B) Expectancy theory supports the idea that grading systems should be challenging but not extremely difficult. In other words, students who do the work should have a reasonable chance of obtaining a good grade; students who exert little effort should be most likely to receive a low grade.

Page Ref: 326

22) Students with learning goals are likely to

   A) have excessive performance goals.

   B) become less motivated when the going gets tough.

   C) feel helpless if they are performing below average.

   D) take difficult courses and seek challenges.

Answer: D

Explanation: D) Students striving toward learning goals are likely to take difficult courses and to seek challenges, while those with performance goals focus on getting good grades, take easy courses, and avoid challenging situations.

Page Ref: 327

23) Compared to those with performance goals, students with learning goals

   A) have higher intelligence.   B) persist in the face of obstacles.

   C) take easier courses.   D) are discipline problems.

Answer: B

Explanation: B) Compared to students with performance goals, students with learning goals are more likely to persist in the face of obstacles. These are individuals who are motivated to improve themselves rather than to obtain recognition or rewards. Thus, they are more persistent and accepting of challenge.

Page Ref: 327

24) Which of the following is true about learning goals?

   A) Instead of encouraging them, teachers should promote performance goals.

   B) Teachers should try to promote learning goals by emphasizing the value of good grades.

   C) Teachers should try to promote learning goals by making lessons interesting to students.

   D) To promote learning goals, teachers should encourage students to make external attributions.

Answer: C

Explanation: C) Teachers should try to promote learning goals by making lessons interesting. In contrast, if they emphasize grades, performance goals will be promoted.

Page Ref: 327

25) Failure avoiders

   A) decrease their efforts following failure.

   B) increase their efforts following failure.

   C) decrease their efforts following success.

   D) increase their efforts when incentive value is zero.

Answer: A

Explanation: A) Atkinson found that some people were more motivated to avoid failure rather than to seek success (failure avoiders), while other were more motivated to seek success than to avoid failure (success seekers). Weiner found that success seekers' motivation is increased following failure, as they intensify their efforts to succeed. Failure avoiders decrease their efforts following failure.

Page Ref: 330

26) Which of the following characteristics is common among failure avoiders?

    A) They tend to choose either very easy or very difficult tasks.

    B) Their motivation increases after a failure.

    C) They attribute their successes and failures to controllable factors.

    D) They respond to tasks in the same manner as success seekers.

Answer: A

Explanation: A) One very important characteristic of failure avoiders is that they tend to choose either very easy or very difficult tasks. For example, a poor reader might choose to write a book report on *War and Peace* but then, when told that was too difficult, might choose a simple children's book.

Page Ref: 330

27) Which of the following statements would a student suffering from learned helplessness be likely to make?

    A) I failed the quiz because I didn't study enough.

    B) I need to adjust my strategy for taking my next driver's test.

    C) It doesn't matter what I do.

    D) If I try harder, I can succeed.

Answer: C

Explanation: C) A student suffering from learned helplessness would be likely to say, "It doesn't matter what I do." This orientation reflects the feeling that one is powerless to avoid failure. Therefore, regardless of behavior, failure is viewed as inevitable.

Page Ref: 330

28) Teachers can help counter learned helplessness by using which of the following general principles?
    1)   Accentuate the positive.
    2)   Eliminate the negative.
    3)   Get a fresh start on new material, without mentioning old ideas.
    4)   Create challenges that actively involve students' capabilities.

    A) 1 and 2 (not 3 and 4).   B) 3 and 4 (not 1 and 2).

    C) 1, 2, and 4 (not 3).   D) All four principles.

Answer: C

Explanation: C) Teachers can help counter learned helplessness by accentuating the positive, eliminating the negative, going from the familiar to the new, and creating challenges.

Page Ref: 331

29) According to the research, teacher expectations

    A) affect student behavior, especially when teachers are unaware of students' actual achievement levels.

    B) are high when teachers' wait times for answers are short.

    C) affect males but not females.

    D) have no significant effect on student achievement.

Answer: A

Explanation: A) Evidence has generally supported the idea that teachers' expectations can affect students' behavior, particularly in the younger grades and when teachers know little about their students' achievement levels.

Page Ref: 332

30) A teachers may communicate positive expectations to a class by doing all of the following **EXCEPT**

    A) allowing students to move between ability groups.

    B) keeping grading a private matter.

    C) waiting longer for students to respond to questions.

    D) calling more often on students who perform well.

Answer: D

Explanation: D) In trying to communicate positive expectations, teachers should not call on students who perform well, more than others. This would communicate to low performers that they are not expected to answer correctly, and accentuate their negative feelings.

Page Ref: 332

31) According to Hill and Wigfield, the main source of anxiety in school is

    A) gangs.   B) fear of failure.

    C) highly structured instruction.   D) being late to class.

Answer: B

Explanation: B) According to research by Hill and Wigfield, the main source of anxiety in school is the fear of failure, and with it, loss of self-esteem. Low achievers are particularly likely to feel anxious in school, but they are by no means the only ones.

Page Ref: 333

32) Mr. Georgopolous is making a special effort to help Steve. When he plans lessons he checks the instructions for learning tasks to make sure they are clear and specific. Mr. Georgopolous also avoids time pressure, gives students a chance to correct errors on their work and fosters an accepting, noncompetitive classroom climate. His emphasis on these strategies for helping Steve suggests that Steve has been having difficulty with

A) the incentive value of success.   B) self-actualization.

C) anxiety.   D) following classroom rules.

Answer: C

Explanation: C) Strategies for reducing student anxiety include comfortable classroom climate, clarity of task instructions and reduction of time pressures.

Page Ref: 334

33) In a study by Lepper et al., students who expected and then received an award for drawing with felt-tipped markers

A) later spent more time drawing with the markers than did students who were not rewarded.

B) drew pictures that were judged higher in quality than did students who were not rewarded.

C) later spent less time drawing with the markers than did students who were not rewarded.

D) drew pictures that were judged lower in quality than did students who were not rewarded.

Answer: C

Explanation: C) Lepper's study showed that students expected and received an award for drawing with felt-tipped markers later spent less time drawing with the markers than did students who were not rewarded. The implication is that extrinsic rewards can sometimes undermine intrinsic motivation.

Page Ref: 335

34) Recent research on classroom rewards, using older students and school-like tasks,

A) clearly supports the earlier finding that material rewards decrease intrinsic motivation.

B) suggests that extrinsic rewards do not necessarily decrease intrinsic motivation.

C) provides unequivocal support for the idea of offering extrinsic rewards on most school tasks.

D) suggests that by the time students reach high school, extrinsic rewards are no longer influential.

Answer: B

Explanation: B) Recent research on classroom rewards suggests that extrinsic rewards do not necessarily decrease intrinsic motivation and may sometimes increase it. Such effects are especially likely when rewards are contingent on the quality of performance.

Page Ref: 335

35) Which of the following statements reflects your textbook author's view of how to use extrinsic rewards?

   A) Do not use them in classroom situations.

   B) Use primary, not secondary, extrinsic reinforcers.

   C) Use them mainly for subjects that have low intrinsic interest.

   D) Use them on most tasks, regardless of their intrinsic interest.

Answer: C

Explanation: C) The textbook author supports using extrinsic rewards for subjects that have low intrinsic interest. In these situations, the rewards can motivate students to engage in activities they would normally try to avoid.

Page Ref: 336

36) The use of rewards often increases intrinsic motivation, especially when rewards are contingent on

   A) the quality of performance.

   B) a student's success in outscoring a certain percentage of classmates.

   C) a high level of intrinsic interest in the task.

   D) participation in the activity, regardless of performance level.

Answer: A

Explanation: A) The use of rewards often increases intrinsic motivation, especially when rewards are contingent on the quality of performance rather than on mere participation in an activity, when the rewards are seen as recognition of competence, when the task in question is not very interesting, or when the rewards are social rather than material.

Page Ref: 336

37) According to research findings, which of the following types of rewards should be **AVOIDED** when rewarding students for performance of intrinsically interesting tasks?

   A) praise

   B) social rewards

   C) feedback on progress toward developing a skill

   D) material rewards

Answer: D

Explanation: D) The research on the effects of extrinsic rewards on intrinsic motivation does counsel caution in the use of material rewards for intrinsically interesting tasks. Teachers should attempt to make everything they teach as intrinsically interesting as possible and should avoid handing out material rewards when they are unnecessary, but they should not refrain from using extrinsic rewards when they are needed.

Page Ref: 336

38) Teachers can enhance intrinsic motivation by

    A) giving tokens.   B) withholding feedback.

    C) personalizing lesson material.   D) giving constant praise.

Answer: C

Explanation: C) Teachers must arouse interest by convincing students of the importance and interest level of the material about to be presented, and show them how it will be useful to them personally. Introducing lessons with examples relating the material to students' cultures can be particularly effective.

Page Ref: 336

39) Which of the following is **NOT** recommended by the text author as a strategy for fostering intrinsic motivation?

    A) games or simulations

    B) employing a variety of presentation modes

    C) student involvement in setting learning goals

    D) using abstract, rather than concrete, examples

Answer: D

Explanation: D) The strategy that is not recommended for fostering curiosity is using abstract examples. Concrete examples make materials more interesting. The other choices (games and simulations, presentation modes and goal–setting strategies) all promote intrinsic interest.

Page Ref: 337

40) One way to enhance students' intrinsic interest is to

    A) provide material rewards over a long period of time.

    B) allow the teacher to make all the decisions.

    C) give them some choice over what they will study.

    D) avoid surprises.

Answer: C

Explanation: C) One way to enhance students' intrinsic interest is to give them some choice over what they will study or how they will study it.

Page Ref: 338

41) The advantage of simulations is that they allow students to learn about a subject

    A) without the help of peers.   B) without interference.

    C) from the outside.   D) from the inside.

Answer: D

Explanation: D) The advantage of simulations is that they allow students to learn about a subject from the inside. Although research on the use of simulations finds that they are generally little or no more effective than traditional instruction for teaching facts and concepts, studies do consistently find that simulations increase student interest, motivation, and affective learning.

Page Ref: 338

42) When assigning material that is not intrinsically interesting to all students, teacher must try to enhance student motivation to learn. To prevent student confusion, teachers must

    A) express clear expectations.   B) read aloud as students follow in texts.

    C) assign simple projects.   D) never assign uninteresting topics.

Answer: A

Explanation: A) Teachers must always try to enhance students' intrinsic motivation to learn academic materials, but not every subject is intrinsically interesting to all students. Students need to know exactly what they are supposed to do, how they will be evaluated, and what the consequences of success will be. Often students' failures on particular tasks stem from confusion about what they are expected to do. Communicating clear expectations is important, and is one incentive that can help motivate students to learn academic material.

Page Ref: 338

43) A student has done well on a test. Which of the following feedback statements from the teacher would be best, based on the discussion in your text?

    A) "Good work, you are still one of the best students."

    B) "You're so smart!"

    C) "Your definitions were very clear."

    D) "You did so well—you really lucked out."

Answer: C

Explanation: C) The most effective feedback statement would be, "Your definitions were very clear." Here the teacher is giving specific information that tells the student what was done well. As a result, the student has direction for future success.

Page Ref: 340

44) A teacher says to a student, "You've done well today." This type of praise may be ineffective because it is **NOT**

A) credible.   B) strong enough.

C) specific.   D) an extrinsic reward.

Answer: C

Explanation: C) Specificity means that the teacher praises students for specific behaviors, not for general goodness.

Page Ref: 340

45) Research on feedback would support the practice of

A) giving many brief quizzes rather than a few long tests.

B) delaying feedback by a few days after an activity is completed.

C) giving feedback that leads students to make external attributions as they try to understand their success or failure.

D) writing only positive comments on returned reports or tests.

Answer: A

Explanation: A) Research on feedback would support the practice of giving many brief quizzes rather than one or two long tests. The quizzes would increase the opportunity for students to obtain information about how they are doing. The informational and motivation value of the feedback would thus be increased.

Page Ref: 341

46) Research on feedback has found that providing information on the results of someone's actions

A) can be an adequate reward if it is specific, clear, and prompt.

B) is most often ineffective as a reward.

C) needs to be accompanied by a material motivator to be useful.

D) is most effective when used infrequently.

Answer: A

Explanation: A) Research on feedback has found that provision of information on the results of one's actions can be an adequate reward in some circumstances. However, feedback must be clear, specific, and given close in time to performance to be an effective motivator.

Page Ref: 341

47) Feedback should be delivered to students

    A) infrequently.   B) on rare occasions.

    C) only when the teacher sees progress.   D) frequently.

Answer: D

Explanation: D) Research has shown that feedback must be clear and specific and given close in time to performance to be an effective motivator. In addition, feedback should be delivered to students frequently.

Page Ref: 341

48) Praise is effective as a student motivator to the extent that it is specific, credible, and

    A) emotionally neutral.

    B) focused on performance of easy tasks.

    C) contingent on the desired behavior.

    D) given to all students in the same words.

Answer: C

Explanation: C) Praise is effective as a classroom motivator to the extent that it is contingent, specific, and credible.

Page Ref: 342

49) A teacher praises a student for good work, but frowns and looks displeased at the same time. By these actions, the teacher is failing to make the praise seem

    A) interesting.   B) credible.   C) specific.   D) contingent.

Answer: B

Explanation: B) The teacher failed to make the praise seem credible. The problem is that the teacher's actions (the frown) are contradicting the words ("good answer"). At this point, the student does not know what to think.

Page Ref: 342

50) Students can learn to mentally give themselves a pat on the back when they finish a task or stop at regular intervals to assess what they have done. What is this called?

    A) integrated learning   B) egocentricism

    C) external attribution   D) self-regulated learning

Answer: D

Explanation: D) There is increasing evidence that students can learn to praise themselves, and that this increases their academic success. For example, students can learn to mentally give themselves a pat on the back when they finish a task, or to stop at regular intervals to notice how much they have done.

Page Ref: 343

51) Experiments comparing ungraded college classes to classes with grades found that

   A) achievement in the two types of cases is about the same.

   B) students in ungraded classrooms achieve less.

   C) the drop rate in ungraded classes is much higher.

   D) performance was higher in ungraded classes.

Answer: B

Explanation: B) Experiments comparing graded to ungraded classes found that students in ungraded classes achieve less. While this is especially true for older students, grades in general serve as incentives to perform well.

Page Ref: 343

52) Although report card grades are not given frequently, they work as incentives for older students in part because

   A) they increase the value of other rewards given closer in time to the behaviors they reinforce.

   B) they decrease the value of other rewards given closer in time to the behaviors they reinforce.

   C) good grades are equally attainable by all students.

   D) they provide feedback that is specific.

Answer: A

Explanation: A) Grades work as incentives in part because they increase the value of other rewards given closer in time to the behaviors they reinforce.

Page Ref: 343

53) What is meant by the "accessibility problem of grades"?

   A) A high achieving student does not see grades as incentives.

   B) Good grades are too easy for some but too difficult for others.

   C) Good grades are equally attainable by all students.

   D) Grades are based largely on effort, not ability.

Answer: B

Explanation: B) The accessibility problem of grades—the fact that good grades are too easy for some students while too difficult for others—may be partially diminished by the use of grading systems with many levels.

Page Ref: 343

54) The goal structure of a classroom refers to the

    A) degree to which competition and cooperation are used.

    B) expectations parents and teachers have for the students.

    C) level of incentive used by teachers and/or parents.

    D) proportion of success seekers vs. failure avoiders in a class.

Answer: A

Explanation: A) The goal structure of a classroom refers to the degree to which competition and cooperation are used. The textbook author strongly favors cooperative goal structures over competitive ones, because the latter necessitate failure by some students, regardless of the effort put forth.

Page Ref: 343

55) A teacher says, "I give the top 20% As, the next 30% Bs, and then decide on Cs, Ds, and Fs for the bottom 50%." This teacher is using what type of goal structure system?

    A) mastery   B) competitive

    C) cooperative   D) criterion referenced

Answer: B

Explanation: B) The teacher is using a competitive grading system by grading on the curve. Regardless of how well or poorly students do, some will receive As and some will receive Bs.

Page Ref: 344

56) Which of the following best reflects the text author's viewpoint on competitive goal structures in classrooms?

    A) advantageous because they raise the status of high achievers

    B) create problems because they restrict the chances of success for low achievers

    C) advantageous because they encourage students to help one another learn

    D) effective because they focus on individual success

Answer: B

Explanation: B) Competitive goal structures have been criticized for allowing low achievers little chance of success.

Page Ref: 344

True/False Questions

1) Motivation varies in both intensity and direction.

Answer: TRUE
Page Ref: 317

2) The motivational value of a reward remains the same, no matter what reward an individual expects.

Answer: FALSE
Page Ref: 317

3) Deficiency needs are those that are critical to psychological, not physiological, well-being.

Answer: FALSE
Page Ref: 319

4) The need to know and understand is a growth need.

Answer: TRUE
Page Ref: 319

5) Attribution theory attempts to show how people explain causes of their own successes and failures.

Answer: TRUE
Page Ref: 321

6) Attribution theory deals primarily with four explanations for success and failure: presence of rewards, feedback, incentive, and time.

Answer: FALSE
Page Ref: 321

7) Confirming Atkinson's theory, recent research has shown that a person's motivation to perform easy-moderately difficult tasks decreases as task difficulty increases.

Answer: FALSE
Page Ref: 322

8) Learning-oriented students are less likely to use metacognitive strategies than are performance-oriented students.

Answer: FALSE
Page Ref: 327

9) Anxious students are likely to be overly self-conscious in performance settings, which distracts attention from the task at hand.

Answer: TRUE
Page Ref: 333

10) Students' extrinsic motivation generally declines from early elementary through secondary school.

Answer: FALSE
Page Ref: 334

11) It has been observed that when teachers praise low-achieving students for good work, they often contradict their words with tone, posture, or other nonverbal cues.

Answer: TRUE
Page Ref: 340

12) There is increasing evidence that students can learn to praise themselves, and that this increases their academic success.

Answer: TRUE
Page Ref: 343

13) Competitive goal structures have been recognized for encouraging students to help one another learn.

Answer: FALSE
Page Ref: 343

Short Answer Questions

1) An internal process that activates, guides, and maintains behavior over time.

Answer: motivation
Page Ref: 317

2) According to Maslow, this is a person's ability to develop to her or his full potential.

Answer: self-actualization
Page Ref: 319

3) Maslow's category of needs that are basic requirements for physical and psychological well-being. Motivation to satisfy them decreases when they are satisfied.

Answer: deficiency needs
Page Ref: 319

4) A theory of motivation that focuses on how people explain the causes of their own successes and failures.

Answer: attribution theory
Page Ref: 321

5) A concept central to attribution theory that points to one's belief that success or failure is due to causes within, or to outside of, oneself.

Answer: locus of control
Page Ref: 322

6) In attribution theory, the label given to perceived causes that are seen as constant—that are expected always to have the same effect on success or failure.

Answer: stable attribution
Page Ref: 322

7) The formula for this theory is: Motivation (M) = Perceived probability of success (Ps) × Incentive value of success (Is).

Answer: expectancy valance
Page Ref: 325

8) The desire to experience success and to participate in activities in which success depends on personal effort and abilities.

Answer: achievement motivation
Page Ref: 326

9) The motivational orientation expressed by parents when their child comes home from school and they say "How d'ya do?" or "What d'ya get?"

Answer: performance goals
Page Ref: 327

10) The expectation, based on experience, that one's actions will ultimately lead to failure.

Answer: learned helplessness
Page Ref: 330

11) Rewards for learning that are not inherent in the material being learned, ranging from praise to grades to recognition to prizes.

Answer: extrinsic incentives
Page Ref: 335

12) The only incentive in this type of reward is the subject being learned, itself.

Answer: intrinsic incentive
Page Ref: 335

13) The degree to which students are placed in competitive or cooperative relationships in the earning of classroom rewards.

Answer: goal structure
Page Ref: 343

Essay Questions

1) How would a behavioral theorist explain motivation? Briefly explain the relevance of the schedules–of–reinforcement concept to motivation.

   Write a brief explanation of a concept that theorists such as Maslow and Weiner would include in their theories, but that a behavioral theorist would not. On what grounds would the behavioral theorist object to this concept?

   Answer: The concept of motivation is tied to the principle that behaviors that have been reinforced in the past are more likely to be repeated than are behaviors that have not been reinforced or that have been punished.

   Motivation affects the intensity and direction of behavior. A schedule of reinforcement may affect the direction of behavior by establishing a more effective pattern of reinforcement for one response, than for another. The schedule also affects intensity of behavior, as reflected in frequency of response.

   Maslow and Weiner include components in their theories that are not directly observable. Needs such a self–actualization, and processes such as the effect of type of attribution on expectations for success, would not appear in a behavioral theory.

   Page Ref: 318

2) Jim Grover's eighth graders are engaged in a cooperative learning task. He expected a high level of interest, but the students are restless. Jim's observations are puzzling.

   In the "wolves" group, Mick and Rick are whispering with their backs to the group. In the "manatees", Ginger is looking out the window, and she is very pale. The "hyenas" are discussing the topic, but keep getting sidetracked in arguments over who came up with the good ideas. Finally, two of the three "otters" who are not absent today are sitting staring at Marty, the third, who keeps standing up and then sitting down, at a rapid pace.

   Jim's students may have current needs that are getting priority over his learning objectives. Identify four of those needs, based on the students' behavior. Using at least two levels of Maslow's hierarchy, explain how the students needs affect their motivation to be on–task in Jim's lesson.

   For one of Jim's groups, suggest a motivational strategy that would address the problem, and explain why Maslow would expect it to work.

   Answer: There is not necessarily a correct "need" for each behavior. For instance, Ginger, who looks pale and distracted, could be ill, or she could be feeling a need for acceptance. In either case a basic need is interfering with her motivation to learn—a higher need. Jim Grover can quietly question Ginger, to find out if she needs attention from an adult. If not, he could motivate the group to involve her by asking them to update their goals, communicating positive expectations for all group members, or by providing them with more frequent feedback.

   Page Ref: 319

3) Using the attribution theory of motivation, describe a situation in which a person attributes success to each of the following: ability, effort, task difficulty, and luck.

   For each of these situations, quote the specific attribution made, and indicate the attribution's locus of control, and whether it is stable or unstable.

   Answer: Ability: A student believes she is smart, therefore, she will do well in school. Effort: Having done well on an exam, a student attributes his success to hours of preparation. Task difficulty: A student thought the assignment given to her by her teacher was too easy.
   Luck: Even though a student did not prepare well for the exam, he did well, which he attributes to good guessing.
   Example: "I passed the test because I'm good at science." —internal; stable.

   Page Ref: 321

4) Suzanne and Pedro got Ds on their quizzes. To Suzanne Mr. Banister says "What happened to you? Did you forget to study?" To Pedro he says "Okay, that's a pretty good score for you." The two students then make attributions: influenced by the teacher's comments, they explain their poor performance to themselves.

   Which student is more likely to make an ability attribution? an effort attribution? For each of the students, explain how the teacher's comment influenced the type of attribution made. Then explain how the type of attribution made will influence the student's expectations for success in the future.

   Answer: Suzanne makes an effort attribution (or other unstable attribution) because Mr. Banister implies that she could do better if she tried. Pedro makes an ability attribution, because Mr. Banister implies that he's doing as well as his ability allows.
   Suzanne can expect to do better in the future. She'll believe she can change the cause of her failure, because it is unstable—subject to change. Pedro is likely to believe he cannot change his ability—seen as stable—so he can only expect more of the same performance.

   Page Ref: 322

5) How might students who are motivated by learning goals behave differently from students who are motivated by performance goals?

   Answer: Students with learning goals and those with performance goals do not differ in overall intelligence, but their classroom performance can differ markedly. When they run into obstacles, performance-oriented students tend to become discouraged and their performance is seriously hampered. In contrast, when learning-oriented students encounter obstacles, they tend to keep trying and their motivation and performance may actually increase.

   Page Ref: 327

6) What is learned helplessness? What are its causes? How can teachers alleviate it?

Answer: Learned helplessness is a perception that no matter what one does, one is doomed to failure. It can arise from an individual's upbringing but also from inconsistent, unpredictable use of rewards and punishments by teachers, leading students to believe that there is little they can do to be successful. Learned helplessness can be avoided or alleviated by giving students opportunities for success in small steps, immediate feedback, and most important, consistent expectations and follow through. Also, focusing on learning goals rather than performance goals can reduce learned helplessness, since all students can attain learning goals to one degree or another.

Page Ref: 330

7) Mr. Joon, a middle school health teacher, heard many horror stories about Stuart from his colleagues over they years. "Just wait until you get Stuart!" they said. It has finally happened. Stuart's name appears on Mr. Joon's class roster for the fall term. As Mr. Joon makes out the seating chart for his first period health class, he puts Stuart in the front center row where he can keep close watch. How might Mr. Joon's behavior create the discipline problem he is trying to avoid?

Answer: Teachers can establish expectations for their students and these expectations can be self-fulfilling. If Mr. Joon expects Stuart to misbehave, and he lets Stuart know this by placing him in the front, center desk, Stuart might try to live up to Mr. Joon's expectation and misbehave.

Page Ref: 331

8) Make a list of ways that teachers can enhance intrinsic motivation. Illustrate three of your strategies with specific classroom examples.

Answer: 1. Arouse interest. 2. Maintain curiosity. 3. Use a variety of interesting presentation modes. 4. Help students set goals.

Page Ref: 334

9) One principle of providing incentives to learn is to provide clear and specific feedback. Make a list of feedback statements that would fit the definition of clear and specific feedback. For each item on the list write a contrasting example, illustrating feedback that is not clear and specific.

Answer: Clear Feedback: I like the way you used the guide words in the dictionary to find the words on your worksheet. Your topic sentence is well stated. You followed through on that serve.
Unclear Feedback: Good job. Nice going. Excellent.

Page Ref: 340

10) What is contingent praise? Give an example of how it might be used to increase student motivation.

Answer: Contingent praise depends on student performance of well defined behaviors. For example, if a teacher says, "I'd like you all to open your books to page 279 and work problems 1 to 10," then praise would only be given to the students who follow directions. Praise should be given only for the right answers and appropriate behaviors.

Page Ref: 342

11) What are the advantages and disadvantages of using grades as incentives for students to do well?

Answer: Grades can serve as incentives, especially for older students, because they increase the value of other rewards given closer in time to the behavior they reinforce. However, grades are given too infrequently to by very useful as incentives and are based on ability rather than effort.

Page Ref: 343

12) Explain the meanings of "goal structure", "cooperative goal structure" and "competitive goal structure." Compare cooperative and competitive goal structures with regard to their effects on student motivation.

Answer: Goal structure is the degree to which students are in cooperation or competition with each other. Motivational concerns noted for competitive goal structures are that low–achieving students may have little chance for success, a pecking order in the classroom is encouraged, and students are discouraged from helping one another.

Page Ref: 343

13) Mary Resnick is teaching creative writing as part of her first teaching assignment. She wonders how her students will react to this being her first year of teaching, but not her first year as a working adult (she decided to become a teacher after raising her own children). Because her daughters had teachers who Mary considered weak, she decided she was going to be firm, but fair. "This is not a popularity contest," Mary reasons. "All students should work hard and if they do, I'll reward them with good grades."

Mrs. Resnick stands by the door as her first period students enter. When they are settled into their desks, she says that she expects them to write well by the end of the school year. She also tells them that if they don't, they will fail her class.

Each week, as the school year progresses, Mrs. Resnick reviews her students' essays. As a motivational technique, she writes comments such as "below average work" or "unacceptable" on the top of their papers. "This will get them to try harder," she rationalizes. However, while the writing skills of some of the students improve, most seemed to be giving up. "This is not what I expected to happen," Mary tells her mentor teacher, Annie Jasperson. "Maybe I can explain how your students might be feeling," replies Annie.

Using the motivational theories from the chapter (e.g., behavioral, human needs, attribution, and expectancy theory), write Annie's response.

Answer: Behavioral theory: The students are not being reinforced for what they are doing right. Instead, they are being punished for trying.
Human needs theory: The students need to be loved and to belong may not be met; therefore, their need to know and understand is less meaningful.
Attribution theory: The students may be attributing their failure to the task difficulty or bad luck rather than attribute their success to effort or ability.
Expectancy theory: If students' probability of and incentive for success is low, they will not be motivated to do well.

Page Ref: 317

14) Below is a model of Maslow's Hierarchy of Needs. Study it, then make changes so that it is correct.

       safety needs
       esteem needs
       aesthetic needs
       physiological needs
       belongingness needs
       self-actualization needs
       need to know and understand

Answer: self-actualization needs
          aesthetic needs
          need to know and understand
          esteem needs
          belongingness needs
          safety needs
          physiological needs
Page Ref: 319

Chapter 11   Effective Learning Environments

Multiple-Choice Questions

1) Strategies for providing effective learning environments include
    1)   using class time well.
    2)   creating an environment conducive to interest and inquiry.
    3)   permitting students to engage in activities that activate their imaginations.
    4)   stopping lessons to address student misbehavior.

  A) 1, 2 and 3 (not 4)   B) 1, 2 and 4 (not 3)

  C) 1, 3 and 4 (not 2)   D) 2, 3 and 4 (not 1)

Answer: A

Explanation: A) Providing an effective learning environment includes strategies that teachers use to create a positive, productive classroom experience. These strategies not only include using time well, creating an atmosphere conducive to student interest and inquiry, and permissive activities that engage students' minds and imaginations, but also prevents and responds to misbehavior in effective ways.
Page Ref: 351

2) Research indicates that the most important time variable affecting student learning is the

  A) length of the school day.

  B) number of school days districts add, above and beyond state requirements.

  C) allocated time.

  D) amount of time students actually spend learning.

Answer: D

Explanation: D) Studies report that the most important element affecting the learning achievement of students is the amount of time spend actually learning. This time measure, called engaged time, represents actual learning activity as opposed to instructional or allocated time, which simply represents the time made available for learning.
Page Ref: 352

3) A teacher wants to improve student achievement by increasing the time that students spend learning. Which type of time would be most valuable to increase for that purpose?

A) seatwork time

B) engaged time

C) time spent on procedures (e.g., distributing materials) throughout the year.

D) allocated time

Answer: B

Explanation: B) It would be most valuable for the teacher to increase engaged time, which constitutes the time students spent actually learning. In contrast, allocated time, which is the time made available for learning, may not be used productively by students.

Page Ref: 352

4) Time during which students have the opportunity to learn, but may or may not actually learn, is called

A) engaged time.   B) allocated time.

C) time out.   D) time-on-task.

Answer: B

Explanation: B) Allocated time is a term for available instructional time, which is the time during which students have an opportunity to learn.

Page Ref: 353

5) In a study by Salganik (1980), a third-grade teacher continued to work with students instead of merely waiting in the hallway to use the library. This teacher helped students develop the perception that

A) teachers need to manage their time better.

B) patience is a virtue and that schools need to help teach it.

C) school is for learning, not for marking time.

D) learning need not be organized.

Answer: C

Explanation: C) In studying an outstandingly effective inner city Baltimore elementary school, Salganik described a third grade teacher who took her class to the library, which she found locked. She improvised a learning activity, giving the students the message that school-time is valuable learning-time.

Page Ref: 353

6) A great deal of allocated instructional time is lost because the teacher does not start teaching at the beginning of the period. This can be a problem in self-contained elementary classes, especially, because

    A) the class may be out of control.

    B) the teachers lack "withitness."

    C) there are no bells or fixed schedules to structure the period.

    D) waiting for everyone to fill a seat is time consuming.

Answer: C

Explanation: C) A certain amount of allocated instructional time is lost because the teacher does not start teaching at the beginning of the period. This can be a particular problem in self-contained elementary classes where there are no bells or fixed schedules to structure the period, but it is also a problem in departmentalized secondary schools, where teachers may spend a long time dealing with late students or other problems before starting the lesson.

Page Ref: 354

7) Which of the following statements concerning engaged time and allocated time is correct?

    A) Engaged time is usually greater than allocated time.

    B) Engaged time differs for every student while allocated time is usually constant for the entire class.

    C) To increase engaged time, it is always necessary to increase allocated time.

    D) Engaged time has only indirect effects on learning while allocated time has direct effects.

Answer: B

Explanation: B) It is true that engaged time differs for every student while allocated time stays about the same for the entire class. Allocated time is the time a class is given for learning. How much of that time is actually used, or engaged time, is up to the individual student who may be active or inattentive.

Page Ref: 355

8) A teacher wants to increase students' engaged time. The most effective strategy would be to

    A) have classroom rules clearly posted.

    B) increase the amount of independent practice assigned.

    C) make lessons interesting to students.

    D) increase the length of lectures by five minutes per lesson.

Answer: C

Explanation: C) The teacher's best approach would be to make the lessons interesting to students. If students are attentive, engaged time will increase. Simply giving longer lectures will not necessarily translate into longer engaged time. In fact, it may decrease engaged time if students become less involved.

Page Ref: 355

9) A teacher notices how listless and bored students seem when they enter class after lunch. Misbehavior seems to increase as a result. Based on the discussion by the textbook author, the best strategy for reducing such misbehavior is likely to be

    A) using moderate punishment such as time-out or a verbal reminder.

    B) a daily report card system.

    C) discussing the problem with individual students.

    D) making the lessons more interesting to students.

Answer: D

Explanation: D) The teacher should try to make the lessons more interesting to students. The main cause of their misbehavior appears to be boredom.

Page Ref: 355

10) A teacher wants to maintain group focus during seatwork. The teacher should consider using all of the following strategies **EXCEPT**

    A) providing students with brief opportunities for individual help.

    B) circulating around the classroom.

    C) finding those students who have not fully understood the lesson, and may be practicing incorrectly.

    D) giving students extended individual attention in responding to their questions.

Answer: D

Explanation: D) The teacher should not give students a lot of individual attention in responding to their questions. The more time spent with individuals, the greater the chances that others will tune out. Consequently, group focus will be reduced.

Page Ref: 358

11) Which strategy does calling on students at random exemplify?

    A) demonstrating withitness   B) transition management

    C) group alerting   D) maintaining momentum

Answer: C

Explanation: C) Calling on students at random is group alerting. When the teacher asks the class a question out of order, the students need to be focused and ready to be called upon.

Page Ref: 358

12) What is the term used to describe the degree to which the teacher is vigilant, and continuously responsive to student behavior?

    A) skill at managing transitions   B) withitness

    C) smoothness   D) momentum

Answer: B

Explanation: B) According to Kounin, withit teachers communicate through their actions that they are constantly aware of what is happening in the classroom. They respond immediately to misbehavior and know who did what.

Page Ref: 359

13) The situation in which students appear to be on-task, but are **NOT** engaged in learning, is called

    A) cooperative learning.   B) mock participation.

    C) active communication.   D) time on task.

Answer: B

Explanation: B) An overemphasis on engaged time rather than engaging instruction can produce what Bloome et al. call "mock participation"; it can be detrimental to learning.

Page Ref: 361

14) Management in a student-centered classroom is

    A) oriented toward few choices for the students.

    B) unlikely to involve students in setting standards of behavior.

    C) more directed at individual work than cooperative projects.

    D) more participatory than in a traditional classroom.

Answer: D

Explanation: D) It is important to note that most research on classroom management has taken place in traditionally organized classrooms in which students have few choices over what they do and few interactions with each other. Classroom management is more participatory in a student-centered classroom, with students centrally involved in setting standards of behavior.

Page Ref: 361

15) Evertson and Emmer (1982) studied teachers' actions at the beginning of the school year and correlated them with students' behaviors later in the year. They found that effective teachers expected students to

    A) get right to work on the first day of school.

    B) already know classroom procedures, from experience in previous years.

    C) do their most difficult assignments within the first few days, so that the rest of the year would seem easy.

    D) work in small groups the first day of school.

Answer: A

Explanation: A) In the research by Evertson and Emmer, students were asked to get right to work on the first day of school and were then given instructions on procedures gradually, to avoid overloading them with too much information at one time.

Page Ref: 362

16) In the research on teachers as effective managers, it was found that during the first days of school effective teachers

    A) work with individual students as much as possible.

    B) work with the whole class.

    C) divide the class into groups.

    D) separate the class into high, average, and low achievers.

Answer: B

Explanation: B) Most effective managers worked with the whole class initially. They were involved with the whole class at all times, rarely leaving any students without something to do or without supervision.

Page Ref: 362

17) The research indicates that effective managers teach students specific procedures in the first days of school. For example, some had students

    A) take tests.

    B) help the teacher prepare teaching materials that would be used in the first few weeks.

    C) practice jigsaw, rehearsing the transition from expert groups to regular groups.

    D) learn the meaning of signals, by responding to stimuli like the flick of a light switch.

Answer: D

Explanation: D) Effective managers taught students specific procedures. Some had students practice lining up quickly and quietly; others taught students to respond to a signal, such as a bell or a flick of the light switch.

Page Ref: 363

18) There are three principles that govern the process of setting class rules. First, they should be few in number; second, they should make sense and be seen as fair; and third, they should

   A) be specific enough that each rule covers only one or two behaviors.

   B) be in alphabetical order for easier recall.

   C) be clearly explained and deliberately taught to students.

   D) always be the same as the previous year's rules, for continuity.

Answer: C

Explanation: C) One of the first management-related tasks at the start of the year is setting class rules. Three principles govern this process. First, class rules should be few in number. Second, they should make sense and be seen as fair by students. Third, they should be clearly explained and deliberately taught to students.

Page Ref: 363

19) A teacher has developed a class rule that covers: listening when the teacher or other students are talking, working on seatwork, continuing to work during any interruptions, staying in one's seat and following directions. Which of the following would be the best wording for this rule?

   A) "Always listen."   B) "Stay on task."

   C) "Never get out of your seat."   D) "Don't get off task."

Answer: B

Explanation: B) Being on-task includes listening when the teacher or other students are talking, working on seatwork, continuing to work during any interruptions, staying in one's seat, being at one's seat and ready to work when the bell rings, and following directions.

Page Ref: 363

20) Which of the following is one of the most important classroom management principles?

   A) Drastic misbehaviors call for drastic measures.

   B) Three strikes and you are out.

   C) Refer to the administration.

   D) Use the simplest intervention that will work.

Answer: D

Explanation: D) Many studies have found that the amount of time spent disciplining students is negatively related to student achievement. The most important principle is that misbehaviors should be corrected using the simplest intervention possible, according to the text author.

Page Ref: 365

21) In classroom management, boredom–caused behavior problems need to be addressed using

    A) mock participation.   B) prevention.

    C) a little frustration.   D) extinction.

Answer: B

Explanation: B) Varying the content of lessons, using a variety of materials and approaches, displaying humor and enthusiasm, or using cooperative learning or project–based learning, can all prevent boredom–caused behavior problems.

Page Ref: 365

22) In the context of classroom management, what is the name of the class of preventative measures that includes eye contact, gestures, physical proximity, or light touching?

    A) overlapping   B) nonverbal cues

    C) verbal reminders   D) applying consequences

Answer: B

Explanation: B) Eye contact, gestures, physical proximity, or touching are types of nonverbal cues. Teachers use them to communicate without interrupting verbal discourse.

Page Ref: 366

23) According to the principle of least intervention, which of the following strategies would normally be tried sooner than the others, following minor misbehavior?

    A) nonverbal cues   B) apply consequences

    C) verbal reminder   D) repeated reminders

Answer: A

Explanation: A) Nonverbal cues are the simplest, least disruptive responses a teacher can make to misbehavior.

Page Ref: 366

24) A student who frequently taps a pencil loudly during seatwork stops the tapping behavior. The teacher praises the quiet behavior. Which intervention strategy is being used?

    A) repeated reminder

    B) simple verbal reminder

    C) praise of incompatible, correct behavior

    D) nonverbal cues

Answer: C

Explanation: C) The teacher is using praise of incompatible, correct behavior with the student —communicating what is appropriate behavior and, hopefully, reinforcing that behavior in the process.

Page Ref: 367

25) A student who usually behaves well is not paying attention during class. Which of the following management strategies would be most effective?

    A) deprive the student of privileges   B) implement a daily report card system

    C) time out   D) praise other students.

Answer: D

Explanation: D) It is often possible to get one student to behave by praising others for behaving. The teacher has been successful in using this technique by getting the student to pay attention in class.

Page Ref: 367

26) The "broken record" strategy is equivalent to which of the following intervention techniques?

    A) repeated reminders   B) simple verbal reminder

    C) praise of other students   D) applying consequences

Answer: A

Explanation: A) The "broken record" strategy is associated with the use of repeated reminders. Teachers decide what they want students to do, state it clearly, then repeat it until they comply.

Page Ref: 367

27) In applying consequences for routine misbehavior, the most important factor is _____ of the punishment.

    A) sufficient delay   B) complete certainty

    C) long duration   D) adequate severity

Answer: B

Explanation: B) In applying consequences for routine misbehavior, the most important factor is the certainty of the consequences. Unless students believe that consequences will really follow, they may fail to take the rules seriously.

Page Ref: 368

28) The most common reinforcer for misbehavior in the classroom is

    A) attention.   B) escape from cooperative groups.

    C) removal from the learning setting.   D) tangible rewards.

Answer: A

Explanation: A) The most common reinforcer for misbehavior tends to be attention. The attention may come from the teacher, peers, or both.

Page Ref: 369

29) According to behavioral learning theorists, all of the following are disadvantages of scolding students **EXCEPT**

    A) Scolding is not conducive to a happy, healthy classroom.

    B) Scolding has no effect on student behavior.

    C) Scolding may cause the student to become resentful.

    D) Scolding may reinforce the undesirable behavior.

Answer: B

Explanation: B) According to behavioral learning theory, the major problem with scolding students is that it gives them attention and may actually reinforce the misbehavior. As a result, the tendency to repeat the misbehavior will increase. Scolding may also harm classroom climate and produce resentment.

Page Ref: 369

30) Which of the following steps are part of any applied behavior analysis program?
    1) Identify target behavior.
    2) Establish a baseline for the target behavior.
    3) Choose a reinforcer and criteria for reinforcement.
    4) Start with infrequent reinforcement; increase the rate of reinforcement when the desired behavior is established.

    A) 1 and 4 (not 2 and 3)   B) 1, 2, and 3 (not 4)

    C) 2 and 3 (not 1 and 4)   D) All four steps.

Answer: B

Explanation: B) In applied behavior analysis program, the teacher should observe behavior at the beginning of program implementation by identifying the targeted behavior, establishing a baseline, and choosing a reinforcer and criteria for reinforcement.

Page Ref: 371

31) O'Leary and O'Leary (1972) list seven principles for the effective and humane use of punishment. Of the following principles, which is **NOT** one of the seven?

    A) Use punishment sparingly.

    B) Punish when the student finishes a behavior.

    C) Make it clear to the student why he or she is being punished.

    D) Avoid physical punishment.

Answer: B

Explanation: B) Research indicates that you should punish when behavior starts rather than when it ends.

Page Ref: 374

32) One of O'Leary and O'Leary's (1972) seven principles for the effective and humane use of punishment indicates that, along with giving punishment, you should reinforce the student for

   A) behaviors incompatible with those you wish to reduce.

   B) behaviors compatible with those you wish to reduce.

   C) stating a reasonable excuse.

   D) mock participation.

Answer: A

Explanation: A) The research work of the O'Learys indicates that you should reinforce a student for behaviors incompatible with those you wish to weaken (e.g., if you punish for being off-task, also reinforce for being on-task).

Page Ref: 374

33) A student plays the role of the class clown. The teacher isolates the student from peers using time out. Which of the following statements about this practice is true?

   A) The strategy is inappropriate because the student will continue to misbehave out of class.

   B) The strategy is inappropriate because the student will receive sympathy from the class.

   C) The strategy is appropriate because it deprives the student of an audience.

   D) The strategy is appropriate because it directly applies the Premack principle.

Answer: C

Explanation: C) The strategy of isolating is basically appropriate because it deprives the student of an audience. As the class clown, the student is evidently motivated to misbehave in order to receive peer attention.

Page Ref: 374

34) A teacher starts a home-based reinforcement program. Over time, the student responds positively with increased frequency of good behavior. Given this result, the reinforcement should now be

   A) kept at the same level indefinitely.   B) gradually increased.

   C) reduced gradually.   D) terminated.

Answer: C

Explanation: C) The frequency of the reinforcement should be reduced over time. The rationale is to make students self-motivated rather than dependent on the tangible rewards.

Page Ref: 374

35) Which of the following types of rewards are recommended for home-based reinforcement programs,?

    A) release from a homework assignment   B) extra credit points

    C) receiving a special gift or privilege   D) change of a grade

Answer: C

Explanation: C) Given the philosophy of home-based reinforcement programs, an especially appropriate reward would be a special privilege such as going on a special outing with a parent. One goal of the programs is to increase positive contacts between students and their parents.

Page Ref: 375

36) A teacher looks at the class and says, "We'll be dismissed as soon as everyone is quiet, sitting in their seats, and prepared." The teacher is using

    A) a group contingency program.   B) overlapping.

    C) a token economy.   D) the principle of least intervention.

Answer: A

Explanation: A) The teacher is using a group contingency that, in this case, requires all students to be quiet and prepared in order for anyone to be dismissed.

Page Ref: 377

37) In discussing the ethics of behavior modification techniques, your text author suggests that these methods

    A) are ethical, but not powerful enough to use with disruptive students.

    B) can lead to overcontrol of student behavior.

    C) frequently injure students' self-esteem through excessive use of punishment.

    D) should only be used under supervision of a clinical or school psychologist.

Answer: B

Explanation: B) In discussing the ethics of behavior modification techniques, the text author suggests that such methods can lead to overcontrol of student behavior. Teachers may begin to focus more on managing behavior than they do on improving learning.

Page Ref: 378

38) Applied behavior analysis strategies use rewards in a systematic way and

    A) avoid punishers as much as possible.

    B) use punishers for routine classroom misbehavior.

    C) use punishers for prevention of discipline problems.

    D) use punishers for being off-task.

Answer: A

Explanation: A) Applied behavior analysis methods should be used only when it is clear that preventative or informal methods of improving classroom management are not enough to create a positive environment for learning.

Page Ref: 379

39) Pellegrini (2002) found which type of schools to reduce bullying and violence?

    A) larger, consolidated schools   B) schools with "zero tolerance" policies

    C) smaller, less impersonal   D) sports-focused schools

Answer: C

Explanation: C) Creating democratic, participatory classrooms can give students ways of achieving recognition and control in a positive environment, reducing the need to act out. Smaller, less impersonal schools have been found to reduce bulling and violence.

Page Ref: 380

40) Which of the following statements regarding adolescents' delinquent acts is accurate?

    A) They are normal for secondary students.

    B) They are usually performed in groups.

    C) They are common among middle class individuals.

    D) Peers play a minor role in motivating delinquent behaviors.

Answer: B

Explanation: B) Delinquent acts are usually performed in groups. For this reason, the role of the delinquent peer group in maintaining delinquent behaviors cannot be overstated.

Page Ref: 380

41) Studies of truancy among delinquents have shown that

    A) rigorous academic programs can significantly increase attendance.

    B) behavior modification programs have been successful at increasing school attendance.

    C) the few successes realized in decreasing truancy have been with borderline rather than more serious delinquents.

    D) there are no effective methods for reducing it, once truancy is established.

Answer: B

Explanation: B) Studies of truancy among delinquents have shown that behavior modification programs have been successful at increasing school attendance. Exemplary strategies are giving students with good attendance tickets for a drawing, parties, or recognition.

Page Ref: 380

42) The Check and Connect attendance program has documented significant improvement in elementary school attendance and on dropout and overall middle school success by

    A) demanding parental involvement in supervision of students.

    B) systematic checks, phone calls, monitoring, and watching of students' whereabouts at all times, and reporting to parents.

    C) fostering mutual trust and open communication, checking signs of withdrawal, and providing support and commitment to students and families.

    D) committing to move in with a student and family for at least two years.

Answer: C

Explanation: C) Check and Connect is a model that provides school-based "monitors" to work with students, families, and school personnel to improve the attendance and engagement of students in schools. The program has documented significant gains on attendance in elementary schools, and on dropout and overall school success in middle schools. Check and Connect includes fostering mutual trust and open communication, checking signs of withdraw, and providing support and commitment to students and families.

Page Ref: 381

43) Tracking (between-class ability grouping), according to research, should be

    A) a significant part of the regular curriculum.

    B) provided for students based on their parents' wishes.

    C) offered in conjunction with the regular curriculum.

    D) avoided if possible.

Answer: D

Explanation: D) According to the research of Howard, tracking (between-class ability grouping) should be avoided if possible. Low track classes are ideal breeding grounds for antisocial delinquent peer groups.

Page Ref: 381

44) Group contingencies can be especially effective with predelinquent students because

    A) they reverse the effects of tracking.

    B) they can deprive students of peer support for misbehavior.

    C) these students need to be singled out for special treatment.

    D) they involve the students' families.

Answer: B

Explanation: B) Group contingencies can be especially effective with predelinquent students because their peers are so influential.

Page Ref: 382

45) If misbehavior persists, parents should be

    A) notified after the third misbehavior.

    B) contacted by letter.

    C) instructed to punish the student at home.

    D) involved in establishing a program to decrease the problem.

Answer: D

Explanation: D) Involve the student's home in any response to serious misbehavior. When misbehavior occurs, parents should be notified. If it persists, they should be involved in establishing a program such as a home–based reinforcement program.

Page Ref: 382

46) When schools use severe penalties as punishment

    A) they effectively prevent most classroom misbehavior.

    B) the students should not be allowed to reenter the classroom for several months.

    C) students have little difficulty getting back on track.

    D) they risk pushing students into the antisocial, delinquent subculture.

Answer: D

Explanation: D) Overly harsh penalties, or penalties that do not allow the student to reenter the classroom on an equal footing with others, risk pushing students into the antisocial, delinquent subculture.

Page Ref: 382

47) A gang of friends is caught on three occasions breaking into school, causing minor damage. The principal should consider all of the following discipline strategies **EXCEPT**

    A) suspending the friends from school.

    B) trying to establish a home-based reinforcement system.

    C) having the friends repair or pay for school property that has been damaged.

    D) implementing behavior modification strategies at school.

Answer: A

Explanation: A) The principal should probably not suspend the gang of friends from school. Suspension often increases truancy problems, while making it even more difficult for students to be successful academically when they return.

Page Ref: 383

True/False Questions

1) The most important aspect of classroom time is the one that is under the teacher's direct control.

Answer: TRUE
Page Ref: 353

2) Class interruptions may be externally imposed or they may be caused by teachers or students themselves.

Answer: TRUE
Page Ref: 354

3) Overlapping refers to the teacher's ability to attend to interruptions or behavior problems while continuing a lesson or other instructional activity.

Answer: TRUE
Page Ref: 359

4) In a student-centered classroom, students have little chance to participate in classroom management.

Answer: FALSE
Page Ref: 361

5) Research indicates that the first days of school are critical in establishing classroom order.

Answer: TRUE
Page Ref: 362

6) Many studies have found that the amount of time spent disciplining students is positively related to student achievement.

Answer: FALSE
Page Ref: 365

7) Nonverbal cues include eye contact, gestures, physical proximity, and touching.

Answer: TRUE
Page Ref: 366

8) One strategy for reducing misbehavior in class is to be sure to praise students for behaviors that are compatible with the misbehavior.

Answer: FALSE
Page Ref: 367

9) Delayed verbal reminders are usually effective.

Answer: FALSE
Page Ref: 367

10) Before presenting a student with a consequence for noncompliance, teachers must be absolutely certain they can and will follow through with enforcement.

Answer: TRUE
Page Ref: 368

11) In classrooms where most students are well-behaved but a few have persistent behavior problems, individual behavior management strategies can be effective.

Answer: TRUE
Page Ref: 375

12) Research has shown that daily report cards dramatically reduce misbehaviors and increase academic output.

Answer: TRUE
Page Ref: 392

13) Delinquent acts among adolescents and preadolescents are usually supported by peer norms that are prosocial.

Answer: FALSE
Page Ref: 380

14) "Zero tolerance" policies have often been found to be highly productive.

Answer: FALSE
Page Ref: 380

15) When punishment is applied it should be brief.

Answer: TRUE
Page Ref: 383

16) Research indicates that suspension (and expulsion) should be used to keep students in line.

Answer: FALSE
Page Ref: 383

Short Answer Questions

1) Time students spend actually on-task or actively learning.

Answer: Engaged time
Page Ref: 352

2) Time during which students have an opportunity to learn.

Answer: allocated time
Page Ref: 353

3) An important source of lost allocated time for instruction.

Answer: interruptions
Page Ref: 354

4) Seams of class management at which order is most likely to come apart

Answer: Transitions
Page Ref: 357

5) Refers to questioning strategies designed to keep all students on their toes during a lecture or discussion.

Answer: group alerting
Page Ref: 358

6) Teachers' actions that indicate awareness of students' behavior at all times.

Answer: withitness
Page Ref: 359

7) Teachers' ability to attend to interruptions or behavior problems while continuing a lesson or activity.

Answer: overlapping
Page Ref: 359

8) Strategies such as making eye contact with a misbehaving student, which work to prevent minor discipline problems.

Answer: nonverbal cues
Page Ref: 366

9) This management strategy, named by Canter and Canter, includes repetition of reminders, and ignoring of any irrelevant excuse or argument.

Answer: broken record or repeated reminders
Page Ref: 367

10) Method of giving a clear, firm, unhostile response to student misbehavior.

Answer: Assertive discipline
Page Ref: 367

11) Strategies in which the entire class is rewarded on the basis of everyone's behavior.

Answer: group contingencies
Page Ref: 370

12) A program that requires following a series of steps that proceed from the observation of the behavior, through program implementation, to program evaluation.

Answer: applied behavior analysis
Page Ref: 369

13) Removal of a student from a situation in which misbehavior was reinforced

Answer: Time out
Page Ref: 374

14) Strategies whereby parents are instructed to provide special privileges or rewards to students on the basis of teacher reports.

Answer: home-based reinforcement strategies
Page Ref: 374

Essay Questions

1) Having completed your first year of teaching, with its ups and downs, you are planning for great success in your second year. You want to prevent behavior problems by doing what effective teachers do, so you take a second look at Kounin's findings, and come up with four resolutions to follow in your classroom. These are four rules for yourself, not for students. You will monitor your teaching daily to make sure you implement these resolutions.
   Describe your set of four "rules for teachers" based on the strategies Kounin derived from observations of effective teachers. Explain why a teacher should follow each directive. What challenges do you think you would encounter in following your plan?

Answer: Based on Kounin's work, a set of directives for teachers might include Maintaining momentum, maintaining smoothness, managing transitions, group focus, withitness, and overlapping. Teaching engaging lessons is approach that would complement Kounin's concepts.
Page Ref: 356

2) How do management strategies differ between student-centered and traditional classrooms?

Answer: Most research on classroom management has taken place in traditionally organized classrooms, in which students have few choices over what they do and few interactions with each other. In more student-centered classrooms, students are likely to be spending much of their time working with each other, doing open ended projects, writing, and experimenting. Therefore, classroom management is more participatory in a student-centered classroom, with students centrally involved in setting standards of behavior.
Page Ref: 361

3) Make a list of rules (for students) you will include in your classroom and explain why you believe they are necessary. How does your set of rules reflect the principles for setting rules described in the textbook?
For two of your rules write a less effective version of the rule, and explain why you consider it less effective.

Answer: A list of classroom rules could include: 1) Be courteous to others. 2) Respect others' property. 3) Be on task. 4) Raise hands to be recognized. Principles used to evaluate sets of rules are: short, make sense, can be clearly explained to students.
Page Ref: 363

4) You are a teacher who is in the middle of a short lecture when you notice two students whispering at the back of the room. Using the principle of least intervention, what would you do?
The principle of least intervention has been described as the Ladder of Discipline. Teachers start at the lowest rung, and reserve the highest rungs for the most extreme behaviors. Describe a ladder of discipline with at least six rungs. Make each rung one very concrete, specific action. Explain how each rung works. Briefly compare the implementation of your ladder by an experienced teacher, to how it might go for a new, unpracticed teacher.

Answer: If at all possible, the lesson must go on while any behavior problems are dealt with. Give nonverbal cues, move closer to the students, or praise incompatible behavior.
Page Ref: 365

5) Explain what this statement means: When applying consequences, certainty is more important than severity.

Answer: It is most important that students understand that there will be consequences when rules are broken, not that the consequences will be severe, which may cause resentment in a student. Also, it may be difficult to follow through on severe or long lasting consequences. Mild but certain consequences communicate, "I cannot tolerate that sort of behavior, but I care about you and want you to rejoin the class when you are ready."
Page Ref: 368

6) Derek, in his first year of teaching, is having difficulties with his German 3 class. The students are very capable, but don't seem to buy into Derek's goals and standards of behavior. Derek is puzzled because what he remembers from Behavioral Theory is that responses that are reinforced grow more common, and responses that are not reinforced, extinguish. He has been ignoring some undesirable behaviors, but they've gotten even worse!

Using behavioral concepts that address how student misbehavior is maintained, develop some advice for Derek. In particular, explain why misbehavior in Derek's class is escalating, and make two specific suggestions that he could implement. Explain why you're suggestions should work. Finally, use your imagination to anticipate what might go wrong when Derek gives your suggestions a try; briefly describe 2 difficulties he might encounter.

Answer: The behaviors Derek is ignoring are not going away because they are being reinforced by peers' attention. He may have a student leading the disruptions, who is playing to the class "audience", and drawing them off Derek's learning tasks. Derek might remove the ring leader, try group contingencies, and work at making his lessons more engaging, developing withitness, and applying the principle of least intervention.

Page Ref: 369

7) You have a student who has difficulty getting to your class on time, which you find unacceptable. Using principles from applied behavior analysis, explain how you would set up a program for the student. Use concrete examples to illustrate each step of analysis.

Answer: First, identify the targeted behavior(s) and reinforcer(s). Establish a baseline for the target behavior. Choose a reinforcer and criteria for reinforcement. If necessary, choose a punisher and criteria for punishment. Observe behavior during program implementation and compare it to the baseline. When the behavior management program is working, reduce the frequency of reinforcement.

Page Ref: 372

8) Give an example of each of the following applied behavior analysis programs: home–based reinforcement, individual daily report card, and group contingency.

For each example, state an advantage or benefit of using the technique. Then, state one difficulty a teacher might encounter in implementing the technique (in other words, what could go wrong?).

Answer: A home–based reinforcement strategy might be teachers who give students a daily or weekly report card to take home, and parents are instructed to provide special privileges or rewards to students on the basis of these teacher reports. An individual daily report card example might be to identify the behaviors to be included in the report, explain the program to parents and how they are to participate; then, when behavior improves, reduce the frequency of the report. A group contingency program example would be to set up a reward system in which an entire group is rewarded on the basis of the behavior of the group members.

Page Ref: 374

9) "A quiet class is a learning class." This is a fallacy, according to your text author. Explain how this viewpoint relates to applied behavioral analysis. In other words, in what ways is the use of this behavioral technique subject to the "quiet class" fallacy?

Answer: There is a danger that teachers may use behavioral analysis techniques to overcontrol students. They may be so concerned about getting students to sit down, stay quiet, and look productive that they lose sight of the fact that school is for learning, not for social control. Behavior modification is being misused if teachers mistakenly believe that a quiet class is a learning class.

Page Ref: 378

10) Why do students misbehave?

Answer: Some students misbehave because they perceive that the rewards for misbehavior outweigh the rewards for good behavior. For example, students who do not experience success in school may perceive that the potential rewards for hard work and good behavior are small, so they turn to other sources of rewards.

Page Ref: 380

11) What strategies are useful for preventing serious behavior problems?

Answer: Enforce rules and practices, enforce school attendance, avoid tracking, practice intervention, request family involvement, use peer mediation, and judiciously apply consequences.

Page Ref: 379

12) Given what he had heard about last year's fourth graders, Mr. Christenson expected to have a tough time this year in fifth grade. But, little did he imagine how bad it would get. Thirty seconds into the science lesson, noticing Tim looking lost, he shouts, "Tim, where is your textbook? You know you're supposed to have it." Tim shrugs. Mr. Christenson looks down at his notes

"Okay, now let's pick up with Mercury." Just then laughter erupts in the back of the room. Glaring at the offenders, Mr. Christenson asks, "Maria, really, is Mercury humorous? Write 25 times 'Mercury is the closest planet to the sun.'" Mr. Christenson glances at his notes to remember his place, but is distracted by Billy leaning on his arms.

"Billy, what is our rule about the proper way of sitting? Explain to the class how posture affects our attentiveness." Billy mumbles something inaudible about not feeling well. Mr. Christenson walks over to Billy's desk so that he can hear the explanation better. Meanwhile, Alicia and Marti, at the front, start giggling. They will be visited by Mr. Christenson next. Discuss the origins of Mr. Christenson's management problems and their probable impact on learning.

Answer: The case can be analyzed using the following ideas: 1) Kounin's withitness and overlapping; 2) principle of least intervention; 3) behavior modification; 4) group contingency programs; or 5) prevention.

Page Ref: 352

13) A teacher attends an education association meeting and fills out the following questionnaire (responses are made with an X on the continuum). After analyzing the responses, what would you say about this teacher's management abilities?

I teach classroom rules during the first days of class.	___X_____	I attend to problems in class as they come up.
When students move around, they disrupt others.	_____X____	Students can move around to help each other.
Students rely on me to stop inappropriate behavior.	_____X__	Students monitor their own behavior.

Answer: The teacher sets rules during the first days of class, allows for students to interact with each other in appropriate ways, and works with students on monitoring their own behavior. She or he is likely to be an effective classroom manager.

Page Ref: 361

Chapter 12   Learners with Exceptionalities

Multiple–Choice Questions

1) Which of the following is the best example of people–first language?

   A) "I have one of those mentally retarded people in my class."

   B) " In my class I have one student with mental retardation."

   C) "In my class I have one mentally retarded student."

   D) "I have one of the retarded in my class."

   Answer: B

   Explanation: B) People–first language mentions the disability only after referring to the person.
   Page Ref: 392

2) Because labels for special needs have a tendency to be difficult to change once placed on students, education professionals must

   A) avoid using labels unless they are intended to stigmatize students.

   B) avoid using labels that segregate students from their peers socially.

   C) only use labels that intentionally discriminate against them.

   D) never use labels that are not dehumanizing.

   Answer: B

   Explanation: B) Labels tend to stick, making change difficult, and the labels themselves can
   become handicaps for the students. Education professionals must avoid using
   labels in a way that unintentionally stigmatizes or dehumanizes students,
   segregates them socially from their peers, or encourages discriminations against
   them in any form.
   Page Ref: 392

3) Physical disabilities such as deafness, blindness, and orthopedic handicaps are

   A) increasing at a rapid rate.   B) relatively rare.

   C) relatively difficult to diagnose.   D) decreasing at a rapid rate.

   Answer: B

   Explanation: B) Physical disabilities such as deafness, blindness, and orthopedic handicaps are
   relatively rare compared to other categories of students who need special
   education services. Learning problems, speech disorders, and emotional
   disorders are considerably more common.
   Page Ref: 393

4) A teacher has a class of 25 students. On the average the teacher might have one with a speech impairment and how many with learning disabilities?

   A) 1–2   B) 7–8   C) 15–18   D) 20–23

Answer: A

Explanation: A) In a class of 25, a classroom teacher might, on average, have one or two students with learning disabilities and one with a speech impairment. In contrast, only about one class in 40 is likely to have a student who has hearing or vision loss or a physical disability.

Page Ref: 393

5) The overall percentage of students receiving special education in 1999–2000 was about

   A) 5 percent.   B) 13 percent.   C) 20 percent.   D) 28 percent.

Answer: B

Explanation: B) The overall percentage of students receiving special education in 2000–2001 was about 13 percent; one out of every 8 students aged 3–21 was categorized as exceptional.

Page Ref: 393

6) Of all students with disabilities, approximately what percent of students ages 3–21 are considered to have specific learning disabilities?

   A) 5 percent   B) 12 percent   C) 26 percent   D) 45 percent

Answer: D

Explanation: D) The percentage of students ages 3–21 with specific learning disabilities, according to statistical information (2001) is 45.2% of all students with disabilities.

Page Ref: 394

7) Dave took an intelligence test and received an IQ score of 62. He was classified as mentally retarded. Of the following, which is the best-informed reaction to Dave's classification?

   A) Dave was correctly classified.

   B) The classification is incorrect because Dave's IQ is in the normal range.

   C) The classification cannot be considered valid unless adaptive skills are also assessed.

   D) The classification is invalid because measurement of IQ is irrelevant.

Answer: C

Explanation: C) Dave's IQ is consistent with the classification, but IQ alone does not determine that a student has mental retardation.

Page Ref: 395

8) Because IQ tests can be culturally biased, educational professionals should

    A) interview students' parents only.

    B) never use an IQ test.

    C) take into account students' age and grade.

    D) take into account scores on other tests, and cultural background.

Answer: D

Explanation: D) Consistent with AAMR recommendations, education professionals do not rely only on IQ scores to determine severity of cognitive impairment. They take into account a student's school and home performance, scores on other tests, and cultural background.

Page Ref: 395

9) A teacher is told a particular child has been diagnosed with mental retardation at the age of seven. It is most likely that the child has what type of disability?

    A) mild   B) moderate   C) severe   D) profound

Answer: A

Explanation: A) You can be reasonably certain that the child is mildly retarded. If there were more serious impairments, a diagnosis would have most likely been made much earlier in the child's life.

Page Ref: 395

10) Which of the following matchings between two classification systems of mental retardation is correct?

    A) educable: moderate   B) trainable: moderate

    C) custodial: mild   D) trainable: severe

Answer: B

Explanation: B) The correct matching is Trainable: Moderate. Students with "moderate" retardation (IQs 40–55) are classified as trainable—able to learn independent self–care and job skills for sheltered workshops.

Page Ref: 395

11) Sheila is in fourth grade but is still reading at the first grade level. She has normal intelligence and is able to understand concepts and contribute to class discussions. When Sheila is given a written quiz, however, she hands in a blank paper. Which of the following best describes Sheila's underlying difficulty?

    A) Sheila has autism.   B) Sheila has a behavioral disorder.

    C) Sheila has mental retardation.   D) Sheila has a learning disability.

Answer: D

Explanation: D) A learning disability in reading can adversely affect the academic performance of a student with normal intelligence.

Page Ref: 399

12) All of the following are characteristics of students with learning disabilities, **EXCEPT**

    A) below normal intelligence

    B) distractibility and hyperactivity

    C) lower academic self-esteem than students who are not disabled

    D) as a group, more likely to include boys than girls

Answer: A

Explanation: A) Students with learning disabilities often have normal, or above normal intelligence.

Page Ref: 400

13) At-risk kindergarten students who might have been categorized as learning disabled have been substantially impacted by

    A) traditional treatments.   B) exotic treatments.

    C) experimental diets.   D) research-based interventions.

Answer: D

Explanation: D) Studies (Francis, Shaywitz, Shaywitz, Stuebing, and Fletcher, 1996; Metsala, Stanovich, and Brown, 1998; Stanovich, Siegel and Gotland, 1997) have undermined the idea that there is a sharp-edged definition of learning disabilities as distinct from low achievement (see Hessler, 2001). The studies point to a very different emphasis for prevention and treatment. The long tradition of searching for exotic treatments are based on the assumption that there is something qualitatively different about the brains of children with learning disabilities, yet few show evidence of neurological dysfunction. Use of research-based interventions for at-risk kindergartners have had substantial impacts on children who might have been categorized as learning disabled.

Page Ref: 401

14) Mr. Welch understands that Tommy sometimes means to obey, but fails to control his behavior. Tommy loves to play with his peers, but tends to annoy them with impulsive actions. Mr. Welch avoids using long time-outs at recess to discipline Tommy, because he wants Tommy to have a chance to be active. Mr. Welch helps Tommy by making rules extra clear, adjusting seating arrangements as needed and sending home daily report cards. Which of the following disabilities best fits Tommy's characteristics?

    A) autism   B) ADHD

    C) hearing impairment   D) withdrawn behavior

Answer: B

Explanation: B) The characteristic that differentiates students with ADD from those with ADHD is that students with the latter classification cannot remain still for long. This differentiates them from students with learning disabilities who have attention deficits for other unknown reasons.

Page Ref: 403

15) A student is classified as having ADHD. Which of the following is true?

A) The student will qualify for special education services because he or she has ADHD.

B) The student is probably female.

C) The student will have difficulty attending to the teacher.

D) The student's IQ will probably be in the 80–95 range.

Answer: C

Explanation: C) The student will have difficulty attending to the teacher. ADHD refers to attention deficit hyperactivity disorder. This disorder in itself does not constitute eligibility for special education services. The student may have normal intelligence and is more often a boy, than a girl.

Page Ref: 403

16) Children with ADHD

A) are usually impulsive.

B) are always inattentive.

C) may find it difficult to sit still.

D) are always medicated.

Answer: C

Explanation: C) Children with ADHD may be impulsive without regard for the situation they are in, and often can be inattentive. They may find it difficult to sit still. Medications for ADHD are widely prescribed.

D)

Page Ref: 403

17) A child has difficulty pronouncing the "r" sound and also says "tham" instead of "Sam." The child probably has a(n) _____ disorder.

A) incurable   B) articulation   C) stuttering   D) voice

Answer: B

Explanation: B) The child appears to have an articulation disorder. Such problems are represented by difficulties in pronouncing words (e.g., substituting one sound for another).

Page Ref: 404

18) Which of the following statements concerning speech disorders is correct?

    A) Most mild speech disorders improve with time.

    B) Language and speech disorders are really the same.

    C) Teacher's should help students with speech disorders by calling on other students to help them finish sentences more quickly.

    D) Therapy should always be delayed until the secondary grades.

    Answer: A

    Explanation: A) Most mild speech disorders improve with time. The lasting damage is more often psychological, since students with these problems often undergo a great deal of teasing and social rejection.
    Page Ref: 404

19) To help a student with a mild speech disorder, a teacher should

    A) accentuate the way a word that is often mispronounced by the student should sound.

    B) avoid finishing the student's sentences when he or she is having difficulty pronouncing words.

    C) call on the student less frequently than others, to avoid embarrassment.

    D) ask the student to write instead of speak.

    Answer: B

    Explanation: B) To help a student with a mild speech disorder, a teacher should avoid finishing the student's sentences when he or she is having difficulty pronouncing the words. The teacher, in general, should not accentuate the student's problems or put her or him in high-pressure situations.
    Page Ref: 405

20) Adriana seems anxious and depressed and stays home with a stomachache when her class does group projects. Adriana may be diagnosed as having an emotional disorder if

    A) these symptoms have grown steadily worse over the past year.

    B) these symptoms are new and are accompanied by mispronunciations of certain words.

    C) she is found to have an IQ lower than 100.

    D) she also has poor motor coordination and difficulty solving problems.

    Answer: A

    Explanation: A) Longstanding symptoms is one of the criteria for emotional disorders.
    Page Ref: 405

21) A student is withdrawn and immature. In general, the most appropriate treatment approach to use is

    A) drug therapy.   B) suspension from school.

    C) teaching of social skills.   D) group contingencies.

Answer: C

Explanation: C) Some of the more effective treatments for withdrawn and immature students is the direct teaching of social skills that other students absorb without special instruction. Such programs have improved the social behavior of withdrawn, friendless students and increased their acceptance by classmates.

Page Ref: 406

22) Students with serious emotional and behavioral disorders are far more likely to be

    A) males than females.

    B) learning disabled than are students from other populations.

    C) under 12 than over.

    D) middle class than lower class.

Answer: A

Explanation: A) Students with serious emotional and behavioral disorders are far more likely to be males than females. It is most prevalent among elementary school students.

Page Ref: 405

23) Students exhibiting socialized–aggressive behaviors such as fighting, stealing, destroying property and refusal to obey teachers may benefit from

    A) rigorous academic programs.   B) behavior management strategies.

    C) home–based reinforcement.   D) aversive academic strategies.

Answer: B

Explanation: B) Students with conduct disorders and socialized–aggressive behaviors typically do no respond to punishment or threats. Aggressive children pose a threat to the school, their peers, and themselves, and usually are boys. Effective approaches for these children include behavior management strategies.

Page Ref: 406

24) A child who is autistic would be **LEAST** likely to

    A) know how to count.   B) spin the wheels on a toy truck.

    C) make friends in class.   D) appear self–absorbed.

Answer: C

Explanation: C) Children with autism are unlikely to have the communication skills to readily make friends in class.

Page Ref: 407

25) Which of the following statements regarding visual impairments is true?

   A) Individuals who are labeled legally blind have no sight.

   B) Partially sighted people must use Braille in order to read.

   C) A person whose field of vision is significantly narrower than a normal person's could be considered legally blind.

   D) When a vision loss is correctable it is still a disability.

Answer: C

Explanation: C) A person whose field of vision is significantly narrower than a normal person could be considered legally blind if the vision loss is not correctable.

Page Ref: 407

26) Which of the following strategies is **NOT** appropriate in trying to help an individual with hearing loss learn in your classroom?

   A) Use exaggerated lip movements when speaking.

   B) Try to speak at the student's eye level.

   C) Seat the student at the front of the room.

   D) Write important information on the chalk board.

Answer: A

Explanation: A) Using exaggerated lip movements is not appropriate in helping hearing–impaired students function in a regular classroom. It is desirable to seat such children toward the front, write important information on the chalkboard, and speak at the student's eye level.

Page Ref: 408

27) Parents of a child who is gifted are wondering what the child will be like as an adult. Based on Terman's classic study, they might expect their grown child to be _____ other adults.

   A) about the same as   B) better adjusted than

   C) less athletic than   D) less socially skilled than

Answer: B

Explanation: B) Based on Terman's classic study, you would expect students who are gifted to be better adjusted as adults than peers. In general, Terman found that his high IQ children were superior as adults in many areas.

Page Ref: 410

28) The researcher Renzulli suggests an emphasis on three types of activities for enrichment programs. One is exploratory activities, the second is individual and small group investigations of real problems, and the third type of activity is

    A) programmed instruction.   B) individualized seatwork assignments.

    C) teacher-focused activities.   D) group training activities.

Answer: D

Explanation: D) Renzulli suggests an emphasis on three types of activities for enrichment programs. One is exploratory activities while the second is individual and small group investigations of real problems. The third type is group training activities.

Page Ref: 410

29) Research on the effects of gifted programs on achievement has indicated that

    A) acceleration outcomes are too difficult to measure, making comparisons to enrichment invalid.

    B) neither acceleration nor enrichment is effective.

    C) acceleration programs are more effective than enrichment programs.

    D) enrichment programs are more effective than acceleration programs.

Answer: C

Explanation: C) Research on the effects of gifted programs on achievement has indicated that acceleration programs are more effective than enrichment programs. Part of the reason may be that the outcomes of enrichment programs are difficult to measure.

Page Ref: 410

30) One criticism of programs aimed at enriching the educational experience of students who are gifted is that

    A) these students already receive too much attention from their teachers.

    B) an enriched educational experience will inhibit their ability to get along with their peers.

    C) all students could benefit from an enriched educational experience.

    D) students who are gifted do not take advantage of such programs.

Answer: C

Explanation: C) A criticism of programs aimed at enriching the educational experience for students who are gifted is that every student could benefit from an enriched educational experience. In this regard, acceleration might be a more beneficial option.

Page Ref: 411

31) What is the term used to describe any program provided for children and adolescents with disabilities instead of, or in addition to, the regular classroom?

   A) IDEA   B) special education

   C) enrichment programs   D) P.L. 95–628

Answer: B

Explanation: B) Special education is any program provided for children and adolescents with disabilities instead of, or in addition to, the general education classroom.

Page Ref: 411

32) Which of the following is an effect of the extension of P.L. 94–142 beyond its original focus?

   A) Mainstreaming has been eliminated.

   B) Students with special needs are now labeled "children with handicaps."

   C) IEPs are now the sole responsibility of the regular education teachers of those needing special services.

   D) Preschool children needing special services can receive them more readily.

Answer: D

Explanation: D) As a consequence of a 1986 extension of P.L.94–142, preschool children needing special services can receive them more readily. This extension, called P.L.99–457, also added programs for infants and toddlers who are seriously disabled.

Page Ref: 411

33) The "least restrictive environment" provision of P.L. 94–142 provides a direct legal basis for

   A) each student who needs special education being entitled to it.

   B) parents having a right to file a grievance if they are dissatisfied with the services their children are receiving.

   C) inclusion of individuals with disabilities in regular classes.

   D) full inclusion.

Answer: C

Explanation: C) The least restrictive environment provision of P.L. 92–142 provides a direct legal basis for inclusion of individuals with disabilities in regular classes. This provision is often called mainstreaming.

Page Ref: 412

34) The concept that provides a legal basis for placing students with disabilities beside their nondisabled peers for as much of their instructional program as possible, is referred to as

A) grouping.

B) cooperative learning.

C) least restrictive environment.

D) integration.

Answer: C

Explanation: C) Least restrictive environment is the legal basis for the placing of students with disabilities with nondisabled peers for as much of their instructional program as possible.

Page Ref: 412

35) Which of the following is the least restrictive environment?

A) special day school

B) special–education class placement with part–time inclusion

C) self–contained special–education classroom

D) resource room placement

Answer: D

Explanation: D) The resource room placement is the least restrictive of the choices here, because it gives the student the largest amount of time with nondisabled peers.

Page Ref: 412

36) Which of the following educational services is most restrictive?

A) consultation

B) self–contained special education

C) resource room placement

D) itinerant services

Answer: B

Explanation: B) The most restrictive educational placement of the choices listed is self–contained special education. It provides few contacts with students in regular classes and, thus, would not be used unless considered necessary.

Page Ref: 412

37) An Individualized Education Program (IEP) is usually written by

A) a special services committee made up of teachers, psychologists and other concerned staff members.

B) the school principal.

C) the regular education teacher.

D) the district special education department.

Answer: A

Explanation: A) An IEP is usually prepared by a special services committee.

Page Ref: 412

38) An Individualized Family Service Plan (IFSP) is a specialized plan focusing on a child and family members, when the child with special needs is

    A) under the age of three.   B) between the ages of four and six.

    C) between the ages of seven and nine.   D) over the age of ten.

Answer: A

Explanation: A) Individualized Family Service Plan (IFSP) is a specialized plan for children with special needs who are under the age of three, which focuses on the child and his or her family.

Page Ref: 414

39) Individualized Transition Plans are written for which of the following groups of students with disabilities?

    A) infants

    B) preschool children between the ages of two and five

    C) children in elementary school

    D) adolescents before their 17th birthdays

Answer: D

Explanation: D) Individualized Transition Plans (ITP) are often written for adolescents with special needs before their 17th birthday. The ITP anticipates the student's needs as he or she makes the transition from school to work and to adult life.

Page Ref: 414

40) Students with learning disabilities are likely to spend most of the school day in a

    A) special class.   B) special school.

    C) general education class.   D) one-to-one tutoring situation.

Answer: C

Explanation: C) Students with learning disabilities are likely to spend most of the school day in a general education class. Learning disabilities usually do not necessitate removing the student from class for any extensive amount of time. The general education class would be the least restrictive placement.

Page Ref: 415

41) Research finds that well designed consulting models can be effective in assisting teachers to keep disabled students in general education classes. To which group of students does this finding best apply?

    A) students with severe disabilities

    B) students with cerebral palsy

    C) students with severe emotional problems

    D) students with mild disabilities

Answer: D

Explanation: D) Research finds that well-designed consulting models can be effective in assisting teachers to maintain students with mild disabilities.

Page Ref: 415

42) A student who is assigned to a general education class for most of the day works away from that classroom for an hour each day, on reading and mathematics, in a small group, with a special education teacher. This type of placement is called

    A) consultation.

    B) special-education class placement.

    C) special-education class placement with part time inclusion.

    D) resource room placement.

Answer: D

Explanation: D) Resource room placement involves working on particular subjects such as reading and mathematics for a period of each day, while spending most of the day in a regular classroom. Such programs usually involve a small number of students working with the special education teacher.

Page Ref: 415

43) An itinerant (or traveling) teacher would be most likely to provide help for a student with

    A) a speech disorder.   B) a hyperactivity problem.

    C) a learning disability.   D) cerebral palsy.

Answer: A

Explanation: A) A traveling (itinerant) teacher would be most likely to provide help for a student with a speech disorder. The other disabilities listed (hyperactivity, learning disability, cerebral palsy) would probably require more intensive or at least more regular interventions.

Page Ref: 415

44) Many students with disabilities are assigned to special classes taught by a special education teacher but are mainstreamed with nondisabled students part of the day. Most often these students join other students for music, art, and

    A) reading.   B) writing.

    C) science.   D) physical education.

Answer: D

Explanation: D) Many students with disabilities are assigned to special classes taught by a special education teacher, but are mainstreamed with nondisabled students part of the day. Most often these students join other students for music, art, and physical education. To a much lesser degree they join them for social sciences, science, and mathematics.

Page Ref: 416

45) Someone who supports full inclusion would advocate

    A) keeping students with disabilities in separate classes for an entire day.

    B) use of pull-out strategies as the primary intervention.

    C) hiring only teachers who are certified in special education.

    D) mainstreaming without pull-out.

Answer: D

Explanation: D) Someone who supports full inclusion would advocate mainstreaming without pull-out. The rationale is that pull-out strategies are disruptive and stigmatizing to the student with disabilities.

Page Ref: 423

46) Research shows that individuals with mild retardation who are placed in regular classrooms

    A) learn less than they would if placed in special classrooms.

    B) perform at the same level as the typical student.

    C) learn about the same as they would if placed in special classrooms.

    D) learn more than they would if placed in special classrooms.

Answer: D

Explanation: D) Research shows that individuals with mild retardation who are placed in general education classrooms learn more than if placed in regular classrooms. It seems likely that the regular classroom provides a more stimulating learning environment.

Page Ref: 425

47) According to research, what effect do techniques such as STAD have in inclusive classrooms?

   A) achievement of nondisabled students drops

   B) achievement of students with disabilities drops

   C) social acceptance of students with learning disabilities increases.

   D) students with disabilities are unable to function as team players.

Answer: C

Explanation: C) A problem in inclusive classes is the social isolation of students with academic disabilities. One strategy for reducing this problem is to involve the students in cooperative learning programs such as STAD which increases social acceptance.

Page Ref: 426

48) A special education teacher suggests that an extra step be added to instructions for a science task, to make the task clearer to a student with a learning disability. This modification is an example of

   A) a format adaptation.

   B) a content adaptation.

   C) full inclusion.

   D) an adaptation in modes of communication.

Answer: A

Explanation: A) In a format adaptation teachers change the format in which a task is presented without changing the actual task.

Page Ref: 427

49) According to the text author, what is "neverstreaming"?

   A) It is synonymous with mainstreaming.

   B) It is the result of adopting early intervention practices so that special education services are unnecessary.

   C) It is an arrangement whereby students who have disabilities or are at risk receive all their instruction in a general education class.

   D) It is the process in which professionals work cooperatively to provide educational services.

Answer: B

Explanation: B) Slavin proposed a policy of "neverstreaming," which avoids the mainstreaming/special education dilemma by focusing attention on intensive early intervention that is capable of bringing at-risk learners to performance levels high enough to remove any need for special education services.

Page Ref: 429

50) Which of the following statements are true regarding the use of computers for instructing exceptional students?
   1) Computers can help individualize instruction in terms of method of delivery and level of instruction.
   2) Computers can give immediate feedback and emphasize the active role of students in learning.
   3) Computers can hold the attention of learners who are easily distracted.
   4) Computer instruction is motivating and patient.

   A) 1, 2, and 3 (not 4).   B) 1, 3, and 4 (not 2).

   C) 2 and 4 (not 1 and 3).   D) All four statements.

Answer: D

Explanation: D) All of the statements are true. Computers can help individualize instruction in terms of method of delivery and level of instruction; computers can give immediate feedback and emphasize the active role of children in learning; and they can hold the attention of students who are easily distracted.

Page Ref: 429

51) In a buddy system, a student with special needs works with

   A) the regular classroom teacher.

   B) another student with special needs.

   C) an adult volunteer from the community.

   D) a student without special needs.

Answer: D

Explanation: D) In a buddy system, a student with special needs works with a student without special needs. The buddy can provide assistance (taking notes, reading directions) geared to the disability of her or his partner.

Page Ref: 430

52) Peer tutors must be taught how to provide assistance by explaining and

   A) criticizing.   B) modeling.   C) lecturing.   D) role playing.

Answer: B

Explanation: B) Teachers who use peers to tutor in their classroom should ensure that these tutors are carefully trained. This means the peer tutor must be taught how to provide assistance by modeling and explaining and how to give specific positive and corrective feedback.

Page Ref: 431

53) Communication between the classroom teacher and special education personnel should begin

    A) any time after the first day of class.

    B) after students are placed in the classroom.

    C) at the time that students are placed in the classroom.

    D) before students are placed in the classroom.

Answer: D

Explanation: D) Communication between the classroom teacher and special education personnel should begin before students are placed in the classroom.

Page Ref: 431

54) The classroom teacher is the expert on how the general classroom operates on a day-to-day basis. The special educator is the expert on the

    A) curriculum of the general education classroom.

    B) standards for grade-level performance .

    C) characteristics of a particular group of people.

    D) organization of the general education classroom.

Answer: C

Explanation: C) The special educator is the expert on the characteristics of a particular group of people while the classroom teacher is the expert on the classroom organization and operation on a day-to-day basis.

Page Ref: 431

55) You are told that two students with mild disabilities will attend your class. Which action would probably best further their social integration into your class?

    A) Ignore the differences between them and the rest of your class, and allow them to be accepted at their own speed.

    B) Use peer tutoring on occasion to help them with learning problems.

    C) Suspend classroom rules concerning social interaction in class, allowing the students with disabilities to communicate with their peers at any time.

    D) Use within-class ability grouping in most subjects.

Answer: B

Explanation: B) In teaching students with disabilities, you should consider using peer tutoring to help them with learning problems. This strategy will put them in direct contact with peers rather than isolate them as would occur with ability grouping.

Page Ref: 431

True/False Questions

1) The overall percentage of students receiving special education is less than ten percent.

Answer: FALSE
Page Ref: 393

2) Mental retardation refers to substantial limitations in present functioning.

Answer: TRUE
Page Ref: 394

3) Mental retardation is a subcategory of learning disabilities.

Answer: FALSE
Page Ref: 394

4) Hyperactivity is particularly common among students with learning disabilities and is much more frequently seen in boys than girls.

Answer: TRUE
Page Ref: 403

5) Children with Attention Deficit Hyperactivity Disorder (ADHD) qualify for special education as a learning disability.

Answer: FALSE
Page Ref: 403

6) Severity is a defining characteristic of a behavioral disorder, but duration is not.

Answer: FALSE
Page Ref: 405

7) It is incorrect to assume that individuals who are legally blind have no sight.

Answer: TRUE
Page Ref: 407

8) Aspergers Syndrome is a mild form of an emotional–behavioral disorder

Answer: FALSE
Page Ref: 407

9) Acceleration programs for the gifted often involve the teaching of advanced mathematics to students at early ages.

Answer: TRUE
Page Ref: 410

10) Public Law 99–457, which added programs to P.L. 94–142, extended services to children ages five to nine, who have serious disabilities.

Answer: FALSE
Page Ref: 411

11) An Individualized Education Program (IEP) describes a student's problems and delineates a specific course of action to address the problem.

Answer: TRUE
Page Ref: 412

12) Proponents of full inclusion argue that pull-out programs discourage effective partnerships between general and special education teachers in implementing IEPs.

Answer: TRUE
Page Ref: 423

13) A key element in effective inclusion is maintaining close coordination between classroom and special teachers.

Answer: TRUE
Page Ref: 426

14) Reliance on computers alienates students with disabilities from their peers and does more harm than good.

Answer: FALSE
Page Ref: 429

15) Social skills training has been found to have no effect on the social acceptance of individuals with disabilities.

Answer: FALSE
Page Ref: 431

Short Answer Questions

1) A functional limitation that interferes with a person's physical or cognitive abilities.

Answer: disability
Page Ref: 392

2) Any individual whose physical, mental, or behavioral performance is so different from the norm—either higher or lower—that additional services are needed to meet the individual's needs.

Answer: Learner with exceptionalities
Page Ref: 392

3) A condition imposed on a person with disabilities by society, the physical environment, or the person's attitude.

Answer: handicap
Page Ref: 392

4) An intelligence test score that should be near 100 for people of average intelligence.

Answer: intelligence quotient (IQ)
Page Ref: 395

5) A general term for a diverse group of disorders characterized by significant difficulties in the acquisition and use of listening, speaking, reading, writing, reasoning, or computing.

Answer: learning disability
Page Ref: 399

6) A condition characterized by extreme restlessness and by a short attention span relative to that of peers.

Answer: attention deficit hyperactivity disorder
Page Ref: 403

7) Impairments of the ability to understand language or to express ideas in one's native language.

Answer: language disorders
Page Ref: 405

8) A disorder that limits social interaction and communication, and is characterized by activities such as spinning objects for long periods of time.

Answer: autism
Page Ref: 407

9) A term now used to describe a broad range of severity of a specific disability including a mild form called Asperger's Syndrome.

Answer: Autism Spectrum Disorder
Page Ref: 407

10) Students who are identified as possessing demonstrated or potential abilities that give evidence of high performance capabilities in areas such as intellectual ability, creativity, or talent.

Answer: giftedness
Page Ref: 408

11) An important requirement of IDEA is that every student have one of these that describes a student's problems and delineates a specific course of action to address these problems.

Answer: Individualized Education Program
Page Ref: 412

12) Name for Public Law 94-142 as it was extended to include free, appropriate education, and transition plans for students with I.E.P.s

Answer: Individuals with Disabilities Education Act (IDEA)
Page Ref: 412

13) Placing **all** students in general education classes with appropriate assistance.

Answer: full inclusion
Page Ref: 423

14) The clause of P.L.94–142 that revolutionized the practice of special as well as regular education. It is the legal basis for the practice of inclusion.

Answer: least restrictive environment
Page Ref: 412

15) Process in which professionals work cooperatively o provide educational services.

Answer: collaboration
Page Ref: 415

Essay Questions

1) What physical, emotional, or cognitive conditions must exist before a student can receive special education services?

Answer: To receive special education services, a student must have one of a small number of categories of disabilities or disorders. These general labels such as learning disability, mental impairment, or orthopedic disability cover a wide range of problems.
Page Ref: 392

2) Define the terms disability and handicap, and explain the difference. Are they synonymous?

Answer: A disability is a functional limitation a person has that interferes with the person's physical or cognitive abilities. A handicap is a condition imposed on a person with disabilities by society, the physical environment, or the person's attitude.
Page Ref: 392

3) Incorporating the text author's viewpoint on labeling, write a response to the following statement "Labels are harmful and should be eliminated from schools."

Answer: Labels can be harmful, but they facilitate important communication about student's needs. Labels must be used carefully, with understanding of their limitations.
Page Ref: 392

4) Distinguish speech disorders from language disorders. Use specific examples to illustrate your explanation.

Answer: Language disorders are disabilities in communication. "Speech disorders" is a narrower category, including difficulties in forming and sequencing sounds. Failure to understand one's native language is a language disorder; inability to articulate common words is a speech disorder.
Page Ref: 404

5) Manisha makes no trouble in class, but she has an emotional disorder. Describe the disorder she might have; indicate how her teacher would know that she has the disorder; and explain how it would be decided that her symptoms reflect a disorder, not a normal emotional problem.

   Answer: Manisha could have the disorder of withdrawn behavior. A teacher might easily overlook her problem, but would need to notice that this student seemed withdrawn, depressed, anxious or friendless. Manisha's problem would be considered a disabling disorder if it interfered with her educational performance over a long period of time, and met the psychologist's criterion for severity.
   Page Ref: 406

6) Some students with hearing loss can be accommodated by an advantageous seating assignment. Describe three other classroom or teaching modifications that could benefit a student with hearing disability. Use specific examples in describing how you would implement your suggestions.

   Answer: Accommodations include speaking at the student's eye level, facing the class while giving instructions, and assisting with a child's hearing aid.
   Page Ref: 408

7) A teacher wants to start a gifted and talented program. According to the 1978 Gifted and Talented Act, who could be included in such a program? On what grounds might someone argue against the teacher's plan?
   How can the teacher respond to a taxpayer who says "Gifted students are emotionally unstable kids with high IQs that need more social contact."

   Answer: The teacher would include students who are identified as "possessing demonstrated or potential abilities that give high performance capabilities in areas such as intellectual, creative, specific academic or leadership ability, or in the performing or visual arts." An argument against gifted and talented programs is that most of the activities suggested for this population would benefit all students.
   Page Ref: 409

8) Why was Public Law 94–142 passed? Describe how historical events led to its adoption.

   Answer: Thirty years ago education of exceptional learners was quite different from what it is today. Students with disabilities generally received no special services and those who did usually attended separate schools or institutions. In the late 1960s this system came under attack. Critics argued that people who had serious disabilities were too often institutionalized with inadequate services or were left at home with no services at all. Those with less severe disabilities were isolated in special programs that failed to teach them the basic skills needed to function in society.
   Page Ref: 411

9) Every school district offers students with special needs an array of services. Make a list of these services beginning with the least restrictive, and ending with the most restrictive. Illustrate each service with a concrete example, specifying a child's grade level, disability, placement and specifics of where and with whom the child spends the day.

Answer: 1. Direct or indirect consultation, support for the regular education teacher. 2. Special education up to one hour per day. 3. Special education one to three hours per day, resource program. 4. Special education more than three hours per day, self-contained special education. 5. Special day school. 6. Special residential school. 7. Home or hospital.

Page Ref: 414

10) A student in your third grade class participates actively in class, and is a class leader in mathematics. As the year goes on, you have noticed this student checking fewer books out of the school library and his grades slowly falling in subjects heavily dependent on reading such as social studies.

Tell what approach you would take to help this student, and if, as his educator, you have any particular responsibility.

Answer: Since education professionals have the responsibility of distinguishing students with learning disabilities from peers without learning disabilities, this classroom teacher must begin the process. If the student has displayed a significant discrepancy between his ability and performance, the teacher may request testing to determine if a disability exists. In the classroom, the teacher may adjust activities to paired- or group-activities to accommodate this student (and others) who may be struggling. Other adaptations may include shortening reading assignments, or asking parents to read aloud to their child. The teacher may also do read-alouds to the class. For written assignments, spacing may be adjusted to allow students to focus on the most important aspects. Direction may be simplified.

Page Ref: 418

11) According to the text, there are four advantages to using computers for students with disabilities. What are the advantages? Describe two ways that you think problems or disadvantages might arise when students with disabilities are using computers (a disadvantage could be a specific problem that might occur when use of computers is implemented).

Answer: The use of computers to help exceptional students learn has four major advantages. First, computers can help to individualize instruction in terms of method of delivery, type and frequency of reinforcement, rate of presentation, and level of instruction. Second, computers can give immediate feedback and emphasize the active role of the student in learning. Third, computers can hold the attention of children who are easily distracted. Fourth, computer instruction is motivating and patient.

Possible disadvantages might be: difficulty in finding the right program for an individual student's strengths and weaknesses; a student might prefer computer time to time developing social skills; some students may need accommodations because of difficulty using keyboards; some students may suffer adverse effects (e.g., absence seizures) from looking at computer screens.

Page Ref: 429

12) Give three examples of how a buddy system involving a student with disabilities and a student without disabilities might work.

Answer: A student who volunteers to be a special education student's buddy can help that student cope with the routine tasks of classroom life. For example, a buddy can guide a student with vision loss, help a student who is academically disabled when directions are not understood, or deliver cues or prompts as needed. Buddies can also take notes for a student with a hearing loss or learning disabilities.
Page Ref: 430

13) You are a teacher who will have a student with learning disabilities in your class. How are teaching responsibilities divided between you and the special-education teacher? In other words, what responsibilities do you have to the student and others in your class? What responsibilities does the special education teacher have to the student?

Answer: As the classroom teacher, you are responsible for the organization and operation on a day-to-day basis, the curriculum of the classroom, and the expectations placed on students for performance. The special education teacher is the expert on the characteristics of a particular group of students with disabilities, the learning and behavioral strengths and deficits of the mainstreamed students, and instructional techniques for a particular type of disability.
Page Ref: 431

14) How will you help to foster the social integration of students with disabilities into your classroom?

Answer: Be caring and accepting. Explain to students that everyone is capable of learning and some learn in different ways. Use IEPs to guide instruction. Use cooperative learning strategies and peer tutors. Set aside time for students to communicate with each other.
Page Ref: 431

15) Lee Thurston, a fifth grade teacher at Washington Elementary School, has had seven very successful years of teaching. His students love him and parents of students who are in the fourth grade classes request that their children be placed with him during their fifth grade experience. And last year Lee was voted "Teacher of the Year" by the faculty in the district.

In the spring of the year, Lee is told that, because he is such a good teacher, he will be getting David Spears as a student in next year's class. David, during his fourth grade year, had been identified as having a behavior disorder after confronting another student with a knife.

Lee had some concerns about David, but decided he was willing to try to help. He would come up with some ideas for working with David as he attended graduate school over the summer.

A week before school started, Lee met with Ellen Lansing, Washington School's principal. "It's been a busy summer," remarked Ellen. "I'm afraid some of your students' parents have requested to have another teacher since you will have David Spears in your class. They are worried that you won't be able to control him or that at some point you won't be available to help if things get out of hand."

With inclusion, situations are going to come up like this more and more," replied Lee. "What do you think we should do?"

Discuss the advantages and disadvantages to full inclusion, mainstreaming, and other options related to student placement. What would you do to solve Lee's problem?

Answer: Advocates of David Spears would argue that he has the right to a public education and that the school can provide services to help with his emotion and behavioral problems. Parents who do not want their children to be in class with David would argue that everyone has the right to a safe classroom environment.
Page Ref: 423

16) Order the following special education services from least restrictive (1) to most restrictive (5).

_____ home or hospital
_____ resource program
_____ self–contained special education
_____ inclusion into regular education
_____ special day school

Answer: _5_ home or hospital
_2_ resource program
_3_ self–contained special education
_1_ inclusion into regular education
_4_ special day school
Page Ref: 412

Chapter 13   Assessing Student Learning

Multiple-Choice Questions

1) Which of the following terms refers to a statement of the skills or concepts that students are expected to have mastered by the end of some period of instruction?

    A) assessment   B) instructional objective

    C) course prerequisite   D) taxonomy

Answer: B

Explanation: B) An instructional objective, sometimes called a behavioral objective, is a statement of skills or concepts that students are expected to know at the end of some period of instruction. Typically, an instructional objective is stated in such a way as to make clear how the objective will be measured.

Page Ref: 440

2) Which of the following verbs would Mager find **LEAST** acceptable for use in an instructional objective?

    A) sing   B) list   C) know   D) define

Answer: C

Explanation: C) Mager would find the verb "to know" least acceptable. It represents what he might call a slippery description of what the student is expected to learn.

Page Ref: 441

3) Which of the following words would be most acceptable, to Mager, for expressing an instructional objective?

    A) sort   B) enjoy   C) discuss   D) appreciate

Answer: A

Explanation: A) The most acceptable verb for an instructional objective would be to sort. This verb makes the nature of the performance expected much clearer than do verbs such as enjoy, discuss, or appreciate. The latter are open to varied interpretations.

Page Ref: 442

4) A teacher uses task analysis in designing a lesson. A benefit that the teacher is likely to realize from this process is

  A) gaining increased awareness of the subskills students need for mastering more complex skills.

  B) allowing students to make important decisions about what they should and should not attend to.

  C) discovering creative ways to make a subject relate to students' lives.

  D) encouraging students to work and learn independently.

Answer: A

Explanation: A) A benefit of performing a task analysis is gaining increased awareness of the subskills needed to master a more complex skill. Consequently, teachers can plan instruction so that the subskills are taught first and then assembled into the final skill.

Page Ref: 443

5) What is the first step in the process of planning a task analysis?

  A) Assemble the subskills into a hierarchy.

  B) Identify what skills students should have before the new lesson is taught.

  C) Discover what portions of the lessons are likely to interest students.

  D) Find adequate means to measure the attainment of the desired skills.

Answer: B

Explanation: B) The first step in the task analysis should be to identify what skills the students should already have before the new lesson is taught. The next two steps are identifying the component skills and planning how they will be assembled into the final skill.

Page Ref: 443

6) Which of the following steps would come first, in backward planning?

  A) Establish individual unit objectives.   B) Construct the final exam.

  C) Establish course objectives.   D) Plan specific lessons.

Answer: C

Explanation: C) The first step in using backward planning is to establish broad course objectives. Then unit objectives are established, followed by the development of specific lessons.

Page Ref: 444

7) A teacher uses a backward-planning strategy in designing a course. The teacher should plan individual lessons

    A) after constructing the final exam.

    B) as the first step.

    C) after establishing course and unit objectives.

    D) after establishing course objectives but before establishing unit objectives.

Answer: C

Explanation: C) The teacher should plan individual lessons after establishing course objectives and then establishing unit objectives. The rationale is that unless the objectives are defined, teachers would not know what content to teach.

Page Ref: 444

8) Increasingly, states are establishing standards for subjects and assessments. These standards should

    A) guide parents in selecting schools for their children.

    B) guide school boards in hiring new staff members.

    C) guide teachers' planning of objectives and lessons.

    D) guide teachers and parents during conferences.

Answer: C

Explanation: C) Increasingly, states are establishing standards for each subject, and these standards should guide teachers' planning, especially if there are also state assessments based on the standards.

Page Ref: 444

9) Which of the following is a recommended use of testing in conjunction with backward planning?

    A) Construct a preliminary version of the unit test before the unit has been taught.

    B) Base your course objectives on ready-made unit tests that are provided by textbook publishers.

    C) If you construct a test as part of backward planning, use exactly the same items when you give the test at the end of your actual course unit.

    D) Be sure that each objective used in developing the unit test is covered by the same number of items.

Answer: A

Explanation: A) In using backward planning, it is recommended that a preliminary version of the test be constructed before the unit has been taught. The rationale is that writing the test in advance helps the teacher to focus on the important topics to be covered. The test can later be revised if necessary.

Page Ref: 445

10) The final step in backward planning is to

    A) estimate the amount of class time to spend on each unit objective.

    B) plan daily lessons.

    C) establish long-term course objectives.

    D) write objectives for large units of instruction.

Answer: B

Explanation: B) The final step in backward planning is to plan the daily lesson, which consists of an objective, a plan for presenting information, a plan for giving students practice, a plan for assessing student understanding, and, if necessary, a plan for reteaching students if understanding is inadequate.

Page Ref: 446

11) A measure of the degree to which instructional objectives have been attained is called

    A) assessment.   B) comprehension.

    C) backward planning.   D) task analysis.

Answer: A

Explanation: A) A measure of the degree to which instructional objectives have been attained is called assessment.

Page Ref: 446

12) Because objectives are stated in terms of how they will be measured, it is clear that objectives are closely linked to

    A) analysis.   B) knowledge.

    C) assessment.   D) comprehension.

Answer: C

Explanation: C) Because instructional objectives are stated in terms of how they will be measured, it is clear that objectives are closely linked to assessment. An assessment is any measure of the degree to which students have learned the objectives set out for them. Most assessments in schools are tests or quizzes, or informal verbal assessments such as questions in class.

Page Ref: 446

13) Which of the following statements is a critical principle of assessment?

A) Affective objectives must be assessed.

B) Everything that is taught must be assessed.

C) Standardized tests should be used to measure general classroom learning.

D) Assessment and objectives must be clearly linked.

Answer: D

Explanation: D) One critical principle of assessment is that assessments and objectives must be clearly linked. Students learn some proportion of what they are taught; the greater the overlap between what was taught and what is tested, the better students will score on a test and the more accurately any need for additional instruction can be determined.

Page Ref: 446

14) Which of the following is the lowest level of objectives in Bloom's taxonomy of educational objectives?

A) comprehension   B) knowledge

C) synthesis   D) application

Answer: B

Explanation: B) The lowest level of objectives in Bloom's hierarchy, knowledge, refers to objectives such as memorizing math facts or formulas, scientific principles, or verb conjugations.

Page Ref: 448

15) Ms. Dickson observes that after reading a research report, her students can use principles of good experimental design to point out flaws in the researchers' procedures and conclusions. What is the highest-level objective from Bloom's taxonomy, that Ms. Dickey's students have met?

A) application   B) evaluation

C) knowledge   D) comprehension

Answer: B

Explanation: B) Evaluation objectives require making value judgments based on a criterion or standard; for example, being able to compare strengths and weaknesses of two products based on performance, reliability, and cost.

Page Ref: 448

16) Mr. Madison's unit test assesses students' understanding at Bloom's knowledge and comprehension levels. Based on this assessment, he should assume that his students will be able to do all of the following **EXCEPT**

A) recall specific information.

B) summarize the material learned.

C) apply concepts they have learned.

D) paraphrase definitions they have learned.

Answer: C

Explanation: C) Application objectives require students to use knowledge.
Page Ref: 448

17) The purpose of a behavior content matrix is to

A) identify affective outcome levels.

B) facilitate the collection of reinforcement data.

C) show the levels of learning that each part of a lesson addresses.

D) organize a lesson presentation.

Answer: C

Explanation: C) The purpose of a behavior content matrix is to show the different cognitive (levels of learning) that different parts of a lesson support. As a result, teachers are in a better position to consider objectives about the knowledge and comprehension levels.
Page Ref: 449

18) The key idea that Bloom's taxonomy offers to teachers is that

A) assessment is an exact process.

B) in planning a lesson on a given topic, there are many levels of skills to consider.

C) higher-order skills should be reserved for college-level classes.

D) lower-level skills should replaced by higher-order skills.

Answer: B

Explanation: B) Bloom's taxonomy helps teachers to appreciate that there are many levels of skills in a particular task. Thus, lessons that emphasize only lower-level objectives might be reexamined.
Page Ref: 449

19) Student evaluations serve many purposes, including all of the following **EXCEPT**

    A) providing information for accountability.

    B) providing feedback to parents.

    C) making information available for selection and certification.

    D) providing incentives for intrinsically motivated behaviors.

Answer: D

Explanation: D) Student evaluations serve six primary purposes: 1) feedback to students; 2) feedback to teachers; 3) information to parents; 4) information for selection and certification; 5) information for accountability; and 6) incentives to increase student effort.

Page Ref: 451

20) Which of the following is true regarding evaluation as feedback?

    A) It should be as specific as possible.

    B) It should not be critical of a student's work.

    C) It should consist of a letter grade.

    D) It should encourage the student to make external attributions.

Answer: A

Explanation: A) To be useful as feedback, evaluations should be as specific as possible. For example, students who receive written feedback in addition to letter grades are more likely than other students to believe that their efforts, rather than luck or other external factors, determined their success.

Page Ref: 451

21) Collecting information for selection of students (for programs, schools, tracks) is a purpose of evaluation that is most closely tied to which other purpose of evaluation?

    A) incentive to increase student effort   B) accountability of teachers and schools

    C) certification for occupations   D) feedback to teachers

Answer: C

Explanation: C) Closely related to selection is certification, a use of tests to qualify students for promotion or for access to various occupations.

Page Ref: 452

22) The purpose of evaluation that provides data for judging teachers, schools, districts, or states, is called

    A) incentives to increase student effort.   B) information for accountability.

    C) information for certification.   D) feedback.

Answer: B

Explanation: B) Often evaluations of students are used to evaluate teachers, schools, districts, or even states. Most states have testing programs that allow them to rank schools in terms of student performance.

Page Ref: 452

23) Which of the following are true in the context of the reporting function of evaluation?
1) Grades and other evaluations set up informal home–based reinforcement systems.
2) Routine measures such as test scores and stars can keep parents informed about their children's school work.
3) Evaluations such as report cards inform parents about their children's school work.
4) When pressured intensely by school administrators, parents will reinforce their children for bringing home good grades.

    A) 1, 2 and 3 (not 4)   B) 1, 2 and 4 (not 3)

    C) 1, 3 and 4 (not 2)   D) 2, 3 and 4 (not 1)

Answer: A

Explanation: A) Routine school evaluations of many kinds—such as test scores, stars, and certificates, as well as report cards—keep parents informed about their children's school work. Grades and other evaluations set up informal home–based reinforcement systems. Parents do not need to be pressured to reinforce good grades, since most parents naturally reinforce their children without much prompting.

D) Parents do not need to be pressured to reinforce good grades. Without much prompting, most parents naturally reinforce their children for bringing home good grades, thereby making grades more important and more effective as incentives.

Page Ref: 452

24) According to the text author, which of the following evaluation strategies would be **LEAST** effective in increasing student effort?

    A) giving recognition for improvement, not just for meeting absolute performance standards

    B) being generous in giving students time to complete tests

    C) varying grading standards according to student differences

    D) giving frequent quizzes rather than infrequent long tests

Answer: C

Explanation: C) According to the text author, an inappropriate strategy for using evaluations to increase student effort is to vary grading standards according to student differences. Evaluations will be effective to the degree that students perceive them to be equal for all.

Page Ref: 453

25) Mrs. Rubeo will be giving a unit test in three weeks. At present she is giving students daily problem sets to find out which material needs reteaching before the unit test. Mrs. Rubeo's use of the problem sets is an example of

    A) task analysis   B) summative evaluation

    C) formative evaluation   D) evaluation as incentive

Answer: C

Explanation: C) The teacher is using formative evaluation. Its purpose is to discover strengths and weaknesses in instruction so that improvements can be made. In contrast, summative evaluations look at finished products.

Page Ref: 453

26) A summative evaluation asks which of the following questions?

    A) What are you doing?   B) Why are you performing as you are?

    C) How well are you doing?   D) How did you do?

Answer: D

Explanation: D) A summative evaluation asks the question: How did you do? Summative evaluation refers to final tests of student knowledge. Summative evaluation may or may not be frequent, but it must be reliable and, in general, allow for comparisons among students.

Page Ref: 453

27) Which of the following descriptors best characterizes the results of a norm-referenced test?

    A) helps teacher revise lessons covered on the test

    B) shows the achievement differences between students

    C) gives teacher feedback on how well students can perform a set of skills

    D) yields a list of remediation strategies to help low achievers

Answer: B

Explanation: B) Norm-referenced tests will provide information on the amount of differences between students in degree of learning. Criterion-referenced tests focus on students' degree of mastery of specific skills.

Page Ref: 453

28) Which of the following practices illustrates norm-referenced evaluations?

    A) Students are given the average of their five tests as a final grade.

    B) Students' lowest test grade is omitted and the other grades are averaged to obtain a final grade.

    C) The five highest-scoring students receive As, the next five receive Bs, and so on.

    D) Different letter grades are awarded on the basis of students reaching specific cutoff scores.

Answer: C

Explanation: C) An example of norm-referenced evaluation might be the first five students receive an A, the next five a B, and so on. The critical feature is that students are being evaluated in comparison to one another rather than relative to performance standards.

Page Ref: 453

29) Criterion-referenced evaluations focus on

    A) selected-response test items.

    B) comparisons of a student's scores to those of other students.

    C) assessing student mastery of specific skills.

    D) affective and psychomotor objectives.

Answer: C

Explanation: C) Criterion-referenced evaluations focus on assessing students' mastery of specific skills, regardless of how other students did on the same skills. Criterion-referenced evaluations should be closely connected with the curriculum being taught and with the lesson or course objectives.

Page Ref: 453

30) After considering the goals and strategies of evaluation, the text author concludes that teachers must choose different types of evaluation for different purposes. At a minimum, how many types of evaluations should be used to assess student learning?

   A) one   B) two   C) three   D) four

Answer: B

Explanation: B) At a minimum, two types of evaluation should be used, one directed at providing incentives and feedback and the other at ranking individual students relative to the larger group.

Page Ref: 454

31) A teacher wants to use evaluations to increase student effort. Which of the following strategies would be desirable?

   A) Reduce the difficulty of the test so that 90 percent of the students reach mastery quickly.

   B) Employ different grading standards for different students, based on ability levels.

   C) Keep students guessing about what they have to do to get a good grade.

   D) Evaluations should be given frequently, with clear criteria.

Answer: D

Explanation: D) Evaluations or quizzes should be given more often. Also, criteria should be clear, standards should be consistent, and evaluations should be challenging.

Page Ref: 455

32) A teacher is discouraged by students' lack of interest in class. If the teacher decides to use grades as motivators, which of the following strategies would be most useful?

   A) reduce the number of tests given

   B) use clear criteria so that students can understand how grades are earned

   C) give students a few weeks to get a test off their minds, before giving them test feedback

   D) use comparative standards for grading

Answer: B

Explanation: B) The teacher should consider grading on the basis of effort and improvement. This strategy is likely to increase effort and interest by making it possible for all students, regardless of ability, to succeed.

Page Ref: 455

33) Which of the following statements concerning comparative grading is correct?

   A) Comparative evaluations are currently considered unnecessary.

   B) Comparative evaluations must be conducted frequently.

   C) The grading of comparative evaluations on course content should make some provision for effort.

   D) Comparative evaluations must emphasize fair, reliable assessment of student performance.

Answer: D

Explanation: D) In using comparative grading, the reliability and fairness of the tests are highly important. Otherwise, the information obtained about what a student can do might well be inaccurate, leading to inappropriate decisions.
Page Ref: 455

34) In designing an achievement test for students, a teacher's major concern should be that the test

   A) matches the instructional objectives for the material covered.

   B) include items for each of the six levels of Bloom's taxonomy.

   C) measures what students are capable of doing rather than what they have done.

   D) includes both objective questions and essay questions.

Answer: A

Explanation: A) In designing an achievement test for students, a teacher's major concern should be to match the test to the instructional objectives for the material covered.
Page Ref: 456

35) A teacher administers an attitude survey to the same students four times. Each time the results differ. In which characteristic of achievement tests is the survey deficient?

   A) reliability   B) validity

   C) specificity   D) representativeness

Answer: A

Explanation: A) The teacher's test appears to lack reliability. Reliability refers to the consistency of test scores over time and administrations.
Page Ref: 457

36) A teacher wanting to increase the reliability of a test should try which of the following strategies?

    A) Increase the proportion of items that are marginally related to the objectives being taught.

    B) Use more items that none of the students can answer correctly.

    C) Increase the number of test items.

    D) Add more easy test items.

Answer: C

Explanation: C) To increase the reliability of a test, the teacher should increase the number of test items. Other strategies are to use clear, unambiguous items that are of moderate difficulty.

Page Ref: 457

37) Which of the following is one of Gronlund's principles regarding the preparation of achievement tests?

    A) Achievement tests should define clearly measured values.

    B) Achievement tests should be broad enough to fit many uses.

    C) Achievement tests should be as reliable as possible and interpreted with caution.

    D) Achievement tests should include corresponding desired outcomes of learning.

Answer: C

Explanation: C) Gronlund's research indicates that achievement tests should be as reliable as possible and interpreted with caution.

Page Ref: 457

38) Teachers should use the results of tests to do all of the following things **EXCEPT**

    A) guide instruction.

    B) set an appropriate pace of instruction.

    C) locate strong and weak points in student understanding.

    D) retaliate against disruptive students.

Answer: D

Explanation: D) Teachers should use the results of tests to guide instruction, to set an appropriate pace of instruction, and to locate strong and weak points in students' understanding.

Page Ref: 457

39) A teacher's goal is for students to solve real-life problems. What does the text author say about the use of multiple-choice items to measure this goal?

    A) Multiple-choice questions are appropriate as long as they are well written.

    B) Multiple-choice questions are inappropriate because they are not similar enough to real-life problems.

    C) Multiple-choice questions are inappropriate because they do not provide specific feedback.

    D) Multiple-choice items are appropriate because they involve selected response, not constructed response.

Answer: B

Explanation: B) Multiple-choice items may be inappropriate for this kind of exam because in real life we are rarely presented with four options as possible solutions to a problem.

Page Ref: 457

40) Which of the following statements is true about using a table of specifications?

    A) It is unnecessary to construct a table of specifications if the teacher knows the subject matter well.

    B) A table of specifications helps teachers keep track of student progress.

    C) A table of specifications is useful for increasing reliability when scoring essay questions.

    D) Teachers use a table of specifications to distribute test items across different instructional objectives.

Answer: D

Explanation: D) Tables of specification help instructors distribute test items across different instructional objectives. This is done by classifying objectives according to different categories of complexity (Bloom's taxonomy) so that the instructor can allocate test items accordingly.

Page Ref: 460

41) Which of the following evaluation strategies are appropriate for use in assessing student achievement?
    1) checklists
    2) interviews
    3) role-playing activities
    4) simulations

    A) 1, 2 and 4 (not 3).   B) 2, 3 and 4 (not 1).

    C) 3 and 4 (not 1 and 2).   D) 1, 2, 3 and 4

    Answer: D

    Explanation: D) Evaluation restricted to information acquired from paper-and-pencil tests provides only certain kinds of information about student progress in school. Other sources and strategies for appraisal of student work must be used, including checklists, interviews, classroom simulations, role-playing activities, and anecdotal records.

    Page Ref: 461

42) The opening statement of a multiple-choice item, which may be a question or partial sentence, is referred to as the

    A) stem.   B) participle.   C) antecedent.   D) consequence.

    Answer: A

    Explanation: A) A question or partial statement in a multiple-choice test item that is completed by one of several choices is called the stem.

    Page Ref: 461

43) A main goal in writing multiple-choice test questions is to

    A) make the distractors tricky enough to fool about half of the students in a class.

    B) include at least one distractor that a knowledgeable student is likely to regard as correct.

    C) make the distractors appear as reasonable as the correct answer to students who do not know the material.

    D) make the average difficulty index .60 (60 percent).

    Answer: C

    Explanation: C) A main goal in writing multiple-choice test questions is to make the distractors appear as plausible as the correct answer to the uniformed student. Thus, one of the tasks of writing a good multiple-choice item is to devise appropriate distractors.

    Page Ref: 461

44) A recommended procedure for writing multiple-choice items is to

    A) make the stem as short as possible.

    B) list alternatives horizontally rather than vertically.

    C) use letters rather than numbers to identify choices.

    D) include at least one implausible choice for each item.

Answer: C

Explanation: C) A recommended procedure is to use letters rather than numbers to identify a choice. Numbers can cause confusion on tests where the answers or distractors contain actual numbers such as in mathematics or science.

Page Ref: 463

45) Which of the following is a disadvantage of true-false items?

    A) They are suitable only for formative evaluation.

    B) They cover only a narrow range of subjects.

    C) They are susceptible to guessing error.

    D) They are difficult to construct.

Answer: C

Explanation: C) The main disadvantage of true-false tests is that they are susceptible to error caused by random guessing. The 50 percent probability of guessing reduces the reliability of the scores.

Page Ref: 464

46) Which of the following statements about matching items is correct?

    A) Matching items can be used to cover a large number of concepts.

    B) It is inappropriate to allow the alternatives in List B to be used for more than one item in list A.

    C) Possibilities for guessing are virtually eliminated.

    D) Directions on how to respond can be eliminated or made very short.

Answer: A

Explanation: A) Matching items can be used to cover a large amount of content; that is, a large number of concepts should appear in the two lists.

Page Ref: 464

47) A teacher wants to determine how well students can discuss ways in which related concepts differ. Based on the text author's discussion of item types, which of the following is most appropriate for this objective?

    A) multiple choice   B) matching

    C) short essay   D) true-false

Answer: C

Explanation: C) The short essay would be the best choice for the teacher. It would test students' ability to define and differentiate the concepts in their own words, as opposed to selecting multiple-choice answers or recalling isolated terminology.

Page Ref: 466

48) For which type of item would the use of model answers be **LEAST** appropriate?

    A) short essay   B) long essay

    C) problem solving   D) multiple choice

Answer: D

Explanation: D) Model answers would be least appropriate on multiple-choice items. The reason is that grading of multiple-choice items is objective whereas it is subjective on essays and problem-solving items.

Page Ref: 467

49) Some teachers count grammar, spelling, and other technical features when evaluating essays. Is this practice appropriate?

    A) Yes, evaluation of essays should be based on rules of grammar.

    B) No, evaluation should be based on content knowledge only.

    C) Yes, if two separate grades (one for content and one for writing mechanics) are given.

    D) If this practice is used, the teacher should also grade the essays on effort.

Answer: C

Explanation: C) The text author suggests that when teachers evaluate the grammar and spelling on an essay answer, two separate grades—one for content and one for writing—should be given. Students will then know the basis on which their work will be evaluated.

Page Ref: 467

50) Why would a teacher who was planning to evaluate student problem solving, be interested in the following steps: understanding the problem to be solved, attacking the problem systematically, and arriving at a reasonable answer?

   A) Each of the steps should be assessed with a different type of test.

   B) The steps will be useful assessment tools because they are components of problem-solving tasks that apply to varied subject-matter.

   C) The steps show that problem-solving should be assessed at levels 1 and 2 of Bloom's taxonomy.

   D) The steps illuminate the affective objectives of problem-solving tasks.

Answer: B

Explanation: B) In problem solving there are several important components that fit most disciplines. These include understanding the problem to be solved, addressing the problem systematically, and arriving at a reasonable answer. Evaluating problem solving will involve observation of these steps.

Page Ref: 470

51) Mr. Romanowski gives an essay a C. Then he realizes that the essay is not Michael's – it is Michelle's. A grade of C is not what Mr. Romanowski expects of Michelle, so he takes another look and finds some ideas in the essay that he didn't notice before. Now he sees it as a B essay and assigns Michelle a B. Michelle is benefitting from

   A) a halo effect.   B) formative evaluation.

   C) clang.   D) backward planning.

Answer: A

Explanation: A) The teacher's general view of the student creates a grading bias in her favor.
Page Ref: 471

52) What is the term used for evaluations that simulate the use of abilities in real-life situations?

   A) authentic assessment   B) standardized tests

   C) goal setting   D) formative evaluation

Answer: A

Explanation: A) Authentic assessment focuses on what students can actually do.
Page Ref: 472

53) Which of the following best describes what portfolios should contain?

   A) a thoughtfully selected collection of core and optional items

   B) a set of required items selected by the student without teacher input

   C) a set of required items selected by the teacher with minimal student input

   D) a randomly selected set of items chosen by either the student or the teacher

Answer: A

Explanation: A) A portfolio should contain a thoughtfully selected set of core items and optional items. The core items would be ones required of every student; optional items would be additional work samples reflecting the individual student's strengths and weaknesses.

Page Ref: 473

54) Why is the use of portfolio assessment for school accountability controversial?

   A) because a student's product can be greatly influenced by teachers and classmates

   B) because portfolios lack breadth of subject matter

   C) because parents have a hard time understanding the material included in a portfolio

   D) because portfolios can not demonstrate that students can actually do something.

Answer: A

Explanation: A) Innovators have proposed that portfolio assessment be used as part of assessments for school accountability. This use is more controversial as a student's product can be subjective.

Page Ref: 475

55) Which of the following is true about using portfolios for evaluation?

   A) Authentic testing advocates criticize their use.

   B) Student journals should not be included as selected items.

   C) Students should have input in determining what will be included.

   D) Each item selected should address only one objective.

Answer: C

Explanation: C) Students should have input in determining the contents of portfolios. This is an advantage in developing their sense of responsibility. Portfolios would be likely to include journal entries and items that address multiple objectives.

Page Ref: 476

56) For which of the following purposes can portfolios be used?
   1) observe a student's place on a sequence of developing skills
   2) provide insight into student knowledge and skills
   3) document and celebrate student learning
   4) target classroom instruction

   A) 1, 2 and 4 (not 3).   B) 2 and 4 (not 1 and 3).

   C) 1 and 3 (not 2 and 4).   D) 1, 2, 3 and 4.

Answer: D

Explanation: D) Portfolios may be used for information to place students on a sequence of developing skills for insight into students' knowledge and skills, to document and celebrate student learning and to target classroom instruction.
Page Ref: 476

57) Which of the following is **NOT** an example of performance assessment?

   A) a driver's test   B) a doctoral thesis

   C) a performance test in medicine   D) a spelling exam

Answer: D

Explanation: D) A driver's test, doctoral thesis, and medical licensure exam are all examples of authentic assessment, according to the text author.
Page Ref: 477

58) According to researchers, one of the most important criticisms of traditional standardized testing is that it

   A) can focus teachers on a narrow range of skills that happen to be on a test.

   B) uses items that lack reliability.

   C) give students too much input into which content is assessed.

   D) relies on the judgments of many different scorers, who may produce a wide range of ratings for work of the same quality.

Answer: A

Explanation: A) According to researchers one of the most important criticisms of traditional standardized testing is that it can focus teachers on teaching the narrow range of skills that happen to be on the test.
Page Ref: 477

59) One of the observations made by researchers (Shavelson, et al., 1992) regarding how well science performance assessments work, is that student scores from the performance assessments were

   A) more closely related to student aptitude, than to what students were actually taught.

   B) consistently related to what had been taught previously, than to aptitude.

   C) not reliable.

   D) too low to make a valid interpretation.

Answer: A

Explanation: A) One of the observations made by researchers regarding how well performance assessments work is that students' scores were still more closely related to student aptitude than to what students were actually taught. They found that student performance on such assessments could be reliably rated, but different performance assessments produced different patterns of scores.

Page Ref: 478

60) Which of the following is a problem that might arise in using relative grading standards?

   A) Students avoid one teacher's course because she never gives an A—her unrealistically high expectations for student-learning are reflected on all of her assessment tasks.

   B) A student whose performance is excellent cannot get an A because he is outscored by too many (for instance, 20%) of his classmates.

   C) Although the students didn't learn very much, they almost all got As because the teacher's newly-developed tests were so easy.

   D) Most of the students in a class received very low quarter-grades because their tests did not reflect the teacher's use of class time.

Answer: B

Explanation: B) With relative grading standards students may be unable to get an A because grades are given according to the student's rank within the class.

Page Ref: 483

61) Which grading practice involves the use of work samples and rubrics, to convey to parents an understanding of what students have learned?

   A) mastery grading   B) relative grading standards

   C) performance grading   D) contract grading

Answer: C

Explanation: C) In performance grading, teachers determine what children know and can do and then report this in a way that is easy for parents and students to understand.

Page Ref: 483

62) Combining scores for grading (such as grades given for homework assignments) causes the important issue of

    A) how to treat extra credit work.

    B) how to treat missing work.

    C) how to treat work obviously done by a parent.

    D) how to treat overachievers.

Answer: B

Explanation: B) An important issue arises when scores are combined for grading; that is, how to treat missing work such as homework assignments. Some teachers assign a "zero" to missing work, but that can be devastating to a student's grade and can only be viewed as a punitive practice. [Example. A student who misses one assignment out of five, but scores 92, 86, 73, and 91 on the others would receive the average scores of 68.4—a "D" in a 60–70–80–90 grading scheme.

Page Ref: 487

63) Martin gets "As" (95–100) on all of the writing assignments that he does, but he has skipped half of the writing assignments. In discussing his grades with a friend, he says "I must have a C in writing, because I have As on half the assignments, and Fs on the other half." But Martin is worse off than he thinks. He actually has an F in writing. His grade is F because

    A) each student's highest and lowest score were omitted from grading.

    B) the teacher's scoring is unreliable.

    C) the teacher assigned a zero for every missing assignment.

    D) the teacher is using absolute grading standards.

Answer: C

Explanation: C) The average of a number of As (95–100) and an equal number of zeroes will be less than or equal to 50, which is usually considered to be an F.

Page Ref: 487

True/False Questions

1) Instructional objectives must be adapted to the subject matter being taught.

Answer: TRUE
Page Ref: 442

2) The process of breaking tasks or objectives down into their simpler components is called skill analysis.

Answer: FALSE
Page Ref: 443

3) Instructional objectives are stated in terms unrelated to and independent of assessment.

Answer: FALSE
Page Ref: 446

4) Bloom and his colleagues categorized objectives in a sequence that proceeds from complex to simple.

Answer: FALSE
Page Ref: 447

5) A behavior content matrix is a chart that classifies lesson objectives according to cognitive levels.

Answer: TRUE
Page Ref: 449

6) Grades will be less effective as incentives for students whose parents pay little attention to their grades.

Answer: TRUE
Page Ref: 452

7) Frequent quizzes given and scored immediately after specific lessons serve as summative evaluations.

Answer: FALSE
Page Ref: 453

8) Formative evaluations are most often criterion-referenced.

Answer: TRUE
Page Ref: 453

9) An achievement test should include items that most appropriately measure the learning outcomes.

Answer: FALSE
Page Ref: 456

10) Considered by some educators to be the most useful and flexible of all assessment item types, multiple-choice questions can be used in tests for most school subjects.

Answer: TRUE
Page Ref: 461

11) The essay item can elicit a wide variety of responses, from giving definitions of terms to comparing and contrasting important concepts.

Answer: TRUE
Page Ref: 466

12) A problem-solving item type involves organizing, selecting, and applying complex procedures that have several important steps or components.

Answer: TRUE
Page Ref: 469

13) Portfolio assessment has important uses when teachers want to evaluate students for reports to parents.

Answer: TRUE
Page Ref: 474

14) Authentic tests involving actual demonstrations of knowledge or skills in real life are called performance assessments.

Answer: TRUE
Page Ref: 477

15) Educators have given up on performance assessments because the difficulty of achieving reliable scoring is overwhelming.

Answer: FALSE
Page Ref: 484

16) Adding explanatory comments to a grade can be very motivating to students needing help in improving their performance.

Answer: TRUE
Page Ref: 451

Short Answer Questions

1) A statement of skills or concepts that students should master after a given period of instruction.

Answer: Instructional objectives
Page Ref: 440

2) The process of breaking tasks or objectives down into their components.

Answer: task analysis
Page Ref: 443

3) Planning instruction by setting long-range goals first, then unit objectives, and finally planning daily lessons.

Answer: backward planning
Page Ref: 444

4) Descriptions of specific behaviors that students are expected to exhibit at the end of a series of lessons.

Answer: learning objectives
Page Ref: 447

5) Bloom's ordering of learning tasks from simple to more complex.

Answer: taxonomy of educational objectives
Page Ref: 447

6) Type of objectives that are related to attitudes and values.

Answer: affective
Page Ref: 451

7) Also known as assessment, these tests and tasks formally measure student performance.

Answer: evaluation
Page Ref: 451

8) This type of evaluation asks: How are you doing?

Answer: formative
Page Ref: 453

9) This type of evaluation asks: How did you do?

Answer: summative
Page Ref: 453

10) Measures that focus on comparisons of a student's scores to those of other students.

Answer: norm-referenced
Page Ref: 453

11) Measures that focus on assessing student mastery of specific skills.

Answer: criterion-referenced
Page Ref: 453

12) A list of instructional objectives and expected levels of understanding that guides test development.

Answer: table of specifications
Page Ref: 459

13) Incorrect responses that are offered as alternative answers to a multiple-choice question.

Answer: distractors
Page Ref: 461

14) Characteristics of writing style or other features of a multiple-choice distractor that make it stand out.

Answer: clang
Page Ref: 463

15) Assessment of a collection of student work in an area, showing growth, self-reflection and achievement.

Answer: portfolio assessment
Page Ref: 473

Essay Questions

1) An instructional objective has three basic parts. What are they? Create two instructional objectives for lessons you could teach, incorporating the three basic parts. For each objective, identify the three parts and explain how they will help in designing assessments.

   Answer: An instructional objective has three parts: a condition, performance, and criterion. Conditions refer to resources needed (e.g., calculator, map, dictionary). Performances are what the students are to do, specified by the verb in the sentence (e.g., calculate, locate, define). Criteria refer to the degree to which the student is to perform (e.g., 15 of 20, 75 percent, all). The conditions, tasks and criteria specified in each example narrow down the choices to be made in designing measures for evaluation.
   Page Ref: 441

2) Identify the highest level of Bloom's taxonomy represented by each of the following objectives.
   a. Students will critique a piece of artwork.
   b. Using a map of the United States, students will label all state capitals.
   c. Given a calculator, students will compute the area of rectangles.

   For objective "a" , above, name any additional levels of Bloom's taxonomy that the task incorporates. In other words, although the task is classified at a certain level, a student who performs the task may, in the process, meet some lower-level objectives. An informal task analysis will lead you to aspects of the task that address lower-level objectives. Using objective "a", illustrate how one lower-level objective is met by this task (which is focused on a higher level).

   Answer: a. evaluation; b. knowledge; c. application.
   The critique calls for evaluation, but also for knowledge, comprehension, and probably application and analysis. The student must comprehend principles of, for instance, shading or color, in order to critique the work of art. Thus, the higher level task meets lower-level objectives, as well as the higher-level objective—evaluation.
   Page Ref: 448

3) Student evaluations serve six purposes. What are they? Using an example, illustrate how two or more of these six functions can be at cross purposes. In other words, illustrate how two of these purposes could call for conflicting evaluation strategies.

   Answer: 1) feedback to students; 2) feedback to teachers; 3) information to parents; 4) information for selection and certification; 5) information for accountability; 6) incentives to increase student effort.
   One example might be: Accountability could conflict with Incentives to students. Assessing for accountability may call for norm-referenced strategies, for the purposes of comparing schools or teachers. But for low-achieving students, norm-referenced measures may be detrimental to motivation.
   Page Ref: 451

4) How do summative evaluations and formative evaluations differ?

Answer: A formative evaluation, given to discover strengths and weaknesses in learning and to make mid-course corrections of instructions, asks the question: How are you doing? A summative evaluation, given after instruction is complete to assess knowledge, asks: How did you do?

Page Ref: 453

5) Drawing on Gronlund's six principles, describe three points that need to be considered when preparing achievement tests. For each of your three points, illustrate a problem that would result if Gronlund's principle were not observed.

Answer: Achievement tests should: 1) measure clearly defined outcomes; 2) measure a representative sample of the learning; 3) include appropriate test item types; 4) fit the particular uses that will be made of the results; 5) yield reliable results; and 6) improve learning.

One example of failure to observe these principles might be that a math test does not measure all learning objectives. The objectives may include problem-solving, but the test items are limited to computations. The consequences are that students may not learn problem-solving, and the teacher has no feedback on whether the problem-solving objective is met.

Page Ref: 456

6) What is a table of specifications? How is it used in evaluating student achievement?

Answer: A table of specifications is a list of instructional objectives and expected levels of understanding that guide test development.

Page Ref: 459

7) Select a familiar topic. On scrap paper, list several learning objectives you you would use in teaching this topic. Be sure your objectives represent a variety of levels from Bloom's taxonomy.

Design three multiple choice items to assess some of your objectives. For each question, state the objective, and identify the level at which Bloom would classify it. Design your multiple choice questions so that each reflects a different level of Bloom's taxonomy.

Use the guidelines on pp. 484-486 to evaluate your multiple choice questions. Note three flaws in your questions, or pitfalls that you avoided in writing them.

Answer: Objectives might include knowledge, comprehension, application, analysis or evaluation. Students may find it very difficult to write questions at the analysis or evaluation levels.

Applicable guidelines include specific stem, brief stem, grammatical fit, no-exception words, qualification in alternatives, options that include other options, absurd options, and clang.

Page Ref: 461

8) Mr. Zhou has given his unit test in Social Studies, and his students obtained the following scores (in percentages):

38 38 59 62 67 67 71 72 74 74 77 78 78 80 82 82 87 86 87 89

Mr. Zhou's absolute grading standards apply a 90% cutoff for an A, an 80% cutoff for a B, etc. Mr. Zhou is questioning his grading system after examining these grades. Describe the problem he faces. Describe Mr. Zhou's alternative for interpreting these test scores. In other words, what other basic approach to grading standards could he apply to the test results? How would the letter grades be affected? Describe one drawback to this change in grading standards.

Answer: Mr. Zhou's students performed poorly on his test. No student received an A, possibly because the test was inappropriately difficult.

Mr. Zhou could apply relative grading standards, assigning As to students scoring in the high 80s, Bs in the 77–82 range, and so on. If Mr. Zhou's test was actually not difficult, though, the relative grading standards may inflate the grades; and if everyone scores high on the next test, there may be students who receive low grades, for high scores, under the relative grading standards.

Page Ref: 481

9) Ms. Frisch is feeling despondent and frustrated as she looks at the chemistry mid–term exam results. The average score was only 68 percent, less than the C cutoff. Only four students scored in the 80 percent range, and just two in the 90 percent range —only four Bs and two As out of 28 students. "Maybe I made the exam too hard," she thinks. "I'm sure the students will be deflated when they see their grades.

If Ms. Frisch came to you to discuss her problem, what would you tell her?

Answer: Discussion might center around grading systems, including advantages and disadvantages of criterion–referenced and norm–referenced measures.

Page Ref: 481

10) For each of the behavioral objectives listed below, circle the behavior, underline the condition, if applicable, and place parenthesis around the criterion, if applicable.

Using the appropriate tools and materials, create a piece of art.

Select, read, and interpret a piece of poetry.

Calculate the diameter of circles.

Without error, perform each step of cardiopulmonary resuscitation.

Identify the planets of the solar system.

Answer: Using the appropriate tools and materials, create a piece of art.
    behavior: create
    condition: tools and materials

Select, read, and interpret a piece of poetry.
    behavior: select, read, interpret

Calculate the diameters of circles.
    behavior: calculate

Without error, perform each step of cardiopulmonary resuscitation.
    behavior: perform
    criterion: without error

Identify the planets of the solar system.
    behavior: identify
Page Ref: 441

11) Describe the advantages and disadvantages of relative grading standards.

Answer: Absolute grading standards are grades given according to a student's rank in his or her class or grade. Relative grading standards have the advantage of placing students' scores in relation to one another. A disadvantage is that the number of As and Bs are held constant, so students in a class of high achievers must get higher scores to earn and A or B than students in low achieving classes.
Page Ref: 483

Chapter 14   Standardized Tests

Multiple–Choice Questions

1) The SAT and the ACT are categorized as which of the following types of tests?

   A) knowledge   B) standardized

   C) diagnostic   D) criterion–referenced

   Answer: B

   Explanation: B) The SAT and ACT are both standardized tests. Both are used for selection and placement, specifically for college admissions.

   Page Ref: 495

2) Typically, standardized tests are carefully constructed to provide accurate information reflecting

   A) the highest achieving students' abilities clearly to set goals for all other students.

   B) clear demarcation between ability levels to define tracking levels.

   C) each student's level of performance.

   D) each student's intelligence quotient.

   Answer: C

   Explanation: C) Standardized tests are typically carefully constructed by curriculum professionals to provide accurate information about students' levels of performance.

   Page Ref: 495

3) Standardized test items are evaluated, and then may be eliminated for all of the following reasons **EXCEPT**

   A) almost all students respond correctly.

   B) almost all students respond incorrectly.

   C) high scoring students respond correctly and low scoring students respond incorrectly.

   D) low scoring students respond correctly and high scoring students respond incorrectly.

   Answer: C

   Explanation: C) A good item selection is one that is answered correctly by students who do well on most other items. If all students answer it correctly or incorrectly, it would not be good because it would not discriminate between or among individuals.

   Page Ref: 496

4) For which of the following purposes are standardized tests **LEAST** useful?

    A) diagnosing learning problems or strengths

    B) evaluating teachers' and schools' effectiveness

    C) improving school processes such as student placement and curriculum development

    D) evaluating student performance in a particular course

Answer: D

Explanation: D) Standardized tests would be least useful for grading in a particular course. Grades in a course should be based on curriculum-specific tests. Typical uses of standardized tests are diagnosing weaknesses, evaluating a program, and selection and placement.

Page Ref: 496

5) Which of the following statements about standardized tests are accurate?
    1)   They contribute to improving the schooling process
    2)   They provide information regarding appropriate student placement
    3)   They play a role in guidance and counseling
    4)   They are used to evaluate instructional programs and strategies

    A) 1 and 4 (not 2 and 3).   B) 2 and 4 (not 1 and 3).

    C) 1 and 2 (not 3 an 4).   D) All four statements.

Answer: D

Explanation: D) Standardized test scores can contribute to improving the schooling process, provide information regarding appropriate student placement and diagnostic information important to remediation, play a role in counseling, and have some administrative roles such as program evaluation.

Page Ref: 497

6) A current problem with standardized achievement testing used for accountability is that

    A) the tests have low reliability.

    B) minimum competency tests focus too much on higher-level objectives.

    C) teachers may teach to the test by varying the curriculum.

    D) the public does not take the tests seriously.

Answer: C

Explanation: C) A concern is that schools will narrow what is taught to match what is tested, such as reading and math, or easy-to-measure skills.

Page Ref: 498

7) A problem for standardized testing that is especially prevalent in lower socio-economic status urban area schools is

    A) high infant mortality.   B) low student mobility.

    C) high student mobility.   D) low child measurability.

Answer: C

Explanation: C) High student mobility, especially prevalent in low-SES urban areas, might mean that schools are held accountable for students they have only had for a few weeks or months.

Page Ref: 498

8) An advantage of holding schools accountable for students' success in learning is that

    A) states are decreasingly reporting "disaggregated" scores.

    B) students of all ethnic groups are making progress.

    C) schools can refuse to use outside innovative techniques.

    D) teachers are pressured to pay attention to school board demands.

Answer: B

Explanation: B) One advantage of accountability is that it does increase the pressure on schools and teachers to pay attention to students who may otherwise fall through the cracks. States are increasingly reporting "disaggregated" scores, meaning they are separately held accountable fo gains of students of each ethnicity, limited English proficiency, and so on. This is a means of ensuring that all groups are making progress.

Page Ref: 499

9) The No Child Left Behind (NCLB) legislation passed by Congress requires all "subgroups" of students in all schools to make

    A) significant quarterly progress.   B) adequate weekly progress.

    C) significant yearly progress.   D) adequate yearly progress.

Answer: D

Explanation: D) All subgroups in all schools are now expected to make "adequate yearly progress" (AYP) on all state assessments. This is defined differently in each state.

Page Ref: 499

10) Some of the criticisms of No Child Left Behind (NCLB) include

   A) the state-to-state standards vary greatly and NCLB is underfunded.

   B) the testing is too infrequent and broad to be effective.

   C) the states have too much authority and too little accountability.

   D) the entire nation receives the same test despite student differences.

Answer: A

Explanation: A) NCLB has been criticized by educators and others. The main criticisms are that NCLB requires excessive and narrow testing, that state-to-state standards vary greatly, and that, despite the heavy requirements of NCLB, it is underfunded.

Page Ref: 501

11) Which of the following descriptions is most characteristic of norm-referenced tests?

   A) They have a high difficulty level.

   B) Scores are compared to a representative group of prior test takers.

   C) Students are not expected to finish the entire test.

   D) The content assessed is curriculum-specific.

Answer: B

Explanation: B) In a norm-referenced test, scores are compared to those for a representative group of students who have also taken the test. Since the norms are established for nationwide use, the test usually cannot be very specific.

Page Ref: 503

12) Which of the following is true regarding norm-referenced achievement tests?

   A) They cannot be highly curriculum-specific because educational programs vary between states.

   B) They evaluate students on all the content areas they have covered.

   C) They provide little information on which to rank students according to their knowledge of a given subject.

   D) They are typically given only in high school, not elementary.

Answer: A

Explanation: A) Norm-referenced tests cannot be highly curriculum-specific because they are designed for nationwide use even though the curricula for any given subject may vary from district to district.

Page Ref: 503

13) A criterion-referenced achievement test is designed to measure the degree to which a student

 A) compares to his or her peers.   B) performs simple tasks.

 C) has mastered well-specified skills.   D) has improved.

Answer: C

Explanation: C) A criterion-referenced achievement test assesses a student's knowledge of subject matter, but is designed to measure the degree to which the student has mastered well-specified skills.

Page Ref: 503

14) The primary purpose of the Scholastic Aptitude Test (SAT) is

 A) predicting aptitude, for purposes of selection and placement.

 B) personality assessment.

 C) diagnosis.

 D) evaluating the effectiveness of a program.

Answer: A

Explanation: A) The primary purpose of the Scholastic Aptitude Test (SAT) is selection and placement. Specifically, it is used to assess students' aptitudes for college studies.

Page Ref: 506

15) When would it be most appropriate for a school psychologist to employ an aptitude test rather than an achievement test?

 A) to yield information on how well a student has learned a skill

 B) to identify or assess students for possible placement in special programs

 C) to suggest ways to remediate specific deficits in knowledge

 D) to identify styles of cognition and learning

Answer: B

Explanation: B) The school psychologist would want to use an aptitude test to predict how a student would perform in a special program. An achievement test would be a better choice for assessing mastery of a particular set of skills.

Page Ref: 505

16) An achievement test is primarily designed to assess

    A) general learning potential.

    B) vocational and academic interests.

    C) skills or abilities that have traditionally been taught in schools.

    D) specific academic deficits, for diagnosis of disabilities.

Answer: C

Explanation: C) Whereas aptitude tests focus on general learning potential and knowledge acquired both in and out of school, achievement tests focus on skills or abilities that are traditionally taught in schools.

Page Ref: 506

17) What is the term for a test that is designed to measure general learning potential?

    A) criterion-referenced achievement test   B) aptitude test

    C) norm-referenced achievement test   D) summative test

Answer: B

Explanation: B) A test that is designed to test a student's general abilities is an aptitude test. In contrast to an achievement test, the aptitude test is designed to predict how students will perform on particular types of tasks rather than measure how much they have already learned.

Page Ref: 503

18) A training department wants to know whether prospective plant employees can operate different types of heavy machinery that are now available. What would be the best type of test to give?

    A) norm-referenced aptitude   B) norm-referenced achievement

    C) criterion-referenced aptitude   D) criterion-referenced achievement

Answer: D

Explanation: D) The department would want to use a criterion-referenced achievement test. The reason is that they are interested in employees' performance on a particular skill. They are not interested as much in predicting future performance or comparing employees to norms.

Page Ref: 507

19) Eighty-three percent of the students in a class can name five countries in South America. Such a statement is probably based on the results of

   A) a norm-referenced achievement test.

   B) an aptitude test.

   C) a criterion-referenced achievement test.

   D) a diagnostic test.

Answer: C

Explanation: C) The statement is probably based on the results of a criterion-referenced achievement test. Such tests are used to provide specific information about what a student or group can do.

Page Ref: 507

20) The establishment of cutoff scores for criterion-referenced tests

   A) relies on the professional judgment of teachers and other school personnel.

   B) employs an 80 percent criterion for difficult objectives and a 90 percent criterion for easy ones.

   C) is set by the school psychologist.

   D) is at a point above which 50 percent of the norming sample fall.

Answer: A

Explanation: A) The determination of cutoff scores for criterion-referenced tests is usually based on the judgment of teachers and other qualified individuals. The decision involves estimating the probabilities that students who have accomplished the content area would answer individual items correctly.

Page Ref: 507

21) Which of the following questions can be best answered by a criterion-referenced test?

   A) Which students would be the best candidates for the advanced placement program?

   B) How do children at a particular elementary school compare with the national norm in reading?

   C) What is the cause of a student's difficulties in mathematics?

   D) How many students can translate a paragraph of text from Spanish to English?

Answer: D

Explanation: D) A criterion-referenced test might indicate, for example, how many students can translate Spanish to English. Such tests typically do not diagnose aptitude problems or compare students to norms; rather, they indicate students' performance with regard to specific objectives.

Page Ref: 507

22) The scoring reports for a criterion-referenced achievement test would show

    A) students' rankings compared to all students who took the test.

    B) the number of test items a student answered correctly for each objective.

    C) students' confidence ratings of their performance on each test item.

    D) a student's normal curve equivalent score on each test item.

Answer: B

Explanation: B) The scoring reports for a criterion-referenced achievement test would probably show the number of items a student answered correctly for each objective. The teacher can use this information to gauge whether the student has met the objectives.

Page Ref: 507

23) If a student scores at the median on a test, her or his percentile rank is

    A) 0.   B) 25.   C) 50.   D) 100.

Answer: C

Explanation: C) If a student scores at the median on a test, the percentile rank would be 50. The median is the halfway point in a distribution—50 percent score above it and 50 percent score below it.

Page Ref: 507

24) If you ranked a group of 40 students from bottom to top on test scores, the 15th student from the bottom would score at what percentile?

    A) 10   B) 22   C) 38   D) 63

Answer: C

Explanation: C) A percentile score, or percentile rank, indicates the percentage of students in the norming group who scored lower than a particular score. Applying the equation to the question demands that you divide the place of the 15th student from the bottom by the total number of students and then multiply by 100 to give you the 37.5 percentile (38 percent).

Page Ref: 508

25) A fourth grade student earns a grade-equivalent score of 6.1 in reading comprehension. One can conclude that the student

    A) is performing about two years above grade level.

    B) has a percentile rank of 61.

    C) should be moved to the sixth grade.

    D) is in need of special services.

Answer: A

Explanation: A) A fourth grader who earns a grade-equivalent score of 6.1 in reading comprehension is performing about two years above grade level. The student's score was comparable to that of the norming group about two years older.

Page Ref: 508

26) Which of the following is true regarding a grade-equivalent score?

    A) It tells a teacher the grade at which a particular student belongs.

    B) It tells a teacher how many students scored above and below the mean score.

    C) It compares a particular student's score to the average scores of the norming groups.

    D) It compares a particular student's score to the stanine scores of other students.

Answer: C

Explanation: C) A grade-equivalent score compares the student's score to the average scores of the norming groups at a particular grade level. It does not mean that the student is necessarily ready to do work at the indicated grade.

Page Ref: 508

27) A grade-equivalent score should be interpreted as a(n)

    A) accurate measure of the student's knowledge of the curriculum of more advanced grade levels.

    B) rough approximation.

    C) accurate reflection of a student's raw score.

    D) predictor of how quickly a student will progress through the year's curriculum .

Answer: B

Explanation: B) Grade-equivalent scores should be interpreted as a rough approximation. For one thing, students do not gain steadily in achievement from month to month. For another, scores far from the expected grade level do not mean what they appear to mean.

Page Ref: 508

28) The average amount that scores in a distribution differ from the mean is indicated by the

    A) stanine score.   B) standard deviation.

    C) standard error of measurement.   D) median.

Answer: B

Explanation: B) The standard deviation indicates the average amount that scores in a distribution differ from the mean. It is a measure of the amount of variability or dispersion in a distribution.

Page Ref: 509

29) One class has a mean achievement raw score of 60 with a standard deviation of 15. A second class has a mean of 58 with a standard deviation of two. Which of the following inferences can be made?

    A) The scores in the second class are more varied than the first.

    B) Whole-group instruction will work with the first class.

    C) Each student in the first class has a score at least 13 points higher than the top-scoring student in the second class.

    D) Adapting instruction to individual differences will be more difficult in the first class.

Answer: D

Explanation: D) Adapting instruction to individual differences will be more difficult in the first class. While the first class has a mean score that is slightly higher than that of the second class, the standard deviation, indicating variability between students, is substantially higher.

Page Ref: 509

30) A student scores at the 90th percentile. It can be concluded that, on this particular test, the student's

    A) grade-equivalent score is above 60.   B) stanine score is higher than seven.

    C) raw score is higher than 85.   D) normal curve equivalent score is 50.

Answer: B

Explanation: B) If a student scored at the 90th percentile, the stanine score would be above seven. A stanine distribution has a mean of five and a standard deviation of two. A stanine of seven is, therefore, one standard deviation above the mean —not nearly as high as the 90th percentile.

Page Ref: 510

31) A particular test has a mean of 50 and a standard deviation of five. A student who scores one standard deviation above the mean will have a score of

    A) 10.   B) 50.   C) 55.   D) 75.

Answer: C

Explanation: C) If a mean were 50 and the standard deviation five, a student who scores one standard deviation above the mean would have a score of 55 (50 + 5 = 55).

Page Ref: 510

32) A z–score is a standard score that has a mean of _____ and a standard deviation of
_____.

   A) 0; 1   B) 50; 5   C) 100; 10   D) 500; 100

Answer: A

Explanation: A) The Wechsler Intelligence Test for Children-Revised and the Stanford–Binet are
both intelligence tests administered to one individual at a time. Although more
costly and time consuming than group–administered tests, they are likely to
yield more accurate IQ scores.

Page Ref: 511

33) A measure of the match between the information on a test and the information taught in a
lesson is referred to as

   A) convergent evidence of validity.   B) predictive evidence of validity.

   C) content evidence of validity.   D) reliability.

Answer: C

Explanation: C) By saying that results have instructional validity and curricular validity, the
speaker is most likely referring to content validity. This type of validity implies
that the results of the test reflect knowledge of content.

Page Ref: 517

34) The validity of test results would be best reflected in response to which one of the following
questions?

   A) Are the test results consistent?

   B) Are there enough items on the test?

   C) Does the test yield the type of information desired?

   D) Is there enough similarity among the items?

Answer: C

Explanation: C) The validity of test results are reflected in the question: Does this test yield the
type of information desired? Validity means that the results are an accurate
measure of what was learned.

Page Ref: 517

35) A teacher designs a survey to assess students' test anxiety. In field testing it, the teacher finds that students score the same from one testing to the next, and that scores correlate with dropout rates, although the test scores do not correlate with those of three standardized tests on test anxiety. The teacher's test is most **DEFICIENT** in

    A) predictive evidence of validity.
    B) convergent evidence of validity.

    C) reliability.
    D) content evidence of validity.

Answer: B

Explanation: B) The teacher's anxiety test results appear deficient in convergent evidence of validity. The scores do not seem to relate to scores on similar measures (i.e., measures of the same trait).

Page Ref: 518

36) A class is given a test of mechanical ability. Results show that those who scored high did well in an industrial technology course while those who scored low did poorly. The test can be said to have high

    A) discriminant evidence of validity.
    B) internal reliability.

    C) content evidence of validity.
    D) predictive evidence of validity.

Answer: D

Explanation: D) The mechanical–aptitude test results appear to have predictive validity. The reason is that the scores are related to future performance in the area of concern.

Page Ref: 518

37) Which of the following can be inferred from the text author's description of validity and reliability?

    A) Test results with low reliability can still be valid.

    B) Test results with high reliability always yield valid results.

    C) Test results with low reliability cannot be valid.

    D) Validity and reliability are synonymous terms.

Answer: C

Explanation: C) Based on the text author's description of validity and reliability, it can be inferred that test results with low reliability cannot be valid. That is, a test that does not yield consistent scores (low reliability) can hardly assess what it is supposed to (high validity).

Page Ref: 518

38) How can the reliability of test results be increased?

    A) Make items easy.

    B) Make items difficult.

    C) Replace multiple-choice items with essay questions.

    D) Increase the length of the test.

Answer: D

Explanation: D) To increase the reliability of the test, the teacher should consider increasing the length of the test. The longer the test and the greater the range of items, the higher the reliability because chance scores that deviate from true scores become less likely.

Page Ref: 518

39) Jerry's old mechanical bathroom scale used to tell him weights that always agreed with the scale at the doctor's office. Then one day the dial on his old scale was damaged and the numbers got scrambled. The scale still operates the same way—it gives him the same weight from day to day. But the weight it gives him now is 27 pounds. Jerry's scale is now

    A) reliable, but not valid.   B) valid, but not reliable.

    C) both reliable and valid.   D) neither reliable nor valid.

Answer: A

Explanation: A) The scale measures Jerry's weight consistently, so it is reliable. It does not measure what it's supposed to measure, so it's not valid.

Page Ref: 518

40) Mr. Bono's seventh graders complain that they studied the class material, but that material wasn't on the test. Mr. Bono should examine his test for evidence of

    A) convergent validity.   B) content validity.

    C) reliability.   D) gender bias.

Answer: B

Explanation: B) Content evidence of validity is found in the overlap between what was taught and what was tested.

Page Ref: 518

41) Mr. Parikh is giving quizzes on current events. A quiz has five questions about what's been in the news. Carly got 100% on one quiz (0 wrong) and 60% on the next quiz (2 wrong). Performance seems to be inconsistent throughout the class. What would help most to improve the reliability of these quizzes?

    A) rephrasing the questions

    B) comparing the content of questions to what was discussed in class

    C) increasing the number of questions

    D) use computer administration

Answer: C

Explanation: C) One way to increase reliability of a measure is to increase the number of questions.

Page Ref: 518

42) Which of the following best represent recent commentary on traditional standardized tests?
    1) Tests give true and accurate information about the status of learning in the nation's schools.
    2) Tests are unfair to some groups of students.
    3) Tests tend to corrupt the process of teaching and learning.
    4) Tests focus time, energy, and attention away from high–order thinking skills.

    A) 1 and 3 (not 2 and 4).   B) 2, 3, and 4 (not 1).

    C) 1 and 2 (not 3 and 4).   D) 1, 2, and 4 (not 3).

Answer: B

Explanation: B) One criticism of traditional multiple–choice standardized tests is that they give false information about the status of learning in the nation's schools. They are also said to be unfair, promote teaching to the test and neglect higher–order skills.

Page Ref: 519

43) What innovation does computer–adaptive testing offer?

    A) Students write their own items as the test progresses.

    B) Items are presented on–screen

    C) Reliability coefficients are computed at the completion of each test.

    D) Selection of items is responsive to ongoing student performance.

Answer: D

Explanation: D) Responsive selection of items tailors the test to the individual student's abilities.
Page Ref: 520

True/False Questions

1) Standardized tests are sometimes used to determine eligibility for grade-to-grade promotion.

   Answer: TRUE
   Page Ref: 496

2) Standardized tests are rarely used to diagnose learning problems or strengths.

   Answer: FALSE
   Page Ref: 496

3) A growing trend since the mid-1970s has been the effort to hold teachers and schools accountable for what students learn.

   Answer: TRUE
   Page Ref: 497

4) The accountability movement stems in part from the public's confidence in the U.S. public school system.

   Answer: FALSE
   Page Ref: 497

5) Under No Child Left Behind (NCLB), states must report test scores for every school according to each subgroup within the school.

   Answer: TRUE
   Page Ref: 499

6) The term "subgroup," as used in No Child Left Behind (NCLB), is defined uniformly throughout the country.

   Answer: FALSE
   Page Ref: 499

7) Under No Child Left Behind (NCLB), all subgroups in all schools are now expected to make adequate yearly progress.

   Answer: TRUE
   Page Ref: 499

8) Achievement tests are used to assess students' general intellectual abilities.

   Answer: FALSE
   Page Ref: 503

9) The measurement of intelligence quotient (IQ) was introduced in the early 1900s by Alfred Binet.

   Answer: TRUE
   Page Ref: 504

10) A percentile rank indicates the percentage of students in the norming group who scored higher than a particular score.

Answer: FALSE
Page Ref: 507

11) Grade-equivalent scores are standard scores that relate students' raw scores to the average scores obtained by norming groups at different grade levels.

Answer: TRUE
Page Ref: 508

12) A frequency graph of a normal distribution produces a disk-shaped curve.

Answer: FALSE
Page Ref: 509

13) A normal curve equivalent may range from 1 to 99.

Answer: TRUE
Page Ref: 511

14) The most important mark of the usefulness of a test—especially an achievement test—is whether it assesses what the user wants it to assess. This quality is called predictive evidence of validity.

Answer: FALSE
Page Ref: 517

15) Test scores are used to make inferences about the students being tested.

Answer: TRUE
Page Ref: 519

16) One major criticism of traditional multiple-choice standardized tests is they give false information about the status of learning in the nation's schools.

Answer: TRUE
Page Ref: 519

Short Answer Questions

1) Tests that are usually commercially prepared for nationwide use and designed to provide accurate and meaningful information on students' performance relative to others, at a particular age or grade.

Answer: standardized tests
Page Ref: 495

2) Standards derived from test scores of a sample of individuals who are similar to future test takers.

Answer: norms
Page Ref: 496

3) Standardized tests measuring how much students have learned in a given context.

Answer: achievement tests
Page Ref: 503

4) The score that is designated as the minimum necessary to demonstrate mastery of a subject.

Answer: cutoff score
Page Ref: 507

5) A derived score that designates what percentage of the norming group earned raw scores lower than a particular score.

Answer: percentile score
Page Ref: 507

6) Standard scores that relate students' raw scores to the average scores obtained by norming groups at different grade levels.

Answer: grade-equivalent
Page Ref: 508

7) A concept, related to normal distribution, that describes dispersion of scores.

Answer: standard deviation
Page Ref: 509

8) A standard score that sets the mean of a distribution at zero and the standard deviation at one.

Answer: z-score
Page Ref: 511

9) A measure of the degree to which a test is appropriate for its intended use.

Answer: validity
Page Ref: 517

10) The evidence of validity that shows the degree of overlap between what is taught and what is tested.

Answer: content evidence of validity
Page Ref: 517

11) The evidence of validity that shows its relationship to a measure of future performance.

Answer: predictive evidence of validity
Page Ref: 518

12) A type of evidence about validity that exists when scores on a test are related to scores from another measure of the same or a very similar trait.

Answer: concurrent evidence
Page Ref: 518

13) A measure of the consistency of test scores obtained from the same students at different times.

Answer: reliability
Page Ref: 518

Essay Questions

1) In what ways are standardized tests used to select and place students into special groups, classes, or institutions?

Answer: Standardized tests such as the Scholastic Aptitude Test (SAT) are often used to select students for entry or placement in specific programs, admission to special programs for the gifted, and placement in special education programs.
Page Ref: 496

2) Using specific examples, illustrate how standardized tests are used for purposes of diagnosis, and of accountability.

Answer: Examples might include diagnostic reading tests such as the Gray Oral Reading Test, to assess a student's strengths and weaknesses, and to help determine whether the student has a reading disability. An example of testing for accountability might be the use of "high stakes" tests, such as minimum competency tests that a child may need to pass in order to be promoted to the next grade.
Page Ref: 496

3) Distinguish aptitude tests from achievement tests, comparing their general purposes, describing an example of each (identify a specific test) and indicating an advantage of each in a specific context.

Answer: Aptitude tests: focus on general learning potential to predict performance; Wechsler Adult Intelligence Scale is an example; an aptitude test could be helpful in determining a student's need for special services. Achievement tests: focus on what students have learned; an example is an SAT subject-test; achievement tests can be helpful in evaluating the success of instructional programs.
Page Ref: 503

4) Norm-referenced achievement tests fall into several categories: achievement batteries; diagnostic tests; and subject area achievement tests. Describe and give an example of each.

Answer: Achievement batteries are used to measure individual or group achievement in a variety of school subjects. These survey batteries include several small tests, each in a different subject area, and are usually administered to a group over a period of several days. Diagnostic tests differ from achievement batteries in that they generally focus on a specific content area and emphasize the skills that are thought to be important for mastery of the subject matter. Subject area achievement tests are made up by teachers to asses skills in specific subjects.

Page Ref: 506

5) Explain how criterion-referenced achievement tests are different from norm-referenced achievement tests.

Answer: Criterion-referenced tests differ from norm-referenced standardized tests in that they are often constructed around a well-defined set of outcomes. Criterion-referenced tests may take the form of a survey battery, a diagnostic test, or a single-subject test. They are also scored differently than norm-referenced tests, and scores are interpreted with respect to specific criterion for adequate performance.

Page Ref: 507

6) A student completes a series of standardized tests. On one test, the student scores at the 50th percentile. On another test, the student scores at the 5.0 grade equivalent. And, on yet another, the student's stanine score is 5. What do you know about this student?

Answer: A score at the 50th percentile tells you that there were an equal number of students who scored better or worse than this student. A grade-equivalent score tells you that the norming group at grade 5.0 would receive this score, on the average. A stanine score of 5 tells you that the student scored at the mean.

Page Ref: 507

7) Mrs. Espadas' classes scored as follows on her first unit Biology test:
1st period: 73 80 80 80 82 82 85 86 86 87 88 88 88 89 90
mean = 84.3   standard deviation = 4.7

8th period: 56 60 75 75 80 84 87 88 88 92 95 96 96 99 100
mean = 84.7   standard deviation = 13.4

Explain why the 8th period scores produce a larger standard deviation. Describe three characteristics of students or situations that could be underlying causes of these differences in standard deviations.

Mrs. Espadas is planning lessons for her next unit in Biology, which depends heavily on prerequisite skills from the first unit. What problems might arise if Mrs. Espadas planned her next unit for these two classes on the basis of their average performance, but ignored the difference in standard deviations?

Answer: The 8th period scores are more spread out or dispersed; on the average these scores range farther from their mean, which produces a larger standard deviation. The larger spread might be caused by individual differences in ability, amount of engaged time, motivational differences or time of day.

Because some of the 8th period students have not learned the prerequisites for the next unit, they will have problems unless Mrs. Espadas plans some reteaching before the next unit.

Page Ref: 509

8) Why are reliability and validity important issues in standardized testing?
Considering the issues of reliability and validity, criticize three of the following claims:
"My test has a very large number of items; it must have strong evidence of content validity."
"This is a highly reliable test, so it is unquestionably valuable for measuring our students' achievement."
"This student cannot be considered for the gifted program—his IQ is not above 135."
"The scores on these art assessments are identical every year—the test must be valid."
"We screen all of our chefs using an elaborate test of their knowledge of recipes. This test is valid, even though many chefs who score high on it make awful food, and those who score low on it sometimes make the best dishes."

Answer: A test cannot serve its intended purpose unless it is both reliable and valid. The statements quoted can be criticized by applying concepts of: content evidence of validity, the relationship between reliability and validity, and predictive evidence of validity.

Page Ref: 517

9) Criticisms of standardized tests often center around bias. Describe two specific examples of test bias.

Answer: Critics of standardized tests argue that tests give false information about the status of learning in the nation's schools, are unfair to some groups of students, and tend to corrupt the process of teaching and learning, often reducing teaching to testing.

Page Ref: 519

10) Jim Bagley, principal of West High School, opened the morning paper before starting to work for the day. He read that East High School, the other secondary school in a large suburban community, scored higher on the Pre–Scholastic Achievement Test (Pre–SAT) than did West high. The story Jim read noted that East High scored third in the state while West High scored seventh. The principal from East High was quoted as saying, "We're very pleased with our test scores. They certainly show the public that we're doing a good job."

Jim was concerned about the public's reaction to such a story and vowed to find a way to improve standardized test scores at West High.

As test time rolled around again, Mr. Bagley had a plan. In past years, all of West High students were notified of and allowed to take the Pre–SAT, and many of them did. This time Mr. Bagley and the school counselor went to all of the advanced placement classes to announce that the test would be offered. No one else was told about the test.

Mr. Bagley was pleased on test day as most of the school's "best and brightest" were there, but few others.

Today, Jim Bagley opens the paper and reads the headlines: West High Is Best In State.

Discuss some of the issues brought forth in the case, including reporting and interpreting standardized test scores.

Answer: Discussion might focus on reporting and interpreting standardized test scores, making comparisons from student to student, school to school, or state to state, and effects of such reporting on public awareness and understanding of how test scores are compared.

Page Ref: 509

11) Emily took a standardized test of individual ability differences in 8th grade. The test assessed aptitude for a wide range of skills, classified according to career paths. Emily's parents were eager to find out what careers Emily was best suited for. When the results arrived, they were reported in stanine scores. Emily's parents anxiously studied the scores, but found that they were all sevens, from mechanical aptitude, to artistic ability, to language skills, to math computation.

Emily's reaction was "I guess I can be anything I want, but that doesn't really help much." What could you tell Emily's parents that might help them make sense of Emily's scores? Is Emily very talented in all areas? How could a different scoring system shed light on Emily's profile of abilities?

Answer: While Emily's stanine scores are high, they give only a rough idea of how well any of her abilities would qualify her for a profession. She has scored one standard deviation above the mean, which means that her ability is well above average. It might be helpful for Emily's parents to look at the corresponding percentile score of 84, which makes it clear that Emily's performance is very high, but that there may be a substantial number of individuals whose ability may be greater.

Page Ref: 510

Teaching Tips for First-time Instructors and Adjunct Professors

Teaching Tips Contents

1. How to be an Effective Teacher
Seven principles of good teaching practice
Tips for Thriving: Creating an Inclusive Classroom

2. Today's Undergraduate Students
Traditional students
Nontraditional students
Emerging influences
What students want from college professors
Tips for Thriving: Be a "Facilitator of Learning"

3. Planning Your Course
Constructing the syllabus
Problems to avoid
Tips for Thriving: Visual Quality

4. Your First Class
Seven goals for a successful first meeting
Tips for Thriving: An Icebreaker

5. Strategies for Teaching and Learning
Getting participation through active learning
Team learning
Tips for Thriving: Active Learning and Lecturing

6. Grading and Assessment Techniques
Philosophy of grading
Criterion grading
Tips for Thriving: Result Feedback

7. Using Technology
Advice on using the web in small steps
Tips for Thriving: Using Videos

8. Managing Problem Situations
Cheating
Unmotivated students
Credibility problems
Tips for Thriving: Discipline

9. Surviving When You're Not Prepared
Contingency plans

10. Improving Your Performance
Self evaluation
Tips for Thriving: Video-Recording Your Class

1   How to be an Effective Teacher

(Adapted from Royse, *Teaching Tips for College and University Instructors: A Practical Guide*, published by Allyn & Bacon, Boston, MA, ©2001, by Pearson Education)

A look at 50 years of research "on the way teachers teach and learners learn" reveals seven broad principles of good teaching practice (Chickering and Gamson, 1987).

1. Frequent student-faculty contact: Faculty who are concerned about their students and their progress and who are perceived to be easy to talk to, serve to motivate and keep students involved. Things you can do to apply this principle:

- ✓ Attend events sponsored by students.
- ✓ Serve as a mentor or advisor to students.
- ✓ Keep "open" or "drop-in" office hours.

2. The encouragement of cooperation among students: There is a wealth of research indicating that students benefit from the use of small group and peer learning instructional approaches. Things you can do to apply this principle:

- ✓ Have students share in class their interests and backgrounds.
- ✓ Create small groups to work on projects together.
- ✓ Encourage students to study together.

3. Active learning techniques: Students don't learn much by sitting in the classroom listening; they must talk about what they are learning, write about it, relate to it, and apply it to their lives. Things you can do to apply this principle:

- ✓ Give students actual problems or situations to analyze.
- ✓ Use role-playing, simulations or hands-on experiments.
- ✓ Encourage students to challenge ideas brought into class.

4. Prompt feedback: Learning theory research has consistently shown that the quicker the feedback, the greater the learning. Things you can do to apply this principle:

- ✓ Return quizzes and exams by the next class meeting.
- ✓ Return homework within one week.
- ✓ Provide students with detailed comments on their written papers.

5. Emphasize time on task: This principle refers to the amount of actual involvement with the material being studied and applies, obviously, to the way the instructor uses classroom instructional time. Faculty need good time-management skills. Things you can do to apply this principle:

- ✓ Require students who miss classes to make up lost work.
- ✓ Require students to rehearse before making oral presentations.
- ✓ Don't let class breaks stretch out too long.

6. Communicating high expectations: The key here is not to make the course impossibly difficult, but to have goals that can be attained as long as individual learners stretch and work hard, going beyond what they already know. Things you can do to apply this principle:

- ✓ Communicate your expectations orally and in writing at the beginning of the course.
- ✓ Explain the penalties for students who turn work in late.
- ✓ Identify excellent work by students; display exemplars if possible.

7. Respecting diverse talents and ways of learning: Within any classroom there will be students who have latent talents and some with skills and abilities far beyond any that you might imagine. Understanding your students as individuals and showing regard for their unique talents is "likely to

facilitate student growth and development in every sphere – academic, social, personal, and vocational" (Sorcinelli, 1991, p.21). Things you can do to apply this principle:
- ✓ Use diverse teaching approaches.
- ✓ Allow students some choice of readings and assignments.
- ✓ Try to find out students' backgrounds and interests.

✓ **Tips for Thriving: Creating an Inclusive Classroom**

How do you model an open, accepting attitude within your classroom where students will feel it is safe to engage in give-and-take discussions? Firstly, view students as individuals instead of representatives of separate and distinct groups. Cultivate a climate that is respectful of diverse viewpoints, and don't allow ridicule, defamatory or hurtful remarks. Try to encourage everyone in the class to participate, and be alert to showing favoritism.

---

2   Today's Undergraduate Students

(Adapted from: Lyons et al, *The Adjunct Professor's Guide to Success*, published by Allyn & Bacon, Boston, MA, ©1999, by Pearson Education)

Total enrollment in all forms of higher education has increased over 65% in the last thirty years. Much of this increase was among part-time students who now comprise over 70% of total college enrollment. The number of "nontraditional" students, typically defined as 25 years of age or older, has been growing more rapidly than the number of "traditional" students, those under 25 years of age. Though there is a great deal of common ground between students of any age, there are some key differences between younger and older students.

Traditional students: Much more than in previous generations, traditional students are the products of dysfunctional families and have had a less effective primary and secondary education. Traditional students have been conditioned by the aftermath of high-profile ethical scandals (such as Watergate), creating a mindset of cynicism and lack of respect for authority figures – including college professors. Students of this generation are quick to proclaim their "rights". Many of today's students perceive professors as service providers, class attendance as a matter of individual choice, and grades as "pay" to which they are entitled for meeting standards they perceive as reasonable.

Nontraditional students: Many older students are attending college after a long lay-off, frequently doubting their ability to succeed. The other time-consuming challenges in their lives – children, work, caring for aging parents – often prevent adequate preparation for class or contribute to frequent absences. While traditional students demand their "rights," many older students won't ask for the smallest extra consideration (e.g., to turn a project in a few days late). Most older students learn best by doing, by applying the theory of the textbook to the rich set of experiences they have accumulated over the years.

Emerging influences: Today, a fourth of all undergraduate students are members of minority groups. Obviously, ethnicity, language, religion, culture, and sexual orientation are each significant issues to which a professor should be sensitive. The successful professor sees these differences as an opportunity rather than a threat to learning.

✓ **Tips for Thriving: Be a "Facilitator of Learning"**

Be energized by students who "don't get it" rather than judgmental of their shortcomings. View yourself as a "facilitator of learning" rather than a "sage on a stage."

What students want from college professors: While each student subgroup has particular characteristics that affect the dynamics of a college learning environment, students consistently need the following from their college instructors:

- ✓ Consistently communicated expectations of student performance that are reasonable in quantity and quality
- ✓ Sensitivity to the diverse demands on students and reasonable flexibility in accommodating them
- ✓ Effective use of classroom time
- ✓ A classroom environment that includes humor and spontaneity
- ✓ Examinations that address issues properly covered in class and are appropriate to the level of the majority of the students in the class
- ✓ Consistently positive treatment of individual students

The new paradigm of "colleges and universities as service providers to consumer-oriented students" is now firmly entrenched. The successful professor will do well to embrace it.

3   Planning Your Course

(Adapted from Royse, *Teaching Tips for College and University Instructors: A Practical Guide*, published by Allyn & Bacon, Boston, MA, ©2001, by Pearson Education)

Constructing the syllabus: The syllabus should clearly communicate course objectives, assignments, required readings, and grading policies. Think of the syllabus as a stand-alone document. Those students who miss the first or second meeting of a class should be able to learn most of what they need to know about the requirements of the course from reading the syllabus. Start by collecting syllabi from colleagues who have recently taught the course you will be teaching and look for common threads and themes.

Problems to avoid: One mistake commonly made by educators teaching a course for the first time is that they may have rich and intricate visions of how they want students to demonstrate comprehension and synthesis of the material, but they somehow fail to convey this information to those enrolled. Check your syllabus to make sure your expectations have been fully articulated. Be very specific. Avoid vaguely worded instructions:

Instruction	Students may interpret as:
"Write a short paper."	Write a paragraph.
	Write half a page.
	Type a two-page paper.
"Keep a log of your experiences."	Make daily entries.
	Make an entry when the spirit moves me.
	At the end of term, record what I recall.
"Obtain an article from the library."	Any magazine article.
	An article from a professional journal.
	A column from a newsletter.

✔ **Tips for Thriving: Visual Quality**

Students today are highly visual learners, so you should give special emphasis to the visual quality of the materials you provide to students. Incorporate graphics into your syllabus and other handouts. Color-code your materials so material for different sections of the course are on different colored papers. Such visuals are likely to create a perception among students that you are contemporary.

(Adapted from: Lyons et al, *The Adjunct Professor's Guide to Success*, published by Allyn & Bacon, Boston, MA, ©1999, by Pearson Education)

Success in achieving a great start is almost always directly attributable to the quality and quantity of planning that has been invested by the course professor. If the first meeting of your class is to be successful, you should strive to achieve seven distinct goals.

Create a Positive First Impression: Renowned communications consultant Roger Ailes (1996) claims you have fewer than 10 seconds to create a positive image of yourself. Students are greatly influenced by the visual component; therefore you must look the part of the professional professor. Dress as you would for a professional job interview. Greet each student entering the room. Be approachable and genuine.

Introduce Yourself Effectively: Communicate to students who you are and why you are credible as the teacher of the course. Seek to establish your approachability by "building common ground," such as stating your understanding of students' hectic lifestyles or their common preconceptions toward the subject matter.

Clarify the Goals and Expectations: Make an acetate transparency of each page of the syllabus for display on an overhead projector and using a cover sheet, expose each section as you explain it. Provide clarification and elicit questions.

Conduct an Activity that Introduces Students to Each Other: Students' chances of being able to complete a course effectively is enhanced if each comes to perceive the classmates as a "support network." The small amount of time you invest in an icebreaker will help create a positive classroom atmosphere and pay additional dividends throughout the term.

✓ **Tips for Thriving: Icebreaker**

The following activity allows students to get acquainted, exchange opinions, and consider new ideas, values or solutions to problems. It's a great way to promote self-disclosure or an active exchange of viewpoints.

Procedure

1. Give students one or more Post-it™ notes
2. Ask them to write on their note(s) one of the following:
   a. A *value* they hold
   b. An *experience* they have had recently
   c. A *creative idea* or solution to a problem you have posed
   d. A *question* they have about the subject matter of the class
   e. An *opinion* they hold about a topic of your choosing
   f. A *fact* about themselves or the subject matter of the class
3. Ask students to stick the note(s) on their clothing and circulate around the room reading each other's notes.
4. Next, have students mingle once again and negotiate a trade of Post-it™ notes with one another. The trade should be based on a desire to possess a particular value, experience, idea, question, opinion or fact for a short period of time. Set the rule that all trades have to be two-way. Encourage students to make as many trades as they like.
5. Reconvene the class and ask students to share what trades they made and why. (e.g., "I traded for a note that Sally had stating that she has traveled to Eastern Europe. I would really like to travel there because I have ancestors from Hungary and the Ukraine.")

(Adapted from: Silverman, *Active Learning: 101 Strategies to Teach Any Subject*, published by Allyn & Bacon, Boston, MA, ©1996, by Pearson Education).

Learn Students' Names: A student who is regularly addressed by name feels more valued, is invested more effectively in classroom discussion, and will approach the professor with questions and concerns.

Whet Students' Appetite for the Course Material: The textbook adopted for the course is critical to your success. Your first meeting should include a review of its approach, features, and sequencing. Explain to students what percentage of class tests will be derived from material from the textbook.

Reassure Students of the Value of the Course: At the close of your first meeting reassure students that the course will be a valuable learning experience and a wise investment of their time. Review the reasons why the course is a good investment: important and relevant content, interesting classmates, and a dynamic classroom environment.

5   Strategies for Teaching and Learning

(Adapted from: Silverman, *Active Learning: 101 Strategies to Teach Any Subject,* published by Allyn & Bacon, Boston, MA, ©1996, by Pearson Education)

Getting participation through active learning: To learn something well, it helps to hear it, see it, ask questions about it, and discuss it with others. What makes learning "active"? When learning is active, students do most of the work: they use their brains to study ideas, solve problems, and apply what they learn. Active learning is fast-paced, fun, supportive, and personally engaging. Active learning cannot occur without student participation, so there are various ways to structure discussion and obtain responses from students at any time during a class. Here are ten methods to get participation at any time:

1. **Open discussion**. Ask a question and open it up to the entire class without further structuring.
2. **Response cards**. Pass out index cards and request anonymous answers to your questions.
3. **Polling**. Design a short survey that is filled out and tallied on the spot.
4. **Subgroup discussion**. Break students into subgroups of three or more to share and record information.
5. **Learning partners**. Have students work on tasks with the student sitting next to them.
6. **Whips**. Go around the group and obtain short responses to key questions – invite students to pass if they wish.
7. **Panels**. Invite a small number of students to present their views in front of the class.
8. **Fishbowl**. Ask a portion of the class to form a discussion circle and have the remaining students form a listening circle around them. Bring new groups into the inner circle to continue the discussion.
9. **Games**. Use a fun exercise or quiz game to elicit students' ideas, knowledge, or skill.
10. **Calling on the next speaker**. Ask students to raise their hands when they want to share their views and ask the current speaker to choose the next speaker.

(Adapted from Royse, *Teaching Tips for College and University Instructors: A Practical Guide*, published by Allyn & Bacon, Boston, MA, ©2001, by Pearson Education)

Team learning: The essential features of this small group learning approach, developed originally for use in large college classrooms are (1) relatively permanent heterogeneous task groups; (2) grading based on a combination of individual performance, group performance, and peer evaluation; (3) organization of the course so that the majority of class time is spent on small group activities; (4) a six-step instructional process similar to the following model:

1. Individual study of material outside of the class is assigned.
2. Individual testing is used (multiple choice questions over homework at the beginning of class)
3. Groups discuss their answers and then are given a group test of the same items. They then get immediate feedback (answers).
4. Groups may prepare written appeals of items.

5. Feedback is given from instructor.
6. An application-oriented activity is assigned (e.g. a problem to be solved requiring input from all group members).

If you plan to use team learning in your class, inform students at the beginning of the course of your intentions to do so and explain the benefits of small group learning. Foster group cohesion by sitting groups together and letting them choose "identities" such as a team name or slogan. You will need to structure and supervise the groups and ensure that the projects build on newly acquired learning. Make the projects realistic and interesting and ensure that they are adequately structured so that each member's contribution is 25 percent. Students should be given criteria by which they can assess and evaluate the contributions of their peers on a project-by-project basis (Michaelsen, 1994).

 Tips for Thriving: Active Learning and Lecturing

Lecturing is one of the most time-honored teaching methods, but does it have a place in an active learning environment? There are times when lecturing can be effective. Think about the following when planning a lecture:

Build Interest: Capture your students' attention by leading off with an anecdote or cartoon.
Maximize Understanding and Retention: Use brief handouts and demonstrations as a visual backup to enable your students to see as well as hear.
Involve Students during the Lecture: Interrupt the lecture occasionally to challenge students to answer spot quiz questions.
Reinforce the Lecture: Give students a self-scoring review test at the end of the lecture.

6   Grading and Assessment Techniques

(Adapted from Wankat, *The Effective, Efficient Professor: Teaching, Scholarship and Service*, published by Allyn & Bacon, Boston, MA, ©2002, by Pearson Education)

Philosophy of grading: Develop your own philosophy of grading by picturing in your mind the performance of typical A students, B students and so on. Try different grading methods until you find one that fits your philosophy and is reasonably fair. Always look closely at students on grade borders – take into account personal factors if the group is small. Be consistent with or slightly more generous than the procedure outlined in your syllabus.

Criterion grading: Professor Philip Wankat writes: "I currently use a form of criterion grading for my sophomore and junior courses. I list the scores in the syllabus that will guarantee the students As, Bs and so forth. For example, a score of 85 to 100 guarantees an A; 75 to 85, a B; 65 to 75, a C; and 55 to 65, a D. If half the class gets above 85% they all get an A. This reduces competition and allows students to work together and help each other. The standard grade gives students something to aim for and tells them exactly what their grade is at any time. For students whose net scores are close to the borders at the end of the course, I look at other factors before deciding a final grade such as attendance."

 Tips for Thriving: Result Feedback

As stated earlier, feedback on results is the most effective of motivating factors. Anxious students are especially hungry for positive feedback. You can quickly and easily provide it by simply writing "Great job!" on the answer sheets or tests. For students who didn't perform well, a brief note such as "I'd love to talk with you at the end of class" can be especially reassuring. The key is to be proactive and maintain high standards, while requiring students to retain ownership of their success.

7 <u>Using Technology</u>

(Adapted from: Sanders, *Creating Learning-Centered Courses for the World Wide Web*, published by Allyn & Bacon, Boston, MA, ©2001, by Pearson Education)

The Web as a source of teaching and learning has generated a great deal of excitement and hyperbole. The Web is neither a panacea nor a demon, but it can be a valuable tool. Among the many misunderstandings about the use of Web pages for teaching and learning is a view that such efforts must encompass an entire course. Like any other tool in a course (e.g. lectures, discussions, films, or field trips) online material can be incorporated to enhance the learning experience.

The best way to start using the Web in a course is with small steps. Developing a single lesson or assignment, a syllabus, or a few well-chosen links makes more sense than trying to develop a whole course without sufficient support or experience. Testing Web materials with a class that regularly meets face-to-face helps a faculty member gauge how well a lesson using the Web works. Making adjustments within the context of a traditional class helps fine-tune Web lessons that may be offered in distance education without face-to-face interaction.

✔️ **Tips for Thriving: Using Videos**

Generally a videotape should not exceed half and hour in length. Always preview a video before showing it to ensure the content, language, and complexity are appropriate for your students. Include major videos on your syllabus to encourage attendance and integrate them into the context of the course. Plan to evaluate students' retention of the concepts on exams or through reports. Avoid reinforcing the common student perception that watching a video is a time-filler.

By beginning with good practices in learning, we ask not how the new technology can help us do a better job of getting students to learn, but rather we ask how good pedagogy be better implemented with the new technology.

8 <u>Managing Problem Situations</u>

(Adapted from Wankat, *The Effective, Efficient Professor: Teaching, Scholarship and Service*, published by Allyn & Bacon, Boston, MA, ©2002, by Pearson Education)

Cheating: Cheating is one behavior that should not be tolerated. Tolerating cheating tends to make it worse. Prevention of cheating is much more effective than trying to cure it once it has occurred. A professor can prevent cheating by:

- Creating rapport with students
- Gaining a reputation for giving fair tests
- Giving clear instructions and guidelines before, during, and after tests
- Educating students on the ethics of plagiarism
- Requiring periodic progress reports and outlines before a paper is due

Try to develop exams that are perceived as fair and secure by students. Often, the accusation that certain questions were tricky is valid as it relates to ambiguous language and trivial material. Ask your mentor or an experienced instructor to closely review the final draft of your first few exams for these factors.

✓ **Tips for Thriving: Discipline**

One effective method for dealing with some discipline problems is to ask the class for feedback (Angelo & Cross, 1993) In a one-minute quiz, ask the students, "What can I do to help you learn?" Collate the responses and present them to the class. If behavior such as excessive talking appears in some responses (e.g. "Tell people to shut up") this gives you the backing to ask students to be quiet. Use of properly channeled peer pressure is often effective in controlling undesired behavior

---

(Adapted from Royse, *Teaching Tips for College and University Instructors: A Practical Guide*, published by Allyn & Bacon, Boston, MA, ©2001, by Pearson Education)

Unmotivated Students: There are numerous reasons why students may not be motivated. The "required course" scenario is a likely explanation – although politics in colonial America is your life's work, it is safe to assume that not everyone will share your enthusiasm. There are also personal reasons such as a death of a loved one or depression. Whenever you detect a pattern that you assume to be due to lack of motivation (e.g. missing classes, not handing assignments in on time, non-participation in class), arrange a time to have the student meet with you outside the classroom. Candidly express your concerns and then listen.

Motivating students is part of the faculty members' job. To increase motivation professors should: show enthusiasm for the topic; use various media and methods to present material; use humor in the classroom; employ activities that encourage active learning; and give frequent, positive feedback.

(Adapted from Baiocco/Waters, *Successful College Teaching*, published by Allyn & Bacon, Boston, MA, ©1998, by Pearson Education)

Credibility Problems. If you are an inexperienced instructor you may have problems with students not taking you seriously. At the first class meeting articulate clear rules of classroom decorum and comport yourself with dignity and respect for students. Try to exude that you are in charge and are the "authority" and avoid trying to pose as the students' friend.

9   Surviving When You're Not Prepared

(Adapted from: Lyons et al, *The Adjunct Professor's Guide to Success*, published by Allyn & Bacon, Boston, MA, ©1999, by Pearson Education)

Despite your thorough course planning, your concern for students, and commitment to the institution, situations will arise – illness, family emergencies – that prevent you from being fully prepared for every class meeting. Most students will excuse one flawed performance during a term, but try to develop contingency plans you can employ on short notice. These might include:

- Recruiting a guest speaker from your circle of colleagues to deliver a presentation that might interest your students.
- Conducting a carousel brainstorming activity, in which a course issue is examined from several perspectives. Divide the students in to groups to identify facts appropriate to each perspective. For example, you might want to do a SWOT analysis (Strengths, Weaknesses, Opportunities, Threats) on a particular organization or public figure.
- Dividing the class into groups of three or four and asking them to develop several questions that would be appropriate for inclusion on your next exam.
- Identify a video at your local rental store that embellishes material from the course.
- Assign students roles (e.g. press, governmental figures, etc.), and conduct a focused analysis of a late-breaking news story related to your course.
- Divide students into groups to work on an assigned course project or upcoming exam.
- As a last resort, admit your inability to prepare a class and allow students input into formulating a strategy for best utilizing class time.

In each case, the key is to shift the initial attention away from yourself (to permit you to gather your thoughts) and onto an activity that engages students in a new and significant way.

10   Improving Your Performance

(Adapted from: Lyons et al, *The Adjunct Professor's Guide to Success*, published by Allyn & Bacon, Boston, MA, ©1999, by Pearson Education)

The instructor who regularly engages in systematic self-evaluation will unquestionably derive greater reward from the formal methods of evaluation commonly employed by colleges and universities. One method for providing structure to an ongoing system of self-evaluation is to keep a journal of reflections on your teaching experiences. Regularly invest 15 or 20 introspective minutes following each class meeting to focus especially on the strategies and events in class that you feel could be improved. Committing your thoughts and emotions enables you to develop more effective habits, build confidence in your teaching performance, and make more effective comparisons later. The following questions will help guide self-assessment:

> *How do I typically begin the class?*
> *Where/How do I position myself in the class?*
> *How do I move in the classroom?*
> *Where are my eyes usually focused?*
> *Do I facilitate students' visual processing of course material?*
> *Do I change the speed, volume, energy, and tone of my voice?*
> *How do I ask questions of students?*
> *How often, and when, do I smile or laugh in class?*
> *How do I react when students are inattentive?*
> *How do I react when students disagree or challenge what I say?*
> *How do I typically end a class?*

✔ **Tips for Thriving: Video-Recording Your Class**

In recent years a wide range if professionals have markedly improved their job performance by employing video recorders in their preparation efforts. As an instructor, an effective method might be to ask your mentor or another colleague to tape a 10 to 15 minute mini-lesson then to debrief it using the assessment questions above. Critiquing a videotaped session provides objectivity and is therefore more likely to effect change. Involving a colleague as an informal coach will enable you to gain from their experience and perspective and will reduce the chances of your engaging in self-depreciation.

References

Ailes, R. (1996) *You are the message: Getting what you want by being who you are*. New York: Doubleday.

Chickering, A.W., & Gamson, Z.F. (1987) Seven principles for good practice in undergraduate education. AAHE Bulletin, 39, 3-7.

Michaelson, L.K. (1994). Team Learning: Making a case for the small-group option. In K.W. Prichard & R.M. Sawyer (Eds.), *Handbook of college teaching*. Westport, CT: Greenwood Press.

Sorcinelli, M.D. (1991). Research findings on the seven principles. In A.W. Chickering & Z. Gamson (eds.), *Applying the seven principles of good practice in undergraduate education*. New Directions for Teaching and Learning #47. San Francisco: Jossey-Bass.